CANADIAN
MILITARY
HISTORY

NeW ✛ CANADIAN READINGS

SERIES EDITOR
J. L. GRANATSTEIN

Titles currently available

Michael D. Behiels, ed., *Quebec Since 1945: Selected Readings*

David J. Bercuson, ed., *Canadian Labour History: Selected Readings*

Carl Berger, ed., *Contemporary Approaches to Canadian History*

Hartwell Bowsfield, ed., *Louis Riel: Selected Readings*

Bettina Bradbury, ed., *Canadian Family History: Selected Readings*

Kenneth S. Coates and William R. Morrison, eds., *Interpreting Canada's North: Selected Readings*

Terry Crowley, ed., *Clio's Craft: A Primer of Historical Methods*

Robin Fisher and Kenneth Coates, eds., *Out of the Background: Readings on Canadian Native History*

J.L. Granatstein, ed., *Canadian Foreign Policy: Historical Readings, Revised Edition*

J.L. Granatstein, ed., *Towards a New World: Readings in the History of Canadian Foreign Policy*

Norman Hillmer, ed., *Partners Nevertheless: Canadian–American Relations in the Twentieth Century*

Michiel Horn, ed., *The Depression in Canada: Responses to Economic Crisis*

B.D. Hunt and R.G. Haycock, eds., *Canadian Defence: Perspectives on Policy in the Twentieth Century*

Douglas McCalla, ed., *The Development of Canadian Capitalism: Essays in Business History*

Douglas McCalla, ed., *Perspectives on Canadian Economic History*

R.C. Macleod, ed., *Lawful Authority: Readings on the History of Criminal Justice in Canada*

Morris Mott, ed., *Sports in Canada: Historical Readings*

Fernand Ouellet, *Economy, Class, and Nation in Quebec: Interpretive Essays*, ed. and trans. Jacques A. Barbier

Michael J. Piva, ed., *A History of Ontario: Selected Readings*

John Saywell and George Vegh, ed., *Making the Law: The Courts and the Constitution*

Gilbert A. Stelter, ed., *Cities and Urbanization: Canadian Historical Perspectives*

Veronica Strong-Boag and Anita Clair Fellman, eds., *Rethinking Canada: The Promise of Women's History*, 2nd edition

Joseph Wearing, ed., *The Ballot and Its Message: Voting in Canada*

Graeme Wynn, ed., *People, Places, Patterns, Processes: Geographical Perspectives on the Canadian Past*

CANADIAN MILITARY HISTORY

SELECTED READINGS

Edited by

Marc Milner

University of New Brunswick

Copp Clark Pitman Ltd.
A Longman Company
Toronto

ISBN: 0-7730-5257-7

editing: Andy Carroll, Pamela Erlichman
design: Susan Hedley, Liz Nyman
cover design: Kyle Gell
cover illustration: Alex Colville, *Infantry Near Nijmegan, Holland*,
  C.N. No. 12172. Copyright Canadian War Museum, Canadian Museum
  of Civilization. Photos for CWM by William Kent.
maps and illustrations: Allan Moon
typesetting: April Haisell
printing and binding: Webcom Limited

Canadian Cataloguing in Publication Data

Main entry under title:

Canadian military history :

(New Canadian readings)
Includes bibliographic references.
ISBN 0-7730-5257-7

1. Canada—History, Military.   I. Milner, Marc.
II. Series.

FC226.C35 1993   335'.00971   C93–094055–5
F1028.C35 1993

Copp Clark Pitman Ltd.
2775 Matheson Blvd. East
Mississauga, Ontario
L4W 4P7

associated companies: *Longman Group Ltd., London* •
Longman Inc., New York • *Longman Cheshire Pty., Melbourne*
• *Longman Paul Pty., Auckland*

Printed and bound in Canada

  2 3 4 5   5257-7   97 96 95 94 93

FOREWORD

○

Military history has been the orphan child of Canadian history for at least a generation. Although some of the country's best professional historians—Charles Stacey and George Stanley, to cite only two—wrote about Canadians at war, the great majority of professional historians scorned this area. It was the "ride to the sound of the guns" style of so much military history that turned them off, and such events as the Vietnam War also assisted in the widespread revulsion against the history of war. Now this is changing dramatically. Military history courses at such universities as Acadia, Wilfrid Laurier, and Calgary draw packed classrooms with long waiting lists. A new journal (*Canadian Military History*) has begun publication. And new scholars have entered the field, bringing great sophistication in method and, not to be understated in importance, the benefits of access to all the records of Canada's role in the two world wars to their books. The result has been a rush of new work of high quality.

    This volume, edited by one of the major figures in this most recent generation of military historians, presents some of the best work—new and old—in an accessible format. When read with the articles collected in *Canada's Defence: Perspectives on Policy in the Twentieth Century*, also published in this New Canadian Readings series, this volume cannot fail to tell us much about Canadians' roles in war and cold war. There is heroism here, but not a little bungling and incompetence too. Much still remains to be written, however, and there is no field in Canadian history with as much room for innovative research and high quality writing.

J.L. Granatstein
General Editor

CONTENTS

○

FOREWORD _____ *v*

INTRODUCTION _____ *1*

section 1   1 8 6 7 – 1 9 1 3 _____ *3*

G . F .   S T A N L E Y   ○   The Northwest Rebellion ____ *6*

D E S M O N D   M O R T O N   ○   Canada's First
Expeditionary Force: The Canadian Contingent in
South Africa, 1899–1900 _____ *26*

S . J .   H A R R I S   ○   The Permanent Force and
"Real Soldiering," 1883–1914 _____ *35*

section 2   1 9 1 4 – 1 9 1 9 _____ *53*

R O N A L D   G .   H A Y C O C K   ○   Recruiting,
1914–1916 _____ *57*

R E G I N A L D   H .   R O Y   ○   The Journal of
Private Fraser: Courcellette, 14–17 September 1916 __ *82*

A . M . J .   H Y A T T   ○   Corps Commander:
Arthur Currie _____ *97*

S . F .   W I S E   ○   The Aerial War, 1917 _____ *120*

R O G E R   S A R T Y   ○   Hard Luck Flotilla:
The RCN's Atlantic Coast Patrol, 1914–1918 _____ *144*

section 3   1 9 1 9 – 1 9 4 5 _____ *167*

C . P .   S T A C E Y   ○   The Raid on Dieppe,
19 August 1942_____ *171*

F A R L E Y   M O W A T   ○   Crossing the Moro _____ *197*

D. GRAHAM AND S. BIDWELL ○
Operation Olive _____ 206

JOHN ENGLISH ○ Operation Tractable _____ 224

J. TERRY COPP ○ Battle Exhaustion and
the Canadian Soldier in Normandy _____ 238

W. DENIS WHITAKER AND
SHELAGH WHITAKER ○ The Guns of
Woensdrecht _____ 250

MURRAY PEDEN ○ Operational
Flying—Apprenticeship _____ 268

W.S. CARTER ○ Strike Hard, Strike Sure:
The Dortmund Raid of 6–7 October 1944 _____ 284

MARC MILNER ○ The Implications of
Technological Backwardness: The Canadian Navy
1939–1945 _____ 298

ALAN EASTON ○ Close Quarters _____ 313

section 4   POST-1945 _____ 327

J.L. GRANATSTEIN AND
D. BERCUSON ○ Peacekeeping: The Mid-East
and Indo-China _____. 331

PETER HAYDON ○ The RCN and the Cuban
Missile Crisis _____ 349

DAVID A. CHARTERS ○ From October to
Oka: Peacekeeping in Canada, 1970–1990 _____ 368

FURTHER READINGS _____ 395

INTRODUCTION

o

George Stanley subtitled his seminal book *Canada's Soldiers, 1604–1954* as "The Military History of an Unmilitary People." The book itself ran to 400 pages and Stanley only managed to skim the highlights. For members of his generation, the extent of Canada's military experience was not a revelation, nor indeed was his underlying theme that war had been a formative influence on the history of Canada itself. It was, after all, with force of arms that French dominion was secured over vast areas of North America, with force that the French dominion was ended, with force that British North America was defended from republicanism, and it was the threat of force that brought the colonies to confederation. It was, moreover, with force of arms that Canadian independence on the world stage was asserted in two catastrophic global conflicts. Canadians, it would appear, were an "unmilitary" people because they shunned large, permanent military establishments, not because they shunned war itself.

For a decade after the appearance of Stanley's book in 1954, war remained part of the mainstream of Canadian history. By the 1960s, however, war had become socially unacceptable because of the nuclear holocaust it threatened—of the wars of the period most were redeemingly categorized as "wars of national liberation." The impolitic nature of war extended into Canada's universities. In the 1960s Reserve Officer Training Programs were harried off campuses, courses in Canadian military history abandoned, and the study of war itself was passed off to social scientists intent on eliminating it completely.

Influenced by social movements, the historical profession was turning in directions which rejected virtually all forms of military history as it had been practised. Academic historians had come to see each event as unique and complete unto itself, and increasingly rejected history formulated as a study of progress or as the march toward nationhood. National history was abandoned for regional, social, economic, and quantitative interpretations of history. War as a driving force in history was buried by "macro-" studies of economic and industrial patterns, and crushed beneath the weight of annual coal and steel production figures. "Micro-" historians, at the other end of the scale, threw themselves into unearthing, to use Joe Clark's infamous words, the "totality" of their subjects' daily lives. Scholars who specialized in fields such as Black, native, women's, and Third World history, applying, among others, quantitative, social, and Marxist interpretations redefined acceptable academic history. The very idea of "nation" seemed lost in the welter of new fields, new ideologies, and new methodologies.

The authority of nationally oriented military history was also undermined by some of its own authors. Although their range of methods and approaches varied considerably, traditional narrative or operational military history was generally written by retired officers and focused on battles. It bordered on the sensational and smacked, to many, of "Boys Own" adventures. Academic historians rejected much military history for these reasons or because it was written for didactic purposes—to train future soldiers.

Not surprisingly, Canadian military history—both impolitic and inherently nationalist—fell from grace, a trend evident elsewhere in the western world. It did not disappear, but by the 1970s the idea of war as part of the mainstream of Canadian history had become anathema to virtually all university programs. A generation of Canadians have grown up with little, if any, knowledge of their own military past or even of the major wars of this century.

Despite its lower profile, Canadian military history as a discipline has expanded and developed, adding new methodologies and exploiting new sources. Practitioners of the "new military history" are again exploring the links between the military experience and the larger society. For many this is labelled institutional or social history, but it is, nonetheless, a form of military history that is acceptable within the halls of academe. This same comprehensive approach to research and writing has been applied to the study of military operations by the new generation of historians. For these scholars, most of whom have never experienced war, it is no longer sufficient to write that, "the battalion was thrown across the river and after heavy casualites secured a bridgehead." The new operational history seeks to examine not only what happened, but how and why, going back to the social and doctrinal origins of the war. In the process, modern Canadian military historians have mastered many other fields, from social history to the history of technology, and apply all disciplines in their interpretations. In some cases, the analyses led to pioneering work in distinctly non-military fields, such as the history of psychiatric medicine.

The intent in this book is to provide an overview of issues and some examples of different methodologies covering Canadian military history from Confederation to 1990, and to do so by focusing on that most quintessential of military activities, actual operations or the organization of the armed forces for the purpose of fighting. The closely related subject of defence policy is covered in B.D. Hunt and R.G. Haycock's *Canada's Defence* in this series.

I would like to thank Bill Acheson, Bill Carter, David Charters, Jack Granatstein, Stephen Harris, Ron Haycock, the late Barry Hunt, Roger Sarty, and Brent Wilson for their help in selecting the readings, the various publishers for permission to reprint, and Elizabeth Heatherington, Gayle Day, and Bobbi Milner for putting portions of the manuscript on disk. Thanks also to Andy Carroll for an excellent editing job. This project was also supported by the Department of National Defence through the University of New Brunswick's Military and Strategic Studies Program.

section

1

1867–1913

T he Canadian military experience up to 1914 was limited almost entirely to militias raised to defend land frontiers; securing maritime approaches was Britain's responsibility. The first Militia Act of 1868 engendered a force of some 40 000 "Active Militia," really volunteer corps receiving regular training, and a reserve militia (never mobilized) encompassing every able-bodied male between the ages of eighteen and sixty. The Active Militia's task was primarily to aid the civil power and to augment whatever British regular troops were deployed for operations, as they did in response to the Fenian Raids and the 1870 Northwest Rebellion. In 1871 though, the final inland British garrison withdrew from Quebec, leaving local defence (apart from the Imperial naval stations at Halifax and Equimalt) in Canadian hands.

Over the four decades following 1868, three themes dominated the course of Canada's military development. The first was the enduring debate over the extent to which the militia was to remain a social institution or to become a professional military one. This was largely—although by no means exclusively—a struggle between senior militia officers and their minister on the one side, and the senior British officer sent out to command the Canadian army on the other. The debate was complicated after 1885 by the formation of the first "regular" units of the Canadian army, whose initial function was to train the militia. The extent to which the militia was to be professionalized and the role of what had become, by 1914, the first regiments of the regular Canadian army was settled before the First World War by the Minister of Militia, Sam Hughes. A consummate politician, long service militiaman and Boer War veteran, Hughes mobilized the militia in 1914 for overseas service his own way (in flagrant defiance of his professional staff's mobilization plans), and sent the regular force regiments to garrison British naval bases in the West Indies.

The second theme that dominates the first decades of the Canadian defence establishment is partly a spin-off of the first, and that is the role of French Canada in the forces of the new Dominion. The concept of a popular militia was part of French-Canadian culture prior to 1867, and the new system of Active Militia units was well received in Quebec. However, somewhere between 1867 and 1914, French Canadians were alienated by the Canadian militia, with serious consequences for enlistment and Canada's role in the First World War. In part, the alienation was the result of increased professionalism, and also in part because of the "anglicization" of the Canadian military. The Canadian militia modelled itself more and more in the image of English country regiments, with allowances for kilts, tartans, animal skins, and "Prussian" fashion but not for French forms of dress. Professional competence depended increasingly on fluency in English and courses taken in schools in the UK. Perhaps the situation would not have been unsalvagable by 1914, had anyone but Sam Hughes been minister of militia.

The third theme that runs through this period concerns the role of the new military establishment. The traditional role of providing aid to the civil power remained, as it does today, but after 1871 and the dispatch of the British battalion from Quebec, the Active Militia became the force of first resort. The need to improve its professional competence led to the founding of schools in 1885, and in that same year two other portentous events occurred. One was the first distinctly Canadian campaign, the 1885 Northwest Rebellion, in which the Canadian militia—with a bit of luck and considerable enthusiasm—managed to beat Riel's insurgents in a series of small skirmishes and the Battle of Batoche. The second was the first Canadian overseas expedition: 386 voyageurs sailed for Egypt to support relief forces headed for Khartoum. They got there too late, but Canadians have been going overseas ever since.

Indeed, fourteen years later Canada mounted her first "major" overseas military adventure, to the veldt of South Africa, when troops were sent to put down the Boers. The decision to do so left Canada deeply divided, and not for the last time. Some Canadians wondered why the British needed colonial troops to handle a few Boer farmers while French Canadians saw not a little of the Boer predicament in their own situation. Many English Canadians, however, responded with zeal for Queen and Empire. Sir Wilfrid Laurier, caught between the two, vacillated, but agreed to send the 2nd (Special Service) Battalion of the Royal Canadian Regiment, which arrived in time to participate in the battle of Paardeberg in February 1900. As the war drifted into its guerrilla phase, Canadian cavalry, including a regiment raised in the west by Lord Strathcona and a young militiaman named Sam Hughes (who by his own reckoning won two VCs), and artillery also saw action. In all, 8300 Canadians fought in South Africa: 89 were killed in action.

A precedent was thus set for overseas expeditions. For the next forty years politicians attempted to control the urge of Canadian militiamen to take up arms and go where the war was, without much luck. Their attempts to re-focus at least some of that energy on the defence of Canada's coastline prior to 1914 were only partially successful. Pushed by the desire to assert the prerogatives of nationhood and prodded by the anxieties in Britain over the growing German fleet, the Royal Canadian Navy was founded in 1910. Crewed largely with British officers and Newfoundland sailors, the fledgling RCN was eviscerated by the general election of 1911 and quickly became the orphan child of the Canadian defence establishment. Imperialists saw it as a wasted effort, Canadians saw it as a magnet for off-shore trouble. Caught between two resolute positions, the government bought two aging cruisers for training purposes and then let the RCN languish. By 1914 there had been more desertions from the Canadian Navy than there were personnel in it. Not surprisingly, when Britain went to war in 1914 it asked Canada to send troops.

THE NORTHWEST REBELLION[✧]

G.F. STANLEY

o

On the evening of 27 March [1885] the people of eastern Canada were startled by the news that the mounted police had been defeated in battle by a mixed force of Métis and Indians. That the Riel agitation should have developed into a serious rebellion was totally unexpected. During 1884 few of the complaints from the Northwest plains had filtered into old Canada. News of Riel's reappearance was announced, but not discussed, of so little importance was it deemed. Throughout the winter the embers of discontent smouldered unsuspected. Early in March a few dispatches and private letters, referring to the growing discontent among the half-breeds, Indians and whites, appeared in the eastern press, but the possibility of revolt was never seriously considered. Following the news of the seizure of certain stores and the retention of prisoners by the Métis the *Gazette* of Montreal expressed the general feeling when it wrote:

> That this rebellion will assume any serious proportions or cause any difficulty in its suppression is not for a moment to be supposed . . . the incident cannot attain proportions of serious significance, being merely local in its character and of no more consequence than a petty riot in any well settled part of old Canada.[1]

The government, however, had already taken steps to suppress the incipient rising by force. On 14 March, following the information that the half-breeds intended preventing settlers from entering the country after the 16th, the prime minister telegraphed to the lieutenant-governor: "You must assume responsibility for peace of District as Governor." He also suggested that the lieutenant-governor, or Hayter Reed, the assistant Indian

---

✧ From "The North-West Rebellion, Part Two," chap. 16 of *The Birth of Western Canada* (Toronto: University of Toronto Press, 1966), 350–73.

commissioner, should visit the locality, and asked "Would Lacombe or Hugonard be of any service?"[2] Five days later a reinforcement of police was dispatched to Prince Albert under Colonel Irvine, but as the situation appeared to grow worse, Dewdney appealed to the prime minister for military support. On 22 March, four days before the disaster of Duck Lake, Dewdney wired Macdonald: "Situation looks very serious. Think it imperative able military man should be on staff in event of militia going north."[3] Macdonald replied with a promptitude which had scarcely characterized his previous dealings with the Northwest Territories: "General Middleton to proceed to Red River to-night. Order sent to Winnipeg Militia to be ready to move."[4] In accordance with this order Major-General Frederick Middleton, commanding the militia of Canada, at once departed for the Northwest. On the 25th, one company of the 90th militia battalion of Winnipeg proceeded to Troy and two days later the remainder of the battalion followed with the major-general. March 28, 29, and 30 were spent in arranging the transport and commissariat services, and by 2 April the whole force had reached Qu'Appelle which had been chosen as the base of operations.

In the meantime the Métis victory had altered the whole situation. What had been up to Duck Lake little more than a riotous assembly, then became open rebellion against constituted authority. Middleton, realizing that the mounted police were insufficient in number to cope with a rebellion which threatened to develop into a general native rising, asked for an immediate force of 2000 men. Troops were accordingly summoned from every province of the Dominion. . . .

The total number of soldiers officially mobilized during the Northwest Rebellion amounted to 5334 added to which were 2648 staff, transport, commissariat, medical, and other corps, totalling in all 7982 men.[5] The mounted police, who are not included in this total, numbered about 500. The artillery consisted of nine guns and two machine guns.

The eastern regiments were despatched to the Northwest with great rapidity considering the time of year, the absence of a standing force, and the lack of stores and equipment for the citizen soldiery. Moreover, the Canadian Pacific Railway line was not yet completed from east to west. North of Lake Superior there were several gaps in the line, aggregating nearly one hundred miles, over which men and supplies had to be transported by sleighs. Nevertheless "A" and "B" Batteries, the only corps constituting a permanent military force in Canada, arrived at Winnipeg on 5 April, ten days after the battle of Duck Lake. Several militia regiments followed within a few days, having been mobilized, equipped, and dispatched over two thousand miles, in less than a fortnight.

While the mobilization was being carried out precautions were taken to guard against the possibilities of incursions by Indians or half-breeds sympathetic to the rebels from south of the international boundary. The governor general immediately put himself into communication with the British minister at Washington, requesting that the necessary steps be taken to prevent men or munitions of war being sent across the frontier.[6] In contrast to

1869–70, the government of the United States, in this instance, co-operated loyally with the British authorities. Secretary of State Bayard at once replied to Sackville-West's request:

> I shall use every endeavour to obtain the earliest knowledge in relation to the revolt in Winnipeg (sic) and this Government will take all available precautions to prevent the dispatch of hostile expeditions, or of arms and munitions of war, from within the jurisdiction of the United States to aid the insurgents in the North-West provinces.[7]

Thus, although there were constant rumours of Fenian invasions and Indian incursions, nothing ever came of them. On 11 April Bayard assured the British minister that the military authorities in Dakota discredited the truth of reports of movements towards Canada by hostile Indians, stating: "The Commanding General adds that he has enjoined the utmost vigilance upon the commanders of the posts along the boundary, and that the reports which he has received indicate that they are zealously carrying out their instructions."[8] Constant vigilance was thus maintained throughout the rebellion by the American authorities, and Canada, protected from the danger of any serious attack from the south, was free to concentrate her efforts in the north.

The seriousness of the rebellion lay not in the actual numbers which the rebels were able to bring into the field against the forces of the federal government, but in the potential danger of a general native rising. Although the rebels who took up arms numbered scarcely over 1000, the number of Indians in Treaties 4, 6, and 7 totalled about 20 000. There were, moreover, numerous Métis settlements scattered throughout the Northwest from Wood Mountain to St. Albert, which might easily provide nuclei for revolt. The first object of the government was, therefore, to localize the rebellion. This was accomplished by the immediate dispatch of men to Qu'Appelle, even prior to the fight at Duck Lake. The rapidity with which these and subsequent troops were thrown into the Northwest from eastern Canada kept quiet the disaffected Indians and Métis in the Qu'Appelle valley who might otherwise have joined the insurgents after their initial success. The early and rapid movement of the troops was one of the decisive actions of the campaign; it practically settled the issue of the rebellion before it had fairly begun.

At the same time the government took steps to remove the grievances of those who had not yet risen in arms. Extra supplies were immediately rushed to the wavering Indian bands. Two car loads of flour and 15 000 pounds of bacon were ordered to Indian Head. The allowances of rations were increased. Tea and tobacco were given to working Indians and requests for oxen and cattle complied with. The cost was considerable, but the Indian commissioner realized that the extra expense would probably prevent a general Indian rising. "We are impressing upon all our officials," he wrote to Macdonald, "the necessity of economy, but at this time it is essential that the Indians be kept busy and contented, and it would be false economy to be too sparing of provisions and other articles that tend to that end."[9] It was to be regretted that the wisdom of this advice had not been recognized during 1883 and 1884 and the unfortunate Indian rising of 1885 thus, possibly, avoided.

As far as the half-breed claims to patents and scrip were concerned, the government, having ignored the Métis petitions for ten years, virtually admitted their culpability for the rebellion by hastily appointing a commission to investigate these claims. The commission had been decided upon as early as January 1885,[10] but it was not until eleven days after Riel had formed his "Provisional Government of the Saskatchewan," that Messrs. Street, Forget, and Goulet, the last-named a Métis from Manitoba, were instructed to report upon the claims preferred by the Northwest half-breeds, and not until 6 April, that the commissioners were authorized to issue scrip in extinguishment of the half-breed title.[11] Had this action been taken during 1884 or earlier, it is more than probable that the Métis rising would never have been precipitated. But belated justice though it may have been, it was an expedient move to localize the half-breed rising to the district of St. Laurent, by removing elsewhere the grievances which had contributed so powerfully to Riel's rising on the North Saskatchewan.

The object of localization achieved, the second object was to crush the armed resistance of the Métis and the Indians by military force. The original intention of the major-general had been to move against St. Antoine or Batoche, the rebel headquarters, with two separate columns, but with the rising of Poundmaker and Big Bear it was deemed advisable to despatch three different columns against the three principal centres of disaffection, Batoche, Battleford, and Fort Pitt. The three bases of operations were fixed at Qu'Appelle, Swift Current, and Calgary. From the first General Middleton planned to take Batoche, thus relieving Prince Albert; from Swift Current Colonel Otter was to relieve Battleford; and from Calgary General Strange was to move against Big Bear via Edmonton and the valley of the North Saskatchewan, effecting a junction with Middleton at Fort Pitt.

The general strategy of the campaign was well conceived but poorly carried out. The movements of the troops were slow, their disposition inadequate, and their principal success fortuitous. The general in command had seen service against the Maoris in New Zealand and in the Indian Mutiny, but, in spite of the plaudits heaped upon him at the time, his management of the Northwest campaign was marked by undue deliberation and hesitancy. His was not the nature to descend to consultation and his lack of confidence in his men was apparent at every engagement. Trained in the theory of the impregnable British square he relied entirely upon infantry, thus forfeiting the advantage of mobility in a country which lent itself to rapid movement. His cavalry were stationed in the rear to protect the line of communications when they should have been at the front. Moreover, when cavalry were finally summoned to the front they were ordered there in inverse order of training! For mounted troops Middleton relied solely upon local corps, such as French's Scouts and Boulton's Scouts; even summoning to the critical centre at Batoche a hastily improvised mounted corps known as the Dominion Land Surveyors Intelligence Corps in preference to the Governor-General's Body-Guard—a well-trained cavalry corps under the command of Colonel G.T. Denison, one of the foremost cavalry officers of

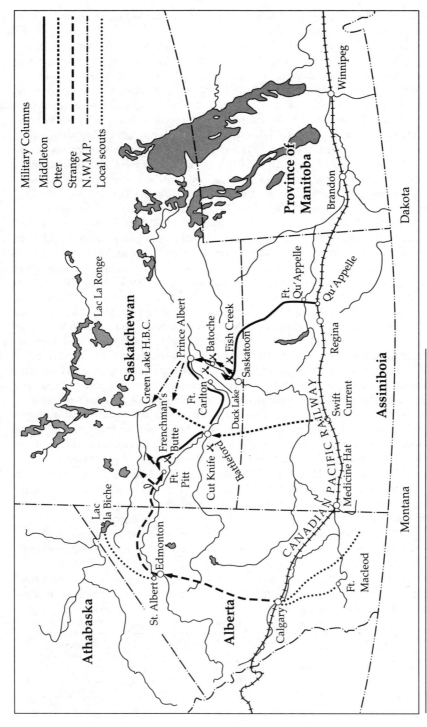

BATTLES OF THE NORTHWEST REBELLION, 1885

this time—the Quebec Cavalry School or the Winnipeg Cavalry, who remained in the rear doing the work ordinarily allotted to infantry. Had it not been for the fact that Riel overruled Dumont's plan to take advantage of the superior mobility of the Métis, Middleton's lack of horse might have proved an expensive blunder.

On 6 April Middleton set out from Fort Qu'Appelle, having halted there four days "to enable the 90th Battalion to fire blank and ball ammunition, as I found that many of the men had never pulled a trigger."[12] The march proceeded slowly. The weather was unfavourable. The winter snow was beginning to melt and the nights were "fearfully cold." On the first evening "the thermometer . . . fell tremendously, and at sunrise it was 23 degrees below zero, and all the tent pegs had to be cut out of the ground with axes next morning."[13] Moreover, Middleton's column was not yet complete in numbers, and the transport services, having been hastily improvised, left much to be desired. Finally, on the 17th Middleton reached Clarke's Crossing on the South Branch of the Saskatchewan river, about forty miles from the rebel headquarters, having covered approximately 180 miles in eleven days. Here he was overtaken by the Royal Grenadiers, bringing the total strength of the column to about 800 men.

At this point Middleton halted, and the next few days were spent in executing what later turned out to be an unnecessary and inadvisable manoeuvre. The force was divided into two columns, the second of which was transported with difficulty across the river to march parallel with the first column down the South Branch towards Batoche. Middleton was perfectly acquainted with the geographical position of Batoche, and the policy of dividing a small force on approaching the enemy country and placing an effective barrier between the two wings was, to say the least, questionable. If the left division was intended to carry out a flanking movement against the rebel stronghold its action would have been rendered useless by the impossibility of effective co-operation across an unbridged river. This move, in the end, not only served to delay the advance of Middleton's force thus giving valuable days to Riel to strengthen his position, but it deprived Middleton of the service of nearly half of his troops at the battle of Fish Creek on 24 April.

In the meantime the Métis were making every preparation to resist the troops. They had been in touch with Middleton's force ever since it had left Fort Qu'Appelle, by means of Indian and half-breed scouts, one of whom, Jérome Henry, accompanied the troops as a government freighter![14] In view of their reports Dumont, the Métis military leader, determined to harass the infantry column by a series of attacks under cover of the darkness. In his account of the campaign Dumont wrote:

> Une vingtaine de jours après,[15] on a appris, par nos éclaireurs qui étaient allés jusqu'à Qu'Appelle, à 260 milles environ de Batoche, que Middleton était en marche.
>
> Nous étions alors 350 hommes en tout, dont 200 étaient armés. J'ai proposé d'aller au devant des troupes et de les harceler pendant la nuit, en les empêchant surtout de dormir, persuadé que

c'était un bon moyen de les démoraliser et de leur faire perdre tout courage. Mais Riel n'y a pas consenti, disant que c'était trop sauvage et que d'ailleurs on s'exposait ainsi à tirer sur nos amis canadiens. Moi, j'aurais été déterminé à le faire sans scrupule, et même j'aurais volontiers fait sauter les chemins de fer, car je ne considérais pas comme des amis ceux qui s'unissaient aux Anglais, pour nous tuer et nous piller. Riel me disait; si vous les connaissiez, vous ne chercheriez pas à les traiter ainsi.

Quoiqu'il en soit, nous avons dû renoncer au projet d'aller rencontrer les ennemis sur un terrain avantageux pour nous, et j'en suis sûr, nous les aurions tellement abrutis qu'au bout de trois nuits ils se seraient entretués les uns les autres.[16]

Thus, in spite of his better judgment, Dumont gave in to Riel, such was his confidence in the former president of the provisional government: "J'ai cédé au conseil de Riel, quoique persuadé que humainement mon dessein était meilleur; mais j'avais confiance dans sa foi et dans ses prières, et que Dieu l'exaucerait."[17]

Riel, however, feared to weaken Batoche by allowing Dumont to carry out his plan of night attacks. The mounted police under Colonel Irvine were stationed at Prince Albert only forty miles north of Batoche, and constituted, in Riel's mind, a constant threat to the Métis capital. Riel had, moreover, been shaken by the fact that Dumont had been wounded at Duck Lake, and was loth to permit his military leader to expose himself unduly to danger. In a memorandum on the defence of Batoche, written on 22 April, Riel stated:

If anything happened to Dumont, it would not only be a misfortune for his friends, but an irreparable loss for the army and to the nation. If my Uncle Gabriel were cured of his wound I should be more willing to see him start on an expedition of this kind. If we get reinforcements I might change my opinion, I think, to a certain extent. Under present circumstances, I know, I understand, that it would be of great benefit to us to go and attack and harass the Mounted Police on the other side of the river, at Clarke's Crossing; but that would weaken us here, and I am afraid that in the meantime there might come from Prince Albert or elsewhere a force which would take all ours to repel.[18]

Such advice, although not unreasonable under the circumstances, was fatal to the Métis cause. Their chief hope of military success lay in taking advantage of Middleton's immobility by a series of rapid demoralizing thrusts against an untried column of infantry, not in the attempted defence of a single position against unfavourable odds.

Finally, however, Dumont could no longer be restrained. He informed Riel "que je ne pouvais plus suivre ses conseils humanitaires, et que j'étais decidé d'aller tirer sur les envahisseurs, et en cela, j'étais approuvé par mes gens."[19] On 23 April, with a mixed force of two hundred Métis, Cree,

Saulteaux, and Sioux, he advanced towards Middleton's position. Riel accompanied the force, conducting religious services during the halts. No sooner had they proceeded a few miles from Batoche when the news reached them that the mounted police from Prince Albert were on their way to make a sortie against the rebel headquarters. Riel at once returned with fifty men to reinforce the small garrison which had been left at Batoche. On the following morning Dumont with twenty men advanced to within half a mile of Middleton's camp. The main body, numbering 130, he stationed in a small ravine or coulée known as Fish Creek, which cut directly across Middleton's road and emptied into the river on his left. Dumont's plan was to draw the troops into the coulée and then to fire on them from behind the shelter of the trees. "Je voulais les traiter comme on traite les buffles," he declared.[20]

In many respects the half-breed tactics were similar to those used by the Boers. The rolling prairie, like the South African veldt, offered extensive cover to the defending force which invariably appeared to be much stronger than it really was. Like the Boers, the Métis kept to the valleys, coulées and hollows, thus placing their adversaries against the skyline whenever they attempted to advance down the slopes. Silhouetted against the sky the troops were admirable targets for the Métis marksmen, many of whom were old buffalo hunters and all of whom were familiar with every foot of the ground upon which they fought. The wonder is, not that the small numbers of half-breeds and Indians were able to check Middleton and Otter, but that the casualties of the citizen militia were not more numerous.

On the morning of the 24th General Middleton broke camp and resumed his deliberate progress towards Batoche. As the troops were entering what was recognized to be the enemy country, added precautions against surprise were taken. Boulton's Scouts were thrown out well in advance of the main body. Middleton, attended by his staff officers, accompanied them. As they approached the ravine the scouts discovered traces of camp fires; at the same time some of the Métis among Dumont's advance party betrayed their presence by firing upon the scouts. Boulton's men dismounted and returned the fire, while Dumont's force hastily retreated towards the edge of the coulée.[21] Middleton ordered the troops to advance and a heavy fire was exchanged. Although they had lost the inestimable advantage of surprise, the Métis had, nevertheless, the advantage of position. From behind the trees and brush of the ravine they were able to fire upon the enemy as they came over the horizon. As the battle progressed, however, the Métis became hard pressed. They attempted to drive back the troops by setting fire to the prairie but without success.[22] The pressure of numbers and the heavy fire of the soldiers, particularly from the artillery, discouraged many of Dumont's men and deserters from the Métis ranks became numerous. At the conclusion of the engagement the Métis numbered only fifty-four men.[23] Nevertheless, they were able to check effectively Middleton's advance, and at the end of the day remained in possession of the coulée. The half-breed success was due largely to the unorthodox tactics employed; although, according to Maxime Lépine, "We prayed all the day, and I think prayer did more than the bullets."[24]

On the whole the result of the battle was indecisive. Middleton was by no means defeated but he had failed to gain a victory. Only the eagerness of the half-breeds had prevented him from walking into a serious ambush. Had Middleton's left wing been in a position to participate in the battle and turn the Métis flank, in place of remaining helpless within the sound of the guns on the opposite side of the river, it is possible that Dumont's force might have been surrounded and captured. Instead, Dumont was given the opportunity to administer a severe check to Middleton which delayed for over a fortnight the attack upon Batoche.

While the first column under Middleton was thus engaged against the Métis on the South Saskatchewan, the second column under Colonel Otter succeeded in relieving the town of Battleford. Superintendent Herchmer of the mounted police had been ordered as early as 29 March to proceed north, but, unfortunately, the ice in the river having given way at Saskatchewan Landing, no further progress was possible for the time being. Herchmer then proceeded to Medicine Hat, where the steamer *Northcote* was being prepared to carry troops to the trouble area. On 11 April Colonel Otter, the officer commanding the second column of militia, was ordered to relieve Battleford "with as little delay as possible."[25] Herchmer then joined Otter, and the combined mounted police and militia force, numbering 543 men with three guns, left Swift Current on the 13th. Considerable difficulty was experienced in crossing the river at Sasktachewan Landing and it was not until the 18th that the march was definitely begun. The progress made by Otter's column was rapid and contrasted favourably with Middleton's deliberate movements. The country traversed in each case was rolling prairie presenting no serious obstacles; but Otter added a wagon train of some 200 men to his force and was thus able to provide transport for the greater number of his troops. The column averaged over thirty miles per day, and on 23 April, five days after leaving Saskatchewan Landing, Otter camped within three miles of his destination. On the following day the troops marched into Battleford amid the shouts of welcome of five hundred inhabitants who had been, for nearly a month, pent up inside an enclosed stockade some two hundred yards square.

The object of the third column, which was formed at Calgary, was to overawe the Indians of Alberta, to protect the outlying settlements, and to move via Edmonton and the North Saskatchewan valley against Big Bear. The protection of southern Alberta was important. Here the Blackfoot confederacy, composed of the strongest and most warlike tribes of the Northwest, held the balance of peace and war. If these Indians elected to join the rebels, a general Indian rising from Manitoba to the Rocky Mountains was not an improbability. Although the Blackfoot were treated with greater consideration on account of their warlike tradition, they too, like the other Indians of the plains, were embittered by the grim experience of civilization. As early as 1877–78 the head chief had been in communication with Louis Riel in the United States.[26] During 1884 the Indian agent reported that Riel's half-breed emissaries were again among the Blackfoot Indians, and that, as a result, their former friendly demeanour had given way to one of sulkiness and hostility. A half-breed, suspected of inciting the aborigines, was arrested by the mounted police but managed to escape and sought refuge in Crowfoot's lodge. The man was re-arrested but only in the face of manifest hostility of Crowfoot and the Blackfoot chiefs.[27]

When the news of the rebellion reached Ottawa the Canadian government, realizing the absolute necessity of placating the southern Alberta Indians, acted promptly. On 24 March, two days before Duck Lake, Macdonald telegraphed to Father Lacombe, a missionary greatly beloved by the Indians, asking him to see Crowfoot and endeavour to ensure the loyalty of the Blackfoot.[28] Lacombe went to the reserve, and on the 31st, replied to the prime minister that Crowfoot "promised me to be loyal no matter how things may turn elsewhere."[29] To assist Father Lacombe in his efforts, and to remove any possible cause for complaint among the Indians, Macdonald advised Dewdney that extra rations should be issued to the Indians.[30] In addition to complying with this request, Dewdney also recalled Agent Denny, who had resigned as a result of the economy cuts, and himself visited Blackfoot Crossing for assurance as to the sincerity of Crowfoot's professions. . . .

To discourage any inclination upon the part of the Blackfoot to go back on their word and to reassure the panic-stricken settlers, troops were quickly dispatched to southern Alberta. Calgary had already formed a troop of scout cavalry and a home guard under the command of Major-General Strange, a retired artillery officer ranching near the town, and on 8 April Strange was appointed to command the third column to move against the rebels. The local force was soon reinforced by the arrival of the 65th Rifles of Montreal, the Winnipeg Light Infantry, and the 9th Voltigeurs of Quebec. Provision was made for the defence of the southern part of the territory by volunteer companies and later by the 9th Voltigeurs, and on 20 April Strange proceeded north to Edmonton with the first division of his force.

Every precaution was taken against attack. Father Lacombe and the Reverend John McDougall of Morley went in advance of the troops to reassure the Indians, and to inform the settlers at Edmonton that the troops were advancing with all speed. The cavalry scouts under the command of Major Steele were detailed to protect the convey. Nothing that caution could dictate was neglected.

The march was not without its difficulties. The horses, with few exceptions, had seldom been ridden and bucked whenever mounted. At Red Deer Crossing the river was in flood and only one small skiff available as a ferry. To cross the swollen ford the wagon boxes had to be raised to prevent the supplies from getting wet and their contents damaged, and some of the carts were swept away. The cannon presented the most formidable problem. Finally a raft was constructed to carry the gun with picket ropes to serve as a ferry cable. The cable parted and the raft was salvaged with the greatest difficulty.[31]

On 1 May the first division of the column reached Edmonton, having covered about 210 miles in ten days. The other divisions followed in the course of the next few days. Small garrisons were placed on the line of communications at Red Deer and at Government Ford near Edmonton. Another force was sent to overawe the Indians on the Bears' Hill reserve, while the remainder advanced down the North Saskatchewan towards Big Bear and Fort Pitt.

While Otter and Strange were leading their respective columns against the Indians on the line of the North Saskatchewan, Louis Riel was endeavouring to bring about a concentration of those who had taken up arms against the government. The check administered to Middleton at Fish Creek enabled Riel and Dumont to dispatch urgent appeals for help to Poundmaker and Big Bear. Immediately after the engagement, runners were dispatched to the reserves to urge upon the Indians the necessity of joining the Métis force at Batoche. McLean stated in his *Reminiscences* that towards the end of April Big Bear received a letter from the half-breeds asking him to join Poundmaker without delay and promising, in the event of his agreeing, to send one hundred wagons and horses to assist him to move quickly. This junction was to be followed by an assault upon Battleford, after which the combined forces of the Indians would join Riel at Batoche.[32]

This plan was excellent strategy. The union of the three rebel forces would have brought their numbers to nearly one thousand and would have enabled Riel to prolong the rebellion, if not to inflict a decisive defeat upon the Canadian troops under Middleton. It was, however, rendered ineffective by the procrastination and lack of purpose which characterized the Indians as a fighting force. The demands of their . . . democracy rendered them incapable of rapid decision and much valuable time was lost in factional disputes.

Big Bear's band, it will be remembered, was composed of the allied forces of the Wood Cree and the Plain Cree. The former, less warlike and less affected by the advent of the white man, were well satisfied to have secured a large quantity of provisions in the pillage of Frog Lake, Cold Lake and Fort Pitt. The Plain Cree, harbouring a greater resentment against the whites, were determined to carry on a war of extermination. Thus the latter were anxious to move towards Battleford to join forces with Poundmaker, while their allies consistently opposed the plan. In this they were abetted by the white prisoners in the camp who fully realized the importance of preventing the junction. The result was a continual bickering and disputation. . . . The Plain Cree chiefs, however, made every effort to preserve the alliance and to convince their reluctant allies of the advantage to be gained from the half-breed proposal, and finally, about 1 May, Big Bear's camp began to move, by short marches, from Frog Lake towards Fort Pitt and Battleford.

In Poundmaker's camp a similar dissension prevailed. The chief himself, like Big Bear, was by no means heart and soul in the rebellion;[33] but the Assiniboines or Stonies, who had murdered their farm instructor and a neighbouring farmer before joining the Cree at Battleford, were inveterate in their hatred of the whites. Like Big Bear's Plain Cree they were strongly in favour of joining the Métis. Poundmaker was unwilling to move from his reserve. He suspected that all was not well in the Métis camp. The early messengers had conveyed the impression that Riel would carry all before him but now they asked for help. Moreover, nothing had been heard of the assistance which Riel had promised would be forthcoming from the United States. Poundmaker accordingly temporized. He replied to Riel's overtures with the statement that "he would send to Fort Pitt, to Big Bear's camp, and he would wait for him a while before he would go down to Riel."[34] On 29 April Poundmaker addressed a long letter to Riel. He informed him of the progress of the Indian rising, but instead of promising to join Riel at Batoche he asked the Métis leader to send men and ammunition to Battleford. His doubts as to Riel's position are apparent from this letter:

> I want to hear news of the progress of God's work. If any event has occurred since your messengers came away, let me know of it. Tell me the date when the Americans will reach the Canadian Pacific Railway. Tell me all the news that you have heard from all places where your work is in progress. . . . Here we have killed six white men. We have not taken the barracks yet, but that is the only entire building in Battleford. All the cattle and horses in the vicinity we have taken. We have lost one man, Nez Percé killed, he being alone, and one wounded. Some soldiers have come from Swift Current, but I do not know their number.[35] We have here guns and rifles of all sorts, but ammunition for them is short. If it be possible, we want you to send us ammunition of various kinds. We are weak only for the want of that. You sent word that you would come to Battleford when you had finished your work at Duck Lake. We wait still for you, as we are unable to take the fort without help. If you send us news send only one messenger. We are impatient to reach you. It would give us—encourage us much to see you, and make us work more heartily. Up to the present everything has gone well with us, but we are constantly expecting the soldiers to visit us here. We trust that God will be as kind to us in the future as he has in the past.[36]

Riel was not in a position to assist Poundmaker; rather he needed Poundmaker's assistance. Riel, therefore, replied in a fulsome strain telling the Indians of the "victory" at Fish Creek at which "nos volontaires . . . se conduisèrent . . . je ne dirai pas seulement commes des braves mais commes des héros." The letter, however, betrayed the critical position of the Métis when it asked:

> Nous vous demandons au nom du Bon Dieu de nous envoyer aussitôt que vous pourrez et si vous le voulez entre deux à deux à deux cent cinquante hommes et même trois cent s'il se peut, afin que non seulement nous puissions venir à bout de Middleton mais que nous puissions même après avoir anéanti, par la puissance de Dieu, une partie de son armée, faire prisonnier l'autre moitié; et la tenant en

otage amener le gouvernement d'Ottawa à traiter avec nous, et à lui faire reconnaître et respecter nos droits, les droits des Métis et des sauvages, Courage! Venez-vous en tous.[37]

This message was not received by Poundmaker until after his Indians had been attacked by Colonel Otter at Cut Knife Hill.

The engagement at Cut Knife was a failure. Otter's object was to prevent, if possible, the junction of Big Bear and Poundmaker and their union with Riel.[38] Although Poundmaker had made no deliberate assault upon the fort at Battleford, his men had raided and fired the town, murdered several white men and waylaid a mounted police patrol several days before Otter's arrival. That Poundmaker's intentions were by no means pacific is shown in his letter to Riel—quoted above—in which he asked for assistance to take the fort. Moreover, the Assiniboines in his camp had set up a "soldiers' lodge," and under the influence of a half-breed agitator, were anxious to join the Métis at Batoche. Otter was therefore justified in an attack, which, had it been successful, would have been considered as a master stroke rather than a blunder.

Otter did not consult General Middleton as to the advisability of the attack upon Poundmaker.[39] Instead he telegraphed to the lieutenant-governor for his approval, a breach of military etiquette that may be explained by the mistaken belief that it was necessary to consult the civil authority responsible for the administration of Indian affairs before launching the attack. On 26 April, two days after his relief of Battleford, Otter wired to Dewdney: "I would propose taking part of my force at once to punish Poundmaker, leaving one hundred men to garrison Battleford. Great depredations committed. Immediate decisive action necessary. Do you approve?"[40] Dewdney wired his approval on the same day, adding a note of warning: "Think you cannot act too energetically or Indians will collect in large numbers. Herchmer knows country to Poundmaker's reserve. Sand hills most dangerous ground to march through. Be sure to secure good reliable scouts."[41] Otter therefore dispatched his scouts to reconnoitre. They reported on the 29th that some two hundred Cree and Assiniboine were camped near Poundmaker's reserve, about thirty-eight miles from Battleford. Otter informed Dewdney on the 30th that he was prepared to move and on the afternoon of the following day set out with a force of 325 men, forty-eight wagons, two seven-pounder guns and a Gatling machine gun.[42] They pushed forward during the night hoping to surprise the Indians at sunrise on May 2nd.

The Indians were encamped on the western slope of Cut Knife Hill where Poundmaker and the Crees had, many years before, defeated the Sarcee warrior, Cut Knife. Poundmaker was daily anticipating an attack from the troops and had obviously chosen his position accordingly. The surprise which Otter had planned was, therefore, only partial. An Indian camp can scarcely ever be said to be asleep, and Otter's column was discovered at daybreak as it was descending the hill opposite and preparing to cross Cut Knife Creek. At once the troops and the Indians raced towards

Cut Knife Hill. As the mounted police and the gunners gained the crest of the hill the Indians fell back into the coulées surrounding it. Taking advantage of the cover thus afforded by the trees and shrubbery, they worked their way around until they had practically surrounded the troops and from their concealed position poured a rapid cross-fire upon the soldiers as they lay exposed upon the hill. For seven hours the fight continued. Finally, with his men exhausted by the all-night march and the hunger and fatigue of the engagement, and realizing that his position would become more and more untenable as the darkness descended, Otter gave the order to retire. The line of retreat was cleared by a charge, and the column, under cover of fire from the cannon and machine gun, made its way over the creek and up the hill on the opposite side. The retreat might easily have developed into a rout. Poundmaker, however, held back his victorious warriors and prevented them from cutting the retreating column to pieces.[43]

Although the troops outnumbered the Indians by three to two and acquitted themselves nobly under fire, Otter's force accomplished nothing. It is possible that, had Otter taken advantage of the surprise, and hurled his few cavalry directly at the Indian camp, instead of being awed by a few casualties, the Indians might have surrendered in order to save their women and children. The Indians' weakest point was their anxiety to keep the fighting as far as possible from the camp, but they were allowed to choose their own fighting ground. The battle of Cut Knife taught the Indians a lesson; but not the lesson which Otter had hoped to teach them. Had he succeeded he would have put an end to any possibility of the junction of the Indians with the half-breed force. Instead his failure rendered it more probable.

On the same or following day the messengers arrived from Batoche with Riel's appeal for help, and with the war party in the ascendant, Poundmaker's Indians began to move towards the half-breed headquarters. On 14 May the Indians, having reached the Eagle Hills, intercepted a supply train en route to Battleford. They were thus able to renew their stock of provisions and took twenty-two prisoners. Later in the same day a skirmish occurred between a small party of Indians and a scouting party from the fort. The scouts suffered one killed and one wounded and beat a hasty retreat to Battleford.[44] Three days later a messenger arrived with the news that the Métis and the soldiers were engaged in a battle at Batoche and with another urgent appeal for assistance from Riel. The Indians, however, did not begin to move until it was too late. On 19 May Poundmaker learned that the Métis had been defeated by the troops after a three days' engagement and that Riel and Dumont were fugitives.[45]

Following the check at Fish Creek, Middleton remained for nearly a fortnight in camp at that place. He had to make provision for his wounded and hesitated to advance without reinforcements. The division which had been so laboriously transported to the left bank of the river at Clarke's Crossing now rejoined the main column and two companies of the Midland Battalion, The Surveyors' Intelligence Corps and a Gatling gun were ordered to join the General's force. It is difficult to understand why Middleton did not order up either the Governor-General's Body-Guard or the Quebec Cavalry from the Qu'Appelle trail: both of these were better mounted and better trained than the improvised Surveyors' Corps.

On 7 May Middleton began to move towards Batoche, his force numbering approximately 850 men.[46] On board the steamer *Northcote*, which had brought the reinforcements from Swift Current, were placed thirty-five men from the Infantry School. The steamer had already been fortified, the object being to use her in a combined attack upon Batoche. On the 9th the troops advanced slowly towards their objective. It had been previously arranged that the *Northcote* should drop downstream to co-operate in the attack which had been scheduled to begin at eight a.m. The General, however, either miscalculated the marching speed of his column or misunderstood the proposed course of action, as the troops, unfortunately, did not arrive until nine a.m., one hour after the *Northcote* had opened fire on the rebels.[47] Hence the advantages of co-operation were lost. The steamer drifted down the river, her mast and funnels carried away by the steel ferry cable which had been lowered by the half-breeds to stop her, and was soon out of range of the battlefield.

Middleton found the rebel position well chosen and strongly entrenched. On the left the South Saskatchewan river flowed westerly for about three-fourths of a mile, then turning sharply it ran almost due north. The bank on the easterly side was bold and steep and well covered with timber and undergrowth. Nearing Batoche it gradually flattened out, rising again lower down the river. The approach to the village was defended by a line of rifle pits or trenches along the edge of the bank. These extended down the river for nearly a mile and were placed at short intervals from each other. The main position of the rebels extended along the edge of a range of hills running parallel with the river and forming the eastern slope of the valley. The slopes of these hills were fairly well wooded and cut by several coulées which afforded excellent protection to the defending force. Independent of the main line of rifle pits, which extended along the brow of the hill, were many others, placed at various points on the face of the hill, which might possibly become a commanding position. The pits were admirably constructed for their purpose. They were about three or four feet deep with breastworks of earth and logs channelled for the rifles. From these pits a constant fire could be directed against the enemy with more or less impunity. The effectiveness of these fortifications is shown by the fact that the Métis sustained no serious casualties during the first three days of the engagement. Middleton himself declared "on inspecting the scene of action after it was over, I was astonished at the strength of the position and at the ingenuity and care displayed in the construction of the rifle pits."[48]

On the first day of the battle Middleton received a definite check. The rebels kept up a steady fire from their trenches as the troops and batteries approached the crest of the hill. Only the rapid fire from the machine gun offered any covering for the movements of Middleton's force. The rebels, it will be observed, were using the same tactics as at Fish Creek and Cut Knife, namely, firing from naturally protected hollows upon an enemy advancing over an unsheltered horizon; unorthodox tactics but eminently successful. Towards evening Middleton's men retired into a zareba which had been formed about a mile to the rear of the battlefield. The same operation was repeated the following day and again on the 11th.[49] The troops, under cover of an artillery barrage, advanced to the edge of the hill, engaged in skirmishes with the rebels, suffered a few casualties and then retired into the fortified zareba for the night.

This policy of delayed action had two important results. In the first place it wore down the resistance of the Métis. They were not prepared to undergo a long siege. The majority of the half-breeds were armed, not with rifles, but with smooth-bore shot guns. On the second day the Brigade Surgeon stated that the rebels were using slugs and duck shot in their shot guns. On the third day their fire became noticeably less, and Bishop Grandin later stated that they were reduced to using small stones and nails for ammunition.[50] It must be remembered, moreover, that many of the Métis were only half-hearted in their resistance, having been forced to take up arms by the militant party amongst them.

But while Middleton's persistence discouraged the Métis, his inaction irritated the troops. The militia officers felt that the General had no confidence in his men and they began to lose confidence in him. The men were indignant at the constant rumours that British Regulars would have to be sent for, but saw little hope of redeeming themselves by Middleton's tactics. It was, therefore, with a feeling of restlessness that the battle was resumed the following day.

On 12 May Middleton planned a great combined movement. Following a reconnaissance on the previous day, he determined to move around to the north-east of Batoche with 150 men, one cannon and the Gatling machine gun, in order to engage the line of rifle pits to the right of the village. In the meantime the main body of troops under Colonel Van Straubenzie were to attack from the south. Owing to a misunderstanding, however, Van Straubenzie remained quiet, waiting to hear Middleton's force engaging the enemy on the right. The misunderstanding turned out to be a fortunate one. The silence on the left apparently convinced the Métis that Middleton's move was genuine and that the main attack would come from that direction. They were, therefore, unprepared for what happened.

Middleton was thoroughly displeased and the Midlanders and the Grenadiers were sent to take up their old position on the left flank as on the previous day. But upon this occasion there was no holding the men. Led by Colonels Williams and Grasset they advanced with a cheer, driving the enemy out of the first line of rifle pits. Pushing on they dashed down the slope towards the village of Batoche scattering the Métis before them. In the meantime the General rushed forward his support. The 90th, Boulton's Scouts, the Surveyors, the machine gun, and the batteries followed the charging line, and in a few moments Batoche had fallen. The Métis fled to the woods; any hope of a further resistance was at an end.[51]

On 15 May Riel was taken prisoner. . . .

On the 26th Poundmaker and his men came in, "the most pathetic and picturesque procession I have ever seen," wrote an observer.[52] Middleton, fresh from his victory, refused to take the Indian chief's hand in greeting, disarmed his followers, lectured them severely, and imprisoned Poundmaker and his head men.

With the surrender of Riel and Poundmaker, the only remaining rebel in the field was Big Bear. . . .

NOTES

1. *Gazette* (Montreal), 25 March 1885. The *Mail* (Toronto) of 24 March stated, "It is a monstrous exaggeration to say that rebellion is afoot. Riel, who is never happy except when he is posing as the hero of some desperate cause, has talked war for months; but no one acquainted with the ex-President will credit him with either the courage or the capacity to make serious trouble." The *Times* (Winnipeg), 23 March 1885, expressed a similar view.

2. Macdonald to Dewdney, telegram, 14 March 1885, Macdonald Papers, vol. 4. Fathers Lacombe and Hugonard were Roman Catholic priests with great influence over the Indians and the Métis.

3. Dewdney to Macdonald, telegram, 22 March 1885, Dewdney Papers, vol. 5.

4. Macdonald to Dewdney, telegram, 23 March 1885, Dewdney Papers, vol. 5.

5. Jackson, "Report on Questions Relative to the Suppression of the Insurrection in the North-West Territories in 1885, 24 Dec. 1886," Canada Sessional Papers (hereafter CSP) 1887, vol. 8, no. 9c.

6. Sackville-West to Bayard, 28 March 1885, Notes from the British Legation, vol. 111, mss., Department of State.

7. Bayard to Sackville-West, 28 March 1885, Notes to the British Legation, vol. 19, mss., Department of State.

8. Bayard to Sackville-West, 11 April 1885, Notes to the British Legation, vol. 19, mss., Department of State.

9. McGirr (pp. Dewdney) to Macdonald, 24 April 1885, Department of Indian Affairs, Ottawa (hereafter ID), file 19550–1.

10. Report of a Committee of the Privy Council, 28 Jan. 1885, CSP 1885, vol. 13, no. 116.

11. Burgess to Street, 30 March 1885 and Macpherson to Street, telegram, 6 April 1885, ibid. Oliver is in error when he writes "it was after the granting of the scrip in March 1885 . . . that Riel formed his provisional government" (Oliver, *Saskatchewan and Alberta, General History 1870–1912,* Canada and its Provinces, 19:210). Riel's government was formed on 19 March. The commission was not appointed until 30 March nor the issue of scrip authorized until 6 April.

12. Middleton, Special Report upon the Military Operations in the North-West, 30 Dec. 1885, CSP 1886, vol. 5, no. 6a.

13. Ibid.

14. Henry, "Report, 23 April 1885" and Carrière, "Report, 22 April 1885," Dewdney Papers, vol. 8. Carrière reported that the troops had three cannon "and another machine with a handle that fires 100 shots a minute."

15. After the engagement at Duck Lake.

16. Dumont, *Le Récit de Dumont,* in Ouimet, *La Verité sur la Question Métisse au Nord-Ouest,* 127.

17. Ibid.

18. Riel, "Advice on the defence of Batoche, 22 April 1885," Dewdney Papers, vol. 8.

19. Dumont, *Le Récit de Dumont*, 130.

20. Ibid., 131.

21. Boulton, *Reminiscences of the North-West Rebellions*, 225–26; Dumont, *Le Récit de Dumont*, 132.

22. Middleton, "Report on the Engagement at Fish Creek, 1 May 1885," app. A, CSP 1886, vol. 5, no. 6a.

23. Middleton stated in his "Report on the Engagement at Fish Creek" that the Métis numbered 280 men. Begg, basing his account on Middleton, gives the same figure. (*The Creation of Manitoba or a History of the Red River Troubles*, 3:213.) According to Dumont, the Métis reached Fish Creek with 150 men. Dumont then went ahead with 20 and stationed 130 in the coulée. At the end of the engagement Dumont had only 54 men when Edouard Dumont arrived with a reinforcement of 80 horsemen. (Dumont, *Le récit de Dumont*, 134.) This is corroborated by reports by Maxime Lépine and Charles Trottier on the engagement. Trottier stated that he counted 48 men and then 6 more came out of the wood, making a total of 54. Dumont's casualties consisted largely of deserters from the Métis ranks. As Middleton had no means of telling the exact numbers of his opponents his estimate is very likely exaggerated.

24. Lépine, "Report on the Battle of April 24th," Dewdney Papers, vol. 8.

25. Otter to Major-General Middleton, 26 May 1885, app. E, CSP 1886, vol. 5, no. 6a.

26. L'Heureux, "Report, 1 Nov. 1886," Macdonald Papers, vol. 7. L'Heureux was the interpreter on Crowfoot's reserve.

27. Steele, *Forty Years in Canada*, 183–84.

28. Macdonald to Lacombe, telegram, 24 March 1885, ID file 1955-1.

29. Lacombe to Macdonald, telegram, 31 March 1885, ID file 1955-1.

30. Macdonald to Dewdney, telegram, 1 April 1885, ID file 1955-1.

31. Strange, "Report of Operations of Alberta Field Force from March 1885, to July 2nd, 1885," app. G, CSP 1886, vol. 5, no. 6a; Perry to Irvine, 19 Aug. 1885, app. F, CSP 1886, vol. 6, no. 8; Steele, *Forty Years in Canada*, 214.

32. McLean, *Reminiscences of the Tragic Events at Frog Lake and in Fort Pitt District with some of the Experiences of the Writer and his Family during the North-West Rebellion of 1885*, mss., Hudson's Bay Company, London, 20.

33. On 14 May Indian Agent Macrae wrote to Dewdney: "I learn that that chief has twice been serious of sending a messenger to us—once to treat—and subsequently to desire the garrison to leave the country. It would seem . . . that his camp has been divided into a peace and war party; if this is so, it is to be greatly regretted that we have been unable to cause a separation of the two." ID file 19550-3.

34. Desjardins, "Evidence, The Trial of Poundmaker," CSP 1886, vol. 13, no. 52. See also Jefferson's evidence.

35. This was Otter's force.

36. Poundmaker to Riel, 29 April 1885, Confidential Papers, Department of Justice. See also Desjardins, "Evidence, The Trial of Poundmaker," CSP 1886, vol. 13, no. 52.

37. Riel to Poundmaker, 1 May 1885, Confidential Papers, Department of Justice.

38. Otter, "Report on the Engagement at Cut Knife Hill, 5 May 1885," app. B, CSP 1886, vol. 5, no. 6a.

39. Middleton disclaimed any responsibility for the attack. "The movement which led to the engagement was made without my orders, though Lieutenant-Colonel Otter had the approval of Lieutenant-Governor Dewdney, to whom however he should not have applied on such a purely military matter." Middleton, "Suppression of Rebellion in the North-West Territories," *The United Service Magazine* (Jan. 1894), 380.

40. Otter to Dewdney, telegram, 26 April 1885, Dewdney Papers, vol. 2.

41. Dewdney to Otter, telegram, 26 April 1885, Dewdney Papers, vol. 2.

42. Otter, "Report on the Engagement at Cut Knife Hill, 5 May 1885."

43. Bigonnesse, letter, 7 June 1885, *Missions of the Oblates of Mary Immaculate* (hereafter *Missions des OMI*), vol. 23 (1885), 336; Jefferson, *Fifty Years on the Saskatchewan* (Canadian North-West Historical Society publications, vol. 1, no. 5), 143; Cochin, *Reminiscences of Louis Cochin* (Canadian North-West Historical Society publications, vol. 1, no. 2, 1927), 17–18. Both Jefferson and Father Cochin were prisoners in Poundmaker's camp.

44. Otter to Middleton, 26 May 1885, app. E, CSP 1886, vol. 5, no. 6a.

45. Cochin, *Reminiscences of Louis Cochin*, 19.

46. Middleton, "Special Report upon the Military Operations in the North-West, 30 Dec. 1885."

47. Captain Smith, who was in charge of the *Northcote* stated in his "Report, 13 May 1885" (app. C.1, CSP 1886, vol. 5, no. 6a), that Middleton ordered him to reach Batoche at "the hour named by you, 8 a.m." Middleton, on the other hand, stated in his report ("Report on the Capture of Batoche and the Surrender of Riel, 31 May 1885," app. C, CSP 1886, vol. 5, no. 6a) that the time was fixed at 9 a.m. The only other testimony on this point is that of Colonel Houghton, deputy adjutant general, who stated in a letter to the Montreal *Gazette* (*Gazette*, 31 March 1894) that the steamer was under orders to be at Batoche at 8 a.m., and that its failure to connect with the troops was due to the fact that Middleton was an hour late in reaching the point of attack.

48. Middleton, "Report on the Capture of Batoche and the Surrender of Riel, 31 May 1885."

49. In his account of the fighting of 11 May, Middleton wrote, "though as yet we had not made much progress I resolved, to use a historical expression, 'to peg away' until I succeeded in my object of taking Batoche, which I was sure I should do."

50. Mgr. Grandin to T.R.P. Supérieur-Général, 17 Oct. 1885, *Missions des OMI*, vol. 24 (1886), 23.

51. The responsibility for the charge at Batoche has been a matter of considerable dispute. Middleton in his "Report" and Van Straubenzie (Van Straubenzie to the Montreal *Gazette*, 22 July 1885, the *Gazette*, 27 July 1885) both claimed to have ordered the charge. Other evidence seems to show that the charge was a spontaneous development and was led by Colonel Williams of the Midland Battalion. In the first place, as Colonel Denison points out (*Soldiering in Canada*, 297), General Middleton was at lunch, the 90th and the two mounted units as well as the machine gun and batteries were resting in the zareba. Only 260 men were opposite the enemy, while the remainder, about 470, were behind the lines. "But who ever heard," wrote Denison, "of a General commencing an action with one-fourth or one-third of his men, with only thirty rounds of ammunition each, and with his artillery and cavalry unharnessed and unsaddled!" Denison attributed the charge to Williams. Captain Kirwan, assistant transport officer in the *Gazette* (Montreal), 8 July 1885, and W.P.E., a member of the Surveyors' Intelligence Corps, in the *Mail* (Toronto), 6 June 1885, support this statement. Colonel Houghton, deputy adjutant general, declared that the Canadian militia officers charged the rifle pits on their own initiative. "Had they been unsuccessful, they would have been tried by court-martial and shot, but being in close touch with their men, and knowing their metal, they drove the rebels from cover and broke the back of the rebellion" (Black, *A History of Saskatchewan and the Old North-West*, 322).

The half-breed tradition of the charge at Batoche is interesting. The half-breeds claim to have run out of ammunition and "in a bravado gesture of defiance they drove home their last charge of powder into their muzzle loaders and fired their ramrods at the troops. Some of the militia, seeing these rods flying amongst them, guessed that the ammunition of their enemies was exhausted and advanced with more boldness. The movement spread along the line and developed into the final spontaneous charge that broke the rebel defence." Jefferys, "Fifty Years Ago," *Canadian Geographical Journal* (June 1935), vol. 10, no. 6.

52. Kennedy, *The Book of the West*, 112.

CANADA'S FIRST EXPEDITIONARY FORCE: THE CANADIAN CONTINGENT IN SOUTH AFRICA, 1899–1900 ⋄

DESMOND MORTON

○

"Never since 1899," wrote Charles Stacey, the great Canadian military historian, speaking of one of Canada's later conflicts "has the outbreak of a war found the national government so deeply and gravely divided."[1] The circumstances surrounding the decision to send an official contingent to the South African War contained a warning of the deep divisions that war in the twentieth century would bring to Canadian society. Canadian historians have dealt more than adequately with the political facets of that decision which led to Canada's first direct contribution to an imperial war, but they have tended to forget the force once it dropped down the St. Lawrence on 30 October 1899.[2] This indifference has obscured other precedents that would set patterns repeated in two world wars and in Korea. In South Africa, for example, in spite of the wishes of at least some members of the Laurier government, Canadians fought as a unit under their own commander. Their military reputation was acquired without a period of intensive training and acclimatization when green troops, rushed into battle, might well have disgraced themselves. Even later problems of inappropriate equipment, symbolized by the notorious Ross rifle of the First World War, were presaged in South Africa by the Oliver equipment, a worthless water bottle and canvas uniforms that either chafed the wearer or disintegrated.[3]

Canada's militia had never been involved in overseas expeditions. Its ostensible purpose was to engage in any renewal of the War of 1812; its actual role was intermittent aid to the civil power, ranging from "strike duty" to the 1885 Campaign. Militia colonels, "anxious for excitement or notoriety," in Sir John A. Macdonald's phrase, might offer their battalions for imperial service but neither Ottawa nor Whitehall would approve.[4]

⋄ *Canadian Defence Quarterly* 15, 3 (Winter 1985/86), 41–46.

During his period in command of the force, 1890 to 1895, Major-General Ivor Herbert turned the tiny permanent force into regiments in the hope that as Canada's "regulars" they might, one day, serve as imperial reinforcements. By 1898, however, at the insistence of Major-General Edward Hutton, they had reverted to their role as training schools for the militia.[5]

The approach of war in South Africa changed Hutton's priorities. As the eager servant of British imperial policy, he understood the wishes of the colonial secretary, Joseph Chamberlain. How convenient it would be if the crisis produced "spontaneous" demonstrations as evidence to the world of the devotion of the self-governing dominions. Not only did Hutton draft a plan for a contingent of 1200 men; he also helped organize the "spontaneity." Not until early September, 1899, did he share his plans with his minister, Dr. Fred Borden. By then, events in South Africa had hurried along their course. As tensions built, the two Boer republics decided to attack before the British could reinforce their garrisons in Natal and at the Cape Colony. On 2 October, the Boer commandos struck deep into Natal. In Whitehall, British activity redoubled. Identical telegrams from the Colonial Office welcomed each dominion's offer of troops and instructed that 125-man units would be welcome, "infantry most preferred, cavalry least."[6]

In Canada, the crisis fired a jingo spirit among English-speaking communities. The Boer invasion broke the last moral scruples about making war. In French Canada, there was cool neutrality, tinged with resentment at the racial arrogance the moment provoked among the majority. The Colonial Office telegram caused consternation in Ottawa. No Canadian offer had been made and none was planned. When Hutton's plan appeared in the 2 October issue of the *Canadian Military Gazette*, a corrosive suspicion spread that it was he or his friend, Lord Minto, the governor general, who had made the offer.[7] What certainly became clear to a shaken Sir Wilfrid Laurier was that even fellow Liberals were telling him to send a contingent or get out. On 14 October, an order-in-council, composed with all the painful indirection of any compromise, explained that the government would help the many Canadians who wanted to volunteer by sending eight of the small units Chamberlain had requested.[8] It was Lord Minto who then persuaded his prime minister that Canada's dignity demanded nothing less than a proper regiment of infantry under Canadian officers. Lieutenant-Colonel William Otter, a grizzled veteran of forty years in the militia and permanent force, including the Fenian Raids and the 1885 Campaign, was the only possible choice for the command.[9]

The British deadline to recruit, equip, and dispatch a contingent was 31 October. One company was raised in the West, three in Ontario, and two each in Quebec and the Maritimes.[10] By the end of the month, they gathered at the Citadel in Quebec to put on the rifle-green uniforms provided for them. Only on 27 October, after would-be officers had exerted their last ounce of political influence, were positions gazetted. Otter's immediate subordinates were Major Lawrence Buchan, a Liberal from Manitoba who had once served as his adjutant in the Queen's Own Rifles, and Major Oscar Pelletier, the son of the Speaker of the Senate. The *Sardinian*, an elderly Allan Line steamer chartered for the voyage, was soon crammed with

1061 passengers, including 62 officers, nurses, chaplains, war correspondents, and an "Official Recorder." It departed on 30 October with a day to spare.[11]

Promptly nicknamed the "Sardine," the ship would have been crowded with half the number, to say nothing of the improvised stables, latrines, and extra lifeboats. In impossible conditions, Otter had to organize his battalion, issue kit, and do whatever training was possible. Only a handful of non-commissioned officers and British army veterans could help. Most of the officers foisted on him and even some he had chosen himself proved to be little help. Like Canadians in later wars, Otter's men were confident that they were ready to meet the enemy.[12] Otter knew differently. At Ridgeway in 1866 and at Cut Knife Hill in 1885, he had seen raw troops under fire. That experience, and his own personality, convinced Otter that only discipline, training, and hardship made a soldier.[13]

This would have been a hard doctrine at any time. On an overcrowded, broiling troopship and later at Belmont in the Karroo desert, the circumstances drained away the wit and resilience which help any soldier to endure.[14] At 57, Otter was physically equal to the ordeal but his temper was not. He forbade the exuberant cheering and the fraternization of officers and men as equally "volunteerish". He ordered drill and route marches when British troops rested in the shade. When officers complained, he ignored them.[15] A good many found their health compelled them to retire to Cape Town. "Otter is a martinet, pure and simple," complained a soldier in the *Toronto World*, "always trying to stand upon a dignity which is altogether above him."[16] Even Hart McHarg, a future CEF colonel, complained of Otter's "supercilious indifference" to the welfare of his men.[17] "Please do not worry about these complaints," Otter himself advised his wife, "as the men have not the least reason for them as far as I am concerned." Influential friends in Toronto made sure that editors suppressed most of the grumbling letters from the front.[18]

The Boer War had gone far worse for the British than anyone had expected. Modern weapons and a mobile, venturesome enemy produced a series of humiliating defeats. Far from being symbolic, the colonial contingents would be needed. In December, a second official Canadian contingent—two mounted rifle battalions and three artillery batteries—was raised.[19] Nevertheless, the 2nd (Special Service) Battalion of the Royal Canadian Regiment kept drilling and waiting. Fortunately for its morale, the war shifted west to the Cape Colony. A new British commander-in-chief, Lord Roberts, and his chief of staff, Sir Herbert Kitchener, passed through Belmont on 8 February 1900. They found the Canadians fit for service. As part of Major-General Horace Smith-Dorrien's 19th Brigade, they would share in a plan to envelop and destroy the Boer army besieging Kimberley.[20] For the Canadians, that meant five days of marching through blinding dust and blazing heat, with only a rare muddy waterhole as oasis. The ordeal was almost in vain. Piet Cronje broke off his siege, gathered his men and the vast carts, families, and flocks that had accompanied the Boers to war, and raced for safety. On 17 February, he was almost clear when a handful of British cavalry caught and held him at Paardeberg.[21]

At dawn on the 18th Smith-Dorrien's brigade joined the battle. The Canadians forded the Modder River, moved cautiously forward and then lay, thirsty, hungry, and exhausted, behind anthills and boulders as Boer bullets cracked overhead.[22] Meanwhile, a furious General Kitchener rode around Cronje's perimeter, ordering a series of futile frontal assaults in the hope of capturing the Boer *laager*. Late in the afternoon, he found Smith-Dorrien's reserve battalion. Its colonel was all too eager for a fight. Smith-Dorrien, watching the action from a convenient hill, was horrified to see his men cross behind the Canadians, turn and charge through their lines. Otter's men rose and joined the rush. Boer marksmen had an easy target. The eager British colonel died. So did many of his men. Most of the twenty-one Canadian dead and sixty-five wounded fell in that hopeless assault.[23]

At nightfall, the survivors withdrew, secretly content that they had passed their baptism of fire. For a week they waited while British heavy artillery was collected to pulverize Cronje's *laager*. Huge geysers of smoke and dirt rose as British artillery pounded the Boer camp. At intervals, the Canadians rested and filled their waterbottles from the only source, an evil-smelling Modder River, whose slow current now carried the putrescent bodies of horses, cattle, and men.[24] On 26 February, it was the Canadian turn to man the trenches. It was also the eve of Majuba Day, the Boer celebration of their triumph over the British in 1881. The Canadians would help prepare vengeance. At 2:00 a.m. on the 27th, Otter's men climbed out of their trenches and moved cautiously forward. Half an hour passed. Suddenly two shots rang out. The troops threw themselves to the ground as a furious fusillade broke overhead. "Retire and bring back your wounded," a voice shouted. Most of the Canadians got up and raced back to their positions. Two companies on the right, better shielded and perhaps unaware of the panic, stayed put. When dawn broke and Cronje passed the order to his men to surrender, the Canadians could claim the victory at a cost of twelve dead and thirty-three wounded.[25]

Reality hardly mattered. The night attack, as so often happens, was a misadventure. Cronje had decided on surrender already. Symbolism mattered very much. The Canadians had avenged Majuba and won the first unequivocal British victory of the war. The British House of Commons rose to cheer the Canadians. So did the Canadian Parliament. A more tangible sign of pleasure was the government's decision to make up the difference between British and Canadian pay scales.[26] Indeed, with an election year upon them, Liberals and Conservatives were eager to make the war an issue. Tories denounced government incompetence for failing to provide details of the Paardeberg casualties—and then for letting the pro-Liberal Toronto *Globe* reveal the names. Why were there no reinforcements for a battalion that, by June, was reduced to a mere 438, all ranks? Best of all was the "emergency ration" scandal—the son of a prominent Montreal Liberal sold the government near-worthless products.[27]

The reverberations added enormously to Otter's burdens. From Paardeberg, Roberts had marched his victorious army to Bloemfontein, capital of the Orange Free State. He planned a brief rest. Instead, a typhoid epidemic and attacks by Boer commandos tied down the army for a month and a half. Drinking from the Modder guaranteed that Canadians shared in the sickness. Careful nursing and adequate medical supplies would have saved most of the sick but Roberts had cut medical services to make his army more mobile and the field hospitals at Bloemfontein became a scandal.[28] The hot weather also ended and Canadians were cold, wet, and hungry as they waited in their bivouacs. Meanwhile, a weary Otter sat under his ox-cart in the rain, struggling with the help of a single clerk to deal with the demands for reports, returns, explanations, and justifications that poured in from Ottawa as well as from his British superiors. Canadian officers, scattered across South Africa, added to their burdens. To his wife, at least, Otter made no secret of his misery: "No one has any idea of the troubles I have in serving two masters, the Imperial people and our own. I would not undertake such a thing again for a great deal more than I shall ever get out of it."[29]

On 23 April, when the campaign resumed, Canadian morale improved. A more dashing division commander, Sir Ian Hamilton, helped Smith-Dorrien's brigade win a reputation as "the very finest in the whole army," according to Sir Arthur Conan-Doyle.[30] At Israel's Poort on the 25th, when the battalion's front line was pinned down by Boer fire, a few men dodged back to safety. Sensing panic, Otter raced to the spot and drove them back to their line. A bullet through his chin and neck almost ended Otter's life. His successor was the plump and popular Major Buchan.[31] A month later, when Otter returned, his battalion had reached the Vaal. On 29 May, the Canadians joined in the attack on Doornkop. On their left, the Gordon Highlanders lost ninety-seven dead and wounded; Otter's men list only eight wounded, thanks to the terrain and more cautious tactics.[32]

Doornkop should have been the last victory. On 5 June, Pretoria fell. The Boer generals met to discuss surrender. The Canadians were homesick and fed up with South Africa and soldiering. Even their colonel agreed; "blood and sand and everything that is disagreeable all for a bit of riband and a piece of silver."[33] It was not to be. Instead of giving up, Boer commandos swept down on Lord Roberts' rear, cut the rail line and took seven hundred prisoners. The war would last another two years until 31 May 1902 at Vereeniging. Instead of triumph, Roberts had to adjust to the ugly business of guerilla war. Far from cutting his forces, he needed troops to guard every village and railway station and to form the mobile columns that could chase the evasive Boer commandos. Instead of going home, the Canadians were sent to the dreary mining town of Springs for a month and a half of garrison duty.[34] On 2 August, they were loaded on trains but not for home. This time they were dumped off at Wolvehoek as part of a massive attempt to encircle the wily Christian de Wet. For three weeks, the heavily-laden infantrymen trudged after the Boer horsemen. In the end, to no one's great surprise, de Wet escaped. Surely that would be the end. Instead, the shrunken battalion was sent to garrisons along the Delangoa Bay railway.[35]

Otter knew as well as his men that their enlistments expired on 15 October. British commanders ignored his reminders: real soldiers did not quit a war. Ottawa had no answer to his anxious enquiries.[36] Finally, he had to approach Lord Roberts himself. The British commander knew that thousands of his men—colonial and British alike—were in the same position. Perhaps the Canadians would set an example: "It would be a great pity for any of them to leave now that the end seems near."[37] To Otter, that sounded like a direct command. To most of his men, it meant nothing. They wanted to go home and their officers did little to change their minds. A humiliated Otter had to go back to Roberts to confess that he had misjudged his troops.[38] Eventually, the promise of a triumphal march through Pretoria and a royal review in Britain helped persuade about three hundred men to stay. The main body, under Pelletier, left Cape Town on 1 October.[39]

The rest followed soon after. On 25 October, they shared in the annexation ceremonies as a defeated Transvaal rejoined the British Empire. A last appeal by Roberts fell on deaf ears.[40] Not even Otter dared challenge his men's verdict. A month-long voyage to England, in a troopship shared by the Household Cavalry was marred for Otter by fears that Canadian discipline might not be proof against British beer and hospitality. Pelletier's men, he was warned, had returned in a wash of drunkenness. Complained the Canadian adjutant general, "It is a great pity and rather disgusting to many people who are otherwise proud of what had been accomplished by our troops."[41] This time, Otter's men did not upset him. From Queen Victoria's review at Windsor to a luncheon at Kensington Palace, where Sergeant McHarg sang a stirring "Land of the Maple Leaf," the Canadians proved to be impeccable guests, and a proud Otter led them through a crowd of fifty thousand people at Liverpool to take ship for home.[42]

Other Canadians had followed him to South Africa and more would go. In all, 8372 served in the war though only 3499 served in official Canadian contingents. Strathcona's Horse was raised at the expense of Canada's wealthy high commissioner in London and other contingents were raised by the British themselves. A 3rd Battalion of the Royal Canadian Regiment replaced the British infantry of the Halifax garrison.[43]

In some ways, Canada's role in South Africa seemed like a brief aberration. Hutton's successors continued to prepare the militia for a wholly improbable war with the United States. Aid to the civil power flourished as never before between 1900 and 1914. Yet that was also the Canadian experience after 1919 and 1945. The precedent was set. Canadian soldiers knew what they would be doing in the next war. Training, tactics, and organization all grew closer to the British model. Otter and other officers who had served in South Africa filled key appointments in the years before 1914 and their experience of that war and the prestige Canadians had gained from their service gave the militia both a heritage and a sense of future purpose. The unresolved issues remained too—the problems of equipment, authority, and discipline. Were Canadians natural soldiers or did they need the austere discipline and the remorseless training that William Otter had demanded?[44]

Another eighty years of military experience have brought Canadians no closer to a resolution.

NOTES

1. C.P. Stacey, *Canada and the Age of Conflict*, vol. 1 (Toronto, 1977), 61.

2. See C.P. Stacey, *Canada and the Age of Conflict*, 1:57–68; Norman Penlington, *Canada and Imperial, 1896–1899* (Toronto, 1965); R.A. Preston, *Canada and "Imperialism Defense"* (Toronto, 1967), 260–82. A somewhat dated survey of the literature is by W.C.B. Kerr, "A Survey of the Literature on Canada's Participation in the South African War," *Canadian Historical Review* 4 (Dec. 1937).

3. See Desmond Morton, *Canada and War: A Political and Military History* (Toronto, 1981), 43ff. On equipment problems, see Canada Department of Militia and Defence, *Supplementary Report, Organization, Equipment Despatch and Service of the Canadian Contingents During the War in South Africa, 1899–1900* (C.S.P. 3sa, 1901), 12–13; W. Hart McHarg, *From Quebec to Pretoria with the Royal Canadian Regiment* (Toronto, 1902), 69–70, 56–57; A.S. McCormick, "The Royal Canadians in South Africa" (unpublished ms., Directorate of History, NDHQ), 3.

4. Macdonald to Tupper, 12 March 1885 in Sir Joseph Pope, *Correspondence of Sir John Macdonald* (Toronto, n.d.), 338. On earlier views of Canadian contributions, see Alice R. Stewart, "Sir John A. Macdonald and the Imperial Defence Commission of 1879," *Canadian Historical Revue* 35, 2 (June 1954); C.P. Stacey, "Canada and the Nile Expedition of 1884–85", *Canadian Historical Revue* 33 (Dec. 1952); Preston, "Imperial Defense," 160–69.

5. On Herbert and Hutton, see Desmond Morton, *Ministers and Generals: Politics and the Canadian Militia, 1868–1904* (Toronto, 1870), 95–111, 129–37; Guy R. Maclean, "The Canadian Offer of Troops for Hong Kong, 1894," *Canadian Historical Review* 38, 4 (Dec. 1957).

6. Colonial Office to Governor-General, 3 Oct. 1899 in *Correspondence Relating to the Despatch of Colonial Military Contingents to South Africa, November, 1899*, Comd. 18, 1899. (The preference for infantry was not as absurd as some historians have claimed, and owed much to the experience of the New South Wales Lancers at Suakin in 1885. See E.B. Pennell memorandum to War Office from Colonial Office, 16 Feb. 1885, Public Record Office, C.O. 42/783, 47–48.)

7. On Hutton and the South African contingent, see Norman Penlington, "General Hutton and the Problem of Military Imperialism in Canada," *Canadian Historical Review* 24, 2 (June, 1943), and a somewhat different view in Desmond Morton, *Ministers and Generals*, 153–55.

8. P.C. 1618k 14 Oct. 1899; See Stacey, *Age of Conflict*, 65; Sir John Willison, *Reminiscences, Political and Personal* (Toronto, 1919), 304–305.

9. On Minto's pressure, see Minto to Chamberlain, 14 Oct. 1899, C.O. 42/769; on Otter see Desmond Morton, *The Canadian General: Sir William Otter* (Toronto, 1974); and Otter Papers, "The Battle of Paardeberg," 1.

10. Companies recruited in western Ontario and for French-speaking Quebeckers had to be reinforced by drafts from Toronto and Ottawa respectively. See Desmond Morton, *Canadian General*, 165; Borden to David Mills, 25 Oct. 1899, F.W. Borden Papers, 5883, Public Archives of Nova Scotia.

11. *Supplementary Reports*, pt. 1, pp. 13–14, 22, pt. 2, p. 407; Borden to Lord Landsdowne, 10 Nov. 1899, F.W. Borden Papers, 6014, Public Archives of Canada.

12. For accounts of the voyage and soldier attitudes, see T.G. Marquis, *Canada's Sons on Kopie and Veldi: An Historical Account of the Canadian Contingents* (Toronto, 1900), 72; Stanley McKeown Brown, *With the Royal Canadians* (Toronto, 1900), 62ff.; Russell G. Hubley, *"G"*

Company or Everyday Life of the R.C.R. (Montreal, 1901), 28; W. Hart McHarg, *From Quebec to Pretoria*, 54–55; A.S. McCormick, "Royal Canadians," 2–3.

13. Otter's philosophy is reflected in his book, *The Guide: A Manual of Interior Economy* (Toronto, 1883). See also Desmond Morton, *The Canadian General*, 172ff.

14. On conditions, see W. Hart McHarg, *From Quebec to Pretoria*, 52–55, 64; Russell G. Hubley, *"G" Company*, 44–48; O.C.C. Pelletier, *Mémoires, Souvenirs de famille et récits* (Quebec, 1940), 311–12; R.C. Featherstonehaugh, *The Royal Canadian Regiment, 1883–1933* (Montreal, 1936), 91–92; Otter to Molly Otter, 12, 21 Nov. 1899, Otter Papers.

15. Otter to Molly Otter, 8 Feb. 1900, 5 April 1900, Otter Papers. See Russell G. Hubley, *"G" Company*, 89, on Buchan; McCormick, "Royal Canadians," 10. (Even Otter's own choices were not infallible. A Toronto captain "lacks force and backbone, and once or twice has given way to temptation in the form of tippling." Otter to Molly Otter, 8 Feb. 1900.)

16. *World*, Toronto, 27 Aug. 1900.

17. W. Hart McHarg, *From Quebec to Pretoria*, 67.

18. Otter to Molly Otter, 22 April 1900, Otter Papers; W. Hart McHarg, *From Quebec to Pretoria*, 67; G.A. Sweny to Otter, 28 April 1900, Otter Papers.

19. On the Second Contingent see Minto to Chamberlain, 21 Nov. 1899, C.O. 42/289; War Office to Colonial Office, 23 Dec. 1899, C.O. 323/447; *Supplementary Report*, pt. 2 pp. 67–163.

20. Otter to Molly Otter, 8 Feb. 1900, Otter Papers. On Smith-Dorrien, see Sir Horace Smith-Dorrien, *Memories of Forty-Eight Years' Service*, (London, 1925).

21. On Paardeberg, see Desmond Morton, "The Battle of Paardeberg," *OMMC Journal*, 8 (1980).

22. Desmond Morton, *The Canadian General*, 188–90; W. Hart McHarg, *From Quebec to Pretoria*, 83–85; Hubley, *"B" Company*, 60–61; Pelletier, *Mémoires*, 321; Otter Papers, "Paardeberg Campaign," 34.

23. Desmond Morton, *Canadian General*, 191–93; Horace Smith-Dorrien, *Memories*, 152–53. W. Hart McHarg, *From Quebec to Pretoria*, 111–13; *Supplementary Report*, pt. 2, 57–60.

24. Otter to Molly Otter, 25 Feb. 1900, Otter Papers.

25. *Supplementary Report*, 46–47; Otter to Molly Otter, 4 March 1900, Otter Papers; Horace Smith-Dorrien, *Memories*, 159–60; L.S. Amery, *The Times History of the War in South Africa*, vol. 3 (London, 1905), 482–83; Desmond Morton, *The Canadian General*, 196–201.

26. *Globe* (Toronto), 28 Feb. 1900; Canada, House of Commons, *Debates*, 27 Feb. 1900, 1013 and *passim*; Col. Foster to Otter, 22 March 1900, Otter Papers. (The original administrative arrangements, passing the full cost of the contingent to the British from the moment it reached Cape Town, remained. Otter's regiment was paid at permanent force rates; members of the Second Contingent were paid at the far higher rate for the North West Mounted Police. Since Canadian officers on the whole earned less than their British counterparts, they gained nothing from the transaction. Otter received $4.75 a day as a Canadian lieutenant-colonel; a British equivalent earned $7.21.)

27. On criticisms, see Desmond Morton, *The Canadian General*, 206–208; Desmond Morton, *Canada and War*, 43.

28. See *Times* (London), 27 June 1900 and reprint in *Mail & Empire* (Toronto), 14 July 1900. On the hospitals, see W. Hart McHarg, *From Quebec to Pretoria*, 153–55; Marquis, *Canada's Sons*, 311–12; Otter to Molly Otter, 26 Aug. 1900, Otter Papers. (Of 29 Canadians who died of disease, 25 perished from typhoid, 12 of them at Bloemfontein.)

29. Otter to Molly Otter, 5 April 1900, Otter Papers; see also 22 March 1900, ibid.

30. Sir Arthur Conan-Doyle, *The Great Boer War* (London, 1903).

31. Desmond Morton, *The Canadian General*, 215; *Supplementary Report*, pt. 2, pp. 48–49. W. Hart McHarg acknowledged that Otter had always been "very cool under fire and inspired confidence wherever he happened to be." W. Hart McHarg, *From Quebec to Pretoria*, 172. A more coarse-grained veteran only wished that the bullet had been better aimed. Russell G. Hubley, *"B" Company*, 88.

32. Desmond Morton, *Canadian General*, 219–20; *Supplementary Report*, 54–55.

33. Otter to Molly Otter, 5 April 1900, Otter Papers; Otter to Agnes Otter, 1 May 1900, Otter Papers.

34. Otter to Agnes Otter, 1 May 1900, Otter Papers; Otter to Molly Otter, 11, 26 June, 10, 24 July 1900, Otter Papers; A.S. McCormick, "Royal Canadians," 8.

35. Otter to Agnes Otter, 9 Sept. 1900, Otter Papers; C.F. Winter, "Some Recollections of Service with the Imperials," *Canadian Defence Quarterly* 4, 4 (July 1927); *Supplementary Report*, 25.

36. Otter to Chief Staff Officer, 12 July 1900, 24 Aug. 1900, Otter Papers. On mood, see W. Hart McHarg, *From Quebec to Pretoria*, 233: "We had been daily expecting to get the news that we were to return to Canada, as we thought that, as the hostilities proper were practically over, and the fighting had developed into guerilla tactics pure and simple, the regular army ought to be able to deal with it."

37. *Supplementary Report*, 27.

38. On the controversy, see Desmond Morton, *The Canadian General*, 226–29.

39. On Otter's view, see Otter to Agnes Otter, 1 Oct. 1900, Otter Papers; Otter to Molly Otter, 7 Oct. 1900, Otter Papers. On the men's opinion, see *Globe* (Toronto), 2 Nov. 1900; *Evening Telegram* (Toronto), 3–4 Nov. 1900.

40. Desmond Morton, *The Canadian General*, 230–31.

41. Adjutant-General (Lord Aylmer) to Otter, 15 Nov. 1900, Otter Papers.

42. Desmond Morton, *The Canadian General*, 232–35; W. Hart McHarg, *From Quebec to Pretoria*, 259 and passim; *Supplementary Report*, 36–40.

43. C. P. Stacey, *Age of Conflict*, 69–70.

44. Desmond Morton, *A Military History of Canada* (Edmonton, 1985), 118–222 and passim.

THE PERMANENT FORCE AND "REAL SOLDIERING," 1883–1914 ◇

S.J. HARRIS

o

Caron's reforms had far less impact than Luard anticipated. Although the schools created in 1883 would inevitably help the militia, there was a crucial difference between them and the artillery batteries at Quebec and Kingston. In addition to their instructional duties, the latter were also quasi-operational units responsible for the upkeep and defence of their fortresses, and they practised this role even while they trained militia gunners. The same could not be said of the infantry and cavalry schools. Indeed, when the Liberals criticized the government for breaking with tradition and creating a standing army, Caron rightly retorted that this was not at all the case. The school companies, he explained, were much too small to be considered the nucleus of a field army; and besides, their job was not to fight, but to instruct the militia. For better or worse, then, the officers and men who joined the infantry and cavalry school corps would be teachers in uniform.[1]

Just how far removed from "real soldiering" life in the permanent force would be was soon evident. Although the commanding officers originally appointed to these units were sent to England to spend time with the British army (the rest trained at Halifax), they were left more or less on their own once they returned home. There were no promotion examinations to pass, and few tests of their military competence. Furthermore, the courses offered to the militia demanded very little of the regulars. Based on British guidelines prepared in the 1860s, the curriculum consisted in the main of lectures presenting repetitive lists of the duties involved in rudimentary administration, with some time for parade square drill. Tactics, and field operations in general, received little or no attention, either as part of the militia course of instruction or to improve the practical knowledge of the instructional staff.[2]

◇ *Canadian Brass* (Toronto: University of Toronto Press, 1988), 22–39.

Indeed, the permanent force probably became less experienced as the years passed. A few of the new subalterns appointed each year attended the Royal Military College [RMC], but many joined the infantry and cavalry with no previous military background or, at best, a few score parades with their local militia unit. And since these officers were not sent to England or Halifax for training, the only place they could learn their trade was within the school itself, where the level of military knowledge and experience was already low. By all accounts, moreover, superiors rarely delegated authority to their younger lieutenants and captains, leaving them with little opportunity to learn even the habit of command or the fundamentals of military administration. Finally, apart from those lucky enough to see active service during the Riel Rebellion in 1885, few had a chance to practise tactics and fieldcraft; they were either preoccupied with their own essential upkeep and administration—feeding and clothing the men; looking after horses and equipment; supervising the orderly room, drill, and pickets; and holding disciplinary parades—or such training was prohibited. Yet, because there were no promotion examinations, these untrained junior officers could count upon being promoted eventually to the rank of lieutenant-colonel, at which point they would be responsible for training the next generation of subalterns. Given such a cycle of mediocrity, conditions could get only worse.[3]

These developments should have come as no surprise to anyone who, during the summer of 1883, paid close attention to the way Caron had set out to man the infantry and cavalry schools in the first place. Unknown to the minister, since early 1881 General Luard had been compiling a list of British army veterans and RMC graduates suitable for permanent employment against the day when a regular army would be established in Canada. But when he forwarded this list to Caron in June 1883, its receipt was not even acknowledged. Instead, as the weeks passed by and the press discussed the candidates under serious consideration, it appeared that blatant political jobbery was playing a major part in the selection process.[4] Appalled that patronage should loom so large in the regular force's crucial formative years, Luard pleaded with Caron to protect the army's credibility by rigorous application of the merit principle, but again received no reply.[5] Now desperate, the GOC [general officer commanding] turned to the governor general and Colonel Walker Powell for help, but their efforts were equally fruitless.[6] In the end, Caron made his choice without once speaking to Luard and even announced his decision while the GOC was away from Ottawa on an inspection tour. Taken to task for this by Walker Powell, Caron justified the affront with the disingenuous remark that the matter had been delayed long enough.[7]

Luard was horrified when he saw the minister's selection. Although some of the twenty-one nominees had the GOC's approval—Colonel W.D. Otter of the Queen's Own Rifles was one, as were six RMC graduates—some seemed entirely unworthy of their appointment. Nine had no military experience and had undoubtedly been put forward to ensure that the officer corps enjoyed a balanced regional representation. Others had served in the militia but had not done well, and their appointment could only be explained in terms of their political or social connection. Captain Charles J.Q. Coursol, for example, who had been arrested for drunkenness while on a course at A Battery, was the son of a member of Parliament and the grandson of Sir Etienne Taché, a former premier and father of Confederation. It was not the best of beginnings.[8] Still, things could have been worse. Three officers—B.A. Vidal, G.J. Maunsell, and J. Freer—had British experience, and J.F. Turnbull, in the militia since 1855, had attended cavalry manoeuvres in Europe at his own expense several times during his career. Moreover, the prime minister had already forced Caron to remove even more objectionable candidates from his original list, and to stipulate that all appointments would remain provisional until each individual passed the appropriate qualifying examination in Great Britain or Halifax. For this reason Macdonald asked the governor general to persuade Luard to tone down his criticism and to do the best he could with those who had been selected for political reasons.[9]

Luard did as he was told, but he remained far from happy. Although he had always been reconciled to the fact that Canada's regular officers would be mediocre until they gained experience, he had not counted on individuals owing their position to the minister alone. That challenged the twin pillars of military discipline and subordination. More to the point, the GOC despaired of improvement in the future. Why should Canadian officers better themselves professionally, he wondered, when any promotions they received were likely to depend on their political connections? For that matter, why should they pay attention to the general officer commanding when his opinions obviously meant so little?

Luard was right. Patronage dominated the permanent force for the next thirty-five years as minister after minister proved all too ready to "drive a coach and six through the Militia Act"[10] to play favourites. Able men, such as George Mutton (Otter's choice as quartermaster in Toronto) who supported the wrong political party, or who lived in a part of the country already well represented in the army, were ignored, while political friends were rewarded with preferential treatment and accelerated promotion. More pernicious still, the prevalence of such partisan behaviour enhanced the development of a self-serving ethos totally at odds with the corporate loyalties normally expected of a professional military organization. Judging from the experience of Colonel Otter, commander of Canada's Boer War contingent, this activity extended even to the battlefield. Time and again he felt compelled to look over his shoulder as his subordinates jockeyed for position to replace him. Pandering to the political system that had created them, Canadian officers routinely sought personal gain at the expense of their comrades-in-arms through direct appeals to friends in Parliament and party.[11]

Furthermore, the ethical decay of the permanent force became well known. The *Canadian Military Gazette*, self-styled "Organ of the Canadian Army," habitually published diatribes against the regulars, but nothing moved it to complain so loudly or for so long as the patronage connected with the permanent corps. Most officers were denounced as "influential incompetents," products of the "political grab-bag" who had found a career without the least regard to "qualification and merit." How, the *Gazette* asked, could the militia look up to such men with confidence when they clearly knew so little about the army![12] Bad publicity like this simply reinforced traditional Canadian antipathy to the standing army—a sentiment that was never far below the surface.

Although not quite so widespread in the early 1880s as it had been only a decade before, the hostility to the permanent force grew markedly in the 1890s when the militia budget had to be trimmed for the sake of economy. For the first time, it seemed, the regulars were actually beginning to usurp the role of the part-time citizen force as the nation's first line of defence, and this was a development that could not be tolerated. "We have held, and always will hold," the *Canadian Military Gazette* proclaimed, "that our permanent corps owe their existence wholly to the educational requirements of the militia force, and what prouder or more honourable distinction could the officers and men of the permanent corps wish for?" But, the *Gazette* continued, the regulars had "fallen short of their mission just so far as they have allowed their ambition to be considered a standing army or a separate fighting machine . . . to get the better of their desire to provide the best instruction possible . . . " to the militia. The *Gazette's* editor promised that he would "not cease to expose the absurdly false position taken by those . . . who, like jackdaws in peacocks' plumes, want to be something they are not, and never cease bewailing the fate which 'makes officers nothing but merely school masters.'" To have greater ambitions was ludicrous for members of a "one-horse service."[13]

Another perceptive and respected critic was Thomas Scoble, a long-time militia officer responsible for organizing the first volunteer company of engineers, who warned that the "arrogant attempt to secure . . . the position and reputation of a 'permanent force' . . . [was] subversive of its own best interests."[14] The greater the pretensions of the regulars, the worse was their public image, and the louder the complaints made against them. An accommodation between the permanent corps' natural desire to be "real soldiers" and the popular view that they were teachers first, administrators second, and fighting men perhaps a distant third, might have been possible had they been able to impress the militia with their knowledge and expertise. But as long as so little was required of the regular officer[s] and so little was offered to [them] in the way of professional education and training, it was next to impossible for [them] to earn the genuine respect of [their] citizen force colleagues. Indeed, it would have taken a great deal of consistently high-calibre work for the regulars to overcome their tarnished image as second-rate political hacks.

The poor reputation of the permanent force was not helped by the conditions of service in the infantry and cavalry schools. These were scarcely conducive to attracting the best and brightest young Canadians to the army or, for that matter, to fostering a spirit of initiative and self-motivation among the officers who did join up. Pay was initially pegged at the comparable British rates without taking into account the higher cost of living in Canada, so that military service in the Dominion was both less exciting and more of a financial sacrifice than in the mother country.[15] By the 1890s the comparison was even less favourable. Canadian rates were now marginally lower than in the United Kingdom, but substantially below the salaries offered by the North West Mounted Police and the United States army.[16] Furthermore, no pension was offered for service in the permanent force. But perhaps more debilitating was the simple truth that no officer could be confident of promotion even if he performed his duties better than his colleagues. For one thing, the school companies were so small, and retirement ages so flexible, that vacancies in the more senior ranks were long in coming. For another, advancement increasingly depended upon ministerial whim, so that neither seniority nor merit eventually counted for much. In terms of promoting professional competence, therefore, there was no carrot—and no stick.

The physical amenities of military life were no more appealing. Many of the barrack blocks and officers' quarters had been built to British garrison standards many years before, and so provided less in the way of creature comforts than Canadians were accustomed to. The hutments at Winnipeg, for instance, occupied by the cavalry school in the 1890s, were legacies of the 1870 Manitoba Field Force, had not yet been winterized when they were taken over, and offered a miserable existence. This was an extreme case, of course, but there were problems even in established stations such as Toronto. In 1888, to take another example, Colonel Otter's wife found it necessary to petition the minister directly, asking him to delay long-overdue repairs to the other ranks' quarters in order that she and her husband might finally have a furnace.[17]

At least Colonel Otter had married quarters. Many others were not so lucky because, as in almost all late-Victorian armies, little provision had been made for officers with wives and families. Yet when they requested living-out allowances to help them find suitable accommodation in town, most were turned down coldly by the militia department. Indeed, in 1886 the deputy minister decreed that henceforth all available living space was to be divided equally among the officers at each station so that none could complain that they had no official place to stay, no matter how unsuitable and uncomfortable one room measuring fifteen feet square may have been for raising a family. Sons of wealthy parents were not bothered by such parsimony: they could afford town houses, country homes, and summer retreats. However, the number of applications for various forms of financial relief on the departmental files (as well as the biographical evidence available) strongly suggests that Canadian regular officers did not come from the monied or landed classes.[18]

Sam Hughes, a militia officer and future minister, put the case against them as bluntly as anyone. Failures at everything else they tried, he wrote, the regular officers looked upon the permanent force as their employer of last resort. Yet even then they could not succeed on their own merit, but required the assistance of a patron. As a result, he grumbled, it was "no compliment to very many prominent . . . Militia Officers to be compared with [the regular] officers as a class."[19] In all fairness it must be said that Hughes went too far. The system which the Conservative government had instituted in 1883 and would not readily change was responsible for much of the permanent force's inadequacies. Still, neither Hughes nor his fellow

critics were wrong to think that the conditions of service, the lack of opportunity to do real soldiering, the financial insecurity, and the continuing
importance of party political considerations crimped the development of a
self-disciplined, cohesive, and professional military force. A few good officers consistently stood out from the rest—T.D.B. Evans, Victor Williams,
Henry Burstall, T.D.R. Hemming, George Maunsell, and W.D. Otter—but
when so little happened to improve the public's image of the army as an
institution there was no reason to expect a popular outcry for change.

That the permanent force did not stagnate altogether was due almost
exclusively to the perseverance of the British officers sent to command the
militia between 1883 and 1904, and to the three chiefs of the general staff
who succeeded them. Indeed, what they were able to accomplish for the
permanent force marked their only real achievement in this era. For, as we
shall see, most of the GOCs had foreshortened careers in Canada, largely
because they ran afoul of the political process in futile attempts to root out
patronage in the militia and to forge closer military ties with the mother
country. They also failed to train or equip the part-time militia to take the
field. But almost all were able to improve the lot of the regular force in one
way or another.

Luard's successor as GOC was Major-General Frederick Middleton, a
portly man in his sixties who realized very quickly that it did not pay to criticize the militia strenuously or to interfere with Caron's designs for his
department. This was true even during the Riel Rebellion of 1885 from
which Middleton emerged victorious (but later tainted by a scandal involving allegedly stolen furs). For although the minister played an energetic role
in Ottawa, making the best of a flawed military machine that had not been
designed for so quick and sudden a mobilization, he had also been faithful to
tradition by carefully employing political friends not only to command
frontline battalions but also to purvey military supplies of all kinds. The
lessons Middleton learned from this experience were evident in his post-
rebellion reports, which treated the militia far more kindly than it deserved.
Nevertheless, when it came to the permanent force the GOC was adamant
that its career system must be based on merit. Although he failed to convince
Caron to make all future appointments from among the graduates of the
Royal Military College, he was at least able to dissuade the minister from
permitting militia officers who transferred to the regular army to retain their
militia rank.[20] As a result, the permanent corps were protected against an
influx of unqualified part-time officers in relatively senior positions. At the
same time Middleton was forcing the government to acknowledge, even if
subtly, that there was a distinction to be made between the country's amateur militiamen and those who had made the army a career—a small, yet
essential, step in improving the credibility of the permanent force.

But this was as much as Middleton could do during his years in Canada.
In 1886, for example, his proposal to lead the infantry and cavalry school
companies into the Northwest to manoeuvre over the ground where the field
force had recently been in action was turned down. Lack of money, and fear
of the popular reaction to any increase in the regulars' share of the defence
budget, was one reason for this decision; but it also seems likely that the

politicians wished to avoid giving any credence to the view that the permanent force might one day have a legitimate fighting role.[21] Three years later the government rejected a well-reasoned proposal to introduce a retirement and pension plan based on the British model and aimed at providing the regular officer with some reward for his services. Money again was a key consideration, but the fact that a similar scheme had recently been adopted for the North West Mounted Police made the rebuff all the more frustrating.[22]

The man who followed Middleton was made of sterner stuff. An officer of private means who had passed staff college, and who was known for his temper, Ivor Caradoc Herbert would not accept continuing decay in the militia without a struggle. But he also perceived that he could not improve the part-time force without first transforming the regular army into something that could win the respect of the country's citizen soldiers. The enormity of this task was apparent on his first tour of inspection. In British Columbia, for example, he found the drill of C Battery of artillery, formed at the Esquimalt fortress in 1887, well below the standard set for the British militia, while the school in Winnipeg was so badly organized and so poorly led that the mounted infantry were eventually amalgamated with the dragoons.[23] However, it was the state of the permanent force officer corps in general that disturbed him most. Few of those now holding senior appointments had qualified for their rank, while the majority of subalterns seemed to have been selected without regard for their "natural fitness . . . or educational qualifications."[24] Most, indeed, had come to regard their jobs as sinecures and, prevented from undertaking realistic training, were satisfied with instructing their men to form fours and with making up regimental accounts. Lacking all "higher sentiment of duty," and oblivious to or ignorant of the responsibility to improve their knowledge and expertise, they exerted themselves only out of self-interest. Little wonder, Herbert concluded, that insubordination and disloyalty to superiors were so prevalent in the force.[25] When added to the stifling routine, low pay, and the high cost of buying out of the service, it was hardly surprising that the desertion rate among the other ranks sometimes approached 50 percent.[26]

Moulded in particular by his experience in the Guards, where esprit de corps and a sense of noblesse oblige were everything, the GOC decided to transform the independent school companies into miniature regiments, in the hope that a family atmosphere might reduce petty bickering and jealous competition while fostering regimental spirit and pride in the greater whole. He also hoped that the change would permit a broadening-out of the army's training syllabus. For although the government could oppose field exercises for the scattered instructional cadres on the grounds that company-sized units did not fit conveniently into the active order of battle, it would be difficult to make the same case against complete regiments of infantry, cavalry, and artillery. Finally, Herbert reasoned that linking the dispersed and independent school companies by way of over-arching regimental headquarters would be the best way to produce uniformity in their approach to training, discipline, and administration.[27]

It was clear, however, that mere reorganization would not correct all the faults Herbert had discovered. The new regiments could easily slip back into their old routine unless something was done to reform an environment that tolerated, and even encouraged, indolence and indifference. The GOC acted quickly and decisively where he could. Concerned particularly about the under-employment of junior officers, Herbert directed that they take over the day-to-day administration of their units in order to gain experience in leadership and management. To ensure that this actually happened, he further ordered commanding officers to submit monthly reports on the progress their subordinates were making.[28] Finally, the GOC planned to use his hybrid regimental system to insist upon compulsory postings from one station to another. For he had discovered that there was a tendency to leave officers in one place, where all too often they neglected their military duties in order to make their mark in local business and social circles. Herbert eventually won his fight to create the Royal Canadian Dragoons and the Royal Regiment of Canadian Infantry (later the Royal Canadian Regiment), and he was able to institute some exchange of personnel, although never to the extent he desired.[29]

The GOC realized that these reforms would have little more than cosmetic value as long as the majority of officers remained unqualified for their appointments and yet were not forfeiting the possibility of promotion. Eager to raise standards, but aware that he dare not risk wholesale change which would threaten powerful vested interests, Herbert had struggled for some time to find an acceptable rationale for forcing these officers to qualify or retire. His solution was brilliant, and carefully couched in terms any Canadian politician would understand and respect. Having already secured a promise that all officers would eventually have to pass fitness tests, Herbert simply calculated the financial implications of waiting until they had moved up a step or two before sending them away (with the pay of their new rank) to take a course in Britain. He then posed an embarrassing question. Why should the government bear the additional expense involved if officers continued to be promoted before they were qualified when the extra funds could be used to increase drill pay for the part-time militia? The tactic worked. Although the government declared that it would not cease making provisional appointments altogether, or dispatch all unqualified officers to England immediately, those without any formal training were to attend the nine-month RMC long course as soon as possible or risk being retired.[30]

At the same time that he was demanding more of the regulars than any previous GOC, Herbert also strove to offer them more. It was only as a result of his efforts, for example, that permanent force rank was accorded a distinct place in the official table of Canadian precedence—an inconsequential achievement in practice, perhaps, but one that acknowledged further the separate status of regular army service.[31] Of more consequence was his success in convincing the government to be more generous in its provision of living allowances to married personnel for whom no suitable official quarters were available. Acting true to form, the minister rewarded political favourites first, but in time all benefited from the change.[32] Somewhat later, after having failed to persuade the government to underwrite pensions for the regulars, Herbert secured a gratuity of one year's pay for all permanent force officers upon their retirement.[33]

Herbert always justified his support for the regulars on the grounds that the permanent force had to be improved before it could serve the militia well. There were, however, many who doubted his motives. "The latest move made by [General Herbert], viz the transformation of the School Corps into a Regiment of Regular Infantry, I confess, I do not understand," wrote one rural militia officer, but there was definitely "a suspicious look about them." The new regiment appeared to be the first step toward creating a standing army which, the writer continued, was "an evil thing . . . born in sin and conceived in iniquity."[34] Lieutenant-Colonel Davis's suspicions were undoubtedly correct. Explaining his purpose to the minister in April 1892, the GOC freely acknowledged that combining the infantry and cavalry companies into regiments would "reflect more accurately their actual organization" because they were more than mere schools of instruction.[35] He had already intimated as much the summer before, when he brought the regular companies together under his personal command for field training at Lévis, Quebec, to show them "what a regiment is."[36] That this occurred in a year when militia training had been cancelled for lack of money enraged those who, like Colonel Davis, already feared the worst. But one brief manoeuvre, or even a succession of summer camps, could not produce real regiments ready for battle—there was no solid foundation upon which to build.

Herbert was also concerned that training the Canadian regulars in splendid isolation from the British army was not preparing them to defend the empire, which was the ultimate goal of the Colonial and War Offices. Accordingly, in May 1894 he proposed that the British garrison at Halifax should serve as the training centre for the permanent force just as the regulars were models for the militia. Canadian officers could "go through the mill of regimental life" while they were still young and then proceed to the United Kingdom for courses, attachments, examinations, and manoeuvres, all of which would fit them to command Canadian forces in the field.[37] The government accepted all these recommendations, and in due course the British army once again became directly involved with training the Canadian military. More important, the Dominion had at last decreed that permanent force officers and men could legitimately aspire to be real soldiers as well as instructors to the militia.

Herbert had achieved much by the end of his tenure, but the reforms he had implemented were actually less well entrenched than he had imagined. In fact, they were products of a historical accident. The death throes of Macdonald's Liberal-Conservative coalition and the succession of administrations from 1891 had thrown up a series of militia ministers too weak or preoccupied to resist the GOC's initiatives, but such conditions would not last.[38] At the same time, so many of Herbert's reforms came at the expense of the militia that they produced an unusually hostile reaction against both the GOC and the permanent force. Led in Parliament by Sam Hughes, the newly elected member for Victoria, Ontario, the critics launched a concerted attack on the regulars, denouncing them as poor cousins of the British army that had been so badly mauled by the Boer commandos at Majuba Hill in 1881.[39]

The frailty of Herbert's program was clear within a year of his departure. Despite the threat of war with the United States over the Venezuela boundary dispute in 1896, the permanent force was reduced in strength from over 900 to 732 all ranks. At the same time the VRI clubs, sponsored in the regular regiments by Herbert to foster a sense of unit pride and identity, fell into disarray once his active support was withdrawn.[40] And sadder still, the interest shown by permanent force officers in attending training courses in Britain declined sharply. In short, within twelve months conditions and attitudes within the regular force were distressingly similar to what they had been before Herbert's arrival in Canada.

The irony, of course, is that such deterioration took place in an era that has been correctly identified as a period of major military reform in Canada.[41] Frederick Borden, the minister of militia in the new Liberal government, was the catalyst for this renaissance, but the ideas he brought to his portfolio did not bode well for the regulars. The Swiss concept of a national army involving the country's total male population was Borden's ideal; however, as this was far-fetched, the minister was determined at the least to see that militia training was more realistic and that the part-time force was better equipped. In this context he had no doubt about the role the permanent force should play. In total opposition to what Herbert was trying to achieve, Borden demanded that the regular regiments concentrate on providing instruction in the militia schools even if this interfered with their own training and threatened their aspirations to be "real soldiers." "Let the permanent force understand that their office is to teach," he declared; "we have no standing army and do not need to have one."[42]

Major-General William Gascoigne, who had replaced Herbert, believed that Borden's priorities were fundamentally wrong; an efficient militia would develop only after a strong and capable regular army had been created. But Gascoigne knew that to contest the minister on this matter so early in the game would be wholly counter-productive. Accordingly, he complied with the minister's directive without comment, and established a number of transient provisional schools across the country—schools which took men away from, and thereby weakened, the permanent force units to a greater extent than ever before. Still, Gascoigne had reason to hope. If the provisional schools persuaded militia officers of the importance of good instruction, and if the regulars did their job well, the image of the permanent force might improve. And in time Canadians might even be reconciled to the need to allow the permanent units to conduct their own training.[43] Meanwhile, the GOC found a way to exploit Borden's program to benefit the regulars. Arguing that they should work more closely with the British garrison at Halifax—ostensibly to become better teachers, but in fact so that they would obtain experience in the field—Gascoigne won approval for an exchange between the Canadian infantry at Fredericton and one company of the Berkshires. The results were gratifying. Lieutenant-Colonel George Maunsell, commanding the former, reported that the experience had been good for all concerned. Not only had the warm welcome by their British hosts raised the RCRI's sense of pride and self-esteem, but it had moved the Canadian company to greater efforts after returning to its home station. His officers and men were not only better teachers, Maunsell concluded; they were also better soldiers.[44]

Gascoigne's hopes were misplaced, however. There was only one such infantry exchange, while most of the other recommendations the GOC submitted to assist the regular force were either rejected or ignored. Borden could not be convinced to limit new officer appointments to graduates of the military college; political connections continued to influence promotions; and all requests to allow the permanent companies to conduct operational training on their own were denied. The edict that there would be no standing army was as strong as ever. Gascoigne had, in a sense, gambled and lost. He had failed to parlay his early efforts at co-operation with Borden into reforms that improved the permanent force; in fact, lacking Herbert's drive and energy, and unable to force them to believe in themselves, the GOC may have caused the regular regiments to deteriorate during his tenure.

All this was known to Major-General E.T. Hutton when he arrived to take over as general officer commanding in 1898. But where Gascoigne had blamed the Canadian political system for his lack of progress, Hutton placed responsibility squarely on the shoulders of the regular officers themselves. Despite Herbert's example, he pointed out, they had lapsed into easy-going indolence, whining about the lack of material comforts instead of getting on with the job. As a result, the new GOC made it clear that he would do nothing to improve conditions of service until the regulars accepted a "higher standard of professional knowledge."[45]

Hutton's ill-concealed [con]tempt for the permanent force reflected his own military philosophy as much as it did frustration and anger with the regulars' self-induced shortcomings. For unlike both his predecessors, who aimed at building up the permanent force before anything was done for the militia, Hutton believed that a national army of citizen soldiers, well-trained, well-equipped, and well-led, was "the true form for an army for an Anglo-Saxon state to possess." By contrast, "a considerable standing army was an unnecessary and unwarranted expense" and was of little use "except for military instruction and the maintenance of law and order within the nation's domain."[46] Under Hutton, therefore, priority would go to the militia, while the regulars would concentrate on teaching.

It is plain to see that although their terminology differed, Borden and Hutton were saying almost the same thing, especially where the permanent force was concerned. But once the possibility arose of sending a Canadian contingent to fight the Boers in South Africa Hutton began to reconsider his position. Despite all that was wrong with them, the regulars were the most competent soldiers in his command. Accordingly, both before and after the Laurier government arrived at its painful decision to commit the Dominion to military intervention in South Africa, Hutton made every effort to ensure that, if troops were sent, the Royal Canadian Regiment, the Royal Canadian Dragoons, and the regular artillery would be among the first to see action. He also insisted that officers from these regiments receive all the senior appointments in the expeditionary force. Borden was less sure—he remained loyal to the militia as the country's first line of defence—but in the end he was persuaded despite the fierce opposition from the militia's supporters in Parliament.[47] Permanent force officers shouldered the burden of leadership in the early months of the fighting.

Not satisfied with this victory, Hutton remained convinced of the need to build a "national army," divorced from party politics, for the future, and it was here that he and Borden parted company. For although Borden championed reform, he still believed that politics and military service could be mixed in the militia. An open conflict with Borden over the officers selected for advanced militia training, coupled with rumours about the GOC's work behind the scenes to secure Canadian involvement in South Africa, eventually cut short Hutton's career in the Dominion, and he therefore had no opportunity to build upon the experience the regulars had gained in South Africa. However, his comments from the front after he was sent to South Africa suggest that he was pleasantly surprised by what he saw. Not only was the overall performance of the Canadian contingents more than acceptable, but the permanent force officers had done quite well indeed.[48] Accordingly, there is little doubt that had he returned to Canada and participated in the discussion of what had been learned from the war, he would have sided with those who saw the result as a victory for the British regular army, rather than with Sam Hughes, who not only extolled the performance of the Boer commandos, but went so far as to argue that victory was possible only after the arrival of British and Dominion citizen soldiers.[49]

Borden had also become more sympathetic to the regulars after the Boer War perhaps because, following the death of his son on active service, he finally understood the ultimate risk of a military career. Victory—and the casualty lists—produced a similar reaction across the country, and the results of this conversion were soon apparent in Parliament. Where only three years before there had been outright hostility to the regulars, after 1901 there was a veritable stampede to pass legislation to improve their conditions of service. A pension scheme was introduced in 1901; rates of pay were increased the next year; and in 1903 all but the most junior officers became eligible for living allowances to offset the cost of housing when suitable government quarters were not available.[50] Even so implacable a foe as Sam Hughes was moved to support these measures, although he could not let the moment pass without reminding the Commons that the defence of Canada rested on the militia, not the permanent force.[51]

Yet if militia headquarters or the government believed that the new spirit of generosity had increased the attractiveness of a military career, they were sadly mistaken. When five vacancies in the officer corps opened up because of casualties suffered in South Africa, there was no rush to join. Not one RMC graduate was interested; and of the very few militia officers who expressed an interest most were unqualified.[52] Despite recent events, the regular force apparently still lacked the prestige and drawing power of continuous active service, army pay remained low enough to cause complaints, and the desertion rate among the other ranks was still high. The situation was likely to improve only when there was widespread acknowledgment of the regulars' claim to be Canada's military elite.

This was the goal of the next GOC, Major-General Lord Dundonald. Of much the same temperament as Hutton but more orthodox in his views,

Dundonald quickly discovered the chimera in his predecessor's vision of a "national army." For although there was reasonable material among the militia officers and non-commissioned officers, the talent was not distributed evenly throughout the force; many units were too poorly led to even bother working with in the field. Accordingly, Dundonald chose to concentrate on leadership, on producing good officers and NCOs, and to worry about the men later.[53] The process would take longer than Hutton had forecast, but in time Dundonald was convinced that he could create a one-hundred-thousand-man army of which Canada would be proud.

Everything depended on the availability of a highly trained and motivated instructional staff and this, to Dundonald, meant a regular force trained and educated to British standards. It is Dundonald, therefore, who may be regarded as the father of Canada's first systematic—and lasting—program of officer education. As a first step he directed the commanding officers of the Royal Canadian Regiment and the Royal Canadian Dragoons to send all their unqualified subordinates to the next RMC long course without fail.[54] Then he worked out rigid criteria for future officer appointments in the regular army: graduates of the Royal Military College would have first priority, then those who had attended university and finished the militia long course, and finally those who had qualified for a commission in the militia. But anyone who had not attended RMC would be on probation for five years, and their performance would be judged by both the commandant of the military college and the GOC.[55] The intention was that ultimately no one "not in every way eligible for a commission in Her Majesty's Army" would be accepted into Canadian service.[56]

That was the first step in Dundonald's master plan. To ensure that officers could not rest on their pre-commissioning laurels, he also insisted that they write the British army's examinations for promotion to captain and each step in rank thereafter, including a trip to the United Kingdom to take the "Tactical Fitness for Command" test before their appointment at the lieutenant-colonel level. Furthermore, any officer still serving who had not earned an RMC diploma or a long course certificate would ineligible for promotion beyond his current rank whether or not he had seen service in South Africa.[57] This was harsh, but the GOC was determined to set standards that prevented any deviation from the merit principle.

Borden accepted all of Dundonald's recommendations, adding at the same time that while he still considered the militia to be fertile and legitimate soil for patronage, he would not tolerate the same kind of behaviour from or attitude to the permanent force. At the Militia Council meeting of 27 April 1905, for example, he announced that he would henceforth invoke the War Office regulation which treated letters seeking favours for individual regular officers as if they had been written by the officer himself—and therefore as prejudicial to his career.[58] Subsequently he increased the size of the permanent force to three thousand, raised its pay schedule to bring it in line with that of the mounted police, and then promised the regulars time to conduct their own training.[59] These were important steps, and the fact that they reflected the minister's sincere and genuine interest in the well-being of the permanent force was proved three years later. Told by the finance minister that he must reduce defence expenditures by one million dollars, Borden accepted the advice of his military staff without complaint and slashed the militia's drill pay while leaving the regulars' training budget as it was.[60]

This was an act of political courage in return for which Borden demanded loyalty—to himself, and to the students at the country's military schools. Little wonder, therefore, that he was so bitter when he received complaints that the regulars were showing no interest whatsoever in instructing officers of the militia. In his view such apathy was a betrayal of the bargain he had struck with Dundonald to offer the permanent schools more scope to develop as a professional fighting force. His anger showed in the circular letter he caused to be read to all regular officers in February 1906. Reminded that their future was "indissolubly bound up with the . . . Active Militia," they were warned against any tendency to regard their responsibilities to the citizen force as secondary to the interests of their own regiments. Instead they were to offer the best possible instruction to the volunteers, and to offer it gladly. As an inducement to do so, Borden announced that the annual evaluation of an officer's professional abilities would henceforth be determined primarily by his performance as a teacher.[61]

Dundonald had left Canada by this time, recalled to England because of an indiscreet public challenge to appointments within the militia,[62] but Major-General Percy Lake, his successor as head of the Canadian army, was no more prepared to sacrifice regular army routine for teaching. Accordingly, despite Borden's unambiguous instructions to the contrary, Lake directed the commander of the Western Ontario district, Colonel Otter, to experiment with the British army's new, incremental, training syllabus, which would keep his men busy in individual, platoon, and company drill from October to May, and culminate in a six-week tactical concentration in the field during the summer. Militia training would be fitted into this timetable, not the reverse, and at no time would the RCR interrupt its schedule to accommodate the needs of the volunteers.[63]

These instructions created the obvious impression that militia training was an unwanted intrusion into regular army routine that had to be tolerated for political reasons alone. They also seemed to reinforce the regulars' sense of superiority over the citizen army, an élitist sentiment with which the minister had little sympathy. The regulars were different, Borden admitted, but they should not boast about it. Lake therefore justified his action on the grounds that it was intended to make better teachers of the permanent corps, a dubious rationale at best, yet perhaps because he found the general so congenial and co-operative in other areas, Borden was charitable in this instance, and allowed Otter to proceed. But when he received another deluge of complaints about the way the regulars were shirking their responsibilities to the militia in 1911, his response was immediate and stern: there would be no second chance for officers found guilty of neglect this time.[64]

This episode illustrated the fact that despite the best of good will on both sides—and the most harmonious relationship ever to exist between a Canadian militia minister and his senior military adviser—a fundamental contradiction existed in the roles set out for the permanent force. So long as the regulars were prohibited from training for battle they were in a poor position to offer good training to the militia; yet whenever the regulars were granted permission to exercise in the field they inevitably began to think of themselves as an embryonic standing army that had better things to do than instruct part-time soldiers. Resentment was bound to grow, especially if the regulars continued to view militiamen as rank amateurs unworthy to command in the field or, like Colonel J. Wilson, complained that militia officers were "not gentlemen, [had] no gentlemanly instincts, and never could be made to act and feel like gentlemen."[65] For their part, militia officers persisted in exploiting their political power to thwart the ambitions of the regular force and to challenge its credibility in the class-room and in the field. Frustrated by this pressure, compelled by Borden's two warnings to give higher priority to teaching, and still yearning to soldier, the permanent force mastered no task well.

The answer to the conundrum was worked out, curiously enough, by Major-General Colin Mackenzie, a dour and somewhat unsympathetic Scot who spent the better part of his three years (1910–13) as Canada's senior soldier writing bitter denunciations to the governor general and the War Office about the treatment he was receiving. Seeing at once that the regulars would never improve as long as they maintained a dual identity, Mackenzie put forward the simplest of solutions: divide the permanent force into two parts, designating one as an instructional cadre whose sole duty would be to work with the militia, and allowing the other to adhere to Percy Lake's training regimen as an embryonic professional, standing army.[66] Borden agreed, and the positive effect was apparent within months. Morale in the militia schools improved dramatically, and with it the teaching, because the instructional staff knew that subsequent postings would eventually let them train as real soldiers. The regular companies, meanwhile, enjoyed the freedom to prepare for battle without the administrative and other distractions of running a school.[67]

The compromise worked out between Mackenzie and Borden survived as the basis of permanent force organization for thirty-five years. Of course, it was not a perfect solution. There were no guarantees that the "combat" element of the standing army would be large or adequately equipped, that its training would be realistic, or that all regular force officers would make the most of their opportunities. And as we shall see, there was nothing to prevent individual ministers from reviving the practice of political favouritism in appointments and promotions, or from consciously setting the militia against the permanent force. Still, when combined with the pay increases, the pension plan, the strict qualification standards introduced during Dundonald's tenure, and the growing tendency to appoint junior officers from among the graduates of the Royal Military College—a group of young men who, in the old-fashioned sense, desired only to serve—these latest measures provided the diligent officer with a much better environment in which to learn his job. This was essential if a true profession of arms was ever to be realized in Canada.

NOTES

1. Canada, House of Commons, *Debates*, 10 April 1883, 27 March 1884, 14 May 1886, 4 May 1888.

2. Lieutenant-Colonel George Maunsell to Adjutant General, 10 Jan. 1885, and Lieutenant-Colonel W.D. Otter to Adjutant General, 11 Jan. 1885, RG 9 11B1, vol. 86, docket 08423, Public Archives of Canada (hereafter PAC). Otter, commanding the school at Toronto, set different examinations for first and second class certificates, while Maunsell, commanding at Fredericton, set only one exam, and awarded those who did well a first.

3. Major-General Ivor Herbert, memorandum, 1894, RG 9 11B1, vol. 208, docket 49569, PAC.

4. Luard to Caron, 26 April 1883, RG 9 11A1, vol. 182, docket 09548, PAC; and, for Luard's initial selection, RG 9 11A1, vol. 150, docket 07048, PAC. Caron's first hint that a regular force might be formed came in Caron to Luard, 18 Feb. 1881, Caron Papers, PAC, vol. 1, letterbook, p. 21.

5. Luard to Caron, 12 May 1883, RG 9 11A1, vol. 183, docket 09601, PAC; and Luard to Caron, 13 June 1883, RG 9 11A1, vol. 185, docket 09697, PAC.

6. Luard to Lorne, 21 June 1883, Macdonald Papers, PAC, vol. 83; and Luard to Walker Powell, 23 June 1883, RG 9 11A1, vol. 185, docket 09697, PAC.

7. Walker Powell to Caron, 27 July 1883, Caron Papers, PAC, vol. 64, letter 3086.

8. RG 9, 11A1, vol. 315, docket A9473, PAC; ibid., vol. 353, docket A11869; ibid., vol. 410, docket 16373, PAC; RG 9 11B1, vol. 408, docket 1476/02, PAC; and Luard to Lorne, 21 June 1883, Macdonald Papers, PAC, vol. 83.

9. Macdonald to Lorne, 10 July 1883, Macdonald Papers, PAC, vol. 83.

10. Mackenzie Bowell to Macdonald, 11 Sept. 1889, Macdonald Papers, PAC, vol. 201.

11. See Desmond Morton, *The Canadian General: Sir William Otter* (Toronto: Hakkert, 1974), 206ff.

12. *Canadian Military Gazette*, 1 Nov. 1893, 207; ibid., 1 April 1895, 1; ibid., 15 April 1896, 2; and ibid., 15 Dec. 1893, 355.

13. *Canadian Military Gazette*, 15 Feb. 1895, 4–5.

14. Thomas Scoble to Hutton, 8 Nov. 1898, RG 9 11B1, vol. 284, docket 77730, PAC.

15. Commandants received $4.00 a day in 1883, captains $3.00, and lieutenants $2.50. By 1889 pay had increased by only fifty cents.

16. In 1893 majors in the United States army earned $209–$291 Canadian a month, majors in the British army $117, and majors in the Canadian permanent force $90–$105. Officers in the mounted police having the status of majors were paid $133. All but Canadian militia officers qualified for some form of pension. RG 24, vol. 6564, file HG 1064-1, PAC.

17. Mary Otter to Caron, 21 Aug. 1888, Caron Papers, PAC, vol. 116, letter 12082.

18. Deputy Minister to General Officer Commanding, 11 June 1886, RG 9 11A1, vol. 250, docket A3826, PAC.

19. Hughes to Hutton, 18 Aug. 1899, RG 9 11B1, vol. 404, docket 1091/02, PAC.

20. Middleton to Caron, 26 Jan. 1888, Caron Papers, vol. 115, letter 11997, PAC.

21. Middleton memorandum, 4 Feb. 1886, RG 9 11B1, vol. 113, docket 13865, PAC.

22. Middleton to Caron, n.d., Caron Papers, PAC, vol. 113, letter 13215.

23. Herbert to Minister of Militia, 19 Feb. 1891, RG 9 11B1, vol. 191, docket 35537, PAC; ibid., 11 Oct. 1892, RG 11B1, vol. 190, docket 43294, PAC.

24. Herbert to Minister of Militia, 10 May 1894, I.J.C. Herbert Papers, PAC, vol. 12, "Memorandum file"; ibid., June 1895, RG 9 11B1, vol. 76, docket 05464, PAC.

25. Herbert minute on Lieutenant-Colonel J. Homes to Herbert, 25 Jan. 1892, I.J.C. Herbert Papers, PAC, vol. 2, 255.

26. Canada Department of Militia, *Annual Report* (Ottawa: King's Printer), (hereafter *Militia Report*). See this report for each year.

27. Herbert to Caron, 27 April 1892, RG 9 11B1, vol. 185, docket 40731, PAC.

28. Herbert memorandum, Jan. 1894, RG 9 11B1, vol. 208, docket 49569, PAC.

29. Herbert to Minister of Militia, 10 May 1894, I.J.C. Herbert Papers, PAC, vol. 12, "Memorandum file."

30. Herbert to Minister of Militia, 4 April 1892, RG 9 11B1, vol. 184, docket 40365, PAC.

31. Herbert to Colonel Gorden, 18 April 1894, I.J.C. Herbert Papers, PAC, vol. 5, letter-book 1, 455–56.

32. Colonel Percy Lake (Quartermaster General) to Minister of Militia, 14 May 1895, RG 9 11B1, vol. 227, docket 56061, PAC.

33. Minister of Militia, memorandum, 5 Aug. 1893, RG 9 11A2, vol. 15, docket 9654, PAC.

34. Lieutenant-Colonel R.H. Davis, "The State and Condition of Rural Battalions of Infantry," *Selected Papers from the Transactions of the Canadian Military Institute*, vol. 6 (1984–85), 52 (hereafter cited as *Selected Papers, CMI*).

35. Herbert to Minister of Militia, 27 April 1892, RG 9 11B1, vol. 185, docket 40731, PAC.

36. Herbert to Minister of Militia, 10 May 1891, I.J.C. Herbert Papers, PAC, vol. 5, letter-book 1.

37. Herbert to Minister of Militia, 10 May 1894, I.J.C. Herbert Papers, PAC, vol. 12, "Memorandum file."

38. Desmond Morton, *Ministers and Generals: Politics and the Canadian Militia, 1868–1904* (Toronto: University of Toronto Press, 1970), 100–101.

39. Canada, House of Commons, *Debates*, 30 March and 8 April 1892, 6 June 1895.

40. Morton, *Ministers and Generals*, 106, 117.

41. Carmen Miller, "Sir Frederick Borden and Military Reform in Canada, 1896–1911," *Canadian Historical Review* 50 (Sept. 1969), 265–84.

42. Quoted in Morton, *Ministers and Generals*, 122.

43. Gascoigne minute, 8 June 1893, RG 9 11B1, vol. 271, docket 73432, PAC.

44. Maunsell to Adjutant General, 21 Sept. 1897, RG 9 11B1, vol. 247, docket 64737, PAC.

45. Hutton to Adjutant General, 16 Jan. 1899, RG 9 11B1, vol. 285, docket 78290, PAC; Hutton to Borden, 18 July 1899, RG 9 11B1, vol. 287, docket 18661, PAC.

46. Hutton to Theodore Roosevelt, 17 Oct. 1901, Hutton Papers, PAC, microfilm reel C1218, 774–75.

47. Hutton to Borden, 21 Dec. 1899, RG 9 11B1, vol. 210, docket 86765, PAC.

48. Hutton to Minto, 14 April 1900, Minto Papers, PAC, vol. 60, box MM #33, 11–16.

49. Canada, House of Commons, *Debates*, 26 June 1900, 15 April 1902. See also C.F. Winter, "Some Reflections upon Recent Experience and How Our Militia May Profit Thereby," *Selected Papers, CMI*, vol. 12 (1902), 45–65.

50. A.K. Blackadar, Inspector of Insurance, to Borden, 8 March 1901, RG 9 11B1, vol. 667, docket 97263, PAC. Bill C-133 was introduced on 2 May 1901. O'Grady-Haly to Minister of Militia, 30 Dec. 1901, RG 9 11B1, vol. 396, docket 200/02, PAC.

51. Canada, House of Commons, *Debates*, 15 April 1901.

52. RG 9 11B1, vol. 379, docket 4296/01, PAC; and *Canadian Military Gazette*, 12 Sept. 1905, 26.

53. *Militia Report*, 1903.

54. Adjutant General circular, 20 Nov. 1902, RG 9 11B1, vol. 447, docket 6038/02, PAC.

55. Adjutant General report, n.d., RG 9 11B1, vol. 448, docket 6120/02, PAC.

56. Adjutant General to Commandant, RMC, 23 June 1903, RG 9 11B1, vol. 665, docket C1/03, PAC.

57. Minutes of Militia Council, Report 3, 3 Jan. 1906, and Report 47, 28 Nov. 1906, RG 9 11A2, vol. 25, PAC.

58. Minutes of Militia Council, Report 24, 27 April 1905, RG 9 11A2, vol. 24, PAC.

59. *Militia Report*, 1905, 12–15.

60. Minutes of Militia Council, Report 27, 24 Dec. 1890, RG 9 11A2, vol. 27, PAC.

61. Minutes of Militia Council, Report 4, 30 Jan. 1906, RG 9 11A2, vol. 25, PAC; Minister of Militia, circular letter, 1 Feb. 1906, RG 24, vol. 4468, files HQC 372 and C11-5-1, PAC.

62. Morton, *Ministers and Generals*, 188ff.

63. Lake to Otter, 9 Feb. 1906, Otter Papers, PAC, vol. 2, file 7, "Jan. 1901–Dec. 1906."

64. Minister of Militia, circular letter, 18 Oct. 1911, RG 24, vol. 4469, file C/11-5-1, PAC.

65. Wilson to Chief Staff Officer, 5 Feb. 1906, RG 9 11J2, vol. 49, PAC.

66. Chief of the General Staff to Minister of Militia, 10 April 1911, approved 2 May 1911, RG 24, vol. 6504, file HG 31-9-13, part 1, PAC.

67. Lieutenant-Colonel Victor Williams to Secretary, Militia Council, 26 March 1912, RG 24, vol. 6504, file HG 313-9-13, part 2, PAC.

section

2

1914–1919

T he First World War was one of the great formative events in Canadian history. Mobilization affected every facet of Canadian life, and accelerated the pre-war trend away from a rural agriculture and resource based economy towards an urban industrial society. The intrusiveness of centrally managed economic policy lingered on after the war, personal income tax (introduced in 1917 as a temporary wartime measure) being just one example. The demands of war reshaped the nation and brought the government closer to the lives of individual citizens.

Mobilization for modern total war required the dispatch of expeditionary forces overseas, and the maintenance of those forces in the face of heavy losses. The debate over the scale of Canada's commitment to fighting polarized around the extent to which the war was seen as Canada's or Britain's—to Britain's war Canada need send little more than a token force. The debate cut across many seams within Canadian society: rural versus urban; new immigrant versus Canadian born; and the most pronounced, English versus French Canadian. In the main, urban English Canada pushed for maximum military effort as the honourable course in a war for peace and democracy. French Canada, largely rural and long settled in North America, not unnaturally showed much less enthusiasm for what was seen as a European war. French-Canadian alienation from the war effort was enhanced by the gross mishandling of recruitment during the first two years of the war. Under Hughes's enthusiastic and utterly misdirected attention, Canada raised nearly 250 battalions for overseas service: only 48 ever saw action in France and only one of these, the 22nd, was French-Canadian. By the middle of the war the wreckage of Hughes's administration lay strewn from Victoria to Dover.

The French-Canadian preference for a small military effort clashed with the increasingly ardent imperial nationalism of English Canada. The crisis came in 1917 when the casualty bill from 1916 and the failure of all attempts at negotiated settlement made it clear that the war would only be ended by more fighting. To maintain the four Canadian divisions at the front, conscription for overseas service was deemed necessary. Even as Canada's great victory at Vimy Ridge was celebrated, the fabric of the nation was rent over the government's plans for compulsory service. Opposition to the plan was intense, particularly in Quebec. While the Canadian Expeditionary Force (CEF) toiled in the mud of Flanders, cavalry from Ontario swept protesters from the streets of Quebec City, and infantrymen with machine guns guarded key buildings. Some French Canadians observed, not without justification, that they did not have to go to Europe to fight "Prussians." The ghosts of 1917 would haunt the nation in the next great war.

It was natural in 1914 for Canada to limit its military effort to land forces. The navy was in a decrepit state and until 1917 Canada's coastline was secured by Britain's preponderant command of the sea. The Royal Canadian Navy's (RCN) one chance at glory came the week war was declared, when the aged cruiser HMCS *Rainbow* was sent to search in the Pacific for a squadron of modern German cruisers. Ottawa admonished Commodore Walter Hose, as he led Canada's entire Pacific fleet to certain destruction, to "remember Nelson and the British Navy." Fortunately for Hose and *Rainbow*, the Germans "escaped" and a potentially great and noble disaster—well suited to the romantic notions of the Edwardian Empire—was avoided. Instead, the RCN's war was largely one of dreary patrolling, and in 1917–18 its small coastal forces were unprepared for the intrusion of large German submarines into Canadian waters.

Canada did, though, have a navy, even if it was unprepared for war. During the First World War there was no Canadian air force to speak of (one was formed in the last weeks of the war). Canadians who wanted to undertake military flying did so as part of the Royal Flying Corps, the Royal Naval Air Service or, after April 1918, the new Royal Air Force. Many thousands did, and they established an enviable reputation. Much has been written about Canada's "knights of the air"—Bishop, Collishaw, Barker, and many others—but the airwar from 1914 to 1918 was far more complex than the fighter ace literature indicates. Indeed, the aces flew so that other, more prosaic tasks such as aerial mapping, reconnaissance, artillery control, and the like, could be employed to assist the army. It was no accident that success at Vimy in 1917 coincided with major advances in air support and the period of the greatest Canadian aces, Bishop and Barker.

The real Canadian military story from 1914 to 1918 was, of course, the growth and development of the Canadian Corps into one of the most successful fighting forces on the Western Front. It was a complex process, involving radical changes in the organization, administration, training, and command of the expeditionary force. In a war that consumed amateurs and professionals alike at a prodigious rate, Canada's frontline soldiers developed their own unique professionalism during the war. That process began near the Belgian city of Ypres in April 1915 when the Canadians fought their first major battle, a baptism of fire known as "Second Ypres." It is best remembered as the first major use of gas in modern war. The Canadians stopped the local German attack, but the defensive part of Second Ypres was less typical of the Canadian experience on the western front than the hastily prepared and dreadfully executed counterattacks that characterized its second phase. Indeed, for most of the war the Canadians were fated to attack. Before Vimy there was little that the individual Canadian divisions could do to mitigate the awful consequences of poorly conceived frontal assaults. The surreal nature of these rushes through no-man's-land in 1915–1916 was epitomized by the Somme offensive of 1916: the Newfoundlanders were literally wiped-out on the first day and Canadian divisions which followed later in the ordeal fared little better.

The intervention of a radically new weapon, the tank, alongside the Canadians at Courcellette in 1916 seemed to offer hope for ending the deadlock. Solving the riddle of trench warfare, though, required more than the introduction of one new weapon; soldiers and generals needed to learn how to use their existing weapons more effectively. The changes that produced the Canadian victory at Vimy in early 1917 had little to do with either attrition or new weapons and had everything to do with rising professional competence and exploitation of the power granted to the Canadians by the establishment of a separate "Canadian Corps." The corps achieved its high standards in part by rejecting the amateurism of Sam Hughes and the pre-war militia, and by keeping the wreckage of Hughes's muddled administration at arm's length. The extent to which the development of this superb corps belonged to its principal commander, Arthur Currie, remains a major point of debate. But Currie, the gifted amateur turned professional by hard experience, was only one among many in the CEF. The new corps' first success was at Vimy (under Sir Julian Byng), but others continued to follow to the very end of the war: Hill 70 and Passchendaele in 1917, and at Amiens on 8 August 1918.

General Erich Ludendorf, Chief of Staff of the German Army, called 8 August the "Black Day of the German Army," and it marked the beginning of the Hundred Days Campaign that culminated in the armistice of 11 November. On that day the Canadian Corps, at the head of the British advance, liberated the Belgian city of Mons, the site of the British Expeditionary Force's first battle with the advancing Germans four years earlier. That symbolic gesture caused some controversy later because casualties were suffered after the armistice had been signed. But Canadians had long since been fighting for more than ground gained or enemies killed. Their purpose had been to achieve for Canada on the international stage what would otherwise require years of quiet diplomacy and lobbying—recognition of Canada as an independent political player. When the issue of the British Dominions signing the Treaty of Versailles on their own behalf was raised in 1919, French objection was swept aside at the mention that Canada and Australia together had put a million citizens into uniform. Not surprisingly, generations of Canadians believed that their new international stature after 1918 owed something to their military effort during the Great War.

RECRUITING, 1914–1916 ◊

RONALD G. HAYCOCK

○

Military records show that by the end of the Great War 619 636 Canadian men and women had served with the army. It took four years to raise such a number, and well over half enlisted while Sam Hughes was war minister. By late 1916 when he was fired from the cabinet, the army overseas had four divisions and another ready for organization. But Canadians at home had lost much of their enthusiasm for volunteering to feed the field force. However, two years earlier the opposite had been true when the majority of Canadians seemed determined to do their duty. After the first contingent left Valcartier, the prime minister authorized a second one in mid-October. The next month militia headquarters decided to maintain 30 000 men under arms in Canada. By July 1915 the overall total was 150 000 and three months later 250 000. On New Year's Day 1916, the prime minister announced that the national establishment of the Canadian Expeditionary Force (CEF) would be a half million men. It all looked so easy. But by mid-1916, the volunteer system began to falter all over the country. As the war effort stepped up, the demands of the other equally vital forces of industry and agriculture competed for the men. Enlistments slowed down. In English Canada pessimistic conscription rumours turned into open demands; and as enlistments dried up before the mounting casualties in Europe, French Canadians recoiled at the prospect of being drafted for a foreign war, which by 1916 they no longer considered much of their concern.

To avoid a national schism—perhaps even an open rebellion—the government desperately tried other solutions. By the fall of 1916 national registration to co-ordinate the wealth of the nation had come and gone. In early

◊ From *Sam Hughes: The Public Career of a Controversial Canadian, 1885–1916,* Canadian War Museum Historical Publication No. 21 (Waterloo, ON: Wilfrid Laurier University Press in collaboration with the Canadian War Museum, the Canadian Museum of Civilization, and the National Museums of Canada, 1986), 198–224.

1917, amid the crescendo of English-Canadian voices demanding conscription, the harried Borden administration attempted to free volunteers for the front by establishing the Canadian Defence Force for domestic duty, but it too failed. That spring, after the British authorities predicted the need for more and more troops, the prime minister finally resigned himself to military conscription. In May 1917 he announced his intention and padded the blow by promising to bring in conscription through a union government. In the next six months, the declaration split the country along French and English lines, irrespective of party, and by the general election in December 1917, Canada had both coalition government and conscripts.[1] The story of these events involves Sam Hughes, and to a large degree he, like his prime minister, must bear both praise and blame.

Sam Hughes' one-man mobilization effort in 1914 set the tone for recruiting in the next two years. Hughes gave to the recruitment effort nerve-end leadership—spirit, enthusiasm, vigour, hope, and confidence—but little order and less administration. He conceived of Canada's war contributions mainly in terms of fighting troops in a national army. But he never appeared to understand fully the modern needs of such a force. He could not see, first, that national war must have at least a semblance of consensus of the nation's people—both French and English—and second, that limits on the size of the force and the method of keeping it at established strength were problems which eventually would have to be faced. Force size was a political problem that belonged to the government as a whole but one for which Sam Hughes as militia minister must give sound and realistic advice to the cabinet. Maintenance of strength, however, was an administrative question that for the most part belonged to Sam Hughes. Instead of understanding these dimensions, he seemed governed solely by a desire to show Canada's martial prowess on the battlefield in a huge patriotic and volunteer army without regard for the effects of unrestrained recruiting on industry, agriculture, or the combat efficiency of the force.[2] But in 1914 and 1915 the faults of Sam Hughes's recruiting system were not immediately obvious because the demands of war were not known; and in all fairness to Hughes, few of his fellow ministers in the beginning had any more of an accurate conception of how best to respond to the crisis. For months all of them worked in the dark using dilapidated tools of state. Some found both light and better utensils; Hughes never did.

When the first contingent had sailed in October 1914, Hughes had been thankful that Borden had allowed all the volunteers to go, a sure sign that both men agreed in the limited and archaic view that the best way to pursue the war effort was with soldiers in large numbers. When Hughes returned from England early the next month he immediately plunged into the organization of the second contingent, recently announced by the prime minister. In terms of manpower, he swung back to the old decentralized recruiting arrangements that had been with the militia since Confederation. In the scheme, authority rested with the officers commanding the divisions, who in turn gave quotas to each of the militia units of their areas. The quotas were supplied by headquarters, but beyond that there was little help from Ottawa in personnel, funds, or organization. In the first three years of the war, Ottawa spent only $27 000 on recruitment, most of it in 1917. But then little help was expected.[3]

The months from August 1914 to July 1915 are best described as ones of the enlisting rather than recruiting. Nearly 60 000 had joined in 1914 alone. By February 1915 Hughes announced that a third contingent would be sent and optimistically told the Commons that "I could raise three more contingents in three weeks if necessary." As yet there was no perceived shortage of manpower in industry or agriculture. But it was the off-season for agriculture, and others presumed that the recession-induced unemployed were being conveniently siphoned off into CEF units. By June 1915 the overseas force had 100 247 officers and men. During the special session of Parliament the year before, Hughes had made it clear that as far as he was concerned this war would be one of volunteers, not conscripts. The prime minister had agreed when he told a Halifax audience in December that "there has not been, there will not be compulsion or conscription." The only technique Hughes applied during this period was to keep close watch on who got the commands of each new battalion.[4] Sometime the divisional commanders asked that units be allowed to organize in their districts; other times—and increasingly so—Hughes made arrangements himself with specific individuals, then informed the divisional organization to expect a new unit in the area. True to his romantic view of war, the minister was convinced that in a crisis a citizen's patriotic sense of duty would be sufficient to supply all the volunteers necessary. All he had to do was constantly remind them of it. As soon as he recovered sufficiently from the illness that had put him in the hospital in late December, Hughes took to his private rail car late in January to encourage volunteering. He had to get back to Ottawa by the opening of the new session on 5 February but before that he covered seven thousand miles in two weeks and delivered over twenty-five recruiting speeches across the country.[5]

Hughes gave out the stuff that many wanted to hear: the Empire was threatened; Canada had to do its duty. Canadians could do it and would do it; it was the moment of national greatness; Canada was a principal in the war, not a colony. Hughes's battle message, mixing national pride and imperial obligation, was contagious. No wonder Castell Hopkins considered him during those early days to be the single most visible and enthusiastic recruiting agent in the country.[6] The minister's confidence, pride, and cajoling also added to the impression that manpower resources were infinite and no other government facilities except Sam Hughes's sermons were necessary in raising the country to war.

The illusion was substantially aided by patriotic citizens themselves. The fervour seemed so great that the problem was not in stirring it up but in controlling it. The various gifts of money and food sent to the Belgian Relief Fund and to the British government in the early days were ample evidence of that spirit; so were the campaigns in many communities to contribute to the well-being of the soldiers. Local councils quickly arranged for gifts of money, clothing, and the small amenities like cigarettes and socks.

Many churches and women's organizations across the country did their bit as well. The Ontario government donated a half million dollars to the Imperial War Fund in Great Britain. The same special session of Parliament that brought the ominous War Measures Act into being in August 1914 also created the Canadian Patriotic Fund, of which Hughes was one of the honorary vice-presidents. This group was dedicated to raising and distributing money to soldiers' families and it expanded and carried out this function throughout the war. In fact, the general shortage of equipment produced such a spontaneous public response of private donations, like "the machine gun movement," that militia officials and Borden were so embarrassed by the summer of 1915, they refused to accept such gifts. Hughes, however, had no such pangs. His role, he knew, was to encourage the people on to new heights of patriotic effort. In fact, Robert Borden's biographer claims that this sort of decentralized war responsibility was a calculated "policy decision at the beginning of the war." Hughes's activities in recruiting, therefore, were not out of tune with the rest of the government's general view of its role in promoting active citizen participation in the war effort.[7]

However, by the spring of 1915 there were signs that these time-honoured concepts were not adequate. There were thirty-six thousand Canadians already overseas, with an entire division in the trenches after February 1915. The war had lasted longer than the predicted six months; Christmas had come and gone and there were yet no victories. Then in mid-March, the British reported thirteen thousand casualties, including one hundred Canadians, at Neuve Chapelle, and bungled the opportunity for the elusive "breakthrough" on the western front to regain the magic mobility every general sought. Even though few Canadian were victims, the twenty-five thousand lost on both sides was a terrible omen for Canadians. The CEF did not have long to wait: a few weeks later the Canadians held a bulging section of the line near Ypres in Belgium. Late in the day of 22 April, the Germans smashed into the French colonial troops to the left of the Canadians with artillery and the dreaded chlorine gas. In a ferocious defensive battle lasting nearly a week, Canada's tenacious amateurs restored the line at the terrible price of nearly six thousand men. They won the admiration of all. Their effort was quickly followed by smaller but similarly expensive defences at Festubert in May and Givenchy in June. The Germans torpedoed the supposedly unarmed British liner *Lusitania* off the coast of Ireland on 8 May. It took twelve hundred lives, one hundred of them from Ontario. This was indeed war; Canadians were stunned.[8]

Back home the successes of the CEF in these battles stirred the Canadian soul; but they also were a rude awakening to the true sacrifices. The Canadian Ross rifle, it was reported, had not worked well. Some said gunners had not had enough artillery shells to give adequate support to the Canadian infantry. But the most shocking revelations were the casualty lists. An increasing number of Canadian homes mourned the loss of loved ones; and it was not likely to stop. At the end of May the British government announced, largely as a result of the jolt to its own complacency caused by the German spring offensive, that "His Majesty's Government would accept with deep gratitude" any number of troops the Canadians could send.[9] Hughes took it as a personal signal.

But would Hughes's non-system of recruiting provide the reinforcements? Even before Ypres there were signs that the rural militia units were having trouble filling their enlistment quotas. *Globe* columnist Peter McArthur demanded that it was time the militia minister co-ordinate his actions with the Agriculture Department in some definite recruiting policy. Part of the flash of enthusiasm which had given nearly sixty thousand volunteers in 1914 was that most of the ranks—over 70 percent in the first contingent—were not Canadians, but British-born immigrants. Initially native Canadians had little enthusiasm to fight for king and Empire in Europe. This fact made no impression on Hughes, at least not one that he nor anyone else admitted publicly. Yet suspicions indicated something extra was needed. Other citizens began stepping into the breach with or without Sam Hughes. The same month as Neuve Chapelle, the Speakers Patriotic League, the joint brainchild of H.A. Ames, a Quebec Conservative MP, and N.F. Davidson, an Ontario Tory organizer, was created in Toronto. It was the first of many private civilian associations designed to promote all facets of the patriotic response to the war, including a more systematic recruiting organization. From this point, private recruiting leagues appeared all over English Canada. Their proliferation in Ontario was so rapid that by November 1915 they combined into a central organization—the Ontario Recruiting Association with branches throughout the province working hand in hand with local militia authorities.[10]

Hughes was all for the local organizations and a personal approach to the war effort, as he had been since he had sent out his famous 226 night telegrams mobilizing the first contingent shortly after the war started. After that he had used the existing local militia structure to funnel into the CEF whole battalions closely associated with particular areas. But he did not do it without opposition. Since September 1914, the chief of the general staff had warned Hughes that he could not keep adding such units to the overseas force. What should be done, Gwatkin had then protested, was to establish modern centrally located depots providing basic training for the unbrigaded troops before they were syphoned off as reinforcements for the veteran line units. Before the war Sir Ian Hamilton had also warned Hughes about this lack of depots. Their reasons were solid. More efficient training and use of manpower and a smaller casualty rate were three important ones. As well, authorities would have some accurate idea of available resources on hand, a fact not always present in the anachronistic and decentralized method which Hughes had followed since the outbreak of hostilities. The American Civil War, of which Hughes claimed to be a student, had pointed out the perils of constantly raising new battalions, then sending these fresh but green troops into battle. But the minister did not believe it was so; the Boer war needed no such elaborate and soulless depots to produce good fighting men, so he ignored his staff.[11]

After the spring battles of 1915, the shocking casualties and increased demands reaffirmed Hughes's resolve to secure more men. The second contingent had lingered long in Canada awaiting transport and billets in England. Hughes was anxious to get it overseas. By the middle of June it sailed, but the recruiting news at home, while gratifying, was not as spectacular as it had been. It seemed that just as the manpower demands were rising remarkably, the will to supply them was faltering. The possibilities of a substantial short-fall were obvious after it became clear at the end of June that Hughes wanted to form a Canadian corps of two divisions. The thought horrified Connaught; he secretly confided to Kitchener that the move was a ruinous one contrived by Hughes for no other reason than to satisfy his ego for a Canadian national force "possibly with a view of obtaining the command . . . himself." The Duke also suffered from his own form of exaggeration: he was afraid of an invasion by German-Americans from the still neutral United States, and even more of a revolt in the west by recent immigrants from enemy countries. Troops should therefore be kept in Canada. More accurately, Connaught worried about the disastrous effect on vital agricultural and industrial production caused by Hughes's wholesale recruiting. Connaught protested to Lord Kitchener that it was "extremely doubtful" if the Dominion could "keep an Army Corps in the field up to its proper establishment."[12]

It was not probable that Hughes had duped Borden into supporting the formation of a Canadian corps, as the governor general also imagined. The prime minister was himself determined to send more troops. Nevertheless, the governor general had put his finger on the exact point that caused the regular soldiers so much anxiety. An army corps meant at least fifty thousand troops in France. A corps was also the natural precursor of an army. Gwatkin and Deputy Minister Fiset had been greatly alarmed at the wastage of the CEF in the spring of 1915. At that time, Canada had to contend only with one division. The possibility of twice as many casualties came with the formation of a corps. An army, if it came out of that, would be impossible to maintain. Gwatkin wanted no more than a corps, and certainly not an army. In June when he told Borden that Hughes's grandiose plans were a "mistake," it had made no impression. A few days later, in responding to an enthusiastic militia colonel, who like many of the patriots wanted many more men sent, Gwatkin bluntly stated that it was wrong "to go on adding to the number of regiments, batteries, and battalions at the front." Better, he thought, to train reinforcements and produce war material rather than to be drawn into an intolerable and exhausting war effort because of a commitment to an unrealistic combat force.[13] The true import of his and the Duke's message was that Sam Hughes's vision of a massive field effort was courting ruin, and that there were different ways to make war other than by sending warriors. Also implicit was that Hughes should advise Borden that a realistic establishment had to be determined and then adopt an efficient method of maintaining it that was in tune with national capabilities.

It was not to happen. On 8 July 1915, Robert Borden increased the CEF force to 150 000.[14] The new figure meant more recruits. While the monthly enlistments had gone up in June, they were not sufficient to allow for even normal wastage in the new national goal.

In response Hughes remained largely on the old personal course. But a few weeks earlier, he had made some small concessions in applying direct government aid for recruiting when he decided that central rather than regimental recruiting offices would be set up and that recruiting would be continuous. In August, as a further inducement for volunteers, he approved from afar a national recruiting poster campaign; one hundred thousand of them were distributed from coast to coast. After that no other national advertising went on out of the militia headquarters for over a year, and even then the minister rejected the Canadian Press Association's offer to co-operate in a national newspaper campaign to stimulate recruiting.[15]

In the summer of 1915, Hughes spent two months in England. Like the prime minister who was also there, Hughes went to the front where he saw the magnitude, the horror, and the deadlock of the war situation. When he got back to Canada in early September, what he had seen and heard only cemented his determination to step up the national effort. Canada now had a corps, but victory was not close; the British had not handled the first year at all well. What was needed was more and more troops. At the end of September, enlistment figures dipped threateningly. Hughes told reporters about his new local battalion and billeting plans. Modelled in part on Lord Derby's battalions in England, Hughes promised to house and train troops in any centre that could raise twenty-five or more district recruits. Surely, he reasoned, it would help the citizens realize the importance of the war as well as comfort men anxious about doing initial duty in a strange place. But the other aspect of the scheme had its roots in the traditional local unit structure of the non-permanent militia. Indeed, that was its very essence and the sum of Sam Hughes's forty-one years of experience in the Canadian volunteers. Hughes believed in the time-honoured technique of raising citizen-soldiers by appointing prominent politicians and business-men as lieutenant-colonels to enlist battalions in their own local areas.[16] Sometimes these men were the minister's personal and political friends who had no particular military knowledge. Over the next year, because recruiting "was continuous" and the men were penny-packeted across the country, the training was a hit and miss affair. The first man to enlist trained most, the last man hardly at all. Often those early volunteers, in effect, immediately became recruiters themselves in the desperate rush to get other men. The local billeting made the plan costly. In some cases supervision was nearly impossible and consequently discipline was often poor. Evidently the plan also deviated from the central recruiting centres set down earlier in the summer. Implicit in Hughes's scheme was the suggestion that recruits raised from the same locality would go overseas and fight together. As it turned out, the units were broken up in England to maintain the strength of the corps in France. A.M.J. Hyatt and Desmond Morton have called Hughes's scheme variously a "confidence trick" or a hoax. Since the labels both imply deliberate intent to defraud, such charges are not fair to Hughes any more than they are to Borden who supported the methods. Yet continuous recruiting until the moment of departure made retraining in England almost a certainty. Nevertheless, these problems were not Hughes's concern; and even though they should have been, his mind could not handle those sorts of details, if he saw the flaws at all. He wanted men, and at October's end, Borden followed Hughes's lead, again raising the national commitment to 250 000.[17]

Why Borden did this is not clear. His biographer suggests the cause was rising casualties, more and more demands, poor leadership in London and Ottawa, and the lack of decisive victory. The papers of Captain Harold Daly, Hughes's assistant, explain more:

> Once toward the end of 1915, he [Hughes] decided to raise another 100 000 men. He went over to see Sir Robert Borden, got authority for it, and told me to send over and get an atlas showing the different [political] constituencies. He then dictated about a hundred telegrams to different people, one in each constituency and out of that I think we got 60 000–70 000 men. He knew everybody all over the country who was popular and who could raise men.[18]

If Daly's memory is correct, the comment epitomizes the personal improvised nature of Hughes's recruiting ideas. But more than that, Daly's observations point out the scope of political party organization; with its emphasis on patronage as the means, the party system had traditionally performed many of the social duties that, in later days, Canadians expected the state to undertake. When war was declared this party machinery geared up to help solve the country's recruitment problem.

Hughes was one of the chief supporters and users of this traditional party system. In 1914 it was at the root of his 226 night telegrams; it was present in his retention of control over military offices and later recruiting. As represented by Sam Hughes, the government provided the impulses to the party structure to secure volunteers. What was in the interest of the party was good for the country. On that October day in 1915, when he told Daly to get out the constituent map, he was really calling for a stepped-up effort by the old party system as one of the normal pieces of machinery running that portion of the war effort. The episode also illuminates the relationship and similarity of ideas between Hughes and Borden. For a short time at least, it appeared that Hughes's recruiting rationale was paying off. With the new establishment set that October, enlistments jumped by five thousand in November, and again in December.[19]

While men like Daly may have thought the minister's recruiting accomplishments "wonderful," the other powerful reasons for the success remained the loyal and hard work of the volunteer citizens, recruiting leagues, and sufficient men who were willing to join. Yet Hughes remained, with his continuous touring, speeches, and inspections, the most visible single national recruiting figure in the entire improvised scheme. The apparent success of the combination, which he believed was mostly due to his own efforts, stirred the minister to make bigger promises and more boastful claims. Already on record the previous February as claiming that he could raise three more contingents in three weeks, a little later he told a Montreal audience that he could "send a fifth [division] a sixth, a tenth or a twentieth." In Toronto in October, he declared to an enthusiastic recruiting rally: "We are coming General Kitchener, 500 000 strong." By the end of the year,

Borden had translated that optimism into a half-million-man establishment for the CEF.[20]

On 30 December, when Hughes and two other cabinet colleagues, White and Reid, met with Borden, the prime minister proposed that the overseas forces' establishment should be raised to five hundred thousand. The move, Borden was convinced, would be welcomed by English Canadians who were beginning to think that the Conservative administration, except for Hughes's activities no doubt, was not fighting the war vigorously enough. He also believed that the larger the physical contribution the greater would be Canada's influence over British war policy. With the way events were going at the front, the prime minister went on to reason, surely such a force would be needed. If all three visitors were surprised by the proposal, Hughes at least expected and wanted the new commitment; and he supported it fully. By 12 January, the establishment of the CEF was put at five hundred thousand men. The question was: Could it be done?[21]

By now there were even Canadians who felt that it was too dangerous and too difficult a task; and as for others, maybe because they were Englishmen or professional soldiers or both, no one had bothered to consult General Gwatkin, the governor general, or the people at the War Office; all of them were opposed. Borden also ignored R.B. Bennett, his parliamentary secretary, who had complained earlier that December that the new figure was impossible. Evidently few other ministers were consulted before Borden's decision was made. The new goal had been an impulse supported by Hughes, by White and Reid, and indirectly endorsed by Sir George Foster in the trade department, who naively thought that if 40 percent of the population of about eight million was of military age then a five hundred thousand man CEF was not unrealistic. Ironically, Foster also thought that Hughes's recruiting methods were unrealistic and chaotic.[22]

But there was no doubt in the militia minister's mind that they could get the half million. Neither a challenge to the prime minister's judgment nor a doubt of its subsequent effect on other vital sectors of the war effort came from Hughes. Privately he told Borden, "we can easily live up to your offer, if right systems are pursued." Immediately he plunged into the new challenge by commissioning more local battalions and more local prominent citizens, friends, and businessmen. In 1915 alone, beyond the elements of the second contingent, Hughes had already approved of 141 CEF units; in 1916 the same method added 79 more; and as the local sources were no longer as fruitful, Hughes encouraged special interests, which encouraged the proliferation of Highland battalions, "Pals" and "Bantams" formations, and Irish regiments. Early in 1916 Hughes also promised that he would bring the best of the overseas officers home from the front to raise new units, a proposal which must have alarmed CEF commanders already suffering from serious shortages of reinforcements and experienced officers. As before, the minister rejected using only the regular military structure; what he sought, he said, was "strong men who have successful business or professional training . . . the best soldiers are such men as engineers, barristers, contractors, large businessmen with military training. . . . They far surpass the professional soldier."[23]

Ministerial optimism knew no bounds. In January 1916 Hughes easily convinced Borden to approve the establishment of a fourth Canadian division; the announcement sparked Max Aitken, the minister's chief overseas agent, to wire flatteringly: "Your exertions may save the Empire." Certainly the accolade spurred the militia minister on; in February he told a New York *Times* reporter that he could raise one and three-quarter million men without compulsion in a matter of a few months. In Ottawa he laid out an elaborate plan to raise nearly twenty more divisions. It was unrealistic. Toronto was to give five, Ontario four; Manitoba and Saskatchewan, Quebec, British Columbia, and the Maritimes each gave two.[24]

By then the magnitude of Hughes's plans started to frighten his cabinet colleagues. Frequently council meetings, already stormy, became even more bitter. Thomas White was now alarmed. Hughes, he complained, "wants to press recruiting regardless of other considerations." It was true. Even the prime minister was finally having doubts about his own national pledge in the hands of Sam Hughes. He asked the militia minister not to recruit so that it dislocated other national priorities or denuded some localities of their manpower. Hughes paid little heed, but continued to cajole the country into sending more of its sons. From January to March 1916 over ninety thousand Canadians joined up.[25]

But in the spring of 1916 there were pressing public arguments against unrestrained enlistments. Ironically much of the discontent came from those groups which had often been the minister's most fervent recruiting aids—the civilian recruiting leagues. Dissatisfied for some time, they all agreed that the government could no longer count on volunteering to provide the resources. Now that Canadian industry, agriculture, timber, and mining resources were beginning to feel the strains of full wartime employment, the government had to impose a centralized and integrated recruiting policy to avoid harming the effort of the home-front. Moreover, the burden had to be distributed so that all parts of the Dominion were sharing it equally; and many identified Quebec as delinquent in doing its share. To some, what was needed was a national registration of the manpower, to others, an inventory of all wealth of the nation including human, and to even others, compulsion if necessary. But they all agreed that the Borden government could no longer avoid direct involvement in recruiting and national mobilization.

Two of the most prominent critics were Lord Shaughnessy, president of the CPR, and Senator James Mason, the seventy-three-year-old former commanding officer of the 10th Royal Grenadiers. Both men had been great supporters of the war effort. But by March they were sceptical about meeting the new national pledge of half a million men. When Shaughnessy spoke out in Montreal about the goal's harmful effect on national production, Hughes scornfully dismissed the warning as a "piffle," and publicly told Shaughnessy to mind his own business. Privately Borden agreed, choosing to believe that Shaughnessy's statement was nothing more than a political conspiracy against his administration. But then James Mason laid bare for his senate colleagues the hard realities of Borden's goals and the weaknesses of Hughes's improvised recruiting. "This large number [500 000]," he told a hushed chamber, "means that we shall have to provide each month . . . at least 25 000 new men—or 300 000 a year. There can be no question that the additional 250 000 to bring our quota up to 500 000 and the 300 000 if required annually to keep it at that figure will not be obtained under the present system of enlistment."[26] To Hughes it was still "piffle."

But it was not so to others. Many of the provincial governments had organized their war effort far better than Hughes had his own department. The Canadian Manufacturers' Association followed up Shaughnessy's predictions in a memorandum critical of Hughes's unlimited and unorganized recruiting. Various patriotic and recruiting leagues called for conscription or at least creation of a national register of wealth. So did Sir John Eaton, and executives of the Nova Scotia Steel Company, Consumers Gas, and the Dominion Steel Corporation. In April the New Brunswick Legislature passed a resolution asking Borden to employ "scientific means" in recruiting to protect industry and agriculture; and many national newspaper editorials carried similar messages. The old Tory, Castell Hopkins, sadly reported to readers of his *Canadian Annual Review* that during these months "the arbitrary policy and personality of Sam Hughes sometimes worked against recruiting as his enthusiasm and efforts worked for it." There was more alarming evidence long before the year was through. By April the monthly recruiting figures started to plummet from over thirty-four thousand in March to a low of about six thousand by September 1916, where they remained for some time. However, the previous spring while the protest was rising and the enlistments falling, Borden had done little publicly to change Hughes's improvised methods. In April the prime minister refused to hear a delegation of recruiting league members who had come to him hoping that he would do something in terms of registration and compulsion. When he refused to act, as Sir George Foster confessed to the delegates the next day, it was because the cabinet was afraid of riots in Quebec. In the same month, the frustrated recruiters formed the Canadian National Service League and openly lobbied for the draft.[27]

While Hughes remained in effective control of his department through 1915 and 1916, he continued to ignore the criticisms that his method of recruiting did not work. But many of his newly minted colonels who were raising local battalions were increasingly aware that there were serious problems. Frequently Hughes had authorized several units in the same area, and the battalion commanders ended up in cut throat competition for men. Many used any method they could to secure the quotas; and it varied from bribing to shaming the individual into enlisting. None of it encouraged the hesitant volunteer. Two examples seem typical of those who had problems. Late in 1915 the militia minister let his old friend, William Price, raise a unit, the 204th, in Quebec's Eastern Townships. After spending three months and a great deal of his time and money, and still never forming much of a battalion, Price lost his enthusiasm. His complaints to Hughes's aide in February 1916 sum up many unit commanders' frustrations and the minister's inability to give recruiting some structure:

I can now see that there will be difficulty in raising many men in this province. The organization is rotten and there is a complete misunderstanding of how to get French-Canadians to recruit. Each battalion should be given a certain district and should be forced to recruit from there and not allowed outside. This would force the battalions to recruit their localities thoroughly; at present, they do as they like and steal from each other. The way things go I am going to have a hard time to raise my men. . . . You might tell Sir Sam after what I have, it is impossible with the present organization to raise twenty thousand men from the district. To do so requires a complete new system and some slave driver at the head with the power of sacking.[28]

This unit never completed its establishment. Further west, where recruiters did not have to contend with reluctant French Canadians, Lieutenant-Colonel W.A. Griesbach, commanding officer of the 49th (Edmonton Regiment), had much more success. But he still complained of the lack of organization and the disastrous effects of interbattalion competition.[29] One of the problems was that Hughes would not establish a centrally controlled system. The "slave driver," as Price said, also needed to be one who was willing to delegate authority and to pay close attention to routine detail.

But it was not only the home-front that suffered under Hughes's recruiting improvisations. Once in England the supposedly trained Hughes battalions were mercifully broken up and retrained by the British, then transferred to France as drafts. Consequently, now unemployed, bitter, and increasingly vocal officers were an embarrassment to the Canadian government. Hughes ignored, then denied their existence as a problem, but the complaints continued to embarrass all. So too did the slowly emerging realization that Hughes's labyrinth of an overseas organization was starving the front of desperately needed reinforcements. One side-effect was to encourage Hughes to try to add more divisions to the Canadian corps as a simple solution. Yet the corps commander, General Alderson, knew that this was not the answer; steady and adequate reinforcement of his existing divisions was. By mid-February 1916, he actually returned to England to try to solve the reinforcement bottleneck. But with little help from Hughes's appointees there, and desperate in the expectation of huge casualties in the spring and summer fighting, the frustrated Alderson circumvented Hughes by placing his grievances directly before his old army friend, the Duke of Connaught. The facts, he told the governor general, spoke for themselves: of the 1476 officers and 25 087 men in the Canadian camp at Shorncliffe, only 75 and 2385, respectively, were trained to go to France. The problem, according to Alderson, was due not only to Hughes's multi-headed overseas administration, but also to the poor state of the recruits coming from Canada.[30]

By then Hughes was not insensitive to the reinforcement problem, but he would not let anyone else try to resolve it. In March, when Parliament was halfway through its 1916 session—and at a time when rumours of Militia Department scandals were growing steadily—Hughes decided to rush over to England to straighten out personally the problems in reinforcement and administration. In the meantime, Gwatkin, who had likely been alerted by Connaught, informed Hughes's temporary replacement, A.E. Kemp, of the dangerous reinforcement situation due to the minister's snafu in training. If Kemp had hoped to improve things during Hughes's absence, a severe political storm focusing directly on Hughes prevented it. Before he could solve anything in England, the attacks on his administration became so acute that Borden had to order him back to Canada in April. It left the situation in England and at the front unresolved. On his return Hughes commissioned General Lessard to make a confidential inspection of training depots in England. After touring the camps for several weeks in April and May, Lessard confirmed Aldersons's and Gwatkin's charges. But Hughes never made public Lessard's damning report. To do so would have been to admit the failure of the minister's local recruiting and training program. If the prime minister knew about it, there [were] also certain benefits for the government in keeping silent on Lessard's findings. Opposition attacks during the parliamentary session, which had ended in mid-May, were very heavy. Most of them were focused on the militia minister and, thereby, the entire Conservative administration. Two royal commissions also were still pending; and both were concerned with Sam Hughes's office. With the recent high casualties coming from the Battle of St. Eloi in March and April, Lessard's news would not be welcomed by the public. But whatever the motives for suppressing the report, the problems of the surplus officers and the quality and training of the troops continued for more months—the months of Mount Sorrel and the Somme.[31]

If Sam Hughes's recruiting policy caused problems in English Canada where the majority viewed the war as a national crusade, then it proved calamitous in French Canada where there was no such passion. As the war progressed, the difference in attitudes between French and English Canada became more and more obvious; and with the imposition of conscription in 1918, it led to near open rebellion that spring. During the previous three years, with a population of about two million, French Canada had given far fewer soldier to the overseas battalions than had English Canada. Soon there were charges that Quebec was not doing its duty. In response, the province became increasingly more sullen: it was a foreign war; Canada was not threatened; there were more pressing problems at home, especially when English Ontario was trying to take away the French-language school rights of her French-speaking citizens. There was also little attraction for most Quebecois in giving their lives for either Great Britain or France. Of the fourteen thousand or so French Canadians who actually joined during Hughes's tenure, many did so not because of patriotism, but for economic and other practical reasons. Yet in the end, the Quebecois in particular—for French Canadians in other parts of the Dominion had enlisted in about the same proportion as their English-speaking confrères—were more seriously divided from the rest of the nation than they had ever been since Confederation. Whose fault was it? As Desmond Morton has pointed out, since Confederation the militia had become increasingly anglicized in men, manners, and equipment. Consequently fewer French Canadians joined its ranks.[32]

Sam Hughes was an important part of the process that led to that alienation. It did not matter much in peacetime, but it did in war. The minister had always been remarkably insensitive to French Canadians. For a long time Hughes foolishly believed that his remote Huguenot ancestry and his friendship with nationalists like Armand Lavergne made him acceptable to Quebec. He was peculiarly unaware that his previous campaigns against separate schools, French priests, Canadian Papal Zouaves, French-Canadian military representation in Catholic ceremonies, and his Orange Lodge activities had overpowered the limited attractions of ancestry or friendship. Nor was he aware that his image as an imperialist, however nationalistic, was not attractive to many French Canadians, who were not at all concerned about defending the Empire outside of Canada.[33]

None of it augered well for a war in 1914. It was not that Sam Hughes did not want to recruit French Canadians. He did. But he did not realize that by scrapping the Gwatkin mobilization scheme, which gave a balanced national representation to French Canada in the form of their own units, he scuppered separate French-Canadian battalions in the first contingent. Still he wanted Quebec's numbers. One of the first things he did was visit Cardinal Bégin of Quebec in September 1914 in an attempt to secure priests for the initial force, but the Cardinal gave him little hope of obtaining any number for overseas service.[34] With this warning, the minister should have seen that Quebec was going to need special care if recruiting for a foreign war was to succeed in the province.

Yet the outbreak of the war did produce some initial sympathy in Quebec for participation; and Hughes wanted a national effort. That had been part of the rationale behind his nationalistic "fiery-cross" call to arms in August. But as the response to it poured into Valcartier he allowed for no separate identity by giving privileges as well as responsibilities to members of the various French-Canadian regiments who turned out. Instead units like the Carabiniers Mont-Royal, the Chausseurs Canadiens, the Voltigeurs de Quebec, and the Carabiniers de Sherbrooke were absorbed into the 12th and 14th Battalions, both of which were English-speaking. Only the 14th went to France where it was reinforced by French Canadians from the 12th Battalion. When Liberal MP and former cabinet minister Rodolphe Lemieux requested the creation of a separate French-Canadian unit with its own officers in the first contingent, Hughes refused. Even the attestation documents were worded in such a fashion that no French-Canadian volunteer could record his racial origin. There were over twelve hundred French Canadians at Valcartier in 1914, sufficient to assemble one complete battalion including officers.[35]

At the beginning of the war, the militia minister had two ready-made native sons of Quebec and generals at his disposal to rally the Canadiens: François Lessard and Oscar Pelletier. Both were regular soldiers of substantial experience. But while Hughes was in office, no meaningful role was ever given them, in spite of pleas by prominent English-Canadian Tories, like Toronto MP and patronage co-ordinator Edmund Bristol, who wanted Lessard to command the second contingent. All Hughes gave him was public abuse over his Toronto mobilization trials and a bitter ministerial squabble over inspection services. As late as 1916, Hughes again refused to make him an overseas brigadier, or even use him in the disastrous Quebec recruiting drives of that year. Only after Hughes was fired did Lessard get a Quebec battalion to recruit. But by then it was too late; he secured only ninety-two men, and he had no battle experience, so was unsuitable for overseas command. As for Pelletier—the son of a Liberal senator and the man whom Hutton had chosen as commander of one of his Boer war infantry columns—in 1914 the minister could only give the major-general command of a half dozen troops guarding a wireless station on Anticosti Island—and that was all.[36]

If Sam Hughes made little use of individual French Canadians, he had not much greater concern for their units. Once the first division got into the fighting, it was this bloody experience that trained many of the future officers of the subsequent divisions. Because the first contingent had few middle and senior level French-Canadian officers beyond the company level, there never would be enough of them to lead other units of their own culture, even if Hughes had wanted to send them. He seemed to think of Quebec with its two-million population only as a place to get numbers, not French Canadians. But the Canadiens themselves had been concerned in September 1914. Then Rodolphe Lemieux and Dr. Arthur Mignault, a wealthy Quebec pharmaceutical manufacturer, led a delegation of fifty-eight influential Liberal and Conservative Quebecois to Ottawa to make sure that at least the second contingent had an identifiable battalion. They warned Borden that if care was not taken to give Quebec representation on the national fighting force, there was a strong risk of losing its active support. Apparently with hardly more sympathy than Hughes, Borden only consented after the militia minister had sailed for England. The result was the formation of the 22nd Battalion commanded by F.M. Gaudet, which went to France with the second contingent the next spring. By then even it was having trouble: 10 percent of the number were English-speaking, and French-Canadian troops had to be transferred from two other battalions recruiting in Quebec before it could sail. In the first two contingents, then, French Canadians were represented only by one battalion and it was to remain the only official one in the Canadian Corps during the entire war.[37]

There was hardly any doubt about the potential enthusiasm for enlistment in French Canada just before and after the 22nd was announced. However, Hughes appeared unappreciative of it. In February 1915 he could only give vague answers about establishing a French-Canadian brigade when questioned in the Commons, and he even seemed unsure of the number of French Canadians who by then had enlisted. Just before the second division sailed for France in mid-1915, a French-Canadian lawyer and militia soldier, Colonel J.P. Landry, who had been given command of one of its brigades as a small conciliation to Quebec, was removed. To replace him came a Tory journalist friend of the minister, Brigadier David Watson, fresh from the First Division. It was inevitable that Landry should lose out. His fate was one of the earliest consequences of Hughes's not including French

Canadians of middle and high command in the first contingent the previous year. Landry had no battle experience, and no one willingly was going to jeopardize lives and efficiency with an untested brigadier. Watson had nearly a year under his belt. Back in Canada, however, no one in Quebec would question Landry's competence. To them there was another obvious reason for his removal. The deposed brigadier's father, Conservative Senator Philippe Landry, had been a major spokesman in the defence of the Franco-Ontario's fight against their Tory government's infamous Regulation 17 denying them French-language rights; to many French Canadians Hughes, the vengeful Orangeman, had simply retaliated.[38]

After mid-1915 when Hughes was trying to recruit the Third and Fourth Divisions, to encourage Quebec enlistments he brought home some of the few French Canadians who had served with the corps overseas. But there were never enough veterans even to begin the job. Mostly he had to use the same method employed in the rest of Canada—prominent citizens and promises of local battalions.[39] From October until the summer of 1916, twelve such groups canvassed in various areas of the province. Most of them had little success. By then an unmoved or lukewarm clergy, stories of the horrors waiting on Flanders' battlefields, and the general shortcomings of the militia minister's recruiting system, all made the Canadiens stubbornly resist any foreign military service. The new munitions industries with their steady and lucrative employment represented a far safer calling. The sneers and accusations of English Canada and the relentless antiwar campaign of Henri Bourassa and his nationaliste allies were strong inducements for many Quebecois to stay away from the colours. Nevertheless Hughes pressed for the numbers.

Wealthy French Canadians were not so willing to become some of Sam Hughes's recruiting colonels as were many in English Canada. As a result, many whom Hughes chose were less than worthy and their units were often doomed. One such example was the 41st Battalion. After a scandalous record both in Canada and England, which included desertion, two murders, and many court-martials, the unit was finally broken up to feed the 22nd in France.[40] Others were little more successful. In the fall of 1915, Hughes asked Armand Lavergne to raise a unit in Montreal. The year before he might have done it, but now his response was an embarrassing public letter in the columns of Bourassa's *Le Devoir* in which he refused to accept what he said was nothing more than an interesting adventure in a foreign country. Unexpectedly, the offer was then accepted by Olivar Asselin—an ardent nationaliste. Whatever his real motives for doing it, Asselin had a little more success than many others. His energy, popularity, and discipline got recruits and better officers, but not full ranks. Only too quickly Asselin discovered that Hughes had authorized a Conservative lawyer, Tancrède Paquelo, to raise the 206th Battalion in the same area. Paquelo was a former commanding officer of the 85th militia regiment and was representative of the declining quality of French-Canadian officers brought about by increasing anglicization in the militia. While Asselin brought men into his unit by hard work and discipline, Paquelo seduced his by appealing to baser values and promises of being "le dernier regiment à parter, le premier à profiter de la victoire." Asselin was so frustrated at the cutthroat competition between the two rivals, he demanded that Hughes get rid of Paquelo's battalion. Asselin's unit was transferred to Bermuda, not France; and Paquelo's was disbanded, with the bulk of them being transferred to the distraught Asselin. When the furious Paquelo heard what was to happen, he paraded his men and told those few who had not already disappeared to desert. For this he was court-martialled, and during the trial it was found that he and some of his officers had also defrauded the unit of funds. Paquelo went to jail.[41]

On other occasions, when Hughes could not get suitable French-Canadian colonels, he chose English-Canadian ones to recruit in Quebec. William Price was one. In spite of the general popularity the Price family had had in Quebec for years, there was little attraction to serve an imperialist "English" colonel in a foreign war; and Price, already encumbered by Hughes's bad system, added his own insensitivities, and so failed. According to Price: "I tell them what no politician dare tell them, that they are away behind all the other provinces and that though they have a double duty, one to the Empire and one to France, yet they are laggards and that they should as a matter of fact furnish more than any other province."[42]

In the summer of 1916, the half dozen battalions still trying to reach their quotas were really only fragments of military units. With a lack of discipline and equipment and ranks thinned by desertion and drafts to other battalions, few were sent to England. Of those who got there, they were broken up to reinforce the 22nd in France. In all, by 1916 the possibility of having a French-Canadian brigade, native sons in senior command, or any serious encouragement for national war participation had all but disappeared under Sam Hughes. Instead the spectacle of most of those French-Canadian battalions stumbling incompetently and often dishonestly through a vain quest for full establishments caused the Quebecois to withdraw further into demoralized and sullen inaction in the province; outside of it, the show reaffirmed the belief that French Canadians were incompetent and unpatriotic.

If Hughes was a major cause of the situation, others must also share the guilt with him. During the first two years, Borden in particular had little more appreciation of cultural politics than did Sam Hughes. Since the prime minister had scant support in the province even after the 1911 election, he should have realized that Quebec would be a special case in a national crisis. Just before the war, he and Monk had parted. The prime minister's failure to respond to the Quebec delegation that wanted a French unit in the first force, his failure to find any post for Lessard, his securing the resignation of two of his three French-Canadian cabinet ministers in the fall of 1914—all these actions held little evidence of an understanding of French Canada. His position on the imperialist side in the naval debate in 1910, and in 1913 the question of cash contributions to the Admiralty only confirmed the nationalistes' charges after 1914 that French Canada was being tossed into a foreign war. So did Borden's quick acceptance of sending more and more troops thereafter. Even after the reshuffle in 1914, his cabinet had no French Canadians with any credibility to defend war participation. Nearly all of them had campaigned for votes in the 1911 election by attacking Laurier's naval bill as conscriptionist. After 1914, how could these same men persuade their confrères that they must participate in a British war? Similarly, Borden and his cabinet seemed to be incapable of or unwilling to support the Franco-Ontarians against the English-speaking "Boches" in the Ontario schools question.[43]

Like Hughes, Borden tried to enthuse Quebec. Early in 1916 he told Hughes that he should be sure that French Canadians who had distinguished themselves at the front were rewarded with decorations that the French government had put at his disposal. The prime minister also suggested that, if Hughes would authorize a Quebec unit for service in the French army, recruiting would be greatly encouraged. But General Gwatkin knew better and so advised against it; he recognized that French Canadians had no particular loyalty to France and that pay difference between the two forces would discourage any chance of success. No one seemed to listen to Gwatkin. Overseas Max Aitken, the government "Eye-Witness" in France, offered Hughes and Borden "a French mission . . . sent to Canada by the Jesuits or other religious orders for religious purposes but really to assist recruiting in Quebec." In all, these schemes represented the bankruptcy of Hughes's and Borden's attitudes to French Canadians. To them France was never an attraction; Canada was. But in order to gain French Canada's support of an external policy, national leaders first would have to give the minority a definite, identifiable, and responsible role and to ensure its well-being at home. Neither Hughes nor his prime minister seemed aware of this. What came from them came too little and too late.[44]

But one of the most objectionable things about Borden for French Canadians was that he would not or could not control Sam Hughes. Most of the time Hughes continued to proclaim his belief that French Canada would measure up to his expectations, or, as Mason Wade puts it, Hughes kept his honest opinion about French Canada to himself. That may be true, but from time to time he made some stupid public moves, often in themselves small but collectively lethal, concerning recruiting in Quebec. When again unsuccessful in obtaining support from Cardinal Bégin in mid-1916, the minister uttered his infamous statement in Lindsay that Quebec had not done its duty. Earlier he had countered questions from an opposition MP, asking why western French Canadians were not organized into a battalion, by saying that their numbers were too small, that they would be better off in English-speaking battalions, and that the local French-Canadian officer of the proposed unit was incompetent. When the same member confronted Hughes with the 1911 census figures indicating that there were over forty thousand French Canadians in the west, Hughes replied that he would order two French-Canadian "half-breed" battalions to be raised. Perhaps the most celebrated and distorted case of Hughes's neglect of sympathetic organization in French Canada occurred in August 1916 when the minister was again out of the country. Military authorities wanted a new enlistment drive in the Montreal area to be jointly headed by two clergymen as representatives of both cultures and faiths. By that time, however, no French Canadian priest would accept the post. But the campaign proceeded anyway, headed by a Methodist clergyman, Reverend C.A. Williams. Williams was hardworking and far more tolerant of French Canada than many have given him credit for. But predictably his efforts ended in failure. The Williams affair was not as it was portrayed by extreme nationalists—an example of Hughes's anti-Catholicism. Nor was Williams a bigoted Orangeman sent by the minster to ride herd on French Canada. The entire episode represented what was tragic about the minister's methods. He could not understand that French Canada required a different approach than the rest of the population. Quebec, because it provided the basis of Laurier's power, was suspect to an old party politician like Hughes. In the past two years he had given Quebec nothing except discrimination to be enthusiastic about. Soon the province was not interested and soon Hughes and his local military officers had run out of prominent French Canadians for such duties; authorities had to use whomever they could get. So they got men like Williams. Common sense, however, should have dictated that it not be a Methodist clergyman. But by then it was a vicious circle.[45]

The militia minister showed more creative imagination in recruiting foreigners for military duty than he did French Canadians. For example, there was the minister's "American Legion" scheme. Soon after the war began, Hughes offered and had accepted for overseas service a battalion of American citizens living in Canada; the offer was a substantial mental somersault for Hughes's usual anti-Americanism. A few weeks later, he extended the project to three "corps of splendid fighters," numbering "sixty thousand," which now included Russians and Serbs.[46]

The British authorities could not co-ordinate their reaction. The Colonial Office authorities were hesitant because they said that such a force would violate the US Foreign Enlistment Act of 1818, and that they did want to keep relations as cordial as possible with the neutral republic. By the same token they did not want to tread on Canadian sensitivities, especially those in the hands of the prickly Sam Hughes. Consequently, the British referred the question back to the governor general, whom they said was free to act as he saw fit. Connaught, who had never seen the first communications between Hughes and Kitchener, and did not like being left out, was puzzled. So he enquired at militia headquarters. The deputy minister said he knew nothing about the scheme either; nor did the Militia Council, but if such a proposal had been made by Hughes, they recommended it be quickly dropped. Meanwhile Kitchener, supported by the king, Churchill, Sir Richard McBride, and Acting High Commissioner Perley gave Hughes permission to send at least one American unit, providing no recruiting went on outside of Canada.[47]

Hughes did not move on the issue until domestic volunteering started to slow down in the fall of 1915. Then he allowed the limited acceptance of American citizens resident in Canada to mushroom ultimately into plans for a full-fledged American brigade of five overseas battalions. The minister had created a special cap badge with an American flag surrounded by clusters of maple leaves. As the first of these units, designated the 97th Overseas Battalion, quickly filled up its ranks during the winter of 1915–1916, Hughes got the idea that he could recruit unlimited numbers. As a result he authorized four more by the late spring (the 211th, 212th, 213th, and the 237th) and labelled them the "American Legion." Their cap badge was a variation of the 97th and all of them wore American Legion shoulder flashes. As was the case elsewhere, none of these units had much success. The minister created each new battalion long before the others finished recruiting, and so they competed, often viciously, with each other for volunteers and none of them ever reached establishment—most of them reached less than half of it. During June 1916, 20 percent of the legion deserted. Hughes also used the typical special agent to organize the entire scheme. C.W. Bullock, who had suggested the brigade idea to the minister, was an American citizen and a Unitarian minister whose military career, as General Gwatkin scornfully commented, "is remarkable. Appointed chaplain with the honorary rank of captain in October last [1915], he is now a lieutenant-colonel commanding an overseas battalion." Whether Hughes ordered it or not is not known, but recruiting took place on American soil. Certainly the minister aided it by making a personal arrangement with customs officials to turn a blind eye to these recruits when they were brought across the border.[48]

These frequent abuses of American neutrality aggravated and embarrassed the Washington and London authorities equally. Every time Connaught confronted Hughes about the foreign recruiting, the minister denied it and then blatantly let it continue. American authorities increasingly objected to the continued use of the US flag displayed at various Canadian recruiting offices; and so there were several stiff diplomatic notes exchanged with British diplomats over Hughes's scheme. In Ottawa, Gwatkin, Fiset, and the governor general had no more success in stopping the plan. For their part, the British would not let the legion come to England until all outward connections with the United States were cut.[49]

By the mid-spring 1916, tired of the long wait, endless changes in officers, and constant haggling, the legionnaires were frustrated. Desertions and resignations mounted while enlistments nearly stopped. Like some of the other battalions Hughes had authorized, the legion had its share of scandal. The Toronto chief of police described the 97th as the "worst behaved battalion in the city." Drunkenness, fraud, embezzlement (including the decamping of the 97th's first commanding officer with all the unit funds), and incompetence plagued the force. In May Fiset said he would be pleased to send the legion overseas before "they all desert," but not until they got rid of American insignia. Connaught's constant complaints and Hughes's lack of response finally brought the prime minster into the picture.[50]

Like many others, Borden was totally surprised at what had so far taken place. Hughes had not told him much in the previous two years and precious time was now wasted while he tried to sort through the minister's mess. In the process, it involved Borden in a first-class row with the governor general, whom the prime minster felt was exerting far too much pressure in a domestic Canadian matter. By late July, when Hughes was out of the country, Borden ended the affair by consolidating the legion's five battalions into one, the 97th, and sending it overseas, shorn of all its insignia. The process only added to its further demoralization. With financial and leadership problems still festering in its ranks, in the end it was broken up to feed the corps' battalions in France.[51]

The prime minister's decision on the American Legion was part of a larger judgment on Hughes's entire domestic administration. In August 1916 he took recruiting out of Sir Sam's hands. First Borden tried a director-general of recruiting to give order to the chaos and to secure the vital enlistments; then in the autumn he tried the National Service Board which was responsible to the cabinet and dedicated to the same causes. Both had little success. By the spring of 1917, large numbers of casualties and the conviction that it was essential to have a Canadian voice in imperial councils made a reluctant prime minister believe that only conscription could do it. By year's end compulsory service had arrived at the hands of the newly elected union government. The war would be pursued to bitter victory. But over a year before, Borden had got rid of Hughes, a major cause of his bad luck; and before Hughes had gone in 1916, he too had come out hotly for conscription—typically without consulting anyone and apparently oblivious to its party or national cost.[52]

By the end of 1916 there were over 250 overseas battalions. Hughes had authorized most of them while he was minister. But earlier that summer, the Canadian Corps was complete at 48 battalions. Except for some reinforcements, it remained at that level in spite of Hughes's attempts to add two more divisions before he left office. The remaining battalions either suffered collapse before they left Canada or were doomed to be broken up in England. Over the previous two years, Sam Hughes had taken the declaration of war as a personal challenge to lead a national crusade to raise as many men as possible. In doing so, he had little regard for dislocation, or for the advice of his professional staff, or for responsibility to his government. He showed no more awareness of the cultural politics of French Canada. While trying to heighten patriotism and enlistment by throwing responsibility to the citizens, he left them confused and adrift when the war demands transcended the ability of individuals, of the party structure, and of local groups to handle them on a national scale. Yet he constantly interfered even in this process because he could neither delegate the necessary authority nor apply himself to the daily routine of co-ordinating a national effort. Moreover, the local battalions ended up being destroyed by the same spontaneity that created them and that helped sour and alienate the two cultures, both from the government and one from the country. Certainly Hughes's prime minister must bear some of the blame. In part Borden put up with Hughes's recruiting ways because in those early years the militia minister gave the most vitality to a pale and hesitant war administration. But neither man checked each other with sound advice or firm control. That Sam Hughes demonstrated initiative, confidence, and an unrelenting energy, which helped rally many Canadians to the early war effort, cannot be doubted. But there was also overwhelming evidence that he lacked the skills of sound administration which the larger war—the one of 1916 and after—demanded. Ironically he was a major force in creating the particular size of the Canadian war effort but he could not cope with its demands. He was a spirited improviser, intolerant of criticism, jealous of power, and imbued with the philosophy of the citizen-solider in a conflict which no longer belonged to the individual citizens. He did not see that Canada had created, with the masses of his recruits, professional demands and a professional modern army. As long as the spirit and manpower were in abundance, and the sophisticated needs few, Sam Hughes's local talents remained unchallenged. When these lagged, Hughes's regime collapsed.

NOTES

1. Desmond Morton, *Canada and War: A Military and Political History* (Toronto: Butterworth's, 1981), chap. 3.

2. *Hansard*, 1917, pp. 261, 269–70 for Hughes's own description of his recruiting methods.

3. R.C. Brown, *Robert Laird Borden, a Biography*, vol. 2, *1914–1937* (Toronto: Macmillan, 1979), 27–28; and Barbara M. Wilson, *Ontario and the First World War 1914–1918: A Collection of Documents* (Toronto: Champlain Society, 1977), xxxi.

4. *Canadian Annual Review of Public Affairs* (hereafter *CAR*), 1915, p. 188; J.L. Granatstein and J.M. Hitsman, *Broken Promises: A History of Conscription in Canada* (Toronto: Oxford University Press, 1977), 34; *Hansard*, special session, 1914, pp. 17, 95; Col. A.F. Duguid, *The Official History of the Canadian Forces in the Great War 1914–1919* (Ottawa: King's Printer, 1938), app. 55; and Address, 18 Dec. 1914, Sir Robert Laird Borden Papers, Public Archives of Canada (hereafter PAC), MG26, p. 34672.

5. *CAR*, 1915, pp. 187–88.

6. Murray Donnelly, *Dafoe of the Free Press* (Toronto: Macmillan, 1968), 76.

7. Wilson, *Ontario and the First World War*, xxi, xxix–xlii; G.N. Tucker, *The Naval Service of Canada* (Ottawa: King's Printer, 1952), chap. 13; note on Canadian Expeditionary Force, Edmund Bristol Papers, Public Archives of Ontario (hereafter PAO),

283, Armour file; *CAR*, 1915, pp. 213–14; and Brown, *Borden*, 2:68–69.

8. John Swettenham, *To Seize Victory: The Canadian Corps in World War One* (Toronto: Ryerson Press, 1965), 71–95; Wilson, *Ontario and the First World War*, xxx.

9. Perley to Borden, 29 May 1915, in Canada, Department of External Affairs, *Documents on Canada's External Relations 1909–1918*, vol. 1 (Ottawa: Queens Printer, 1967), 73–74.

10. *Globe* (Toronto), 22 Jan. 1915, 6; Wilson, *Ontario and the First World War*, xxxv–1, 6–8, B4; Duguid, *The Official History of the Canadian Forces*, app. 86; Canada, Senate, *Debates*, 1916, p. 406; Granatstein and Hitsman, *Broken Promises*, 23–24; and R. Mathew Bray, "Fighting as an Ally: The English-Canadian Patriotic Response to the Great War," *The Canadian Historical Review* 61 (2 Nov. 1980), 147–49.

11. Gwatkin to Hughes, 21 Sept. 1914, W.G. Gwatkin Papers, PAC, MG30, G13, F4; PAC, Pamphlet, no. 4039, p. 8; Gen. Charles F. Winter, *Lieutenant-General the Hon. Sir Sam Hughes, K.C.B., M.P., Canada's War Minister 1911–1916* (Toronto: Macmillan, 1931), 88–89.

12. Connaught to Kitchener, 1 July 1915, Lord Kitchener Papers, Public Records Office, London, 30/57/56, FNG 43A and B.

13. Gwatkin to Mason, 3 July 1915, Gwatkin Papers, f2; and Gwatkin to Christie, 24 May 1915, Borden Papers, p. 109601.

14. Brown, *Borden*, 2:28.

15. Wilson, *Ontario and the First World War*, xxxii, 8, B5, Militia Order no. 340, 12 July 1915; Basset to Winter, 19 Aug. 1915, John Basset Papers, PAC, MG 30, E 302; *CAR*, 1915, p. 190; and P.D. Ross, *Retrospects of a Newspaper Person* (Toronto: Oxford, 1931), 206–11.

16. "Memorandum on Recruiting in England Prior to the Derby Recruiting Scheme," Borden Papers, OC313, claims Hughes's method was similar to that in Britain; an improvised, local volunteer response with little government planning. Also see G.W.L. Nicholson, *Official History of the Canadian Army in the First World War: The Canadian Expeditionary Force, 1914–1919* (Ottawa: Queen's Printer, 1962), 109; and PAC, RG 24, vol. 6999, 593-1-40.

17. *Hansard*, 1916, pp. 3288–89; "Report on the work of the Department of Militia and Defence to Feb. 1, 1915," Memorandum no. 1, Gwatkin to the Prime Minister, 1 Feb. 1915, PAC, RG 24, vol. 413; Memorandum no. 3, Gwatkin to the Prime Minister, 1 Dec. 1916, PAC, RG 24, vol. 413; McCurdy to Borden, 7 Oct. 1916, Borden Papers, OC313; *Hansard*, 1917, p. 263; Canada, National Defence Headquarters, Ottawa, Directorate of History, Historical Section, *Canadian War Records*, vol. 1, *A Narrative of the Formation and Operations of the First Canadian Division, to the End of the Second Battle of Ypres, May 4, 1915* (Ottawa: Historical Section, General Staff, King's Printer, 1920), 3; and Desmond Morton, *A Peculiar Kind of Politics: Canada's Overseas Ministry in the First World War* (Toronto: University of Toronto Press, 1982), 44.

18. "Memoire notes," Harold Mayne Daly Papers, PAC, MG 27, III, f9, D.

19. Nicholson, *Official History of the Canadian Army in the First World War*, 213–14, 546; and John English, *The*

Decline of Politics: The Conservatives and the Party System, 1901–1920 (Toronto: University of Toronto Press, 1977), 95–105.

20. *CAR*, 1915, pp. 187–93, 222–27; and *Hansard*, 1915, p. 438.

21. Canada, Department of the Secretary of State, *Copies of Proclamations, Orders-in-Council and Documents relating to the European War* (King's Printer, 1915 and 1917), no. 556; PC 36, 12 Jan. 1916; and Brown, *Borden*, 2:32–34.

22. Bennett to Borden, 7 Dec. 1915, Sir George Perley Papers, PAC, MG27, II, D12, vol. 5; Stanton to Blount, 31 Dec. 1915, in Sir Robert Laird Borden, *Robert Laird Borden: His Memoirs*, ed. Henry Borden, vol. 1 (Toronto: Macmillan, 1938), 529; 10 Aug. 1915, Sir George Foster Diaries, PAC; Memorandum no. 3, PAC, RG 24, vol. 413; and Brown, *Borden*, 2:33–35.

23. *Hansard*, 1917, pp. 269–71; Sir Robert Laird Borden, *Private Diaries*, 18 Jan. 1916, PAC; Desmond Morton, *Canada and War* (Toronto: Butterworth's, 1981), 60; Wilson, *Ontario and the First World War*, xxxvi, xlv; *Free Press* (Winnipeg), 29 May 1916; and *CAR*, 1916, p. 256.

24. *Times* (New York), 27 Feb. 1916, 3; *CAR*, 1916, p. 303; and General Hughes, no. 2, Lord Beaverbrook Papers (BBK), The House of Lords Record Office, Westminster, Great Britain; Hughes to Aitken, 15 Jan. 1916, IP; and Aitken to Hughes, 19 Jan. 1916, IP.

25. Borden, *Private Diaries*, 18 Jan. 1916 and 5 Feb. 1916, PAC; Flavelle to W.E. Rundle, 14 June 1916, Joseph Wesley Flavelle Papers, Queen's University, Douglas Library, C25, B2, pp. 1500–502; and *Hansard*, 1917, pp. 269–70.

26. Senate, *Debates*, 1916, pp. 127–32; Borden to Perley, 14 March 1916, Perley Papers, vol. 5; *CAR*, 1916, p. 319; *Hansard*, 1917, pp. 269–71; and *Daily Herald* (Calgary), 11 March 1916, 6.

27. For instance, in Ontario see Wilson, *Ontario and the First World War*, li–lii. Also see *Hansard*, 1916, pp. 145, 440, 498–500, 3550; Nicholson, *Official History of the Canadian Army in the First World War*, 219; *CAR*, 1916, pp. 310–24; *Citizen* (Ottawa), 14 April 1916, 1; *Globe* (Toronto), 28 June 1916, 6; *Daily Herald* (Calgary), 29 March 1916, 6.

28. Price to Bassett, 25 Feb. 1916, Bassett Papers, vol. 5. On the recruiting methods in Ontario, see Wilson, *Ontario and the First World War*, xlii–liii.

29. Griesbach to Hughes, 13 May 1915, Major-General W.A. Griesbach Papers, PAC, MG30, E15, vol. 1.

30. Report of IG (Imperial) on Canadian Troops, no. 47/560/MT2, 16 June 1915, app. A, in Lessard to Hughes, May 1916, F.L. Lessard Papers, PAC, MG 30, G 47; Hughes to Lessard, 16 April 1916, F.L. Lessard Papers; Nicholson, *Official History of the Canadian Army in the First World War*, 202, 225; Duguid, *Official History of the Canadian Forces in the Great War*, app. 8; Alderson to Governor General, 17 Feb. 1916, Sir Edward Kemp Papers, PAC, MG27, II, D9, vol. 110; McCurdy to Hughes, 21 July 1916, and Hughes to Borden, 2 Aug. 1916, Borden Papers, OC318. When Hughes was fired, Perley resolved the problem of surplus officers by sending them home or letting them go to France with a lesser rank. Nicholson, *Official History of the Canadian Army in the First World War*, 223–24.

31. Gwatkin to Kemp, 1916, Kemp Papers; Hughes to Lessard, 16 April 1916, and Lessard to Hughes, May 1916, Lessard Papers; Borden to Hughes, 19 Aug. 1916, Borden Papers, OC318; and Gwatkin to Christie, 27 June 1916, Borden Papers, OC322.

32. For an overview, see Granatstein and Hitsman, *Broken Promises*, 22–34; Desmond Morton, "French Canada and the War, 1868–1917: The Military Background to the Conscription Crisis of 1917," in *War and Society in North America*, ed. J.L. Granatstein and R.D. Cuff (Toronto: Nelson, 1971), 84–103.

33. Mason Wade, *The French Canadians, 1760–1967*, vol. 2 (Toronto: Macmillan, 1968), 640–41. See ibid., 640–726 for the trials of French Canadians during the war. Also Elizabeth A. Armstrong, *The Crisis of Quebec, 1914–1918* (Toronto: McClelland and Stewart, 1974), 35–160.

34. Winter, *Lieutenant-General the Hon. Sir Sam Hughes*, 140.

35. Duguid, *Official History of the Canadian Forces in the Great War*, app. 85, "Composition of Provisional Infantry Brigades and Battalions, Valcartier Camp, Sept. 3, 1914," app. 88, "Questions to be put before attestation," and app. 86; Morton, "French Canada and the War, 1868–1917," 96; *Hansard*, 1916, p. 3283; Gwatkin to Sladen, 27 Aug. 1915, Gwatkin Papers, F2.

36. Bristol to Borden, 17 Oct. 1914, and Bristol to Hazen, 17 Oct. 1914, Bristol Papers, PAO, 285, political 1914; *Hansard*, 1916, p. 3281; Morton, "French Canada and the War, 1868–1917," 102; and Wade, *The French Canadians, 1760–1967*, 2:668, 708, 709; and Oscar Pelletier, *Memoires, Souveniers de Famille et Récits* (Quebec, 1940), 382–90.

37. Duguid, *Official History of the Canadian Forces in the Great War*, apps. 74, 711, 843; and Armstrong, *The Crisis of Quebec*, 70, 83–84.

38. Department of Militia and Defence, *The Militia Lists of the Dominion of Canada, 1875–1920*, Sept. 1914, p. 204; Henry James Morgan, ed. *The Canadian Men and Women of the Time: A Handbook of Living Characters* (Toronto: Briggs, 1912), 436, 447; Morton, "French Canada and the War, 1868–1917," 97.

39. Desmond Morton, "The Limits of Loyalty: French Canadian Officers and the First World War," in *Limits of Loyalty*, ed. Edgar Denton (Waterloo: Wilfrid Laurier University Press, 1980), 92–93.

40. Gwatkin to Sladen, 27 Aug. 1915, Gwatkin Papers, F2; and Desmond Morton, "The Short, Unhappy Life of the 41st Battalion CEF," in *Queens Quarterly* 81, 1 (1974), 70–80.

41. *CAR*, 1916, p. 194; *Hansard*, 1916, p. 3283; Oliver Asselin, *Pourquoi Je m'enrole* (Montreal, 1916), esp. 32; and Morton, "The Limits of Loyalty," 92–94.

42. Price to Bassett, 24 Feb. 1916, Bassett Papers, vol. 5.

43. Granatstein and Hitsman, *Broken Promises*, 30.

44. Aitken to Borden, 17 May 1916, Beaverbrook Papers, E, 7–8; Borden to Hughes, 25 Jan. 1916, Borden Papers, OC68; Gwatkin to Kemp, spring 1916, Gwatkin Papers, F1; and *CAR*, 1916, p. 258.

45. Wade, *The French Canadians, 1760–1967*, 2:727; E.M. MacDonald, *Recollections: Political and Personal* (Toronto: Ryerson Press, 1939), 335; *Current Opinion* (Sept. 1917), 158; *Free Press* (London), 12 June 1916, 4; *Daily Herald* (Calgary), 18 July 1916, 6; *Hansard*, 1916, pp. 1373–74; Mason Wade, *The French Canadian Outlook* (Toronto: McClelland and Stewart, 1964), 52; Nicholson, *Official History of the Canadian Army in the First World War*, 221; and Morton, "French Canada and the War, 1868–1917," 98–99.

46. Law to Governor General, 30 Aug. 1914, and Kitchener to Hughes, 7 Sept. 1914, Borden Papers; and Duguid, *Official History of the Canadian Forces in the Great War*, app. 87, Hughes to Kitchener, 29 Aug. 1914.

47. Fiset to Sec. External Affairs, 24 Oct. 1914, and McBride to R.L. Borden, 25 Nov. 1914, Borden Papers, OC322, vol. 70. Also see W.S. Churchill memo, 5 Sept. 1914, Edwin Pye Papers, Directorate of History, National Defence Headquarters, Ottawa (hereafter DHist), F1, f5; and Perley to Borden, 2 Dec. 1914, First Viscount Harcourt Papers, Oxford University, Box 465, p. 49.

48. Minute of Militia Council, 13 Jan. 1916, PAC, RG 24, vol. 1542, 684-1-174-1; Gwatkin to Sladen, 31 July 1916, PAC, RG 24, vol. 14071, vol. 461; Gwatkin to Christie (HQC 1562), 18 June 1916, Connaught to Borden, 25 June 1916, and DMD memo, 4 July 1916, Borden Papers, OC322, vol. 70; J.G. Mitchell, Department of Interior to Sam Hughes, 3 Nov. 1915, Pye Papers, DHist, F1, f5; and PAC, RG 24, vol. 1383, 593-6-1-93.

49. F? to Spring-Rice, 17 July 1916, Beaverbrook Papers, E/18, 97th Battalion; Spring-Rice to Connaught, 2 May 1916, US Department of Justice to US Secretary of State, 17 Jan. 1916, Beaverbrook Papers, RG 7, 14071, vol. 452; Spring-Rice to Governor General, 1 July 1916, Beaverbrook Papers, RG 7, 14071, vol. 455; and *Free Press* (Detroit), 19 Dec. 1915, 24 Dec. 1915, and 6 Jan. 1916, editorial.

50. "Notes by Pye," CGS to AG, 3 March 1916, Pye Papers; and Fiset to Christie, 27 March 1916, Borden Papers, OC322, vol. 70.

51. R.G. Haycock, "The American Legion in the Canadian Expeditionary Force, 1914–1917: A Study in Failure," in *Military Affairs* 43, 3 (Oct. 1979), 115–19.

52. Morton, "The Limits of Loyalty," 91; Hughes to Borden, 23 Oct. 1916, Borden Papers, OC318; and CAR, 1916, pp. 265–66. For a review of Borden's course after 1916, see Brown, *Borden*, vol. 2, chaps. 8–10. As early as August 1914, Sir Charles Ross had protested the loss of his skilled machinists in Hughes's "fiery cross" mobilization. See Ross to Hughes, 6 Aug. 1914, Sir Charles Ross Papers, PAC, MG30, A95, vol. 5.

THE JOURNAL OF PRIVATE FRASER: COURCELLETTE, 14–17 SEPTEMBER 1916 [*]

REGINALD H. ROY

○

Thursday, 14 September 1916

Cpl. Steel was badly wounded today while working on Major Splane's dug-out. He received shrapnel in the face, disfiguring him badly, and was returned to Canada. Hannah, a new man, was also placed "Hors de Combat."

A number of us were detailed to carry Stokes bombs[1] up the line to a dump for tomorrow's attack. I was in charge of a small party. A guide had been allotted to direct us to the required dump newly constructed off the front line. Scrambling along we piloted ourselves with our precious and dangerous cargo up the communications [trench] a considerable distance until the guide acknowledged that he had lost his bearings. Deciding to remain where we were until he found the route to the dump, we stuck around the trench while he went forward. Minutes passed and he did not return. The men became impatient and anxious so I decided to push on and find the dump myself, the others following. Getting up to what appeared to be the front line, and the trench becoming shallow, convinced me that we must be in the vicinity of the dump. A newly dug trench on the right a few yards further on gave me the cue and crouching I stole along about one hundred and fifty yards to the end which finished off in a circle of about ten feet in diameter. Depositing the bombs I called on the others to come along. About five followed, laid down their bombs and hurried back. Finding no more coming I retraced my steps. After proceeding thirty yards or so I came across a couple of "Stokes," a few yards further on came across some more, at intervals of a few yards, more were seen. At once it was observed the back of the party had developed nerves, got rid of their bombs and fled.

[*] From Reginald H. Roy ed., *The Journal of Private Fraser, 1914–1918: Canadian Expeditionary Force* (Victoria, BC: Sono Nis Press, 1985), 199–215.

Gathering them up I carried them to the dump then went back for more, repeating the trip several times, until I found the distance between the dump and bombs getting greater and greater. By this time I got "fed up," hopped over the remaining bombs, turned into the main trench and beat it out of the line myself.

Word had just eked out that we are in for our third engagement: first, St. Eloi; second, Third [sic] Battle of Ypres; and now the Somme, this time not as defenders, but as aggressors primed up for the event. The announcement that at 6:20 tomorrow morning we would make a charge, co-operating with the British and French created quite a stir. Some looked upon the matter in a serious light, others were indifferent while the remainder treated the whole affair in a humorous vein. A few discussed the mode of attack, chances of success, but the knowing felt and knew that the result depended upon the artillery. Exaggerated tales had reached us that the attacks on the Somme were a series of walkovers and there was nothing for us to do but gather in the spoils. I believe most of us hearing such stories, treated the defences with, if not contempt, at least with levity.

Personally, I did not sense the full amount of danger, though I realized it quickly when I was twenty yards over the parapet. Cpl. Recknell, who partnered me in the dug-out, was not feeling in the best of form, and apparently had a grudge at being sent up the line instead of Cpl. Woods. At this time the practice was to hold back in reserve a certain number of the battalion, particularly N.C.O's., so that if the worst happened, the battalion would have a nucleus to fall back upon. Woods did not require to go up this trip, but apparently it would not have mattered, for Recknell was killed the following day and Woods a week later.

Tomorrow was a fitting day for the attack for it marked the first anniversary of the Second Division's entry into France. The attack was planned on a large scale. The Canadians were to go over on the north with Courcellette as the objective. Imperials, Scottish troops principally, were to take Martinpuich adjoining in the south, and still further south the French were to carry the fight in the direction of Combles. Our 4th Brigade was to attack on the right of the Bapaume Road and the 6th Brigade on the left, while the 5th Brigade was to remain in reserve. The attacking forces of the 6th Brigade were the 27th, 28th, and 31st Battalions with the 29th in Brigade reserve. It was understood that the 27th Battalion was to take the right sector, the 28th the left sector and the 31st was to act as moppers up to both battalions, though in reality the 31st, or at least certain members, did not adhere strictly to operation orders, but went ahead on their own and penetrated further than their neighbours.

The frontage covered by the brigade was roughly 1800 yards and the objective or furthest points about a mile, involving Sugar trench, Sugar refinery and ridge. Orders called for the 27th as the first attacking wave, followed ten yards behind by 3 and 4 platoons of the 31st Battalion, i.e., as far as our immediate front was concerned. Four waves were to be employed altogether in the first attack. The objective of the left half of the Company to which I belonged was Fritz's front line. We were entrusted with the job of cleaning or mopping up the trench, killing all those who showed fight or defiance, digging out the enemy from dug-outs and passing them out as prisoners; in short, disposing of all opposition and taking complete posses- sion of the enemy front line, manning and consolidating it in event of a counter-attack being launched.

During the afternoon an extra supply of rifle shells, in bandoliers,[2] were handed out to us together with a couple of Mills bombs. With these ban- doliers and a couple of gas masks hanging from our necks together with equipment, speedy manoeuvre was practically impossible. I, therefore, was glad to turn my overcoat over to the Q.M. to be obtained back at billets, rather than carry it during the attack, notwithstanding that it may be badly required later on.

Late at night (9:30) the sergeants in quiet tones softly told us to fall in. There was not much need for preparation, as each one had been ready long beforehand. We were on a mission which required not only alert faculties, but arms and equipment in order so that one could at least get a favourable and comfortable start off. Our attitude was possibly a little more serious and quieter than usual, but the humorists were still around. It was imposs- ible to quell them, and when all is said and done, they are the best men to have in the ranks in modern warfare. A jovial temperament seems to be an antidote to morbid thought, fear or cowardice. Cutting to the left, platoon after platoon, in single file steal across the dip to the communication trench, while all around were scores of khaki clad men apparently bent on support- ing the attack. The Field Artillery had crept up closer than ever. They had not much to be afraid of for the German airmen and sausage balloons were non-existent during the battles of the Somme. The British completely domi- nated the air and it was a rare sight to see the "eyes" of the enemy.

Skirting Pozières movements up the trench was slow. The communi- cations were badly blocked, through parties coming down. Shelling, although intermittent, in no way delayed us. At last we reached the assembly trench on the right and filed along, allowing each soldier three or four yards space. It soon began to drizzle and rain and we became cold and numb, lying in the damp trench, trying to obtain forty winks. Several of us could have done with our overcoats. To make matters worse Fritz was indulging in scattered shelling. Fortunately, the range was long though a few fell in front and nearly rocked the trench. The shelling was sufficient, however, to keep us on edge.

As we lay shivering there in the darkness, the mind had every oppor- tunity to run riot. I believe Thiebot, a dark-skinned Channel Islander, and one of our "tough guys" who always took a great delight in taunting and scaring the "drafts" with the remarks that they would last like a "snowball in hell" when Fritz got after them, and so forth, took a very serious, religious view of things, going even so far as to say that he knew he was going to get it, and turned over personal effects to one of his comrades. His premonition turned out correct for he was dead in No Man's Land a few hours later.

Shivering to the bone, we were glad to get the news about 3:30 a.m. to move out to the front line preparatory to attack. Stretching our limbs, we moved upwards, jumbled together with other units, to near the junction of trenches, when Charlie Knight appeared on the scene from the left trench in a great state, his face covered with blood, and his hands holding his chin and neck, elbowing his way, passed us in hot haste, his eyes staring wildly out of his head. It looked as if he had been hit a moment before and had not yet realized to the full what happened.

A few yards further on we became choc-a-bloc. It was impossible to move backward or forward. The trench was a jumble of soldiers. Our wrath as usual began to rise and imprecations were showered upon those in charge. The next moment saw those in the lead climb out of the trench into the open on the left, trying to make for our jumping off position in the line. The ground was a quagmire of shell holes and one had to move rapidly to keep up with his predecessor. Fritz, nervous and apparently under the impression that we were going to pull something off, was firing wildly over No Man's Land, and the bullets whistled around as we scrambled from shell hole to shell hole. Joe Saunders who was following a few paces behind me, was shot in the abdomen. Breathing heavily, he expired a few moments later, Fardell watching over him. Poor Joe, who was a 56th man, often remarked that Heiny would never get him. His death thoroughly angered us. It looked as if word had been given to every unit to make for their positions at the same time with the resultant jam that caused us to get out in the open in the vicinity of the front line. In the end we got into the trench, moved along a bit and got stuck once more. As it was becoming light, word was finally given to back up and remain where we were, mixed with the men of the 29th Battalion. Behind the parados, in shell holes, lay a number of 4 Platoon. My own platoon, No. 3, lost several in the scramble for position.

Two or three hundred yards ahead, and slightly down a slope, Fritz's line threaded its way along our front. The ground over which the attack was to be made was an expanse of pasture land torn by incessant shell fire and dotted closely with shell holes. Of growth there was nothing to be seen excepting tree trunks alongside the road running back from the enemy trench. There was the usual formidable support line, Sugar and Candy trenches, and the Sugar Refinery stronghold, several hundred yards in the German rear.

Our artillery preparation, I understand, took place the day before and ceased during the early morning of the 15th. I cannot recollect particularly heavy gunfire, and the concentration was certainly not on Fritz's front line in our vicinity, for when we entered it, it was absolutely intact. The opposition Fritz put up also pointed out that he had been severely left alone by the artillery until the last minute.

Whatever Fritz's thoughts were, they certainly were not of jubilancy. Since 1 July, regiment after regiment of Huns had been flung in the breach to stem the ever forward march of British battalions. From week to week and in some cases, day to day, he was recoiling backwards, squelched by an avalanche of iron and ground into the mire. With desperate efforts, goaded by the Higher Command, he tried to hold on, but all in vain, and unposted letters taken from the dead and captives bitterly told the tale of despair.

Their letters were full of hunger, cold, and death, with upbraidings of their airmen, who as one said, were spending their time in the theatres of Lille.

It was the same repetition in each letter—the British gunners are shelling their positions and communications so persistently and methodically that they dare not move backward or forward. No food or reserves are reaching them and they are gradually being killed off. The cry was, will we ever be relieved, will we ever emerge alive? Their letters were full of pathos, hopelessness, and at times bitterness at their helplessness against us. Those opposed to us, however, were allowed to remain in their trenches without much molestation since the first week of August and in consequence had their lines in fine shape and dug-outs fairly deep.

The morning was opening out into a typical autumn one, sharp and slightly cloudy. No Man's Land badly furrowed and scarred afforded fairly firm footing but the innumerable shell holes and general unevenness of the surface foretold difficulties in crossing.

As zero hour approached I glanced around looking for signs to charge. The signal came like a bolt from the blue. Right on the second the barrage opened with a roar that seemed to split the heavens. Looking along the right, about forty yards away, I caught the first glimpse of a khaki-clad figure climbing over the parapet. It was the start of the first wave, the 27th Battalion. More Winnipeg men followed. Then glancing back over the parados I saw Sgt. Teddy Torrens rise up from a shell hole and wave his platoon forward. So quick, however, were the men of the 31st on the heels of the 27th that when I turned my head, those of my platoon beside Sgt. Hunter were actually up and over the parapet with a good five to ten yards start ahead of me. In a hurry to overtake them and carry the line as even as possible, I was up and over in a trice, running into shell holes, down and up for about twenty yards, until I found that if I continued this procedure and rate, loaded up as I was, I would be exhausted before I could get to grips with Fritz.

It was at this juncture that instinct told me to avoid the shell holes and move along the edges. I raised my head for the first time and looked at the Hun trench, and to my astonishment, saw Heiny after Heiny ranging along the line, up on the firing step, blazing wildly into us, to all appearances unmolested. Seriousness and grim determination took possession of me as I stared hard and menacing at those death-dealing rifles. Strange to say they all seemed to be pointing at me, an illusion but nevertheless that is how it appeared. My eyes were for a moment glued a little ahead to the right on Sgt. Hunter, who was leading with little Lt. Newlands beside him. He appeared a picture, heroic in the extreme; his rush had dwindled to practically a walk, and he strode forward with body erect, right in the forefront, a target for innumerable shots. As I was fast levelling up on the left, it seemed a thousand miracles that he was not laid low.

My wits sharpened when it burnt deeply into me that death was in the offing. At this stage an everchanging panorama of events passed quickly before my gaze, and my mind was vividly impressed. The air was seething with shells. Immediately above, the atmosphere was cracking with a myriad of machine-gun bullets, startling and disconcerting in the extreme.

Bullets from the enemy rifles were whistling and swishing around my ears in hundreds, that to this day I cannot understand how anyone could have crossed that inferno alive. As I pressed forward with eyes strained, to the extent of being half closed, I expected and almost felt being shot in the stomach. All around our men were falling, their rifles loosening from their grasp. The wounded, writhing in their agonies, struggled and toppled into shell holes for safety from rifle and machine-gun fire, though in my path the latter must have been negligible, for a slow or even quick traverse would have brought us down before we reached many yards into No Man's Land.[3] Rifle fire, however, was taking its toll, and on my front and flanks, soldier after soldier was tumbling to disablement or death, and I expected my turn every moment. The transition from life to death was terribly swift.

Halfway across the first wave seemed to melt and we were in front, heading for Fritz, who was firing wildly and frantically, and scared beyond measure as we bore down upon him. Their faces seemed peculiarly foreign to me. Their trench was full and firing strong and as the remnants of us were nearing bombing reach, we almost, as one man, dropped into shell holes, a move wisely done and swiftly executed. Further progress and it is more than likely that we would have stepped into a volley of grenades. At this time, I had the shell hole to myself and took cover behind the left front edge, which was higher than any other part of the lip, and I could see without being seen from the immediate front, the flanks to the Hun line and the left rear right back to our trench. I was hardly down, when a man around the forty mark, medium-sized, well built, with a heavy sandy moustache, of Scandinavian appearance, came up on my left and stopped not a yard away. He seemed to be nonplussed as if wondering what came over those who were ahead of him a moment ago, as it suddenly dawned upon him that he was the nearest moving soldier to Fritz. I will never forget the look of bewilderment which came over his face, but it quickly changed to puzzled thought, as if wondering what to do next, when a rifle bullet caused him to shudder as if he had received an electric shock. In a flash another must have tore into his vitals for he winced with the shock, then his eyes opened wide and a terrified look of despair and helplessness crept over his features, his eyes rolled, and with a heart-rending shriek as he realized his end had come, he fell forward flat on his face, stone dead, almost on top of me.

It all happened in a twinkling, his death practically instantaneous, but that fatal moment, the wincing, the hopeless, piteous look, were indelibly printed on my mind forever. Glancing back I saw waves of men coming on, right away back to the parapet, but they were collapsing right and left and not a single one got as far forward as the remnants of our own Company. I saw one poor fellow stretched out, apparently dead, with a bullet wound in the head beside the ear, with a face waxen white, and a line of blood tracing down his cheek and neck. The moment after dropping into shell holes we started sniping. The target was so easy it was impossible to miss. The Huns, not many yards ahead, were up on the firing step, blazing in panic at the advancing men behind us, seemingly with only one thought, namely to stop those moving, and in their fright and fear, forgot our little band lying close at hand. Heiny after Heiny fell back in a heap as we closed upon the triggers.

On my left at the edge of the shell hole, a few inches from my shoulder a little ground flew up, and at once I saw I was observed and that a Fritz had just missed me. Pulling in my rifle I lay quiet. Looking back not a man was moving, the attack had stopped. By this time, Cross and Judge, formerly of the 56th Battalion, had jumped into the shell hole one after the other. Fritz finding no movement across No Man's Land, turned his attention to those nearest his line. Cpl. Recknell, who was in a shell hole about ten yards away on my right and very slightly ahead, got up on his knees and stretching his head, curious to see what was happening ahead, got slung in a second by a rifle bullet, quivered, doubled up and dropped forward, killed instantaneously. He appeared to have been struck in the body. Bobby Bisset, a stocky little Scotsman, who was lying in the same shell hole, crawled up on Recknell, caught him by the shoulders, as if to speak and shake him, and immediately his head fell and he practically lay dead on the top of Charlie. The next instant, adjoining Recknell, still further to the right, another soldier was killed as he peered over the shell hole. It looked like Thiebot. Nearer still and on my right was Grewzelier. He was sniping steadily. I saw him get shot also. Just when he was on the point of firing, a bullet got him and he rolled completely round on his back, stone dead. They were killed within a few moments of each other and I think by the same Hun.

At this time a strange incident happened; a German, without arms and equipment, climbed over the parapet on my right and ran into No Man's Land, shrieking and waving his arms, apparently stark, staring mad. He ran about twenty-five yards, wheeled round in a circle several times, the circles narrowing each time, then flopped dead. It was a weird and uncanny spectacle and I was held spellbound, watching his cantrips. I do not think any of our men shot him when he was in the open. He seemed to be in his death throes when he clambered over the parapet and reeled into No Man's Land. Thrilling sights passed before my eyes, during what must have been seconds though they could easily have been construed into hours, so great was the tension, and so miraculous was it that I and a few others in this vicinity escaped destruction.

Lt. Newlands rose up a little from me and gallantly endeavoured to signal us forward by a sweep of his hand, but the time was inopportune and no one moved. He himself was hardly up, when he was wounded and fell back into the shell hole. In the adjoining shell hole, almost touching ours, Lt. Foster got up almost simultaneously with Newlands and promptly collapsed back again, having been hit in the upper arm or shoulder. Freudemacher jumped in beside him to render first aid. It seemed that Foster was painfully hit, for I could see for a minute or two, an arm waving back and forward above the shell hole, as if he was in pain.

As the attack subsided and not a soul moved in No Man's Land save the wounded twisting and moaning in their agony, it dawned upon me that the assault was a failure and now we were at the mercy of the enemy. It was suicide to venture back and our only hope lay in waiting until darkness set in and then trying to win our way back. During this period of waiting, I expected we would be deluged by bombs, shrapnel, and shell fire, and when darkness set in, ravaged by machine-gun fire, altogether a hopeless outlook, especially for our lot, who were lying up against his trench. The situation seemed critical and the chances of withdrawal to safety nigh impossible. So many things had happened, so many lives were snuffed out since I left the comparative safety of our front line, that I lost completely all idea of time.

Lying low in the shell hole contemplating events with now and then a side glance at my sandy moustached comrade, lying dead beside me, his mess tin shining and scintillating on his back, a strange and curious sight appeared. Away to my left rear, a huge grey object reared itself into view, and slowly, very slowly, it crawled along like a gigantic toad, feeling its way across the shell-stricken field. It was a tank, the "Creme de Menthe,"[4] the latest invention of destruction and the first of its kind to be employed in the Great War. I watched it coming towards our direction. How painfully slow it travelled. Down and up the shell holes it clambered, a weird, ungainly monster, moving relentlessly forward. Suddenly men from the ground looked up, rose as if from the dead, and running from the flanks to behind it, followed in the rear as if to be in on the kill. The last I saw of it, it was wending its way to the Sugar Refinery. It crossed Fritz's trenches, a few yards from me, with hardly a jolt.

When first observed it gave new life and vigour to our men. Seeing away behind men getting up, and no one falling, I looked up and there met the gaze of some of my comrades in the shell holes. Instinctively I jumped up and quickly, though warily, ran to where I could see into Fritz's trench, with bayonet pointing and finger on the trigger. Running my eyes up and down his trench, ready to shoot if I saw any signs of hostility, and equally on the alert to jump out of view if I saw a rifle pointing at me, it was a tense and exciting moment but I felt marvellously fit and wits extremely acute, for any encounter. I expected opposition and was ready for danger, but a swift glance, and to my amazement, not a German was staring at me, far less being defiant. Down the trench about a hundred yards, several Huns, minus rifles and equipment, got out of their trench and were beating it back over the open, terrified at the approach of the tank. Only a moment sufficed to show that it was safer in the German trench than being up in the open, where one may be sniped, so with a leap I jumped into the trench, almost transfixing myself with [my] bayonet in the effort.

In several seconds a few more of the Company were into the trench. With two others, I proceeded south to clean up the line. Going about fifty yards without encountering any opposition, and meeting some more of our fellows, we retraced our steps and ran back forty yards or so beyond where we entered the trench when we connected up with some more of our men. There was not a single German capable of offering fight. To the south in the open, I saw Sgt. George West driving about ten prisoners towards our line. A little fellow, I forget his name, a draft to No. 4 Platoon, was busy in the open and extremely keen on his job rounding up another batch of prisoners. Further away on the flanks more Germans were seen hurrying back to our lines, apparently quite anxious to be taken captive. Finding the trench completely in our possession, we started shaking hands and telling each other who was killed and wounded. Young Hayden arrived on the scene and overhearing that his brother was killed commenced sobbing, but controlled himself when his brother suddenly appeared in our midst. The latter complained of being hurt in the eye and beat it out shortly afterwards. The danger of being shot by the front line Germans being now over, several of us set about collecting souvenirs.

I tried to cut off buttons from the coat of a dead German but it was a tough job, as I found they were wired on. I chased up and down the trench looking for Iron Crosses. Two dead Heinies had the black and white ribbons, one with black and yellow also. I went through their pockets but could not locate them, so contented myself with taking a ribbon. Later I heard the crosses were usually attached to a chain, worn round the neck. One dead Heinie, doubled up in the trench, had attached to his belt a dagger, with a fancy tassel hanging therefrom, which appealed to me. I had quite a job loosening the belt from his body. He was equipped with a revolver, which I handed to Sgt. West, who appeared on the scene at the moment. Another dead German I rifled yielded a purse containing seventeen marks in paper and currency. A further one supplied a watch of the cheap variety. I got two helmets but discarded them later. I also passed up field glasses, but changing my mind I returned to Fritz to find, however, that somebody else got there in the meantime. I also took possession of a couple of Heiny Caps, one split new, and the other with a hole through it, and saturated with blood. The heavier stuff I placed in a sandbag and the smaller and lighter stuff I carried on my person. In a dug-out was found a raft of papers, letters, and postcards. Three or four of us congregated and were examining the contents, when a soldier with a couple of sandbags appeared upon the scene, said he belonged to [the] Intelligence Department, and became thoroughly delighted when he saw the capture. When I moved away he was busy stuffing his sandbags. Ten to one Headquarters would have been so much enraptured with his booty that a D.C.M.[5] would be earmarked for him. From one dead Fritz, I took a postcard. It showed his name was Wilhelm Diercks, that he belonged to the 45th Reserve Division, Reserve Infantry Regiment 21, and what appeared to be 2nd Battalion, F Company. It was posted on 9 September 1916, and sent by his sister, Vreda; the post stamp bore the Altrahlstedt.

The first thing that struck me was that this trench was hardly touched by our bombardment. It was deeper and much better constructed than ours, and that it had several dug-outs, one or two fairly deep. The trench was scrupulously clean, not a particle of filth, tins, paper, or refuse of any kind was to be seen. Contrary to information handed out to us, Fritz himself was splendidly equipped. His uniform was in good condition and nothing was lacking in the way of equipment. Nearly every fourth man had a pair of glasses, revolver, or trench dagger, the latter decorated with a tassel. There was no evidence of starvation. The trench and dug-outs disclosed all sorts of supplies. Brown bread was lying around, also cylindrical tins of meat paste. Boxes of dark, cheap looking cigars were here and there in the dug-outs and seltzer water was to be obtained in plenty. I was rather chary about tackling his eatables but I did not pass up his white Rum. It was greatly appreciated but for taste, strength, or quality, it was no match for our S.R.D. [Service Rum Diluted]. We were surprised to see Fritz so comfortable and well equipped and we so ragged and often pinched in our rations. Mr. German, however, got a rude awakening. In perfect health half an hour ago, he was now wallowing in death.

When I jumped into the trench, the sight I beheld, for sheer bloodiness and murder, baffles description. Apparently our artillery had sent over a last minute shrapnel barrage, for the Huns were terribly mangled about the head and shoulders which coupled with our sniping, completely wiped out every Heiny in the bays in front of us. Everyone of them was either dead or dying and the trench literally was running blood. As each bay contained three to five men, it required no imagination to picture the carnage. In the middle of a bay, a Heinie with a dark, stiff moustache, completely doubled up, was suspended, stuck between the parapet and parados. It seemed a peculiar and strange sight to see this Hun, head and knees almost touching, blocking the trench. A few feet north, at a corner, another Hun lay in the bottom of the trench, his head and face terribly lacerated, feebly groaning to death. Every soldier practically stepped on his face when passing south along the trench. Lying around a bend he was trod on before one was aware of his presence. Several times I ran over him. He appeared to be unconscious and was gasping his last breaths. A German with ruddy face, clean shaven and intelligent looking, was lying on his back on the firingstep, minus equipment, as if he had been placed there. At first I wondered what happened to him for he appeared unmarked. His feet, however, were torn to shreds. He had a pleasant countenance and looked as if he was smiling in death. It was off him that I took the Iron Cross ribbon. A typical Hun, big, fat with a double chin, was sitting on the parapet in the south corner of the bay, his stomach so protruding over his thighs that very little of the latter could be seen, stone dead, and not a mark to be seen. There was no shell hole near him, so I conjecture he must have died of fright and not concussion. In the other corner of the bay, reclining back against the parapet, lay a young German, a bullet wound in the head, his face ashen white and with a look as if he sickened to death. How deadly the sprays of metal had done their work, how effective our sniping had been, was plainly discernible. In every bay lay dead and dying Germans, lying in grotesque shapes, and some huddled on the top of each other. Most of them had fearful wounds and the whole line resembled a shambles.

The survivors of the 27th and 28th Battalions, with odds and ends of the 31st, jumped over Fritz's front line, and continued their way to the objective. The last I saw of them they were on the skyline, going over the ridge, their numbers pretty well thinned out. A few patrols of the 31st penetrated to the outskirts of Courcellette.

After we reached Fritz's front line a lull developed and during this period the timid found courage to come across and the stretcher bearers got breathing space to evacuate the wounded. Ridiculous instructions were issued to dig a communication trench in the direction of the enemy, commencing from the front line, by whose order I do not know. Lts. Newlands and Foster were wounded and Major Splane and Lt. Sharples, who were with 1 and 2 Platoons, were killed, the Major, I understand, being shot within seventy-five yards of our parapet. The only officers that appeared in our vicinity were Norris and Kennedy and they were attached to other Companies. Sgt.-Maj. Lawson put in an appearance, but had not a word to say, while Sgt. Wheatley lay in Fritz's trench feeling pretty sick. Sgt. Hunter was the active and most alive head. Spades were found and soon the dirt began to fly, but it was difficult to arouse much enthusiasm for the job, knowing there was a communication trench a little to the north and doubtless another one not very far south. We tackled a stretch of about 150 yards and got down to two to three feet, when a number of bullets came whistling in our direction. Thinking Heiny had found his bearings and was coming back on us we retreated into the trench, ready for defence. It was, however, a false alarm, so we returned to the digging.

The Hun command apparently realized the extent of our attack for shortly afterwards the hostile artillery opened up on his front line, right away back to our communications and belaboured these parts for a considerable period, sending us back for the second time and compelling us to seek safety in the snuggest portions of the trench. Holding our breath as shell after shell burst in and around, Fritz ultimately ceased. A party was organized to go forward and lend assistance further on. Sgt. Hunter led the way, while I took up the rear. Proceeding up the new trench we had dug we soon stopped and laid down, one behind the other. After a few minutes, I passed up the word, "Why the delay?" information coming back to the effect that so and so, the fourth man, had failed to connect up with those in front as they emerged into the open, so he lay down, the rest following suit. On enquiring what direction they took, another fellow and self set out after them, but could see no signs of either Hunter or the other two, so retraced our steps, expecting they would return and pick us up.

A few minutes later an officer of the 27th Battalion appeared on the scene, asked me what we were doing here and cursorily ordered us up ahead to help the 27th dig in. He was as drunk as a piper. I told him who we were and showed him a copy of operation orders, drawing his attention to the fact that our duty was to man Fritz's front line after it had been mopped up. He grabbed the sheet, looked at it upside down, muttered and cursed and commanded us to go ahead. It was most amusing; while this conversation was going on, one after another of our men, overhearing what had been said, quietly slid out of the road, back to the trench. He became angry and I annoyed, so I blurted out, in any case we could not go forward until I reported back to our officer in the trench. (We had no officer in the trench). "All right," he blurted out, then threateningly he fired back at me, "see you come back." Just as I reached the trench the balance of the company was filing out, going north, Sgt. Alec McDonald bringing up the rear, carrying a Heinie dress helmet. I asked him what was the matter. He responded, "Hurry out, we are relieved." Returning I told the officer that our lot was relieved and they were passing out at the moment. "Get up there," he said, pointing towards Fritz. Being sore and disgusted as the dickens, I flashed back, "All right, show us the way." He looked around, was at a loss for an answer, and at the moment a corporal of the 27th appeared on the scene and inquired about a supply of ammunition for the men. Without a word, the officer went away with the corporal. I stood, furious, looking at them hiking back over No Man's Land, then turning to young Hayden, who stuck to me like a leech, the others using discretion got out of the road one by one, said "To H—— with him, come on, beat it," and flung my spade as far as possible, utterly fed up with the gall of this strange intoxicated officer.

We chased back to the front line. Upon proceeding south a Hun shot his head above a shell hole, but promptly dropped it again as I caught a glimpse of him. By this time, I was passing three men of the relieving battalion lounging around the bay, and pointing told them that there was a very much alive Heiny in the shell hole over there. As I passed hurrying to overtake McDonald and the party, they stood up preparing to account for their shell hole neighbour. There was no signs of our men to be seen. All the information the newcomers could give us was that they had gone out. We struck a side trench which led into a circular machine-gun emplacement in No Man's Land, when we encountered a fellow, minus equipment, lying on his back yelling and kicking up a deuce of a row. At first I thought he was badly wounded; who did it turn out to be but Mackintosh of No. 4 Platoon, helplessly full of Fritz's rum, as happy as a lark, and trying to sing for all he was worth. Kennedy, a new officer, formerly of the 66th Battalion, I think, had lost himself, so joined Hayden and self at this point. I told him that we had been relieved and were going out. He seemed to be uncertain what to do and was half afraid to go out in case he might get a slating from the colonel. He mentioned that this was his first engagement and he hoped he was doing right. We retraced our steps and made a fruitless attempt to find 31st men, and we got in contact with Sewell, a runner. Satisfied that they had gone out we made up our minds to return. By this time, Fritz recommenced shelling and we crossed No Man's Land, running from shell hole to shell hole, narrowly escaping disaster several times. One shrapnel bullet hit the field dressing at the corner of my tunic as we lay in a shell hole, getting ready for a run between the bursts. A number of our dead were passed and we heard one fellow yelling a considerable distance away.

Reaching our old front line we came across some of our machine-gunners. At this point we witnessed a fine sight. About 3:30 p.m. in extended order and in the middle of a bombardment the 42nd Battalion and the Princess Pats swept across our front, angling off to the left in great style and causing us to halt for a few minutes on our way back to witness this unexpected and alluring spectacle. One would have thought that Fritz was expecting them for the shelling was very severe at the moment, and though a number were falling, they moved evenly across in unbroken waves, apparently making for the northern flank, no doubt to protect the 5th

Brigade. On the right, the latter was sweeping forward irresistibly on Courcellette, enveloping it and having it safely in their possession an hour and a half later.

Going down the trench we came across [Sgt.-Maj.] Lawson and a few others taking refuge in the narrowest and most secure looking part of the communications. While here, an officer, a little, middle-aged man, badly shell shocked, his mouth quivering, like a child crying, was being led out by a private, the latter holding his hand. He was a pitiable object. It was hard to believe that he could be reduced to such a state. Asking Lawson why they were staying there, I was told that Fritz was shelling the trench lower down badly and apparently they thought it was safer to remain where they were. Leaving the officer and telling Hayden to come on and take the risk, we beat it down in a series of spurts, flopping with each shell burst, ultimately reaching a deep dug-out at Pozières, pretty well pumped out. We waited here for several minutes, picking up Stretcher-Bearer Bamforth, and finally got out of the bombardment area, after experiencing several narrow squeaks and landed down at the position we vacated on the evening of the 14th, where we met the bulk of the survivors of the assault. After obtaining something to eat, Stretcher-Bearer Bamforth and self paired off into a little unoccupied dug-out, let the gas blanket down, and slept long and sound.

We awoke in the morning, made for the cook's limber with mess tins, and to our surprise found our limber had vanished and in its place was the cook limber of another battalion. At the moment our Company was on its way out to Albert. Minus breakfast we packed up and hiked along the valley towards Contalmaison, meeting MacNair of the police, who was left to inform the stragglers of the whereabouts of the battalion. Above Contalmaison we met the Company finishing their midday meal, and tried to obtain some scraps without success. I was rested not much more than ten minutes when Sgt.-Maj. Lawson appeared asking on behalf of the colonel for four volunteers to return to No Man's Land and bring in Major Splane's body. When he reached me nobody had volunteered, and apparently had anticipated trouble, for he looked rather wistfully at me after explaining his mission. I said offhand he could put my name down if he could not scratch the number. Returning later he intimated that he had been round the Company and only got one man. I told him I was ready, and the next minute collared Simmons as he was passing and said, "Come on, you'll come with me." "Sure," he said, "what for." And he did. Later another fellow was dug up. Simmons was originally a 66th man and was killed later on in the campaign. The other two were drafts named Campbell and Graham.

Informing us that we would go out under the white flag, we kicked over this, as we had not sufficient faith to believe that Fritz would pay much attention to any flag, if he had an opportunity to kill. So in the end we went fully armed. Talbordet, who knew where Major Splane was lying, was to accompany us. At the last moment we found out that four representatives from the other companies were on a similar errand to bring in their commanding officers who were killed: Capt. Boucher of "B" Company,

Capt. Pinkham of "C" Company, the name of the officer of "D" Company I do not remember. Capt. Soley, an officer lately attached to the battalion, was in charge of our strange outfits. We returned to the line by way of Pozières and saw full evidence of the wreckage of the last twenty-four hours. At the side of the road were two of our men with their arms and legs broken and almost detached, mere trunks of men, and much more ghastly looking than the general run of dead. At the other end of Pozières we went off the road into a trench on the right and worked our way south. Parts of the trench were completely wrecked; the parapets being blown down, it was impossible to pass along without exposing yourself. At these points, Fritz was sniping and we had a deuce of a time getting along and keeping contact. The going was so hard and risky that one Company's representatives turned back and left us. Not content sniping with rifle fire, it appeared as if Fritz was trying the same with whiz-bangs for they seemed to be following us as we struggled along. The whole thing was ridiculous. How we expected to get into No Man's Land and pick up the major when we had all we could do to handle ourselves in the trench, was hard to comprehend. At last we halted beside some Red Cross men and they asked us what we were doing here. Upon being informed of our mission they mentioned that they were up on a similar errand since an hour or two and found it hopeless to show themselves above the parapet. Returning, we had the job of dodging shells for several hundred yards and passed one of the tanks stuck in the communications [trench]. Our party scattered. Near La Boiselle I got a lift from a truck to Albert, where I hiked to the Brick Fields, arriving too late for supper, so crossed over the road to the canteen a little before closing time and had a scramble to get something to eat. I emerged, however, with a big tin of fruit and a couple of packets of biscuits and ate the lot, the first bite I had since twenty-four hours.

On reaching the camp, I made steps to obtain my pack and found the Q.M. [Quartermaster] busy sorting out those belonging to casualties. My attention was aroused when I overheard the remarks, "Look what Recknell has been packing around" and saw their eyes open wide when a sixteen pound iron ball was fished out of the pack. They looked surprised and wondered what the idea was. I suddenly remembered that Malcolm Maclean, myself, and a few others, found the ball on the camping ground before we left for the Somme, had several putts at it, and then for devilment shoved it into Recknell's pack.

Sunday, 17 September 1916

Today we took stock of the casualties of the battalion and found 247 were put out of action, 78 belonging to "A" Company, a rather high percentage for a few hour's offensive. 7 officers were killed, 5 wounded, and 1 missing. Of the rank and file of "A" Company, 19 were listed as killed, 11 missing, and 37 wounded. The missing with few exceptions may be regarded as killed, while several of the wounded succumbed later. The killed to wounded showed an abnormally high ratio.

NOTES

1. These would be the cast iron bombs for the 3-inch Stokes trench mortar. Production of this mortar began late in 1915. It was simple to construct, weighed about 36 pounds, and was a very practical weapon for trench warfare.

2. A cloth bandolier contained 60 rounds of .303 ammunition, the total weighing seven pounds. Each Mills grenade weighed a pound and a half.

3. Firing at a rate of over 300 rounds per minute, the German Spandau machine-gun, if moved from side to side on its mounting, could act like a steel scythe cutting down exposed infantry advancing over open ground.

4. The tremendous casualties caused by the combination of machine-guns, trenches, and barbed wire spurred the Allies into devising some sort of machine which would overcome all three. The result was the tank. The one seen by Fraser was a Mark I. It weighed 28 tons, had a speed of about 4 m.p.h., and was equipped with either machine-guns or two 6-pounder guns. It had a dramatic effect on the battlefield.

5. D.C.M.—Distinguished Conduct Medal.

CORPS COMMANDER: ARTHUR CURRIE *

A.M.J. HYATT

o

The success at Vimy Ridge was encouraging, but Currie remained convinced that there was still hard fighting ahead. In January 1917 he had predicted that the enemy would "fight desperately until beaten absolutely. I do not think that he can be beaten this year; and I believe that next year he will fight more desperately than ever. The most foolish thing any of our people could do would be to imagine victory is so close that their efforts can be relaxed."[1] After Vimy Ridge there was little reason, so far as Currie was concerned, to revise his earlier appreciation, and he maintained a healthy scepticism of predictions of an early peace. The summer of 1917, however, was to prove even more difficult than expected in Currie's cautious estimate. The Canadian attack at Vimy, in fact, had been only the most successful part of a much larger British operation, planned as a preface to an enormous French thrust, The Battle of the Aisne. This attack, the French high command had predicted, would knock Germany out of the war. Conceived by General Nivelle, who had replaced Joffre as French commander-in-chief in December 1916, the plan for the battle was one of the most flatulent plans of the entire war. When the French struck, the success achieved was a "ludicrous fraction of what had been promised . . . Instead of being miles behind the German lines, the French were barely clinging to toeholds in the enemy defences . . . Unsaid, but fully understood by the whole Army, was the fact that Nivelle had failed to make good on even one of his grandiose promises."[2] As a result, General Pétain became the third French commander-in-chief within a period of six months, and his first task was to quell the mutinies that began to break out in the French army. It was now the turn of the British to make great plans.

---

* "Corps Commander," chap. 5 from *General Sir Arthur Currie: A Military Biography* (Toronto: University of Toronto Press in collaboration with the Canadian War Museum, the Canadian Museum of Civilization, and the National Museums of Canada, 1987), 68–89.

General Haig had agreed to co-operate with Nivelle's offensive, but he had long wanted to launch an attack further north, if only, as the editor of his diaries put it, "because a success in Flanders would have had the effect of rolling back the whole of the German right wing; whereas success further south all too often merely meant the creation of a dangerous salient in the enemy line."[3] To mask his intentions and also to meet Pétain's urgent plea that pressure be taken off the French until the mutinies could be subdued, Haig ordered that the Canadian Corps and adjacent British formations keep pushing the Germans in the Vimy area. As a consequence the 1st Canadian Division continued to move east of Vimy and captured the towns of Arleux and Fresnoy, small but intricate and frustrating operations.

Currie and his soldiers were soon to be involved more intimately in the British plan for 1917, but in the meantime other, seemingly unrelated events occurred that were to make this involvement more difficult for Arthur Currie. In April 1917 the British government decided to replace the commander-in-chief in Palestine. This decision on a remote theatre of the war was to have a direct and profound effect on Currie's career. General Allenby, commander of the Third British Army in France, was the choice for Palestine. Haig decided to replace Allenby with Byng which, of course, meant that yet another man had to be placed in charge of the Canadian Corps. Sheer chance, or perhaps fate, kept Currie in the running for this selection; for it was luck that saved his life on 2 June. Normally the divisional commander handed his messages to a runner, who would take them to the signals centre for transmission, but on 2 June no runner was available, and Currie himself took a message across to signals. As he did so, his headquarters received a direct hit. Currie was thrown to the ground, covered with earth, and received a nasty graze on his head from flying shrapnel. Those still in the headquarters were not so lucky: two were killed and sixteen wounded. The day after his "lucky" accident Currie learned that he had been awarded a KCMG in the Birthday Honours list; three days later Byng told him that he was to command the Canadian Corps.

Such a promotion, after Byng's recommendation and Haig's approval, in any other case would have been a routine matter. In Currie's case the situation was not so simple. His promotion, in the first place, was embarrassing for the minister of overseas military forces, Sir George Perley. It will be recalled that when Richard Turner had been appointed CGS in England, he had insisted that if a Canadian were ever to be appointed commander of the corps, he, as senior major-general in the Canadian forces, would be considered. Perley was quite aware of his promise to Turner but probably was even more concerned that his efforts to untangle the Canadian administrative jungle in England should not go awry. To have Currie's appointment announced before it was confirmed by Canadian authorities was a direct threat to Perley's reorganization. This problem was easily resolved by a letter from Haig's military secretary which indicated that all arrangements and promotions in France were "temporary" until confirmed by Canadian authority.[4]

On the question of who should be selected to command the Canadian Corps, Sir George Perley had few doubts. Turner, he knew was doing satisfactory work in England and was "rather out of touch with the front after a six month absence." Currie, on the other hand, was "considered most suitable for the Corps by higher command and also by the larger half of [the] troops."[5] These views he immediately wired to the prime minister. Before Borden's answer arrived, Perley had come to his own solution. Turner would remain as CGS, but with powers extended to include a "certain measure [of] authority over administrative matters at [the] front particularly on lines [of] communication." Meanwhile both Currie and Turner would be promoted simultaneously, which would "preserve Turner's seniority."[6] Perley's solution was not unreasonable, since it would keep both Turner and Currie at the jobs they did best. He was relieved when the prime minister concurred, recommending that Perley should take the "advice of higher command unless you see strong reason to the contrary."[7]

While these negotiations proceeded, Currie's position was extraordinarily complicated. In the first place, he had been given very little warning to prepare himself for taking over his new command. Henceforth, he would be accountable for the entire corps, and so long as any part of it was in combat he always felt responsible for his men. The communiqué indicating that he was to step up reached him on 6 June, and two days later he was at corps headquarters struggling with the problems of the larger formation. Still to be settled was the issue of who would take his place as commander of the 1st Division.[8] Currie had recommended and Byng had accepted the commander of the 7th Canadian Infantry Brigade, Brigadier-General A.C. Macdonnell, as his replacement at 1st Division headquarters. Macdonnell, popularly known as "Batty Mac," was one of the few pre-war Canadian permanent force officers who gained general's rank during the First World War. His promotion to brigadier had been fiercely opposed by Sir Sam Hughes.[9] Though Sir Sam was no longer minister of militia, further promotion for Macdonnell was to prove not easy.

Currie was convinced that Macdonnell was the best qualified for divisional commander of the senior officers at the front and thus was enthusiastic about his appointment. Sir Robert Borden, who had little knowledge of performance in France, believed that the appointment to the 1st Division of Major-General Garnet Hughes might well dampen the fire of criticism from Sir Sam. Perley had only recently settled an extremely awkward situation that had resulted when Sir Sam's brother, St. Pierre Hughes, was dismissed from the command of the 10th Brigade. Perley, therefore, could hardly be against something that would reduce the attacks of the former minister. Thus he concurred with the prime minister's recommendation that Garnet Hughes be given the 1st Division. When Currie discovered that Hughes was being considered for command of the 1st Division, he immediately objected.[10] Perley called him to London on 14 June. The resulting interview, according to Perley, produced a "most pleasant undertaking" among Currie, Turner, and himself.[11] The issues discussed, apparently, were command of the corps, new administrative arrangements between OMFC [Overseas Military Forces of Canada] and the corps, and command of the 1st Division.[12] Unquestionably, Currie was easily satisfied on the relationship between himself and Turner. The real issue was Macdonnell's appointment. Currie interpreted the offer to Garnet Hughes of the 1st Division as a quid pro quo for his own appointment to command of the corps and refused to accept it. In his diary he noted that in the interview with Perley "it was decided that I take the Corps and my attitude toward the appointment of Garnet Hughes was fully explained."[13] It was not only explained, it was accepted by Perley. (Indeed, even before his meetings with Currie on 14 and 15 June Perley had supported the nomination of Macdonnell.) In the words of Desmond Morton, Perley "had seen enough of the aftermath of Hughes's patronage and cronyism to recognize its price."[14] Borden had stronger feelings about appointing Garnet Hughes, though he was not adamant about the matter. On 13 June he had wired Perley: "If Garnet Hughes is acceptable for Division Commander, I would like to see him appointed but leave the question to your judgement."[15] Later Borden would attempt to deny any involvement.[16]

In a letter written after the war, Currie too placed a rather different interpretation on the events in question. Then he argued not only that his own appointment was conditional on his acceptance of Garnet Hughes, but that this point of view was put forward, in Morton's words, with "ruthless and irresponsible pressure."[17] "I refused," Currie wrote, "to accept command . . . on any conditions which I thought would embarrass me." He added that the "main condition was that I should accept as my successor in the 1st Division Major-General Garnett [sic] Hughes." Finally, he claims to have been "importuned, coaxed, threatened and bullied. I was told that Garnett Hughes would have to get the 1st Division, that there was a combination in England and Canada for him that neither I, nor any man could beat; that his father wanted him to get the position and that God help the man who fell out with his father."[18]

There are two puzzles here. One is the reason for which Currie rejected Garnet Hughes, which he never committed to paper. The other mystery that is undocumented is why Currie rationalized an interpretation of the negotiations over his appointment which was different than close inspection of the event suggests. Garnet Hughes, it should be remembered, was well known to Currie. Only five years younger, Garnet had been a friend in Victoria; Currie liked the younger man, and the affection seemed reciprocal.[19] However, Currie's biographer argues that the corps commander did "not admire Hughes as a leader in the field."[20] John Swettenham in his history of the Canadian Corps indicated that Currie considered Garnet "an indifferent front-line soldier."[21] In fact, there was a single occasion on which this opinion could have been based—Hughes's performance as brigade major during the gas attack of 1915. There can be no doubt that Hughes was confused in that situation. Equally there is little doubt that there were mitigating circumstances—an extremely difficult action, Hughes's first experience under fire, and other senior officers equally confused. This episode bothered Currie at the time, but it is impossible to be certain that it was the sole or even the main reason for his rejection of Garnet Hughes. Currie did not ever in writing accuse Hughes of being a poor leader in battle. He did, on the other hand, make it absolutely clear that he did not want him. When Hughes was given command of the 1st

Brigade, Currie had argued that he was not sufficiently experienced as a combat commander. By 1917 it was still possible to make this argument, but it was much less cogent than it had been in 1915. Hughes had served for less than four months as a brigade major, he had been a divisional staff officer for nearly three months, and for almost sixteen months he had served creditably as GOC of the 1st Canadian Infantry Brigade.

With such a record, one could scarcely claim that Garnet was inexperienced, though it could still be claimed that his record was less impressive than those of other divisional commanders in the Canadian Corps. Major-General Henry Burstall of the 2nd Division had been a pre-war permanent force officer and a graduate of staff college. He had come overseas in charge of the 1st Divisional Artillery. When the Canadian Corps had been formed, he became GOC of the Corps Artillery, served in that position for fifteen months, and then had taken over the 2nd Division. General Lipsett, commander of the 3rd Division, came overseas as commanding officer of the 8th Battalion, followed Currie as GOC of the 2nd Brigade, and after ten months had taken over the 3rd Canadian Division. When the 4th Division had been formed in April 1916, Brigadier-General David Watson of the 5th Brigade was selected as commander. Watson too came overseas with the first contingent as commanding officer of an infantry battalion. He served for almost a year in the position before taking over the 5th Brigade, where he remained for eight months before becoming GOC of the 4th Division. Brigadier-General Macdonnell, the man Currie picked as his replacement in the 1st Division, was a pre-war permanent officer who had served in South Africa. Macdonnell came overseas as commanding officer of the Lord Strathcona's Horse and had served as GOC of the 7th Brigade since its formation in December 1915, except for three months spent recuperating from wounds. Each of these men had splendid records, but simply counting months in various positions of command would not be sufficient in itself to disqualify Garnet Hughes.

Perhaps Currie was negative towards Hughes partly because the suggestion for his appointment did not come from corps headquarters. Currie's subsequent correspondence with Sir George Perley confirms that he believed strongly that there ought to be "no interference with my prerogatives in the matter of recommendations" for appointments.[22] On this matter the corps commander was unfair to Perley.[23] In any event, Currie believed that it was his right to make initial recommendations on appointments within the Canadian Corps, and he was particularly touchy about suggestions for appointments that came from England or Canada.

Probably, and the evidence is inferential, a key factor in Hughes's disqualification was his name. Sir Sam Hughes's influence had been so pervasive, his interference in appointments so well known, and his nepotism so obvious, that if Currie had accepted Garnet as GOC of the 1st Canadian Division, few could have believed that the old business of influence determining promotion was dead. When, after the question of the promotion was settled, the deputy minister of the Overseas Military Forces visited France, he found general satisfaction with both the new organization and

Currie's selection of Macdonnell. He then reported to Perley that "there could be no further question of raising Garnet Hughes' prospects."[24] In short, if part of Currie's reason for not accepting Garnet Hughes was that he wanted to make a clean break with the Hughes system, it seems clear that he had done so. But if this was the case, it is quite likely that Currie had pangs of conscience about the matter. He owed his own appointment in 1914 to the influence of his friend Garnet Hughes. With the shoe on the other foot, Currie was not prepared to back Hughes for an appointment in the 1st Division. Thus Desmond Morton's claim that "Currie's sense of martyrdom may have concealed a justifiably bad conscience"[25] seems valid. Given the evidence, this is probably as far as one can go with the puzzle about Currie's reasons for rejecting Garnet Hughes. It also offers a plausible explanation for the second question of why Currie changed his view on the negotiations concerning his own appointment.

On the second issue, however, there is something that should be added. The summer of 1917, as we shall see, was more difficult, frustrating, and disappointing for Arthur Currie than any other period during the war. During this time he took over the corps, dealt with complex military problems, settled his long-standing personal problems, participated in the great conscription issue, and discovered that it would not produce the men it promised. With the passage of time, it is surely not surprising that in his recollection of events one problem should become entangled with others occurring simultaneously. Currie probably did have a guilty conscience about Garnet Hughes. There was pressure to appoint Hughes, but it was not "ruthless and irresponsible." Currie was not "importuned, coaxed threatened and bullied," but it is quite easy to see how in retrospect he came to believe that he had been.

Before leaving England for France, Currie had an interview with Garnet Hughes which was long and heated. Hughes argued that he was the most senior major-general available for the 1st Division, and Currie plainly indicated that he would not back Hughes's appointment. If there were heat and pressure anywhere, it must have been during this meeting wherein former friends disagreed.[26] Hughes left the meeting feeling betrayed, and disappointed and promising revenge. Currie must have left frustrated and guilty, even if convinced of the correctness of his position.

Currie's biographer, Colonel Urquhart, has suggested that as soon as the command arrangements in France became public knowledge, a personal attack was launched on Currie, led by Sam Hughes. This attack, apparently, was based on the financial difficulties that Currie had left behind in Victoria in 1914. Urquhart alleges that Currie's enemies in Canada insisted that the debts be paid at once or legal action would follow.[27] Whatever the state of his debts, Currie, it should be recalled, had left Victoria having used the government uniform allowance to the 50th Regiment for personal purposes. He claimed on 25 June 1917, in a letter to the then commanding officer of the 50th Regiment, "it is impossible for me to tell . . . the efforts I have constantly made to meet the claim but I can tell you that for nearly three years the last thing I thought of at night and the first thing in the morning was this."[28] His statement is probably the literal truth, since it appears that until June 1917 he had made very little effort indeed to redeem this debt. The only record that survives of an earlier attempt to take action is his letter of late September 1914 to Sam Matson asking Matson to get him time to pay. Yet on 25 June 1917, shortly after his interview with Perley that settled the question of command, Currie took the first step to pay off the debt. As commander of the Canadian Corps his pay jumped approximately 71 percent (from $24 to $41.24 per day), which one might assume would make it possible to pay the obligation quickly. In fact, the 50th Regiment was not reimbursed until September 1917, when Currie borrowed money from two of his wealthy subordinate officers, Major-General David Watson of the 4th Division and Brigadier-General Victor Odlum of the 11th Brigade. Subsequently Currie settled with these men by paying instalments which ended in 1919. For an individual caught in the vice of unpleasant circumstances, conspiracy is always a tempting explanation for these circumstances. However, conspiracy does not explain Currie's failure to take action to pay off the obligation, nor does it explain his decision to settle the matter in June. The only conspiracy was the subsequent action of Sir George Perley and Sir Robert Borden to cover up the corps commander's culpability.

After Currie wrote to him in September 1914, the loyal Matson made a substantial effort to help Currie. He sent Currie's letter to Borden, urging that Currie's case was one that merited "generous treatment" and asking that Bordon should do his best "to prevent an investigation until this poor unfortunate fellow has been given the chance he asks for."[29] Matson's efforts to gain time and his subsequent and unsuccessful attempt to raise money for Currie have been carefully examined by R. Craig Brown and Desmond Morton.[30] They demonstrate that in spite of Matson's letter and a later anonymous letter from Victoria, it is not at all certain that the prime minister knew about Currie's action until after he had been appointed corps commander in 1917. They further demonstrate that only the polite and patient efforts of Moore, Taggart, the Glasgow manufacturers of the 50th Regiment uniforms, to secure their money kept the matter alive at all. Indeed, it moved with glacial slowness through the militia bureaucracy, coming to the attention of the militia council only on 15 June 1917. The council, practised bureaucrats all, simply referred the whole matter to the minister of overseas military forces of Canada, and the file that documented Currie's action reached the overseas minister on 21 July. There was no conspiracy of enemies here—only the lethargy of bureaucrats and the accident of the mails. Perley was shocked and appalled. He "understood at once that the only possible outcome of further investigation would be a court martial and certain disgrace [for Currie]."[31] Perley instantly informed the prime minister that the matter would result in a scandal if it became public and offered to pay half of the amount personally if the minister of militia, Sir Edward Kemp, would put up the other half.[32] Borden replied that such action was unnecessary, since Sir Edward Kemp had arranged for the debt to be paid by the Department of Militia and Defence and the money subsequently recovered from Currie.[33] A draft order-in-council was prepared to pay off the Glasgow company but remained unsigned. Professors Morton and Brown have questioned this delay and found no definitive answer. They suggest, however, that the most plausible explanation of the delay is that "someone had quietly intimated that Currie was finally making restitution and the potential scandal could be safely allowed to sink back into the shadows."[34] It seems likely that this is the case, since Currie, as we have seen, had indeed begun to arrange to repay his debt.[35] He had informed the commanding officer of the 50th in June that the affair would soon be settled, and by 10 September he had borrowed the money from his two subordinates, and had begun to have the money transferred to Victoria.

While Currie was at last free of the direct financial obligation, he could never be free of the knowledge of what he had done. There is no evidence that he was aware that his action had been exposed to the militia council, the cabinet, and especially the overseas minister, Sir George Perley. All these people, in Morton's words, "had exercised a beneficial discretion," and had become "accomplices in the cover-up."[36] But they were not Currie's accomplices; he continued to carry his guilty "secret" and to remember that Borden and Perley had had no initial objections to Garnet Hughes.

At the very least Currie's take-over of the Canadian Corps was something less than one might expect from a promotion. It seemed to him that he had earned the command of Canada's largest military formation on the strength of his ability, only to be questioned when he insisted on the right to appoint competent subordinates. Throughout the experience he constantly faced the enormous responsibility of commanding the entire corps. In these circumstances it is perhaps understandable that he occasionally was less generous in his dealings with Sir George Perley than he might have been,[37] and perhaps even more surprising that he carried out his military responsibilities so superbly.

The first major operation that Currie directed from start to finish was an assault on the city of Lens. In this attack Currie was being asked to do two things, and the successful completion of one complicated the achievement of the other. First, he was to create a threat at Lens that would draw German attention away from the operations being conducted further north in Flanders; and second, he was to disrupt German reinforcement plans by destroying as many enemy formations as possible. Possibly because Currie was new at his job, the orders received by Canadian Corps from First Army for the Lens attack were considerably more detailed than usual. These orders dictated that the Canadians should break the German line south of the city and then advance by stages until the city was taken.[38] Such a plan, in Currie's view, took no account of the tactical features of the battleground and made the dual objective very difficult to achieve. Currie met General Horne on 10 July and persuaded him that the First Army plan must be replaced.[39]

Currie pointed out to Horne that Lens was dominated from the north and south by two hills—Hill 70 and Sallaumines Hill, respectively—which were precluded from the attack in the First Army plan. Each of these hills, in Currie's view, was a more important tactical feature than the city of Lens itself, and Hill 70 was the key to capturing the southern hill. Currie's basic idea was a modification of a theory advocated by the general staff officer in charge of planning at general headquarters, Brigadier John Davidson. The goal was to seize a tactical position of vital importance to the enemy which he would then be forced to retake. Once taken, the position would be held largely by preregistered artillery and machine-gun fire. As a modern student of tactics put it, this was "typical of Currie, who used other people's ideas but did them better."[40] Currie, in any event, persuaded the army commander to make Hill 70 the main objective, but Canadian plans were again complicated when the First Army ordered that "all the ground [taken in any raid] must be held by rifle and bayonet alone if no assistance is obtainable from other arms."[41] The order was almost preposterous. If followed, it would heavily handicap the success of the corps, since Currie planned to make a number of preliminary raids to destroy key defensive emplacements. Currie solved the issue merely by ignoring the army order and issuing instructions for immediate withdrawal after the destructive missions were completed.[42]

In order to achieve the objective of pinning down as many German forces as possible, it was essential to mislead the enemy into expecting a much larger attack than that of a single corps. If the Germans did expect a larger attack, then Canadian casualties would inevitably be heavy. Preliminary raids were designed to alarm the Germans and also to destroy key defensive works that would cause Canadian casualties when the real attack was made. Extensive gas shelling and dragging dummy tanks behind the lines served to increase further the enemy's apprehension, but the artillery barrages were carefully designed so that tactical surprise for the main attack could still be achieved. Currie planned for a lightning success and very quickly to consolidate the new position; then he could let the enemy wear himself out making counterattacks.

Currie repeatedly postponed the final assault until weather conditions were perfect. Then, on 15 August, behind the protective fire of nine field artillery brigades, the Canadians attacked. Hill 70 itself was quickly seized and consolidated.[43] German counterattacks continued almost unabated for three days, but the new line remained firm. Currie was delighted as the German attacks continued to be broken by artillery fire and collapse against the Canadian trenches. Between 15 and 18 August, he noted, "there were no fewer than twenty-one counter attacks delivered, many with very large forces . . . Four German divisions were accounted for . . . (and) our gunners, machine gunners and infantry never had such targets."[44] The Germans continued sporadically until 25 August, each attack adding to the success of the operation. The German official history noted lugubriously that "Even though we soon succeeded in sealing off the local penetration at Lens, the Canadians had attained their ends. The fighting at Lens had cost us a considerable number of troops which had to be replaced. The entire preconceived plan for relieving the troops in Flanders had been upset."[45]

Thanks to Currie's careful planning, Canadian losses were less than expected; during July and August the Canadians suffered approximately ten thousand casualties while inflicting between two and three times that number on the enemy.[46] Still, the well-spring of Canadian reinforcements seemed to be rapidly drying up, and the events of autumn of 1917 were to prove costly in numbers of men. The Canadian attack at Lens was a part of the campaign in Flanders, since it was fought to keep German reserves from being sent to the Ypres area. But the Canadians were not to escape a more direct exposure to what Winston Churchill termed a "forlorn expenditure of valour and life without equal in futility."[47] To follow Currie's corps, however, we must have some understanding of the fighting that preceded its action.

The possibility of following up Plumer's success at Messines had been hinted at in the original order for Messines, but for a variety of reasons the possibility was forgone in June. The next phase was to be carried out by General Gough's Fifth Army and would not begin before a long delay. As Haig's biographer remarked, "immeasurable ill flowed from this option." The "Third Battle of Ypres"—the formal name for the Flanders operations— began officially on 31 July, when Gough's army assaulted Pilckem ridge after a fifteen-day preliminary bombardment had pounded the earth to dust. During the week before the assault, sporadic rains mixed with the dust to make the ground very muddy for the attacking troops. On the evening of 31 July the rain became heavy and for four days it fell incessantly, bringing the Fifth Army to a standstill. The results: a maximum advance of three thousand yards and 31 850 British casualties.[48]

"Third Ypres" consisted of eight separate battles and can be divided conveniently into three stages. Stage one, fought entirely under Gough's command, began with the attack on Pilckem ridge and ended with "The Battle of Langemarck," which was coincident with Currie's attack on Lens in the rainiest August for four years.[49] With Langemarck, the casualty total climbed to 68 000.[50] In the second stage Haig decided to switch the main effort from Gough back to Plumer. Hope for a major breakthrough was then abandoned, since Plumer planned a succession of three limited attacks designed to win the southern half of Passchendaele ridge.[51]

Perhaps the supreme irony of the campaign—if not the entire war— occurred in the three weeks between the end of the Battle of Langemarck and Plumer's battle of the Menin Road Ridge. During this interval the prime minister, Lloyd George, who had opposed the approval of the campaign, had ample opportunity to stop it and failed to do so. By the beginning of September it was obvious that Haig's action in Flanders was hardly about to achieve its grandiose objectives. Lloyd George after the war claimed that in June the war cabinet had agreed to Haig's offensive on the "understanding that if the progress . . . made with the operation did not realize the expectations . . . [of the planners], it would be called off and effective help rendered to the Italians to press their offensive."[52] In fact Haig did not get such approval in June; it did not come until July, and unqualified approval of the war cabinet was not given until 25 July. Nonetheless, Lloyd George, who could have stopped the fighting in September, made no move to do so. Perhaps the prime minister really did subscribe to the bloody plan that Sir Henry Wilson, then in charge of the Eastern Command, attributed to him: "I believe," wrote Wilson, "that Lloyd George, knowing that Haig will not do any good has allowed him to keep all his guns, etc., so that he can, later on, say, 'Well, I gave you everything. I even allowed you to spoil the Italian offensive. And now, owing to gross miscalculation and incapacity you have entirely failed to do anything serious except lose a lot of men.' And in this indictment he will include Robertson, and then get rid of them both."[53] In any event, Lloyd George did not stop the offensive. Instead he "submitted with sullen fatalism" and allowed it to continue.[54]

Equally ironically, in Flanders all rain ceased. Cloudless skies and brilliantly sunlit days refined the mud once more to dust. For two idyllic weeks the soldiers in Flanders were warm, dry, and unhampered by malodorous sludge. To the German infantry it "seemed almost inconceivable . . . that even the peculiar British would fight in the rain and rest in the sun."[55] In fact, there was no 'rest' for the British soldiers, who, under Plumer's direction, prepared for the next phase scheduled for 20 September. As darkness set in on 19 [September], it began to drizzle, and by midnight rain was falling heavily. Luckily the rain stopped next morning, and Plumer's attack, meticulously planned, was successful. On 26 September Plumer launched his second thrust (the Battle of Polygon Wood) which was equally successful, but for the third stroke, Broodseinde, it was again necessary to attack in the rain. The consensus of opinion of the Battle of Broodseinde is that it too, despite the rain, was successful.[56] But the village of Passchendaele was still a mile away from Plumer's exhausted troops, and Haig now seemed more determined than ever to occupy the higher ground on which the ruined village sat.[57]

For the third stage of the Flanders campaign Haig planned a further series of three attacks, but the heavens had opened and turned the ground into a "porridge of mud."[58] Both Gough and Plumer recommended that the campaign should be stopped. Yet the line as then held was not good, and Haig insisted on pushing forward. Thus, on 9 October 1917 three assaulting divisions lost seven thousand casualties at the Battle of Poelcappelle, and on 12 October the 2nd Anzac Corps suffered through the mud in the "First Battle of Passchendaele." That day the German commander, Crown Prince Rupprecht, gave thanks in his diary: "A break in the weather. Welcome rain, our strongest ally."[59]

In the last battle of the last stage, Currie's command performed in the centre ring. On 3 October Currie was warned that his corps was to move north towards Passchendaele. He was less than pleased.[60] Canadian losses in the Hill 70 fighting had been heavy, and Currie realized that those in Flanders would probably be even greater. It seemed to him, moreover, that no appreciable good would come from continuation of the campaign. Thus, he protested vigorously against Canadian participation in the northern fighting. "Every Canadian," he later wrote, "hated to go to Passchendaele . . . I carried my protest to the extreme limit . . . which I believe would have resulted in my being sent home had I been other than the Canadian Corps Commander. I pointed out what the casualties were bound to be, and was ordered to go and make the attack."[61]

Aside from the heavy casualties that were bound to result, Currie realized that if his corps fought at Passchendaele, it would be impossible to participate in a forthcoming Third Army attack. General Byng now commanded the Third Army, and over the summer of 1917 he and Currie had discussed the possibilities of making a surprise attack by massed tanks and had drawn up tentative plans for such an experiment.[62] (When Byng, without the Canadian Corps, later made such an attack at Cambrai it proved to be the most successful tank action of the war.) More serious in Currie's mind than missing such an experiment was the possibility that the Canadians at Passchendaele would have to fight in the Fifth Army. Long after the war Currie claimed that he had threatened to resign if he were put under General Gough and the Fifth Army at Passchendaele.[63] There is no doubt that Currie complained about Gough, but the chances of his being placed in the Fifth Army seem quite remote, since the Canadians were to replace the 2nd Anzac Corps which had been under Plumer since the end of August.[64] Currie, in other words, was probably less [op]posed to serving under Gough in 1917 than he still assumed after the war. At the time Currie noted with displeasure the experience of the Canadians at the Somme while under Gough. Later he would also recall the misfortune of the Fifth Army during the German spring offensive of 1918. For the latter Gough's reputation has suffered, though he bore little responsibility for what happened. Regardless of the army in which the Canadians were placed, Currie was strongly opposed to participating in the Passchendaele fighting. The casualties that the campaign had produced so far and the tactical possibilities for continued fighting were more than enough to explain the corps commander's reluctance to move north.

Two facts connected with Currie's distaste for participation at Passchendaele are worth noting; for both are important points of dispute in the literature on this most contentious battle. First, Currie was not the only commander in favour of stopping the battle (we have already noted the objections of Generals Plumer and Gough), yet he ceased his protest and prepared to take part when the commander-in-chief requested him to. This submission was not simply because Haig insisted; rather it is a measure of Haig's influence on senior commanders. Currie later explained that Haig gave no reason for continuing the campaign but merely promised that "some day I will tell you why, but Passchendaele must be taken."[65] Haig was wrong about many things, but one should remember that he at least seemed to have enormous influence on those senior officers who knew him personally—so much so that he could sometimes persuade them to acquiesce in plans that they bitterly opposed. Secondly, even though Currie was opposed to continuing the attack, he was still a firm advocate of fighting the war on the Western Front. His basic objection to continuing at Passchendaele was that the tactical and strategic results of continuing the campaign were simply not worth the cost: more could be gained, still on the Western Front, by using other methods. In any event, when it appeared that his protest would not avert the attack Currie threw himself into the task of making the fight with the minimum cost in casualties.

It should be noted that Currie's attitude on Passchendaele was not formed in a vacuum. As soon as he learned of the possibility that the Canadians would go to Passchendaele, he asked General Lipsett and Brigadier Victor Odlum to go to that sector of the front, make a reconnaissance, and report back to him. Odlum had come overseas as second-in-command of the 7th Battalion and had taken over when his commanding officer, Lieutenant-Colonel Hart-McHarg, had been killed. Like Lipsett, he was a thoroughly experienced, intelligent officer. "All you could see," Odlum reported to Currie, "was shell holes with a group of men in them, and you could look perhaps two hundred yards over and see the Germans in the same position. Both sides were just finished. They were down in the mud and there they were staying and they weren't even fighting."[66] General McNaughton, then a lieutenant-colonel on the corps artillery staff, confirmed the distaste all Canadians shared for going to Passchendaele. "Nobody wanted to go there," he said. "It isn't that we didn't want to fight, but when you fight you like to fight under reasonable conditions, particularly when you've got a good mechanism in which you have confidence. You don't want to be paralysed by mud and terrain difficulties."[67]

During April 1915, before the gas attack, the Canadians had held virtually the same front that they reoccupied in October 1917. But even the veterans of the gas attack found the landscape, which had been reduced to "an unrecognizable waste of ridge and hollow," totally alien.[68] Understandably depressed by the nature of the battlefield, Currie realized that the success of the coming encounter would depend to a large extent on the ability of his engineers and artillery. Consequently, he sent a strong contingent of sappers and gunners ahead of his infantry to the Ypres area.[69] Perhaps even more important, Currie secured the commander-in-chief's consent that the battle should not begin until the Canadian Corps was satisfied that pre-battle preparations had been completed.[70]

Dwarfing all other problems at Passchendaele was the question of the ground. The official historian records that over half of the battle field in front of the Canadians was covered by water or very deep mud.[71] Not only was it almost impossible for men to advance across this ground, but it was equally impossible to bring up supplies, to concentrate men for the attack, to find stable gun platforms for the artillery or to evacuate casualties. During the last attacks launched by the 2nd Anzac Corps at Passchendaele, sixteen men were required to carry one stretcher from the front lines, a job normally done by two bearers.[72] Currie put his entire engineer resources immediately to work, as well as those engineers received under command from Second Army. The corps chief engineer, Major-General W.B. Lindsay, from 17 October until the beginning of the Canadian attacks had "a daily average of ten field companies, seven tunnelling companies and four army troops companies [of engineers] assisted by two infantry and seven pioneer battalions" at work in the Canadian sector.[73] Drainage canals were made wherever possible; road beds were improved; gun positions were stabilized; and supplies were stockpiled, so that a recent critic claimed the Canadian victory to be a triumph of "aquatic engineering" and "sheer courage."[74]

One of the keys to success in Currie's view was to provide adequate support at all times for the assaulting infantry, and he was desperately worried that the artillery would not be able to do its share. He never rejected entirely the notion of a preliminary bombardment before an attack, but he put the greatest emphasis on the barrage that would cover the infantry advance, and on counter-battery fire to silence enemy guns. When, as at Passchendaele, the infantry had to struggle through mud to advance, the artillery task became all the more difficult. The infantry rate of advance could not be predicted accurately, and keeping the barrage just in front of the foot soldiers required not only careful planning but great flexibility in artillery arrangements and close liaison with the infantry. When the advance proceeded beyond the range of the artillery, the guns had to be hauled forward through the mud and placed in new firing positions. For the fire to be continuous, some portion of the artillery would always be moving once the infantry attack had begun. Hence the need for adequate roads and gun platforms well forward of the starting positions prepared before the attack. Indeed, two of the most essential prerequisites for an attack in such complex conditions were very careful planning and close co-operation—qualities in which Currie excelled.[75] Daily conferences with his chief engineer and senior artillery officer became routine.

Immediately after his headquarters arrived in the salient, Currie spent an entire day checking his position. He discovered a number of disquieting facts. General Morrison, his reliable artillery chief, reported that only 220 of the 360 field guns that were to be taken over from the Australians were in working condition. Currie at once went to Second Army headquarters to demand that his deficiencies be made good. Plumer's chief artillery officer contended that if Currie did not have the actual guns, he should have received indents for them during the take-over, and without the indents nothing could be done. The corps commander replied that he "could not fight the Boche with indents" and the dispute was referred to Plumer himself.[76] The army commander came straight to the point, demanding to know how Currie knew the guns were not in position. Currie replied, "I walked over this region, and many of the guns have disappeared altogether in the mud."[77] The incident was typical. Currie learned of the trouble from his staff, then checked it out personally. Currie got his guns because he knew the situation and would not move until it was remedied. Throughout the preparatory phase of the battle Currie was almost continuously in the salient. Stubbornly he demanded reconnaissance and co-operation at all levels. In his post-battle report he wrote, "I am convinced that this reconnaissance and close liaison between the artillery, the infantry units, and the staff, is vital to the success of any operation."[78] Currie planned to secure Passchendaele ridge by three limited attacks which he originally hoped to begin on 24 October. When it became apparent that the engineer preparations were taking longer than expected, he recommended postponement until 29 October but agreed to begin on 26 October when the commander-in-chief insisted that time was crucial.[79] Because of the swampy ground directly to the front, the first attack was planned as a two-pronged advance on the corps' left and right where the ground rose slightly. The object of the attack was to carry the front approximately 1200 yards forward, and one of the points that concerned Currie was that no easily discernible landmark could be selected as an objective for the first attack.

From 15 October the weather had been unexpectedly fine, and the engineers' work was facilitated by the fact that no rain had fallen. During the night of 25–26 October, however, there was a "wet mist" which turned into heavy rain with the beginning of the attack. So far as most of the infantry were concerned, the attack followed the pattern of the previous Passchendaele assault—the "sea of choking fetid mud in which men, animals and tanks floundered and perished hopelessly" still had to be crossed.[80] Casualties were high: 2481 from 26 to 28 October, though less in comparison with other actions than one might expect.[81] There were, however, certain novel features of the battle which are worth noting.

In the first place, the troops making the assault were fresh. Frequently in the past, when new troops had been available for an attack, commanders had kept these soldiers out of the front line until just before zero hour. This meant that the trip to the front lines—almost as enervating and dangerous as the journey across no-man's land—was made just before the actual attack, with the result that at zero hour the assaulting troops were more fatigued than the veterans who had been holding the front line. Currie ordered his men into the front lines slightly early, preferring to risk the possibility of casualties against the certainty that attacking with exhausted troops would produce even greater losses.[82] Secondly, the planning of the artillery barrage paid handsome dividends, because artillery fire did not run away from the infantry during the advance.[83] Although the attack met all the resistance Currie expected, it accomplished its basic purpose of securing the jumping-off position for the next thrust scheduled for 30 October. In the interim the work of the engineers continued unabated.

At 5:50 a.m. on 30 October the Canadian Corps again advanced, this time behind the protective curtain provided by 420 guns and howitzers. More important perhaps than the artillery support was the fact that the morning was clear and cold and no rain fell until late afternoon. Once again the front lurched forward approximately one thousand yards at the cost of 1321 killed, wounded, and missing.[84] Currie now rotated his divisions, replacing the depleted and exhausted 3rd and 4th Canadian Divisions by the 1st and 2nd. Unfortunately, while the Canadians were arranging reliefs, the Germans were doing exactly the same thing along most of the front. On 3 November the German 11th Division arrived from the Champagne area to take up positions along the front from Ypres-Roulers railway to the Mosselmarkt road. Along the rest of the front the 1st and 2nd Divisions faced the same opponents as had the 3rd and 4th Canadian Divisions.[85]

Battlefield communication has always been and still remains one of the key ingredients of tactical success. Throughout the First World War it was a problem with which most commanders struggled. Continuous wave wireless sets had been used with considerable success by the Canadians before Passchendaele. According to one expert the "CW set" would be "put to the supreme test" on the Passchendaele battlefield.[86] The freshness of the Canadian troops, the careful planning of the artillery barrage, and, most critical of all, clear skies, were obvious once the attack began.[87] According to the official account the attack began so quickly that "the enemy's retaliatory fire, opening a few minutes later, fell mainly behind the advancing troops. Afterwards prisoners reported that the infantry followed their barrage so closely that in most cases the Germans could not man their machine guns before the attackers were on top of them. Almost everywhere the attack went well . . . less than three hours after zero the village that had so long been an allied objective was securely in Canadian hands."[88]

The rubble of Passchendaele village was at last captured, but the Canadian Corps was again weaker by 2238 casualties. Haig recorded jubilantly in his diary that the losses were "under 700 men" and the Canadian official history rather generously concludes that Sir Douglas's figures "must have referred only to fatal casualties reported to him up to that time."[89] Haig's most recent biographer, John Terraine, credits the capture to the "brilliant organization and method" of the Canadians.[90]

A final attack was still deemed necessary before the campaign could end. It was designed to gain the remaining high ground north of Passchendaele village. The fact that additional reliefs were undertaken by the Germans does not seem to have operated to the attackers' disadvantage. Indeed, precisely the opposite was the case: the German units were now so disorganized that many were unsure of their own boundaries.[91] Other equalizing factors were the heavy rain that fell when the attack was launched on 10 November and the fact that the Canadians were no longer as fresh as they had been during the previous assaults. In spite of the advance, the results of the attack were hardly salutary, for the entire line about Passchendaele now formed a dangerous salient. "The new tongue of ground" gained on 10 November "jutted out even more awkwardly and now could be fired into not only from three sides but slightly from the rear as well."[92] A final loss of 1094 men by Currie's command ended the Passchendaele campaign. On 14 November the relief began, and six days later Currie once again resumed command of the old Lens front.

Third Ypres has become the most contentious subject in the English literature of the First World War. Yet Arthur Currie has received relatively little attention, in spite of the fact that it was his command that captured Passchendaele and ended the campaign. In the dispute the points of issue are many, and they arise partly from the curious attitude of the British official historian, General Edmonds, who over the years in conversation "might demolish the reputations of the higher commanders—even Haig—but [who] in print . . . was far more circumspect."[93] The tremendous loss of life in the campaign focused popular attention on Passchendaele, as did the abominable conditions under which it was fought. Though the British casualties were actually less than those suffered during the Battles of the Somme in 1916, Third Ypres epitomized to many the extraordinary stupidity and inhuman aloofness of the generals who ordered such slaughter. To those who were appalled by the role of the professional soldier in the First World War, it was a hideous example of unrestrained generalship. Haig has been portrayed by the civilian protagonists in the debate as "a stubborn, fame-hungry, cold-blooded, deceiving oaf, and his [Passchendaele] campaign as a military abortion unparalleled in the history of the western world."[94]

Beyond doubt, the high command made egregious errors in the campaign. In the most ardent defence of Haig, his "gravest and most fatal error" is conceded to be the decision to give the main role to the Fifth Army under General Gough.[95] Many other charges have been levelled against the commander-in-chief, but "since the debate is endless and by its nature cannot lead to a conclusion," one turns to the "repellent but more tangible process of 'counting heads.' "[96] Even here there is much controversy. In the British official history German casualty figures are adjusted from 217 000 to 400 000, and the British loss is placed at 244 897.[97] A Canadian compilation reckons British casualties at approximately 260 000, compared with 202 000 for the Germans, but sidesteps the conclusion that this calculation seems to suggest, claiming instead that the "Somme, costly as it was to the Allies, began the destruction of the German Army. Passchendaele carried the process a long step forward."[98]

The campaign has fascinated historians. It was "a long grim ordeal, its horror forever etched on the minds and hearts of those who fought there."[99] But this assessment has led critics automatically to assume that "tactics were always bad." Actually, the individual battles—those of the Canadian Corps at any rate—were very cleverly conducted and by a commander fully aware of the horror his men faced. Currie's experience goes far in support of the claim that "tactics were never more skilful" than at Passchendaele.[100] One might argue, of course, that Currie's divisional generals or brigadiers should have equal recognition or that the entire credit for the smooth functioning of the Canadian attacks properly belongs to General Plumer. Both Plumer and the Canadian divisional commanders deserve great praise; teamwork was an essential element of Canadian success. Brigadier Odlum of the 11th Brigade later observed that "Currie was a man with remarkable intelligence. And when we gathered together . . . for discussions he would listen to us as we argued amongst ourselves, and we did argue, but . . . in the end, [he] would sum up what was said and draw deductions from it . . . He had that mentality that made it possible for him to pick things up, to listen to others and gather from them."[101] Brigadier-General J.A. Clark of the 72nd Battalion recorded that "Everybody with any common sense was going to conserve his force and protect his men from casualties to the absolute limit and that was Currie's theory. That was instilled by him into every Commander, and the Battalion Commanders, of course, they were the key to it because some Battalion Commanders could conserve lives better than others. The man who wasted lives, well, he would lose his job."[102]

Currie's role in the battle of Passchendaele is also important with respect to the controversy regarding civilians and professional soldiers. Lloyd George saw the campaign as the natural outcome of a war directed by incompetent professional soldiers. He charged that in the British army no pre-war civilian rose above the rank of brigadier-general: "the ablest brains did not climb to the top of the stairs and they did not reach a height where politicians could even see them."[103] Yet the majority of men and regimental officers in the army had been civilians when the war broke out. Thus, claims the British official historian, the British army from 1916 to the end of the war was "an amateur army, with a very small leaven of professionals."[104] This does not substantially answer Lloyd George; as long as the "leaven" was spread evenly over the top, the army was essentially professional. The essence of the charge, moreover, is that the professional soldiers, such as Haig, deliberately suppressed the military careers of promising amateurs or pre-war civilians—presumably because the professionals feared they would lose control of the war. C.E.W. Bean, the Australian official historian, comes closer than General Edmonds to a genuine rebuttal when he argues that "Haig's constant support of Monash [the Australian Corps Commander] . . . throws a vivid light on the inaccuracy of the constant implication . . . made by Lloyd George that Haig was prejudiced against civilian soldiers and tended to suppress them."[105] But Bean's argument itself is not entirely adequate.

In the first place Lloyd George was willing to admit that "the only exceptions" to the suppression of civilian soldiers were "to be found in the Dominion forces . . . General Currie . . . and General Monash . . . were both in civil life when war broke out. Both proved themselves to be brilliant military leaders and went right through to the top. It means that their being officers in unprofessional armies gave full play to their gifts."[106] Secondly, he suggested that if an amateur soldier such as Currie or Monash had been allowed to rise higher, to the command of an army or to the position of commander-in-chief, the course of the war would have been radically different, and the tragic slaughters on the Western Front would have been avoided. In short, an amateur would have followed quite a different strategy for the war—presumably akin to that Lloyd George had advocated.[107] In this view Currie and Monash struggled upwards, in spite of the fact that they were civilians and in spite of their radical notions.

Without examining a multitude of case studies, it is impossible to refute positively the first charge—that within the armies raised in Britain professional soldiers repressed amateurs. Currie's case, however, suggests that Lloyd George's argument is a shaky one. Currie, it should be recalled, started the war as a brigadier-general, mostly because of the paucity of trained regulars in Canada.[108] As a brigade commander, the chances of his surviving while learning of war in France were, relatively speaking, quite good. The same is true of other colonials, such as Monash, who rose to high rank during the war. But in the British armies there were many more senior professional officers to begin with, and so a civilian soldier at the start of the war began his career with a lower rank. The chances of a British amateur who began the war as a captain of surviving the learning period were obviously much lower than those of the colonial who began as a brigadier.[109] In other words, the composition of the British army partly explains the slow promotion of amateur soldiers, without resorting to fanciful arguments concerning "repression." We should recall also that while Currie did not hesitate to oppose higher professional officers if he thought the reasons for such action sufficient, one of his most difficult tasks during the summer of 1917 was to advance a prewar professional soldier to the command of a division. On the question of friction between amateurs and professionals Currie was emphatic. "My first," he afterwards recorded, "was not with the regular officers at all. It was with the Canadian authorities in London."[110]

It is worth noting that after the war Lloyd George's thesis was given considerable support by the stories of returned men, who contributed to the common view of the "military mind"—"by necessity an inferior and unimaginative mind; no man of high intellectual power would willingly imprison his gifts in such a calling."[111] This notion was as common and as overdrawn in Canada and Australia as it was in England and the United States. Frequently citizen soldiers judged professionals on the most picayune personal experiences.[112] Just as frequently they were so revolted by war that a professional soldier became noxious simply by association. For one who had "seen so much death—and brains and blood—and marvellous human machines smashed like Humpty-Dumpties . . . [who] had bound up a man without a face . . . [and] had stood by the body of a man bent backward over a shattered tree while the blood dripped from his gaping head," it seemed natural to hate armies and those whose profession it was to lead armies.[113]

The second part of Lloyd George's claim—that successful amateurs opposed Haig's strategy—is disproved by the 1917 campaign in Flanders. To be sure, Currie was opposed to participating in the campaign and favoured making an end to the battle. But, and this must be stressed, Currie did not oppose Haig's strategy of fighting the war on the Western Front; rather his objections to continuing the campaign were based on tactical grounds. Currie was not the only general who advocated different tactics on the Western Front. Bidwell and Graham in the book *Firepower* show that many British divisional commanders had worked out tactical ideas very similar to Currie's. Currie, however, as commander of the Canadian Corps, was in a better position than his British peers to push such ideas forward. Even after the war Currie maintained that Passchendaele had been an "expensive" operation, but he never opposed Haig's fundamental strategy. In discussing Haig and the Ypres campaign after the war, Currie wrote in a vein that surely would have enraged Lloyd George: "There were always those in authority in England who wanted to fight the war in many places other than on the Western Front, and so he, (Haig) who held strongly that the issue must be decided there, was often very much concerned when Divisions which he badly needed were sent to other places. Much has been written and much has been implied concerning his troubles with those whom we may call the politicians. He had to withstand from them much criticism and much interference, but he never complained bitterly about these things, but always held out with the greatest patience for what he knew to be right."[114]

To recapitulate, Currie commanded an army corps for only the second time in the Passchendaele battle. He was thrust into this position when both his old and his new commands were actively engaged with the enemy and when his personal affairs were in a highly embarrassing condition. When he became corps commander he insisted on the right to appoint his own subordinates, but he did not challenge the ill-defined nature of Turner's "administrative authority" in France, which was to prove the cause of considerable friction during the coming year. In spite of these handicaps, Currie handled his corps with extraordinary tactical skill.

Perhaps a special word on the success of the Canadians is in order; for in the summer of 1917 Currie's command had a record of which, not unnaturally, he was extremely proud. It had been the Canadians who took on elements of five German divisions at Hill 70 and who seized Passchendaele ridge, finishing the campaign. There is little doubt that such success was in large part due to effective leadership and sound planning by Currie and other senior officers. It was, equally, the result of the truly astonishing courage of the men who had to wrestle their way through the mud. But the outcome of Passchendaele rested on other factors as well. The Canadians, after all, were relatively fresh, while the Germans were exhausted. The artillery barrage that covered the Canadian advances was meticulously planned to stay just in front of the attacking troops. And, not to be ignored, the Canadians frequently had the good luck to make their attacks when there was no rain, an advantage the British and Australian troops less often enjoyed. In short, success was not the simple result of Canadian fighting superiority over other forces in the Allied armies. Many people, mostly Canadians, nevertheless came to believe that the Canadian Corps was the only force capable of taking Passchendaele. Unwittingly perhaps, Haig contributed to this notion. Currie later observed that Haig "always left you feeling he had supreme confidence in your ability to carry through successfully the task which he had assigned to you."[115] Currie realized that Haig "seldom showed any emotion," and as a consequence the commander-in-chief's appeal for success at Passchendaele seemed to take on a special significance. In any case Currie came to believe that it was not "too much to say . . . that the victory of the Canadians at Passchendaele kept the Allies in the war."[116]

NOTES

1. Cited in Hugh M. Urquhart, *Arthur Currie: A Biography of a Great Canadian* (Toronto, 1950), 146.

2. Richard M. Watt, *Dare Call It Treason* (New York, 1963), 173.

3. Robert Blake, ed., *The Private Papers of Douglas Haig, 1914–1919: Being Selections from the Private Diary and Correspondence of Field Marshal the Earl Haig of Bemersyde K.G., G.C.B., O.M., etc.* (London, 1952), 225.

4. Perley to War Office, 12 June 1917, Perley Papers, Public Archives of Canada (hereafter PAC).

5. Perley to Borden, 9 June 1917, Perley Papers.

6. Ibid.

7. Borden to Perley, 13 June 1917, Perley Papers.

8. Macdonnell to Borden, 14 Dec. 1934, Borden Papers, PAC.

9. Hughes to Aitken, 28 May 1916, Beaverbrook Papers.

10. Currie Diary, 10 June 1917, Currie Papers, PAC.

11. Perley to Borden, 15 June 1917, Perley Papers.

12. Currie to McGillicudy, n.d., Currie Papers.

13. Currie Diary, cited in Urquhart, *Arthur Currie*, 163.

14. Desmond Morton, *A Peculiar Kind of Politics: Canada's Overseas Ministry in the First World War* (Toronto, 1982), 122.

15. Borden to Perley, 13 June 1917, Perley Papers.

16. Morton, *Peculiar Politics*, 234, n. 58.

17. Ibid., 122.

18. Currie to McGillicudy, n.d., Currie Papers.

19. Urquhart, *Arthur Currie*, 164.

20. Ibid.

21. J.A. Swettenham, *To Seize the Victory: The Canadian Corps in World War I* (Toronto, 1965), 174.

22. Currie to Perley, 4 Aug. 1917, Borden Papers, vol. 72, file 10-8-7.

23. Morton, *Peculiar Politics*, 124.

24. Ibid.

25. Ibid., 122.

26. Ibid., 121; Urquhart, *Arthur Currie*, 164.

27. Urquhart, *Arthur Currie*, 165.

28. Currie to Forsythe, 25 June 1917, Currie Papers.

29. Matson to Borden, 28 Oct. 1914, Borden Papers, vol. 361.

30. Robert Craig Brown and Desmond Morton, "The Embarrassing Apotheosis of a 'Great Canadian': Sir Arthur Currie's Personal Crisis in 1917," *Canadian Historical Review* 60 (March 1979).

31. Morton, *Peculiar Politics*, 123.

32. Perley to Borden, 21 July 1917, Perley Papers.

33. Ibid.; Borden to Perley, 18 July 1917, Perley Papers; Currie to Forsythe, 25 June 1917, Urquhart Papers; J.H.P. to D.W. Oliver, 17 June 1930.

34. Brown and Morton, "Apotheosis," 61.

35. Ibid.

36. Morton, *Peculiar Politics*, 123.

37. Ibid., 124.

38. First Army Order, G.S., 658/1(a), 7 July 1917, PAC; app. 1/1 to W.D., G.S., Cdn. Corps., July 1917, PAC; First Army Order, 137, 10 July 1917, app. 1/2, PAC.

39. Currie Diary, 10 July 1917, Currie Papers.

40. Letter, Dominick Graham to author, June 1986.

41. First Army Order, G.W. 658/13(a), 13 July 1917, app. 1/1, PAC.

42. Cdn. Corps Operation Order 139, 17 July 1917, PAC. app. 2/10 to W.D., G.S., Cdn. Corps, July 1917, PAC.

43. For a detailed account of the battle, see G.W.L. Nicholson, *Canadian Expeditionary Force, 1914–1919* (Ottawa, 1962), 297.

44. Currie Diary, 18 August 1917, Currie Papers. German accounts later revealed that five German divisions were engaged by the Canadians at Hill 70. Nicholson, *CEF*, 292n.

45. Von Kuhl, *Der Weltkrieg 1917–1918*, ii, p. 123, quoted in Nicholson, *CEF*, 297.

46. Currie estimated Canadian casualties at 8000 in the period between 15 and 23 August, while he thought German losses to be between 25 000 and 30 000. Currie to Underhill, 17 Sept. 1920, Currie Papers. A later postwar calculation put the Canadian losses at 10 746 to the months of July and August. A.F. Duguid, *The Canadian Forces in the Great War* (Ottawa, 1946), 6.

47. W.S. Churchill, *The World Crisis*, vol. 4 (New York, 1929), 1177.

48. John Terraine, *Douglas Haig: The Educated Soldier* (London, 1963), 337; and ibid., *The Road to Passchendaele: The Flanders Offensive of 1917: A Study in Inevitability* (London, 1977). Brig.-Gen. Sir James E. Edmonds, *Military Operations France and Belgium: 1917, June 7–November 10. Messines and Third Ypres (Passchendaele)* (London, 1948), 177–179.

49. Haig's intelligence chief, Brigadier-General Charteris, claimed that it was the wettest August for thirty years. Terraine, *Douglas Haig*, 348.

50. Nicholson, *CEF*, 308.

51. 2nd Army Operation Order No. 4, 1 Sept. 1917, app. 21 to Military

Operations: 1917 June–November 10, PAC.

52. Terraine, *Douglas Haig*, 334; Terraine, *The Road to Passchendaele*, 203.

53. C.E. Calwell, *Field Marshall Sir Henry Wilson*, vol. 2 (London, 1927), 14.

54. Churchill, *World Crisis*, 818.

55. Leon Wolff, *In Flanders Fields* (New York, 1958), 157–58.

56. Ibid.

57. Edmonds, *Military Operations*, 325–26.

58. Ibid., 327.

59. *Mein Kriegstagebuch*, 2:271, cited in Cyril Falls, *The Great War* (New York, 1971).

60. Currie Diary, 3–6 Oct. 1917, Currie Papers.

61. Currie to Paterson, 8 March 1920, Currie Papers.

62. Currie to Underhill, 17 Sept. 1920, Currie Papers.

63. Currie to Livesay, 26 Jan. 1933, Currie Papers; Blake, *Papers of Douglas Haig*, 257.

64. Nicholson, *CEF*, 312.

65. Ibid., Currie to Beattie, 8 Feb. 1929.

66. C.B.C., "In Flanders Fields," program 10, p. 2.

67. Ibid.

68. Nicholson, *CEF*, 313.

69. Urquhart, *Arthur Currie*, 175.

70. "Operations of the Canadian Corps during October 1917," Morrison Papers, PAC, p. 2.

71. Nicholson, *CEF*, 313.

72. Terraine, *Douglas Haig*, 369.

73. Nicholson, *CEF*, 313.

74. Terraine, *Douglas Haig*, 369.

75. A.G.L. McNaughton, "The Development of Artillery in the Great War," *Canadian Defence Quarterly* 6, 2 (Jan. 1929), 162–68.

76. Currie to Underhill, 17 Sept. 1920, Currie Papers.

77. Seely, *Adventure*, 272.

78. Cdn. Corps to Second Army, "Passchendaele—Causes of Success and Failure," 20 Nov. 1917, app. to W.D., G.S., Cdn. Corps, Nov. 1917, PAC.

79. Nicholson, *CEF*, 314.

80. Churchill, *World Crisis*, 821.

81. Nicholson, *CEF*, 320.

82. "Instructions for Offensive No. 2," 20 Oct. 1917, app. to W.D., G.S., 3rd Cdn. Div., Oct. 1917, PAC; Nicholson, *CEF*, 318.

83. Nicholson, *CEF*, 319.

84. Ibid., 323.

85. Ibid., 324.

86. W.A. Steel, "Wireless Telegraphy in the Canadian Corps in France," *Canadian Defence Quarterly* (July 1930), 462.

87. Leon Wolff claims that the Canadians attacked "in a typical cold rain" (Wolff, *Flanders Fields*, 22), but on questions of weather Nicholson's account is invariably accurate. "The attack was launched under a clear sky that later became cloudy but shed no heavy rain" (Nicholson, *CEF*, 324).

88. Nicholson, *CEF*, 324.

89. Ibid., 325.

90. Terraine, *Douglas Haig*, 345.

91. Nicholson, *CEF*, 326.

92. Wolff, *Flanders Fields*, 229.

93. Jay Luvaas, "The First British Official Historians," *Military Affairs* 26 (Summer, 1962), 56.

94. Wolff, *Flanders Fields*, 241.

95. Terraine, *Douglas Haig*, 337.

96. Wolff, *Flanders Fields*, 233.

97. Edmonds, *Military Operations*, 361.

98. Nicholson, *CEF*, 329–30.

99. W. Baldwin Hanson, *World War I* (New York, 1962), 103.

100. Falls, *The Great War*, 304.

101. C.B.C., "In Flanders Fields," program 14, 11.

102. C.B.C., "In Flanders Fields," program 14, 12.

103. Lloyd George, *Memoirs*, 6:3422–23.

104. James E. Edmonds, *A Short History of World War I* (London, 1951), 35.

105. C.E.W. Bean, *Anzac to Amiens: A Shorter History of the Australian Fighting Services in the First World War* (Canberra, 1952), 458.

106. Lloyd George, *Memoirs*, 6:3423–24.

107. Lloyd George substantiates the case, especially in regard to Monash, who was "the most resourceful general in the whole of the British Army," but he implies that the same would have been true for any number of other civilian soldiers, including Currie. Of Monash he flatly states that "Professional soldiers would hardly be expected to advertise the fact that the greatest strategist in the army was a civilian when war began and that they were being surpassed by a man who had not received of their advantages in training and teaching". Lloyd George, *Memoirs*, 6:3524, 3382.

108. The establishment of the permanent force at the outbreak of war called for only 247 officers in the entire dominion. Director Canadian Army Historical Section to Author, 15 Feb. 1962.

109. Major-General H. Essame, who fought the battle of Passchendaele as a subaltern, claims that by the end of July 1917, when his battalion entered the Passchendaele fight, there were only thirty of the original 1025 members of his battalion surviving. Major-General H. Essame, "Second Lieutenants Unless Otherwise Stated," *Military Review* 44 (May 1964), 91. Unfortunately the figures for a really meaningful comparison with Canadian battalions do not exist, but a comparison of percentages is at least suggestive. If Essame's figures are correct, his battalion, which he indicates had had a typical casualty record, suffered approximately 97 percent casualties to its original complement. Its total casualties, of course, would be much higher, because many reinforcements had been killed or wounded. In comparison, the total Canadian casualty record by the end of July 1917, which can be calculated very roughly from the total number of soldiers sent to France and the total number of casualties (the total of monthly strengths in France minus the total sent to France), was approximately 87 percent. Though these figures are subject to challenge, they do suggest that a substantially higher proportion of original officers and men survived 1915 and 1916 in the Canadian forces than in the British Army.

110. Currie to Nelson, 9 Dec. 1925, Currie Papers.

111. H.G. Wells, *Outline of History*, quoted in Wolff, *Flanders Fields*, 239.

112. One example of this sort of issue was the Canadian preference for collar harness rather than British general-issue breast harness for draught horses. Canadian teamsters came to think that British generals were fools for not knowing that horses could pull better in a collar. What the men overlooked was that the breast harness was cheaper, easily adjusted to any horse, and more readily repaired than the more sophisticated collar, which had to be fitted to each horse. Other men became dedicated to a general "because he spoke to me at once," or raged that "he never returned my salute."

113. T.M. Papineau to B. Fox, 5 Aug. 1915, Papineau Papers, PAC.

114. Currie to Beattie, 8 Feb. 1920, Currie Papers.

115. Ibid.

116. Currie to Livesay, 24 Oct. 1919, Currie Papers.

THE AERIAL WAR, 1917[*]

S . F .   W I S E

o

At the turn of the year the RFC [Royal Flying Corps] had thirty-nine squadrons available for operations on the Western Front, but only twelve were classed as suitable for escort work, offensive patrols, and general air combat. Only five of these, equipped with Nieuport 17s and Sopwith Pups, were capable of meeting the German *Jastas* on anything like even terms. [Major-General] Trenchard had been promised eleven additional fighter squadrons by March, but as of 10 February none had arrived. On learning from Sir David Henderson that he could expect no more than two by the scheduled date, he wrote to General L.E. Kiggell, Haig's Chief of Staff, explaining once more the gravity of the situation: "There is no possibility of improving matters before operations are likely to commence, and, in view of the hostile aerial activity now being disclosed, our fighting machines will almost certainly be inferior in number and quite certainly in performance to those of the enemy. The success of our aerial offensive will consequently be very seriously jeopardized, and we cannot therefore hope that our Corps machines will be able to accomplish their work as successfully or with as few casualties as during the battle of the SOMME."[1]

The one bright spot in the supply problem was the assistance provided by the Royal Naval Air Service. By the end of 1916 the Board of Admiralty had formally approved Trenchard's request for four additional naval squadrons on the Western Front. He already had 8 (Naval) at his disposal, and the others arrived at intervals between February and May. Three of the squadrons, Nos. 1, 8, and 10, were equipped with Sopwith Triplanes. The triplane structure gave the pilot a wide field of vision, an exceptional rate of climb, and an extremely manoeuvrable aircraft, capable of attaining a speed

[*] From "Stalemate on the Western Front, 1917," chap. 14 of *Canadian Airmen in the First World War: The Official History of the Royal Canadian Air Force*, vol. 1 (Toronto: University of Toronto Press, 1986), 395–419.

of 117 mph. Unfortunately for the RFC the Triplane was flown operationally only by the RNAS.[2]

It was through the naval squadrons that Canadians made some of their
most significant contributions in the spring offensive. Pride of service made
the naval authorities anxious for their squadrons "to put up a good show
with the RFC." One outstanding example was 3 (Naval), commanded by
Squadron Commander R.H. Mulock of Winnipeg and equipped with
Sopwith Pups. During the heavy fighting in March and April it was one of
the few allied squadrons which gave out more punishment than it received.
Its success was attributable in large measure to Mulock's ability as a leader
and organizer and his extensive knowledge of aeroplanes and engines.

To a greater degree than most squadron commanders Mulock made each
of his flight commanders responsible for keeping his flight in fighting trim.
His administrative methods were directly related to operational requirements
because the flight of five or six aircraft remained the tactical air unit, each
patrol being carried out by a flight or section of a flight. One naval officer,
attached to the RFC in France to monitor the performance of the naval
squadrons, reported to his headquarters at Dunkirk that Mulock's "is the best
organized and the best run of any Squadron I have seen down here (including R.F.C. Squadrons)."[3] On his suggestion a study was made of Mulock's
methods, and when the squadron returned to the RNAS in June 1917 after
four-and-one-half months of service with the RFC, he commended Mulock
on its good record: "Your men have done invaluable work, overcoming all
difficulties, and have maintained Machines, Engines, Guns and Transport in
a very high state of efficiency, and it is largely due to their self sacrifice and
hard work that the pilots have been able to gain their undoubted supremacy
in the air."[4] Trenchard, too, expressed his appreciation:

> They [Naval Three] joined us at the beginning of February at a time
> when aerial activity was becoming great and were forced to work
> at full pressure right up to June 14th, when they left us.
>
> Eighty enemy aircraft were accounted for[5] which, with only a
> loss of nine machines missing, alone shews [sic] the efficiency of
> the Squadron as a fighting unit.
>
> The escorts provided by the squadron to the photographic
> reconnaissance and bomb raids enabled our machines to carry out
> these tasks unmolested.
>
> The supremacy in the air which they undoubtedly gained, is
> largely due to the manner in which the machines, engines, guns
> and transport have been looked after by the Flight Commander(s),
> Flying Officers and Mechanics.
>
> The work of Squadron Commander Mulock is worthy of the
> highest praise; his knowledge of machines and engines and the
> way in which he handled his officers and men is very largely
> responsible for the great success and durability of the Squadron.[6]

On 1 February, when Naval Three joined 22 (Army) Wing of V Brigade,
half of its twelve pilots were Canadians and three more arrived later that

month. Besides Mulock the six originals included Flight Sub-Lieutenants R. Collishaw of Nanaimo, BC, P.G. McNeil and A.T. Whealy, both of Toronto, J.P. White of Winnipeg, and Flight Lieutenant H.R. Wambolt of Dartmouth, NS. Collishaw was the most experienced fighter pilot of this group. The three who followed them, Flight Sub-Lieutenant F.C. Armstrong of Toronto, J.S.T. Fall of Hillbank, BC, and Flight Lieutenant J.J. Malone of Regina, were all decorated for service with the squadron during the following months. Fall and Armstrong received the DSC and Malone, who was killed in April, was posthumously gazetted a DSO. Another notable group arrived in March, including Flight Sub-Lieutenant L.S. Breadner of Carleton Place, who succeeded to command of one of the three flights a month later.[7]

More Canadians came in with the other RNAS and RFC squadron reinforcements to supplement those already at the front. Twenty were flying with the seven squadrons of 9 (HQ) Wing at the beginning of April, and three times that number served during the month with III Brigade, half of them with corps and half with army squadrons. In I Brigade, on the left of the Vimy–Arras front, many Canadians flew with 2 and 16 Squadrons, both equipped with BE2s and the only corps units directly involved in the Vimy area. In the fighter squadrons of I Brigade, Naval Eight had several Canadians and so did 40 Squadron flying Nieuport 17s. The other army units, 25 and 43 Squadrons, flying FE2bs and Sopwith $1\frac{1}{2}$ Strutters, respectively, were responsible for long-distance reconnaissance, bombing, and line patrols.[8]

The air plan for the spring attack was based, as always, on the offensive doctrine which Trenchard had adopted from the moment that he first took command, and to which he adamantly adhered throughout his three-year tenure as commander of the RFC in the field. Air superiority was to be obtained by carrying the fight to the Germans over their own territory. This offensive pressure, it was assumed, would enable "our Corps machines to cooperate with the artillery and infantry during the ground operations with as little interference as possible from the enemy." Trenchard expected his fighter pilots to penetrate well behind the lines "seeking out and fighting the enemy over his own aerodromes."[9] "The aim of our offensive," he stressed to his brigades, "will therefore be to force the enemy to fight well behind, and not on, the lines. This aim will only be successfully achieved if offensive patrols are pushed well out to the limits of Army reconnaissance areas, and the G.O.C. looks to Brigadiers to carry out this policy and not to give way to requests for the close protection of corps machines except in special cases when such machines are proceeding on work at an abnormal distance over the lines. The aerial ascendancy which was gained by our pilots and observers on the SOMME last year was a direct result of the policy outlines above, and with the considerable addition to our strength provided by the new type fighting squadrons now available the G.O.C. feels confident that a similar ascendancy will be gained this year."[10]

Within these general directives, on 4 April, five days before the Canadian Corps went into action at Vimy Ridge and the Third British Army began its drive along the Scarpe River, the RFC launched an all-out air offensive, attacking enemy observation balloons, bombing rail centres and aerodromes, and carrying the fighting deep into enemy territory. In order to seal off the battle area and allow the artillery aircraft to operate with as much freedom as possible, a large quadrilateral-shaped intercept zone extending about fifteen miles into enemy territory was established. It was bounded on the west by a line running from Lens to Bullecourt, approximately twenty miles, and on the east from Henin-Lètard to Sains. At times there were as many as fifty single-seater fighters patrolling this area seeking to bring the enemy to combat, while half as many two-seaters, principally $1\frac{1}{2}$ Strutters and FE2bs, patrolled defensively closer to the battle line to protect the artillery aircraft.[11]

The Germans, however, found it relatively easy to penetrate the air screen. Although they also stressed the offensive, they were selective in their application of it. The chief task of the German fighters was to destroy allied artillery and reconnaissance aircraft and bombers which crossed the lines. As a rule they attacked allied fighter patrols only when the situation was particularly favourable and seldom did they carry the fight across the line. Taking advantage of cloud cover and aided by ground observation centres which determined the best time to bring the fighters into action, small enemy formations, usually two or three fighters, slipped past the allied patrols and attacked the vulnerable artillery aircraft. So while allied offensive patrols could count on a scrap only when they were escorting bombers and reconnaissance machines, the corps two-seaters felt the full weight of the German fighters. On the Vimy front in April, of thirty-eight aircraft known to be missing, wrecked on landing after combat, or returned with wounded airmen, thirty-five were two-seaters while only three were single-seater fighters.[12]

A factor which contributed to the heavy losses suffered by RFC corps aircraft during "Bloody April" was the coming into service of a new machine, the RE8, designed to replace the BE2s. As early as the end of 1915 it had been recognized that the BE2c was obsolete (although seventeen squadrons were still equipped with the machine in January 1917), and RFC Headquarters had asked for a new reconnaissance and artillery aircraft that could defend itself. The RE8 was the Royal Aircraft Factory's answer. During tests in 1916 the aircraft acquired an evil reputation which never quite deserted it. The gas tanks were directly behind the engine; if a crash occurred, fuel from the tanks burst into flame on contact with the hot engine. The fuselage had a peculiar upward tilt, intended to increase the angle of attack of the wings on landing. The consequent braking effect made the aircraft at home in small fields. Many pilots, however, failed to adapt to the aircraft's strange attitude, and crashes from overshooting were frequent. Finally, the RE8 was far too stable (a characteristic of Royal Aircraft Factory designs) and it proved an easy target for the fast German fighters. By the beginning of April three corps squadrons had been furnished with the RE8. On 13 April one of them, 59 Squadron, lost six of these unwieldy aircraft and ten pilots and observers killed in a few minutes to a patrol led by Richthofen.[13]

Of the ground operations fought on the British front in April and known collectively as the Battles of Arras, the Canadian Corps' attack on Vimy Ridge was the only one entirely successful. The ridge, rising gently to a height of over two hundred feet above the Douai plain, had been one of the dominating features of the northern sector of the Western Front for more than two years. The Germans had taken possession of it in October 1914 and since then had worked continuously at fortifying it. On the forward slope a system of trenches with inter-connecting tunnels and deep dug-outs barred the way. On the other side of the crest, visible in most places only from the air, a second network of trenches had been constructed. Fortunately for the Canadians, however, plans to introduce the principle of defence in depth were not carried out. The bulk of the defending troops were in the front trench system with orders to hold their ground at all costs. The immediate purpose of the assault on the ridge was to form a defensive flank for the advance of the Third Army along the Scarpe and to deprive the enemy of observation into the valleys running southwest. A secondary purpose, arising from plans for a northern offensive to be undertaken later in the year, was to secure a commanding view of the plains to the north and east and thus threaten the German hold on the Belgian coast.[14]

The Vimy offensive was marked by careful planning, meticulous preparation, and effective air-artillery co-operation. The artillery plan was carried out in two phases—a preliminary bombardment which began on a limited scale twenty days before the attack and gradually increased in weight, with an intense barrage supporting the assault itself. Prior to this much aerial photography had been completed, information obtained, and damage done to trench systems and hostile batteries. By early March air photos of the entire German defence system formed the basis of a new map which was continually brought up to date as enemy dispositions changed. Of 212 hostile batteries deployed on Vimy Ridge and beyond, over 180 were accurately located and plotted by aerial photography and other means.[15]

The most effective work of 16 Squadron, supporting the Canadian Corps, was accomplished during the preparatory period, bad weather restricting flying during the actual assault. Based at Bruay about six miles behind the front and making use of a forward landing field close by the Corps Headquarters at Camblain l'Abbé, the squadron was organized in three flights of eight aircraft each. Two flights were assigned to counter-battery work and one to trench bombardment.[16]

Each flight of BE2s worked with a particular artillery group and also carried out photographic reconnaissance of its own area up to four thousand yards beyond the front-line trenches, where the FE2bs of 25 Squadron took over. Neutralizing fire, intended to silence enemy guns temporarily, was conducted through RFC wireless stations at battery positions, and through an advanced central wireless station which monitored and assisted calls for fire and provided communication between the aircraft and the Canadian Counter Battery Office. Tasks were prepared, targets identified, batteries assigned, and observation schedules issued by Canadian Corps Heavy Artillery. Before and after each shoot aerial photos were taken from which damage assessments could be made and plans adjusted accordingly. A proficient observer was expected to control two shoots simultaneously and complete four during a regular two-hour flight.[17]

The air battle of Vimy Ridge started long before the ground fighting began. Left relatively unprotected by the application of Trenchardian doctrine, 16 Squadron's BE2s were no match for the marauding German fighters. Four Canadians were killed and one wounded during February and March. On 1 February Lieutenant D.J. McRae of St Anne de Prescott was operating a camera when he and his pilot were surprised by Richthofen, who had made Vimy Ridge one of his favourite hunting areas. Twin Spandaus poured a hail of bullets into the aircraft, sending it down into the German trenches near Thélus within view of the troops of the 3rd Canadian Division. The pilot and observer both died from their wounds. Lieutenant J.W. Boyd of Toronto, who was wounded on 4 February and died the next day, and Second Lieutenant A. E. Watts of Fort Frances, Ont., and Lieutenant J.G.O. Brichta of North Battleford, Sask., both killed on 6 March, were the other Canadian fatalities. Lieutenant R.H. Lloyd of Wingham, Ont., was wounded on 28 March. In return, Second Lieutenant F.H. Baguley of Toronto had the satisfaction of sending a Halberstadt down out of control on 6 March; five days later the observer of Lieutenant F.L. Baker damaged and drove off another machine of the same type.[18] The pressure on 16 Squadron became so great that on 19 March III and V Brigades were ordered to help I Brigade by maintaining offensive patrols in the neighbourhood of Douai, the home of *Jasta 11* and the source of much of 16 Squadron's grief. This added measure of protection may have brought some relief because in the first week of April only two of their machines were lost. The enemy remained active, however. After a lull from 17 to 20 April caused by bad weather, air fighting was again severe until the end of the month. The Germans concentrated so effectively on the corps machines that, despite Trenchard's explicit instructions, offensive patrols were forced in closer to the lines to provide direct protection for the artillery aircraft. Nevertheless, the BEs continued to fall. On I Brigade front between 20 and 30 April eight were reported missing, five of them from 16 Squadron, four were wrecked on landing after being damaged in combat, two returned with wounded observers, and in another the pilot was fatally wounded. In all, six Canadians were missing and one wounded in this climactic ending to "Bloody April."[19]

Much of the air fighting took place within full view of the front-line troops and the war diaries of various units of the Canadian Corps contain a number of eyewitness accounts. Understandably, artillery units were most interested in the air battle: "Situation very quiet with the exception of air activity, several air fights took place, one enemy and one British plane came down," the diary of a field artillery formation recorded on 7 March 1917. On 12 March another entry noted that "Two of our planes brought down and one hostile plane."[20] The diarist of the 2nd Canadian Divisional Artillery commented that "enemy machines seem considerably superior to our own": "For the past three weeks enemy planes have had the best of every encounter on our front, & there have been many. The German fast red plane can make circles round our slow F.E. patrol & artillery machines, many of which have been shot down. Our new Sopwith triplanes seem to be useful."[21] Two observation aircraft came down in flames in front of the 3rd Canadian Siege Battery on 6 April, provoking the comment: "A great many of our observing planes have been lost during the past few weeks and it is a wonder to us that some steps are not taken to give them proper protection." Still, the enemy did not always dominate the action. An entry for 3 April in the diary of the 2nd Brigade, Canadian Field Artillery, located near Neuville St Waast, recorded that during the day "Our aeroplanes were very active as many as 35 being counted at one time, while enemy planes were not in evidence."[22]

The danger of being hit by artillery shells was another hazard that the corps squadron crews faced. Major E.O. McMurtry of Montreal and his observer, Lieutenant H.D. Mason of Canton, Ont., were both killed when their BE2 was apparently struck by an artillery shell.[23] Fighter pilots, especially on low-flying missions, also ran the risk of being blown out of the air in this way. In his 1918 book, *Winged Warfare*, W.A. Bishop related: "Over and over again one felt a sudden jerk under a wing-tip, and the machine would heave quickly. This meant a shell had passed within a few feet of you. As the battle went on the work grew more terrifying, because reports came in that several of our machines had been hit by shells in flight and brought down. . . . Yet the risk was one we could not avoid; we had to endure it with the best spirit possible."[24]

The high toll among two-seaters brought into question the efficacy of Trenchard's offensive policy. Corps and divisional commanders, the primary users of the vulnerable corps aircraft, began to press for protective fighter escorts. Their requests, however, were quashed with the support of General Kiggell, Haig's Chief of Staff, who circulated a statement of air policy stressing once more the importance of keeping the offensive patrols well beyond the enemy lines and pointing out the folly of weakening the fighter force by using it in a defensive role. Kiggell's directive, expressing Trenchard's views, claimed that "since our aerial offensive commenced early this month, the losses among fighting machines has been more than five times as many as among Corps machines, and the work of the latter has been very little interfered with."[25] While this statement may have been true for the RFC as a whole, it did not fit the situation in I Brigade. The brigade's loss ratio in April was about one army to two corps aircraft. Eight Canadians were reported killed or missing in corps aircraft as compared with three in fighter and fighter-reconnaissance planes.

South of Vimy in the valley of the Scarpe where the objective of the Third British Army was to drive through to Cambrai and link up with the French forces, more decisive clashes between the rival fighter arms took place. Here the ratio of casualties between co-operation and fighter aircraft was closer to that claimed by General Kiggell. Of the sixty Canadians flying with III Brigade in support of the Third Army, nine were killed, five wounded, and one captured during April. Five of those killed, the prisoner of war, and two of the wounded were members of fighter squadrons.[26]

Three of the Canadian casualties were members of 60 Squadron, whose record exemplifies the struggle of the fighter squadrons in "Bloody April." Its pilots patrolled an area east of Arras, from the slopes of Vimy to Fampoux. This sector was also frequented by Richthofen and clashes between Nieuport and Albatros were frequent. The squadron had its first serious setback on 7 April when three Nieuports were shot down in an encounter with *Jagdstaffel 11*. One of those killed was Second Lieutenant C.S. Hall, address unknown, who had been with the squadron since 6 January. Major J.A. Milot of Joliette, Que., was killed the next day and on the weekend of 14–16 April the squadron lost ten Nieuports out of an establishment of eighteen, including that of Lieutenant J. McC. Elliott of Winnipeg who was wounded on 16 April.[27]

It was during this dark period, one of the most critical that the RFC was to undergo during the war, that W.A. "Billy" Bishop emerged as 60 Squadron's foremost fighter pilot, beginning a career that was to make him one of the most famous airmen of his generation. Of that extraordinary group of Canadian fighter pilots of the First World War—Collishaw, Bishop, MacLaren, Barker, McKeever, Claxton, to name the most prominent—it was Bishop more than any other who caught the public eye. More has been written of him than of any other airman in Canada's history. A decidedly erratic RMC cadet, he left the college to join the Mississauga Horse when war broke out and went overseas in 1915 with the 7th Canadian Mounted Rifles. In September of that year, when his unit crossed to France, Bishop was left behind; he had transferred to the RFC, where he was training with 21 Squadron as an observer. After a brief period on the Western Front with that squadron in early 1916 he underwent pilot training in England. In March 1917 he reported to 60 Squadron at Izel-le-Hameau. By that time, according to his logbook, he had a total of seventy-five hours, and experience on BE2s, BE12s, Avro 504s, and Sopwith Pups.[28]

No 60 Squadron, however, flew Nieuports, and Bishop, a better fighter than he was a pilot, had trouble adjusting to this sensitive aircraft. On 11 March he began practice flying; over the next two weeks he and the groundcrew endured burst tires, strained airframes, and at least one crash-landing. A less discerning squadron commander might well have returned Bishop to the pilot's pool before he had had an opportunity to show what he could do. But Major A.J.L. Scott, one of the RFC's most perceptive leaders, recognized that the ham-fisted young Canadian flew with the calculating aggressiveness that marked the great fighter pilots. After five hours of practice flying in France, he flew his first operational patrol on 17 March. On 25 March he shot down his first enemy aircraft, an Albatros, while flying as rear man in a formation of four Nieuports. The combat began at nine thousand feet near Arras and demonstrated that, whatever Bishop's weaknesses as a pilot, he was a first-class shot with the true killer instinct:

While on D[efensive] P[atrol] 3 Albatros Scouts approached us. One, separating from the rest, lost height and attempted to come up behind our second to the rear machines. I dived and fired about 12 to 15 rounds. Tracers went all around his machine. He dived steeply for about 600 ft. and flattened out. I followed him and opened fire from 40 to 50 yards range. A group of tracers went into the fuselage and centre section, one being seen to enter immediately behind the pilot's seat and one seemed to hit the pilot himself. The machine then fell out of control in a spinning nose dive. I dived after him, firing. I reached 1500 or 2000 ft. My engine had oiled up and I glided just over the line. . . . The Albatros Scout when last seen by me was going vertically downwards at a height of 500 to 600 ft. [29]

On 30 March Scott demonstrated his prescience by sending the still inexperienced Bishop out as the leader of a five-man offensive patrol. Within a month of his first operational flight Bishop had become the squadron's "ace," and Scott was permitting him to fly roving missions by himself in addition to his normal patrol duties.

Like all the great air fighters, Bishop was an expert deflection shot, a skill he maintained by constant practice. His tactics, a subject to which he gave much thought, were built around surprise, which he regarded as the essence of air fighting. In part, his methods were forced upon him because the Nieuport was much slower than the best German fighters; even so, his combat reports from this period show that, once surprise was lost, he was usually willing to break off combat. When that was not possible, his heavy-handedness became a positive advantage in the rough-and-tumble of air combat. He threw the little Nieuport about with complete abandon and a rare tactical sense. As his letters home reveal, he was also driven by an intense urge to win recognition. His personal and family correspondence contains many accounts of his victories, as well as references to his "score," his decorations, and the number of victories registered by RFC and French rivals. Joined to his skill and drive was a relentless courage that impelled him constantly to seek combat. On 30 April, for example, in a space of two hours before noon, he reported eight distinct combats against a total of nineteen aircraft. As Scott noted at the bottom of his report: "Comment, I think, is unnecessary."[30]

Naval Three also acquitted itself exceptionally during the April battles, its Pups usually getting the better of the Halberstadt and Albatros scouts. It was employed principally on escort duty providing protection for BE2s used as bombers. The nature of this work was almost bound to bring on an encounter with the German air force, yet only three of the Pups were lost during the month of April. The squadron had one of its busiest days on 11 April while escorting a formation of BE2s on a bombing raid on Cambrai. L.S. Breadner destroyed one Albatros in the air, forced another out of the fight, and sent an unidentified enemy machine down in flames. J.S.T. Fall scored three remarkable victories for which he was awarded the DSC. He attacked and destroyed one enemy aircraft; he was driven down toward the ground by hostile scouts, but manoeuvred onto one of them from behind and saw his tracers go into the pilot's head; later he brought down another enemy who attacked him. He returned with his own aircraft riddled with bullet holes.[31]

Two weeks later Breadner, described by one of his acquaintances as a "fire-eater,"[32] brought down an enemy aircraft not far from his own aerodrome at Marieux and within an hour or so was back in his room telling about the adventure in a letter to Canada: "I was going down to the aerodrome when I heard the anti-aircraft guns going. On looking up I saw a Hun directly over-head at about 10 000 ft. So I scrambled into my "bus" & after him. He was at 12 000 ft. when I got up to him (a great big double-engined pusher type machine) so I sat right behind his tail where he couldn't shoot at me. I fired 190 rounds at him & shot both his engines."[33]

The German aircraft crashed on the allied side of the lines and Breadner landed in a field close by. He was unable to converse with the occupants of the downed machines, a pilot and two observers who were captured by some "Tommies," since they spoke no English. Their aircraft was still burning, but before it was destroyed Breadner cut away the cross insignia, boasting that "We have it in the mess now." The letter ended with a hurried notation: "I'll have to close now as we are going out on a 'Big Stunt' in a few minutes & I have to put my kit on yet." Breadner then led his flight of five Pups in escorting a formation of six FE2bs en route to bomb Epinoy aerodrome. Soon after crossing the line they were met by two formations of enemy fighters. After making sure that the bombers were back over the British lines the escort turned on their pursuers. J.J. Malone attacked one enemy plane, shooting the pilot, drove down a second, and went after a third. Flight Sub-Lieutenant G.B. Anderson of Ottawa sent another German down out of control. The skirmish attracted other machines from both sides and a free-wheeling battle developed and spread over a large area. During the engagement Malone ran out of ammunition, flew to a nearby aerodrome, reloaded, returned to the fight, and drove down another hostile aircraft. Malone was reported missing the following week. At that time he was credited with seven downed enemy aircraft and was posthumously gazetted for the DSO for his victories.[34]

In April, reflecting the intensity of the fighting, casualties reached an all time high in the RFC. In the four-week period ending 27 April 238 personnel were reported missing or killed and 105 wounded. Known Canadian casualties for the month totalled twenty-six killed, thirteen wounded, and six missing. German losses from 31 March to 11 May were thirty-three killed, sixteen missing, and nineteen wounded. Thirty German aircraft were destroyed in the same period, compared with 122 RFC machines, but the RFC was continually operating over enemy territory and its pilots were much more vulnerable than their German adversaries, who were seldom far from the safety of their own aerodromes.[35]

A classic illustration of this is provided by a letter written by Lieutenant T.W. McConkey of Bradford, Ont., the observer in an RE8 of 59 Squadron engaged on routine corps reconnaissance duties on 11 May. It describes he won the MC ". . . while photographing about 9000 yards into Hunland. We were attacked by five Albatross scouts which broke up our formation. Between us we shot down two of the enemy and drove another down, apparently out of control. My pilot, Captain Pemberton from B.C. manoeuvred the machine in a most excellent fashion, evading the fire of Huns as much as possible and giving me every opportunity to bring my Lewis gun into play. He received a spent bullet in the back, necessitating his spending a week in the casualty clearing station. I came off less fortunately, with four bullet wounds in the right thigh, one in shoulder and one in face."[36]

The bloody operations about Arras, which had originally been intended as diversionary attacks to draw off German reserves from Nivelle's offensive on the Aisne, were prolonged into May because of the collapse of the French assault after the first few days. The French debacle was compounded by widespread mutiny among the troops. Nivelle was replaced by Général Henri Pétain, and the new commander-in-chief was compelled to adopt a defensive stance for the rest of the year, while the morale of his shattered forces was rebuilt. As a result, the major responsibility for offensive action on the Western Front passed to the British, with predictable consequences for the focus of the air war.

Plans for an assault on the Messines-Wytschaete Ridge, which commanded the British position on the right flank of the Ypres Salient, had been included in the original offensive plans for 1917. Its seizure was necessary for a successful offensive in Flanders to free the Belgian coastal region, a course urged by the Lords of the Admiralty who wanted the ports of Ostend and Zeebrugge. But it was to be undertaken only on the condition that Nivelle's master plan failed to achieve a decisive breakthrough. The British, Nivelle had agreed, would then be free to break off the fighting east of Arras and attack in Belgium with the Second British Army supported by the Belgian army and the French forces at Nieuport. Consequently, with the French halted on the Aisne and Pétain asking for time to restore the confidence of his demoralized troops, Haig decided to implement the plans for a British offensive in the north. The first move was to be against the Messines Ridge, whose capture would deprive the Germans of valuable observation points and form a solid right flank for the advance into the coastal region.

The offensive was mounted by the Second British Army and its air arm, II Brigade, which was significantly reinforced for the operation. Two corps squadrons of RE8s and BE2es were added along with two army squadrons, 1 and 10 (Naval) with their Sopwith Triplanes. In addition, 23 (Spad) and 40 (Nieuport) Squadrons of I Brigade were detailed to extend their offensive patrols to cover the II Brigade area, while the fighter, bomber, and reconnaissance squadrons of 9 (HQ) Wing were moved north at the end of May to the Second Army zone. By the beginning of June Trenchard had concentrated twenty squadrons (half of them equipped with single-seater fighters) mustering well over three hundred serviceable aircraft. German reinforcements for the entire Fourth Army front, from Messines to the sea, fell short of this number, and in the battle area further reinforcements did not arrive in time for the fight. Although a detailed German air order of battle has not been found, it seems likely that enemy aircraft on the Flanders Front were out-numbered two to one, and along the Messines Ridge by a much higher margin.[37]

Using its numerical advantage the RFC tried to seal off the battle area by a system of barrage patrols flown by the army squadrons along a line that corresponded approximately with the enemy's line of observation balloons, tethered about a mile behind his front line. This system had brought the Germans little success at Verdun in 1916, but the margin of numerical superiority held by the RFC enabled it to police the barrage line from dawn to dusk, with patrols maintained at two or more levels, and still form an outer screen of distant offensive patrols. The main task of the fighters on the barrage line was to protect the corps aircraft. They were also expected to prevent the enemy from using his own artillery co-operation machines and force him to haul down his observation balloons. Orders were issued that no German planes were to be permitted to cross the barrage line. Some of course did. But it is remarkable, in view of what had happened in April, and a measure of the air superiority established in the battle area, that between 31 May, when the main bombardment began, and 6 June only one corps machine was lost. This was an RE8 of 42 Squadron carrying Second Lieutenant C.J. Baylis of Victoria as observer. He was killed.[38]

The fighter patrols were supplemented by the compass stations installed in each army area late in 1916. These were located at widely separated points, and by obtaining cross-bearings on the wireless transmissions of an enemy artillery-ranging aircraft they could trace its movements with a fair degree of accuracy. By the spring of 1917 the system was in full operation with all the compass stations linked in a single network. When an enemy aircraft was located in this way its position was relayed to the appropriate army wing headquarters and from there by telephone to a squadron or flight on standby for such emergencies.[39] The response bears close resemblance to the fighter "scrambles" of the Second World War. The procedure followed in 60 Squadron was probably typical of the RFC as a whole: ". . . in order efficiently to answer the compass calls, as they were termed, three or four pilots always had to be standing by to leap into their machines and be off the ground, in formation, inside of two minutes. Nevertheless, they became extraordinarily smart at this manoeuvre, and answered to the [Klaxon] hunting horn—doubled blasts of which were the signal at that time—as keenly as a fashionable pack of foxhounds."[40] In the first week of June the army wing headquarters of II Brigade received forty-seven calls from the wireless interception centre at Messines. The net result was one enemy aircraft destroyed, seven estimated to be damaged, and twenty-two enemy artillery shoots abruptly terminated.[41]

The Battle of Messines, like that at Vimy, was based on limited objectives, to be achieved by concentrating an overwhelming weight of artillery fire on a narrow front. The artillery bombardment and counter-battery programme began on 21 May and increased in intensity as the day of the attack, 7 June, approached. Within the security screen provided by the fighters and assisted by good weather the artillery flights were able to direct the British guns on to enemy positions on the far side of the ridge with devastating effect. When the ground attack went in almost a quarter of the German field artillery, and nearly half of their heavy artillery, had been knocked out. The assault itself was preceded by the detonation of nineteen mines, with over 450 tons of explosives, which had been placed under the German front lines more than six months before. Immediately after the mines were blown, at 0310 hrs, the whole of the artillery of the Second Army began to fire at the maximum rate. From the air the ground appeared to be "bouncing up like the surface of water in a heavy storm." Although there was stiff resistance in places, the infantry assault was successful, most of the assigned objectives being taken that same day.[42]

Strong air support was one of the key factors in the victory. The fighter screen was so effective that Maurice Baring, Trenchard's personal aide and secretary, was moved to comment that 7 June was "the finest day in the air we have ever had. Our people entirely prevented the Boche Flying Corps from working, and our artillery work in co-operation with aircraft went without a hitch." Twenty-nine corps aircraft worked along the front of the three attacking corps, a distance of about seventeen thousand yards, almost doubling the highest density employed previously. No. 6 Squadron attached to X Corps was the only corps unit to lose aircraft. Two of its RE8s went missing and in other combats four members of the squadron were wounded. In 42 Squadron on the II Anzac Corps' front Lieutenant W.F. Anderson of Toronto, flying an RE8, was attacked by three fighters while on a photo mission, but his observer sent one of the attackers down in flames and damaged another. Their aircraft "was very badly shot about but neither was injured." Apart from these incidents, the corps squadrons carried on without any interference, adjusting artillery fire on to 157 enemy batteries. Nos. 1 and 41 Squadrons, flying Nieuports and FE8s, respectively, were specifically assigned to provide close ground support over the battlefield while other fighter squadrons were given ground attack as a secondary role. Aerodromes and ground transport were the main targets, but they had a roving commission to strike at anything they saw "in order to harass the enemy as much as possible and spoil the morale of his troops."[43]

During June ninety Canadians served with the squadrons of the re-inforced II Brigade operating in support of the Messines attack, of whom ten were killed, six wounded, and three reported missing.[44] The most dis-tinctively Canadian unit was 10 (Naval) in which thirteen of the squadron's fifteen pilots were Canadian when the unit joined II Brigade in mid-May.

Naval Ten was formed at St Pol (Dunkirk) on 12 February and was shortly thereafter equipped with Sopwith Triplanes. Its original pilots were considered unready for action, however, so in the spring it was restaffed with seasoned veterans, almost all of whom were Canadians. Eight were posted in from Naval Three with the others coming from various sources. Collishaw, for instance, had recently returned from convalescent leave and was available for a new posting. As one of the most experienced pilots he assumed command of "B" Flight[45] and took a leading part in preparing the unit for action. Collishaw remained with the squadron until the end of July and received a DSC and DSO for his service on the Ypres front.[46]

The Canadian pilots soon established the squadron as one of the lead-ing fighter units in II Brigade. In June its aircraft destroyed fifteen of the forty-six enemy machines claimed by II Brigade and twenty-seven of eighty-three others damaged or driven down out of control. Naval Ten's biggest day was 6 June when it claimed five destroyed and five others forced down. Collishaw, whose logbook records sixty missions that month, destroyed or sent down out of control thirteen enemy aircraft.[47] His combat report for 17 June describes one of these encounters:

> Near Armentieres [sic] our patrol [six aircraft] met five Spads,[48] who accompanied us. Over Roulers, we saw and dived on eight enemy Scouts, followed by Spads. After diving on three different Scouts and missing them with my fire, I climbed away each time. I then saw an E.A. [enemy aircraft] attacking one of the Spad machines and dived on him firing about 50 rounds, when the E.A. stalled and fell out of control.
>
> I attached another enemy Scout, which was attacking a Spad, but after 30 rounds my gun jambed and I could not clear it.
>
> I saw Flt. Sub-Lt. Reid close one . . . and fire into it. I was able to see the E.A. go down in a series of stalls and spins, and I am certain he was out of control beyond recovery.
>
> I also saw another machine go down out of control after attack from a Spad.[49]

Notwithstanding the fact that they were rated as generally superior in performance to the Albatros and Halberstadt scouts, the Sopwith Triplanes by no means had it all their own way. Between 15 May and 30 June the squadron lost six of its Canadian members, three killed and three wounded or missing. In addition, at least two other members of the squadron were lost, one being killed and the other taken prisoner.[50]

Although Messines was the main centre of air action in the latter part of May and early June, the most publicized event in the air war was the strafing of a German airfield on the Arras front by W.A. Bishop on 2 June. His action brought him a Victoria Cross, the tenth to be won by an airman and the first by a Canadian flyer. The attack had its origin in Bishop's brief association with Captain Albert Ball, recognized at the time as the most outstanding airman in the RFC. During a visit to 60 Squadron on 5 May Ball had invited Bishop to join him in a surprise raid on a German aerodrome with the object of destroying aircraft on the ground. There were obvious hazards, but the aggressive young Briton felt that surprise, in as much as a low-level attack on an aerodrome had never been attempted and would not be expected, would enable them to turn the trick. A few days later, before anything definite had been organized, Ball was killed in action. But the idea kept churning in Bishop's mind.

By the end of May, with the Arras front relatively quiet, 60 Squadron was mainly occupied with answering compass calls. Bishop disliked this exhausting and unrewarding type of work: there were frequent chases but few combats. Moreover, he found the sound of that "damned Klaxon horn" used to alert the pilots was becoming "hard on the nerves—and the legs." It was in this mood that he determined to carry out the proposal which he and Ball had briefly discussed. He chose a free day, 2 June, for his self-assigned mission and took off before dawn in his Nieuport. At the aerodrome he attacked the Germans as they were getting ready for the day's work.[51]

Always a key factor in his tactics, surprise worked for Bishop here as it did on so many other occasions. His combat report tells what happened during the few minutes he was over the enemy airfield:

> I fired on 7 machines on the aerodrome, some of which had their engines running. One of them took off and I fired 15 rounds at him from close range 60 ft. up and he crashed. A second one taking off, I opened fire and fired 30 rounds at 150 yards range, he crashed into a tree. Two more were then taking off together. I climbed and engaged one at 1000 ft., finishing my drum, and he crashed 300 yards from the aerodrome. I changed drums and climbed E[ast] a fourth H.A. came after me and I fired one whole drum into him. He flew away and I then flew 1000 ft. under 4 scouts at 5000 ft. for one mile and turned W. climbing. The aerodrome was armed with one or more machine guns. Machines on the ground were 6 scouts (Albatros Type I or II) and one two-seater.[52]

A note appended to the combat report by the squadron commander observed that Bishop "was several times at a height of 50 ft. over this enemy aerodrome[53] at least 17 miles East of the lines. His machine is full of holes caused by machine gun fire from the ground." A fellow pilot remembered "clearly seeing a group of about five bullet holes in the rear half of his tailplane, the elevator, within a circle of not more than six inches diameter at the most. Whatever machine was on his tail must have been very close indeed to achieve that group."[54]

Although an isolated event and really an episode in the private war which Bishop, like many another fighter pilot, carried on against the German air force, the action did have a wider significance. As the most daring and successful low-level attack yet carried out, it provided an example which was repeated during the Battle of Messines and later. Thus, the orders issued to 9 (HQ) Wing for 7 June included specific reference to low-flying attacks on aerodromes of a kind which had not been attempted before Bishop's exploit.[55] On the announcement of Bishop's having been awarded the Victoria Cross, more than two months later,[56] General Trenchard removed him from operational flying. He was not to return to the Western Front until 1918, when he came back as a squadron commander. Until he left for England in August, however, Bishop continued to take a prominent part in the air war, which now centred upon a major British offensive in Flanders.

Sir Douglas Haig had been favourable to the idea of a Flanders offensive since January 1916. It had been his alternative to operations on the Somme and now, with the clean, if very limited, success of Messines behind him, and the French incapable of mounting a significant attack, he was in a strong position to push for it as a better choice than the Italian offensive backed by the "Easterners" on Lloyd George's newly-formed War Policy Committee. Strategic justification for the Flanders offensive was given to the committee in a week-long series of conferences attended by Haig starting 19 June. The demoralized French armies needed time to recover from the mutinies of the previous month; Admiral Sir John Jellicoe considered that unless the German submarine warfare campaign could be restricted by the capture of the Channel ports, Britain would have to end the war in 1918 because of shipping losses; any breakthrough in Flanders would threaten the main communication of the German armies there, which ran through bottlenecks north and south of the Ardennes; and if the enemy could be driven from the Belgian coast it would compel his heavy bombers to cross the BEF lines to carry out raids against London.[57]

The War Policy Committee reluctantly accepted Haig's arguments although it still doubted the ability of the BEF to achieve such ambitious goals. Finally, on 16 July, a clear decision was reached "to allow Haig to begin his offensive, but not to allow it to degenerate into a drawn out, indecisive battle of the 'Somme' type." The first phase of the ground offensive was to drive a wedge into the German defences around the Ypres Salient. From the expanded salient the British would then advance northeastwards, with their right on the high ground of the Passchendaele Ridge, to gain the Thourout-Couckelaere line on their way to Bruges.[58]

Prior to the infantry assault, scheduled for 15 July, General Gough's Fifth Army would lay down a massive sixteen-day artillery bombardment. Since the main German defences lay along the crest and reverse slope of the low ridge which dominated the Ypres Salient, the British artillery—especially the heavy guns engaged in counter-battery work—were, as usual, heavily dependent on aerial observation for accurate ranging. This, together with the army's demands for photo-reconnaissance and protection against enemy air observation, required that the RFC establish and maintain aerial superiority for a considerable period. Thus the Third Battle of Ypres really began on 11 July with the opening of an RFC intrusion of enemy reconnaissance aircraft.[59]

The artillery preparation ruled out the possibility of strategic surprise and the air build-up on both sides had become obvious several weeks earlier still. Between the middle of June and the end of July the Allies and the Germans had concentrated every available aircraft into the thirty-mile corridor between the Lys and the sea—the entire Belgian air force, forty strong, some two hundred French and over five hundred British machines (totalling 60 percent of the RFC in France and half of them single-seater fighters), facing about six hundred Germans. Many famous squadrons were gathered there, including the French "Les Cigognes," the American "Lafayette Escadrille," the RFC's 56 and 60 Squadrons, and the RNAS' Naval Ten.[60]

The German force included *Jagdgeschwader I - Jastas* 4, 6, 10, and 11 under the overall command of Germany's top-scoring pilot, Manfred von Richthofen, who had already been credited with fifty-six victories when his "Circus" was formed on 23 June. But the Allies had a clear-cut numerical advantage and they added to it an advantage in morale on 6 July when, in a dogfight between the "Circus" and six FE2ds of 20 Squadron and four Sopwith Triplanes of Naval Ten, Richthofen was shot down by an FE observer, temporarily blinded and paralyzed by a bullet which creased his skull. The enemy's premier fighter ace was thus removed from the battle for six weeks.

By the opening of the offensive the technological superiority so decidedly in the Germans' favour earlier in the year had evaporated. Three new British aircraft were responsible. The first was the Bristol F2A, or Bristol Fighter, a large, powerful, and fast two-seater, designed as a fighter-reconnaissance machine and commonly called the "Brisfit." Its first employment on operations, by 48 Squadron on 5 April, was an unqualified disaster, four of a flight of six being shot down by Richthofen and his companions. Richthofen judged the machine as "quick and rather handy, with a powerful motor," but considered the Albatros D-III "undoubtedly superior." Yet within a few weeks the Brisfit had emerged as a most formidable and versatile aircraft. Its most notable pilot was Lieutenant A.E. McKeever of Listowel, Ont., who demonstrated that the best use of the machine was to fly it as if it were a single-seat fighter, instead of using it in the standard two-seater fashion as a firing platform for the observer. McKeever was thus able to exploit fully the Bristol's flying qualities and the firepower of its fixed, forward-firing Vickers, while his observer was left to cover the tail with a Lewis gun on a flexible ring mounting.[61]

The second new aircraft, beset with engine problems, also had an inauspicious debut in April. The SE5 and its subsequent modification, the splendid SE5a with a 200-hp Hispano-Suiza engine, were among the fastest fighters manufactured during the war, showing top speeds in the 120–130 mph range during 1917 tests. The aircraft was the first British two-gun single-seater fighter, having a Lewis gun mounted on the top plane and a Vickers synchronized to fire through the air-screw.[62]

Finally, in July, some RFC and RNAS squadrons began to re-equip with the Sopwith Camel, a stubby little machine that was to become the most famous of all British fighters. The Camel did not have the speed of the SE5a, but the concentration of weight in the forward section of its short fuselage and the pronounced torque of its engine, which made it unstable and somewhat hazardous to fly, also meant that in the right hands it had a quite startling agility. The Camel mounted a pair of belt-fed Vickers firing through the propeller arc, giving it even greater firepower than the SE5. In 1917 the Germans had no real answer to these aircraft, the Albatros D-V and D-Va, introduced in mid-summer, not being appreciably better than the D III.[63]

Tactically, however, the Germans continued to hold the edge. Their *Geschwader*—Richthofen's Circus was the first of them—were self-contained fighter wings which could be deployed on any part of the front to establish local air superiority, then moved again as the tactical situation demanded. This concept was well ahead of current British tactics. While the RFC was only now enlarging its basic tactical formation from three- to five-machine flights and was endeavouring to maintain such a continuous offensive strategy that "along the whole stretch of the British Front there were seldom more than 25 fighting aircraft in the air together," the Germans usually chose to mass one or more fighter wings at times and places of their own choosing and then make sudden sweeps over the line. Casualties were heavy in the sparse and outnumbered British fighter patrols and even heavier among the relatively unprotected artillery and reconnaissance machines. "If not before, Webb-Bowen [commanding V Brigade, RFC] ought to have changed his policy of withholding escorts at the beginning of July 1917," recalled one former British pilot, "when the new *Jagdgeschwader* moved north . . . and British squadrons . . . faced a much greater concentration of German fighters than before."[64]

On 7 July, for example, a formation of six Sopwith 1½ Strutters of 45 Squadron, returning from a photo-reconnaissance mission to Wervicq, was attacked by eighteen or more Albatros scouts from the *Richthofengeschwader*. Two of the Sopwiths fell in flames, carrying with them their pilots and two Canadian observers, Lieutenants J.B. Fotheringham of Ottawa and F.C.H. Snyder of Kitchener, Ont. On this occasion Lieutenant C.R.T. Ward of Lennoxville, Que., flying as observer in the formation commander's machine, was able to bring back twenty-one exposed plates, but fifteen days later another formation of eight aircraft from the same squadron, sent to photograph Menin, was much less successful. Attacked by the Circus before it reached the objective, the formation was quickly broken up, three of its aircraft shot down, and the remainder driven back without any photographs. It was small consolation that a Canadian crew, piloted by Lieutenant E.F. Crossland of Toronto with G.W. Blaiklock of Montreal as observer, claimed one enemy machine driven down out of control.[65]

Meanwhile, the fighter squadrons which might have been protecting these obsolescent fighter-reconnaissance machines or defending their ground forces against enemy bombing raids[66] were dissipating their strength flying distant offensive patrols far over the enemy lines. Arthur Gould Lee, then a junior pilot of 46 Squadron, later an RAF air vice-marshal, has eloquently recorded the fighter pilot's disillusion with this interpretation of the offensive spirit:

> The futility of such wasteful losses was the deeper because if a D[istant] O[ffensive] P[atrol] were weak in numbers . . . it could easily be overwhelmed, but if the patrol were strong, the Germans could, and frequently did, ignore it, leaving us with a debit of forced-landed aeroplanes, wasted engine hours and wasted petrol.
>
> Had there been a specific object in our deep penetrations, such as covering a bombing raid or a photographic reconnaissance, we would have thought nothing of it, but we could see no rational purpose in our coat-trailing D.O.P.s. . . . Was it to lower the morale of the German Air Forces? This notion we found laughable, for ours was the morale that suffered.
>
> Then did we find more fights or shoot down more Huns? . . . On the contrary, combats were fewer, for the really intensive fighting was always near the Lines, within reach of the artillery-spotting and other patrolling two-seaters.
>
> Unfortunately High Command held to the illusion that D.O.P.s not only produced bigger and better combats but were an important instrument of offensive policy, which was a meaningless slogan, for an offensive spirit in the air meant attacking the enemy

with resolution, not showing the flag over Tournai. The consequence was that fighter pilots built up a deep resentment. . . . These
insubordinate notions did not all come unbidden in the air but later
on the ground, when there was time and mood to reflect.[67]

Despite being frequently outnumbered things did not always go so
badly for the fighter pilots of the RFC. McKeever in 11 Squadron started his
remarkable record of success by claiming his first victim on 26 June. He and
his observers—"gunners" might have been a more appropriate term—were
credited with their eighth victory only eighteen days later. On 21 July
Raymond Collishaw and four other Canadians from Naval Ten—Flight
Commander J.E. Sharman of Oak Lake, Man., Flight Lieutenant W.M.
Alexander of Toronto and Flight Sub-Lieutenants E.V. Reid of Toronto and
G.L. Trapp of New Westminster, BC—dived on about twenty enemy scouts
over Passchendaele. Collishaw claimed three out of control in the course of
a long general combat.[68] This struggle for air superiority imposed a considerable physical strain on the pilots, as "Mel" Alexander recalled in tranquil-
lity many years later. At nineteen years of age he was an experienced pilot
in perhaps the most successful of all British air formations, the famed
"Black Flight" of Naval Ten.[69] "Butterflies in your stomach is what you call
it—nervous tension. You're almost panicky . . . " he remembered, and after
most patrols his jaws ached from the prolonged muscular tension.

On 24 July the staff of V Brigade could confidently report that "the
number of decisive combats had considerably decreased during the last few
days which is a sure sign that the German morale is breaking down," but
the truth of the matter was that the enemy, subject to similar strains, was
holding up about equally well. This brief lull in the air battle had more to
do with re-deployments in the air arm of the Fourth German Army and the
difficulties of finding sufficient airfields on the watery Flanders plain than it
had with German morale. In an air battle over Polygon Wood two days
later a German force of about fifty fighters engaged almost as many British
scouts, while down below four German two-seaters successfully reconnoitred the British line in front of Ypres. That neither side was able to shoot
down a single opponent in such a large dogfight suggests that they were
very well-matched, rather that that the German morale was breaking down.
Throughout this period, too, enemy reconnaissance machines were able to
keep a satisfactory watch on the two-and-a-half mile wide main zone of
traffic which ran parallel to the front some three miles behind. A single
reconnaissance machine, flying at high speed, could cover the whole corridor of the British front in less than an hour. The observed volume and regu-
larity of ground traffic contributed greatly to the enemy's understanding of
the British build-up.[70]

On the other hand, the German scouts were even less able to prevent the
RFC's reconnaissance and artillery observation aircraft from fulfilling their
functions. The weekly intelligence summary of the Fourth German Army
recorded on 18 July that "the number of [enemy] reconnaissance formations
has doubled," although "these mainly confined themselves to close reconnaissance; the line Courtrai-Tourcoing was reached only once." Reconnaissance

on this scale meant that the Germans could keep few secrets, and it could only have been a slight consolation to them that forty-five British machines were claimed to have been shot down in the week under review, twenty-two of them falling within the German lines. By the end of the month 9 Squadron, attached to the Fifth Army's XIV Corps in the tip of the salient, was flying fifteen counter-battery and twenty or more trench shoots a day despite all attempts to stop them.[71]

After several postponements the ground attack was finally scheduled for the morning of 31 July. As had happened earlier at Vimy, however, the most effective air operations had been conducted prior to the ground assault. The weather deteriorated so badly on the 29th that the air war virtually ceased until dawn on the 31st. In late afternoon the weather again closed in and flying had to be postponed. In the interval overcast skies and drizzling rain severely limited air operations. The artillery machines were unable to conduct a single shoot, contact patrolling was ineffective, and neither bombing nor close ground support missions could claim much success. For their marginal efforts the RFC paid dearly; thirty machines were rendered unserviceable (mostly by ground fire) during the day.[72]

It continued to rain intermittently for ninety-six hours while the poor British infantry carried the line forward to a maximum depth of three thousand yards at the cost of some 31 000 casualties. Every small British advance was met by a determined German counter-attack, in which the German *Schlachtstaffeln*, unlike their British opponents, used large formations of close support aircraft to aid their ground forces in tactical arrangements which had been carefully worked out and rehearsed beforehand.[73] With only half of the planned territorial gains actually in British hands, Haig temporarily called off the ground attack, explaining to the British government that "The low-lying, clayey soil, torn by shells and sodden with rain, turned to a succession of vast muddy pools. The valleys of the chocked and overflowing streams were speedily transformed into long stretches of bog. . . . In these conditions operations of any magnitude became impossible, and the resumption of our offensive was necessarily postponed until a period of fine weather should allow the ground to recover."[74]

The aerial battle could not so easily be stopped and restarted. . . .

NOTES

1. Trenchard to Chief of Staff, 11 Feb. 1917, Air 1/522/16/12/5.

2. Admiralty to Air Board, 20 Dec. 1916, Air 1/520/16/12/1; J.M. Bruce, *British Aeroplanes, 1914–1918* (London, 1957), 563–68. The Fokker Dr-I was the German response to the Sopwith Triplane. It was powered by a French-designed Le Rhône rotary engine, obtained from a Swedish firm which had built them under licence. An extremely agile aircraft, the Dr-I did not appear on the Western Front until August; its most famous pilots were Richthofen and Werner Voss. It remained in service until mid-1918.

3. Collishaw to Grange, 30 Oct. 1965, Raymond Collishaw Papers, Directorate of History, National Defence Headquarters, Ottawa (hereafter DHist), 78/132, 1-A, folder

101; Chambers to Hallahan, 10 April 1917, R.H. Mulock Papers, DHist, document 43.

4. Chambers to Mulock, 13 June 1917, Mulock Papers, DHist, document 53.

5. The claim of eighty enemy aircraft being accounted for by the Squadron may be taken as an instance of the general tendency to exaggerate enemy losses. Naval Three was credited with twenty aircraft destroyed and twenty-four damaged in RFC communiqués during the period under review, but even these figures are questionable in the light of admitted German losses.

6. Trenchard to Senior Officer, RNAS Dunkirk, 27 June 1917, Mulock Papers, DHist, document 57.

7. Collishaw to Grange, 21 May 1965, Collishaw Papers, DHist 78/132, 1-A, folder 101; letters home, 9 March and 11 April 1917, L.S. Breadner Papers, DHist 74/707, files 32 and 34; DHist squadron lists.

8. DHist squadron lists; H.A. Jones, *The War in the Air: Being the Story of the Part Played in the Great War by the Royal Air Force*, vol. 3 (London, 1931), map facing 330, app. 12.

9. RAF Staff College précis, "Air Warfare," nd, 45, Air 1/2385/228/10; HQ RFC to all brigades and 9 Wing, 26 March 1917, Air 1/1008/204/5/1283.

10. HQ RFC to all brigades and 9 Wing, 26 March 1917.

11. Ibid.; Jones, *War in the Air*, 3:334, 360.

12. Jones, *War in the Air*, 3:354–55, 360; RAF Staff College précis, "Air Warfare," 44–45; I Brigade work summary, April 1917, Air 1/768/204/4/252.

13. Bruce, *British Aeroplanes*, 426–38.

14. James E. Edmonds, *Military Operations: France and Belgium, 1917*, vol. 1 (London, 1940), 300–305; Report of Canadian Corps operations, Vimy, folder 52, file 7, Public Archives of Canada (hereafter PAC), RG 9 III, vol. 3846.

15. Report of Canadian Corps operations, Vimy; Edmonds, *Military Operations: France and Belgium, 1917*, 1:311, 314; C. à C. Repington, *The First World War, 1914–1918*, vol. 1 (London, 1921), 530.

16. I Brigade to HQ RFC and attached plan, 26 March 1917, Air 1/1008/204/5/1283.

17. "Notes on Counter Battery Work in connection with the Capture of Vimy Ridge," Canadian Corps General Staff, folder 46, file 2, "Instructions for Co-operation Between Divisional Artillery, Heavy Artillery and RFC during Trench Destruction," app. E to Artillery Instructions for Vimy Ridge, 28 March 1917, Canadian Corps General Staff, folder 46, file 6, PAC, RG 9 III, vol. 3843; Edmonds, *Military Operations: France and Belgium, 1917*, vol. 1, app. 15; Jones, *War in the Air*, 3:311–13, 332, 344–45, app. 12.

18. Floyd Gibbons, *The Red Knight of Germany: Baron von Richthofen, Germany's Great War Airman* (London, 1930), 126–27; I Brigade work summary, 27–28 March 1917, Air 1/767/204/4/251; 16 Squadron air combat reports, 6 and 11 March 1917, Air 1/1219/204/5/2634/16; RFC communiqué nos. 74, 78, DHist 75/413.

19. I Brigade work summary, April 1917, Air 1/768/204/4/252; Jones, *War in the Air*, 3:356, 365.

20. War diary, I Brigade, Canadian Field Artillery, 7 and 12 March 1917, folder 527, PAC, RG 9 III, vol. 4963.

21. War diary, 2nd Canadian Divisional Artillery, 11 March and 5 April 1917, folder 510, PAC, RG 9 III, vol. 4959.

22. War diary, II Brigade, Canadian Field Artillery, 3 April 1917, folder 529, PAC, RG 9 III, vol. 4964; War diary, 3rd Canadian Siege Battery, 6 April 1917, folder 570, PAC RG 9 III, vol. 4976.

23. No. 16 SRB, 9 April 1917, Air 1/1343/204/19/15; I Brigade work summary, April 1917, Air 1/768/204/4/252.

24. W.A. Bishop, *Winged Warfare: Hunting the Huns in the Air* (London, 1918), 93–94.

25. "Policy in the Air," attached to Kiggel to distribution, 9 April 1917, Air 1/522/16/12/5.

26. Jones, *War in the Air*, vol. 3, app. 12; DHist squadron lists.

27. A.J.L. Scott, *Sixty Squadron R.A.F.: A History of the Squadron from its Formation* (London, 1920), 30, 38, 44–45, app. 2.

28. W.A. Bishop biographical file, DHist.

29. No. 60 Squadron air combat report, 25 March 1917, Air 1/1225/204/5/2634/60.

30. Ibid., 30 April 1917; W.A. Bishop biographical file, DHist.

31. RCF war diary, 11 April 1917, Air 1/1185/204/5/2595; J.S.T. Fall biographical file, DHist.

32. "Some Notes on Officers who served in RFC and RAF Canada," app. D, Allen to Dodds, 5 Dec. 1962, D.L. Allen Papers, DHist 76/199.

33. Letter home, 23 April 1917, L.S. Breadner Papers, DHist 74/707, file 35. Presumably the enemy machine was either a Friedrichshafen G-III or a Gotha G-IV or V. All of these bombers were in service at that time.

34. Ibid.; RFC war diary, 23 April 1917, Air 1/1185/204/5/2595; J.J. Malone biographical file, DHist.

35. "Number of Machines Employed on Each Front and Casualties in France Only," nd, Air 1/516/16/6/1; DHist squadron lists; "Functions and Tactics of German Air Service, Spring of 1917, Particularly During Arras Battle April–May, 1917," [1924], Air 1/9/15/1/22.

36. Canadian Bank of Commerce, *Letters from the Front: Being a Record of the Part Played by Officers of the Bank in the Great War, 1914–1919*, ed. C.L. Foster and W.S. Duthie, vol. 1 (Toronto, 1921), 210.

37. Edmonds, *Military Operations: France and Belgium, 1917*, vol. 2 (London,

1948), 42, 93–94; Trenchard to Advanced GHQ, proposals for organizational changes, 9 May 1917, Air 1/1008/204/5/1283; Jones, *War in the Air*, vol. 4 (London, 1934), 111–13, app. 3. See also Sir Gordon Taylor, *Sopwith Scout 7309* (London, 1968), 103–18.

38. II Brigade work summary, 6–7 June 1917, Air 1/768/204/4/254; Jones, *War in the Air*, 4:114–15, 118. Jones, *War in the Air*, 4:119, states that until 7 June no artillery planes were shot down. Since the RE8 in which Baylis was flying was reported missing on the evening of 6 June, after the day's entry had been made in the Squadron Record Book, the casualty was counted as occurring on 7 June.

39. Correspondence and instructions on wireless intelligence of hostile aircraft, 24 Oct. 1916–25 May 1917, Air 1/526/16/12/38.

40. Scott, *Sixty Squadron RAF*, 59.

41. Ibid., 58–59; Jones, *War in the Air*, 4:119–20.

42. G.W.L. Nicholson, *Official History of the Canadian Army in the First World War: Canadian Expeditionary Force, 1914–1919* (Ottawa: Queen's Printer, 1962), 302; Taylor, *Sopwith Scout*, 111; Edmonds, *Military Operations: France and Belgium, 1917*, 2:41, 43–49, 55.

43. Edmonds, *Military Operations: France and Belgium, 1917*, 2:70; "Resumé of the Wireless Organization of the 2nd Wing, RFC Previous to and During the Offensive Operations of the Second Army in June, 1917," 11 June 1917, Air 1/1007/204/5/1271; II Brigade work summary, 6–7 June 1917, Air 1/768/204/4/254; 42 Squadron air combat report, 7 June 1917, Air 1/1222/204/5/2634/42; Jones, *War in the Air*, 3:310, 410, 413; Maurice Baring, *Flying Corps Headquarters, 1914–1918* (London, 1968), 228.

44. DHist squadron lists.

45. "B" Flight was nick-named "Black" Flight because the engine cowlings and top and side fuselage panels were painted black to enable the flight mechanics to recognize their

own aircraft and go immediately to their assistance as they returned from patrol. "A" and "C" Flights used red and blue colour schemes respectively to identify their aircraft. Raymond Collishaw with R.V. Dodds, *Air Command: A Fighter Pilot's Story* (London, 1973), 81.

46. R.V. Dodds, historical sketch of 210 Squadron RAF [10 (Naval)], DHist 73/1552; Raymond Collishaw biographical file, DHist; letter to Vice-Admiral Dover Patrol, 19 April 1917, Lambe to RNAS Dunkirk, 16 May 1917, Lambe to Vice-Admiral Dover Patrol, 23 Aug. 1917, Air 1/637/17/122/142.

47. Collishaw's air combats and logbook, Collishaw Papers, DHist 78/132, 1-A, folder 35; RFC communiqué nos. 91–94, June 1917, DHist 75/413.

48. There were no Spad squadrons in II Brigade and the five that joined Collishaw's patrol must have been from 23 Squadron of I Brigade or from a French Squadron.

49. No. 10 (Naval) Squadron air combat report, 17 June 1917, Air 1/1219/204/5/2634/10.

50. DHist squadron lists; Collishaw and Dodds, *Air Command*, 79, 100.

51. William Arthur Bishop, *The Courage of the Early Morning: A Son's Biography of a Famous Father* (Toronto, 1965), 97–100.

52. No. 60 Squadron air combat report, 2 June 1917, Air 1/1225/204/5/2634/60.

53. The location of the airfield Bishop attacked has never been definitively established. Arthur Bishop identified Estourmel as the airfield attacked, on the basis of his father's recollections and a study of the ground. Bishop, *The Courage of the Early Morning*, 100. The combat report gives the location as "either Esnes Aerodrome or Awoignt," but by Bishop's own admission he didn't know where he was. All three airfields were clustered within a few miles of each other southeast of Cambrai.

54. No. 60 Squadron air combat report, 2 June 1917, Air 1/1225/204/5/2634/60; William Frye, *Air of Battle* (London, 1974), 136.

55. Jones, *War in the Air*, 4:129–30.

56. "This must surely be a very unusual case of a Victoria Cross or any high honour being awarded on the word of the recipient only as to his exploit and without any witnesses or participants. Our CO knew Bishop so well as to believe in him implicitly, as did the whole squadron and higher authority." Frye, *Air of Battle*, 136.

57. M.P.A. Hankey, 1st Baron Hankey, *The Supreme Command, 1914–1918*, vol. 2 (London, 1961), 677–80.

58. Ibid., 683; Edmonds, *Military Operations: France and Belgium, 1917*, 2:124.

59. Edmonds, *Military Operations: France and Belgium, 1917*, 2:133–34; V Brigade order, 8 July 1917, Air 1/1592/204/83/17; Jones, *War in the Air*, 4:145, 148.

60. Jones, *War in the Air*, 4:141, 418; Edmonds, *Military Operations: France and Belgium, 1917*, 2:134.

61. Bruce, *British Aeroplanes*, 126–30.

62. Ibid., 445–55. As well as engine problems, the SE5 had initial difficulties with the synchronizing gear. In a letter home on 22 July W.A. Bishop wrote: "Yesterday we did our first jobs on S.E. 5s and my gun was the only one that fired. It shot holes through my propellor." Nevertheless, the strength, speed, and firepower of the aircraft was ideally suited to Bishop's heavy-handed flying and his tactical approach; he himself soon termed the SE5 "the best machine in the world." In a period from 28 July to 16 August, when he was taken off operations, Bishop and his SE5 were credited with bringing down eleven aircraft, nine of them Albatros fighters. This brought his score to forty-seven. See Bishop biographical file, DHist.

63. Bruce, *British Aeroplanes*, 573–76; Peter Gray and Owen Thetford,

German Aircraft of the First World War (London, 1962), xxx, 52–55.

64. Raymond Collishaw's Staff College essay, 23 Sept. 1924, Air 1/2387/228/11/40; Bruce Robertson, ed., *Von Richthofen and the Flying Circus* (Letchworth, Herts., 1959), 64–65; Karl Bodenschatz, *Jagd in Flanderns Himmel* (München, 1942), 13–14; Norman Macmillan, *Into the Blue* (London, 1969), 125.

65. Macmillan, *Into the Blue*, 125–26.

66. "Enemy planes visited us that week. . . . We looked up to see not one visitor but a fleet of them, great bombers riding the skies in battle formation. There were twenty-four of them, flying in perfect order and making straight for us. . . . Then there was a soft whirring noise and the first bomb fell with a thud and crash of flame. Then came the deluge—CRASH! CRASH! CRASH!—down they came, thick and fast." Aubrey Wade, *Gunner on the Western Front* (London, 1959), 85.

67. Arthur Gould Lee, *Open Cockpit: A Pilot of the Royal Flying Corps* (London, 1969), 91–92.

68. Extracts from III Brigade war diary, June and July 1917, V Brigade war diary, July 1917, Air 1/721/48/2; H.E. Creagan, "W.M. Alexander of Black Flight, Naval 10," *CAHS Journal* 3 (Fall 1965), 64.

69. The commander of this all-Canadian flight, Raymond Collishaw, with twenty-seven victories to his credit by 5 July, added ten more to his score and was shot down himself twice in three days before going on two months well-earned leave in early August. "Pilots soon wear out as such," recorded General Trenchard on 30 August 1917 when offering GHQ some points concerning the formation of a separate air service. "There are not enough ground billets for all worn out pilots. Arrangements should be made for them to be received into the Army or the Navy if they desire such employment." Air 1/521/16/12/3.

70. Brigadier-General Commanding V Brigade to 15 and 22 Wings, 24 July 1917, Air 1/1592/204/83/17; Jones, *War in the Air*, 4:157; Hans Arndt, "Die Fliegerwaffe," in F. Seesselberg, *Der Stellungskrieg, 1914–1918* (Berlin, 1926), 339–40, 342, DHist SGR I 196, Set 88.

71. Translation of "weekly intelligence summary of the German Fourth Army," 12–18 July 1917, DHist SS 582; G.S.B. Fuller, "Reminiscences of Lieut. G.S.B. Fuller, No. 9 Sqdn., RFC," *Cross and Cockade Journal* 10 (Spring 1969), 41.

72. Jones, *War in the Air*, 4:161–62; John Charteris, *At G.H.Q.* (London, 1931), 238.

73. H. von Bülow, *Geschichte der Luftwaffe* (Frankfurt, 1937), 95; Arndt, "Die Fliegerwaffe," 343–46, sketches 225a and b.

74. Douglas Haig, 1st Earl Haig, *Sir Douglas Haig's Despatches*, ed. J.H. Boraston (London, 1919), 116.

HARD LUCK FLOTILLA: THE RCN'S ATLANTIC COAST PATROL, 1914-1918 ⋄

ROGER SARTY

○

In 1918 the Royal Canadian Navy—a tiny service that had nearly been scuttled by political controversy—suddenly had to protect Canada's waters against raids by three large U-boats. The events of these difficult months have been virtually forgotten. Most strikingly, they are not mentioned in the official history of the naval service.[1] It was an experience that senior Canadian sailors preferred not to dwell on, for although the flotilla that was hastily assembled kept losses of merchant vessels to a minimum, individual officers and ships performed very poorly at critical junctures. Much of the fault lay with the virtual absence of thoroughly trained sea-going personnel, suitable vessels, and shore bases to support them. Yet British and Canadian officers had pressed the Canadian government to establish an appropriate naval organization on the east coast for nearly a decade before the outbreak of war, and that made the legacy more bitter still. Paradoxically, in 1917–18, when Sir Robert Borden was asserting national control over the Canadian army fighting in Europe, the defence of the Dominion's home waters depended upon the meagre resources Great Britain and the United States chose to provide.

Prior to the First World War no one, aside from a few imaginative individuals like H.G. Wells and Admiral Sir John Fisher, anticipated that submarines would prove to be a decisive weapon against merchant shipping. The British Admiralty's great fear was that fast enemy cruisers or armed merchant ships would evade the Royal Navy's squadrons to strike at the Empire's trade and ports, much as Confederate warships like the CSS *Alabama* had done in the face of overwhelming United States naval superiority during the American Civil War. It was against this threat that Great

⋄ From *The RCN in Transition, 1910–1985*, ed. W.A.B. Douglas (Vancouver: The University of British Columbia Press, 1988), 103–25.

Britain repeatedly advised Canada to develop naval defences, but these would have been equally effective against the U-boats that arrived off Nova Scotia in 1918.[2]

Britain threw the whole of the responsibility for local Canadian naval defence onto the Dominion government in 1904–1906 with the closure of the dockyards at Halifax and Esquimalt, the withdrawal of the army garrisons from these fortified ports, and the reduction of the North America and West Indies squadron to a single cruiser based on Bermuda. The government of Sir Wilfrid Laurier immediately provided Canadian troops for the fortresses, but both British services advised this was not enough. Modern torpedo craft—torpedo boats, destroyers (in effect, large torpedo boats) and submarines—were now an indispensible adjunct to fortifications on shore. These relatively economical vessels would at least provide an early warning of an attack, and might effectively counter raids on shipping or coastlines a hundred miles or more beyond the range of coast artillery.[3]

The Laurier government would have been content to organize such a coast defence flotilla when it founded the naval service in 1910. Under pressure from the Admiralty, which also wanted support on the critical north Atlantic shipping routes, the Canadians agreed to do considerably more. The programme of 1910 included not only six large destroyers, but four light cruisers for trade defence on the high seas.[4] Robert Borden's cancellation of this programme when his Conservative government came to power in 1911, and his attempts to provide more direct support for the Royal Navy in the form of financial grants for the construction of dreadnoughts, are famous events in Canadian political history. Less well known is that in 1912 the Admiralty advised that Canada should also carry on with a version of the Laurier fleet for trade and coast defence. Forces required for the local protection of the Halifax approaches and the Gulf of St. Lawrence included a small cruiser, 18 torpedo boats and a dozen submarines. In June 1914 the prime minister responded to efforts by the Admiralty and the Canadian naval staff to revive these proposals with a note that he would not have time to look at the papers for a few weeks. By then it was too late.[5]

When war broke out the RCN was incapable of undertaking a seagoing role. The total strength of the service was only 350 regular personnel and the 250 slightly trained members of the Royal Naval Canadian Volunteer Reserve (RNCVR). Resources on the east coast amounted to the old cruiser, *Niobe*, for which an adequate crew could not be mustered, and the small, out-dated and poorly maintained dockyard at Halifax. The Canadian government placed *Niobe* under British control; the Royal Navy completed the crew and she put to sea with the North America and West Indies squadron, now expanded to about a dozen cruisers. With a handful of small vessels borrowed from other government departments and chartered from commercial firms, the RCN was only able to examine merchant ships entering Halifax, sweep the harbour's immediate approaches for mines that might have been dropped by German raiders, and mount the occasional lookout patrol along the coast of Nova Scotia. Even these services could not be properly carried out.[6]

At the urging of the Canadian naval staff and the British commander-in-chief of the North America and West Indies Station, Borden began to press the need for destroyers and submarines on the Admiralty in November 1914. He wanted to build the warships in Canada, and borrow others from the Royal Navy in the meantime. The success of U-boats against merchant shipping during the first half of 1915, and persistent intelligence from German circles in the United States that the campaign would soon extend across the Atlantic, seemed to strengthen Borden's case. These would be excellent anti-submarine vessels; the commander-in-chief warned that his unmanoeuvrable cruisers could only run for cover in the face of U-boat attacks.[7]

The Admiralty held to the opinion Winston Churchill, the First Lord, had given in October 1914: Canada should restrict her effort to the raising of land forces.[8] No torpedo craft could be spared from European waters, and production in Canada was not practicable because armament, specialized equipment and skilled manpower would have to be obtained in the United Kingdom, thereby disrupting British shipbuilding. In any case, the U-boat threat to Canada was potential rather than actual; the only immediate requirement was for coastal patrols to ensure that German agents or sympathizers did not establish fuel caches in isolated areas to support long-range submarine operations. During the summer of 1915 the RCN accordingly established the Gulf of St. Lawrence patrol, which normally included seven ships that had been obtained by purchasing private yachts in the United States and borrowing additional vessels from other departments. Operating from an improvised base at Sydney during the navigation season, the force returned to Halifax during the winter months.[9]

It seemed that the RCN's major contribution would be the supply of personnel to the British service. In 1916 the overseas division of the RNCVR was organized; by the spring of the following year nearly twelve hundred recruits, most of them with seafaring backgrounds, had been sent to the United Kingdom. By that time, too, some forty-seven RCN officers were serving with the Royal Navy, including the best of the young officers in the service.[10]

Events in late 1916 and early 1917 thrust much larger responsibilities on the RCN. Germany commenced a renewed U-boat offensive to cut the Atlantic shipping lanes that sustained the Allied war effort with men and materiel; intensified with the declaration of "unrestricted submarine warfare" on 31 January 1917, the campaign nearly succeeded. Visits to the United States by the merchant submarine *Deutschland* in July and November 1916 proclaimed the trans-Atlantic capability of the U-boat arm. More disturbing were the exploits of the fighting boat U-53 which on 7 October 1916 appeared at Newport, Rhode Island, cast off without refuelling, and sank five Allied merchant ships off Nantucket the next day. In November the Admiralty informed the Canadian government that its flotilla of twelve vessels should be tripled in size, but the only assistance the Royal Navy could offer would be the services of an experienced officer to organize and command the expanded patrol. During the 1917 shipping season purchases of civilian vessels and further transfers of other Canadian government ships increased the strength of the patrols to about twenty-two vessels. Early in

February the government had also placed orders with Polsons in Toronto and Canadian Vickers in Montreal for the construction of twelve trawlers.[11]

Much larger shipbuilding orders came from the Admiralty that same month. Possibly influenced by bitter Canadian remonstrances that the Dominion was being asked greatly to increase its anti-submarine effort after Great Britain had drained the country of suitable ships and men and refused to sanction warship construction in Canadian yards, the Admiralty asked Ottawa to place contracts for thirty-six steel trawlers and one hundred wooden drifters. Orders were accordingly given to shipyards on the St. Lawrence and Great Lakes. Although the vessels were being built at British expense, the Admiralty suggested rather obliquely that they would be used on Canada's Atlantic coast. Confusion on this point in Ottawa bred a good deal of correspondence and discussion in which the Admiralty left open the possibility that the vessels might have to be used elsewhere. This was reasonable in view of the gravity of the crisis the Royal Navy faced in European waters, but created serious difficulties for the RCN in planning for the expansion of the Canadian patrols. In July 1917, the Admiralty asked Ottawa to place orders for a further twenty-four trawlers. Unlike the twelve Canadian trawlers, which were named for battles of the war (*Arras, Arleux*, and so forth), the vessels building on imperial account were merely numbered, 1–60 in the case of the trawlers, and 1–100 for the drifters.[12]

Although a large number of anti-submarine vessels were now building in Canadian yards, these were modest craft. The trawlers measured about 130 feet in length and displaced 130–140 tons; they mounted a single 12-pounder gun, and could make a speed of ten knots. The wooden drifters were only 84 feet in length, carried a 6-pounder, and could move at no more than nine knots. In fact, the most capable of the Canadian vessels were seven "auxiliary patrol ships" (*Canada, Cartier, Acadia, Hochelaga, Lady Evelyn, Margaret*, and *Stadacona*) acquired in 1915 and 1917 from other government departments and through the purchase of yachts in the United States. Good sea boats, each of these vessels displaced from 700 to 1050 tons, measured 170 to 210 feet in length, and could make from eleven to sixteen knots. All ultimately carried at least two 12-pounder guns; four of the vessels mounted a single 4-inch, albeit not of the latest and most powerful type. Normally operating out of Sydney in the Gulf and in the waters to the south of Newfoundland, they formed the backbone of the Canadian patrols until the end of the war.[13]

While the Canadian government struggled to expand the Atlantic coast patrols, the U-boat crisis of 1917 was reshaping naval operations in North American waters. On 6 April the United States declared war on Germany as a direct result of U-boat attacks on American shipping. Having no idea of how close the U-boats were to winning the battle on the shipping lanes, the United States Navy had made no special effort to expand its anti-submarine forces. On learning from the Admiralty of the desperate state of affairs in European waters, the American navy department began to send overseas every suitable vessel that could be spared. Thus, although the Canadian government hoped that the Americans could offer substantial assistance in patrolling off the southern tip of Nova Scotia and in the Bay of Fundy, the Navy Department was only willing to undertake occasional visits with larger ships to the deep waters off the Bay of Fundy.[14]

So severe were Allied shipping losses at the time of the American entry into the war, that the Admiralty soon decided to sail merchantmen in defended convoys. This ancient method was thought to have been impracticable or even suicidal with modern steamships, but it proved to be the key to victory. Trans-Atlantic convoys began to sail from Hampton Roads, Virginia, New York City, and Sydney, Nova Scotia, in July 1917. As the system developed, the Sydney convoys, known as the HS series, were reserved for slow cargo carrying vessels from Canadian and American ports. In September the HX series of fast troopships and merchantmen started to sail from Halifax. A reorganization of the convoy system in March 1918 transferred the HX series to New York, and instituted the HC series, for troopships and cargo vessels of medium speed ($11\frac{1}{2}$ knots), from Halifax. Meanwhile, with the freeze-up of the St. Lawrence in December 1917, the HS series had assembled at Halifax, until navigation opened again at Sydney in July 1918. British and American cruisers escorted the convoys through their entire passage to guard against the ever-present danger of German surface warships breaking out of the North Sea; anti-submarine vessels joined as the convoys approached the zone of intense U-boat operations off Britain and the west coast of France.[15]

Successful as the convoy system proved to be, it did inject yet another naval authority into the already confused organization on the Canadian east coast. Rear Admiral B.M. Chambers, RN, and his staff arrived at Sydney in August 1917 to organize the Canadian convoys; Chambers reported directly to the Admiralty. Control of all other shipping that sailed from Canadian ports was, however, under Canadian naval staffs at Montreal, Quebec, Saint John, New Brunswick, Sydney, and Halifax that reported to naval headquarters in Ottawa. In charge of the establishments at Halifax, and the local naval defences of the port to a distance of about ten miles from the harbour mouth, was the superintendent of HMC Dockyard, who also reported to naval headquarters. From December 1917 the appointment was held by Vice-Admiral W.O. Story, RN (retired), an employee of the Canadian government. The patrols organization based at Sydney was another separate command, directly under naval headquarters; the division of responsibility between the patrols and Admiral Story for the seaward defence of Halifax became a source of continuing controversy as the Canadian flotilla began to expand in 1917.

Co-ordination of the many authorities at convoy ports in both Canada and the United States fell to the commander-in-chief North America and West Indies, Vice-Admiral M.E. Browning who was succeeded by Vice-Admiral W.L. Grant in February 1918. It was an enormous task, and an extremely frustrating one because the commander-in-chief's power of command was restricted to British warships operating in the western Atlantic and the Royal Navy's base at Bermuda. Although Browning and Grant were normally at Washington liaising with the Navy Department, they both visited Halifax and Ottawa regularly. On many of the most important questions they, rather than Admiral C.E. Kingsmill, director of the Canadian naval service, acted as the senior naval advisors to the Canadian government.[16]

Much less successful was the officer sent out by the Admiralty in March 1917 to command and reorganize the Canadian patrols. Earlier in the war Vice-Admiral Sir Charles H. Coke had flown his flag at Queenstown on the coast of southern Ireland; he appears to have been remembered primarily for the fact that *Lusitania* was lost within his command. Having accepted the rank of commodore second class for the Canadian appointment, he nevertheless behaved as if he were the senior admiral of the RCN, interfering in a wide range of matters outside of his mandate, and giving little attention to the questions he had been hired to tackle. In June the Admiralty agreed to recall Coke, observing that "his advancing age has seriously told on him."[17]

The commodore's departure did not immediately improve understanding between London and Ottawa. In July, naval headquarters concurred in the selection of Captain J.O. Hatcher, RN, as Coke's successor, and at the end of the month the Admiralty appointed him "Captain in charge of Patrols." Kingsmill, however, in an obscurely phrased cable, had left open the question of whether Hatcher would actually command or merely assist with the organization of the patrol. While Hatcher was on passage, naval headquarters appointed Captain Walter Hose, RCN, to the patrols command. Greeted with this development on his arrival, the British officer nevertheless agreed to serve as an advisor, and set to work on a plan for the employment of the trawlers and drifters building on Imperial account.[18]

In September the Admiralty threw a spanner into the works, announcing that the first sixteen trawlers and fifty drifters completed would be employed overseas. Hose, who misunderstood the function of drifters, believed that the remaining fifty vessels of that type would be too few in number to do anything useful and should be offered to the Admiralty in return for some additional trawlers. Hatcher and the commander-in-chief disagreed, but Kingsmill supported Hose. Whatever the merits of the technical argument, Kingsmill realized that planning was futile until the Admiralty made a firm allocation of vessels. In November the Department of the Naval Service asked the Admiralty for a statement of the specific threat to Canadian waters and for "some definite scheme" of defence.[19]

The Admiralty responded, on 3 January 1918, with a paper that became the blueprint for the development of the Atlantic coast patrols until the end of the war. "It is considered very probable," their Lordships wrote, "that an attack by one of the new submarine cruisers may be expected at any time after March. . . . Whether in the future more than one submarine or not operates on the Canadian coast at a time, the measures necessary to protect shipping will be the same, based on the assumption that at any moment one submarine may be in a position to attack every outgoing convoy." Because mines were an uneconomic load for submarines crossing the Atlantic, the most likely form of attack would be by torpedoes and deck guns. Minelaying by surface raiders was only a "possibility," although one that had to be guarded against.[20]

This appreciation was the basis for a fundamental recasting of the operations of the Atlantic patrols. Both the Hatcher and Hose schemes had merely strengthened the forces allocated to the flotilla's existing tasks: protection of the approaches to Sydney and Halifax, and the maintenance of a watch along the shores of the Maritimes and Gulf of St. Lawrence. Intensified coastal patrols would not be very useful, the Admiralty advised. Additional ships should instead be concentrated at Halifax and Sydney where their principal role would be to screen convoys as they formed up, and provide an anti-submarine escort during the first hours of passage. As well, separate escort forces would be required to provide two anti-submarine vessels for the protection of each convoy out to a distance of 200–300 miles. Finally the St. Lawrence patrol should be strengthened so that it could also serve as a mobile striking force, "available to be sent anywhere." In February Hose drafted a detailed scheme that, closely following the Admiralty's paper, allocated thirty-three vessels to Halifax for escort and local defence duties, forty-six to Sydney for the same tasks, and thirty-one to the St. Lawrence force, also based on Sydney. The Admiralty and the Canadian government readily approved these proposals.[21]

The appeal to London had had the desired result of bringing a more generous and well-considered allocation of resources to the Canadian patrols. The Admiralty was now willing to turn over all thirty-six of the first batch of trawlers building in Canada on imperial account, and thirty-six of the drifters. Before the close of navigation on the St. Lawrence at the end of 1917, the first three Admiralty trawlers and thirty-eight drifters had arrived at Halifax. Fifteen drifters departed for imperial service, but the other vessels joined the Canadian patrol.[22]

Manpower inevitably created difficulties. About 2300 personnel, it was estimated early in 1918, would be needed for the ships and bases of the expanded flotilla; slightly over 1500 were then available. Arrangements by the Admiralty to man the imperial trawlers and drifters slated for Canadian service provided essential reinforcements. At least 230 and perhaps as many as 330 ratings from the Newfoundland Royal Naval Reserve ultimately served in the vessels, as did some 200 members of the RNCVR's Overseas Division who were returned from the United Kingdom. That still left a substantial shortage, especially for billets that demanded experience and extensive training. The Admiralty admitted a moral responsibility to give further help, but could spare a very limited number of officers and technical ratings. In February 1918, for example, the Canadians asked for 25 skippers to command patrol vessels and 100 engine specialists; the British could offer only 4 of the former and 28 of the latter. There was no alternative but to place unqualified personnel in key positions and rush recent recruits into service.[23]

Finding the faster and more heavily armed warships needed to protect shipping and chase down U-boats beyond the reach of the local defence flotillas at Halifax and Sydney was an insuperable problem. The Admiralty's scheme included six sloops or destroyers and six "fast trawlers" (probably P-boats with a speed of twenty knots and modern 4-inch guns) to form the bulk of the long-range escort forces and the striking group of the

St. Lawrence patrol. In March word came from London that fast trawlers could not be provided for "some months" owing to delays in the construction programme, and that no destroyers could be spared; Canada should, therefore, appeal to the United States Navy for assistance. The commander-in-chief was in a difficult position: for the past year the British government had been minimizing the threat to the western Atlantic while urging the United States to send its best anti-submarine vessels overseas. On pointing this out to the Admiralty, he received the distinctly unhelpful reply that "there is no intention to propose any alteration in policy." Admiral Grant responded that he could not but "concur in the view generally expressed this side that we are very open to a sudden attack and sinkings possibly of large troop transports and am afraid that this would very probably cause great popular commotion in Canada and the United States."[24] Captain Hose was more blunt. Without the destroyers or fast trawlers there would be "not one gun" in his force "which would be able to get within range of a U-cruiser before the patrol vessel would, in all probability, be sunk."[25]

Plans for the RCN's submarines, CC-1 and CC-2, to reinforce the east coast patrols came to naught. The British Columbia government had purchased these American H class boats from their Seattle builders at the outbreak of war, and turned them over to the navy for operations from Esquimalt. In the spring of 1917 the Canadian government complied with the Admiralty's request that the vessels go overseas where they would be much more useful than in British Columbia. The submarines arrived at Halifax, with their tender, HMCS *Shearwater*, in the fall of 1917 after a harrowing trip by way of the Panama Canal during which their machinery repeatedly broke down. Once the vessels were refitted, the Admiralty now suggested, they should remain on the Canadian coast because of the growing danger of trans-Atlantic U-boat raids. Poorly equipped and swamped with work, the ship repair facilities at Halifax were unable to make the boats fully operational, however. Their principal emloyment was for anti-submarine exercises with patrol vessels on the Bras d'Or Lakes beginning in August 1918.[26]

Air patrols were another method of dealing with U-boats. Although effective aerial anti-submarine weapons had not yet been developed, aircraft had afforded nearly perfect protection to convoys they accompanied as escorts. U-boats inevitably submerged in the presence of aircraft, whose crews might score a lucky bomb hit, or would most certainly summon anti-submarine warships. Unable to move at a speed of more than a few knots while submerged, the U-boat soon lost contact with the shipping it was pursuing and had no opportunity to attack. On 7 March the Admiralty urged the Canadian government to organize an air service on the Atlantic coast as soon as possible, but could offer no equipment of any type.[27]

With Canadian complaints about the lack of British help ringing in his ears, Admiral Grant appealed to the United States Navy in mid-April. Destroyers could not be spared but the Americans were prepared to send six submarine chasers and two torpedo boats, all fully manned, for operations under Canadian control. Grant also arranged meetings between American, British, and Canadian officers at Washington on 20 April, and

Boston on 23 April to secure further help for the RCN. Rear-Admiral Spencer S. Wood, commandant of the 1st Naval District at Boston, agreed that his forces would assume full responsibility for both sea and coastal patrols as far as the 65th meridian, (Lockeport, Nova Scotia), including the mouth of the Bay of Fundy. The Americans would also supply aircraft and personnel for Halifax and Sydney, while the Canadian Naval Air Service organized. Captain Hose brightened, believing that the aircraft would provide the offensive power his little ships lacked, but it soon emerged that the USN could not make good on the offer until mid-August.[28]

The eight American vessels arrived at Halifax during the latter part of May. Although the two old torpedo boats, *Tingey* and *DeLong*, were suitable only for patrols close in to port, the submarine chasers proved to be extremely useful. Their 110-foot long wooden hulls carried powerful engines that delivered an impressive speed of sixteen knots. For that reason, they were employed as the long-range escort force; three of the vessels moved to Sydney when the HS series began to sail from that port again at the beginning of July. Their armament, however, was light, including six depth charges and only a single 6-pounder gun.[29]

During May as well, the delivery of additional drifters and trawlers began as the ice cleared from the St. Lawrence. By the end of July the last of the thirty-six drifters from imperial contracts and all but three of the forty-eight trawlers from Canadian and imperial orders had arrived on the east coast. About sixty vessels were based at Sydney, including those allocated to the St. Lawrence patrol, and forty at Halifax. But grand totals can be deceptive. Most of the trawlers and drifters had only recently been commissioned, and their machinery needed a good deal of "shaking down" before it could be depended upon. Hasty construction under wartime conditions had also taken a toll; five of the named trawlers, for example, experienced such chronic engine trouble they were seldom sent on patrol. The Admiralty, moreover, had not yet delivered guns to arm several of the trawlers. Most seriously, ships' companies throughout the flotilla included a large proportion of personnel with little training.[30]

Progress was being made, however, in the fitting of depth charges and hydrophones. In February, 140 depth charges had been on hand, and a further 700 were ordered. These were issued on a scale of 6 per auxiliary patrol ship and 5 for each trawler and drifter. It appears that additional charges were carried as they became available; in mid-June, for example, *Trawler 30* stowed a total of 10, while a later report shows that *Cartier* had 8. In early 1918 there had been 27 non-directional "general service hydrophones" available on the east coast, and orders had been placed in England for the more capable Mark II directional hydrophones. In mid-August, the latter equipment had already been installed on five vessels and was being fitted in at least three others.[31]

Slight as was the material help available from the United Kingdom, the Admiralty was able to give full and timely intelligence about trans-Atlantic U-boat operations through the interception and decryption of German wireless traffic. The information was supplied to the United States Navy through Rear-Admiral W.S. Sims, commander of American naval forces in

Europe, and by cable to the commander-in-chief North America and West Indies who passed it by telegraph to Canadian authorities.

On 3 and 16 May the first intelligence reached the Canadian service: a U-boat had sailed from Germany about 19 April to strike at shipping off United States ports and could be expected at any time after 20 May. The boat was a converted mercantile submarine of the *Deutschland* class: the new long-range types of which the Admiralty had warned the Canadian government in January were still incomplete. Earlier operations by the *Deutschlands* showed that because their lightly built hulls were more vulnerable to depth charges than those of fighting boats, they were less likely to make submerged attacks or strike at convoys. However, the converted merchantman had a formidable gun armament, including two 5.9-inch, for surface operations, and carried about forty mines.[32]

The campaign in the western Atlantic opened, as the Admiralty had warned, on 25 May when U-151 attacked three American schooners south of the Delaware. By 23 June, when the submarine was homebound, she had destroyed twenty-two vessels of some fifty-two thousand tons off the central Atlantic states. This cruise set the pattern for U-boat operations in North American waters during the rest of the 1918 season. The boat made no attacks on escorted shipping, and reserved her torpedoes for submerged attacks on large steamers that carried defensive armament. Otherwise the submariners sank their victims with gunfire, or boarded vessels and placed time-fused charges. Perhaps the most notable victory, however, was the destruction of the tanker *Herbert L. Pratt* which on 3 June ran into a minefield the submarine had laid off the mouth of Delaware Bay.[33]

By the end of June the Admiralty knew that another converted mercantile submarine, U-156, was on her way to North American waters. Within a week German wireless traffic revealed that the recently completed "cruiser" U-140 was following her.[34] Precisely where the boats would operate was not yet clear, but the Admiralty asked Admiral Grant what could be done if the Halifax approaches came under attack. Grant replied that although the 1st US Naval District was prepared to reinforce the Canadian patrols, the force would still be too weak to prevent a U-boat from operating close in to the port, or to provide convoys with long-range anti-submarine escorts. Ships en route to Halifax for convoy should be redirected to New York, the New England ports, and to Sydney. This proposal was related to a larger scheme for diverting shipping from threatened ports, but Grant was particularly worried about Halifax. The lightness of the forces there created special dangers because the troopships that sailed from the port were very desirable targets, and the great width of the continental shelf off that part of Nova Scotia made it possible for the enemy to plant mines up to 130 miles from the harbour mouth.[35]

As Grant considered the Halifax problem, U-156 was approaching American waters. On 7–8 July she destroyed two large sailing vessels some four hundred miles southeast of Sable Island. Running in along forty degrees latitude, U-156 then laid mines near the Fire Island light vessel. During the late morning of 19 July the 13 000-ton cruiser USS *San Diego* struck one of the mines and sank in twenty minutes with the loss of six of her crew. Two days later, the submarine came out of a fog bank within sight of vacationers on the beaches of southeastern Cape Cod and bombarded a tug and four barges under tow.

The first warning that U-boats would soon strike further north appears to have reached Canadian naval authorities on 26 July. Instructions for U-156 to operate in the Gulf of Maine had been decrypted at the Admiralty, but the news was not timely: on 27 July headquarters learned that the boat had already sunk an American schooner there five days before. The Admiralty also passed word that another U-boat had been assigned to the Gulf of Maine. This was derived from the earliest intelligence that yet a third submarine, the large purpose-built minelayer U-117, had been assigned to North American waters; U-140 was at the time approaching the central Atlantic states, the area to which she confined her operations. On 2 August, the Canadian shipping control and intelligence staff at Halifax broadcast a warning to all vessels that U-boats might be encountered anywhere between the latitudes of Cape Hatteras and Halifax.[36]

The danger to Canadian waters materialized very quickly. After sunrise on 3 August the crew of the four-master schooner *Dornfontein* came ashore in lifeboats at Gannet Rock at the mouth of the Bay of Fundy, with the news their ship had been stopped and set afire by U-156 the day before. The trawler *Festubert*, then at Saint John, proceeded to search the area, but found no trace of the submarine.[37] By that time U-156 was east of Seal Island, off the southern tip of Nova Scotia, where she set charges in four small American fishing schooners. The next day, the submarine destroyed the Canadian schooner *Nelson A.* twenty-five miles off Shelburne, and on the morning of 5 August, bombed the schooners *Agnes B. Holland* and *Gladys M. Hollett* near the Lahave Banks. Like the *Dornfontein*, none of these vessels was equipped with wireless, so word of the sinkings did not reach Halifax until the crews rowed to shore and notified authorities, at least twelve hours after the event.[38]

While U-156 advanced along the south shore of Nova Scotia, the flotilla at Halifax was hard pressed to carry out its basic mission of convoy escort and patrol in the harbour approaches. Engine defects had laid up five vessels in addition to those undergoing long-term refits and routine maintenance, while guns had not yet arrived to arm two of the recently delivered trawlers. When convoy HC-12 sailed in the early afternoon of 4 August, therefore, the warships available for service were fully occupied in providing the routine protecton laid down in standing orders; under the charge of the flotilla were seventeen merchantmen laden with cargo and over 12 500 Canadian and American troops.[39]

In the morning the minesweeping division had swept to about fifty miles beyond the harbour mouth. Following were the three American submarine chasers who preceded the convoy by two hours to make an anti-submarine patrol. Sailing with the convoy was the "forming up escort and outer patrol force," which was organized in three divisions, each including one trawler and two drifters (there was probably a second trawler in one division). As the submarine chasers took over the van outside the harbour, the trawlers and drifters did their best to remain in company until dusk, but must have fallen back as their patrol speed was only eight knots. One division then returned to port, while the others cruised in the outer patrol areas, one towards Shelburne and the other towards Sable Island.

Next morning, shortly after sunrise on the fifth, the British tanker *Luz Blanca* left port bound for Mexico. Her master had ignored instructions from the shipping control staff to wait until dusk and to zig zag. At 1140, local time, when the ship was about thirty-five miles south of the Sambro light vessel, a heavy explosion shook the after section. One tank flooded, but she was still able to make way and turned for port. Twenty minutes later U-156 broke the surface, but then apparently dived. At 1400 the submarine reappeared and opened gunfire at a range of approximately four miles. The ship's RNR gun crew gamely returned fire, even though the torpedo hit had damaged the training gear on their 12-pounder. During the gun battle, which lasted for a full hour, the tanker sustained at least two serious hits, one of which wrecked the lower bridge, killing two crew members; the other stopped her screw and settled the issue. At about 1500 the crew took to the boats, while U-156 continued to shell the hulk which soon burst into flames. The ship was then seventeen miles south of the Sambro light vessel.[40]

Word of the attack was first received at HMC Dockyard shortly before 1345. (*Luz Blanca's* wireless had been damaged in the torpedo explosion; the message presumably came from the American steamer *F.Q. Barstow* who was within visual distance of the attack.) Commander P.F. Newcombe, RN, who commanded the patrol depot at Halifax and, under Hose's direction, exercised operational control over the outer patrol and escort vessels, had the information broadcast to the trawler-drifter division still at sea, the USS *Tingey*, then on the inner patrol, and the submarine chasers who were returning from HC-12 (one of these, SC-247, was short of fuel and had returned to port). *Tingey* was closest to the scene, but did not receive the wireless broadcasts until 1630 (wireless procedures throughout the flotilla showed up badly that day). The trawler-drifter division, on the other hand, responded promptly to the first signals. These vessels should have arrived while U-156 was still on the surface, but did not find anything in the hazy, thick weather. Newcombe subsequently blamed the division's senior officer for the failure. Thus it was the submarine chasers which were first on the scene, apparently at about 1700. They picked up two boatloads of survivors, and made a hydrophone search for U-156 without result. Meanwhile, Newcombe hustled SC-247 and the remaining two trawler-drifter divisions back out to sea; he also pulled the trawler *St. Eloi* out of dockyard hands and despatched her. At 2000 these vessels began to scour the vicinity of the attack. By the next morning (6 August 1918) the Halifax ships were making a general search of the Nova Scotia coast in co-operation with two trawler-drifter divisions from Sydney.

Admiral Kingsmill, in Ottawa, soon intervened. A report from Sydney on the sixth revealed that five of the auxiliary patrol ships were engaged in "domestic" tasks, assisting in the removal of cargo from a wrecked merchant ship, carrying coal and supplies to isolated light houses, and inspecting life-saving stations. Naval headquarters instructed Hose to recall the vessels for anti-submarine duty, and asked what special orders he had given on learning of U-156's thrust into Canadian waters. None, came the answer from Sydney, because the standard patrols had been organized expressly to meet this contingency. Kingsmill's reaction has not come to light, but he was obviously unhappy, having already delivered an admonition about the necessity of deploying every vessel possible in an emergency. At the end of the month, headquarters handed virtually complete operational control of the Halifax outer patrol and escort flotilla over to Vice-Admiral Story, superintendent of the dockyard; Commander Newcombe, Hose's subordinate, was now responsible only for training and discipline. This was an attempt to clear up longstanding difficulties created by the muddled lines of authority at Halifax, but events on 5 August undoubtedly contributed to the outcome.[41]

U-156's appearance had the furthest reaching impact on the convoy system. Control over shipping on the coastal routes between Newfoundland, Nova Scotia, the Bay of Fundy, and the Gulf of Maine was greatly tightened; merchant vessels were often gathered into small convoys at Halifax, Sydney, and St. John's under the escort of whatever warships were at hand. Certainly this system was neither rigorously organized nor complete, for the meagre strength of the flotilla made it impossible to maintain a regular schedule of sailings. The surviving logs of the auxiliary patrol ships and trawlers leave no doubt, however, that escort of coastal shipping was a major commitment for the vessels from August 1918 until the end of the war.[42]

Still more important were changes in the trans-Atlantic convoys. Within hours of the attack on *Luz Blanca*, Admiral Grant began to make the diversions he had suggested the previous month. Ships from the St. Lawrence for HC-13, the next medium convoy due to sail, would assemble at Sydney rather than Halifax, while those from American ports would gather at New York. The two sections would then rendezvous at sea, clear of the danger area. Hose scrambled to provide what little protection he could for the ships coming down from Montreal, and the Sydney section sailed on 14 August, only two days later than the normal eight-day cycle. Meanwhile, on 8 August, the Admiralty informed naval headquarters that in future all ships for HC convoys would assemble at Quebec City. Wireless intelligence received that same day that another converted mercantile submarine would soon sail to mine the approaches to Halifax and St. John's, Newfoundland, in mid-September possibly influenced the decision. By 10 August, the Admiralty was also aware that the minelayer U-117 would strike off Halifax and Cape Race after her initial operations in American waters.[43]

Estimates that U-156 was still lurking in the Halifax approaches were wrong. Actually, the U-boat had immediately headed to the southwest and sank the Swedish steamer *Sydland* about 180 miles off Cape Cod on 8 August. British submarine trackers did not correct their appreciation, believing the culprit to be U-117, expected to arrive at this time. U-117 had indeed turned up on schedule, and ran amok among the Georges Bank fishing fleet, about 100 miles from Cape Cod, on 10 August before continuing on to the southwest. Meanwhile U-156 sank two more steamers in American waters before heading back towards Nova Scotia on the homeward leg of her voyage.

Although not as successful as her first sojourn in Canadian waters, U-156's second appearance caused at least as great a stir. During the early hours of 21 August the crew of the steam trawler *Triumph* landed in boats at Canso and told a startling story: the previous day their ship had been overtaken by a U-boat whose commander had put a crew, two light guns, wireless equipment and a supply of bombs aboard the Canadian vessel. Hose despatched three auxiliary patrol ships, two trawlers, and three American submarine chasers from Halifax to search the fishing banks off Canso and warn the fishing fleet there. Submarine chasers and trawlers from Sydney joined the hunt later in the day. Word soon came from the commander-in-chief that an American destroyer and eighteen submarine chasers, promised as reinforcements for Halifax after the sinking of *Luz Blanca*, were on their way and would search east of Nova Scotia during the passage. In addition, the USN despatched two patrol vessels to the Grand Banks.[44]

Triumph had set to work as soon as her new crew ran up the German naval ensign. The trawler and the submarine sank five schooners on 20 August and two on 21 August. Nothing more was heard from the raiders for three days; *Triumph's* coal would have been exhausted in that period and evidence suggests the Germans scuttled her. In the early hours of 25 August U-156 reappeared off the Newfoundland coast, about seventy miles west of St. Pierre where she sank the small British steamer *Erik*. Later that morning the U-boat fell in with a group of four fishing schooners about forty-five miles southwest of St. Pierre and proceeded to sink the vessels with charges.

At about 1345, when U-156 was finishing off the last of the schooners, a Canadian patrol arrived from the northwest. *Trawler 22, Cartier, Hochelaga,* and *Trawler 32* were proceeding line abreast at intervals of three to four miles, on a southerly course. *Hochelaga's* crew sighted two schooners at a distance of six miles, and the ship altered to an intercepting easterly course, intending to warn the fishermen about the U-boat threat. *Trawler 32* followed, but the other vessels continued on the original line of advance. At approximately 1400, when the distance was about four miles, *Hochelaga's* crew saw a U-boat near the schooners—one of which instantly disappeared. The patrol vessel's commanding officer then altered course away from the submarine and back towards *Cartier* and *Trawler 22* ordering *Trawler 32* to follow.

> On seeing *Hochelaga* make this last alteration in course and hoist a flag, Lieutenant McGuirk in *Cartier* altered course to North 25° East (Magnetic) to meet her. The time during which *Hochelaga* was steering towards *Cartier* was approximately seven or eight minutes. At the expiration of this period, when the vessels were about a mile apart, *Cartier* signalled to *Hochelaga* "What is your signal and what have you seen?" *Hochelaga* replied "Submarine bearing East," *Cartier* then altered course to the East, *Hochelaga* and Trawler No. 32 altering to the same course and coming up *Hochelaga* on *Cartier's* port quarter, and Trawler 32 on *Hochelaga's* port quarter. *Cartier* then signalled to *Hochelaga* to increase to full speed. Shortly after *Hochelaga*

signalled to *Cartier* "Do you see reinforcements astern, don't you think it better to wait for them?" *Cartier* replied "Negative."

The Submarine had by this time submerged while the schooner which had been seen from *Hochelaga* to disappear had capsized and could be seen on her side. *Cartier*, *Hochelaga*, and Trawler No. 32 came up to her and cruised round; some empty dories were seen, but no signs of the submarine.[45]

Hochelaga's captain had had a failure of nerve. Instructions issued by Admiral Kingsmill to the east coast patrol a few weeks before had stressed that although the U-boats had a great advantage over the ships of the Canadian flotilla in gun power, the submariners, unwilling to risk even slight damage at such a great distance from home, were unlikely to stand and fight. Patrol vessels should therefore not hesitate to attack, especially if additional ships were within supporting distance. The U-boat would probably dive, thereby enabling the surface vessels to conduct a hunt with hydrophones and depth charges; if the Canadian ships inflicted any damage with their guns or underwater weapons it would greatly reduce the submarine's chances of returning to base through the Royal Navy's defences in the North Sea and English Channel. There could be no excuse for *Hochelaga's* captain. He had been on active service with the navy since September 1914, received a commission in the RNCVR in June 1915, and held ship commands since January 1917. A court martial at Halifax on 5 October 1918 found that he "did not, from negligence or other default, on sight of the enemy which it was his duty to engage use his utmost exertion to bring his ship into action." He was immediately dismissed from the service.[46]

As it happened, U-156's good fortune had also run out. After the encounter with *Hochelaga* the boat was able to destroy only one small schooner before shaping course for home on 30 August. On about 25 September U-156 was sunk in the Anglo-American minefields between Scotland and Norway; she was the only raider that failed to return from North American waters.

During the last week of August U-117 had also come up from American waters as the Admiralty had warned. Between 24 and 30 August she sank four schooners and a steamer. the first of them south of Sable Island and the last about 150 miles southeast of St. John's, as she headed for Germany. Because U-117 operated further off the coast than U-156, the shipwrecked crews were not able to reach shore and give word of the sinkings until 24 hours or more after the event. Some precautions had already been taken, however. In response to the intelligence received on 10 August that the submarine might lay mines in the vicinity of Cape Race, the RCN had despatched two trawlers equipped with sweeps to St. John's, while the auxiliary patrol ships and trawlers escorting shipping to that port and patrolling the fishing banks also kept a watch on the area.[47]

Additional resources had become available during August to assist the Canadian flotilla in meeting its expanded commitments. With the delivery of 12-pounder guns early in the month, it was possible to arm seven trawlers that had recently arrived at Sydney and Halifax; no guns were available, however, for two of the last three Admiralty trawlers nearing completion at Great Lakes shipyards. Although the American destroyer and eighteen submarine chasers that patrolled off Nova Scotia on 22–24 August soon departed for operations in the United States sector west of 65 degrees west, on 24 August the USS *Yorktown*, an old gunboat of 1710 tons with 5-inch guns, arrived at Halifax and appears to have remained on station there until at least the latter part of September. More important was the arrival on 19 August of a United States Navy air detachment at the seaplane station the Canadian government was building at Bakers Point near Dartmouth. Hastily assembling four HS2L flying boats, the American aviators made their first flights on the 25th. By the last week in September a similar detachment was ready for operations from North Sydney. The seaplanes provided cover for convoys at distances of up to eighty miles from port, and performed coastal searches, supplying much needed support for the outer patrol and escort divisions at Halifax and Sydney.[48]

Any increment in the strength of the anti-submarine forces on the Canadian Atlantic coast was more than over-balanced by the RCN's responsibility for the defence of HC convoys from the new assembly port of Quebec. The route from that city to the open ocean, either through the Cabot Strait or the Strait of Belle Isle, was some 600 miles in length, and convoys had to be protected over the whole of it. U-boats could readily evade hunting forces in the deep channels and broad waters of the Gulf but could easily locate and attack shipping which was confined to restricted routes by the Magdalenes, Anticosti Island and the mouth of the St. Lawrence River. Naval headquarters explained these difficulties to the commander-in-chief at the end of August, but he responded that "the Admiralty would not hear of any alteration." Admiral Grant did arrange for the release to the RCN of fifteen additional drifters and five trawlers from the second batch of twenty-four building in Canada on imperial account. Because of delays in construction only two of the new trawlers ultimately joined the Canadian flotillas, but during September eighteen drifters took up station. The bulk went to form patrols at Gaspé and the Strait of Belle Isle (a trawler from the St. Lawrence patrol supported each of these forces), two operated from Rimouski, PQ, and two reinforced the trawler-sweepers at St. John's.[49]

Because Halifax was now being used primarily to escort coastwise shipping, Admiral Grant hoped that much of the force there could be sent to the St. Lawrence. The Canadians were understandably reluctant to make substantial cuts at their main naval base. In the end, three auxiliary patrol ships that had operated from Halifax in the wake of U-156's first visit, three or four trawlers and a few drifters moved to Sydney.[50]

HC-16, the first convoy to assemble at Quebec, sailed on 3 September. From that time the auxiliary patrol ships assumed a greatly increased importance as the only vessels in the Canadian patrols with the speed and endurance necessary to escort the medium convoys through the Gulf. When the convoys went by way of the Cabot Strait, as did HC-16, the American submarine chasers based at Sydney reinforced the escort, while trawlers and drifters of the Sydney flotilla mounted extra patrols in the strait and its approaches.[51]

The last submarine to operate in Canadian waters was the *Deutschland* herself, renamed U-155 after conversion into a long-range raider. As already noted, German signals decrypted in early August had revealed her mission and sailing date. When on 13 September the boat made an unsuccessful torpedo and gun attack on the British steamer *Newby Hall* about 100 miles southeast of Sable Island, the Admiralty immediately warned the naval authorities on the Canadian east coast to expect minelaying off St. John's and Halifax, and attacks on shipping on the routes between those ports. Four days later U-155 slipped in off Halifax to lay eight mines close to the Sambro light vessel, and six approximately ten miles southeast of Peggy's Cove. One mine that immediately broke away from its moorings was discovered floating and destroyed with gunfire by the patrol vessel *Grilse* on 18 September. None of the others was either swept up before the end of the war or did any damage, presumably because the fields were clear of the war channels into Halifax where the minesweeping flotilla performed daily searches. Although this also meant that mines did no damage, the patrol vessels which used Sambro light vessel as a rendezvous were lucky to have escaped unharmed.[52]

Lingering in Canadian waters for at least a week after laying the mines, U-155 was rewarded only with the destruction of a single fishing trawler south of Sable Island. Once again Canadian warships patrolled the banks and warned fishermen, but this effort was not allowed to interfere with the protection of ocean convoys and the sailing of convoys on the coastal routes. As a further precaution the medium convoys from Quebec were now routed through the Strait of Belle Isle; plans had been made for a similar diversion of the Sydney convoys but were never carried out.[53]

Depite U-155's failure to inflict significant damage, the senior officers of the RCN and their political masters were profoundly unhappy about the course of events in 1918, and even more worried about what would happen in 1919. U-boats of the powerful new cruiser class would undoubtedly turn up, and operate with the benefit of complete intelligence about the shipping and defences in Canadian waters. In September, C.C. Ballantyne, Minister of the Naval Service, had written personally to Admiral Lord Weymss, First Sea Lord at the Admiralty, to ask once again if Great Britain could supply equipment and armament for the construction of destroyers in Canada. Ballantyne was also dissatisfied with the performance of naval headquarters during the crises of August, and believed a fundamental shake up was necessary.[54]

At the end of September, Hose reported that the shortage of personnel was having such a grievous effect on the efficiency of the patrols that the system of manning and training would have to be entirely revamped for 1919. The requirements for manpower laid down in early 1918 had been for the bare minimum needed actually to serve in the ships and shore establishments. In fact a "considerable reserve" of both officers and ratings was essential to cover temporary vacancies, and to allow systematic training. At the best of times the crews of the patrols spent only eight days out of 20 in port, and however energetically the instructional staffs worked, "it will be realized that it is impossible to fit in Hydrophone, Signal, Minesweeping, Depth Charges, and Gunnery Instruction, clean and refit, coal and store the ships, and also provide working parties." The result was that, although the officers and ratings of most crews were experienced seamen, they were "untrained, not only in the technical knowledge required to handle the weapons and offensive appliances on board the ships, but also in service discipline."[55]

The dearth of qualified personnel also placed an enormous burden on the handful of professional officers who commanded the shore establishments. Subordinates could not carry out even the most routine tasks without close supervision. Kingsmill was deeply worried during August and September that the health of some of the key officers might collapse under the strain. Certainly, they were so overwhelmed by administrative duties that it was impossible for them to maintain a firm grasp of developments at sea.[56]

Senior officers, too, often worked at cross purposes. As the war ended, Admirals Story and Hose were again arguing over who controlled which parts of the Halifax flotilla. This was symptomatic of organizational difficulties that bedevilled the whole of the British and Canadian organization for the control and defence of shipping that had grown up in North America under the sporadic guidance of a remote and distracted Admiralty.

Most galling for the RCN was the lack of suitable ships. Hose vented his frustration at the end of October 1918 with a far-fetched scheme for the following summer. Observing that the existing ships of the patrols were "powerless to prevent the enemy from acting when and where he pleases against the shipping off Canadian Coasts," he advised that thirty-three destroyers and four submarines was the "minimum defence force required." Commander J.P. Gibbs, RN, Director of Operations at headquarters, observed that this was "quite outside the realm of practical politics," but he did believe that Canada should construct six large destroyers and eight submarines in her own yards. In any case, Gibbs warned, it would be "useless to build good ships . . . if there was not a thoroughly efficient Dockyard to keep them in repair." The existing facilities at Halifax had failed to keep pace with the maintenance requirements of the existing flotilla, technically unsophisticated as those vessels were. It was scarcely worth refurbishing the damaged and decrepit buildings at the dockyard; an entirely new complex should be constructed. Kingsmill forwarded Gibbs' paper to the minister, with a sharp reminder that the Laurier programme projected in 1909–10 would have provided much of what was now needed. In fact, Ballantyne received a note from the British First Sea Lord at this same time that once more discouraged the construction of destroyers in Canada, but promised that the United States would supply six of the warships early in the new year. All of this correspondence became irrelevant the moment it was completed; on 5 November Ballantyne called a halt to planning for 1919 in view of Germany's impending collapse.[57]

The encounter with the U-boats in 1918 contributed nothing to the fighting tradition that a young service, buffetted by political controversy and nearly bereft of public support, so desperately needed. On the two occasions when Canadian warships were in a position to strike back at the enemy, their officers had fumbled badly. Gilbert and Sullivan might have written the script. The U-boats faced such slight danger of retribution that, in contrast to the deadly battle being waged in the eastern Atlantic, they were able to conduct freewheeling operations with not a little flair, rather like good-natured pirates. In most cases the submarines could make surfaced attacks and take full precautions for the safety of ships' crews. When it emerged that the steamer *Erik* lacked sufficient boats for her people, U-156 took them on board, while searching for another victim with a surplus of boats. But the schooner *Willie G.*, the submarine's next target, was short of dories, so U-156 spared her and put *Erik's* crew on board. Earlier in August, a German-speaking member of *Dornfontein's* crew had had a chance to chat with one of the submariners; the latter produced a photograph of himself, with the address of his mother in Hamburg on the back, and asked the Canadian seaman to mail it if he heard that U-156 had been sunk. Although the American and Canadian press in reporting the U-boat attacks emphasized Hun brutality, such vignettes as these brought some papers to refute a growing sentiment that the U-boat crews were actually gentlemen, forced by difficult circumstances to do a nasty job. The German officers had been hoping for such an effect. They explained to many of the seamen they cast adrift that the object of the attacks was not to inflict death and injury, but to sink ships as a warning to President Wilson (they never mentioned Sir Robert Borden) of the futility of continuing the war.[58]

Yet the Germans had expended a good deal of effort in Canadian waters for very meagre returns. Only two substantial vessels—*Luz Blanca* of 4868 tons, and the steamer *Bergsdalen* of 2500 tons—had been destroyed, the latter by U-117 in a torpedo attack on 27 August. The fishing vessels of 250 tons or less that accounted for the bulk of the submariners' victories were attacked largely because the U-boats could not find more worthwhile targets. U-156 reported by wireless that although there was plenty of shipping between New York and Halifax, little could be found to the north of the latter port; the captain of U-117 was reduced to asking the masters of ships he sank where the steamer routes were located, and showed his exasperation by threatening to take one of them prisoner if he did not co-operate. Here lay the great achievement of the Canadian flotilla. During late August more than a dozen steamers had travelled between Sydney and St. John's through the waters patrolled by U-156 and U-117, but they had sailed in groups under the protection of trawlers and auxiliary patrol ships; as a recent author put it, the great virtue of convoy was that "the ocean suddenly seemed to the U-boats to be devoid of shipping."[59]

The ultimate object of the Royal Navy's operations during the First World War was to ensure the "safe and timely" arrival of the merchant shipping upon which Britain's survival depended. All-out efforts to hunt down and destroy U-boats failed to reduce their numbers; in the end, convoy proved to be the only way to secure the Atlantic sea lanes. The

Canadian patrols made a small but significant contribution to the success of the convoy system. That contribution must be measured not only by the number of merchantmen that sailed safely and on schedule, but also by the fact that Great Britain did not have to divert one major anti-submarine warship from the critical battle in the eastern Atlantic to protect the coastal waters of Canada and Newfoundland.

NOTES

This paper could not have been completed in its present form without the material gathered and narratives written by the members of the Naval Historical Section, which, in 1966, combined with the Army and Air Force Historical Sections to form the Directorate of History at National Defence Headquarters in Ottawa. I must express my appreciation to the late E.C. Russell, formerly the naval historian, and to J.D.F. Kealy, the late Thor Thorgrimsson, Hartley Brown, and Philip Chaplin of his staff. Philip also read a draft of the manuscript and caught many slips, a service for which I am most grateful.

1. Gilbert Norman Tucker, *The Naval Service of Canada: Its Official History*, vol. 1, *Origins and Early Years* (Ottawa, 1952).

2. B.M. Ranft, "The Naval Defence of British Sea-Borne Trade 1860–1905" (unpublished Ph.D. thesis, Oxford University, 1967); A.J. Marder, *From the Dreadnought to Scapa Flow: The Royal Navy in the Fisher Era, 1904–1919*, vol. 1., *The Road to War, 1904–1914* (London, 1961), 358–67.

3. See, for example, Colonial Defence Committee, no. 399M, "Defence of Halifax against Torpedo Attack," 27 Feb. 1908, National Archives of Canada (hereafter NAC), Record Group (hereafter RG) 7 G-21, box 234, file 343(8).

4. Richard Howard Gimblett, "'Tin-Pots' or Dreadnoughts? The Evolution of the Naval Policy of the Laurier Administration, 1896–1911" (unpublished MA thesis, Trent University, 1981).

5. Roger Sarty, "Silent Sentry: A Military and Political History of Canadian Coast Defence 1860–1945" (unpublished Ph.D. thesis, University of Toronto, 1982), 172–73, 221–22.

6. Ibid., 275–76.

7. Ibid., 276-77; Gaddis Smith, *Britain's Clandestine Submarines 1914–1915* (New Haven, Conn., 1964), 76–77, 101, 103, 108–10; NAC, RG 24, box 4020, files 62-12-1, 62-12-2.

8. Tucker, *Naval Service*, 1:219.

9. Perley, memorandum, 2 July 1915, Graham Green to Borden, 12 Aug. 1915, NAC, Manuscript Group (hereafter MG) 26 H, Sir Robert Borden papers, vol. 76, p. 39492; Kingsmill to minister, 11 Aug. 1915, extracts from file 62-13-4 in Directorate of History (hereafter DHist), Naval Historical Section files (hereafter NHS), 1440-11.

10. Historical Records Officer to Senior Canadian Naval Officer (London), 12 Jan. 1944, DHist, NHS 1700–1903.

11. United States, Navy Department, Office of Naval Records and Library, Historical Section, *German Submarine Activities on the Atlantic Coast of the United States and Canada* (Washington, 1920), 15–23; NHS, "Ships and Vessels of the RCN on the Atlantic Coast in the Great War 1914–1918," 17 July 1963, 16–21; "Information Regarding Marine Defences of Defended Ports . . . in Canada," 1 July 1917, NAC, RG 24, box 3809, file 10-11-1 lists the vessels then in commission.

12. NHS, "Ships and Vessels," 22–24; extracts from file 65-7-2 in DHist, NHS 1440-11; Borden to Blount, telegram, 30 March 1917, NAC, MG 26H, reel C-4314, p. 35454; Anderson, minute, 4 Feb. 1917, Great Britain, Public Record Officer (hereafter PRO), Adm 116/1400 case 620.

13. "Information regarding Marine Defences," 1 April 1918, NAC, RG 24, box 3810, file 10-11-1; NHS, "Ships and Vessels"; see also Fraser McKee, *The Armed Yachts of Canada* (Erin, ON, 1983), chaps. 2–3.

14. David M. Trask, *Captains and Cabinets: Anglo-American Naval Relations, 1917–1918* (Columbia, MO, 1972), chap. 2.

15. C. Ernest Fayle, *Seaborne Trade*, vol. 3, *The Period of Unrestricted Submarine Warfare* (London, 1924), 134, 139–40, 313.

16. Long to Governor General, telegram, 7 July 1917, Transports Sydney to Naval Ottawa, signal 7991, 3 Aug. 1917, Graham Green to Chambers, 20 July 1917, NAC, RG 24, box 5645, file 48-48-1, vol. 1; the final reports of the naval control of shipping staffs are in NAC, RG 24, box 3981, file 49-2-40; for a detailed account of the byzantine Canadian command structure on the Atlantic coast see NHS, "RCN Shore Establishments on the Canadian East Coast, 1910–1919," 1961; Commander-in-chief, North America and West Indies, general letter, 1 Oct. 1918, PRO, Adm 137/504, f. 427.

17. Patrick Beesly, *Room 40: British Naval Intelligence 1914–18* (London, 1982), 120; quote from Long to Governor General, telegram, 22 June 1917, NAC, RG 24, box 4031, file 65-7-3.

18. Kingsmill to minister, 1 Aug. 1917, NAC, RG 24, box 4031, file 65-7-3.

19. NAC, RG 24, box 3832, file 17-10-3; Kingsmill to secretary of the Admiralty, Nov. 1917, NAC, RG 24, box 3831, file 17-10-1, vol. 1.

20. Admiralty to Colonial Office, 3 Jan. 1918, NAC, RG 24, box 3831, file 17-10-1, vol. 1.

21. Deputy minister, Department of the Naval Service to under secretary of state, Department of External Affairs, 8 March 1918, enclosing "Memorandum on Organization of Atlantic Patrols," NAC, RG 24, box 3831, file 17-10-1, vol. 1.

22. Ibid.; NHS, "Ships and Vessels," 30–31.

23. NAC, RG 24, box 5662, file 58-53-30; deputy minister, Department of the Naval Service to under secretary of state, Department of External Affairs, 23 May 1918, Admiralty to Naval Ottawa, signal 793, 4 July 1918, NAC, RG 24, box 4031, file 66-7-6.

24. Commander-in-chief, North America and West Indies, general letter, 1 April 1918, PRO, Adm 137/504, f. 331.

25. Hose to secretary, Department of the Naval Service, 25 March 1918, NAC, RG 24, box 3832, file 17-10-4; Sarty, "Silent Sentry," 327–28.

26. NAC, RG 24, box 4027, file 62-18-2, vols. 1–3; extracts from file 47-19-4, DHist, NHS 1440-6, "Halifax 1905-20."

27. On the east coast air patrols see J.D.F. Kealy and E.C. Russell, *A History of Canadian Naval Aviation 1918–1962* (Ottawa, 1965), 1–10; S.F. Wise, *Canadian Airmen and the First World War: The Official History of the Royal Canadian Air Force*, vol. 1 (Toronto: University of Toronto Press, 1980), 603–608.

28. Commander-in-chief, North America and West Indies, general letter, 3 May 1918, PRO, Adm 137/504, f. 348; Hose to Kingsmill, 20 April 1918, NAC, RG 24, box 3833, file 17-10-7, vol. 1.

29. Hose to secretary, Department of the Naval Service, 22 May 1918, Submarine chaser division commander to Admiral Superintendent Halifax, 19 June 1918, NAC, RG 24, box 4031, file 65-7-6.

30. Hose to secretary, Department of the Naval Service, 1 Aug. 1918, NAC,

RG 24, box 4031, file 65-7-6; Department of the Naval Service, *Navy List*, Aug. 1918.

31. Kingsmill to minister, 21 Feb. 1918 forwarding Hose, memorandum, n.d., NAC, RG 24, box 3831, file 17-10-1, vol. 1; Notes from file 47-2-4, DHist, NHS 1440-6, "Halifax 1905-20"; *Trawler 30* log, 12 June 1918, NAC, RG 24, vol. 7953.

32. Washington to Naval Ottawa, signal, 2 May 1918, and Washington to Naval Ottawa, signal, 16 May 1918, NAC, RG 24, box 4021, file 62-13-2, vol. 3.

33. USN, *German Submarine Activities*. Unless noted otherwise, all descriptions of U-boat operations are derived from this source. William Bell Clark, *When the U-Boats Came to America* (Boston, 1929) contains some additional information.

34. Robert M. Grant, *U-Boat Intelligence 1914–1918* (London, 1969), 152.

35. Washington to Naval Ottawa, signal 27, 5 July 1918, NAC, RG 24, box 3773, file 48-38-1, vol. 3.

36. Grant, *Intelligence*, 153–54; Navinet Halifax to Naval Ottawa, signal 922, 26 July 1918, NAC, RG 24, box 4021, file 62-13-2, vol. 3.

37. Report of attack on *Dornfontein*, NAC, RG 24, box 4023, file 62-13-10, vol. 5; Transports Saint John to Naval Ottawa, signal 515, 3 Aug. 1918, NAC, RG 24, box 4021, file 62-13-2, vol. 4.

38. Signals, 4–6 Aug. 1918, NAC, RG 24, box 4021, file 62-13-2, vol. 4.

39. Patrols Sydney to Naval Ottawa, signal, 5 Aug. 1918, NAC, RG 24, box 4031, file 65-7-6; Newcombe to Captain of Patrols, 13 Aug. 1918, DHist, NHS 8000, "Niobe" (the account of the movements of the Canadian and American patrol vessels is primarily based upon this report); logs of *Canadian Drifter (CD)14*, NAC, RG 24, vol. 7155; *CD 15*, ibid., vol. 7157; *CD 19*, ibid., 7158; *CD 33*, ibid., vol. 7171; *St. Eloi*, ibid., 7919.

40. Report of attack on *Luz Blanca*, NAC, RG 24, box 4023, file 62-13-10, vol. 4.

41. Sydney-Ottawa signals, 5–7 Aug. 1918, NAC, RG 24, box 4031, file 65-7-6; NHS, "RCN Shore Establishments," 27–28.

42. In addition to the First World War logs in the 7000 series of volumes in NAC, RG 24, see the final reports of the Canadian control of shipping staffs, NAC, RG 24, box 3981, file 49-2-40; notes from file 57-4-30, DHist, NHS 8000, "Trawlers and Drifters," vol. 2.

43. USN, *German Submarine Activities*, 11; Washington to Naval Ottawa, signals 101 and 104, 6 Aug. 1918, Admiralty to Naval Ottawa, signal 42, 8 Aug. 1918, NAC, RG 24, box 3773, file 48-48-1, vol. 4; Grant, *Intelligence*, 154.

44. Report of attack on *Triumph*, NAC, RG 24, box 4023, file 62-13-10, vol. 4; signals, 21–3 Aug. 1918, NAC, RG 24, box 4023, file 62-13-2, vols. 4–5.

45. Quote from McKnight to Captain of Patrols, 17 Sept. 1918, DHist, NHS 1440–6 "Halifax 1905–20"; also see extracts from file 47-5-1, DHist, NHS 8000 "Stadacona (Ship Afloat)."

46. Quote from extracts from file 47-23-164, DHist, NHS "Halifax 1905–20"; Kingsmill, memorandum, 7 Aug. 1918, DHist 81/520/1000-973, vol. 1.

47. Signals, 10–12 Aug. 1918, NAC, RG 24, box 4031, file 65-7-6; notes from file 57-4-30, DHist, NHS 8000, "Trawlers and Drifters," vol. 2; Signals, 27 Aug.–8 Sept. 1918, NAC, RG 24, box 4021, file 62-13-2, vol. 5.

48. Naval Ottawa to Transports Sydney, signal 44, 6 Aug. 1918, NAC, RG 24, box 4031, file 65-7-6; *Laurentian* log, 11 Aug. 1918, NAC, RG 24, vol. 7450; Notes from file 57-4-31, DHist, NHS 8000, "Trawlers and Drifters," vol. 2.

49. Director of Operations Division to Director of the Naval Service, 29 Aug. 1918, Department of the Naval Service, "Drifters Built in Canada," 3 March 1919, NAC, RG 24, box

4031, file 65-7-6; NHS, "Ships and Vessels," 35–37.

50. Naval Ottawa to Navyard Halifax, signal 974, 19 Aug. 1918, Story to Director of the Naval Service, 20 Aug. 1918, NAC, RG 24, box 4031, file 65-7-6.

51. Naval Ottawa-Patrols Sydney signals, 3–5 Sept. 1918, NAC, RG 24, box 4031, file 65-7-6.

52. Navinet Halifax to Naval Ottawa, signal 732, 14 Sept. 1918, NAC, RG 24, box 4021, file 62-13-2, vol. 5; NAC, RG 24, box 3970, file 47-30-2, vol. 2.

53. *Margaret* log, 14–26 Sept. 1918, NAC, RG 24, vol. 7493; Notes from file 57-4-31, DHist, NHS, "Trawlers and Drifters," vol. 2; Patrols Sydney to Naval Ottawa, signal 430, 21 Sept. 1918, Washington to Naval Ottawa, signal 410, 31 Oct. 1918, NAC, RG 24, box 3773, file 48-48-1, vol. 4.

54. Ballantyne to Wemyss, 11 Sept. 1918, NAC, RG 24, box 3831, file 17-10-1, vol. 1; G.J. Desbarats diary, 16 Sept. 1918, NAC, RG 30E89, vol. 5.

55. Hose to secretary, Department of the Naval Service, 24 Sept. 1918, NAC, RG 24, box 4032, file 65-7-12.

56. Naval Ottawa to Britannia, signal 2023, 29 Aug. 1918, NAC, RG 24, box 5651, vol. 2; Newcombe to Captain of Patrols, 13 Aug. 1918, DHist, NHS 8000, "Niobe."

57. Hose to secretary, Department of the Naval Service, 21 Oct. 1918, NAC, RG 24, box 4032, file 65-7-12; Kingsmill to minister, 5 Nov. 1918 forwarding Gibbs to Director of the Naval Service, 28 Oct. 1918, Ballantyne to Kingsmill, 5 Nov. 1918, NAC, RG 24, box 4029, file 65-1-1.

58. Report of attack on *Erik*, NAC, RG 24, box 4023, file 62-13-10, vol. 4; clippings from *The Standard* (Saint John, NB) in NAC, RG 24, box 4021, file 62-13-2, vol. 4.

59. Grant, *Intelligence*, 155; *German Submarine Activities*, 99; see also report of attack on *Kingfisher*, NAC, RG 24, box 4023, file 62-13-10, vol. 4; quote from Arthur Hezlett, *The Submarine and Sea Power* (London, 1967), 94–5.

section

3

1919 – 1945

○

After the First World War Canada's armed forces contracted, but there was no return to the pre-war status quo. The RCN even enjoyed a brief period of growth until 1922, when financial constraints forced sharp reductions. In the mid-twenties the fortunes of the RCN were restored modestly when the government ordered the destroyers *Skeena* and *Saguenay*, the first warships ever built for Canada. From 1935 onwards, under Mackenzie King's administration, the fleet grew to a respectable "half flotilla" of six modern destroyers. The RCN was seen by the Liberals as a way of doing something "military" without too many Canadians getting killed.

By the end of the 1930s the same view prevailed about the air force. The Royal Canadian Air Force, founded in 1924, devoted most of its first decade to exploring and mapping the north. Like the navy, the RCAF too was put on more of a war footing in the last years before 1939, but it had very few first-line aircraft and clear home defence priorities.

The army soldiered on despite the best efforts of successive governments—particularly Liberal ones—to sharply curtail its ambitions. Attempts immediately after the war to introduce peacetime conscription as the basis of a massive mobilization plan for the militia came to nought. However, a substantially larger permanent, and much more professional, force characterized the interwar army establishment. The real problem was figuring out just what the army should train for. Overseas operations were the only "real soldiering" Canadian soldiers could expect, but the government had no plans to participate in British adventures or another major European war. As war clouds gathered over Europe, however, some improvements were made. The absurdly large number of militia units was dramatically reduced, a number of ostensible "armoured" units were designated, and some new equipment was acquired. Despite these efforts, the army was little better prepared for war in 1939 than it had been in 1914.

The Second World War can be neatly divided into several distinct phases, each of which brought its own unique challenges. The Phoney War, from September 1939 to the spring of 1940, was viewed by the Canadian government as a limited European war that called for maximum industrial and economic effort and minimum military involvement. The fleet was kept close to home, the army overseas limited to one division, and the air force tied as closely as possible to home defence and to the British Commonwealth Air Training Plan.

The collapse of western Europe in the spring of 1940 left Canada as Britain's most important ally and with that the flood gates of effort were opened. The overseas army quickly grew to become the "First Canadian Army," consisting of five divisions and two armoured brigades. The navy's expansion, still seen by King as both safe and economically beneficial, since many of the ships would be built in Canada, gathered momentum. And the RCAF broke its fetters: Canadian squadrons were expanded in number overseas, largely paid for by the British taxpayers. Apart from the First Canadian Army, which threatened to embroil Canada in heavy losses, there was little in this expansion to cause King's government alarm—provided the army could be kept well away from the fighting.

The entry of the United States into the war in 1941 and the widening of the war's scope both eased and complicated the Canadian government's task. Active American involvement guaranteed an Allied victory, so there was little purpose in the Canadians charging headlong into a battle which US manpower would ultimately decide. Moreover, defence of the Canadian west coast and conscription for home defence gave at least momentary vent to clamouring for more Canadian action—as did the two ill-fated actions at Hong Kong and Dieppe. Two battalions were lost in the debacle at Hong Kong in December 1941. One of the great tragedies of Canadian history followed the next August, when the Second Division was hurled against the defended beaches of Dieppe in the largest amphibious raid of the war. Five thousand Canadians took part in the raid: by the end of the day 3367 were dead, wounded, or prisoner, the largest single-day casualty toll of the war for Canada.

Despite these figures, in this early phase of the war it was the RCN that carried the burden of Canadian military operations. Using primarily small Canadian-built ships, the navy expanded rapidly and soon found itself, alongside RCAF squadrons, engaged in important convoy escort duty in the North Atlantic—work no Canadian planner had foreseen. Not surprisingly, the performance of Canada's expansion fleet, particularly in convoy battles in 1941 and 1942, frequently left something to be desired. The Canadian fleet, however, reflected the strengths and weaknesses of Canada itself, and no other campaign was so affected by distinctly Canadian issues.

If the navy's operations were well focused in both purpose and locale, the same cannot be said of the other two services. The RCAF mushroomed at home and abroad, and was primarily responsible for Canada's massive share of the British Commonwealth Air Training Plan. At home the air force came of age as an institution during the war years, building bases, infrastructure, and administrative experience that would stand it in good stead in the post-war world. Overseas, however, RCAF aircrew and formations operated as part of a much larger RAF. It fielded nearly fifty overseas squadrons and Canadians made up nearly a quarter of RAF aircrew by 1944–45. Canadian squadrons and personnel could be found in all types of operations, from fighter missions, to maritime patrols, to, especially, the efforts of Bomber Command. It was rather ironic that the air force, which the government had fostered as a means of fighting with few casualties, suffered heavily in the bomber offensive—10 000 Canadian deaths. However, by the time the RCAF losses began to mount, the army had finally been committed to sustained operations—four years after the outbreak of the war.

For political and professional reasons it was necessary to commit the army to sustained fighting by 1943, so they went to the Italian campaign. The First Division and the First Armoured Brigade took part in the Sicilian operations in July and August, and landed in Italy proper in September. Before the end of 1943 the Fifth (Armoured) Division joined them and with its arrival the I Canadian Corps was established. There they would remain until March 1945: "The D-Day Dodgers" being their self-adopted label.

Much of the glamour—if there was any—of the Italian campaign evaporated once the landings in France occurred on 6 June 1944. Indeed, operations in Northwest Europe were, by implication then and now, Canada's real war. The assault, by the Third Division and the Second Armoured Brigade, went well. Of the Allies, the Canadians pushed the deepest inland and over the next few days stopped fierce German counterattacks on the beachhead. The war in Normandy over the next two months became a grinding war of attrition, more reminiscent of the western front in the previous war than anything generally envisaged of the Second World War. Sustaining operations at the required pace took a heavy toll in personnel, particularly infantry, and placed an enormous burden on those who carried on from day to day. Third Division had the highest casualty rate of any Allied division in Normandy, and the Second Division, which joined in July with the establishment of the II Canadian Corps, was not far behind. Thus by the summer of 1944 the Canadian army was fully engaged in serious and sustained fighting.

After four months of sustained fighting in both Italy and northwest Europe, the need for trained infantry precipitated a crisis, and the nation debated once again the issue of conscription for overseas service. The ghost of 1917 stalked the land. By the time the issue was resolved the army had spent a relatively quiet winter and few of the "Zombies" saw action. The First Canadian Army reached the peak of its professional development in early 1945, and when I Canadian Corps joined from Italy in March the First Canadian Army became truly Canadian.

Between 1939 and 1945 Canada put more than a million men and women into uniform. Military and industrial effort had made Canada a "middle power" by 1945, and Canadian statesmen used that position to help establish the United Nations and, in time, the North Atlantic Treaty Organization. The Canadian Second World War effort increased Canada's influence on the global scene to a level which has not yet been surpassed.

THE RAID ON DIEPPE, 19 AUGUST 1942 [*]

C.P. STACEY

○

DISASTER AT PUYS

The bad luck of No. 3 Commando on the extreme left extended to the Canadian unit closest to it: The Royal Regiment of Canada at Puys. The beach here, and the gully behind it in which the little resort village lay, were both extremely narrow and were commanded at very short range by lofty cliffs on either side. Success depended entirely upon surprise and upon the assault being made while it was dark enough to interfere with the aim of the German gunners. Neither of these conditions was achieved. The German garrison at Puys was only two platoons, one of the army and one of the Luftwaffe, plus some technical personnel; nor does it appear to have been reinforced during the morning. In the circumstances, it was quite enough for the work in hand.

The Royal Regiment of Canada had attached to it three platoons of The Black Watch (Royal Highland Regiment) of Canada, and detachments of the 3rd Light Anti-Aircraft Regiment and the 4th Field Regiment, R.C.A. The artillerymen were to assist in capturing enemy guns in the area and subsequently to man them. The Royals' general task is best described in the words of the *Combined Plan*:

> The Royal Regiment of Canada at BLUE beach will secure the headland east of JUBILEE [Dieppe] and destroy local objectives consisting of machine gun posts, heavy and light flak installations and a 4 gun battery south and east of the town. The battalion will then come into reserve, and detach a company to protect an engineer demolition party operating in the gas works and power plant.

[*] From *The Official History of the Canadian Army in the Second World War*, vol. 1, *Six Years of War: The Army in Canada, Britain and the Pacific* (Ottawa: The Queen's Printer, 1957), 363–86.

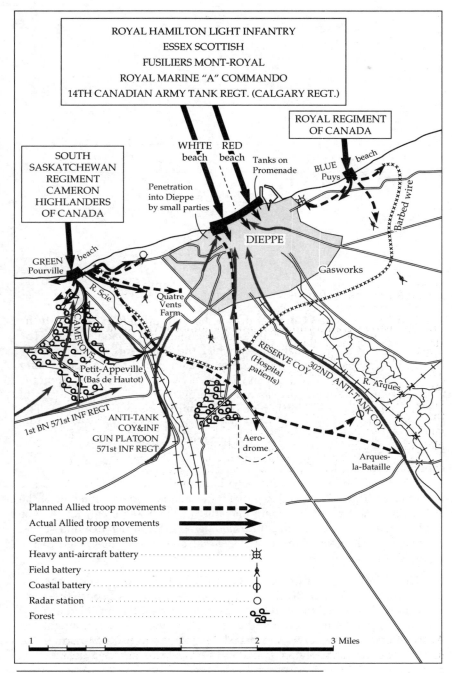

ROYAL HAMILTON LIGHT INFANTRY
ESSEX SCOTTISH
FUSILIERS MONT-ROYAL
ROYAL MARINE "A" COMMANDO
14TH CANADIAN ARMY TANK REGT. (CALGARY REGT.)

ROYAL REGIMENT
OF CANADA

WHITE   RED
beach   beach   Tanks on
Promenade

SOUTH
SASKATCHEWAN
REGIMENT
CAMERON
HIGHLANDERS
OF CANADA

BLUE   beach
Puys

Barbed wire

Penetration
into Dieppe
by small parties

DIEPPE

GREEN   beach
Pourville

Gasworks

R. Scie

Quatre
Vents
Farm

CAMERONS

RESERVE COY
(Hospital
patients)

302ND ANTI-TANK COY

R. Arques

Petit-Appeville
(Bas de Hautot)

1st BN 571st INF REGT

ANTI-TANK
COY&INF
GUN PLATOON
571st INF REGT

Aero-
drome

Arques-
la-Bataille

Planned Allied troop movements
Actual Allied troop movements
German troop movements
Heavy anti-aircraft battery
Field battery
Coastal battery
Radar station
Forest

1   0   1   2   3 Miles

THE RAID ON DIEPPE, 19 AUGUST 1942

Source: Based on map by Captain C.C.J. Bond opposite p. 386 in C.P. Stacey, *Six Years of War*.

This task was of special importance, since if the East Headland was not cleared the numerous weapons there would be able to fire on the main beaches in front of Dieppe.

Although the Detailed Military Plan does not assist us, and none of the Canadian infantry units issued separate written orders, individuals in positions to know[1] state that the Royal Regiment was to land in three waves: the first to consist of three companies and an advance group of battalion headquarters; the second, consisting of the remaining rifle company and the balance of the headquarters, to land ten minutes later; while the third, formed mainly of the attached platoons of the Black Watch, was to go in when signalled by the force already landed.

Unfortunately, the naval landing arrangements for Blue Beach went awry. No operation of war is harder than landing troops in darkness with precision as to time and place, and the danger of reckoning upon exactitude in such matters was well illustrated at Dieppe. The Royals were carried in the landing ships *Queen Emma* and *Princess Astrid*, while the Black Watch detachment was in the *Duke of Wellington*. (The last-named ship's landing craft flotilla was almost entirely manned by Canadian sailors, and a Canadian officer, Lieut. J.E. Koyl, R.C.N.V.R., took command of it after the Flotilla Officer was wounded.)[2] There was delay in forming up after the craft were lowered from the ships; this was mainly, apparently, the result of *Princess Astrid*'s craft forming on a motor gunboat which, having got out of station, was mistaken for the one which was to lead them in.[3] The Flotilla Officer of *Queen Emma* states that the delay made it necessary to proceed at a greater speed than had been intended, and as a result the two mechanized landing craft (L.C.M.) which formed part of this ship's flotilla, and were carrying 100 men each, could not keep up. Ultimately, according to this officer, these two L.C.M.s, with four assault craft which had been astern of them, landed as a second wave. In fact, one of the L.C.M.s developed engine trouble and consequently touched down in due course quite alone.[4]

Thanks to these mischances, the first group of craft carrying the Royal Regiment struck the beach late. The situation is thus described in the record of a conference held on 13 September 1942 by the senior Canadian officers confined in Oflag VIIB, one of whom was Lt.-Col. Catto of the Royals:

> Only part of three leading assault companies were landed in first wave and these were brought 35 minutes late by Navy. Remainder of companies finally reached beach nearly one hour late. Effect of darkness and smoke screen entirely lost.

Princess Astrid's Flotilla Officer states that touchdown was at 5:07 a.m., which would make it seventeen minutes late. The time given by the Oflag VIIB conference is only one of many widely varying estimates made by Army officers and men. On a point of this sort it seems best to accept the naval evidence, the more so as that of the Germans agrees with it pretty closely: their 302nd Division gives the time of the first landing as 5:10. Whatever the exact time, the unit was certainly placed upon the beach so late as to make its task far more difficult than it would have been at 4:50.

The defenders of Blue Beach were fully on the alert. Fire was opened upon the leading craft while they were still well offshore; the *Princess Astrid* Flotilla Officer estimates that it began when they were "about 100 yards from the beach." He states that Major G.P. Scholfield, the senior officer of the Royals with the first wave, was slightly wounded before landing. All accounts agree, moreover, that as this wave touched down and the craft dropped their ramps machine-gun fire was greatly intensified and heavy casualties were suffered immediately. The Flotilla Officer says, "In several cases officers and men were wounded or killed on the ramp as they made to leave the boats."[5]

At the head of the Puys beach was a sea-wall ten or a dozen feet high, covered with heavy barbed wire. The wire's presence had not been detected before the operation, but Lt.-Col. Catto, suspecting it, had seen to it that the unit had "Bangalore torpedoes" for blowing paths through such obstacles.[6] Survivors of the Royal Regiment and enemy documents both testify that the German defence was concentrated upon the east cliff.[7] A brick house which stood here had in its front garden a concrete pillbox disguised as a summer-house, whose main slit had a murderous command of the beach and the sea-wall at very short range.[8] This "L.M.G. bunker" (which bore bullet-marks when examined in 1944) was probably responsible for a great number of the Royals' casualties on the beach. It and other positions enfiladed the sea-wall, and caused heavy losses among the men who ran forward from the boats to take shelter there.

Although several Bangalore torpedoes were exploded on the wall to cut the wire, very few men succeeded in passing through the gaps alive. The combination of the absence of surprise with the fact that the assault was made in much broader daylight than had been intended had been fatal to the Blue Beach attack. In the words of Capt. G.A. Browne, the artillery Forward Observation Officer attached to the battalion, "In five minutes time they were changed from an assaulting Battalion on the offensive to something less than two companies on the defensive being hammered by fire which they could not locate."[9]

The second group of craft seems to have landed some twenty minutes later than the first; Canadian and naval estimates of the time vary from 5:25 to 5:35 a.m.[10] Capt. Browne, who was in this group, has described[11] the bearing of the men during the approach and the landing; he and those with him had been intended to land with the first wave, and they did not realize that in fact other troops had gone in before them:

> In spite of the steady approach to the beach under fire, the Royals in my ALC appeared cool and steady. It was their first experience under fire, and although I watched them closely, they gave no sign of alarm, although first light was broadening into dawn, and the interior of the ALC was illuminated by the many flares from the beach and the flash of the Bostons' bombs. The quiet steady voice of Capt. [W.B.] Thomson, seated just behind me, held the troops up to a confident and offensive spirit, although shells were whizzing

over the craft, and [they] could hear the steady whisper and crackle of S.A. [small arms] fire over the top of the ALC. At the instant of touchdown, small arms fire was striking the ALC, and here there was a not unnatural split-second hesitation in the bow in leaping out onto the beach. But only a split-second. The troops got out onto the beach as fast as [in] any of the SIMMER[12] exercises, and got across the beach to the wall and under the cliff.

This second wave of assault, in the circumstances, could accomplish nothing; it simply added to the number of men sheltering on the beach and being pounded by the German machine-guns and mortars. The landing of the third wave proved equally useless. No signal having been received, and no information concerning the situation ashore being available, Lieut. Koyl, in charge of *Duke of Wellington*'s flotilla, and Capt. R.C. Hicks, in command of the troops, jointly took the decision to land. At Hicks' request, the Black Watch company was put ashore under the cliff to the west of the sea-wall, where the main body of survivors of the earlier waves gathered.[13] Virtually every man of the Black Watch who landed ultimately became a prisoner; one officer was killed.

The men on the beach were cheered by close and constant air support. Aircraft went in at clifftop level to lay smoke, and in Colonel Catto's words, "The fighters came in again and again on the batteries while our show was on and later continued their close attacks while the withdrawal was taking place, and they undoubtedly affected quite seriously the fire from the east headland." Only one small party of the Royals is definitely known to have got off the beach.[14] This was not long after 6:00 a.m. The party, numbering about twenty officers and men, was led by Lt.-Col. Catto himself. They cut a path through the wire at the western end of the sea-wall, and the colonel led them up the cliff between bursts of machine gun fire. They cleared two houses on the clifftop, "resistance being met in the first only." The Germans now brought intense fire to bear upon the gap in the wire, and no more men got through it. The colonel's party moved westward above the beach in the hope of making contact with the Essex Scottish; but this battalion had never got off the beach in front of Dieppe. Catto's group lay up in a small wood until it was obvious that the men left on the Puys beach had been overwhelmed, that the landing force had withdrawn and that there was no hope of being taken off. At 4:20 p.m., after equipping a number of active unwounded men with "escape kits" and sending them off in the hope—which proved illusory—that some of them might get clear, the party surrendered.[15]

In the face of the German artillery fire (a troop of four howitzers in position only a few hundred yards south of Puys fired 550 rounds during the morning at craft offshore)[16] it was impossible to organize any systematic evacuation of the beach, although valiant attempts were made by the Navy. Analysis of the naval reports seems to indicate that the only craft which actually touched down on Blue Beach for the purpose of re-embarking troops was L.C.A. 209, commanded by Lieut. N.E.B. Ramsay, R.N.V.R.

Many soldiers made a rush for it under heavy fire, and, overloaded and badly holed, it capsized not far offshore. Lieut. Ramsay was among the killed.[17] Several men clung to the bottom, and two of *Duke of Wellington's* landing craft, largely manned by Canadians, pushed in through a hail of missiles and rescued at least three of them, at the cost however of two or more sailors' lives.[18]

As was inevitable in the circumstances, it is difficult to build up from the naval reports a completely coherent picture of the attempts to evacuate the Royal Regiment. It is clear, however, that Lieut.-Commander H.W. Goulding, Senior Officer Blue Beach Landings, visited H.M.S. *Calpe* shortly after 7:00 a.m. He did not know what was happening on shore, but reported that the Royals had been duly landed. While he was in the headquarters ship a signal arrived, passed through H.M.S. *Garth*, operating off Blue Beach. This untimed message, apparently the only one from *Garth* to *Calpe* which has been preserved, reads: "From Blue Beach: Is there any possible chance of getting us off."[19] Goulding recorded that he was now ordered by the Naval Force Commander "to take an M.L. [motor launch] for close support and make an attempt to evacuate Blue Beach." This was done accordingly, but when Goulding approached the beach heavy fire opened and no craft reached the shore.[20] A signal, sent by him, was logged at 11:45 a.m.: "Could not see provision [? position] Blue Beach owing to fog and heavy fires from cliff and White House. Nobody evacuated."[21] At least one further attempt was made, this time by four craft from *Princess Astrid*, whose Flotilla Officer reported that "Fire from the beach was still terrific," one craft was sunk, and "there was no sign of life on the beach."[22]

In point of fact, the remnants of The Royal Regiment of Canada on the Puys beach had probably surrendered a little before 8:30 a.m., rather more than three hours after the first landing. At 8:35 the 571st German Infantry Regiment informed its divisional headquarters, "Puys firmly in our hands; enemy has lost about 500 men prisoners and dead."[23]

Very few men of the Royals returned to England: all told, two officers and sixty-five men. Practically all of these were in one craft—that L.C.M. which, as described above, had had engine trouble and touched down independently. It pulled back off the beach under murderous fire, only a few men having landed from it and many having been hit on board.[24]

The episode at Puys was the grimmest of the whole grim operation, and the Royal Regiment had more men killed than any other unit engaged. Along the fatal sea-wall the lads from Toronto lay in heaps.[25] The regiment's fatal casualties, including those who died of wounds and 18 who died from any cause while prisoners of war, amounted to 227 all ranks out of 554 embarked. And there is no doubt that the setback at Puys had a most adverse effect upon the raid as a whole, for, as we noted, failure to clear the East Headland was certain to make success in the centre much less likely. The Naval Force Commander reports, "There is little doubt that this was the chief cause of the failure of the Military Plan." It certainly had great influence.

Some indication has already been given of the inadequacy of the information concerning events at Blue Beach which reached the headquarters ship during the early stages. Indeed, this extended to the whole of the eastern beaches, for we have seen that the Force Commanders got no reliable account of what had happened to No. 3 Commando for more than two hours after its encounter with the German convoy. Information about Puys should have been better, for though the only wireless set working on the beach was that of Capt. Browne, the Forward Observation Officer, he was in communication with the destroyer *Garth* offshore. *Garth's* commander confirms that the ship was in touch with Browne from 5:41 to 7:47, "during which time he was held up at the foot of the cliff and most messages received concerned wounded and the fact that they were held up, which were passed to CALPE."[26] The tragic fact is, however, that none of the early messages reached the headquarters ship. The Intelligence Log maintained in *Calpe* notes at 5:50 a.m. that there is no word from the Royals; and the first definite statement recorded concerning Blue Beach is at 6:20 and is extremely inaccurate: "R. Regt C. not landed." Another version appears in the *Fernie* Intelligence Log at 6:25, "Impossible to land any troops on Blue Beach. From Navy." This is probably a garbled version of an untimed message recorded as received by the Naval Force Commander from the Puys naval beach station: "Impossible to land any more troops on Blue Beach." It presumably came from the Beachmaster, who had not succeeded in getting inshore. In any case, the Force Commanders were long left in the belief that the Royal Regiment had not been landed; and as a result of this General Roberts sent out to the Royals, at 6:40 a.m. or a little before, an order directing them to go to Red Beach to support the Essex Scottish.[27]

THE FIGHTING IN THE POURVILLE AREA

The units landed on "Green Beach," at Pourville to the west of Dieppe, had better fortune, on the whole, than any other Canadian troops in the operation. Nevertheless, this success was only comparative, for they attained but few of their objectives.

The Pourville beach, though much longer than that at Puys, is still dominated by cliffs on both sides. Standing in the village of Pourville and looking east towards Dieppe, one faces a lofty and forbidding rampart, the eastern ridge of the valley of the Scie. This obstacle, strongly held by the Germans, proved insuperable on the morning of 19 August 1942.

The South Saskatchewan Regiment was carried across the Channel in the landing ships *Princess Beatrix* and *Invicta*. The trans-shipment to landing craft and the approach to the beach went without a hitch, and the craft touched down within a very few minutes of the time planned (4:50 a.m.); the two ships' Flotilla Officers agree in fixing the time at 4:52. A considerable measure of surprise was achieved. The naval reports indicate that there was no fire as the boats ran in, although it began very soon after the landing. One craft which touched down two minutes late on the extreme right flank was fired upon and the soldiers in it suffered casualties as they disembarked.[28] The whole unit landed as one wave. This was the earliest actual landing of troops in this operation, except perhaps for those of No. 4 Commando on the same flank; we have seen that both the eastern landings, though timed to take place simultaneously with that at Pourville, were considerably delayed.

One misfortune during the disembarkation, however, had considerable effect upon events. The River Scie flows into the Channel near the middle of the Pourville beach, and the intention had been to land the battalion *astride* the river, so that the companies operating against the objectives east of it could deliver their attacks without having to seek a crossing. Although there is no reference to this in the naval reports (indeed, the officers of the landing craft may have been unaware of the fact), accounts by officers and men with The South Saskatchewan Regiment[29] leave no doubt that in the semi-darkness the craft had not been able to strike the precise parts of the beach intended, and almost the whole of the battalion was actually landed *west* of the river. This meant that the companies having the vital task of seizing the high ground to the eastward had first to penetrate into the village and cross the river by the bridge carrying the main road towards Dieppe. The delay thus caused nullified the effect of the surprise that had been obtained, and was probably fatal.

"C" Company, operating to the west of Pourville, promptly occupied all its objectives, including positions on the hills immediately southwest of the village, and killed a good many Germans in the process. The companies working to the eastward had no such success. "A" Company's objective was the radar station on the cliff-edge roughly a mile east of Pourville. "D" Company's was positions on the adjacent high ground to the southward, including Quatre Vents Farm and anti-aircraft guns nearby; it was expected that they would be helped by The Royal Hamilton Light Infantry and a troop of tanks arriving from Dieppe. Before these two companies, having been landed west of the Scie, could get across the bridge and reach the heights, the enemy's posts there were manned and firing. The eastern part of the village, and the bridge, were completely dominated by them. Soon the bridge was carpeted with dead and wounded men and the advance of the South Saskatchewans came to a halt.

At this point, Lt.-Col. Merritt, having established his headquarters near the beach, came forward and took charge himself. Walking calmly into the storm of fire upon the bridge, waving his helmet and calling "Come on over—there's nothing to it," he carried party after party across by the force of his strong example. Other men forded or swam the river.[30] The Colonel then led a series of fierce uphill rushes which cleared several of the concrete positions commanding bridge and village.[31] Nevertheless, in spite of his extraordinary energy and dauntless courage, and the best efforts of his men and of the Camerons who were shortly mingled with them, the posts on the summit, including the trench system of Quatre Vents Farm and the radar station, could not be taken. Apparently some of our men got within a short distance of the radar station, but it was heavily wired and defended and could not be dealt with without artillery support.[32] The enemy handled his mortars and machine-guns skilfully, and our thrusts were all beaten back. One party actually reached the edge of the Quatre Vents position and killed several Germans before being forced out.[33] Attempts to obtain artillery support from the destroyer *Albrighton* were nullified by the Forward Observation Officer's inability to observe and lack of knowledge of the exact positions of our own troops; he did indicate several targets, but was unable to spot the fall of the ship's shells.[34]

The Cameron Highlanders of Canada, who were to pass through the Pourville bridgehead and operate against the aerodrome in conjunction with the tanks from Dieppe, were landed about half an hour late. This was due in part at least to the wishes of Lt.-Col. Gostling, who, according to Commander H.V.P. McClintock, the naval officer in charge, "preferred to arrive late [rather] than early." The idea (a dubious one) apparently was to land ten minutes later than the plan provided; however, miscalculations of speed and course lengthened the delay, and the battalion touched down at 5:50 a.m.[35] During the approach, it was apparent that the South Saskatchewan had not succeeded in opening up their bridgehead in the manner expected; fighting was clearly in progress in the outskirts of Pourville, and shells were bursting in the water offshore. With the Camerons' pipers playing, the craft pushed on; all of them reached the beach and there were almost no casualties on board. As Lt.-Col. Gostling's own craft ran in, he was calling cheerfully to his men, identifying the types of fire that were coming down upon them. When the boat touched down, near the east end of Green Beach, he leaped on to the shingle and went forward to direct the cutting of wire. Fire immediately opened from a pillbox built into the headland on the left, apparently the one position closely covering the beach which the South Saskatchewans had not succeeded in clearing; and the Commanding Officer fell dead.[36] The second in command, Major A.T. Law, took over.

The battalion had been landed astride the Scie, and mainly as a result of this it became divided into two main sections. The larger, which had landed west of the river, consisted of "A" Company, two platoons of "B," and evidently the major part of all three platoons of "C." This main body under Major Law subsequently moved inland and effected the deepest penetration made by any portion of the force engaged that day. The rest of the battalion remained in the Pourville area and fought in parties of varying strength mingled with The South Saskatchewan Regiment.[37]

Pourville was under heavy mortar fire, and this, plus the lateness of the hour, made it desirable that the battalion should move inland as rapidly as possible. It was clear that although the original plan had provided for an advance up the east bank of the Scie and a rendezvous with the tanks from Dieppe at the Bois des Vertus, the South Saskatchewans had not made enough progress for this to be practicable. However, an alternative route, up the west bank, had been planned in case of need, and this Major Law now adopted.[38] He debouched from Pourville with his main body at a time which was not recorded.

At first the battalion followed the main road; then, coming under machine-gun fire from the direction of Quatre Vents, it bore to the right to take advantage of the cover of the woods on the heights overlooking the Scie. It continued to be harassed by German snipers, and would seem to have advanced slowly. After penetrating roughly a mile and a half from Pourville, it moved left again towards the hamlet and bridges of Petit Appeville (Bas de Hautot). Here Law hoped to cross the river and make contact with the tanks.[39]

Looking down on the crossings from the high ground west of the village, Law saw enemy forces beyond the river, including what appeared to be a bicycle platoon (we now know that a German cyclist platoon had been sent at 5:30 to reinforce the ridge near Quatre Vents Farm).[40] There was no sign of the Canadian tanks; none of them had, in fact, got beyond the Promenade at Dieppe. Law had no information beyond what he could see, and as time was getting short he resolved to abandon the attack against the planned objectives, and instead to cross the river and clear the Quatre Vents area. Orders to this effect were issued about nine o'clock. As the companies moved towards the road-bridge, there was contact with the enemy coming from two directions: a party moving south on the road from Pourville (probably a reconnaissance patrol of engineers which was operating in this area)[41] and forces moving up from the south on the west bank of the Scie. Casualties were inflicted on both. The Germans, however, were establishing an increasingly firm hold on the area about the crossings. At 6:10 a.m. their 571st Infantry Regiment had sent an order by dispatch rider to its 1st Battalion, the regimental reserve in Ouville, to move to the Hautot area for an attack against Pourville. This unit in the course of assembling ran into the Camerons (a report of this contact was received by the German divisional headquarters at 9:55 a.m. from a staff officer who had been sent to the battalion). Law saw a detachment of horse-drawn close-support guns arrive from the south, cross one of the Petit Appeville bridges and take up a position on the east side covering the crossings. This was doubtless the infantry gun platoon "in process of formation" which is known to have been stationed at Offranville as part of the regimental reserve.[42] Although its operations are not mentioned in the German documents, the 302nd Division's administrative report speaks of two 75-millimetre infantry guns being in action during the day.

The Camerons' 3-inch mortars having been knocked out in Pourville, they had no weapons capable of silencing these shielded guns at several hundred yards' range. At the same time, they were under machine-gun and sniper fire from the high ground overlooking the crossings. Major Law now decided that it was not practicable to fight his way across the river. About 9:30 a.m. he gave orders for withdrawal. Immediately afterwards he heard that his wireless set had intercepted a message from Headquarters 6th Brigade to The South Saskatchewan Regiment advising of the intention to evacuate from Green Beach and adding, "Get in touch with the Camerons." The message was understood as giving the time of evacuation as ten o'clock; thus a speedy retreat was essential. After sending a message telling the South Saskatchewans what he was doing, Law began his withdrawal by the route by which he had advanced. The unit retired under pressure. On the way it met a South Saskatchewan platoon which had been sent out to make contact with it, and the combined force re-entered Pourville just before ten.[43]

The penetration through Pourville was the most important effected during the day, and it was about this area that the Germans were most apprehensive. The regiment in Corps Reserve was moved up in that direction and was about to attack when the operation came to an end.[44] Moreover, as we shall see, the Germans' intention was to employ the 10th Panzer Division in this area. There has been a tendency to criticize the Military Force Commander for not exploiting the advantage gained here; but the fact is that he knew nothing of the extent of the penetration. No reports about the Camerons' progress appear in the headquarters logs during the period when they were inland.[45] All General Roberts knew was that they "had penetrated some distance inland and . . . were out of wireless touch."[46] In any case, by the time they reached Petit Appeville it was too late to begin exploiting, and the infantry reserves had been expended elsewhere.

The plan had envisaged evacuating all the troops, in the event of success, through the town of Dieppe. In the circumstances actually existing, however, The South Saskatchewan Regiment and the Camerons had to be taken off from the same beach at Pourville on which they had landed. This decision was made and orders given about 9:00 a.m. The time fixed was 11:00 a.m., the same as for the main beach. The boats arrived on schedule, but the South Saskatchewans and the Camerons lost heavily during the withdrawal. The enemy was able to bring fierce fire upon the beach from his lofty positions east of Pourville, and also from the high ground to the west, from which "C" Company of the South Saskatchewan had retired as the result of a misunderstanding (the order from the headquarters ship for the battalion to withdraw and re-embark was apparently passed on to this company and understood by it as an executive order from the Commanding Officer, although it was not so intended).[47] However, the landing craft came in through the storm of steel with self-sacrificing gallantry (one Cameron wrote afterwards, "The L.M.G. fire was wicked on the beach, but the Navy was right in there").[48] The naval reports indicate that probably twelve assault landing craft, one support craft and one *chasseur* took part in lifting troops from Green Beach. In this task at least four, and probably five, assault craft were lost.[49] Several larger vessels gave fire support.

The enemy's troops, who showed little stomach for really close fighting, were kept at arm's length by a courageous rear guard commanded by Lt.-Col. Merritt. Throughout the day, Merritt had been in the forefront of the bitter struggle around Pourville, exposing himself recklessly and displaying an energy almost incredible ("It wasn't human, what he did," said an officer who was with him).[50] Thanks to Merritt's group, the greater part of both units was successfully re-embarked, though many of the men were wounded. The rear guard itself could not be brought off. It held out on the beach until ammunition was running low and there was no possibility of evacuation or of doing further harm to the enemy. At 1:37 p.m. the 571st German Infantry Regiment reported, "Pourville firmly in our hands."[51] Lt.-Col. Merritt subsequently received the Victoria Cross.

The fatal casualties suffered by the Camerons and The South Saskatchewan Regiment were respectively six officers and 70 other ranks, and three officers and 81 other ranks.

THE FRONTAL ATTACK ON DIEPPE

The frontal attack on Dieppe was to be delivered by The Royal Hamilton Light Infantry on the right and the Essex Scottish on the left, with the nine leading tanks of the 14th Army Tank Regiment landing simultaneously with the first infantry. The assault was to be covered by the 4-inch guns of the destroyers and *Locust*; and close-support fighter aircraft were to attack the beaches, the buildings overlooking them, and the gun positions on the West Headland "as the landing craft finally approach and the first troops step ashore on RED and WHITE beaches."[52] There was no hope of surprise here, for the flank landings were scheduled for half an hour earlier; and we have seen that the alarm was given in Dieppe, following the Pourville landing, twenty minutes before the main assault.

The R.H.L.I. and the Essex Scottish were carried across the Channel in the landing ships *Glengyle*, *Prince Leopold*, and *Prince Charles*. The landing craft were lowered and made their approach without untoward incident,[53] and the infantry units touched down on the long beach in front of Dieppe's Promenade—dedicated once to idleness and pleasure—at the exact time appointed or within a minute or two of it.

The naval orders called for intense direct bombardment by four destroyers and *Locust* from the time when the landing craft were one mile from the beach until they touched down. These were carried out, except that *Locust* did not participate; she had been unable to keep up during the passage.[54] The Air Force also played its part precisely as planned. Smoke was laid to screen the East Headland; and at 5:15 a.m. five squadrons of Hurricane fighters made a cannon attack upon the beach defences.[55] This was ending just as the Essex Scottish and The Royal Hamilton Light Infantry leaped from their assault craft and began to scramble through the wire obstacles towards the town. All witnesses[56] agree that the Hurricane attack was excellently timed and most terrifying. It was planned to cease at 5:25, and its effect was of course purely temporary. Naval estimates of the time the first landing craft touched down vary from 5:20 to 5:23;[57] they may thus have been up to a couple of minutes late. If so, the troops were to this extent less able to profit by the air attack.

There was, however, a more serious error in timing. The three craft carrying the first nine tanks "approached from too far to the westward and were about 10 to 15 minutes late in touching down."[58] During this period, between the cessation of the naval and air bombardment and the tanks' arrival, there was no support for the infantry; and the enemy, recovering from the Hurricane attack, was able to sweep the beaches with fire. This happened so rapidly that our infantry were pinned down before they could get through the wire obstacles, climb the sea-wall, and cross the broad Promenade into the town. In any opposed landing, the first minute or two after the craft touch down are of crucial importance; and it may be said that during that minute or two the Dieppe battle, on the main beaches, was lost. The impetus of the attack ebbed quickly away, and by the time the tanks arrived the psychological moment was past.

The enemy had been firing upon the landing craft as they approached the shore. Some reports suggest a temporary slackening at the moment of landing, possibly the result of the Hurricanes' blow, but it was followed immediately by an intensification of machine-gun and mortar fire.[59] Officers of the R.H.L.I. state that "D" Company, which was on the right closest to the West Headland, was almost wiped out immediately after landing.[60] It had, in fact, suffered heavily while still afloat. Two craft, both apparently carrying platoons of this company, were reported lost. A responsible naval officer[61] states that both were "heavily damaged during the approach" but touched down; this seems likely, though an Army witness doubts whether they reached the beach.[62]

At the west end of the Promenade, in front of the town, stood the large isolated Casino. The Germans, we have seen, had begun to demolish it, but only the southwest wing had been destroyed before the raid. The building, and pillboxes and gun emplacements near it, were occupied by the enemy, and clearing them took time and cost lives; but the R.H.L.I. shortly broke into the Casino and rounded up the snipers. "Nearly an hour was needed before all the enemy were either killed or taken prisoners."[63] In this work Lance-Sergeant G.A. Hickson, R.C.E., leading the survivors of a demolition party whose assigned task was the destruction of the telephone exchange, distinguished himself.[64] At 7:12 a.m. a report that the Casino had been "taken" was logged on the headquarters ship; this may indicate when the clearing process was completed.

The Casino constituted a sort of covered avenue between the beach and the Boulevard de Verdun, the street skirting the front of the town. Thanks largely to this fact, at least one party of the R.H.L.I. and another led by a Sapper sergeant were able to get into the town and remain there for some time.

The first party to enter seems to have been a group of about fourteen men under Capt. A.C. Hill. This officer led it from the beach into and through the Casino at about 6 a.m., when our troops had entered the building but not yet cleared it. Covered by Bren gun fire, they ran across the open to the buildings on the front of the town and broke into one which let them into a theatre, through which in turn they got into the town. They circled through several streets, engaging enemy patrols and losing one man killed. Encountering increasingly heavy opposition, they fell back to the theatre, where they were joined by some other men of our force. About ten in the morning, when enemy infantry were seen converging on the theatre, the whole party retired to the Casino, only one man being hit during the rush across the open.[65]

At a fairly late hour in the morning Lance-Sergeant Hickson took a party of about eighteen men into the town,[66] profiting by the fire of one of our tanks which had stopped near the southeast corner of the Casino and had silenced some of the machine-guns in and around the lofty Castle on the West Headland. The party had trouble with snipers and cleared one house held by German infantry before withdrawing to the Casino towards noon.[67] Hickson was awarded the Distinguished Conduct Medal.

On the Essex Scottish beach there was no such feature as the Casino to facilitate infiltration. It was completely open and was commanded by both headlands as well as by the high buildings in front. We have mentioned the French tank dug in near the base of the west mole; and on the mole itself there was a pillbox mounting an anti-tank gun. These two positions remained in German hands throughout the operation, though the enemy records that the one on the mole "suffered a direct hit," possibly from naval fire.[68]

The only party of the Essex Scottish known to have got into the town was led by C.S.M. Cornelius Stapleton. Only a few minutes after the first landing, this stout Warrant Officer led a dozen or so men across the fire-swept Promenade into the buildings fronting the Boulevard de Verdun.[69] The party killed a number of enemy snipers in the buildings and subsequently penetrated through the streets to the harbour. It "accounted for a considerable number of enemy in transport and also enemy snipers"[70] before being overpowered; its action is doubtless reflected in a German report logged at 8:16 a.m., that the enemy had been thrown back "from the harbour station (100 metres from the beach)."[71] C.S.M. Stapleton got back to the beach and reported to Colonel Jasperson. In due course he received the Distinguished Conduct Medal.

Capt. D.F. MacRae, the only officer to land with the Essex Scottish who returned to England after the operation, recorded two attempts to attack across the sea-wall, followed by a third "on a reduced scale." These took place very soon after the landing and were beaten back by heavy fire. His estimate was that between 30 and 40 percent of the Essex Scottish had been killed or wounded by 5:45 a.m.[72] The estimate seems high, but it is clear that at an early stage the unit was, in MacRae's phrase, "unable to continue organized fighting" and was forced on to the defensive, using the line of the wall as a sort of fire-trench. "D" Company had had as one of its tasks the destruction of the Tobacco Factory, which was supposed to contain explosives. It fired grenades into the building, which from this or some other cause caught fire and burned fiercely.[73]

From the time when the first momentum of the assault was lost, the situation on the beach remained largely static. The men of the R.H.L.I. and the Essex found what cover they could and tried to return the fire of a largely invisible enemy who continued to pour down bullets, mortar-bombs, and shells. Casualties mounted steadily. Among those who laboured to assist the wounded during that sombre morning, one was particularly conspicuous: Honorary Captain J.W. Foote, Chaplain of the Hamilton regiment. He worked ceaselessly at giving first aid, and repeatedly exposed himself to carry injured men to the aid post. At the withdrawal, he helped bear the wounded to the boats but disdained to embark himself, choosing rather to continue his work of mercy as a prisoner. At the end of the war he received the Victoria Cross—the first ever awarded to a Canadian chaplain.[74]

The Navy did its courageous utmost to assist the men on the beaches. The Naval Force Commander's account of the work of one flak craft (a converted L.C.T. mounting several anti-aircraft guns) may be quoted. "A brilliant feature of this assault was the support given by L.C.F. (L)2, who remained close in firing at all positions, for a very considerable time. She was straddled continually by enemy batteries and under heavy fire from close range weapons. One by one her guns were put out of action and finally she sank."[75]

THE FORTUNES OF THE TANKS

It is well to consider separately the experience of the Calgary Regiment's tanks. The 14th Army Tank Regiment was the first unit of the Canadian Armoured Corps ever to go into action. This was, moreover, the Churchill tank's first battle, as well as the earliest test of tank landing craft under fire.

It has already been explained that the leading group of tanks, "Flight 1" (nine tanks, carried in three L.C.T.s) was perhaps as much as a quarter of an hour late in landing. Of the three craft carrying this wave, two were lost; one remained on the beach, and another succeeded in withdrawing but evidently sank shortly afterwards. L.C.T. 2, which touched down near the east end of the beach, landed its three tanks, though only after some delay. All three are known to have crossed the sea-wall. The craft got off the beach successfully, intending to land the engineers who were on board farther to the right; but damage to the ramp by shellfire prevented its putting in again and these sappers never got ashore.[76] L.C.T. 1 landed its tanks, but only one got on to the Promenade. The craft itself sank in shallow water offshore; it appears in German photographs close to the base of the west mole. Unfortunately, the leading tank from L.C.T. 3 went off "in very deep water"[77] and was "drowned" and lost. The others landed successfully but did not get beyond the beach. This was the craft that was unable to withdraw.

Flight 1A likewise consisted of three craft, each carrying three tanks. It was due to land at 5:35 a.m., which was approximately the time that Flight 1 actually did land. The naval reports indicate that Flight 1A came in "shortly afterwards."[78] The fortunes of the three craft and their tanks may be briefly stated. L.C.T. 4 landed all its tanks, but none crossed the wall. This craft evidently sank after withdrawing from the beach. L.C.T. 5 on the other hand never got off the beach; German photographs show it directly in front of the Casino. All its tanks landed, but only one got over the wall. L.C.T. 6 likewise landed its tanks, and all three reached the Promenade. This craft survived the operation.

Flight 2, consisting of 12 tanks carried in four L.C.T.s, was due to land at 6:05 a.m., and it appears to have been on time.[79] The regimental headquarters troop was in L.C.T. 8. When this craft touched down the leading tank got ashore but "bellied" in the shingle and blocked the ramp. The craft pulled off and made another approach, but shellfire severed the cables so that its ramp fell and it touched down in perhaps eight feet of water. Lt.-Col. Andrews, receiving a signal from a sailor who doubtless thought that his tank could get off, drove off the craft, and the tank was almost entirely submerged. The young Commanding Officer and his crew got out, and it would seem that Colonel Andrews reached, or nearly reached the shore; but he appears to have been shot down at the water's edge.[80] He was a most promising officer and an agreeable companion; many mourned him.

L.C.T. 8's third tank remained on board. L.C.T. 7 and L.C.T. 9 landed their tanks, and all of them crossed the wall. L.C.T. 10 likewise put all its tanks ashore but only one reached the Promenade. All four craft of this flight survived the landing, but L.C.T. 7 was lost during the withdrawal.[81]

The remainder of the tank regiment (the whole of "A" Squadron and three troops of "C") was not landed.[82]

We have already given some hint of the action of the tanks ashore. It will be noted that the sea-wall did not present an especially serious obstacle. It has often been assumed that it was intended to blow holes in the wall to open a passage for the tanks; but the actual plan was to build timber-crib ramps to enable tanks to cross it in the central section, where it was highest. To give the tanks traction on the beach and assist them in climbing the low end sections of the wall, a track-laying device had been invented by which the leading tank on each craft would lay a path of "chespaling" in front of it.[83] In fact, no ramps were built, nor could they have been built under the conditions that existed. The Germans had had a mechanical excavator at work in front of the central section of the wall, and here it was quite impassable; but at either end it rose less than two feet above the shingle, and the tanks had little difficulty in crossing it at these points.[84]

A total of twenty-nine tanks went off the landing craft; two were drowned, and of the twenty-seven that landed, fifteen crossed the sea-wall. Major C.E. Page, the senior officer of the Calgary Regiment in Oflag VIIB, held a conference of the unit's officers in that camp to decide this point. Collating all their information, they found that thirteen tanks had certainly crossed the wall, but were uncertain concerning two others, which belonged to a troop commanded by Lieut. E. Bennett, who was in a different camp. Correspondence with Lieut. Bennett has since established that these two also crossed.[85] Some infantry officers have given much lower estimates of the number that reached the Promenade, but the evidence of the men who were in the tanks is conclusive. Incidentally, the report of the German 81st Corps states that eyewitnesses reported that "probably sixteen" tanks reached the Promenade. The Commander-in-Chief West, it is true, states that only five got there; this appears to have been the actual number remaining there after the operation. The author of this report presumably did not know that, as stated in the 81st Corps report, as well as in the evidence of the Calgary Regiment officers, many of the tanks that crossed the wall returned subsequently to the beach.

More formidable obstacles than the wall were the heavy concrete road-blocks barring the streets leading out of the Promenade into the town. To breach these with explosives was the engineers' business; but some of the demolition parties had not landed, others had had equipment destroyed, and others had suffered casualties. The officer in charge on White Beach,

Lieut. W.A. Ewener, was badly wounded.[86] Those who could get within reach went forward gallantly, in spite of the deadline fire from the Castle and other flank positions. But none of the blocks was breached. Although some charges were actually placed on a block near the Casino, it appears that the means of detonating them were lacking; and a sharp-eyed French civilian saw one still there on the following day.[87] It was reported after the operation that three or four tanks had penetrated into the town; but none actually got farther than the Promenade.

Further progress being prevented by the road-blocks, almost all the tanks on the upper level returned after a time to the beach, and German propaganda pictures, and our own aerial photographs taken after the raid, led us to underestimate the number that had succeeded in crossing the wall. Information about the tanks' action was long very meagre, chiefly because only one man (Trooper G. Volk) who had been in a tank on shore returned to England.[88] Only when our first prisoners were repatriated (on medical grounds) in 1943 did the real facts begin to emerge.

Most of the tanks were sooner or later immobilized by damage or by bellying in the beach shingle. However, they continued firing, operating in effect as pillboxes, and effectively supporting the infantry, who speak in the warmest terms of the manner in which they were fought. The Calgary Regiment's chaplain, on an L.C.T. offshore, listened to the cool and steady voices that spoke over the tanks' radio telephones and reflected that it might have been a game of bridge.[89] The tank fire certainly contributed to the withdrawal of many infantrymen. The crews did not leave their vehicles until 12:25.[90] By this time evacuation had virtually ceased, and this is the explanation of why almost none of the tankmen returned to England. Thanks to the Churchills' staunchness, however, the regiment had very few fatal casualties: actually, two officers and eleven other ranks. The enemy's anti-tank guns were mainly 37-millimetre, against which the tanks' armour gave complete protection. About nine o'clock the Germans brought into action an anti-tank company armed with 75-millimetre guns; but the road-blocks prevented these from firing on the beach at close range.[91]

THE LANDING OF THE RESERVES

Something has already been said of the inadequacy of the information available to General Roberts about progress ashore. We have noted the false report to the effect that the Royal Regiment had not landed at Puys, which led him to send orders for that unit to come to Red Beach to support the Essex. This was about 6:40. About the same time, Roberts decided to land the main body of his floating reserve. This was done because, as he says in his report, "information received indicated that 'Red' Beach was sufficiently cleared" to permit such action to be properly taken. The "information received" was evidently a message entered in the *Fernie* intelligence log at 6:10: "Essex Scot across the beaches and in houses." This seems to have originated in a message from the Essex to the R.H.L.I. which is recorded elsewhere and which appears to describe the penetration made by C.S.M. Stapleton's little party: "12 of our men in the buildings. Have not heard from them for some time."[92] Reaching the Military Force Commander in the very exaggerated form which has been quoted, it led him to believe that the Essex had made a penetration suitable for exploitation, and he ordered Les Fusiliers Mont-Royal, whose Commanding Officer came on board *Calpe* at 6:10, to land on Red Beach. At 7:00 a.m., accordingly, the unit went in in its twenty-six unarmoured personnel landing craft.[93]

The Germans observed this "major formation of approaching landing craft" and their artillery fired on it for ten minutes.[94] This was not all. In the words of the naval officer in charge (Lt.-Cmdr. J.H. Dathan), when the boats neared the beach "very heavy firing was opened . . . from buildings in front of the beach, machine guns which appeared to be on the boulevard, and from the top of the west cliff further heavy machine gun fire, mortar fire and grenades."[95] A considerable number of casualties were suffered before the craft touched down. But the Fusiliers were not discouraged. Capt. MacRae recalled later how the boats struck the beach at speed, and the dash with which the men rushed ashore and charged up the shingle.

Although General Roberts' intention had been that the unit should land on Red Beach, it was in fact landed along the whole extent of the main beaches, and a considerable part of it was put ashore on the narrow strip of shingle under the cliffs west of the town.[96] The men landed here could of course accomplish nothing. Of those farther east, some were active in and around the Casino, while others were pinned down on the beach along with the greater part of the R.H.L.I. and the Essex Scottish.[97] Various parties were reported to have got into the town, but none is attested by evidence except one including Sergeant P. Dubuc, which penetrated some distance, was captured, but subsequently overpowered its guard. Sergeant Dubuc succeeded in getting back to the beach.[98] Lt.-Col. Ménard was severely wounded immediately after landing, and suffered further wounds later; and in general the Fusiliers' losses were very heavy, their total fatal casualties being 8 officers and 111 other ranks. Of the officers who actually landed, only 2 returned to England, and both were wounded.

After the commitment of the Fusiliers, General Roberts had still available as a reserve (apart from the unlanded tanks) the Royal marine Commando. The original plan to use this unit as a cutting-out force against shipping in the harbour was of course impracticable, and Roberts now decided to utilize it too on the main beaches. Perhaps the General was unwise in persisting in reinforcing the beaches at this stage; yet deceptively encouraging intelligence was still being received. Shortly after 8 a.m. he believed that the situation on White Beach was such that additional troops landed there might be able to penetrate through the town and circle round to clear the East Headland. The *Calpe* intelligence log contains at 8:17 the entry, "Have control of White Beach." It was about this time that General Roberts instructed the Marines to transfer to armoured landing craft and go in "and support the Essex Scottish through White beach . . . the object . . . being to pass around the West and South of the town, and attack the batteries on the East cliff from the South."[99] Some of the remaining tanks were ordered to land in support, but this was cancelled ten minutes later, and the craft carrying the unlanded tanks were ordered back to England about nine o'clock.[100]

The information received had been false and the plan over-optimistic. The Marines, like the Fusiliers, met a most destructive fire as they approached the shore. When Lt.-Col. Phillipps realized the situation, he stood up in his own craft and signalled to the rest to retire into the shelter of the smoke-screen offshore. His action doubtless saved many of his men from landing upon a beach where they could have accomplished nothing.[101] The Commando's report states that of the seven craft in which the unit was embarked, only three actually reached the shore; the rest turned back or had already broken down. Phillipps fell mortally wounded after completing his signal.[102]

The Headquarters of the 4th and 6th Brigades were in tank landing craft, each divided into two groups in different craft. In the case of the 4th Brigade, neither group succeeded in landing. Brigadier Lett was in L.C.T. 8, which, as already noted, touched down twice and was heavily shelled. On the second occasion the Brigadier was badly wounded, and instructed Lt.-Col. Labatt of the R.H.L.I. to take over the Brigade. The order was received, but under the conditions existing on the beach Labatt could exercise little control. On board the L.C.T., Brigadier Lett was still able to give orders as he lay on a stretcher.[103] Of the 6th Brigade's Headquarters the only officer to land was Brigadier Southam himself, who followed the tanks from L.C.T. 7 ashore. Although wounded, he was active on the beach throughout the operation, directing and encouraging the men. He kept in touch with Force Headquarters, reporting progress and giving guidance, through a wireless set in the scout car belonging to Major G.M. Rolfe, the senior signals officer who landed. This car was slightly to the west of the Tobacco Factory.[104]

As the morning progressed, an increasingly fierce battle developed in the air. The Luftwaffe's effort was slow in getting under way—one more indication that the Germans were surprised—but as the hours passed it threw more and more squadrons in. About 10 a.m. it began to use bombers escorted by fighters,[105] and in the end, the Air Force Commander believed, "all his [the enemy's] resources on the Western Front were in action." The war diary of the German Naval Operations Staff states, "According to data compiled by the Air Force, 945 German planes were sent into action over the Channel on 19 August." Despite the fact that our aircraft were frequently fired upon by our ships, whose gunners showed a "low standard of aircraft recognition," the R.A.F. gave most effective cover to the great assembly of shipping off Dieppe.[106] The only major vessel lost was the destroyer *Berkeley*, which "received a direct hit with a heavy bomb" about one o'clock and had to be sunk by British torpedoes. About the same moment, a fighter attack on *Calpe's* bridge caused a number of casualties. The Naval and Military Force Commanders were lucky enough to escape, but Air Commodore Cole was severely wounded.[107]

The air force, in addition to providing the large support programme which had been pre-arranged, and carrying out the special directions of the Fighter Controller in the headquarters ship, received and met many requests from the men on the beaches for special emergency missions.

However, in such cases there was an inevitable time-lag of approximately an hour and a half between the request being made and the aircraft being over the target. To give one example, at 11:48 a.m. Brigadier Mann sent a message to Uxbridge passing on a request for bomber action against the East and West Headlands received from Brigadier Southam four minutes before. This was received at Uxbridge at 12:17 and orders for an attack on both headlands by Hurricane bombers and close support aircraft were issued at 12:43. The attacks were delivered at 1:30 p.m., after our troops ashore had surrendered. General Crerar recalls one case at Uxbridge in which Admiral Mountbatten asked him to intervene by requesting intensive bombing of the East Headland. But since the bombing could not take place for an hour and a half, since there was no telling what might happen in that period, and since General Roberts had not asked for such action, Crerar declined the request.[108]

WITHDRAWAL FROM THE MAIN BEACHES

By nine o'clock, it was evident that the landing of the reserves had been without effect. The enemy still held both headlands and was sweeping the beaches with fire. Since "the military situation was serious, and . . . it was becoming steadily more difficult for ships and craft to close the beaches," Captain Hughes-Hallett advised General Roberts "that the withdrawal should take place with as little further delay as possible, and should be confined to personnel." He considered 10:30 a.m. the earliest practicable time, as it was necessary to warn the Air Force Commander and pass orders to the landing craft. This time was accordingly agreed upon, but shortly afterwards, at Roberts' request, it was changed to 11:00 a.m. The reasons for Roberts' suggestion were the fear that there might not be time to make contact with the Camerons, and advice from Air Commodore Cole that the extra half-hour would ensure more adequate air support for the withdrawal.[109]

At 10:30 the German fighter airfield of Abbeville-Drucat was attacked by Fortress bombers of the United States Army Air Force escorted by R.A.F. Spitfires. Of the twenty-four bombers comprising the four squadrons employed, twenty-two actually bombed. The bombing was reported to be very accurate, and the enemy was probably unable to use this aerodrome for about two hours during the critical stage of the withdrawal.[110]

The arrangements for the withdrawal had largely to be improvised. The original intention, had the raid gone according to plan, was to take most of the troops off the beaches in tank landing craft. In the conditions actually existing, however, it was out of the question to send these large and vulnerable vessels in, and assault landing craft (small bullet-proof boats capable of carrying about a platoon of infantry apiece) had to be used.[111] These circumstances increase the credit due the Navy for an evacuation carried out under conditions probably without parallel in the history of warfare.

At eleven o'clock the landing craft began to go in, covered by naval fire and R.A.F. fighters; the fighter force over Dieppe had now been increased from three squadrons to six, and sometimes was as high as nine.[112] "The wind was onshore and slightly from the west, and an effective screen of smoke prevented the landing craft from being fired upon until they were close inshore."[113] The Germans on the clifftops continued to pour down shells and bullets, taking toll of boats and men alike.

On the Essex Scottish beach, not many craft came in, and of those that did a very high proportion (six out of eight mentioned in a report from H.M.S. *Prince Charles*)[114] were lost.[115] The craft from H.M.S. *Prince Leopold* were intended for Red Beach but actually went in by mistake to Green Beach (Pourville), where they did very useful work. This undoubtedly reduced materially the number of craft available to evacuate the Essex Scottish, but naval records indicate that one of these boats did get to Red Beach later.[116] It appears also that enemy air attacks contributed in some degree to scattering and disorganizing the landing craft. Commander H.V.P. McClintock, the Boat Pool Officer, describes such an attack and its effect; it evidently helped to bring him to the conclusion that further evacuation from Blue, White, and Red beaches was not practicable. At about 12:20 he signalled the Naval Force Commander's Chief of Staff to this effect. General Roberts, however, "asked that a further effort should be made," and Captain Hughes-Hallett, although apprehensive that this might merely mean "greater losses to troops already embarked," decided to give McClintock discretion in the matter. He accordingly replied. "If no further evacuation possible withdraw"; but as received by McClintock the signal read, "No further evacuation possible, withdraw." Since, however, he was already convinced that there was no point in persisting, this error in transmission had no actual influence on events.[117]

The Force Commanders were unwilling to leave the area while any hope remained of bringing off men still on shore. At 12:48 *Calpe* went close to the beach, with a landing craft on either bow, and shelled the breakwaters, "on which machine gun posts were reported to be preventing the troops on Red Beach from reaching the water." Other destroyers had previously gone close in to assist; H.M.S. *Brocklesby* reported that she had actually grounded by the stern for a moment as she turned away.[118] Captain Hughes-Hallett was taking counsel with the shallow-draught gunboat *Locust*, whose people might have better knowledge of the state of things on the beaches, when about ten minutes past one a signal was received from Brigadier Southam's rudimentary headquarters, "Our people here have surrendered."[119]

Thanks to the boundless skill and courage of the Navy and particularly of the crews of the landing craft, a considerable proportion of the force that had landed was successfully brought away. Of the 4963 Canadians who embarked for the operation, 2211 returned to England. Of these, however, it seems likely that nearly 1000 had never landed. Analysis suggests that only between 350 and 400 men were evacuated from the main beaches in front of the town. The larger vessels were full of casualties during the return voyage; the little destroyer *Calpe* brought back 278 wounded soldiers.[120]

By 2 p.m. the operation was over. At 1:58 the German artillery finally fell silent. Its meticulous returns indicate that it had fired 7458 rounds during the battle, not counting anti-tank and anti-aircraft shell.[121] About 2:10 the last craft was reported three miles from the French coast.[122] General

Roberts had already sent by pigeon to Headquarters 1st Canadian Corps a message[123] summing up the grim record of the battle:

> Very heavy casualties in men and ships. Did everything possible to get men off but in order to get any home had to come to sad decision to abandon remainder. This was joint decision by Force Commanders. Obviously operation completely lacked surprise.

Fighter cover was maintained over the force throughout the homeward voyage, and enemy air attacks did no serious damage to the ships. "The coastal craft and landing craft reached Newhaven without further incident, and the destroyers and H.M.S. *Locust* berthed alongside at Portsmouth shortly after midnight."[124] The protection of the flotillas in the final phase had crowned the work of the air forces, which throughout the operation had been beyond praise; General Roberts' word for it was "magnificent."[125]

So ended the brave and bitter day. Under the shaded dockside lights in the English ports, tired and grimy men drank strong tea and told their tales, and the ambulance trains filled and drew slowly out. Back on the Dieppe beaches the Germans were still collecting Canadian wounded, and the Canadian dead in their hundreds lay yet where they had fallen. On both sides of the Channel staff officers were already beginning to scan the record and assess the lessons of the raid; and beyond the Atlantic, in innumerable communities across Canada, people waited in painful anxiety for news of friends in the overseas army—that army which, after three years of war, had just fought its first battle.

NOTES

1. Evidence of Maj. J.C.H. Anderson, 29 May 1943, C.M.H.Q. file 24/Dieppe/1; report of conference at Oflag VIIB, 13 Sept. 1942, paragraph 10.

2. Information from Lieut. Koyl, 27 Nov. 1942.

3. Lt.-Col. Catto remembers a flare being dropped by an aircraft at this point. This is not mentioned by *Queen Emma*'s Commanding Officer or in any other naval report. Certainly no warning reached the Germans at this time.

4. Evidence of Maj. J.C.H. Anderson, 29 May 1943.

5. United Kingdom records.

6. Report of conference at Oflag VIIB, paragraph 10; information from Lt.-Col. Catto, July 1952.

7. Evidence of Cpl. L.G. Ellis.

8. Examination of site by the writer, 5 Sept. 1944.

9. Capt. G.A. Browne, "Report on the Operation at Dieppe, 19 Aug. 1942" (undated, but previous to 11 Nov. 1942).

10. Ibid.; United Kingdom records.

11. Browne, "Report."

12. The code name applied to the special training for the operation.

13. Information from Lieut. Koyl, 27 Nov. 1942.

14. Nevertheless, the report of the German 302nd Division, after mentioning what is evidently Catto's party, adds, "An additional 25 men, suffering losses, scrambled through the wire entanglements reinforced with mine charges; they are annihilated at 0815 hours [7:15 a.m. B.S.T.] by assault detachment

of 23 (Heavy) Aircraft Reporting Company."

15. Comment by Lt.-Col. Catto, 8 July 1952, H.Q.C. 1453-21-5, vol. 2; Browne, "Report"; cf. report of conference at Oflag VIIB, paragraph 10; interview with Lt.-Col. Catto, 9 July 1952.

16. W.D., H.Q. 302nd Div., Quartiermeisterabteilung (C.R.S. 24361/1), 25 Aug. 1942.

17. Personal accounts of several soldiers, particularly Pte. E.J. Simpson; United Kingdom records.

18. Account by Pte. Simpson; information from Sub-Lieut. J.E. Boak, R.C.N.V.R., 24 Aug. 1942.

19. W.D., G.S., H.Q. 2nd Div., Aug. 1942, app. 51.

20. United Kingdom records.

21. H.Q. 1st Canadian Corps file Ops 3-3-1-2 Div.

22. United Kingdom records.

23. 302nd Div. report (Operations Sec.), II (C).

24. Account by Mr. Ross Munro, Canadian Press correspondent who was in this craft, *Globe and Mail* (Toronto), 22 August 1942; cf. his *Gauntlet to Overlord* (Toronto, 1945), 325–28; account by Cpl. F.H. Ruggles.

25. German newsreel film of the operation.

26. United Kingdom records.

27. *Calpe* Intelligence Log.

28. United Kingdom records.

29. See especially account by Capt. H. B. Carswell, F.O.O.; information from Maj. J.E. McRae, 25 Feb. 1943; and various accounts by men of "A" and "D" Companies.

30. Accounts by Lieut. J.S. Edmondson, Lt.-Cpl. H. McKenzie, Pte. J. Krohn, etc.; Wallace Reyburn, *Rehearsal for Invasion: An Eyewitness Story of the Dieppe Raid* (London, 1943), 59–62; recommendation for V.C., Lt.-Col. C.C.I. Merritt.

31. The following information was logged by the 302nd German Division at 8:00 a.m. (7:00 a.m. British time): "At Pourville-East 4.7 cm anti-tank gun position is overrun by enemy. Anti-tank gun unable to continue fire due to jamming of loophole, crew is killed. Enemy advances on height up to orderly room of 6th Company 571st Regiment, is held here. One beach-defence gun and one heavy machine-gun put out of commission."

32. Account by Lt.-Cpl. A.F. Bales.

33. Account by Sgt. K.A. Williams.

34. Account by Capt. H.B. Carswell.

35. United Kingdom records.

36. Information from Maj. A.T. Law, 3 Dec. 1942, Sub-Lieut. J.E. O'Rourke, R.C.N.V.R., 24 Aug. 1942, and Capt. J. Runcie, 11 Dec. 1942; account by Pte. W.J. Coll.

37. Information from Maj. Law, Capt. Runcie, and Capt. R.M. Campbell.

38. Information from Maj. Law, 3 Dec. 1942.

39. Ibid.; see also battalion and company narratives appended to W.D., Camerons of Canada, Aug. 1942.

40. 302nd Div. report (Operations Sec.), II (C).

41. Ibid.

42. Ibid., I (B).

43. Information from Maj. Law, 3 Dec. 1942, and W.D., Camerons of Canada, Aug. 1942.

44. 302nd Div. report (Operations Sec.), II (C).

45. The narrative in the Camerons' war diary states, "We were unable to contact Bde. H.W. at any time during the advance inland and subsequent withdrawal, and it was not until approximately 1005 hrs when we returned to Pourville that this was accomplished."

46. Gen. Roberts to Senior Officer, C.M.H.Q., 11 May 1943, C.M.H.Q. file 24/Dieppe/1.

47. Lt.-Col. Merritt to the writer, 10 March 1947, H.Q.C. 1453-6-5, vol. 1.

48. Account by Cpl. R.R. Hughes.

49. United Kingdom records.

50. Capt. John Runcie, 11 Dec. 1942.

51. 302nd Div. report (Operations Sec.), II (C).

52. Combined Plan, paragraph 25 (iii).

53. Lt.-Col. Labatt states that shells fell near H.M.S. *Glengyle* while craft were being lowered; and, doubtless on the basis of his report, the conference of Commanding Officers at Oflag VIIB on 13 Sept. 1942 recorded that "infantry assault ships . . . came under fire by 0340 hours from shore batteries." But the German documents disprove this, and the report of *Glengyle*'s Commanding Officer makes it clear that the firing was that resulting from Group 5's encounter with the German convoy. He writes, " . . . heavy fire from guns of light calibre was observed (0350) bearing 130°—the direction of 'Yellow' landing—and a few 'overs' of no importance burst near the ship."

54. United Kingdom records.

55. "Detailed Chronological Air Narrative," app. D to Report by the Air Force Commander.

56. Account by Capt. D.F. MacRae, W.D., Essex Scottish, Aug. 1942, app. 6; account by C.S.M. J. Stewart, R.H.L.I.; and United Kingdom records.

57. United Kingdom records.

58. Despatch by Naval Force Commander, Narrative, paragraph 13.

59. See, e.g., accounts by Ptes. C. Johnson and J. Telfer and Sgt. F.B. Volterman, and information from Lieut. L.C. Counsell, 6 June 1944 (all R.H.L.I.).

60. Narrative by Capt. W.D. Whitaker, W.D., R.H.L.I., Aug. 1942, app. 21; information from Lt. Counsell, 6 June 1944.

61. United Kingdom records.

62. Information from Lt. Counsell, 6 June 1944.

63. Narrative by Capt. Whitaker.

64. W.D., 7th Field Coy, R.C.E., 19 Aug. 1942; recommendation for D.C.M., Lt.-Sgt. G.A. Hickson.

65. Information from C.S.M. J. Stewart, 26 Oct. 1942.

66. A narrative written by Capt. W.D. Whitaker states that another party of the R.H.L.I., led by Lieut. L.C. Bell, also penetrated into the town. In the opinion of Lt.-Col. Labatt, this is an error. Lieut. Bell himself was killed during the operation. The present writer however thinks it probable that another party got into Dieppe in the R.H.L.I. area. The German 302nd Division records at 7:45 the capture of a "British assault detachment . . . near Dieppe city hall" (not far from the Casino); and a careful French observer, M. Georges Guibon, relates what seems to be the same incident.

67. Information from Lt.-Sgt. G.A. Hickson, 13 Oct. 1942; cf. account by Spr. W. Price, 2nd Field Coy. R.C.E.

68. 302nd Div. report (Operations Sec.), III.

69. How fierce the fire was is indicated by the evidence of a soldier (Pte. J.T. Fleming, 4 Nov. 1943) who was one of a group who crossed the Promenade at this time and joined Stapleton in the buildings. He testified that of about nine men in his group only two reached the houses.

70. Letter from Lt.-Col. Jasperson, 23 Aug. 1942, C.M.H.Q. file 10/Jasperson F.K./1.

71. 302nd Div. report (Operations Sec.), II (C).

72. Account by Capt. MacRae, Aug. 1942.

73. Information from Pte. J. Maier, 29 Dec. 1942; comment by Col. D.F. MacRae, 23 July 1952, H.Q.C. 1453-21-5, vol. 2.

74. Recommendation for V.C., H./ Capt. J.W. Foote.

75. United Kingdom records.

76. Report by Maj. B. Sucharov, R.C.E., 2 Sept. 1942, C.M.H.Q. file 55/7116/9/2.

77. W.D., 14th Canadian Army Tank Regiment, 19 Aug. 1942.

78. United Kingdom records.

79. Report of Lt.-Col. R.D. King.

80. Comment by Brig. Sherwood Lett, 17 July 1952, H.Q.C. 1453-21-5, vol. 2; information from Cpl. T.L. Carnie (a member of crew of this tank), 29 Oct. 1943.

81. The Naval Force Commander's despatch attributes the damage suffered by the L.C.T.s in part to the long periods they remained on the beach "waiting for the miscellaneous troops that they were carrying in addition to the tanks, to disembark." Only two reports from individual L.C.T.s are available. One (from L.C.T. 8) complains that after the second tank "landed" no effort was made to get the third off. The author (not the craft's commanding officer) evidently did not know of the second tank being drowned or have a clear picture of the circumstances, which are described above. The other report (from L.C.T. 6) states, "All the Infantry except thirty went ashore, and after waiting 15 minutes for the other thirty to go ashore, I came off the beach." In this case, "infantry" presumably means simply "men on foot." There were only thirty-five actual infantrymen in this craft.

82. Sources for account of tank landings: allocations to craft and flights, loading tables in Detailed Military Plan; list of tanks landed (names and troops), W.D., 14th Canadian Army Tank Regiment, 19 Aug. 1942; list of tanks crossing wall, information from Maj. C.E. Page, 6 Nov. 1943; information from various individuals. See also above, notes 76–80.

83. Report of Maj. Sucharov, 2 Sept. 1942.

84. Information from Maj. Page, 29 Oct. 1943.

85. H.Q. 1451-202/14.

86. W.D., 7th Field Coy. R.C.E., 19 Aug. 1942.

87. Accounts by Lt.-Cpl. M.D. Sinasac and Spr. L.W. Laur, and information from C.S.M. J. Stewart, 26 Oct. 1942; G. Guibon, *A Dieppe le 19 Août 1942* (Dieppe, n.d.), 19.

88. Memo of evidence of Tpr. Volk, H.Q. 1st Canadian Corps file Ops 3-3-1-2 Div.

89. E.g., C.S.M. Stewart, 26 Oct. 1942; Capt. Whitaker narrative; "Narrative of Experiences at Dieppe" by Lt.-Col. R.R. Labatt, paragraph 23; Waldo E.L. Smith, *What Time the Tempest* (Toronto, 1953), 77–79.

90. Wireless Log, regimental command net, W.D., 14th Canadian Army Tank Regiment, Aug. 1942, app. 7.

91. 302nd Div. report (Operations Sec.), II (C) and III.

92. Untimed message heard by listening set, H.M.S. *Calpe*.

93. *Calpe* Intelligence Log; United Kingdom records.

94. 302nd Div. report (Operations Sec.), II (C).

95. United Kingdom records.

96. Analysis of 103 questionnaires filled out by individual soldiers, Fusiliers Mont-Royal.

97. Information from Lieut. A.A. Masson, 30 Jan. 1943, P.S.M. L.A. Dumais, 23 Oct. 1942, and other personnel of Fusiliers Mont-Royal.

98. Information from Sgt. Dubuc, 3 Nov. 1942.

99. Report by Capt. P.W.C. Hellings, R.M.; cf. entry of 0818 hours in *Calpe* Intelligence Log.

100. Naval Message, 0837 hrs, W.D., G.S., H.Q. 2nd Div., Aug. 1942, app. 51; despatch by Naval Force Commander, Narrative, paragraph 25; United Kingdom records.

101. The detail, frequently repeated, that Phillipps put on white gloves before making his signal, is not in the Commando's reports. An account by a Marine private who claims to have been in the Colonel's L.C.M. fully confirms the Commanding Officer's gallantry, but makes no mention of the signal. James Spenser, *The Awkward Marine* (London, 1948), 58–66. The reports, however, are much better evidence.

102. United Kingdom records.

103. Narrative by Maj. M.E.P. Garneau, W.D., H.Q. 4th Infantry Brigade, Aug. 1942, app. 15A; account by C.S.M. W. Dean, R.H.L.I.; narrative by Lt.-Col. R.R. Labatt.

104. Memorandum by Maj. G.M. Rolfe, 11 Feb. 1946, H.Q. 1451-202/14; Information from Maj. C.E. Page, 6 Nov. 1943; Brig. W.W. Southam, "Report on Approach, Landing, and Subsequent Events, Dieppe."

105. At 7:11 a.m. British time, nearly two-and-a-half hours after the first landings, the German 302nd Division logged the message, "Corps H.Q. advises that bomber aircraft will be committed to action."

106. Report by the Air Force Commander, and covering letter.

107. Despatch by Naval Force Commander, Narrative, paragraph 33.

108. *Fernie* Messages, app. 63, W.D., G.S., H.Q. 2nd Div., Aug. 1942; "Detailed Chronological Air Narrative"; comment by General Crerar, 7 June 1952, H.Q.C. 1453-21-5, vol. 2.

109. Despatch by Naval Force Commander, Narrative, paragraphs 26–28; Roberts to Senior Officer, C.M.H.Q., 11 May 1943, C.M.H.Q. file 24/Dieppe/1.

110. Information from Historical Division, Air University Library, United States Air Force, 24 May 1950.

111. Despatch by Naval Force Commander, Narrative, paragraph 27.

112. Report by Air Force Commander, paragraph 55.

113. Despatch by Naval Force Commander, Narrative, paragraph 28.

114. United Kingdom records.

115. The report of the Commanding Officers' conference at Oflag VIIB states, "No naval craft came in to evacuate this battalion." In 1952 Colonel Jasperson was still of this opinion, but Colonel MacRae "had the impression that the navy did make attempts." MacRae himself, however, got off with the aid of a small wooden rowboat full of wounded, which he, swimming, pushed for two miles, when he and his party were picked up. (Comments by Lt.-Col. Jasperson, 12 June 1952, and by Col. MacRae, 23 July 1952, H.Q.C. 1453-21-5, vol. 2; recommendation for M.C., Capt. D.F. MacRae.

116. United Kingdom records.

117. United Kingdom records; despatch of Naval Force Commander, Narrative, paragraph 31.

118. Despatch by Naval Force Commander, Narrative, paragraph 33; United Kingdom records.

119. Despatch by Naval Force Commander, Narrative, paragraph 33; W.D., H.Q. 6th Infantry Brigade, Aug. 1942, app. 13.

120. Despatch by Naval Force Commander, paragraph 37; cf. Lt.-Gen. L.K. Truscott, *Command Missions* (New York, 1954), 67–72.

121. 302nd Div. report (Administrative Sec.) and (Operations Sec.), VII (F).

122. Report by Air Force Commander, paragraph 66.

123. Message 1340 hrs, H.Q. 1st Canadian Corps file Ops 3-3-1-2 Div., vol. 2.

124. Despatch by Naval Force Commander, Narrative, paragraph 35.

125. Report by Military Force Commander, 27 Aug. 1942, paragraph 5.

CROSSING THE MORO ✧

FARLEY MOWAT

○

Because of the conditions under which we had been existing for so many weeks, disease had taken a heavy toll. Epidemic jaundice in particular caused many casualties. Among its victims, all evacuated to North Africa, were Alex Campbell and John Tweedsmuir. Both went unwillingly (Alex had to be ordered into hospital) and both were sorely missed. With Tweedsmuir's departure, Ack Ack Kennedy again took over as commanding officer.

On November 25 Kennedy, [the Battalion C.O.,] and I attended a Divisional briefing in Campobasso. A fiery brigadier from Eighth Army Headquarters, backed by an immense map, gave us "the form" from the stage of a warm and well-lit theatre.

"As you may have guessed, gentlemen, our objective remains Rome. Can't let the Hun spend the rest of the winter there all nice and comfy-cosy. So we shall jolly well turf him out. Over on the left . . . here . . . the Yanks will burst through the Bernhard Line and streak up the Liri valley past Cassino and pop into Rome from the south. Our chaps . . . over here . . . will smash across the Sangro and gallop up the coast to Pescara then make a left hook into the mountains and pounce on Rome from the east. Our part of the show will open with a colossal crack at the mouth of the Sangro River. . . . First Canadian Division will spearhead the advance after the breakthrough has been made. We've bags of tanks and guns so it should be plain sailing, what?"

There are some phrases which can chill the veteran soldier's blood more effectively than any polar blizzard—and "spearhead the advance" is one such. Kennedy and I had nothing much to say to one another as our open jeep jounced back to Castropigface [Castropignano] through driving

✧ From *And No Birds Sang* (Toronto: McClelland and Stewart, 1979), 215–29.

sleet. There was no joy in me as I contemplated the prospects. There was even less joy when, two days later, I accompanied Kennedy on reconnaissance, prior to moving the battalion to the Adriatic coast.

Winter had preceded us. The snow that had been steadily building on the inland peaks had been falling just as heavily into the grey valleys of the coastal plains, but melting as it fell. The *torrentes* were bearing eloquent witness to their name, racing and roaring to the sea. Heavy with saffron-coloured muck, they sucked at the shaking supports of the prefabricated Bailey spans with which our sappers had replaced the demolished Italian bridges. From the distant coast of Yugoslavia the infamous *Bora* gale drove black clouds in from seaward almost at ground level, enveloping the wetlands in dark and deathly mist. Everything that was not solid rock seemed to be turning fluid. Lines of olive trees gnarled by a hundred winters stood gaunt as gibbets on dripping ridges above vineyards that had become slimy swamps. In the villages the sad stone houses seemed to have shrunk even closer to one another under the burden of unrelenting rain and sleet.

It was a time for plants to die, for birds to flee, for small animals to burrow deep into the earth, and for human beings to huddle by charcoal braziers and wait the winter out. It was assuredly neither the time nor place for waging war.

Kennedy's disgusted comment as we headed back to rejoin the Regiment was prophetic.

"*Gallop* up the coast to Pescara, will we? Gallop like a goddamn snail more like!"

The first day of December, 1943, found a great convoy of trucks rolling eastward out of the mountains carrying First Division toward the visceral rumble of a singularly savage battle which had then been in progress for three days as two British and one Indian Division delivered the "colossal crack" against the Bernhard Line. The Sangro was crossed and a bridgehead established, but at fearsome cost. A liaison officer from the British 79th Division told me about it with tears—not of sorrow, but of rage—in his eyes.

"We've had five hundred casualties crossing this one flaming river! And for what? Haven't any of the high mucky-mucks looked at their frigging maps? There'll be half a dozen Sangros before we get to Pescara . . . *if* we get to Pescara. Thank God you're taking over, Canada. We've *had* this show!"

The coastal plain north of the Sangro is a narrow shelf between the towering Maiella Mountains and the sea. At intervals of a mile or so, it is deeply gashed from mountains to tidewater by steep-sided ravines and river valleys. In summertime this constrained ribbon of lowland presents a singularly formidable obstacle to an attacking army. Once the winter floods have set in, it becomes almost impassable.

If our high command seemed blind to the nature of the ground and its defensive possibilities, the German staff was not. Even while the Bernhard Line was being breached, the Germans were preparing a new line along the Moro River, a scant nine miles north of the Sangro. And they had already manned it with fresh troops, including another of their more famous formations, the 90th Light Panzer-Grenadier Division which also had been part of Rommel's Army.

By the morning of December 5, 79th Division's Royal Irish Fusiliers had reached the near bank of the Moro. That afternoon we were ordered to relieve them and become the "spearhead of the advance."

It was pelting rain when I went forward with the Fusiliers' intelligence officer to see what he could show me. Long files of soaked and muddy Fusiliers wound their way past us, moving to the rear. Their faces were as colourless as paper pulp and they were so exhausted they hardly seemed to notice the intense shelling the coastal road was getting as they straggled down it.

But *I* noticed, as I never had before. The rancid taint of cordite seemed to work on me like some powerful and alien drug. My heart was thumping to no regular rhythm. It was hard to draw breath, and I was shivering spasmodically though I was not cold. Worst of all, I had to wrestle with an almost irresistible compulsion to stop, to turn about, to join those deathly visaged men who were escaping from the battle that awaited me.

I paused, fumbled for a cigarette and offered one to the Irish lieutenant trudging at my side. He lit a match and held it in cupped hands for me . . . but I turned my face away, for in that instant I realized what was happening to me. I was sickening with the most virulent and deadly of all apprehensions . . . the fear of fear itself.

At length the Irishmen and I reached the edge of the plateau forming the south wall of the valley. We lay on our bellies behind some dripping bushes and I raised my binoculars and hid my face behind them. There was nothing to see through the haze of rain and mist.

" 'Fraid there's not much I can show you." The voice of the man beside me was strained, almost impatient. "Been thick as soup ever since we got here so we've not seen what the far bank looks like, and my chaps were too done-in to go patrolling. Just the same you can stake your soul old Jerry's over there, and good and ready, I'll be bound."

"Well," he added when I did not reply, "nothing more I can do here, eh? Best be catching up to my regiment. Cheer-oh . . . and best of luck."

He scrambled to his feet and vanished into the rain scud with what seemed like indecent haste. I had an almost overwhelming urge to run after him, but fought it down. High-flying shells droned their dirge overhead while I lay on the wet earth, trying to pull myself together.

It was almost dusk when I reached B.H.Q., which was in a *casa* half a mile south of the river mouth. Kennedy was fuming with impatience.

"Where the hell have *you* been? Goddamn it, we're to cross the Moro right away. No preparation. No support. What've you found out?"

"Sorry, sir, not much. The Irish couldn't tell me anything and there's nothing to be seen from our side of the valley."

He grunted angrily.

"Can you get scouts out there and find a crossing place? And get them back inside an hour?"

"Don't know, sir. I can try."

"*Try*? Goddamn you, *do it!*"

Oh Christ, I thought, I'll have to go myself . . . I'll have to go . . . No! . . . I'll send Langstaff . . . He's far the best man for the job . . . I'll send him out . . .

The scouts were brewing tea in a nearby cow byre. They watched me without expression as I briefed George Langstaff and two other men. They knew I had at least glimpsed the valley in daylight and so was the logical one to lead the patrol. What they did not know was that the mere prospect of descending into that ominously shrouded valley was paralyzing me. I was convinced that death or ghastly mutilation awaited me there. The certainty was absolute! The Worm that was growing in my gut had told me so.

Four months earlier I would have welcomed the chance to make a patrol like this. Two months past and I would have accepted it as a risky job that had to be done. But on this December day I would have given everything I was, or ever hoped to be, for a way out.

There was none.

I took the patrol out . . . and nothing happened. The Worm had lied. The darkness was so opaque and the whip of wind and rain so masked our movements that we went and returned unseen and unmolested. We felt our way to the swollen river and waded along its overflowing banks until we found a ford. And we got back to our own lines just in time for Langstaff to become guide for Able Company as it moved into the attack.

After wading the river at the ford, Able, with my old platoon in the lead, had barely begun to climb the far bank when twenty or thirty German machine guns began stitching the darkness with vicious needles of tracer. Flares—some green, some red—burst overhead, and these SOS signals were instantly answered by the distant grumble of enemy guns. Within seconds roaring salvos of artillery and mortar shells were falling on Able Company, the explosions illuminating the bleak valley floor with fluctuating and hellish flames.

I was with Kennedy on the south escarpment when the Germans opened up, and we were appalled by the ferocity of the German reaction. After only a few minutes Kennedy yelled to the signaller manning the radio to call Able back.

As the survivors came straggling out of that inferno, we realized we had never before seen war in its full and dreadful magnitude. Seven Platoon in particular had suffered fearfully. The platoon commander who had succeeded me had been severely wounded, and Sgt. Bates and several other men I had known and led were dead or dying.

All through the rest of that long, wet night the forward troops manned their weapons while all of us tried to avoid thoughts of the morrow. At dawn we heard that Second Brigade had attacked at San Leonardo four miles upstream, and had also been bloodily repulsed.

Shortly thereafter we received orders to force a crossing on our front at whatever cost.

o

The battle that followed began at 1400 hours on December 6 and ended on December 15, barely a mile north of where it had begun. It was a ten-day blood bath that cost the Regiment over a hundred and fifty battle casualties.

The opening attack was made in broad daylight by Charley Company under cover of the strongest artillery support Division could muster. It was a devastating barrage . . . but the enemy replied with equal violence and within minutes Charley was being pounded into the saturated valley floor under a titanic upheaval of mud and steel. Dog, coming up behind, tried to avoid the worst of that holocaust and swung to the left into a smoke screen being laid by our own heavy mortars, and the entire company simply vanished from our ken. When, after nearly an hour, there was still no word from Dog, Kennedy became so distrait that he ordered me and a Battalion Headquarters runner to follow, then flung himself hell-bent down the slope.

My whole being screamed resistance. Three times we were pinned, grovelling in the mud, before we reached the river and struggled through its icy waters. On the far shore we fell into a slimy ditch with the survivors of one of Charley Company's platoons. We tried to find out from them what was happening, but nobody knew. The German counter-barrage had by then become so heavy that platoons and even sections were isolated and out of communication with one another, cowering into the muck as almost continuous explosions leapt about them.

Kennedy led us on in search of Charley Company Headquarters, and we miraculously stumbled on it in a tiny cave at the foot of a steep cliff; but the company commander was missing and a terrified sergeant could tell us nothing. Kennedy realized the situation was hopeless and that we would have to withdraw, but he had no way of issuing the necessary order until he could get to his radio. So he led us back across the valley.

My memory of that return must be akin to what a drowning man feels during the endless, agonizing moments when he is sinking slowly into the depths. My chest felt crushed and I was gasping for air by the time we reached the road which climbed the south slope. There must have been a lull in the shelling then or else Kennedy was just so anxious to reach the radio that he did not care what the enemy might do, for he led us straight up the road in full view of the Germans opposite. We had not gone fifty feet when they bracketed us with a salvo of Eighty-eights.

Something struck my right foot a numbing blow and a stunning concussion flung me face down into the mud. I heard screaming close at hand and, struggling to my knees, saw Kennedy on *his* knees in the centre of the smoking road, shaking his head slowly from side to side like an old and tired dog, but the screaming was not his. Ten feet behind him the runner, a young lad whose name I never knew, was humping jerkily away from his own leg which had been severed at the thigh. In the instant that I saw him, he gave one final bubbling shriek, collapsed, and mercifully was still.

I heard Kennedy's voice as from some distant mountain peak.

"Get up, Mowat! Goddamn you! *Up!*"

He was standing over me, swaying, but apparently unhurt.

"Can't," I said quite calmly. "Hit in the leg, I think."

In a moment he had me by the shoulders and hoisted me to my feet. We stumbled over the crest and fell into the cover of a gully as another salvo of Eighty-eights ploughed into the road behind us.

There was no pain in my foot and glorious euphoria was overwhelming me. *I had a Blighty*! Soon I would be on my way back down the line to a field hospital and then perhaps still farther back for a sea voyage to England or even Canada! The sound and fury . . . and the fear . . . would be behind me. But somewhere within my skull a spiteful voice poured vitriol on my joy. "Coward!" it said. "You gutless wonder!"

A couple of men from Baker Company spotted us and now they helped me to the regimental aid post which the medical officer, Capt. Charlie Krakauer, had pushed forward to the doubtful shelter of a ruined hovel on the very lip of the valley. Kennedy was in a desperate hurry to get on to B.H.Q. but he spared a moment for me.

"Good lad, Squib. You've done okay."

I gave him a lying grin but I was thinking, Thank Christ I'm getting out of here!

Someone helped me onto a stretcher in the dim-lit room and Krakauer was soon bending over my feet. I heard him grunt and felt a tug, then his face was above me, split by a lopsided grin.

"You lucky little prick! Shell cut your boot open from end to end and hardly creased the skin. Wait till we get a band aid on it and you can go right back to work!"

I did not believe him! Outraged, I rolled over and sat up . . . and shrieked as a flame of agony seared deep into my backside. Krakauer's smile faded as with one big hand he pushed me back on the stretcher and rolled me over. Again I heard him grunt as he swiftly scissored off the seat of my trousers . . . then a bellow of raucous laughter burst from him.

It must have been the last laughter heard at the regimental aid post that day and for days thereafter. It was justified. Sticking out of the right cheek of my ass, unnoticed until I sat upon it, was a wedge of steel shell casing which had penetrated to a depth of perhaps half an inch. Charlie yanked it out with his fingers and presented it to me with a flourish.

"Keep this in memory of me," he said.

I departed limping slightly, for feeling had not yet returned to me foot, and with the seat of my pants held together with a large safety pin contributed by a stretcher-bearer. I was not on my way to Blighty. My destination was rear B.H.Q., there to seek out a new pair of boots and a whole pair of trousers. I also had some hopes of being able to hide for awhile in the relatively shellproof gully where rear headquarters was located, but even this was not to be.

I was met by a white-faced and fluttering Jimmy Bird who told me Kennedy had been unable to contact Dog Company on the radio and had therefore decided the attack would have to be renewed in order to rescue Dog. Charley Company, whose survivors had mostly dribbled back by

now, was in no shape for another round; so I was to fetch what was left of
Able and lead it up to take part in a new attack in company with Baker.

There was no time to change either boots or trousers. Physically sickened by the mere thought of going back into the valley, I stumbled down
the road to Able's area where I found Alex's replacement, a newly arrived
captain whom I did not know, and gave him my message. He hardly
seemed to hear.

Al Park was standing nearby, a strange, obdurate look on his face, and
his eyes hooded. He beckoned me off to one side.

"Paddy's bought it," he said in a voice thin with grief or rage—I could
not tell which. "Phosphorous grenade exploded in his face and burned him to
a crisp . . . died in the ambulance on the way out. We just now heard . . . the
company's down to about forty bods still able to pull a trigger. God almighty,
Squib, they can't send us back in now!"

Yes, I thought dully, they can. They will. But I said nothing, and Al's
gaze dropped from my face to the mud at our feet. Memory flickered and I
saw Paddy kneeling beside the dead Italian officer on that dusty road in
Sicily. The Irish Rover . . . gone now for good.

Al uncorked his water bottle and offered it to me. We both took choking gulps of the straight issue rum. It did not restore my failing courage but
at least it helped a little to deaden the throbbing fear.

Kennedy was waiting for us near the aid post, which was now clustered about with jeep ambulances taking out the wounded from Charley
Company. Moments later we were descending into the void again.

The German fire, which had slackened somewhat after Charley's withdrawal, started up anew and, so it seemed, with redoubled weight and fury.
Most of the artillery of the German Corps holding the coast section, augmented by self-propelled guns and an avalanche of mortar bombs and
rocket projectiles, was now concentrated in the valley. However, the very
massiveness of the bombardment served to partially defeat its purpose. It
would not permit us to retreat. We had no choice but to stampede forward
up the enemy-held slopes, for there alone could we hope to find shelter
from the annihilating blast.

I have no recollection of that second crossing until I found myself in the
same little cave that had been Charley Company's Headquarters during
their ill-fated attack, and being roundly cursed by the battalion signals
sergeant who did not recognize me in my mud-caked state and thought I
was one of his signallers. Then Kennedy appeared, wild-eyed and glaring
like a maniac.

"*Jerry's on the run!*" he cried. "But the goddamn radio's gone out!
Mowat! Go back and get what's left of Charley!"

Of *that* crossing of the Moro I have no memories at all. Darkness had
fallen by the time I returned to Kennedy again. By that time a few men from
Able and Baker had thrust forward to the edge of the northern plateau, where
German tanks and a savage infantry counterattack forced them to dig in.

What followed was the kind of night men dream about in afteryears,
waking in a cold sweat to a surge of gratitude that it is but a dream. It was a
delirium of sustained violence. Small pockets of Germans that had been cut

off throughout our bridgehead fired their automatic weapons in hysterical dismay at every shadow. The grind of enemy tanks and self-propelled guns working their way along the crest was multiplied by echoes until it sounded like an entire Panzer army. Illuminating flares flamed in darkness with a sick radiance. The snap and scream of high-velocity tank shells pierced the brutal guttural of an endless cannonade from both German and Canadian artillery. Moaning Minnie projectiles whumped down like thunderbolts, searching for our hurriedly dug foxholes. Soldiers of both sides, blundering through the vineyards, fired with panicky impartiality in all directions. And it began to rain again, a bitter, penetrating winter rain.

December 7 dawned overcast and brought black news. The engorged Sangro River had risen twenty feet in as many hours and washed away the precious pontoon bridges, leaving First and Second brigades isolated from the rest of the army. Worse still, the Germans had smashed a bridgehead which had been established across the Moro at grim cost by Second Brigade near San Leonardo, leaving us holding the sole remaining foothold on the northern bank.

As icy rain squalls swept the smoking valley, things grew worse. A troop of British tanks attempting to cross in our support became hopelessly bogged and were picked off, one by one, by German self-propelled guns. Then came word that despite our success at the mouth of the river, the divisional commander intended to persist with the bloody attempts to make a main crossing at San Leonardo. Therefore, we were not to be reinforced, and much of the artillery support which had been vitally instrumental to our survival was to be switched to the San Leonardo sector. Left on our own, our orders were to "engage the enemy closely" in order to draw his attention away from Second Brigade's assault.

This order was superfluous, for the Germans now proceeded to engage us as closely as they could.

During the next thirty-six hours eleven separate counterattacks were flung against us. Yet somehow we clung to our precarious salient across the Moro, and by drawing upon ourselves the German fire and reinforcements, including a fresh regiment from the First Paratroop Division, enabled our sister brigade to make a new crossing of the river at San Leonardo and consolidate a bridgehead there.

The cost had been appalling. When the firing died down on our sector, stretcher and burial parties scouring the slimy slopes and the tangles of shell-torn debris found one hundred and seventy German corpses. Our own dead and wounded amounted to a third of the four hundred or so Hasty Pees who had gone into the valley of the shadow.

○

For me the Moro is to be remembered as the lair of the Worm That Never Dies—and of one particular victim. He was a stretcher-bearer, an older man—he might have been all of thirty-five—who had been with the Regiment since the autumn of 1939.

By day and by night the bearers had to make their ways across valley, crawling forward to the lead platoon positions, if necessary. Some of them must have made that agonizing passage a score of times. For them there was no rest and no surcease; no burrowing in a slit trench to escape the sound and fury. For them there was only a journey into the inferno, then the withdrawal to momentary sanctuary, and the return to hell once more.

That was the hardest thing to bear. Those who remained under sustained and unremitting fire could partially armour themselves with the apathy of the half-dead; but those who had to come and go, knowing the searing repetition of brief escape followed by a new immersion in the bath of terror—those were the ones who paid the heaviest price.

On the last night of our ordeal I was descending the north slope, numbed and passionless, drugged with fatigue, dead on my feet, when I heard someone singing! It was a rough voice, husky yet powerful. A cluster of mortar bombs came crashing down and I threw myself into the mud. When I could hear again, the first sound that came to me was the singing voice. Cautiously I raised myself just as a starshell burst overhead, and saw him coming toward me through that blasted wasteland.

Stark naked, he was striding through the cordite stench with his head held high and his arms swinging. His body shone white in the brilliant light of the flare, except for what appeared to be a glistening crimson sash that ran from one shoulder down one thigh and dripped from his lifted foot.

He was singing "Home on the Range" at the top of his lungs.

The Worm That Never Died had taken him.

OPERATION OLIVE[✧]

D. GRAHAM AND S. BIDWELL

o

> I am told that the 5th Canadian Armoured Division was excellent . . . though not strong in numbers, the Canadians are right good soldiers.
>
> Von Vietinghoff to Kesselring, 7 September 1944[1]

The pursuit after DIADEM came to a halt in July, with Kesselring's forces, battered but still intact and full of fight, ranged across Italy from the Metauro river on the Adriatic coast along the Arno to the Mediterranean, covering the Pisa-Rimini line according to plan. The long debate over ANVIL (renamed DRAGOON) had gone against Alexander, and he was forced to halt and redeploy to fill the huge gap left in the Fifth Army by the loss of seven divisions. The enforced pause enabled Leghorn to be opened as a forward base and supply port and the infantry were given a much-needed rest, for the pursuit had been a hard-fought affair costing Clark 18 000 and Leese 16 000 casualties.[2] All hope, however, of bursting through the Gothic Line and reaching the plain of Emilia before the summer ended had evaporated and Alexander prepared for an autumn offensive.

His mission, to contain Kesselring, remained the same and Harding once again decided that the best course was an all-out offensive, with the full weight of both armies concentrated and an elaborate deception plan to conceal the point of attack. In the area of Ancona the Apennines turn northwest in a great mountain rampart, rising from the rolling foothills in the east to snowy peaks in Liguria, offering only two avenues of advance. Harding discarded the Adriatic, with its alternation of ridge and river valleys that had so troubled the Eighth Army in the winter of 1943. The most promising, he thought, was the main highway over the passes from Florence to Bologna. This plan, which suited Clark, was short lived.[3]

✧ From *Tug of War: The Battle for Italy, 1943–45* (London, UK: Hodder and Stoughton, 1986), 347–66.

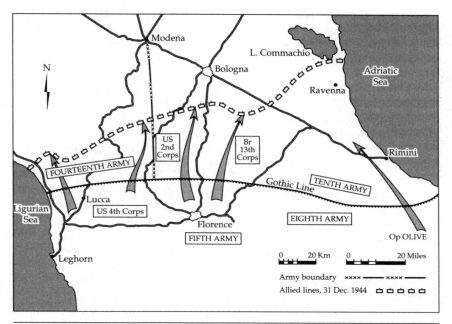

F I G U R E   1   *THE GOTHIC LINE: ALEXANDER'S FINAL*
PLAN FOR THE OFFENSIVE, AUGUST 1944

Kirkman's powerful 13th Corps was halted in line south of the Arno astride Florence and in his view the natural defences of the mountains facing him were strong enough to delay a mechanized army indefinitely. He decided that of two difficult options the eastern end of the Gothic Line was preferable, for only there could the great assets of the Eighth Army, a mass of tanks and thousands of guns, be realized. On 3 August when Leese visited him he pressed for the plan to be changed and found the army commander receptive. Leese, for emotional and personal reasons, had resolved never to fight shoulder to shoulder with Clark again if he could avoid it, and Kirkman now supplied him with a persuasive tactical argument. On the 4th Leese met Alexander and Harding, and Alexander, as compliant as ever, agreed with it.[4]

On the 10th Alexander summoned Clark to discuss the sudden change of plan. Clark agreed in principle with it, but was not prepared to see his Fifth Army reduced to a secondary role. Like Alexander, he was convinced that the correct strategy was to burst into the Po valley and thence into Austria and the Danube basin, and determined that he was going to play the leading part in this great enterprise. The "British," for whom by this time he felt nothing but profound contempt, could not "carry the ball" without his aid. (In DIADEM they had been "nothing but grief.")[5] There was also the danger that if Marshall and Devers thought the Fifth Army was not fully employed they might transfer it to France, a thought Clark could not endure. Keeping all this to himself Clark proceeded to negotiate in calm and masterly style. He brought the argument down to the tactical question of his right flank and who was to control the British division adjacent to it. His price for acquiescence was Kirkman's corps, complete.[6] British troops were better than none, and they would enable him to concentrate his trusted US divisions as his spearhead. Alexander, as ever, concurred. It made sense to put the left-hand corps under Clark so as to allow him to co-ordinate its operations with his own, and free Leese to conduct the battle on the coast, but Alexander's judgment of Solomon deprived Leese of a reserve, ignored the unsuitability of the central sector for tanks and divided his forces instead of concentrating them in one place or the other.

The staff, and the Canadians in particular, performed wonders transferring the Canadian Corps from its position south of Florence to the coast and in reversing the deception plan that had pointed to an offensive being launched on the Adriatic. That proved superfluous, for in Kesselring's opinion the landing of the US Seventh Army in the south of France on 15 August precluded any major offensive in Italy. What worried him was his weakness, for he had suffered some 63 000 casualties and he feared that he might have to transfer some of his elite troops, his trouble-shooting 26th Panzer and 29th Panzer Grenadiers to France, and other divisions as well. Meanwhile the 2nd Polish Corps was pressing uncomfortably hard on the Adriatic flank. He ordered von Vietinghoff to withdraw the 76th Panzer Corps into the "Red Line," or forward defence zone of the Gothic defences in that sector, between the Metauro and the Foglia rivers, and awaited events.

Leese's Operation OLIVE was simple, bold, and enterprising. He was faced by three divisions in the Red Line, the 1st Parachute on the Via Adriatica (Highway No. 16), the 71st and the 5th Mountain inland in the hills. He disposed of ten divisions altogether, and intended to open his attack with three corps in line abreast. Anders [Polish Corps] was to continue on the coast until he had masked Pesaro, and halt. Burns [Canadian Corps] then would extend to the right and Keightley's powerful corps of five divisions, on his left, would press forward. Leese's intention was to overrun the Red Line, the outpost zone of the Gothic defences, in a surprise attack without artillery preparation, bounce both parts of the Green Line, the main battle zone, before it could be properly manned and then use his mass of armour to break through the rear defences, the Rimini Line, into the Romagna, the flat alluvial plain beyond. Following Montgomery's example, he visited as many units as possible, talking to the men and filling them with enthusiasm and confidence that this was to be the final victory in Italy. ("We'll meet in Venice!" was the cry.) Surprise was to be complete, with von Vietinghoff and Heidrich, the parachute commander, both on leave.

There was, however, trouble ahead. Leese had put his strongest corps, the 5th, on the hilly inland route, changing his original plan, since Anders had already found it was less well defended and the strongpoints on the coast could be turned from the higher ground. However, Leese, having given the Canadians what the Poles told him was the toughest route, along the coast, neither reinforced them, nor made arrangements to do so were they to break through on the direct route to Rimini. He had no flexible plan for his mid-battle, the "dog-fight," when inevitably a melee with the panzers and panzer grenadiers rushing up to counterattack would develop, and it was vital to reach the ground with his own armour first.

Leese's third handicap was not of his own making. Deprived of the services of the experienced South African and British 6th Armoured Divisions, he had given Keightley the British 1st Armoured. Now in the course of the war in Italy the armoured divisions, following the German example, had learnt to fight in mixed teams of tanks and infantry, and like the New Zealand Division had added an extra infantry brigade. The 1st Armoured had not been in action since April 1943 in Africa, it was unaware of and untrained in the new tactics, its reorganization on the new model had been only just completed, the armour and infantry were strangers to each other, and Major-General Richard Hull had only recently assumed command. In short, it was not yet battle-worthy. The consequences of all this lay ahead.

The men of the Eighth Army went into battle cheered by the presence of Winston Churchill, and in the best of spirits.

It was a clear night on 25/26 August when the 1st Canadian Division with the British 46th Division on its left passed through a screen of Polish troops and established bridgeheads over the Metauro. In daylight the 1st Canadian Division advanced, the 21st Tank Brigade in support. There was resistance, so they quickly learned that the enemy had not withdrawn. The advance was hindered by cratering and mining which delayed the tanks, radio communication failed here and there and some units lost their way in the confusing country. By the evening of the 26th the division had advanced about five miles.

Next morning the vanguards arrived at the hill-towns of Monteciccardo, S. Angelo, and Ginestreto. In the afternoon Monteciccardo was bombed, unfortunately too early for the Edmontons to attack it at once, but in the small hours of the 28th their A Company entered the town and found it empty. Ten minutes later its forward platoon, having placed Bren guns to command the main street, was amazed to see a company of German infantry in threes marching down it towards them. Opening fire with two machine guns they inflicted about sixty or seventy causalties in less than a minute. Shortly afterwards, a tank appeared behind the Germans and the platoon was soon attacked by the rest of a German battalion; the company prudently withdrew to a ridge outside the town.[7] The Germans were, indeed, in some disarray and still unaware of the weight of the Eighth Army attack. They were playing for time to occupy the Green Line but also unwilling to weaken themselves so that they could not hold it. The Canadians had not attacked in great strength anywhere, and their tanks, delayed by demolitions, had not always been up with their infantry. Fortunately, this served to conceal their real strength from the Germans who did not positively identify their presence and took them for a force that was closing up to the Green Line, not one intent on pushing through it in strength.

By the evening of the 27th Burns felt less confident that he could bounce the Green Line. The 71st Division was giving ground and yielding prisoners, but though the Parachute Division had recently absorbed 2000 half-trained replacements the Canadians found Heidrich's men their usual aggressive selves. When Burns asked Vokes whether he would reach the Foglia on the 28th he replied: "Seems unlikely."

Opinion in Army Group "C" was divided. Kesselring, supported by the staff of HQ Fourteenth Army, considered that the Eighth Army's *Schwerpunkt* would be in the centre, on the Arno front. The Germans had come to regard the Canadians and the New Zealanders as elite assault troops, whose presence on any part of the front was significant. Their intelligence staff was misled by identifications of both on the central front, and reports that the area behind it was buzzing with activity. This was correct, but the Canadians were from the independent 1st Canadian Armoured Brigade, attached to the British 13th Corps, and the New Zealanders were resting. Consequently, when Kesselring heard that Canadian prisoners had been taken on the coastal sector he told Wentzell that he believed that it was a diversion. This impression was strengthened by the fact that as the 76th Corps was already in the process of falling back from its outpost positions to the Green Line it had not felt the full weight of the Eighth Army's opening blow. The Canadians, in the opinion of the German staff, never took risks. Kesselring felt that his only immediate problem was to ensure that the Green Line was fully manned in good time, so he decided to wait for the battle to develop before altering his plans.

Wentzell disagreed. He told Kesselring that if the Canadian attack now under way was in fact the main Eighth Army effort, it was (in his view) on the correct axis. He recalled von Vietinghoff, who was on leave. "Then," in the words of the Canadian official history, "came one of those dramatic finds that sometimes fall to a groping Intelligence." The Germans got hold of a copy of the message sent by Leese to the troops on the eve of the battle. It spoke of "the last lap," secret concentrations of great strength to break the Gothic Line, and bringing the campaign to an end. On the night of the 28th, with von Vietinghoff back from leave, the Germans were at last convinced that the objective of OLIVE was, indeed, the Romagna. "Such was the cost of a single sheet of very inferior paper," wrote Lieutenant-Colonel Nicholson, the Canadian official historian.[8] In fact, Kesselring had already started the 26th Panzer on its way on the 27th and the 29th Panzer Grenadiers were warned to follow it as soon as they could be relieved. The Tenth Army ordered the 98th Infantry to relieve the 71st. On the 29th, the retreating divisions crossed the Foglia, with orders to hurry their occupation of the First Green Line. But despite that, Wentzell thought that the 30th would be a day of crisis, for neither the 98th nor the 26th Panzer Divisions could reach the front until that day at the earliest.

On the 29th Leese, Keightley, and Burns considered whether to pause and mount a set-piece battle, for which fire-plans had been prepared in advance, or to try to bounce the Green Line. The 46th Division had kept almost abreast of the Canadians and patrols from both corps which had penetrated the two-mile-wide flat valley of the Foglia in the evening reported that the Green Line was lightly held. While the wire obstacles were formidable and the minefields well sited, the latter had been bombed and considerably disarranged by the Desert Air Force and so some patrols had passed through them without difficulty. On the morning of the 30th, when more aggressive patrols reached the road connecting the villages of Montecchio on the left, Osteria Nuova in the centre and Borgo S. Maria on the right, battalion commanders recommended that an immediate attack be attempted. By this time Burns had brought his armoured division into the line on the left of the 1st Division which was concentrated on a narrower front. He intended to attack with the two divisions in line, each with one brigade up, whatever form the attack took. After receiving the latest patrol information he recommended to Leese that his corps should attack immediately, pushing forward with companies, followed by battalions to make a lodgement while the Green Line was still only partially occupied.

From this time the "gate-crash battle," as Burns called it, was the responsibility of the "lieutenant-colonels who rose to the occasion and gave notable examples of leadership." This was well said, for the breaking of the Green Line was an occasion when Canadian units were faster to the punch than the Germans, exhibiting excellent minor tactics, out-fighting the parachutists and the 26th Panzer Division and opening the door for the Eighth Army to roll forward into the plain. Major-General Bert Hoffmeister sent his 11th Brigade infantry forward in the late afternoon of the 30th without a preliminary bombardment. Vokes' 3rd Brigade advanced at about the same time. The Cape Breton Highlanders on the left of them were to take Montecchio and Point 120, on the right the Perth Regiment went for Point 111 and then Point 147. Vokes' Princess Patricia's Canadian Light Infantry were to take Osteria Nuova and the West Nova Scotias Point 133. Behind the 11th Brigade, tanks of the 5th Armoured Brigade would cross the river and the anti-tank ditch, pass through the minefields as best they could and support the infantry as soon as possible. They could offer some fire-support even from the midst of the minefields but their direct presence would be required when the infantry fought their way through the German defences.

At first things did not go well because the Germans came to life and reacted strongly. (They had either been lying low or had arrived just in time to meet the advancing Canadians.) The Cape Breton Highlanders were thrown back from Point 120, where the 71st Division had been relieved by the 67th Panzer Grenadier Regiment of the 26th Panzer Division. However, the Perths took Point 111 and the Irish Regiment of Canada were brought across from the left flank and passed through between them and the battling Highlanders to attack Point 120 from the rear. The move took time in the darkness but when their attack with the tanks of the New Brunswick Hussars did go in at midday on the 31st it was entirely successful and freed the left for a further advance. In the meantime the West Novas had a dreadful time in the minefields, especially from the "schu-mines." The "Princess Pat's" persevered, cleared the village of Osteria Nuova of enemy, went on to take Point 115, pushed a company down the road to contact the 11th Brigade, and collected a good haul of prisoners from the Parachute Division.

During the night the tanks of the British Columbia Dragoons worked their way through the minefield with much shouting and cursing and not a little chaos to catch up with the Perths during the morning. The Perths had outflanked and taken Point 147 from the rear and sent a company up the spur beyond leading to the heights behind the Green Line, only for it to be pinned down by fire. The Dragoons were ordered forward to pick up the Perths and make a joint attack on their objective, Point 204 and Tomba di Pesaro, but the Perths were immobilized by "the severest shelling and mortaring that we had ever experienced," and the Dragoons went on alone. So difficult was the climb that the tank commanders dismounted to pick out a route for each tank, to be sniped and ambushed by the parachutists, until they were down to eighteen tanks, but they reached the goal, Point 204 in the very heart of the enemy position. Now the Dragoons could shoot into the rear of the enemy holding up the 3rd Brigade at Pozzo Alto, and had cut the road from the top of the hill to Borgo S. Maria.

It was now vital to get infantry on to Point 204 before dark, when the parachutists would certainly counterattack. Fortunately the tanks of Lieutenant-Colonel McAvity's Lord Strathcona's Horse by then had passed through the minefields and they picked up the Perths' infantry late in the day. Fighting a model action, troop covering troop as they climbed the ridge with the battalion, they relieved the British Columbia Dragoons at nightfall. The BCD had lost their commanding officer, Fred Vokes, brother of the commander of the 1st Division, killed, together with twenty-one others, and forty-nine wounded.

There was no sleep that night for the men on Point 204. Attack followed attack by parachutists and sniping assault guns. A farm cart was driven into the position and set on fire, brilliantly illuminating the tanks. Solid shot flew in all directions and mortar bombs crumped persistently, but the Perths gave as good as they got, chased away their assailants and at sunrise still held the position. Their friends on either side benefited immediately as the Strathcona's tanks were able to shoot at Pozzo Alto and help the 1st Division forward. Had Hoffmeister been able to listen to the agitated telephone calls between the 76th Panzer Corps, Tenth Army, and Kesselring's HQ he would have been greatly encouraged. What the Germans most feared—a thrust from Point 204 to the summit of the ridge at Tomba di Pesaro and M. Peloso—was to be his next step. It would split the German defences and enable the 1st Canadian Division to take M. Luro and drive from there to the sea. The 1st Parachute Division would be cornered in Pesaro and the Green Line rolled up from the east.

The plan was for the Straths and the Perths to take both objectives early in the morning of September 1. However, the Perths had been fighting hard for two days and were too weak to go on. (Their commander Lieutenant-Colonel Reid, twice wounded, was awarded the DSO for outstanding leadership.) Their place was taken by the 4th Princess Louise Dragoon Guards—the "Plugs"—fighting for the first time as infantry, with the Strathcona's tanks. They were not deterred by a sharp artillery bombardment that greeted them as they arrived on Point 204, costing them several men, and at 1 p.m. jumped off together with the tanks supported by an artillery fire-plan. The newly converted infantry scored a great success, recorded blow by blow in the Strathcona's radio log. Working closely together tanks and foot soldiers remorselessly drove the enemy from one

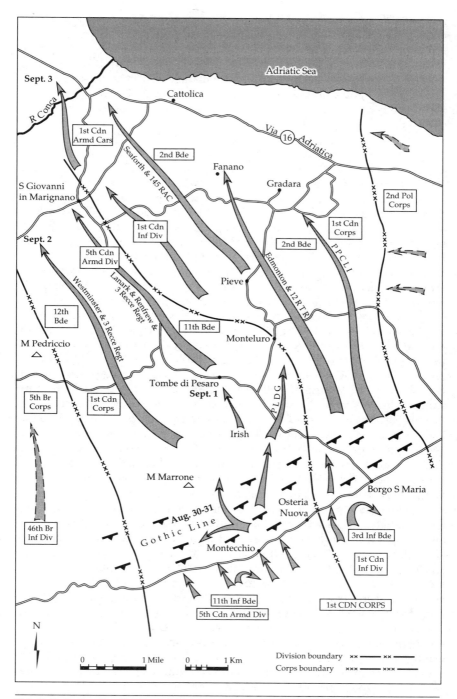

Adriatic Sea

Sept. 3

R Conca

Cattolica

1st Cdn
Armd Cars

2nd Bde

Fanano

Gradara

Via 16 Adriatica

S Giovanni
in Marignano

Seaforth & 145 RAC

1st Cdn
Inf Div

1st Cdn
Corps

2nd Pol
Corps

Sept. 2

5th Cdn
Armd Div

2nd Bde

PPCLI

Pieve

Lanark & Renfrew &
3 Recce Regt

Edmonton & 12 RTR

Westminster & 3 Recce Regt

12th
Bde

11th Bde

Monteluro

M Pedriccio
△

5th Br
Corps

1st Cdn
Corps

Tombe di Pesaro
Sept. 1

PLDG

Irish

46th Br
Inf Div

M Marrone
△

Borgo S Maria

Aug. 30-31

Osteria
Nuova

Gothic Line

3rd Inf Bde

Montecchio

1st Cdn
Inf Div

N

11th Inf Bde

5th Cdn Armd Div

1st CDN CORPS

| 0 | 1 Mile | 0 | 1 Km |

Division boundary   ×× ——— ××

Corps boundary   ××× ——— ×××

FIGURE 2 *THE CANADIANS BREAK THE GOTHIC*
LINE: 30 AUGUST–3 SEPTEMBER 1944

fire position to another; from behind corn stooks, hedgerows, and inside houses until, when all was over, his dead lay in rows and a bulldozer had to be summoned to dig a trench for a mass grave. (Lieutenant-Colonel W.W.G. Darling, the commanding officer of the "Plugs," who controlled the battle, was also awarded the DSO for "sheer gallantry and personal example.") The victors from the grassy slopes of M. Peloso now had a panorama of the Second Green Line: M. Gemmano on the left, Coriano beyond the Conca river, and to Riccione on the Via Adriatica, where the routed enemy was flying in the hope of occupying it during the night.[9]

A wonderful opportunity waited to be seized. If M. Luro fell as well as Tomba di Pesaro, a swift thrust by the 1st Infantry Division would seal the fate of the whole 1st Parachute Division, which had already lost its 4th Regiment; with it eliminated, the Second Green Line could not be held. In the 5th Armoured Division the 11th Infantry Brigade was exhausted and needed time to reorganize, and the armoured troops, equally tired, required time to recover and repair damaged vehicles and to replenish. General Hoffmeister still had in reserve his second infantry brigade, the 12th. Reinforcing it with his 3rd Armoured Reconnaissance Regiment (tanks and armoured infantry), he sent it forward that night.[10] The 11th Brigade followed up in their troop carriers. Hoffmeister's objective was S. Fortunato in the third or reserve German line southwest of Rimini—The Rimini Line— and he had the satisfaction of driving through the Second Green Line before it could be occupied by the enemy. On his right the 1st Division had taken rather longer to get off the mark. It did not capture M. Luro until five hours after M. Peloso had fallen, and then Vokes had to organize a pursuit group with the tanks of the British 21st Tank Brigade, just too late to catch the remnants of the Parachute Division. The Canadians were now in full cry.

Earlier that afternoon General Burns had reported to Alexander and Leese at Eighth Army tactical HQ that the Green Lines had been crossed and his pursuit had begun. Leese and Alexander expressed their delight but seemed startled by the news that the advance had actually started and the speed of Burns' coup. Burns formed the impression that both men were completely at a loss. When he made to leave, Leese called him back. Alexander told him that he would recommend him for the DSO. In the book he wrote later Burns recorded that he took this to mean that at last Leese and Alexander had decided he was fit to handle his command and that "confidence had replaced the doubts that had formerly existed."[11] This was all very well, but Burns' immediate need was not a DSO but another armoured division. Leese's first error, his failure to provide Burns with a reserve division before OLIVE started, was one of judgment. Now, condoned by a passive Alexander, he was guilty of criminal inertia. The door to the enemy position, if not open, was at least ajar. Leese could not have been in any doubt that given the shortest breathing space Herr, like any German commander, would leap to slam the opening door in Hoffmeister's face, nor could he have been in any doubt that according to his own plan the 1st Armoured Division could not reach even the line of the Metauro for twenty-four hours. It was not impossible to improvise a mobile group to

exploit Burns' success. A German or an American general would have gal-
vanized his staff into immediate action. Any action would have been better
than none. Leese did nothing.

On the 3rd, having crossed the Conca river, Hoffmeister's division
pushed on and took Misano but on the 4th, as they were fighting their way
down the ridge which terminated in the village of Besanigo, beyond the
Second Green Line, the New Brunswick Hussars were heavily fired on and
attacked by troops from their left flank. It transpired that the ridge from
Coriano in the north to the villages of Passano and S. Savino in the south was
held by the enemy. The corps boundary ran down the Besanigo stream, the
Coriano ridge was in the 5th Corps sector. What had happened was that the
98th Infantry Division had arrived on the 3rd, and that night the 29th Panzer
Grenadiers' 71st Regiment. It is questionable whether closer action between
the 46th Division, held up at S. Clemente, and the Canadians would have
been able to dislodge the 98th Division which was now supported by the
26th Panzer Division. However, the Irish and the Cape Breton Highlanders
pushed on and took the hamlet of Besanigo on the 5th. Meanwhile on the 4th
the 1st Division was echeloned back on the right of the 5th, held up in the
Second Green Line by parachutists in S. Maria di Scacciano. That night it
threw them out by turning their seaward flank and moved forward to the
Melo stream crossing it on the 5th, but was held up there. The 1st Brigade
lost 300 men in these few hours of fighting. Neither it nor the armoured
division could go any further as long as the Germans were firmly entrenched
in their left rear. Where was 1st Armoured Division, which was supposed to
dislodge the enemy from the Coriano ridge?

It was not until the late afternoon of the 2nd that the 4th Hussars, the
armoured reconnaissance regiment of the division, was ordered forward in
advance of the main body of the division, which had not yet reached the
Metauro, over twenty miles behind the Conca. The 4th Hussars drove all
night over treacherous tracks under the impression that they were to find
crossings over the Conca and then lead an advance through and beyond
Coriano. Next morning they were bogged behind Clemente where they
found the infantry of the 46th Division dug in.[12] On the night of the 3rd/4th
the Hampshires of the 46th Division attacked but were halted by fire from S.
Savino. In the morning they were shelled from the hills on their left flank
and rear where Croce and Gemmano were firmly held by the Germans.
During the 4th General Hawkesworth was still assuring General Hull that he
was holding "the gate" open for him and one of Leese's liaison officers
reported that Hawkesworth had the enemy on the run. All this, the 4th
Hussars discovered, was fantasy, but could not pass the truth back to HQ 1st
Armoured Division. (Presumably because the radio distance was too great.)

For the state of affairs in front of Clemente the 46th Division was not
altogether to blame. The 5th Corps terrain was difficult and Leese had
underestimated the effect of the high ground on the left of the funnel into
which he had committed it. When the 46th Division had been drawn along
in the slip-stream of the 5th Armoured, a gap occurred on their left.
Keightley filled it with the 56th Division and urged it to cross the Conca

quickly. Its commander, Major-General John Whitfield, understood that he was not to be distracted by high ground on his flanks and ordered his leading brigade to push on, leaving a battalion following behind to occupy M. Gemmano. By the time the battalion arrived and climbed the steep hill to the fortified village of that name on top, it found the 100th Mountain Regiment already in occupation and could not dislodge it. Gemmano was the hinge of the Second Green Line and as long as it was in their hands the Germans could hinder an advance on Croce and narrow the corps front to virtually that on which the 46th Division was halted. The general form that the battle on the left had taken could have been anticipated from Leese's plan, given the terrain, even if it could not have been avoided. What was incomprehensible was the failure to bring the 1st Armoured Division to a point close behind the front from which it could exploit the opportunity on September 1 for which Leese had been hoping.

A number of circumstances contributed to the situation. In the first place Leese had been surprised by the speed of the Canadian penetration. Second, he had deliberately kept the 1st Armoured well back to avoid blocking the roads forward. Had he been prepared to commit it to the Canadian Corps that would not have been a problem, for there was plenty of room immediately behind them. Third, Leese's mind worked at infantry pace. At Alamein he had commanded the 30th Corps which had done most of the infantry work to crack the line, for the armour had at first refused to fight its way through the German positions, insisting that its task was to go through "the gap" and "pursue" the enemy. The 1st Armoured Division still held that outdated notion—shared, apparently, by Leese. It was looking for a gap.

Hull could reasonably complain about the way his division had been prepared for battle, particularly of the lack of time to weld the brigades together, but a more alert commander might at least have insisted that his division was positioned closer to the front. How had the 1st Division been briefed for its mission? What did it expect? Keightley emphasised a pursuit. Driving off from one visit with a flourish he called out, "Meet you on the Po," and left the expectation of a "sure-thing gallop." Richard Goodbody, who commanded the armoured brigade, had run a training programme in June to practise the tactics used by the Canadians in the Green Line but for OLIVE he had been briefed for a task which called for the armoured brigade to work alone except for its motor battalion. He and Hull told the officers they would "pass through the Rimini gap after the infantry had broken through the Gothic Line defences and then to go on, and on and on, day and night, until we are too exhausted to see the target."

The plan was to concentrate the division on the Foglia only on the morning of the 3rd. At dawn on the 2nd it was still at Senigallia about forty miles away. The leading elements reached the Metauro in the evening. Driving through the night the wheeled vehicle column reached the Foglia by appallingly difficult tracks on the morning of the 3rd; the drivers exhausted, the columns having been on the move for fifty hours. The tanks had an even worse journey. After a scant two-hour halt at the Metauro they moved on:

The dust flung up by the sliding, churning tank tracks of the Shermans was so thick that drivers in the rear of the column cold not see at all, but drove by listening above the roar of their engines to the bellowing of the tanks in front. Sometimes a tank would slew to the side of the road, one of its tracks ripped from the bogies by some too-exacting strain. Here and there a tank attempted an impossible gradient to try to get round some obstacle while its bruised and shaken crew clung hard to the ammunition racks inside the turret.

By the time that the fighting echelons of the division reached the Foglia on the 3rd men were stupid with exhaustion, and tanks were scattered down the line of march being recovered and repaired. Brigadier Richard Goodbody's own armoured command vehicle over-turned with him in it. He was unhurt but far from fresh when he gave out his orders at about midnight on the 3rd. His 2nd Armoured Brigade would concentrate north of the Conca at S. Savino by first light on the 4th, after yet another night march. They would pass through the 46th Division and advance to the Marano and beyond. They were to start at 2:30 a.m. There was a delay to allow stragglers to catch up and to net radio sets. When the column started the regimental net of the Queen's Bays was superimposed on a BBC channel. Throughout the night the voice of Alvar Liddell reading the news was heard every half hour. Brass bands playing stirring marches cut into every message passed over the net. It was another one of those unsettling and ominous signs that the regiment was engaged in what was called "a nonsense." By 8 a.m. little more than six miles had been covered because of a late start and negotiating diversions around broken bridges and culverts.

At about noon on the 4th the main body of the 2nd Armoured Brigade was across the Conca and Goodbody was still being told that Coriano was "expected to fall soon." He was to attack through the 46th Division even though the infantry brigades in the lorries were far behind. But his leading regiment, the 10th Hussars, with a company of the 1st King's Royal Rifle Corps (the motor battalion) had gone over the S. Clemente ridge and met the Canadians on the Besanigo ridge, where they were told the real situation. The Germans held Coriano and the ridge in front in strength, Croce on their flank, and the hill-fortress Gemmano which overlooked their right rear. Keightley was misinformed and so were they as a result. The 46th Division's attack on the night of the 3rd/4th failed. The battle had slipped out of Keightley's hands, and the front was stalled.

There followed a classical situation in which a commander of a lower formation could not tell his superiors that they were talking through their hats. Goodbody had to change his plan and make what was to have been his jump-off line his objective. The artillery fire-plan was dislocated and the attack delayed. What ensued was the inevitable conclusion to three days and nights of marches and committing semi-trained units to an improvised plan without a proper reconnaissance. The history of the British Army, like others, is marred by such lapses. It was sad, though, that a débâcle like this should have occurred so late in the war.

The 2nd Armoured Brigade—without infantry, which was still south of the Conca—attacked with great courage into a setting sun against an enemy whose location had not been determined across an unsecured start line. It smacked of the Western Desert and what most soldiers then hoped were the bad old days. The attack failed, of course, and at great cost. The Queen's Bays had only nineteen out of fifty-two tanks running at the end of the battle, the 10th Hussars thirty and the 9th Lancers thirty-two. Many of the casualties were recovered, it is true, but the brigade had been thoroughly discomfited. As Kesselring had once caustically observed, "The first battles of green formations are nothing great." (Of the 5th Canadian Armoured Division on the Arielli at the end of 1943.)

The Germans' friend, the rain, fell that evening and continued in torrents on the 5th and 6th. The dust, cursed by everyone, became mud, which was worse. Streams, so easily crossed on the 4th, were impassable on the 5th. The 1st Armoured's infantry did not cross the Conca into action until the 6th, but one factor must be added. The battle was undoubtedly lost because of lack of forethought, bad management, inertia, and the passage of no or faulty information and the failure of what throughout the Italian campaign had proved a second-rate infantry division. It was won by rapid reaction and sound judgment of the German commanders who unerringly sent their reserves to the correct places. The 98th Division, partially trained and untried, rushed its 117th Regiment to help the 1st Parachute Division on the evening of the 2nd, and the rest took over from the battered 71st on the 46th Division's front on the 3rd. A mixed group from the 162nd (Turkoman) Division was thrust into the line opposite the 1st Canadians. The 278th Division appeared in front of the 56th Division to relieve the 5th Mountain, of which the 100th Regiment remained at Gemmano. What remained of the 71st Division, about three weak battalions, took over a narrow front between the 278th and 98th Divisions. The crisis had been on the 3rd when the 98th Infantry Division, with the assistance of the 26th Panzer, stopped the 46th Division and ensured that the left flank of the Canadians would be exposed. When the 29th Panzer Grenadiers were available on the 4th, they used their flank position to strike at the Besanigo ridge. On the coast the 1st Canadians were held for most of September 4 in the Second Green Line by the parachutists, even though the 5th Division had turned the inland flank. Had the line not held the two Canadian divisions might have been able to by-pass the Coriano ridge on the 4th. On the night of the 3rd Kesselring had returned from a visit to the Fourteenth Army to find Herr and von Vietinghoff considering a further withdrawal. "Prolonged plain speaking crackled over the wires till past midnight, when the more even-tempered von Vietinghoff managed to calm his superior by alluding (among other things) to the German casualties, and declaring that he knew of no man who could better the performance of Herr." No retirement was ordered.

On the morning of the 6th Leese, recognizing that a set-piece assault was necessary against the Coriano position, ordered the 5th Corps to carry it out while Burns crossed the Marano and exploited to the Marecchia. For this

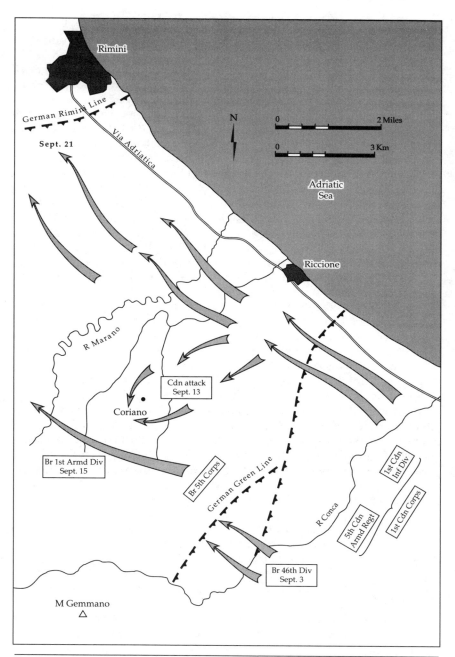

F I G U R E 3 *1ST CANADIAN CORPS: CAPTURE OF CORIANO AND ADVANCE TO RIMINI, 3–21 SEPTEMBER 1944*

Burns was to be given the British 4th Infantry Division and a Greek brigade. The New Zealand Division, under him from the 4th for liaison purposes, was to be fully under his command on the 13th. The attack was timed for the night of the 12th/13th. After discussion with Keightley, Burns suggested that his 5th Armoured Division should be responsible for taking Coriano itself, leaving the 1st Armoured Division to attack from San Clemente.

Judging that the pause in operations marked the maximum shift of German divisions to the Adriatic, Alexander gave Clark the order to attack and directed the Desert Air Force to transfer its main effort to his front. As it happened the 1st Parachute Corps was already slowly withdrawing to the main defence zone in its sector, so the Fifth and Eighth Armies' attack co-incided, marking "the beginning of a week of perhaps the heaviest fighting on both fronts that either Army had yet experienced."

The action against Coriano was highly successful. While the infantry of the 1st Armoured Division drove off the enemy from Passano and San Savino, the 5th [Canadian] Armoured Division took Coriano. The New Brunswick Hussars supported each battalion of the 11th Brigade, the Perths on the ridge south of the town, the Cape Breton Highlanders to the north and the Irish who cleared the houses one by one. Exploitation was done by the Westminster Regiment (Motor Infantry) and Strathcona's Horse. The preliminary bombardment was devastating and smoke screens blinded German observers and their anti-tank guns. The air operations of the Desert Air Force were particularly effective and virtually prevented the movement of German reserves, stifling local counterattacks. In the twenty-four hours ending at sunset on September 13 more than 500 tons of bombs were dropped in 700 sorties against battlefield targets. The town was not finally cleared until the morning of the 14th by which time the 29th Panzer Grenadiers reported "considerable losses" and 14 officers and 775 other ranks were taken by the 1st Armoured Division, which bagged part of the garrison which fled from the Canadians. The 26th Panzer, 98th Infantry, and 71st Infantry lost heavily too. It remained only to exploit the victory.

How shaken the Germans were is evident from a conversation between von Vietinghoff and Kesselring on the evening of the 13th:

Kesselring:	I have just returned and heard the terrible news. Will you please inform me of the situation.
Von Vietinghoff:	The depth of the penetration cannot be ascertained with accuracy as yet. . . . The front has been greatly weakened.
Kesselring:	We must realize that tomorrow will be a day of great crisis.
Von Vietinghoff:	We are certain of that; all day we have been racking our brains about how to help, but we have nothing left . . .

All that Kesselring had to offer were three divisions, none of them immediately available, partly due to their having been held up by air force interdiction, but luck was with him. The 1st Armoured Division found the Fornacci stream swollen by rain and their tanks could not cross. The 4th Infantry Division was held up by shelling while passing through the 5th

Armoured Division and then by Germans on the Ripabianca Ridge. The
Canadians were briefly relieved and did not resume the advance until the
14th. The Germans needed no more time than that to recover. There followed
a week of hard fighting first for the Ripabianca Ridge and then for S. Martino
and finally S. Fortunato by the 1st Canadians with the 4th Division on their
left. The Greek Brigade with the New Zealand Motor Battalion fought its
way along the coast. Rimini fell to it on the 21st, and on the same day the
1st Canadian Division crossed the Marecchia into the Romagna.

In the week the Eighth Army suffered a daily average of 145 killed and
600 wounded. From the beginning of OLIVE the total figure was 14 000
with the Canadians' share being 4511, their highest casualties for any period
of equal length either before or after the Italian campaign.[13] Tanks were
replaceable, the men were not. The 1st Armoured Division was disbanded,
every UK infantry battalion was cut to only three rifle companies. The
Germans were in worse condition. For the period August 26 to September
15 the 76th Panzer Corps reported 14 604 casualties, including 7000 missing.
By the 25th, of the Tenth Army's ninety-two infantry battalions only ten had
a strength of over 400 men, sixteen were over 300, twenty-six were over 200,
and thirty-eight had less than 200.[14]

When the Canadians crossed the Marecchia on the 21st Leese signalled
to Burns: "You have won a great victory. By the bitterest fighting since
Alamein and Cassino you have beaten eleven German divisions and broken
through into the Po Valley. The greater part of the German armies in Italy
were massed against us and they have been terribly mauled. I congratulate
and thank you all. We must now hit hard day and night and force them
back over the Po." To Burns' units he signalled: "Well done Canada!"

It had, indeed, been a great and hard-fought victory. Mauled the enemy
might have been, but not destroyed, for prolonged rain on September 20/21
helped the 76th Panzer Corps to withdraw in good order. The song sung by
the 1st Canadian Division to the tune of "Lilli Marlene"—"We will debouch
into the Valley of the Po"—seemed inappropriate on the 21st, not only
because it was to be the New Zealand Division who would "debouch," but
because the "plain" had proved a soggy disappointment. "Half seen through
the fine drizzle of September 21st it offered a dreary prospect of flat, watery
and characterless land receding monotonously towards a grey horizon" to
the platoons of the Princess Patricia's Light Infantry and the 48th Highlanders
as they crossed the Marecchia, walked cautiously over a road on the other
side, and began to dig in. That was as far as they were to go and they were
not at all sorry. Not many of them may have considered it, but their crossing
"marked the end of an era. . . . Behind lay the memorials of Eighth Army's
past, San Fortunato and the Gothic Line, Florence and the Paula Line,
Cassino and the Gustav and Hitler Lines, Orsogna and Ortona, and farther
back still, beyond the many rivers and hills, the toe of Calabria where the
army had first touched Italy one year and 18 days before."

Of all the divisions fighting in OLIVE, only the 1st Canadians and their
old adversaries, the 26th Panzer and 29th Panzer Grenadiers, had been in
action from the beginning, although the 46th and 56th Divisions, veterans of
Salerno, could claim almost as long a service.

SOURCES

This chapter was originally researched in 1970 by Dominick Graham and Nicholas Straker as part of their battlefield tour in the summer of that year. The documentary support on the British side was sparse since the relevant volume of the Official History had not been commissioned. However, Straker wrote a narrative using what had been prepared by historians in the Cabinet Office, Jackson's *Battle for Italy*, Orgill's *The Gothic Line*, and British regimental histories. By then Nicholson's volume had been published and much of the documentation on which it was based, German as well as Allied, was available at the Directorate of History, Ottawa. Good regimental histories, such as those of Roy and How (BC Dragoons and New Brunswick Hussars), were also published. This ought to have served to balance the accounts of Jackson and Orgill which tend to concentrate unduly on the operations of the British 5th Corps, whereas it was the Canadian Corps that broke the German main defensive line, captured Coriano, and finally broke through.

In 1983 Brereton Greenhous and William McAndrew of the Directorate of History conducted a battlefield tour to study the actions of the Canadian 5th Armoured Division. Many veterans, including the divisional commander, Major-General Hoffmeister, participated. We have used the papers written for the tour which reinforce our view that a great opportunity was lost. The inherent fault in Leese's plan was the lack of a reserve he could dispose of flexibly. As a result when the 5th Corps failed to loosen the strong German defence lines near the coast by a series of left hooks, the Canadians, whose role and strength were incompatible, were unable rapidly to exploit their success and help the 5th Corps forward, instead of *vice versa*.

NOTES

1. G.W.L. Nicholson, *Official History of the Canadian Army in the First World War: The Canadian Expeditionary Force, 1914–1919* (Ottawa: Queen's Printer, 1962), 564.

2. Fisher, 297.

3. Carver, *Harding of Petherton*, 141–42.

4. The accepted version of how the change of plan came about—Carver, Blumenson (*Mark Clark*) and Fisher— is correct as far as it goes. The moving spirit, however, was in fact Kirkman, whose views were respected by all concerned (except Clark). It can be assumed that he had already weighed Harding's plan and found it wanting before 3 August when, according to his diary, he met Leese and discussed "future fighting." In the days succeeding, this discussion was followed up by a telephone call to Leese and meetings with Harding and McCreery. On the 10th Kirkman was summoned to HQ Eighth Army, arriving after the conference between Clark, Leese, and Alexander. "Alex took me aside . . . the [new] plan is entirely according to my suggestion . . . the only snag, and it is I am afraid entirely logical, is the 13th Corps will go under command of 5 Army."

5. Blumenson, *Mark Clark*, 222–26; Fisher, 306–307.

6. 6th British and 6th South African Armoured Divisions; 1st British and 8th Indian Infantry Divisions.

7. War Diary, Loyal Edmonton Regiment, quoted by Brereton Greenhous in a paper prepared for the Canadian Army battlefield tour of 1983.

8. Nicholson, *Official History*, 511–12.

9. Ibid., 521.

10. One lesson of DIADEM had been that armoured divisions in Italy required extra infantry. Canada could spare none for its 5th Armoured Division, so the requirement was met by converting the 4th Princess Louise Dragoon Guards (an armoured reconnaissance regiment) and the Lanark and Renfrew Infantry (Anti-aircraft artillery, reverting to its original role) to form the 12th Canadian Infantry Brigade.

11. Burns, *General Mud*, 189.

12. For a good account of the tribulations of the 1st Armoured Division see Orgill, *The Gothic Line*, chaps. 9–11.

13. Nicholson, *Official History*, 681 and note.

14. Ibid., 563.

OPERATION TRACTABLE ◇

JOHN ENGLISH

○

> We who have spent so many years in England think and speak
> constantly of England and our friends there . . . even to the point of
> appearing disloyal to Canada. The thought of returning there on
> leave sometime soon alone makes life supportable at times.
>
> Canadian War Diary Entry, 31 August 1944[1]

The black day, *Der Schwarze Tag*, visited upon the German army on 8 August
1918 by the Canadian and Australian corps was not repeated in the half-
forgotten summer of 1944. In the final analysis Operation "Totalize" was a
failure. Despite overwhelming air and artillery superiority, five divisions
and two armoured brigades comprising upwards of six hundred tanks could
not handle two depleted German divisions, mustering no more than sixty
panzers and tank destroyers. Contrary to popular belief, the bulk of roughly
eighty 88-mm antitank guns, mostly belonging to three *Luftwaffe* flak regiments, were deployed south of Potigny; only the divisional batteries were
forward. It was thus mainly the 12th SS Division's resourceful handling of
Tigers and Panthers that stemmed the Canadian attack. Yet, while these
Eastern Front leviathans were more than a match for Shermans and
Churchills, the Germans had nothing to compare with the Typhoon or
"Jabo" (*Jagdbombern*) as their troops fearfully labelled it. Then, too, the 17-
pounder in its Firefly, SP, and towed configurations possessed an ample
margin of power over the Tiger as demonstrated since 1943.[2]

To Simonds, the problem was not weapons or machines, but rather a
lack of proper handling of resources within armoured divisions. Troops
also displayed a tendency, traceable back to training in Britain, to stick to
roads and thereby inevitably encounter the antitank guns sited to cover
them. Simonds had also expressly urged his armoured commanders not to
wait for infantry divisions to take out final objectives or "get involved in

---

◇ "Case Hardening," chap. 12 of *The Canadian Army and the Normandy Campaign: A
Study of Failure in High Command* (Praeger, 1991), 289–304.

probing . . . before they called down fire or . . . fighter bombers." If he had given them narrow frontages, he had also allotted each division an AGRA [Army Group, Royal Artillery] of five medium regiments specifically to assist them in getting on quickly.[3] Kitching's reaction, however, was to attack with two brigades up, instead of in depth as per Simonds's operational policy, leaving them pretty much to their own devices. Booth, in turn, delegated tactical responsibility down to battle groups with the result that artillery was never effectively brought to bear against pockets of resistance like that initially, and critically, encountered at Gaumesnil.

That Canadian armour in "Totalize" exhibited both the dashing recklessness and excessive caution of their British brethren is, of course, striking. Such bifurcation no doubt reflected the doctrinal contradictions that grew out of Africa, and which battle experience in the static Italian campaign could hardly have been expected to resolve. Even the failure to employ available artillery resources approximates the British armoured pattern, and one could well say that the operation foundered for not making better use of guns. At the same time, it might have been better had Simonds committed the 3rd Division supported by the 2nd Armoured Brigade to the "second break in" rather than the Poles. This would have at least alleviated communications difficulties due to language and seen two additional infantry brigades in action. It would appear, however, that the El Hamma model appealed more to Simonds than the lesson of Wadi Akarit, so convincingly demonstrated by the Argylls in taking Point 195.

Crerar simply blamed the Poles. The "bog-down" of the 2 Corps attack, as he saw it, was mainly due to the "dog fight" that developed between the 1st Polish Armoured Division and German elements in Quesnay Wood. Had the Poles smoked off and contained the enemy there and pushed on with the bulk of their strength, they would have widened the front and increased the depth for a tactically decisive advance. As it was, when dark came, they had advanced "not more than a few hundred yards."[4] It is worth noting, of course, the later criticism of Hubert Meyer, former first operations officer of the 12th SS, that it would have been wiser to have outflanked the *Hitlerjugend* to the east, an action that conceivably could have been initiated by Crerar himself much as Dempsey had in personally redirecting the 7th Armoured onto Villers Bocage on 12 June. Whether Simonds would have intervened in this manner had he been army commander is an intriguing matter of conjecture.[5]

The commander of the 12th SS, Kurt Meyer, considered "Totalize" an example of "inflexible, time wasting method," whereby staff planning and preparation "succeeded in burying the enemy under several thousand tons of explosives." Never once did speed, "the most powerful weapon of Armoured Warfare," appear to have been a paramount concern. In Meyer's view, the road to Falaise had been open and basically undefended from midnight 7 August to noon 8 August. *Kampfgruppe Krause*, for example, did not arrive from the west until shortly before midnight on 8 August. He attributed Canadian inaction after the initial breakthrough to be "the result of too much planning by the 2nd Corps" related to the employment of bombers. The development of the battle also convinced him that divisional commanders had not placed themselves "in the leading combat group, to see for . . . [themselves] to save precious time, and to make lightning de-cisions" to exploit "given opportunities."[6]

It seems clear that the failure of "Totalize" was less a product of troop inexperience, for Canadian soldiers had performed well when correctly employed, than the result of a flawed concept. Waiting for the second bomber strike guaranteed a loss of momentum. Had the strike been waived and high-command attention turned to the staff problem of getting troops and artillery forward, the tempo could have been sustained. But the strike could only have been cancelled through the First Canadian Army, which had expended so much effort in arranging strategic bomber support that it had become almost bureaucratically entrenched. Notwithstanding the requirement for 24 hours notification, it is highly unlikely that Crerar would have even felt disposed to request a cancellation of "Bomber" Harris, with whom he appears to have struck up a rather ingratiating relationship.[7] Besides, it was the one area in "Totalize" planning that because of its stra-tegic overtones would have remained the sole prerogative of the First Canadian Army headquarters. Crerar no less than Simonds was also attracted to the technological expedient, which the Allied bomber barons at the strategic level had so mistakenly yet skillfully proselytized.

That another more tactical approach was feasible is evident from Meyer's post-war postulation of a "Red Totalize." After three years of combat experi-ence in Russia, he was convinced the Soviets would not have permitted a "battle of phases" with a "first objective only three miles behind the enemy Front Line." The tasks of the 2nd and 51st Divisions would have been to advance behind a concentrated artillery attack "to smash the enemy defence on both sides . . . and open the road to Falaise." The armoured brigades and carrier-borne infantry which accomplished this would have then "automati-cally take[n] over the task of advance force for the two attacking divisions," one brigade pushing toward St. Sylvain while the other seized Bretteville-sur-Laize. At the "first sign" that the road was open, the advance force of the 4th Armoured—a tank battalion with two companies of infantry, a battery of SP howitzers, a reconnaissance company, and an air force controller—would have "plung[ed] onward to the south towards their objective, Falaise."[8]

He went on to suggest that the advance force, commanded by a "young fanatical Communist" and assisted by ground support aircraft, would have stopped at nothing before Falaise. It would have advanced not by tactical manoeuvring, but with guns blazing to either Falaise or "a glorious finish." The main body of the 4th Division would have followed at a steady pace to ensure the success of its spearhead. By attacking during the early morning hours instead of in darkness, which left the tank a "creeping pill-box" with reduced "ram-power" for lack of speed, the Red Army would have been able to strike deeply into the enemy defensive system, leaving the 12th SS absolutely no chance of reaching the Falaise road area north of Bretteville-le-Rabet. Strategic bombers, which in the Canadian case represented overkill anyway, would have been used, since it would have "transferred the initiative from . . . leading combat elements to timetable acrobats of . . . Headquarters." Operation "Totalize" would have been accomplished in 24 hours.[9]

In consequence of the failure of "Totalize," however, Montgomery on 11 August issued a new directive that instructed the First Canadian Army to capture Falaise as "a first priority . . . [to] be done quickly." Argentan to the south was also to be secured with strong U.S. armoured and mobile forces. The object of these two moves was to close the gap between the 21st and 12th Army Groups, thereby trapping German forces in the west now dangerously overextended as a result of operations against the Americans in the Mortain area.[10] This directive officially set in train the short envelopment, an idea hatched by Bradley, enthusiastically endorsed by Eisenhower, but only perfunctorily accepted by Montgomery. His preferred strategy remained to establish a bridgehead across the Seine in a longer envelopment. Indeed, he understood that classic encirclement operations called for a line of circumvallation as well as one of countervallation, which made the envelopment an extremely perilous prospect, especially against Germans well-versed in *Keil und Kessel* operations on a grand scale. Without a blocking force at Trun-Chambois or along the Seine, any force interposed at Falaise ran the risk of being sandwiched between enemy forces breaking out and those sent to their relief.[11]

In any event, Montgomery was quick to give Bradley permission to move north of the interarmy group boundary that was established on 5 August twelve miles south of Argentan. That Bradley developed a similar caution of early encirclement was demonstrated on 12 August when he refused Patton permission to proceed north of Argentan to "drive the British into the sea." As Bradley later explained, better a "solid shoulder at Argentan to the possibility of a broken neck at Falaise." He nonetheless went to his grave blaming Montgomery for his failure to "close the trap by capping the leak at Falaise."[12] Yet, both Bradley and Montgomery appear to have believed at the time that the Canadians, only ten kilometres from Falaise, had to succeed in their second try. It was only subsequently that Bradley criticized Montgomery for not reinforcing the Canadians with the "more battle-seasoned troops of the Second Army."[13]

Within the First Canadian Army planning commenced almost immediately to launch another heavily supported attack toward Falaise, this time east of the road thrusting south from the general line of Estrées-la-Campagne-Soignolles. At 1000 hours 12 August, Simonds held a conference with all three Canadian divisional commanders on Operation "Tallulah," curiously named after Alabama actress Tallulah Brockman Bankhead. In the interests of security, he on 13 August issued only verbal orders for the operation, now more optimistically designated "Tractable." Following his orders group, which included brigadiers, he went on to personally brief all armoured commanders down to unit level. Making known his extreme displeasure with their "Totalize" performance in no uncertain terms, Simonds directed that armor was henceforth neither to balk at movement by night nor expect infantry protection in harboring. He further warned that while there would probably continue to be "cases of . . . mis-employment of armour" in future operations, "this was to be no excuse for non-success." Canadian tank units and formations, in short, were to be pushed to the very limits of their endurance.[14]

"Tractable" was essentially "Totalize" in smoke. It also bore an astounding resemblance to the theoretical operation in *Current Reports From Overseas* described earlier. The principal object of "Tractable" was to dominate the northern, eastern, and southern exits from Falaise so that no enemy could escape. Physical occupation of the town was to be completed by the Second British Army following the success of "Tractable," after which the First Canadian Army was to exploit southeast to capture or dominate Trun. In this attack on Falaise, which aimed to skirt Quesnay Wood and Potigny, 2 Corps was to be assisted by the 2nd Tactical Air Force and Bomber Command.[15] Again Simonds planned to use massed armour and carrier-borne infantry to break speedily through the enemy gun screen, only this time he chose for surprise purposes to cloak their movement with smoke rather than darkness. Once more, preliminary bombardment was dispensed with in order to avoid signalling attack frontage, which enabled the enemy to bring heavy defensive fire to bear on rearward assaulting elements, thus reducing their capacity to penetrate in depth.

As explained by Simonds, the "first step" was to secure the high ground northwest of Versainville and then, during a "second," push through toward Falaise. To accomplish the former, the corps was to attack with two roughly equal divisional groups up: the 4th Division, with the 8th Brigade under command, on the left; and the remainder of the 3rd Division, with the 2nd Armoured Brigade (less the Sherbrookes) under command, on the right. The 2nd Brigade was to capture Point 184 northwest of Epaney while the 4th Division formed a pivot at Perrières, seized the Versainville high ground, and exploited to Eraines and Damblainville. One AGRA was placed in immediate support of each division until the 2nd Armoured Brigade attained its objective, after which both AGRA, less one medium regiment, were to support the 4th Division. The task of the 3rd Division was to clear the intervening valley of the Laison River between Montboint and Maizieres and exploit to form a pivot at Sassy. To assist with this, the 8th Brigade was to revert to 3rd Division command upon reaching the river.[16]

As in "Totalize," 2 Corps assaulting elements were drawn up in densely packed formation with armoured brigades, including special squadrons, to the forefront. Simonds appears to have listened to complaints about narrow frontages, however, for he directed the armoured brigades to attack on a wide front, if possible with three units up, though he stipulated fifteen-yard marshaling intervals between tanks. The armoured brigades were to push straight through to their objectives, advancing at a rate of twelve miles in the hour, the "proper emp[loyment] of armour . . . [being] to pos[itio]n it so that the enemy must drive it out in order to regain his freedom of manoeuvre." A carrier-borne infantry brigade charged with dismounting and clearing the valley of the Laison followed within each divisional column; the 8th Brigade in the case of the 4th Division and the 9th Brigade in the 3rd. Last in the order of march came the marching infantry brigades, the 10th and 7th respectively, whose task it was to pass through and join the armour on objectives.

The forward movement of the columns was to be screened by artillery smoke, of impenetrable density on the flanks and of "mist" density, as controlled by FOOs with armour, on the front (the attack was to be postponed in

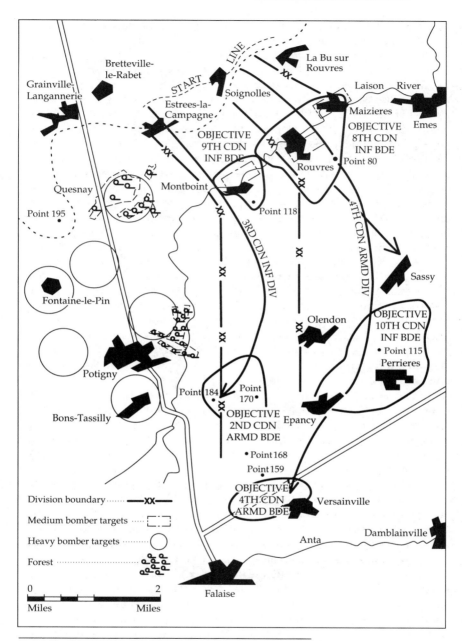

Map labels:

Grainville-Langannerie

Bretteville-le-Rabet

START LINE

Soignolles

La Bu sur Rouvres

Laison River

Estrees-la-Campagne

OBJECTIVE 9TH CDN INF BDE

Maizieres

OBJECTIVE 8TH CDN INF BDE

Emes

Rouvres

Point 80

Quesnay

Montboint

Point 118

Point 195

3RD CDN INF DIV

4TH CDN ARMD DIV

Sassy

Fontaine-le-Pin

Olendon

OBJECTIVE 10TH CDN INF BDE

• Point 115

Perrieres

Potigny

Point 184

Point 170

OBJECTIVE 2ND CDN ARMD BDE

Epancy

Bons-Tassilly

• Point 168

Point 159

OBJECTIVE 4TH CDN ARMD BDE

Versainville

Damblainville

Anta

Division boundary ········ —XX—

Medium bomber targets ····· ⌐ ¬

Heavy bomber targets ········· ○

Forest ·····················

0   2

Miles   Miles

Falaise

PLAN FOR OPERATION "TRACTABLE"

the event of direct frontal winds). Over and above counterbombardment by all available medium artillery, concentrations on call were prearranged on known or suspected enemy 88-mm gun positions, the latter to be engaged during the advance whether they opened fire or not. From fifteen minutes prior to the attack for ten minutes, medium bombers were also to engage enemy tank, gun, and mortar positions up to the Laison valley. Two hours after commencement, heavy bombers were slated to strike Quesnay Wood, Potigny, and German defences astride the Falaise road for one and a half hours.[17]

The enemy position to be assaulted was not considered to be posted in any great depth. It was estimated to comprise a light infantry screen backed up by a large number of 88-mm guns along the general line of the Laison and *Nebelwerfers* behind reverse slopes. While elements of the 271st Division were believed to be joining the newly arrived 85th Infantry in this area, the disposition of the 12th SS Division could not be defined. In fact, the division was but a shadow of its former self, mustering on 12 August seven Panthers and seventeen Panzer IVs, four 88-mm Flak, and six understrength rifle companies of perhaps 500 men.[18] Not surprisingly, both Simonds and Crerar were apparently satisfied that they had sufficient force to deal with the situation. The 1st Polish Division and 33rd Armoured Brigade, for example, were each directed to form a firm base, the former near the start line at Estrées-la-Campagne.

When the Canadians attacked at 1200 hours 14 August, then, it was generally with the rekindled hope that they would secure Falaise the second time round. Again, save for some clear patches in the smoke, everything went well from the beginning and leading elements were on the Laison within an hour. As might be expected on a hot summer's day, however, the kilometre-wide tank phalanxes threw up huge dust clouds that combined with high-explosive concentrations and "vision limiting smoke" to plunge columns into incredible disorder. In "charge of the light brigade" fashion, tanks, carriers, and half-tracks steering only by the sun all vied for the lead as control became virtually impossible to maintain. When they arrived on the river, most units were widely dispersed and in need of reorganization. As if this self-inflicted wound were not enough, the Laison was now found not to be, as Simonds reportedly said, "fordable by tanks at almost all points."[19]

Ironically, a major observation made by Simonds after Exercise "Spartan" was that a corps plan could not await engineer ground reconnaissance, for it would then be unable "to keep up with operations." The best that could be done was to "demand [air] photographic reconnaissance of obstacles well in advance" and through a study of these and the map prepare flexibly "for the worst."[20] Given that corps planning had to look several days ahead, Simonds was essentially correct, but to have misjudged the Laison with its muddy bottom and steep banks was an error of major consequence. The 2nd Armoured Brigade in an after-action report categorized the river as a "definite tank obstacle" and recommended that, in future, tank commanders rather than engineers determine whether an obstacle was a tank obstacle or not.[21] Fortunately, AVREs carrying fascines (bundles of poles for filling ditches and streams) were eventually able to bridge the Laison's six-foot breadth for tanks that had neither bogged nor crossed by improvised fords and demolition-free bridges.

On the 4th Division front the search for crossings forced the armour northeast along the river beyond Ernes "where tanks were lined up for two hours amid scenes of great confusion."[22] Since this formation had the farthest to go to secure its final objective, delay here was critical. Although

Foot Guard tanks were over the river by 1430 hours, they like other units required some reorganization before pushing onward. About this time the brigade commander, Booth, was also mortally wounded and his entire tactical headquarters effectively put out of action. Obviously, no succession of command had been detailed within the brigade, and it was not until after 1900 hours that the CO of the Foot Guards, Lieutenant-Colonel Murray Scott, received notification from Kitching to take over. Suffering from a broken ankle and considering it too late for armour to cover the remaining five kilometres to Versainville, he suspended operations for the day.[23]

First light of 15 August found the 4th Armoured Brigade beyond Olendon, which had been secured by the 10th Brigade. On the 3rd Division front, the 2nd Armoured and 7th Brigades were in possession of the greater part of the Point 184 objective northeast of Souligny; the 8th Brigade, to the east, held Sassy. By the time operations were resumed, however, the First Canadian Army had been directed to capture Falaise as well as close off its eastern exits.[24] It was thus even more imperative that the 4th Division capture its final objective as soon as possible. The 4th Armoured Brigade under the wounded Scott, who was in some pain, accordingly renewed its advance toward Versainville, but not until 0930 hours due to a decision to refuel and replenish. Brigade tactical headquarters only resumed functioning in the early afternoon. Progress was also slowed initially by fierce German resistance from Epaney, which was eventually reduced mainly by the Algonquins of the 10th Brigade and partly by the Lake Superiors.

It was not until midafternoon that the Grenadier Guards and the reconstituted BCR of the 4th Armoured Brigade, now grown cautious for lack of infantry and artillery support, approached the final objective above Versainville. Unfortunately, the more distant Foot Guards at 1650 hours erroneously reported that the two units had taken it, a message that was joyfully and prematurely passed on to Simonds. Kitching shortly thereafter relieved the injured Scott at his own request, replacing him with Halpenny. It was only after having dined with the jubilant Simonds at corps headquarters that Kitching learned that the objective had not been captured. He in turn informed Simonds, much to the latter's understandable disappointment and annoyance. News from the 3rd Division was likewise disconcerting, for after having advanced to Point 168 in a costly action that afternoon, assaulting 7th Brigade troops were thrown out of Souligny before dark.[25] As in "Totalize," the Germans had managed to deny Canadian arms the planned goal they sought.

The ultimate failure of "Tractable" was largely obscured by a contretemps of considerable magnitude, though it had little impact on the battle. In a performance reminiscent of "Totalize," seventy-seven bombers, forty-four of them from No. 6 (RCAF) Bomber Group, mistakenly unloaded short on Canadian rearward units, especially 2 Canadian AGRA, and elements of the 1st Polish Armoured Division. Troop attempts to remedy this blunder by setting out yellow markers and letting off yellow flares and smoke, a procedure rehearsed just for such an eventuality, only brought more bombs as a similar target indicator colour was employed by the air force that day. Regrettably, Bomber Command had never been informed of a Supreme Headquarters Allied Expeditionary Force (SHAEF) directive that authorized the use of this colour for indicating positions of forward ground troops.[26] While in a strict sense SHAEF should have so advised Bomber Command, the fact that all communication with the latter funnelled through Headquarters First Canadian Army suggests, in a practical sense, a degree of accountability on its part.

This was at least the way the COS, Brigadier Mann, initially saw it. In a first draft memorandum to Crerar he "suggested that we (and myself in particular) might be considered as having some responsibility" insofar as "First Canadian Army had erred in some degree by not pointing out the use of yellow smoke and flares" to indicate the positions of troops. Crerar, on the other hand, disagreed. He noted instead that "it was, if anyone's fault, that of AEAF [Allied Expeditionary Air Forces], in not drawing attention of Bomber Command to [the appropriate SHAEF directive]."[27] Clearly, however, a commander and staff at any higher headquarters have an ineluctable responsibility to ensure that all aspects of an operation, especially those related to the safety of their own troops, are thoroughly checked and co-ordinated. It is thus difficult to accept totally the bureaucratic shifting of blame for bombing errors in "Tractable." In any event, when all bombing was ordered stopped at 1520 hours, most of the 769 Lancasters and Halifaxes had delivered on target. With close to 400 Canadian and Polish casualties incurred, however, the raid had a devastating effect on ground force morale.[28]

Another incident that affected later assessment of "Tractable" was the capture by the Germans of an officer of the 8th Reconnaissance Regiment who had accidentally directed his scout car into their lines on the evening of 13 August. The officer was shot dead, but a copy of a 2nd Divison instruction outlining the entire corps plan was found on his body. When Simonds learned what had happened, he was highly angered and quick to claim that this individual act of "carelessness" had compromised surprise and "enabled the enemy to make quick adjustments to his dispositions which undoubtedly resulted in casualties to . . . [Canadian] troops the following day." Simonds also apparently believed that it "delayed the capture of FALAISE for over twenty-four hours."[29] According to Hubert Meyer, however, no redeployment of import took place as there was insufficient time to react. The uncomfortable fact thus remains that roughly 300 tanks and four brigades of infantry supported by massive artillery and air resources failed to overcome some 41 tanks, albeit more than half Panthers and Tigers, and two reinforced infantry regiments many of whose men had not been under fire before.[30] True, the 88-mm gun line remained formidable, but Simonds's expectation that the operation should have accomplished what it set out to do still seems valid. The real seeds of failure, in short, were less extrinsic than intrinsic to "Tractable" itself.

This was most assuredly the view of the 7th Brigade commander, Brigadier Foster, who described "Tractable" as "certainly one of the strangest attack formations anyone ever dreamed up and without a hope . . . of succeeding as planned." In his judgement what "looked good to . . . [Simonds's] precise engineering mind on paper seldom worked in practice once the human element was added."[31] To be sure, just to line up formations in parade square fashion was a complex undertaking that could not possibly have been attempted without absolute air superiority. On the other hand, it solved the potentially disastrous movement problem of getting hundreds of armoured vehicles to the start line in good order. Not to have expected huge amounts of dust to generate mass confusion and associated control problems, however, seems an extraordinary oversight, suggestive even of an unfamiliarity with basic armoured vehicular movement. This, coupled with a misreading of the Laison, was the fatal flaw of "Tractable," from which there was simply no time left for recovery.

The operation also suffered from difficulties in getting artillery forward, for Simonds at 1810 hours had to order the CCRA [Corps Commander Royal Artillery] to get guns into the "valley below Soignolles."[32] While bombing errors doubtless contributed to this problem, artillery insistence on having gun areas absolutely cleared of enemy may also have been a factor. An additional impediment, of course, was the tardy transference of command following Booth's incapacitation, exactly the situation that Montgomery had warned Canadians about in 1942. Since the armoured regiments of the 4th Brigade had continued to progress, an extra hour or two of firm direction from that level would literally have made all the difference. Though lower echelons are often easier to blame than higher command for operational failures like "Tractable," it is impossible to fault the performance of units like the Canadian Scottish who managed, without benefit of intimate tank support, to take Point 168 while being shelled by their own artillery.[33] The performance of many other infantry and even armoured units, incidentally, does not seem to suffer by comparison.

After "Tractable" the initiative that had momentarily resided with the First Canadian Army passed into other hands. It now reacted to higher direction in an increasingly fluid situation as four Allied armies converged upon the "Falaise Gap." The withdrawal of German forces through the Gap reached full flood on 18 August, the very day Falaise finally fell. Ironically, it was taken by the 2nd Division, which since 13 August had been steadily advancing from a bridgehead at Clair Tizon; but only after a most desperate last ditch stand by about 60 *Hitlerjugend*, none of whom surrendered. The 4th and 1st Armoured Divisions had meanwhile been directed toward Trun and Chambois, respectively, to link up with the Americans approaching from the south. Unlike the region of the Caen plain, the rising countryside around Trun east of the Dives was characterized by thickly wooded hills interspersed with hamlets, small fields, and numerous orchards, all ringed by valleys, streams, and winding sunken lanes. Like the area of Villers-Bocage, it was less than ideal tank country, but it was through here that the Canadian and Polish armoured divisions with their insufficient infantry complements fought a series of highly disparate offensive and defensive actions.[34]

Caught in the inexorable crush of Allied forces, the Germans fought back with determination and skill. On 20 August the 1st Polish Division was sandwiched in an *Ostfront*-style operation that saw not only the Seventh German Army breaking out of the Falaise pocket past Canadian elements at St. Lambert and Polish positions at Coudehard, but the 2nd SS Panzer Corps "breaking back" on Polish defences to the east. Between St. Lambert and Chambois up "Dead Horse Alley," the Germans ultimately managed to extricate possibly one-third of their forces. By nightfall 21 August the Gap was nonetheless closed for good and its endless controversy begun. For our purposes, however, but one thing needs to be noted: in this confused fighting, for which reinforcements were never requested by corps or army, individual Canadian soldiers and units, even when outnumbered, appear with few exceptions to have performed well.[35]

The Battle of Normandy, rightfully considered one of the world's most decisive, was over. It had cost the Canadian Army 18 444 casualties, including 5021 dead. The 3rd Canadian Infantry Division also suffered greater losses than any other division within the 21st Army Group. The 2nd Canadian Infantry Division, though it did not arrive in France until 7 July, incurred the next highest. All told, battle casualties slightly exceeded 3000 in June, 5500 in July, and 7400 for the 1–23 August. Fighting in "Totalize" through "Tractable" up to 21 August accounted for 5679 casualties. Significantly, the two British divisions with the highest casualty rates, the 3rd and 51st (Highland), both landed on D-Day.[36] The troublesome thing about these figures is that they cannot simply be explained away in nationalist terms of Canadians being assigned more difficult tactical tasks. As already mentioned, British engagements in the bocage to the west approached Great War proportions in their severity. Fighting in the "Epsom" offensive, for example, "reached a sustained intensity rare even in the Normandy campaign."[37] One might have expected further, from the experience of the Great War, that an all-volunteer army would have performed appreciably better than a conscripted one like the British.

To say that the Canadian government got more than it deserved from the performance of its castaway army in Normandy would nonetheless be an understatement. One cannot escape the feeling that the prime minister of Canada would personally have preferred its troops to have fought and died with as little fuss and bother as possible. That many Canadian soldiers came to look upon Britain as a surrogate homeland is not therefore surprising. After the closure of the Falaise Gap, of course, the First Canadian Army literally marched into a new world order. Whereas the battle for Normandy was directed by a British field commander, the rest of "Overlord" was not. From 1 September onward, Montgomery reverted to command an army group of roughly fifteen divisions. His erstwhile subordinate, Bradley, on the other hand, rose to command close to fifty in what clearly signalled a changing of the guard. The First Canadian Army, whose British composition at one point increased to 80 percent, advanced with the rest of the British Liberation Army into an imperial retreat.

NOTES

1. Record Group (hereafter RG) 24, National Defence 1870–1981, National Archives of Canada (hereafter NAC), Ottawa, vol. 15 271, WD SDG, 31 Aug. 1944.

2. Hubert Meyer, "Report of the Battlefield Study 1987 by Canadian Forces Support Establishment Central Army Group, 20 June 1987," and his *Kriegsgeschichte der 12.SS-Panzerdivision "Hitlerjugend"* (Osnabruck, Germany: Munin Verlag, 1987), 2:620; and MS# P–164, *12th SS Panzer Division "Hitlerjugend" June to September 1944* (HQ U.S. Army, Europe, 1954), p. 102. The 17-pounder was known to have successfully dealt with Tigers at 1500 yards range. It was nonetheless

difficult to manoeuvre and took twelve to fifteen hours to dig in. The Tiger was also vulnerable to 6-pounder fire in the flanks. Brig. A. L. Pemberton, *The Second World War, 1939–1945, Army, The Development of Artillery Tactics and Equipment* (London: War Office, 1951), 162–63, 203, 223.

3. Extracts from lecture given by Simonds, 23 June 1947, DHist 693.013(D2) Ops 2 Cdn Corps, *British Army of the Rhine Battlefield Tour Operation Totalize: 2 Canadian Corps Operations Astride the Road Caen-Falaise 7–8 August 1944*, prepared under the direction of G (Training) HQ British Army of the Rhine (BAOR), 33.

4. Crerar to Stacey, 10 January 1958, Crerar Papers (hereafter CP), NAC, vol. 21.

5. Carlo D'Este, *Decision in Normandy: The Unwritten Story of Montgomery and the Allied Campaign* (London: Pan, 1984), 172; and Meyer, "Report of the Battlefield Study 1987." Dempsey told Bucknall, 30 Corps commander, to switch the 7th Armoured to the Villers-Bocage axis immediately. Crerar might have redirected the 3rd Division in the same manner. He had also given 1 British Corps the role to comply on its right with the intentions of 2 Canadian Corps, "right shoulder up." Public Records Office, Kew, UK (hereafter PRO), CAB 106/1064 Crerar WD, GOC-in-C–1–0–4 Crerar to Crocker and Simonds, 6 Aug. 1944.

6. DHist 73/1302 Interview Kurt Meyer, 3 Sept. 1950, by Maj. James R. Millar, forwarded to Director of Chaplain Service (P) 6 Sept. 1950; and Meyer, *12.SS-Panzerdivision*, 104.

7. Crerar, even as the bombing was in progress 7 Aug., signalled Harris: "Greatly appreciate outstanding contribution your Command. We shall hope to continue and complete this battle as well as you have commenced it." Col. C. P. Stacey, *Official History of the Canadian Army in the Second World War*, vol. 3, *The Victory Campaign: The Operations in North-West Europe 1944–1945* (Ottawa: Queen's Printer, 1966), 218. Harris

later wrote to Crerar: "If, as I consider and believe you think, the heavy bombers from Caen onwards whenever they were called in to assist the army have been an outstanding success in forwarding the military design and in saving a large number of casualties amongst our own troops, then I hope you will agree that the facts should be blazoned abroad." Harris to Crerar, 13 Sept. 1944, CP, vol. 6. At Walcheren, Canadians were said to be "drugged with bombs." W. Denis Whitaker and Shelagh Whitaker, *Tug of War: The Canadian Victory that Opened Antwerp* (Toronto: Stoddart, 1984), 372; and Jeffrey Williams, *Long Left Flank: The Hard Fought Way to Reich, 1944–1945* (Toronto: Stoddart, 1988), 149–150.

8. DHist 73/1302 Interview Kurt Meyer, 3 Sept. 1950.

9. Ibid.

10. 21 Army Group M518 General Operational Situation and Directive 11–8–44.

11. For insight into the sophistication of German operational capacity in such circumstances, see *Operations of Encircled Forces: German Experiences in Russia* (Washington: Department of the Army Pamphlet no. 20–234, 1952); and Maj. Timothy A. Wray, *Standing Fast: German Defensive Doctrine on the Russian Front During World War II, Prewar to March 1943* (Fort Leavenworth: Combat Studies Institute, 1986), 25–33. On to encircle or not to encircle, see Gen. S. M. Shtemenko, *The Soviet General Staff at War, 1941–1945*, trans. Robert Daglish (Moscow: Progress, 1985), 1:243–44, 311–14.

12. D'Este, *Decision in Normandy*, 424–30, 439–60; and Nigel Hamilton, *Monty*, vol. 2, *Master of the Battlefield 1942–1944* (Sevenoaks, UK: Hodder and Stoughton, 1984), 770–75. D'Este covers the controversy related to the closure of the gap very thoroughly.

13. D'Este, *Decision in Normandy*, 426–27, 444–45; and Eversley Belfield and H. Essame, *The Battle for Normandy* (London: Pan, 1983), 225.

14. RG 24, vol. 10 797, GOC's Activities; RG 24, vol. 13 789, WD GS 4 CAD

SEI, 13 Aug. 1944; Stacey, *Victory Campaign*, 236; and Terry Copp and Robert Vogel, *Maple Leaf Route: Falaise* (Alma: Maple Leaf Route, 1983), 112. Had the lady's name been "bridgehead" instead of "bankhead," a diarist commented, "Tractable" would have remained "Tallulah." According to information provided by Dr. Robert L. Fraser, Simonds during his critique of armoured performance on "Totalize" called some commanders yellow and directed them to command henceforth from tanks. Meyer, an infantryman, commanded from a motorcycle.

15. CP, vol. 2, Crerar to Simonds and Crocker on Operation "Tractable," 13 Aug. 1944. The 2nd Tactical Air Force included 2, 83, 84 Groups. "Tractable" was also called the "Mad Charge." Alexander McKee, *Caen: Anvil of Victory* (London: Souvenir, 1964), 335.

16. RG 24, vol. 13 751, WD GS 2 CID "Tallulah" Notes on Corps Comd's Outline Talk 131000 hrs; RG 24, vol. 14 156, WD GS 4 CAD Outline of Instrs Issued by GOC 4 Cdn Armd Div 131230 B, Aug. 1944 Op "Tractable"; and RG 24, vol. 10 800, 2 Canadian Corps "Immediate Report" on 2 Canadian Corps Operations "Tractable"—The Capture of Falaise, 14–16 Aug. 1944, dated 22 Aug. 1944.

17. Ibid.; CP, vol. 2, Op Tallulah Notes Given Verbally by C of S 2 Cdn Corps to GSO 1 Ops First Cdn Army at HQ 2 Cdn Corps 122300B Aug.; RG 24, vol. 14 141, WD HQ 8 CIB 8 Cdn Inf Bde 00 No 17 Op "Tallulah," 14 Aug. 1944; and Stacey, *Victory Campaign*, 236–38. The 3rd Division was deployed with two armoured regiments up, 1st Hussars left, and FGH right, each with two squadrons up and one in reserve; behind these came the 7th Canadian Reconnaissance Regiment (17th Duke of York's Royal Canadian Hussars), the 9th Brigade, and the 7th Brigade. The 4th Division also advanced with two armoured regiments up, the Grenadiers left and Foot Guards right, both with three squadrons up; the Lake Superiors followed left rear and the British Columbia Regiment right rear.

Behind these came the 8th Brigade and the 10th Brigade with the 29th Canadian Reconnaissance Regiment (The South Alberta Light Horse). Reginald H. Roy, *1944: The Canadians in Normandy*, Canadian War Museum Historical publication no. 19 (Ottawa: Macmillan, 1984), 240, 251.

18. RG 24, vol. 13 712, 2 Cdn Corps Intelligence Summaries no. 31 of 11 Aug., no. 32 of 12 Aug., and no. 33 of 13 Aug. 1944; RG 24, vol. 14 141, WD HQ 8 CIB 8 Cdn Inf Bde 00 no. 17 Op "Tallulah," 14 Aug. 1944; Craig W. H. Luther, *Blood and Honor: The History of the 12th SS Panzer Division "Hitler Youth," 1943–1945* (San Jose, Calif.: Bender, 1987), 234, 253–54; and Meyer, *12.SS-Panzerdivision*, 109. Stacey estimated that the 12th SS at this time had 18 Mark IVs, 9 Panthers, and 17 Tigers. Stacey, *Victory Campaign*, 248.

19. RG 24, vol. 13 751, WD GS 2 CID "Tallulah" Notes on Corps Comd's Outline Talk 131000 hrs; RG 24, vol. 13 767, WD GS 3 CID SEI, 14 Aug. 1944; RG 24, vol. 14 141, WD HD 8 CIB 8 Cdn Inf Bde 00 no. 17 Op "Tallulah"; RG 24, vol. 15 098, WD Lake Superiors, 14 Aug. 1944; Maj. Gen. George Kitching, *Mud and Green Fields: The Memoirs of Major General George Kitching* (Langley, B.C.: Battleline, 1986), 216; and Stacey, *Victory Campaign*, 240–41.

20. McNaughton Papers (hereafter MP), NAC, vol. 161, Simonds to McNaughton, 29 April 1943.

21. RG 24, vol. 14 117, WD HQ 2 CAB Op "Tractable," An Account of Ops by 2 Cdn Armd Bde in France, 14–16 Aug. 1944. Canadian intelligence admitted that the "Laison River . . . turned out to be an unexpectedly difficult obstacle that . . . [photographic interpretation and intelligence] failed to estimate correctly." Maj. S.R. Elliot, *Scarlet to Green: "History of Intelligence in the Canadian Army 1903–1963"* (Ottawa: Canadian Intelligence and Security Association, 1981), 271.

22. Kitching, *Mud and Green Fields*, 219.

23. Roy, *Canadians in Normandy*, 240–49, 253–60, 262–63; and Stacey, *Victory*

Campaign, 241. Division did not know until 1615 that Booth was wounded. He and his tactical headquarters may have been lost. Lt. M. O. Rollefson, ed., *Green Route Up* (The Hague: Mouton and Cy, 1945), 321–32.

24. RG 24, vol. 10 797, 2 Cdn Corps COS Telephone Notes, 14 Aug. 1944. The scribbled entry for 1720 hours ends: "Go on with Trun—though Falaise priority."

25. Stacey, *Victory Campaign*, 248–49; Kitching, *Mud and Green Fields*, 220–21; Roy, *Canadians in Normandy*, 269–78; RG 24, vol. 13 789, WD GS 4 CAD SEI, 15 Aug. 1944; RG 24, vol. 14 052, WD HQ 4 CAB SEI, 15 Aug. 1944; and RG 24, vol. 14 130, WD HQ 7 CIB SEI, 15 Aug. 1944.

26. Personal Copies CLFCSC Collection, Operation "Tractable" Bombing Errors in Close Support Operation of 14 Aug. 1944; PRO Air 14/860, XC/A/51202, First Cdn Army COS Memo on Use of Coloured Smoke and Flares to GOC-in-C, 22 Aug. 1944 and Minute by A.T. Harris, 31 Aug.; Report on Bombing of Our Own Troops During Operation "Tractable" by Air Chief Marshal A.T. Harris, 25 Aug. 1944; and PRO Air 14/861, XC/A/51202, RAF Proceedings of a Board of Officers 16–18 Aug. 1944 for the purpose of investigating errors in bombing that occurred on 14 Aug. 1944 in connection with operation "Tractable."

27. CP, vol. 5, Memo COS to GOC-in-C Regarding the Report of the AOC in C Bomber Command, 28 Aug. 1944.

28. RG 24, vol. 10 797, Notes COS 2 Corps 14 Aug.; Stacey, *Victory Campaign*, 243–45; and Roy, *Canadians in Normandy*, 238–39, 263–65. Crerar remained a believer in heavy bombers and accordingly thanked "Bomber" Harris, doubtless the price of continued friendship, not to mention support; he also took pains to point out to troops that most of the bombs that did not land on them hit their targets.

29. Personal copy from CLFCSC Collection, Simonds "To be Read by All Officers" circular, 23 Aug. 1944.

30. Interview Meyer, 6 March 1986, and his *12.SS-Panzerdivision*, 109–10; RG 24, vol. 13 712, Extract from an order of 85 Inf Div, dated 9 Aug. 1944, captured 16 Aug. 1944; RG 24, vol. 13 712, 2 Cdn Corps Intelligence Summaries no. 30 of 10 Aug., and no. 33 of 13 Aug. 1944; Stacey, *Victory Campaign*, 247–48; Copp and Vogel, *Falaise*, 116; and Kitching, *Mud and Green Fields*, 216. The 102nd SS Tiger battalion reinforced the line north of Falaise, coming under command of the 85th Division.

31. Tony Foster, *Meeting of Generals* (Toronto: Methuen, 1986), 368.

32. RG 24, vol. 10 797, Notes COS 2 Corps, 14 Aug.

33. Roy, *Ready for the Fray*, 286–94. The Canadian Scottish had 34 killed and 93 wounded in this battle, more than in any other.

34. RC 24, vol. 10 797, GOC's Activities, 17–23 Aug. 1944; RG 24, vol. 13 789, WD GS 4 CAD SEI, 17–21 Aug. 1944; RG 24, vol. 14 052, WD HQ 4 CAB SEI, 16–20 Aug. 1944; CP, vol. 2, Crerar to Ralston, 1 September 1944; Stacey, *Victory Campaign*, 236, 250–65; Roy, *Canadians in Normandy*, 289–315; Belfield and Essame, *Battle for Normandy*, 231–37; Kitching, *Mud and Green Fields*, 221–25; and Lt. Gen. Sir Brian Horrocks, *Corps Commander* (London: Sidgwick and Jackson, 1977), 53. Kitching was relieved of command by Simonds on 21 Aug. Hutchinson charges that the 4th Armoured Division, which had been given the 2nd Armoured and 9th Infantry Brigades under command, reacted too slowly on 20 Aug. Hutchinson, "Corps Commander," 229–42). It may be that Kitching was also fired for his performance on "Totalize" and "Tractable."

35. Ibid.

36. Stacey, *Victory Campaign*, 271; LHC, de Guingand Papers, 1-IV/3, Notes on the Operations of 21 Army Group, 6 June 1944–5 May 1945; and Copp and Vogel, *Falaise*, 138.

37. Belfield and Essame, *Battle for Normandy*, 130.

BATTLE EXHAUSTION AND THE
CANADIAN SOLDIER IN NORMANDY◇

J. TERRY COPP

o

The fortieth anniversary of the Normandy invasion brought forth a new flood of books each purporting to tell the real story of battle. Strategic questions have been reassessed, the significance of Ultra brought to light and the personalities of the leading figures re-examined. There is a good deal of new information in the recent studies of the 1944 campaign but almost all of it[1] relates to questions which are quite remote from the actual experience of the young men who fought the battle in close contact with the enemy.

The purpose of this paper is to attempt to get some measure of the experience of the Canadian infantry soldier by examining the phenomenon of Battle Exhaustion, the catch-all term used by the Army to describe stress-related neuro-psychiatric casualties. But before attempting to analyze this small part of the story it seems necessary to explain some facets of the organization of the Canadian and British forces who set out to invade Normandy on 6 June 1944 and to make some comments on the nature of the campaign in Normandy.

We must first always remind ourselves that the Allied plan for the invasion of northwest Europe was dependent upon the ability of the Red Army to continue operations which occupied the energies of three-quarters of the German army. The Allies had simply not created a force large enough to confront the bulk of the German army. Indeed British (and thus Canadian) preparations for Operation Overlord were strongly affected by the overall war policy of Great Britain which was based on the desire to defeat the enemy by means other than direct conflict with substantial elements of the German army. In the spring of 1944 the British-Canadian component of the Allied forces, available for the invasion of Normandy, included a formidable

◇ From *The British Army Review* 85 (April 1987), 46–54.

tactical air force, a naval commitment of unparalleled power, and a small army which was rich in every resource except infantry.

Twenty-one Army Group which was charged with the responsibility for the invasion was to have an establishment of some 750 000 men but there were only nine infantry divisions (including two Canadian) available. Fifteen percent of the total troops were infantry,[2] but the designation "infantry" should not be confused with actual commitment to battle in a rifle company. A standard 1944 infantry division contained 915 officers and 17 247 men, but less than half were infantry and of those only 4500 served in the thirty-six divisional rifle companies.[3]

The British had long since determined, as the Germans in Normandy were soon to discover, that artillery was to be the army's principal weapon and fully 18 percent of the troops in the bridgehead were artillerymen.[4] The planners also hoped that the fourteen armoured brigades allotted to 21 Army Group would play a prominent role in cracking the German defences. It was hoped that these two Arms, together with the 2nd Tactical Air Force, would ensure that the Battle of Normandy would not become a bloody replay of the Western Front in World War I.

Viewed in hindsight the Normandy campaign went much better than the planners hoped. Not only were the Germans unable to bring substantial reinforcements from the Eastern Front (the Russian summer offensive which began two weeks after D Day was to cost the Germans close to one million casualties) but the Allied deception scheme "Fortitude" kept large elements of their western forces away from Normandy until it was too late. The Tactical Air Force, naval guns, the heavy bombers, and the artillery struck the German defenders with such a weight of high explosives that it may reasonably be argued that the Germans were blasted out of Normandy acre by acre.

But, and it is a very large but, the skill and resilience of the German defenders meant that the Allied infantry were required to attack, occupy, and hold small parcels of ground under circumstances which fully paralleled the horrors of the fighting on the Western Front in the first World War.

Modern memory has a firm image of "suicide battalions" and long casualty lists in the first World War, but we are not accustomed to thinking of Normandy in these terms, perhaps because of the relatively short duration of the campaign (88 days) and the overwhelming victory which climaxed the battle. A single crude comparison will help to make the point. During a 105-day period in the summer and fall of 1917, British and Canadian soldiers fought the battle known as 3rd Ypres which included the struggle for Passchendaele. When it was over our forces had suffered 244 000 casualties[5] or 2324 a day. Normandy was to cost the Allies more than 200 000 casualties or 2354 a day and 70 percent of these casualties were suffered by the tiny minority of men who fought in infantry rifle companies.[6]

So far what we have been trying to establish is that the fighting in Normandy placed a burden of almost unbearable proportions on one small Arm of the Allied armies—the Infantry. British (and thus Canadian) planners had not, despite the lessons of Italy, been willing to prepare for this eventuality. Well before D Day Montgomery had been warned that reserves of infantry replacements were dangerously limited. The War Office had already calculated that "at least two infantry divisions and several separate brigades might have to be disbanded by the end of 1944 for lack of reinforcements."[7] By early July the character of the Normandy battle had brought this crisis to hand and infantry battalions were frequently operating well below strength. By early August the Canadians, for whom infantry casualties were running at 76 percent of the total,[8] were reporting a deficiency of 1900 general duty infantry[9] or the equivalent of four battalions of riflemen. By the end of August shortages had reached the staggering figure of 4318.[10]

This situation, which was proportionately only slightly less serious among British divisions, forced Montgomery to cannibalize the 59th division. On 14 August he told Alanbrooke, "My infantry divisions are now so low in effective rifle strength they can no longer—repeat, no longer—fight effectively in major operations. The need for action has been present for some time, but the urgency of battle operations forced me to delay a decision."[11]

Perhaps enough has been said to indicate something of the context within which the Infantry fought in Normandy. Let us turn to the impact which the battle had upon the men who fought it as measured by the phenomenon of Battle Exhaustion. Needless to say, Battle Exhaustion was largely an infantryman's problem. More than 90 percent of the known cases were among infantry. The large majority of individuals diagnosed as suffering from Battle Exhaustion exhibited what the psychiatrists described as acute fear reactions and acute and chronic anxiety manifested through uncontrollable tremors, a pronounced startle reaction to war-related sounds, and a profound loss of self-confidence. The second largest symptomatic category was depression with accompanying withdrawal. Conversion states such as amnesia, stupor, or loss of control over some physical function, which had made up a large component of those described as "shell shocked" in World War I, were rarely seen in World War II.[12]

In preparing for Operation Overlord the Canadian Army was able to draw upon its own experiences with Battle Exhaustion in the Italian campaign as well as the much more extensive information available from British and American sources. The assumptions of Canadian military authorities in May of 1944 may be summarized quite briefly.

The most commonly used method of measuring exhaustion rates was the so-called NP ratio which measured neuropsychiatric casualties in relation to total non-fatal battle casualties. Experience in the Mediterranean among British, American, and Canadian units suggested that a NP ratio of 23 percent, more than 1 in 5 of non-fatal casualties, was normal for infantry divisions in combat.[13]

Neither the military planners, frightened by the shrinking pool of General Service infantry reinforcements, nor the psychiatrists, professionally committed to reducing the NP ratio, were very happy with either the quantity or predictability of neuropsychiatric casualties. The military authorities could and did, on occasion, issue directives attempting to forbid soldiers from breaking down. The major impact of such orders was to make life difficult for the Regimental Medical Officer and to make it nearly impossible for historians to compile accurate battle exhaustion statistics. Shortly after

General Burns assumed command of 1st Corps, RMOs were ordered to be very strict and hold all NP cases until it was certain that they could not be returned to unit and regimental CO's were told that battle exhaustion was their responsibility and if it occurred in the coming action "it would be taken as a reflection upon the ability of these officers."[14] General Guy Simonds never went quite that far, but it is evident that he had little patience with the policies of First Canadian Army relating to battle exhaustion.[15]

The psychiatrists in the Canadian Army, fully supported by their Allied colleagues, took a different approach. If battle exhaustion was a psycho-neurosis, i.e.

> an emotional disorder in which feelings of anxiety, obsessional thoughts, compulsive acts and physical complaints, without objective evidence of disease, in various patterns, dominate the personality,

then their training indicated that the neurotic individual must have been predisposed to neurosis by childhood experiences. If enough attention was paid to screening combat units for pre-disposed individuals, then the NP ratio could be significantly reduced. Dr. Arthur Manning Doyle, the First Division psychiatrist (and the only Canadian psychiatrist, in May 1944, with direct experience of battle exhaustion) did admit that "stress of battle" as well as pre-disposition was a variable, but he could only offer advice on the desirability of "weeding" units to remove the pre-disposed.[16]

Doyle's careful investigation of the NP ratio in the various regiments of the 1st Division should have suggested that a more elaborate diagnosis was required. His own figures showed that the Loyal Edmonton Regiment had less than half the NP casualties of some other regiments and that the variation between regiments was very large. It was also evident that 3 Brigade continued to have a much higher NP ratio than other brigades,[17] but no conclusions were drawn or indeed questions raised about these striking differences.

For Overlord the emphasis was on "weeding" and Dr. Gregory, the 3 Division psychiatrist, rejected 150 men—including three officers and one senior NCO—in the weeks before D Day, even though the division's regiments had been repeatedly "weeded" in the long months of assault training.[18] Once in combat the division utilized one of its Field Dressing Stations as an exhaustion unit, treating 208 men in the first two weeks of combat.[19] Exhaustion soon became the "outstanding problem"[20] for the medicals and in early July, Colonel Watson, the division's ADMS, issued instructions asking units to keep what he called "physical exhaustion" cases with the left-out-of-battle personnel. True battle exhaustion cases should come to the attention of the medical services only after they had had a rest.[21]

Colonel Watson and the divisional psychiatrist became convinced that common sense was "the first quality required" in the control of battle exhaustion. The truly neurotic soldier was a "menace to the stability of the force, even during rest periods" and must be removed. But for the rest, common sense meant:

> planned rest periods on a company, unit, brigade or divisional basis with diversions in the form of movies, sports etc. must be arranged. During battle this can only be done on a platoon or company basis.

During these periods, even if bombing or shelling are only remotely possible, adequate protection in the form of solid buildings and numerous slit trenches should be readily available to the soldier. For psychological reasons, the soldier should not be in a position where he is constantly having to search for a place to duck in an emergency; if so, he becomes cowardly; plenty of obvious slit trenches makes him feel secure and he becomes brave and does not require to use them. Troops in rest areas, even where odd shells are falling, should sleep above ground.

(d) The Divisional Psychologist (sic) should be possessed of a degree of common sense well above that of the average officer. It is an essential appointment for the right man. His duty is to discuss with the ADMS all measures which will raise the morale of the fighting soldier as they apply to each separate situation and to examine and classify all casualties which are referred to him. He should not have to make a professional show by having specially allotted Field Dressing Stations or Field Ambulances filled with cases on which he can base statistics and lengthy reports to Headquarters. In fact, if he has many patients and issues long reports, he should be removed at once for failing in his job.

The 'G' staff should be alert to the fact that providing the medicals have done their job, a high incidence of exhaustion cases indicates deficient training, poor leadership with a low fighting ability of the force. Battles are won by causing exhaustion in the enemy's ranks!![22]

All of this was at least an improvement on the preoccupation with childhood neuroses, but it was quite remote from the actual experience of 3 Division rifle companies. In *Maple Leaf Route: Falaise*, Robert Vogel and I reproduced the only battalion casualty report we found that dealt frankly with the problem of Battle Exhaustion. This report by the Officer Commanding the Canadian Scottish Regiment noted that, on 28 July, the regiment (which had begun the campaign with 38 officers and 815 other ranks) had suffered 569 casualties and contained only 15 officers and 321 other ranks who had landed on D Day. Many of the survivors were, of course, not riflemen. Of the 421 men who had been "wounded" to that date, 117 had been evacuated as Battle Exhaustion cases. Not included on the list were "24 men sent down to Corps Rest Camp and a large number (approx. 36) withdrawn from the front line during periods of relative quiet who, in the opinion of the company commanders and Medical Officer, required twenty-four or forty-eight hours of rest."[23]

The Canadian Scottish Regiment was, by any standards, well led, well-trained and was as effective a unit as the Allied armies possessed. Furthermore, unlike a number of its sister regiments, it had yet to experience[24] one of those single day disasters that had scarred units like the Royal Winnipeg Rifles, the North Nova Scotia Regiment or the Highland Light Infantry. The Canadian Scottish had, however, remained in the line continuously under fire and had taken part in some of the most difficult battles.

By late July the Canadian Scottish, like the rest of the division, had reached a dangerous state of nervous tension and Colonel Watson, the senior Medical Officer, "drew the attention of the GOC to the situation in a letter which he in turn discussed with the Brigade Commanders who strongly supported the request for a rest of seven to ten days. . . . "[25] The Third Division was finally pulled out of the line.

The experiences of British 3 Division which fought alongside the Canadians in the first phase of the Normandy campaign was similar with 253 cases in June and 736 cases in July.[26] Overall the exhaustion ratio in 2 British Army rose from 9.5 percent in June to 22 percent in late July.[27] The 2 Army psychiatrist, Major A. Watterson, described the situation in these terms:

> The high optimism of the troops who landed in the assault and early build-up phases inevitably dwindled when the campaign for a few weeks appeared to have slowed down. Almost certainly the initial hopes and optimism were too high and the gradual realization that the "walk-over" to Berlin had developed into an infantry slogging match caused an unspoken but clearly recognizable fall of morale. One sign of this was the increase in the incidence of psychiatric casualties arriving in a steady stream at the Exhaustion Centres and reinforced by waves of beaten, exhausted men from each of the major battles. For every man breaking down there were certainly three or four ineffective men remaining with their units.[28]

The pattern of battle exhaustion casualties in both 3 Canadian and 3 British Division could be understood in the terms outlined by Watson and Gregory—psychiatric casualties would increase over time if units were not relieved. What disturbed Canadian Army authorities was the sudden influx of NP casualties from 2 Division in the early weeks of combat. It must be stressed that no accurate count of NP casualties is possible. Indeed, given the attitude of 2 Canadian Corps headquarters "there will be no evacuation of psychiatric casualties in 2 Corps"[29] and the refusal to accept a divisional psychiatrist on the staff of 2 Division,[30] estimates for 2 Division are even more difficult to arrive at than for 3 Division.

First Canadian Exhaustion unit, which had been activated with 2 Corps, dealt with 2 Division NP casualties during mid-July before divisional recovery centres were functioning. In the period 13 July to 24 July it reported approximately 300 cases from 2 Division, including 13 officers.[31] After 24 July, 4 Canadian FDS [Field Dressing Station] was used as a divisional recovery centre and, in the first seven days, it admitted 118 cases.[32] A similar number were admitted to the Corps Exhaustion unit that terrible week.[33] For the entire period, 13 July to 15 August, First Canadian Exhaustion Unit reported 576 cases from 2 Division and as many as 200 further cases were treated at Field Dressing stations; 23 officers were evacuated to hospital.[34] This indicates a NP ratio well above 30 percent and clearly demonstrates that 2 Division's first weeks in battle were even more horrific than existing accounts of the battles of Verrières Ridge suggest.

The extent of battle exhaustion casualties in 2 Division became a subject of considerable notoriety in the Canadian Army and, after the Battle of

Normandy was over, Dr. Burdett McNeel who had commanded the Corps Exhaustion Centre in July and August, was asked to investigate the situation in 2 Division.[35] By eliminating the first nine days of the division's frontline experiences from consideration, McNeel was able to show that the division's exhaustion rate was no higher than 3 Division's. This did nothing to clarify the situation. However, McNeel's own War Diary and quarterly report covering the entire period do provide some insight.

The first wave of exhaustion cases from 2 Division included truckloads, complete with NCO's, of "dirty, haggard and dejected men"[36] from a regiment whose lead companies were caught by their own artillery barrage. The next day these were joined by more than one hundred cases largely from the three regiments shattered in the dying hours of Operation Goodwood on the rain-drenched and deadly slopes of Verrières Ridge.

In conversation with Dr. McNeel some forty years later,[37] it was evident that he had known nothing of the military situation which precipitated the evacuation of so many men from the 2 Division, either on 20th July or in the aftermath.

It seems quite clear that a detailed knowledge of the events of mid-July provides an adequate explanation of the extent of Battle Exhaustion in 2 Division. The Division was ordered into the Normandy battle in the final stages of an operation (Goodwood) which had already failed. The decision to commit two "green" infantry brigades to a frontal attack on a position which the Germans were steadily reinforcing was not a wise one. The results were horrific. The division suffered 1149 casualties in its first battle since Dieppe and four of its regiments were devastated. Everything was out of control and no one's morale was in very good shape after the battle.

The renewal of offensive operations on 25th July (Operation Spring) was a replay of the disasters of the 19th–20th. The Canadian army experienced a catastrophe of almost Dieppe proportions, losing 1500 men, most of them from 2 Division, in the space of 24 hours. No division could be expected to absorb these kinds of casualties in offensive operations which were clearly failures and maintain high morale. Substantial Battle Exhaustion casualties were simply inevitable.

At the time psychiatrists, wedded to their theories on pre-disposition, could only assume that 2 Division had been less carefully screened than 3 Division. The Exhaustion Units' diagnoses of cases seen in this period suggest just how committed to personality development theory the psychiatrists were. Almost half the evacuees were labelled psychopathic personalities, i.e.:

> a disorder of behaviour towards other individuals or towards society in which reality is clearly perceived except for an individual's social and moral obligations. . . .

Even a layman can be forgiven for doubting that the two harassed psychiatrists who dealt with hundreds of cases in a matter of a few days, would have accurately diagnosed 197 psychopaths![38]

However, McNeel's report on 2 Division which was written in late September reflected his growing awareness of the nature of warfare in

Northwest Europe. He spoke with both medical and line officers in 2 Division and became convinced that casualty statistics and exhaustion ratios were of doubtful value in assessing personnel or performance. He wrote:

> The sources of error in the compilation of statistics and the use of such a figure as an exhaustion ratio are so numerous as to make any conclusion based on statistics alone of very doubtful value. The incidence of exhaustion in any unit is only a part of the picture of that unit's efficiency and is outweighed in a positive direction by a generally high standard of performance and in a negative direction by large numbers of AWOL, POW and trivial illnesses. I have been told that one regiment which has a high exhaustion ratio is always reliable and has never withdrawn from an action, whereas another regiment with a low exhaustion ratio has usually withdrawn from an action whenever the stress became great. . . . The exhaustion ratio will also be altered by the wholesale evacuation of trivial sick or wounded. . . . For these reasons the thoughtful appraisal of a unit's overall performance by responsible officers who know all the factors is of more value than any set of statistics or ratios can ever hope to be. However the latter may be used as a lead.[39]

McNeel gave a further illustration of the problems of using battle exhaustion ratios. He had spoken with a RMO in July about the number of evacuations from his regiment and urged him to keep the men with the unit. Later he had occasion to compliment the RMO on the changed situation only to be told "Well, I don't know—we have 50 men AWOL today."[40]

McNeel's superior officer, Colonel F.H. van Nostrand, was equally dubious about the value of exhaustion ratios. The Colonel, who had been pulled out of regimental duties in 1942 when General McNaughton had become alarmed over the number of psychiatric cases in the Army overseas, assumed responsibility as the Consultant Neuropsychiatrist Canadian Army Overseas. "Van," as he was universally known, brought a degree of common sense and unpretentiousness to psychiatric work that was badly needed. McNeel tells the story of a discussion of NP ratios as predictive tools in which he, McNeel, was fumbling for a statement of his own doubts when Van Nostrand calmly brought the debate to a halt with these lines:

> There was a young man named Paul
> Who had a hexagonal ball
> The square of its weight
> Plus his penis times eight
> Was two-thirds of three-fifths of * * * * - all.[41]

The conclusion of the Battle of Normandy brought an end to the battle exhaustion crisis. Cases were rare during the September pursuit and, when neuropsychiatric casualties began to accumulate again in October, there was no sudden influx of large numbers. There was now time available for more careful diagnosis and treatment.

Dr. Travis Dancey, the new Corps Exhaustion Unit psychiatrist wrote:

The type of NP case seen ... has been much different from that so frequently described in the literature and from that admitted this summer. Although recent reinforcements who break down tend to show gross demoralization characterized by conversion-hysteria or anxiety-hysteria, we are handling an increasing number of men who have carried on under considerable stress for long periods of time. ... We are not dealing with chronic psychoneurotics, or with men who could be called inadequate in any sense of the term.[42]

Dancey, who was not in France during the Normandy battle, was not yet prepared to challenge the literature or to suggest that the Normandy experience be reassessed. It was not until the battles of 1945, when a more elaborate system of diagnosing and treating NP casualties was developed, that new evidence began to accumulate.[43] Many "predisposed" neurotic personalities had functioned very well and many "normal" individuals had broken down. It further became evident that every infantry soldier who remained for any length of time in combat developed neurotic traits which, in civilian life, would have indicated serious personality disturbance. The question was, why some men became incapacitated by stress and why others (often with "weaker" personalities) did not.

William C. Menninger who served as Chief Consultant in Neuropsychiatry to the US Army provided this answer:

The breakdown of the soldier in combat, whether it was during his first week or his fifteenth month, was related to the ability of his personality to maintain further the balance between stress and compensating support. Support was derived from various sources. The external situation which presented the necessity of killing in order not to be killed, was a stimulus to keep the aggression mobilized for action. Fear, if controlled, was a factor in maintaining ... alertness. Very significant aids in the control of this aggression were the approval and command of the leader and the identification and close association with a group of men who shared the same plight.

The same psychological reinforcements which made it possible for the soldier to fight were potential causes of the development of a psychiatric casualty, if they suddenly disappeared. Because of great dependence on them, the ego was left without support in their absence. ... The very occasional soldier might carry on alone. ... More often, as the tension increased, the personality tried to relieve its distress by transforming anxiety into symptoms.[44]

Canadian army psychiatrists never quite went this far, though one study of 544 cases did conclude with the following:

Two thirds of the cases gave no apparent history of neurotic predisposition or previous instability ... only 19% of the total could have been considered as originally unfit ... 30% were sensitized by long service alone (average of 230 days). 23% had an added factor of being previously wounded and 18% had been previously evacuated for exhaustion. ... A further finding of interest was that of the 167 cases with long front-line service . . . 42 cases or 23% had carried on in spite of the fact that they had histories of previous nervous disorders or evident traits predisposing to neurotic breakdown . . . even a neurotic can stand a long period of battle stress when he has good drive, morale and character . . . a man can be "burnt out" due to long exposure to battle conditions even when he is considered quite normal.[45]

Here we are less interested in the education of Canadian psychiatrists than we are with the soldier in Normandy so I will say no more about psychiatric reports. When Canadians and other Allied veterans assemble this June to commemorate the beginning of the campaign to liberate the peoples of Western Europe all of them will be deserving of our gratitude but perhaps it would not be unfair if we kept a special place in our hearts for the rifleman who fought "without promise of reward or relief." For no one, not even a psychiatrist or an historian "however he may talk has the remotest idea of what an ordinary infantry soldier endures."

NOTES

1. See John Ellis, *The Sharp End of War* (London, 1980), which attempts to describe combat in World War II from the point of view of the ordinary soldier. Carlo D'Este, *Decision in Normandy* (London, 1983). This contains a good discussion of infantry manpower problems.

2. The figures adjusted to include Canadian personnel are from L.F. Ellis, *Victory in the West* (London, 1962), vol. 1, HMSO, app. 4.

3. M. Hitsman, *Manpower Problems of the Canadian Army*, Report #63 Historical Section, Department of National Defence, app. L, 352.

4. Ellis, *Victory in the West*, app. 4.

5. John Terraine, *The Smoke and the Fire* (London, 1980), 46.

6. C.P. Stacey, *The Victory Campaign* (Ottawa, 1960), calculates Canadian infantry casualties as 76 percent of the total. The figure of 70 percent appears to be an accepted average for all allied casualties. See Ellis, *The Sharp End of War*, 158.

7. D'Este, *Decision in Normandy*, 252.

8. Stacey, *The Victory Campaign*, 284.

9. C.P. Stacey, *Arms, Men and Government* (Ottawa, 1970), 435.

10. Ibid., 438–39.

11. D'Este, *Decision in Normandy*, 262.

12. There does not seem to be any adequate explanation for this difference.

13. A.M. Doyle, "Report of 1 Cdn. Neuropsychiatrist, period 1 April–20 June 1944," Public Archives of Canada (hereafter PAC), Record Group (hereafter RG) 24, vol. 15, G46, p. 11.

14. W.R. Feasby, *Official History of the Canadian Medical Services 1939–45*, vol. 2 (Ottawa, 1956), 58.

15. On 29 August Simonds in a letter to his divisional commanders urged greater efforts to limit straggling, absenteeism, and battle exhaustion and suggested that the latter problem should not occur under the conditions of fighting in Normandy.

16. It should be noted that by 1945 Dr. Doyle was arguing that:

    the following factors are those that affect the incidence of Neuropsychiatric casualties in order of importance.
    a) Quality of Personnel
    b) Degree and severity of action
    c) Duration of Action

d) Quality of leadership
e) Considerations such as weather, opportunity for rest and recreation and other such items relating to the welfare of the soldier.

Doyle's emphasis on quality of personnel was reflected in his overall conclusion that "the units which have shown consistently high neuropsychiatric ratios are those units who have had in their ranks too many inadequate, neurotic or mentally defective personnel." This judgement was to be challenged by the end of the Northwest European campaign.

See Lt. Col. A.M. Doyle "Psychiatry with the Canadian Army in Action in the C.M.F." *The Journal of the Canadian Medical Services*, vol. 3 (January 1946), 93. I wish to thank Dr. Bill McAndrew (DHist, National Defence) for discussing this point with me and sharing his own research into battle exhaustion in Italy.

17. Doyle may well have been thinking about 3 Brigade in particular when he emphasized quality of personnel but the difficulties encountered by 3 Brigade from training through its first months in combat require a far more complex analysis than this.

18. Dr. Dick Gregory was an unusual individual. Energetic, gregarious and colourful, he won the confidence of the ADMS, Col. Watson, and of the Regimental Medical Officers. He was able to arrange for the officers of each divisional Field Ambulance to attend an American School of Psychiatry and did much to prepare both medical and non-medical personnel for battle exhaustion casualties. Gregory reported that in June and early July he was able to return more than 50 percent of such casualties to their unit after brief treatment at the Field Ambulance recovery centre. This "success rate" was so extraordinarily high that his fellow psychiatrists were frankly dubious. However it is clear that 3 Division, as a whole, was better prepared for dealing with psychiatric casualties

than the other divisions and it may be that early rest and reassurance did work well. R.A. Gregory "Psychiatric Report 3 Division," 18 March 1944, 11 April 1944, and 17 May 1944, PAC, RG 24, vol. 15 661. Interview with Dr. B.H. McNeel (3 Dec. 1982) "War Diary 1 Cdn. Exhaustion Unit," July 1944, PAC, RG 24, vol. 15 659.

19. "War Diary, ADMS 3 Cdn. Inf. Division," June 1944, PAC, RG 24, vol. 15 661.

20. "War Diary, ADMS 3 Cdn. Inf. Division," July 1944, PAC, RG 24, vol. 15 661.

21. Ibid.

22. Ibid.

23. Terry Copp and Robert Vogel, *Maple Leaf Route: Falaise* (Alma, Ont., 1983), 34.

24. The Canadian Scottish were to experience such a day on 15 August when the Regiment took 130 casualties in the space of a few hours at Pt. 168, north of Falaise. The royal Winnipeg Rifles lost 128 men on D Day, 256 on 8 June in the defence of Putôt-en-Bessin and 132 on 4 July in the attack on Carpiquet Airport. The North Nova Scotia Regiment lost more than 200 men on 7 June and a similar number on 25 July. The Highland Light Infantry were reduced to 50 percent of their strength in their first major battle 8 July at Buron.

25. "War Diary, ADMS 3 Cdn. Inf. Div.," July 1944, PAC, RG 24, vol. 15 661.

26. "War Diary, ADMS 3 Division," July 1944, PRO, WO 177/344. There was an extraordinary variance in N.P. ratios among the regiments in the division but the overall ratio was under $10\frac{1}{2}$ for June and over $30\frac{1}{2}$ for July (app. C, August War Diary ADMS).

27. "Report by Psychiatrist attached 2nd Army" for Month of July 1944, app. AI, WO 1777/321.

28. Ibid.

29. Quoted from an interview with Dr. B. McNeel, 3 Dec., 1982.

30. Dr. John Burch had been assigned as 2 Division psychiatrist but he was quickly transferred out. No psychiatrist was appointed to 4 Division.

31. John Burch, "Quarterly Report 1 Cdn. Exhaustion Unit 1 July–30 Sept. 1944," PAC, RG 24, vol. 15 659.

32. "War Diary, 4 Cdn. Field Dressing Station," July 1944.

33. "War Diary, 1 Cdn. Exhaustion Unit," July 1944, PAC, RG 24, vol. 15 659.

34. Burch, "Quarterly Report."

35. B. McNeel, "Report on Exhaustive Cases 2 Cdn. Inf. Division."

36. "War Diary, 1 Cdn. Exhaustion Unit."

37. McNeel Interview.

38. Burch, "Quarterly Report."

39. B.H. McNeel, "Re: Cases of Exhaustion—2 Cdn. Inf. Div. War Diary," app. DDMS 2 Cdn. Corps Oct. 1944.

40. McNeel Interview.

41. Ibid.

42. "Quarterly Report, 1 Cdn. Exhaustion Unit, 30 Sept.–30 Dec. 1944," PAC, RG 24, vol. 15 569.

43. See, for example, B.H. McNeel and Travis Dancey, "The Personality of the Successful Soldier," *American Journal of Psychiatry* 102, 3 (Nov. 1945), 338.

44. William C. Menninger, *Psychiatry in a Troubled World* (New York, 1948), 145.

45. Quoted in J.C. Richardson, "Neuropsychiatry with the Canadian Army in Western Europe, 6 June 1944–8 May 1945." Typescript 17 pages nd (loaned to the author by Dr. Richardson.)

COMMENT BY DIRECTOR OF ARMY PSYCHIATRY, BRITISH ARMY

It may seem easy for a well informed historian to deride the follies of the military authorities who attempted "to forbid soldiers from breaking down" or medical commanders who maintained that the "specially allotted Field Dressing Stations or Field Ambulances filled with cases" were merely a "professional show."

They were, however, guilty of overlooking the clearly established lessons of World War I, a trap into which every new generation is in danger of falling.

Battle exhaustion, battleshock as we now call it, is simply an inseparable concomitant of the kind of ferocious warfare in which "lead companies were caught by their own artillery barrage" and friends are killed and injured on all sides: "1500 men, most of them from 2 Division, in the space of 24 hours."

But that is not the end of the story. It is unfortunate that Professor Copp fails to record crucially important figures which put the whole question in perspective. From the Exhaustion Centres in that same terrible battle for Normandy 70 percent returned to duty of whom no more than 7 percent relapsed. The exhaustion or shock need only be temporary and it is up to everyone from junior commanders to doctors to see that it is so. (See note 18.)

THE GUNS OF WOENSDRECHT◇

W. DENIS WHITAKER AND SHELAGH WHITAKER

○

By October, 1944, an infantry officer reaching the age of twenty-three or -four was considered old. Mostly, the ones that got killed off were the young men, the recent replacements or transferees from other units, men whose training, whose experience, and whose coolness under fire became the unnerving wartime yardstick that measured their chances of staying alive. In that sense, a man was born on the battlefield, and if he didn't know very much about the business of infantry survival, he died there too.

Joe Pigott was one of those seasoned old infantrymen. He was twenty-three. Louis Froggett (of Antwerp dock fame) and Huck Welch, all-star football player, were two more of the wartime "old boys." The fourth man, the senior officer of the quartet, was a survivor too, until the crisis at Woensdrecht.

These were my four company commanders, majors in the Royal Hamilton Light Infantry [RHLI], who led off the attack for Woensdrecht in the black, predawn hours of Monday, the 16th of October. For, by now, the backlash of Black Friday had had its effect on the Rileys, too. The second ultimatum arising from the Black Watch debacle had been issued. This time, it was not from me, but to me. The dead and wounded from Black Friday were still being carried off the Beveland polders when Brigadier Cabeldu called a 4th Brigade Orders Group.

The RHLI was given forty-eight hours to plan and execute an assault; those guns of Woensdrecht had to be silenced, once and for all. Within the hour, the wheels were in motion to formulate a winning plan. I held a battalion "O" Group with my company commanders and supporting arms to fill them in on the broad objectives. Maps and aerial photographs were distributed, and the men were given time to study them.

◇ From *Tug of War: The Canadian Victory that Opened Antwerp* (Toronto: Stoddart, 1984), 179–201.

We needed more information about the enemy numbers and positions, and we needed specifics about the terrain. Recce patrols were sent out on missions that night to get this essential intelligence.

The Rileys were proud of their battalion's reputation during the Northwest Europe campaign of never failing to take an objective and of never being driven off by counterattack. We were determined we would succeed again. We were angry at the terrible waste of life we had witnessed when the Black Watch lost almost half their strength—futilely, without wresting a foot of ground from the enemy.

There was no point in reinforcing their mistakes; we had seen too well how badly the strength and skill of the enemy forces we faced had been underestimated. He was tough, this enemy, professional and brave, skilled in use of weaponry, canny in battlefield intrigue. Looking down from rain-soaked slit trenches in the shelter of Woensdrecht Hill, he could see virtually every living being that breathed on the flats below. All civilians were being evacuated; the Red Cross had informed us of that. The Germans were dug in and fortified, waiting for the attack they knew would come. The Black Watch's daylight attack had met a well-organized and battle-ready enemy.

To achieve some element of surprise, one that could give us an immediate advantage in the engagement as well as limit the number of casualties, we hoped to catch the Germans off-balance with a night attack. The major "catch 22" built into all night attacks is that assault troops lose their sense of direction in the darkness and often miss their objectives. In Normandy, General Guy Simonds came up with an innovative solution to this problem by firing phosphorescent tracers overhead at fifteen-second intervals from Bofors guns to direct the forward advance of the infantry. Theoretically, the men had only to follow the fireworks to find their targets. Even adopting this idea at Woensdrecht, I reckoned the darkness of the Scheldt might make the task a little more difficult. I couldn't imagine just how serious a hazard the darkness would become.

Strong artillery support was essential. My fire plan, probably the most extravagant I'd ever put together, involved 168 guns. Seventy-two of these were field guns (25-pounders) from the 4th, 5th, and 6th Field Regiments, RCA, which normally supported the 2nd Canadian Infantry Division. Forty-eight medium guns (100-pounders) were with Canadian Medium Regiments, RCA. The remainder were 3.7-inch guns of the British Royal Artillery—normally an anti-aircraft weapon, they had been adapted for use in a ground role. Additional support was provided by medium machine guns and heavy mortars from the Toronto Scottish Regiment, as well as a section of Royal Canadian Engineers and a squadron of the 10th Armoured Regiment.

The three regiments of 25-pounder guns fired their high explosive shells at a maximum rate of five shells per gun per minute. Each shell was loaded manually by the gun crew of five men. These regiments formed an integral part of each infantry division and provided the major supporting fire for the infantry both in offense and defence. The mediums were 4.5-inch guns firing a 100-pound shell. The heavy anti-aircraft 3.7-inch calibre guns fired shells which burst in the air just above their target.[1]

Before the RHLI put a foot over the start line, I intended to lay on a dense concentration of shellfire on the German positions to allow our men to close with the enemy under its protective cover. Troops had been taught to get up to within twenty-five yards of where the shells were falling and stay there until the moment the fire was lifted. The object was to be upon the enemy defences before he could recover from the traumatic effects of the shellfire.

So the three essential components in my battle plan were there: determined men, fire and movement, and the element of surprise ensured by a night attack. That fourth component, luck, would determine the winner.

On Sunday afternoon, at 1600 hours, I called an Orders Group to give a final briefing. The shell-battered town hall of Hoogerheide served as RHLI headquarters, its carved, oaken door hanging crazily from its hinges. It was through this door that the dozens of personnel involved in mounting and supporting the attack—infantry, artillery and other supporting arms—entered for the briefing.

"O" Groups were an essential element in the function of a battalion in any military operation. The success of the action would depend upon the efficacy of the plan, and the confidence it instilled in the participants; so, certainly, would the survival of the men who were to execute the battle plan.

At the first battalion "O" Group, the four company commanders and other officers from the supporting arms were instructed in detail about the coming operation. They were given pertinent information about enemy strength and disposition, and a general overview of Canadian action and strength in the area. The all-important intention or objective of the action was clearly defined; then the method of achieving the goal was explained in full detail. Finally, administrative and communication tasks were assigned, and questions and discussion were encouraged.

This nucleus of command would then hold "O" Groups for their own subordinates until every man involved in the battle had been thoroughly briefed on his area of responsibility and activity, however large or small this might be.

The general plan was a simple one, a night attack on a double axis, with the whole unit, including battalion headquarters, moving forward as one onto the objectives. The start line was a track which was halfway between Hoogerheide and Woensdrecht. The rate of advance was one hundred yards in four minutes. The intention: to capture the Woensdrecht feature. H-Hour was 0330, Monday, the 16th of October.

Carefully examining the sandbox contour model prepared by our Intelligence Section to represent the area topography and the enemy dispositions of Woensdrecht, the four company commanders studied their tasks.

The commanders of A and C companies would lead their men to forward positions approximately 1500 yards distant to the hill that rimmed the northern edge of the town. They had reconnoitred the area with me that morning in the small, single-engine Austers which were piloted by officers of the Royal Artillery for low-level observation of the enemy. These gave us a very good view of the land and allowed us to make definite plans as to the best attack.

The remaining companies, under the command of Joe Pigott and Huck Welch, were designated as "mopping up" units, to stay 150 yards behind.

Signallers were instructed to link up all companies by land lines when the objective was reached, so that we would have an alternative to our frequently unreliable radio net. This was a task often made extremely hazardous by enemy shell and mortar fire. The RHLI Intelligence Section under Captain Lyle Doering had the task of laying lines of white tape to mark the start line and the FUP (forming up position). Never was the procedure more important than on this night, when men would have to grope for their positions in total darkness.

Again, Major Jack Drewry, CO's rep, artillery advisor, and my close friend, would have a key role in the coming hours.

Another intrepid individual, Captain Steve Stevenson, an artillery FOO (Forward Observation Officer) was ordered, with his section, to positions with the front-line troops. Steve's job was to register defensive fire tasks and to pinpoint gunnery targets from the highest point of observation. In normal warfare, this would be a tall tree, a steeple, any high building. In Beveland the loft of a barn or house was often the best—or only—observation point the FOO could manage. At Woensdrecht, Steve discovered, this was to prove more dangerous than usual when the Germans were counter attacking: "I was spotting from the bedroom of this funny little red house when a shell hit the wall just below me, just a few feet below the window where I was looking out. Well, next thing I knew, I was crashing through the floor, me, my batman, my radio pack . . . the house just collapsed on me. And we didn't even get scratched."[2]

As orders filtering out of the "O"Group descended down the line, each man silently weighed his chances of still being alive at the end of that day. Of their objectives the ranks had been well briefed. Of the strategy, the understanding of why the hamlet that waited darkly ahead of them should be worth the lives it was about to claim, nobody knew. Or cared. These five hundred Canadians were concerned with two things: survival and success. If the commanding officer had demonstrated an understanding of the task and consideration of the men who would achieve it, and if he had then developed a sound plan, he would win the confidence of the officers and, through them, of the troops.

The morale in the RHLI was high; I think success had brought a good deal of that about. We had seen others fail where we had succeeded. And our officers were strong; that made quite a difference. Through their own qualities of leadership, they could instil confidence in the other ranks.

Air reconnaissance photos had shown German slit trenches and concrete bunkers dug into the slopes, dykes, and houses of the town. The intelligence report also told a grim tale: Dutch Resistance and the Red Cross had reported spotting two thousand German paratroopers in the woods north of Woensdrecht. If this information was correct, we would have to face a formidable counterattack force, five times our number. In reality, it was a military rule of thumb that, to ensure success, the ratio should favour the attacker by five to one. Facing us was the ratio in reverse. It made the hope of winning a long shot.

But H-Hour was crowding in on us and there were still several administrative tasks to assign: cages for prisoners of war, for instance, and dumps for ammunition and petrol, each with map references.

The trenching tool was of particular importance. In this bizarre war, digging-in when objectives were reached had almost more immediate priority for assault troops than firing back. His trenching shovel, as one survivor extolled, had become "a mighty weapon of war, a treasure to be hoarded carefully, lest it be snatched up by some pilferer; being without a shovel left one feeling as naked as a man in Piccadilly without his trousers."[3]

Finally, a hot meal and a substantial four-ounce tot of rum were ordered for all troops at 2359 hours, in the dying moments of Sunday, the 15th of October.

o

From his headquarters in a large white-brick country estate in the densely wooded ridge bordering the northern outskirts of Woensdrecht, Lieutenant Colonel Friedrich Augustus von der Heydte, nineteen years a career officer in the Wehrmacht, studied intently the last drops of wine in his glass. However excellent the vintage, however liberally he had dispatched the bulk of the absentee Dutch owner's cellar to his Bavarian home, it could not distract him long from the business on hand. His "fire brigade" had been rushed to this new trouble spot; he must ensure that it would not fail in its assignment.

On the 5th of October, a runner had brought an urgent message from Chief of Staff, General Student, to von der Heydte's central Holland HQ in Alphen. A strong force of Canadians had been observed moving forward north of the Scheldt Estuary in the direction of Woensdrecht. Von der Heydte was to break off the attack against the Polish Armoured Division and leave immediately for Woensdrecht. The paratroop commander recalls the anxiety at German headquarters:

> I was told that it was of extreme importance that we defend Woensdrecht. General Student advised me that there were three reasons for this: first, to secure the 15th Army retreat; then, it was important to hold open communication from Walcheren through the neck of South Beveland and through to Germany. Finally, the Germans had expected that, after the Arnhem experience, the Allies would attack up the coast in a pincer movement through Rotterdam and east to Germany. That had to be stopped. I realized the urgency of the mission: it was the first time in the whole war I had been ordered to break off a successful attack mid-battle.[4]

That night, four thousand German troops advanced westward toward Bergen op Zoom, some in trucks, most marching on foot through the bitter, rainy night to their newly established headquarters on the main Bergen-Antwerp road just north of Woensdrecht. It was an ideal defensive position.

Part of the property of the estate contained a brickyard, an excellent observation post for von der Heydte's paratroops. From the comfortable quarters of his command post, the commander could easily observe all troop action in the vicinity, as he recounts: "I would take my customary evening stroll, and could walk just a thousand metres away, to the houses over at the top end of the ridge overlooking Woensdrecht. Or, if I wished, I could easily get to the first cluster of farmhouses at Hoogerheide."

The commander could also observe the German occupation force in those towns, and was highly displeased at their undisciplined actions: "We found German troops who were just elements of our occupation forces, and other dispersed groups of German soldiers who were on the march to the north. But we found no German troops able to fight."[5]

However, the 6th Parachute Regiment was independent of these itinerant soldiers. Von der Heydte believed that his trouble-shooting troops had all the skill and ability needed for their new task. They needed no help from this dubious police force to stop the Canadians from sealing off the mouth of the isthmus.

In all, the "fire brigade" comprised a force of over 4000 men, including support staff. In terms of battlefield effectiveness, it had 2600 experienced, well-trained fighting men, four times the number of any Canadian infantry battalion. His companies were at seventy-five percent of normal strength (Canadian companies at that time averaged about forty-five percent strength), numbering 156 soldiers in each of the regiment's seventeen companies. These were divided into three light battalions and one special battalion of engineers, infantry guns, mortars, and anti-aircraft guns. These elite troops had been given high priority from the German high command for all the supplies of arms and ammunition they might need.

As soon as his men were established, von der Heydte received orders to attack the advancing Canadians. But then a new obstacle—evidence of the confusion in the ranks of German occupation troops—delayed the German attack. As von der Heydte explained: "The execution of this order turned out to be impossible because of the supposed existence of unknown minefields which had to be cleared before an attack could be undertaken. No maps could be found in which the mines had been indicated.

However, during the week that followed, the two villages of Woensdrecht and Hoogerheide were fought for very heavily. Some houses changed occupants nearly every day."[6]

During this second week of October, the Canadians were in contact with this force. The Royal Regiment captured the village of Ossendrecht, just a few kilometres south of Hoogerheide. Then the Calgaries fought for three days on the "grim road to Hoogerheide," a bitter, seesaw conflict where Canadian and German met head on in hand-to-hand fighting. On Black Friday, the 13th, the Black Watch met the fury of these paratroopers, and few survived.

Von der Heydte had never commanded his regiment against Canadian troops. Now, fighting alongside his men in the front line, he could observe and evaluate this new enemy. He personally interrogated prisoners from the Canadian regiments, probing for weaknesses he could exploit. It was the outcome of these interrogations that he was pondering in the dying hours of Sunday October 15th:

> I talked to many Canadian prisoners in the past few days. I always asked, "Who do you trust?". I could find out a lot about their units if I could assess their morale. No American, except Patton's men, even said he trusted his general. The Americans had a great mass of material and they trusted that, not their generals. The British had a more sportsmanlike spirit; they trusted their commanders. The Canadians are loyal to their command. And they have the strong artillery, where we have almost none. But they are volunteers. What can they know of battle tactics?[7]

At 0230 hours on the morning of the 16th of October, a disturbing report reached von der Heydte:

> A young lieutenant, one of my company commanders, reported that the scouts had observed some unusual movements in the Canadian position five or six hundred metres south of our front line. There was no indication of any attack at that moment, just a "change of attitude." It was essential to find out just what was happening.
>
> I jumped into the sidecar of my motorcycle and ordered my driver to proceed quickly through the town to the forward observation outpost. My intention was to assess this change and, if it appeared to be an attack forming up, to withdraw my men to the pre-established rear line of resistance. The troops had been briefed on the position on which they were to fall back in the event of attack; from there we could launch strong counterattacks to regain our main line of resistance.
>
> This was the tactic I intended to follow. When I gave an order to defend a certain line, I always gave a second line as a retreat line. The best way to withstand an attack was to withdraw from the position known to the enemy without his being aware of it, and build a new defence line in a position not known to him.
>
> Looking from behind some bushes, I saw that I was too late. The Canadians had begun their attack. I gave the order to retreat to those of my men that I could find; my duty was to bring as many as possible back to the prepared positions.[8]

H-Hour minus 30

The period just before a battle begins can be the most agonizing of an infantryman's life. Your comrades are all around you, and that's reassuring, but still you are completely alone. You want to run, to scream, to pray, to do anything but cross that start line. But you continue to stand there, sweating, praying, hating war, hating yourself for being afraid. One rifleman recalls that the waiting was far worse than the battle ever could be: "When we were on the start line, waiting, I never knew that I could pee so many times, nervous pees. I was that scared. Once you got moving, then it was alright.

We would settle down and just block out all the extraneous nonsense so you could concentrate on what you had to do."[9]

Seeing these men cross the line into battle was a very moving experience, as one Canadian Padre remembered: "My boys move in tonight . . . new boys with fears and nerves and anxiety hidden under quick smiles and quick seriousness. Old campaigners with a faraway look. It is the hardest thing to watch without breaking into tears."[10]

And when the battle begins, with an ear-bursting barrage, you determine not to let the men you lead see how frightened you are. If you're in the ranks, you hope like hell your bosses know what they're doing. You hope they value human life—especially yours.

Demolition Platoon Corporal Arthur Kelly most clearly recalled "that moment when you put in that attack, when you climb out of that slit trench . . . if you were to look around and find that you didn't have an officer, boy, that would have a tremendous effect on you psychologically."[11]

Minutes before H-Hour, an urgent call came through my Tac headquarters. It was the second-in-command of A Company, a young captain named Lyn Hegelheimer.

"Sir, something very strange is happening here. The company commander fell asleep some time ago and we've been trying for an hour without success to wake him."

As 2/I-C, Hegelheimer had on this occasion been posted as LOB (Left Out of Battle), one of several veterans kept back to ensure that the battalion, despite losses, would have an ongoing cadre of seasoned officers and men. He had therefore not attended the battalion "O" Group, although he had later seen some aerial photographs of the position. However, there was no option but to order him to take command, with only a quick briefing on his tasks. His senior officer's bizarre sleep would have to be dealt with at a later time; for now, the battle for Woensdrecht had begun.

H - H o u r : 0 3 3 0 h o u r s

One hundred and sixty-eight guns opened fire in one massive, ear-splitting, earth-shattering barrage. And five hundred Riley riflemen rose as one, hugging the awesome fire curtain, advancing over the start line under its fearful cover. The sky screamed, its blackness ruptured.

It was a night of intense darkness. The phosphorescent tracer fire marked its trail in space to guide the men to their objectives. Its splashes of light spilled eerily onto the fields where they advanced.

The carrier platoon, having begun the attack as foot soliders guarding the start line, suffered the first casualties of the assault. We were upset to discover that one section had got too far forward when the opening artillery barrage began, and, tragically, had incurred seven casualties from our own guns.

Normally, hugging the bombardment was a hazard the veteran troops could understand. Casualties from enemy fire would have been very much greater had they not learned to lean into the barrage. But they were not all seasoned veterans that marched on Woensdrecht that raw October morning. Several were young, ill-trained reinforcements in the battle for the first time, as Carrier Platoon Sergeant Pete Bolus recalls:

We were told at what time the barrage was coming down and that we were to get out and not get caught in it. My section pulled out about a minute before the barrage started, but even then, we had one hell of a time trying to find our way back in the darkness. But Jimmy Ratcliffe's section took a real beating. Seven of the men got hit. They didn't get out in time.

We had had a few reinforcements come up; I didn't even get to know these guys' names that were hit. The older fellows were all in one piece practically; they knew how to look after themselves.

The thing about it was you got a feeling for it; you knew when things were going to go bad and you went under cover. It was a skill that you seemed to develop. The reinforcements would see us walking around but when we went under cover, they thought we were chicken. They were scared but they wouldn't listen. They would say, "There's nothing to it."

We lost a lot of good kids that way. Some of them didn't have more than their basic training. Some of them hadn't even had that. I had a kid who came from the ack-ack regiment, who didn't know how to detonate a grenade.[12]

0 5 0 0   H o u r s

The silent night closed in again on the village. So far, there had been no resistance; Woensdrecht was as a ghost town. Froggett of D Company was the first to report in. "Balmy Beach," flashed the success signal. Thirty minutes later came "Argos," Hegelheimer's A Company salute. Then "Rough Riders" . . . "Tigers" . . . the four companies were on their objectives. Or so they thought.

The commanding officer of C Company, Major Joe Pigott, paced restlessly in the farm cottage, now his headquarters, just above the main road into Woensdrecht. The silence, he thought, was disquieting:

I remembered from fighting in North Africa that a favorite tactic of the Germans, and one of their greatest strengths, was to pull out of strategic positions when the heat was on, and then lay on a well-planned, well-executed counterattack. I warned the men that the present quiet was unnatural and was not to be believed and that we were going to catch hell first thing in the morning.

I had positioned my three platoons the best I could, but it was so black we dug in mainly by feel. We couldn't see Hegelheimer's A Company; there was a rise of high ground between us.

When dawn broke, I discovered to my horror that I had positioned one platoon so far out of line it couldn't even support the other two. We were desperately trying to adjust the thing so that we could put up a reasonable defence when the counterattack came.[13]

0 6 1 5   H o u r s

Pigott wasn't the only company commander running into problems in those pre-dawn hours. Daybreak had some disquieting shocks for all the forward RHLI companies. Like Pigott, the other company commanders found their platoons too dispersed to form a cohesive defence. That was one of the problems of the night attack; it was very difficult to site good defensive positions because it was very difficult to see anything, and the things one did see did not look the same at night as they did in the daytime. Now they were frantically moving their men up to ensure that they were all in slits defensively positioned to repel the expected counterattack. All four companies were now under continuous artillery and mortar fire.

Major Louis Froggett discovered he was a hundred and fifty yards short of his objective, but he soon managed to correct and consolidate his position. He had driven back the Germans so quickly that their candles still burned in their dugouts.

Behind Froggett, Major Welch reported from the centre of the village that B Company was getting a lot of casualties from snipers hiding out in the shadows of houses and barns near the main crossroad of the tidy cottage-lined streets. He was working feverishly to try to clear up the situation.

He was surprised to see emerging from behind the church three of his own men, grinning through soot-streaked faces. They had been sent on recce patrol into the village three nights ago and found themselves trapped. As Sergeant Harold Hall, then nineteen years old, still clearly recalls: "I had a patrol out and I didn't get back before daylight. There was a church in the square and I had to hide behind it. The Germans started coming into the square from all directions; we were cut off. I took two men in through the back door of this little church; I remember standing there with my back against the wall just about ten feet away from the Jerries. Then we hid in the coal bin for about three days. I was missing in action for four days."[14]

The carrier platoon by this time had picked up their vehicles and were being led by their commander, Captain Bill Whiteside, across an open field toward the village. An incident occurred that has Sergeant Bolus still chuckling: "They were shelling the hell out of us, but this was one of the comical things: there were pigs running around and a pig got hit. Whiteside stops the whole convoy of carriers, jumps out and slits its throat. Then he says, 'We'll bleed this one and come back for him later,' and away we went. A day or two later, he held a lecture in the barn while he dissected it; the guy had been to vet school."[15]

Up above, on the northen end of the slope closest of all to the German defensive line, Captain Lyn Hegelheimer was in command of a company for the first time. Few assignments would ever be tougher than this literal baptism of fire. Along with his fellow company commanders, he had slightly misjudged his positions in the intense darkness and had lost communication with his scattered platoons. But, as he sadly recalls, his troubles really started on his initial approach when he overshot his objective and had to backtrack down the road to reach it:

> We still hadn't seen a damn soul since we left the start line. Nobody had fired a round at us. Suddenly we saw a couple of German troopers walking up the road talking to one another. Why they didn't hear us, I don't know. I was at the head of the company so I whipped out my pistol and we took them prisoner. They thought we were Germans because we were coming from the

wrong direction. Finally we arrived at our objective. Then just at daybreak I got the three platoon commanders together to coordinate our defense. ·

At daylight, my senior officer of A Company comes riding up in a carrier driven by the sergeant major. He got out and I said, "Well sir, here's your company." But I don't know what the hell happened to him after that. Later, I could see him standing in front of the carrier and the CSM driving. He had sort of an odd look on his face. Then he just disappeared from my view.[16]

At 0615 hours, while the commanders were consolidating their positions, I moved battalion headquarters forward into Woensdrecht. The white-stuccoed farmhouse, for decades the home of Cornelis van Beek, was now to become my home for some days ahead. The house was on Dorpstraat, the main east-west road through town. Welch was in a house a few blocks west on the same street, with Froggett on the rise above him.

Captain Bob Wight's demolition platoon had been ordered to barricade themselves in a house on the northwest corner of the street a few hundred yards west. Their job was to hold a defensive position guarding that western flank. Meanwhile, my two advance companies, with Pigott and Hegelheimer, were just over the slope to the north of us, out of our sight.

The Scout Platoon had followed the lead companies in, clearing some two dozen Germans from houses and farm buildings around the crossroads where my HQ was to be established.

Six Germans hiding in the van Beek cellar were rooted out, and then four more from a dugout in the yard. These prisoners, plus another fifty or so sent back from the forward companies, were taken to the POW cage, and then transported as quickly as possible to divisional headquarters for interrogation.

Even within Geneva Convention restrictions, we had discovered that trained intelligence interrogators could ferret out information about the strength and disposition of the enemy forces. It was information that could save many Canadian lives and in Woensdrecht we were in urgent need of this help.

I was deeply concerned to note that all our prisoners bore insignia of the 6th Paratroop Division, whom I knew to be specially trained and skilled infantrymen. They already had the reputation of being an elite, hard-fighting battle group who were only committed to major trouble areas.

As I leaned over one wounded prisoner to question him, he glared up at me and spat in my face. Even in captivity, the beast could snarl.

1000 Hours

Shortly before ten o'clock in the morning a private soldier, a young recruit, was squatting at his gun position beside a barn window. It was his first day of war. He peered through the narrow dormer and commented cheerfully to the man next him: "Hey, I didn't know the Americans were fighting here!" The novice, confusing American steel helmets with German "coal skuttles," thus became the first RHLI man to spot the enemy counterattack.[17]

Minutes later, a runner brought the alarming news that Hegelheimer's company was being overrun by German paratroopers with Mark IV tanks and self-propelled guns. Our Piats and antitank guns had been knocked out. Fierce hand-to-hand fighting had ensued. One of our antitank men, Sergeant Alf Southern, fired point-blank at the enemy until finally his 6-pounder was hit by the powerful 75mm weapon and put out of action. Then the FOO, Captain Stevenson of 4 Field Regiment, radioed in that his carrier had been hit and was burning.

It was at about this point that the senior A Company commander turned and left the field. (It was later suggested that he suffered from battle fatigue, having been in continuous action and under heavy pressure since early July.) Unfortunately, when men see their own leaders turn away from battle, it becomes a very natural choice that they shall follow, and that is what happened on Woensdrecht Hill. Pigott and I both had to watch this horrible sight, those wretched men running panic-stricken down the hill toward us.

I pulled out my revolver and stopped some of them at gun point. Further over, Joe stopped the others the same way. We ordered them back to Pigott's C Company to take up additional defensive positions.

We had just minutes to wait for the German offensive to reach Joe's company. Pigott describes the action around him:

> The company in front of me was attacked in force by German para-troops, excellent troops, first-class troops who knew how to handle their weapons and the ground. They overran the A Company men and in the process killed and wounded a lot of them.
>
> Unfortunately, communications between myself and A Company, because of the confusion, were virtually nonexistent and I wasn't aware of the extent of the disaster forward until the first wave of German paratroops accompanied by tanks came into sight about fifty metres away.[18]

Pigott's driver, Private Harry Gram, had been wounded by shrapnel and Joe had been trying to get him to walk down to the Regimental Aid Post. Just as a German SP (self-propelled) gun pulled up, Gram pulled out—in the wrong direction, as Pigott later recalled:

> Instead of walking out the back door and down the street like he should have, Harry decided to take the jeep which was parked in front of the house—it had about forty holes in it and wouldn't run. He got in and tried to start it. It wasn't going anywhere. Cursing . . . I never heard such language in all my life. Here's this tank sitting there with a self-propelled gun, not twenty-five yards away. All of a sudden the turret opened, an officer stood up, gestured to Harry to move on, and poor old Harry got out and walked away down the road. Seconds later, the German was dead. He got a direct hit.
>
> There was no time to organize our own counterattack; the enemy was almost on top of us. My only chance was to contact my commanding officer and through him order a concentration of

artillery to bring all our fire power directly on our position. At the same time I was yelling and shouting at my troops to get down in their slit trenches and pray when our shells started to fall.[19]

Joe's position was desperate; so was his appeal. Our only hope was to direct on his headquarters all of our available artillery strength—a "Victor Target"—a concentration of fire which gunnery men maintain even today was seldom if ever duplicated in World War Two.

There was too much at stake to indulge the thought that this man, my friend, was inviting death, and was asking me to be his executioner. Jack Drewry, CO's Rep, was at my elbow. I yelled: "REFERENCE 'C' HEAD-QUARTERS, VICTOR TARGET, SCALE TEN."[20]

Within seconds, Drewry was on the radio net and brought down a massive concentration of shellfire, almost beyond conception in intensity. It was directed with pinpoint precision on Pigott's own headquarters.

We had pulled off a target of opportunity, a bombardment of four thousand shells, about fifty tons of high explosives, which completely knocked out the enemy tanks and killed, wounded, or dispersed the paratroops involved in the Germans' counterattack. Incredibly, because they were down in their slits, just one of our men was slightly wounded. The Rileys sprang from their trenches and drove off the rest.

Joe Pigott's Citation for the DSO reads in part:

> . . . At this point Major Pigott was wounded by fire from the gun which was still in action. Despite his wound, and with no regard for his own personal safety, he proceeded across one hundred yards of open ground, under heavy machine-gun and shell fire, and personally directed an antitank gun forward into a position from which it was able to destroy the self-propelled gun. The enemy were then forced to withdraw.
>
> Throughout the whole encounter Major Pigott moved from one platoon to another under constant fire, encouraging his men and directing their fire. He was personally responsible for beating off a fierce enemy counterattack which threatened the whole battalion position, and was an inspiration and example to all ranks.[21]

o

For some of the Rileys, the war was now over. Signaller Jimmy Bulmer was captured in the root cellar of A Company headquarters, where he had dived for cover when the counterattack began. Piecing together the kaleidoscopic recollections of his capture, Bulmer tells of his final moments on the battlefield:

> The German tanks were coming down the long road from Bergen op Zoom. I asked my senior officer what we were going to do and

he said, "Dig in and fight them off." The Germans started mortaring. One shell hit the jeep; the horn stuck and the noise went on and on. Then one hit the house and I got into the root cellar.

There were three of us down there, waiting: the intrepreter— young Cyril, the Belgian kid—was down there with this old stretcher bearer called Pop. (We called him Pop because he was so old to us. He must have been thirty.)

Finally, we heard German voices upstairs. I said to Pop: "When that door opens, put the white flag up with the Red Cross." The door opened and two enemy stood looking at us. One had a Schmeizer. He was sweating. Standing right behind him was a guy with a flame thrower. They took us out with our hands up and on the way the watch went, the cigarettes went, and everything else went. I'm glad they didn't look at the watch because I'd got it off a German a couple of weeks before. They got us out into this clearing.

This German lieutenant colonel came over and said (his English was perfect, better than mine), "What are you? American or British?" I said, "Canadian, sir," and he said, "Good. We fought you before. You're good soldiers." Then they pulled out. They were a special hit-and-run outfit.

There were about thirty of us taken prisoner. On the way back we came under shellfire, our own Canadian 25-pounders. Later, we were interrogated, one at a time, about who we were and what our codes were. I pretended I didn't know. That walk started there on Woensdrecht Hill and ended up at a prison camp near Hanover in Germany.[22]

1410 Hours

Twelve hours had passed. Although the immediate crisis had been averted, the Germans showed no inclination to back down; the battle was far from won. We had gained, by incredible effort, the narrowest of fingerholds on Woensdrecht Hill. In this brief time the cost had already been appalling. Rifle companies generally numbered over one hundred; we had been reduced by one half. I contacted Brigadier Cabeldu's 4th Brigade HQ by wireless about our thinness on the ground: "Estimated strengths at the present time are: A Company, one officer, eighteen ORs; B Company, two officers, thirty-nine ORs; C Company, two officers, forty ORs; D Company, one officer, sixty ORs.[23]

Twice that afternoon, help came from the skies. A large force of Spitfires dropped fifty tons of bombs on enemy positions. Later, our friends the "Typhies" joined the fray.

Heavy mortaring and shelling and sniper action continued to harass the Rileys, particularly in the west end of Dorpstraat where Welch was taking a lot of fire. Although I knew he was in agony with a painful knee injury from his football days with the Hamilton Tigers, Huck fought furiously to maintain his position.

o

We were feeling the almost overpowering strength of three columns of paratroops, some two thousand men, as we later learned from von der Heydte. With the professional skill that had already won him a reputation for tenacious fighting, von der Heydte had recovered from the surprise of our assault and had organized a powerful counterattack. He was, as he later told me, as determined to recover his position as we were to hang on to it:

> At first light, soon after the surprise Canadian attack, I gave the respective orders to counterattack. Our aim was to restore our main line of combat. We attacked in three columns: one over the railway embankment west of Woensdrecht; another—with which I fought personally—over a smaller railway embankment northwest of Woensdrecht, and a third smaller one northeast of the town. The first two columns succeeded in joining up in the northwest part of Woensdrecht. We managed to recover some of our old positions, and my men dug in to their old holes.[24]

In fact, it was this strong force of counterattacking paratroopers that converged near the lead companies' positions. It was under von der Heydte's personal command that his men overran A Company and threatened to overrun Joe's. And it was von der Heydte himself who spoke a few sympathetic words to Signaller Jimmy Bulmer when he was taken prisoner. Many decades later, meeting for the first time, we recreated the events of a battle that we both still remember with horror. I had the last word in 1944; he was to have it forty years later: "It was very close fighting. When you attacked, we missed each other by only ten minutes, you and I. I was just above the road on which you began your advance. And our two sides were only a hundred yards apart when we came back in the counterattack. Once," he added with an odd look, "my men shot at you."[25]

o

The guns of Woensdrecht were not to be silenced for five more days of agonizing effort when the battered Rileys were finally relieved by the Queen's Own Cameron Highlanders of Canada on the 21st of October.

After the first eighteen hours of fighting, ninety-one casualties had been evacuated. In just two days, we had managed to hang on to the narrowest of holds, measuring a single kilometre in width and 500 metres in depth. The cost: 167 casualties, twenty-one of them killed. But nothing would ever duplicate that brief moment of horror when men, hysterical with fear, had to be forced at gunpoint to return to battle.

Still, the Germans pummelled the thinning line of Rileys. Froggett's company was infiltrated on several occasions, and one whole platoon was overrun; only six men returned. Nor did the situation ease much during the next day. Thirty-nine reinforcements, almost none with any infantry experience, were sent in. However, one company from the Essex Scottish Regiment took some of the heat off Pigott's position.

Sniping was still heavy in Froggett's area, and infiltration of the enemy was becoming so serious that Lieutenant Bob Wight was ordered to lay trip wires in front of Froggett's line. "We were told not to wait for the dark," Wight later explained. "I was to send men up the ridge in broad daylight, and that would mean that they would be within sight of enemy snipers. Joe Hoonan said, `I'll go by myself. There's no point in having three or four of us milling around there.' It was a brave act."[26]

There were so many brave acts in those treacherous days. On the third day of the action, German infiltration brought the enemy perilously close to the forward lines of the Rileys. Lieutenant Williamson of the scout platoon sent out three snipers to try to relieve the pressure—Corporal Joe Friyia, Privates Heinz Kunzelman and J.S. Whitehead—with startling results, as Williamson recounts: "They noticed that there were some Germans within fairly close distance, about 100 yards or less, in slit trenches, and so they decided to assault them on their own. They dropped right into the slit trenches with the Germans. Each of them had pistols which they used. They killed several and routed the rest."[27]

Corporal Friyia, who was subsequently awarded the Military Medal, was shot in the foot. With Froggett's help, he managed to get back, as did Whitehead. But Kunzelman was lost, believed killed, and was never heard of again.

Days and nights ran into one another, seemingly endless hours of mud and cold and exhaustion. Those that lived, fought. Even when their vision blurred and their hands shook, when fatigue and fear threatened to engulf them, there was always someone to set a new pace.

One night, Major Froggett requested that a section from the carrier platoon set up machine-gun posts in front of his line to prevent further infiltration during the nights. Sergeant Pete Bolus was one of three men who volunteered to dig in on the ridge:

> We were up quite a bit in front of Froggett's position in a sort of a draw, sweeping the area all night with pretty continuous fire so the Germans couldn't come up through it. We used to take up three boxes of ammunition, which is a lot, and we used that much each night. We took all the magazines that we could possibly carry. We must have had about twenty magazines up there, always loaded. You'd let off a magazine and then you'd load it right away. We'd come back there each night and would have to dig in and set up new positions. It was good to get out of there in the mornings.[28]

Night after night, the three men went forward into the silent fields toward the German lines and took up their desperately dangerous task. And the other Rileys, watching, found that the impossible was within reach for them too: "You see these guys, all night long firing their Bren guns, never stopping, and you think, 'If this bloody little Bolus can do this; why can't I?' And that's what kept a lot of us going."[29]

○

A short distance away, just where the road dipped into a hollow, Bob Wight's demolition platoon was also being clobbered by heavy sniper activity.

Taking a couple of men, Wight ducked down the street and into a house were he suspected a sniper was hiding. They burst into the kitchen. Wight stopped short at a scene of domesticity totally incongruous amidst the armed conflict going on around it: a family sat around the table, father and mother and two children, one a toddler. Before them, on a table festive with freshly cut fall flowers and delft china, were plates of food, the morning meal, untouched. Then he realized that the entire family was dead. There were no bullet wounds, no blood, no signs of violence. They just sat on, and on, lifeless.[30]

○

On the 21st of October the weary 4th Canadian Infantry Brigade was given a twenty-four hour rest, and with it, the opportunity to plan the next phase of its advance. The 4th Brigade was relieved by the three battalions of the 6th: the South Saskatchewan Regiment, Les Fusiliers de Mont-Royal and the Queen's Own Cameron Highlanders of Canada—the last taking over the Riley positions.

NOTES

1. The Toronto Scottish account of their part in the bombardment noted: "Two thousand mortar bombs, the biggest show since the Caen break-out." Maj. D.W. Grant, *Carry On: The History of the Toronto Scottish Regiment (MG) 1939–1945*, 107.

2. Personal interview with Capt. W.D. Stevenson.

3. John Ellis, *Sharp End of War: The Fighting Man in World War II* (Newton Abbot, Devon: David & Charles Ltd., Brunel House, 1980), 46.

4. Personal interview with Lt.-Col. von der Heydte.

5. Ibid.

6. Ibid.

7. Ibid.

8. Ibid.

9. Personal interview with Sgt. Peter Bolus.

10. Ellis, *Sharp End of War*, 98.

11. Personal interview with Cpl. Arthur Kelly.

12. Personal interview with Sgt. Peter Bolus.

13. Personal interview with Maj. J.M. Pigott.

14. Personal interview with Sgt. Harold Hall.

15. Personal interview with Sgt. Peter Bolus.

16. Personal interview with Capt. Lyn Heigelheimer.

17. Personal interview with Cpl. James Bulmer.

18. Personal interview with Maj. J.M. Pigott.

19. Ibid.

20. The target was the map reference for C Company headquarters. A Victor Target is one that brings to bear as many guns as are available in the army—in this case, three divisional artillery regiments (each of seventy-two 25-pounder guns), three medium regiments (each of sixteen 4.5-inch guns), and three regiments of heavy anti-aircraft regiments (each of sixteen 3.7-inch guns). This makes a total of 312 guns, firing at ten rounds per gun.

21. Public Archives of Canada.

22. Personal interview with Cpl. James Bulmer.

23. War Diary, RHLI, 16 Oct. 1944.

24. Personal interview with Lt.-Col. von der Heydte.

25. Ibid. This surprising recollection is substantiated in the RHLI War Diary, 18 October, 1600 hours: "The CO [Lieutenant Colonel Whitaker] and IO [Captain Doering] visited D Company and looked over the company defensive position, then to B Company. By error, the CO, driving the carrier, went beyond the FDLs [forward defense lines] and an enemy sniper hit the carrier several times. A hasty retreat was made."

26. Personal interview with Lieut. A.R.G. Wight.

27. Personal interview with Lieut. John Williamson.

28. Personal interview with Sgt. Peter Bolus.

29. Personal interview with Corporal Arthur Kelly; Arthur Kelly, *There's a Goddamn Bullet for Everyone* (Paris, Ontario: Arts and Publishing Co. Ltd., 1979).

30. Personal interview with Lieut. A.R.G. Wight.

OPERATIONAL FLYING — APPRENTICESHIP✧

MURRAY PEDEN

o

For I dipt into the Future, far as human eye could see,
Saw the Vision of the world, and all the wonder that would be;

. . .

Heard the heavens fill with shouting, and there rain'd a ghastly dew
From the nations' airy navies grappling in the central blue;
Tennyson, "Locksley Hall"

We arrived at Chedburgh in the back of a truck at 3:00 p.m. I reported to the adjutant, a bluff, hearty flight lieutenant named George Wright, expecting to spend the remaining half-day chasing about getting quarters and going through the rest of the prosaic routine involved in getting squared away at a new station. I was wrong; the pace was a little different on 214. George put me straight in a few clipped phrases.

"You're flying second dickey tonight, Peden—Wingco's orders. Briefing at 4:00 o'clock, so you've no time to settle in. Leave your trunk and the rest of your kit here; I'll see it gets down to the mess—pick it up there when you get back. Keep the bag with your flying clothing with you. Get your NCOs to report to the station warrant officer; he'll get them fixed up for quarters. Your bomb aimer can step over to the admin officer."

When J.B. and the rest of the boys left, I came back, and George took me in to meet Wing Commander McGlinn, the commanding officer of 214 Squadron. During our two-minute meeting the only impression I was able to form was a vague one of rather distant severity—a cool businesslike gentleman.

Then the adjutant took me over to meet the pilot with whom I was to fly that night. I was naturally more interested in appraising him than the

✧ From *A Thousand Shall Fall* (Toronto: Stoddart, 1988), 242–62.

wing commander. One of the more senior pilots on the station, he struck me as a pretty decent chap; but when he introduced me to his crew I was disappointed. For a team who were supposed to be experienced they came across as a noticeably windy lot. In adolescent style they were playing guessing games as to what the target was going to be—a practice which I decided I did not favour—and I was not at all reassured by the feverish flavour of their conversation. After a short time we joined the steady trickle of aircrew walking over to the briefing room.

Inside, the now familiar tension was easily sensed, razor sharp, despite the casual air assumed by most of the aircrew. Whatever the target was, a maximum effort had been called for; 214 Squadron and its offspring,[1] 620 Squadron, had about twenty Stirlings bombed up and ready to go. All crews carefully emptied their pockets and drew escape kits, which each man then slid into the blouse of his battledress. The wingco entered and we all stood while he and his entourage went to the stage. The time-honoured announcement came crisply as the drapes over the large wall map were drawn back:

"Gentlemen, the target for tonight is Hanover."

I felt a tremor. Hanover struck me as a pretty deep penetration for my maiden effort into the Fatherland. The red tapes ran north and east of our base to a point around Terschelling in the West Frisians, then slanted down across the mainland for most of the remaining two hundred miles on a line which pointed at Berlin and carried the attacking force mid-way between Bremen and Hanover. In the eyes of the assessing German night-fighter controller this line of advance would threaten both those important cities, and Berlin as well. Close to Hanover the tape turned abruptly and went directly to the target.

The attack was to open predominantly as a fire raid, in an attempt to duplicate the devastation visited upon Hamburg a few weeks earlier. The Pathfinders' TI's (Target Indicators) at a later stage were to move from the old residential quarter of the city into the heart of the industrial sector. No. 3 Group aircraft were to open the attack with several hundred tons of incendiaries. The groups following a few minutes behind were to shift the focus of the attack, dropping a much heavier tonnage of high explosive in a pattern designed to spread the fire into the industrial area, then to blast, burn, and flatten as large a sector there as possible. Seven hundred and eleven four-engined aircraft were scheduled to attack the city.

Takeoff was at sunset. I sat up front with the skipper as the line of hulking Stirlings taxied implacably, ponderously, toward the takeoff point. On the way the perimeter track ran within a hundred yards of Chedburgh's pub, before which the locals, knowledgeable in these matters, had assembled for their nightly show. It did not lack interest.

Before our turn came, we watched four others line up, strain briefly against the brakes, then slip the invisible bond and lumber forward. Each plane would accelerate sluggishly until the tail was up, then roar heavily, faster and faster, toward the far end of the runway. The wind was between runways, and gave little help. None of the first four parted company with the concrete until it seemed certain to run off the end and pile in; but just short of catastrophe each one inched reluctantly skyward. When the green Aldis winked at us I could easily have been persuaded to switch places with the casual spectators who had given us a thumbs up with their free hands as we rolled by.

Duplicating the earlier performances, our aircraft staggered off a hundred yards from the end of the runway, and we began our slow climb. As we made a gentle turn to port I noticed that one of the four aircraft ahead of us was smoking. Like the others, he had been circling base to gain height, and I watched, sick and helpless, as the smoke streaming out from the underside of the wing root grew more and more dense, and the plane froze in a gentle dive for the earth. I kept urging the crew silently to jump, but no chutes appeared. It was like watching an impending execution.

In a flash it was over. No one spoke. My thoughts jumped to my crew on the ground: they would undoubtedly have been watching, and for hours they wo⋯ ⋯e field like slow bees ha⋯

Sh⋯ ⋯:irling softly silhouette⋯ ⋯e right, climbing on our⋯ ⋯:pt a wary eye on it. Alt⋯ ⋯just above us, he could⋯ ⋯must have altered cours⋯ ⋯:he skipper expectantl⋯ ⋯a safe crossing, for we v⋯ ⋯aware of the other aircr⋯ ⋯get out of the way. I squ⋯ ⋯ickey to tell the first pilo⋯ ⋯:rt wing slightly and begar⋯ ⋯ne to talk. I grabbed the controls and shoved, realizing⋯ ⋯kipper had not even seen the other plane. It drifted across just above us, missing colliding with us by no more than three or four feet. My skipper was clearly startled at the sudden diving of our aircraft, but the sight of that hulking shadow drifting just over our heads with an almost inaudible hum was all the explanation he required. He resumed control without a word and we carried on.

With that inauspicious start the trip proceeded to deteriorate. On the run in from the Frisians, the navigator computed a new wind and then made the incredible mistake (we later discovered) of "correcting" the drift on the wrong side. When our ETA Hanover arrived there was no sign of the Pathfinders' TI's. The skipper held his course for another ten minutes, getting more and more frustrated, before the rear gunner thought to mention that some city thirty miles behind us had been burning fiercely for most of that period. At that the skipper cursed, reversed our course, and steered for the flaming city, and the navigator, who had already been checking his suspect plotting, simultaneously discovered the glaring error.

By the time we were halfway back to Hanover the raid was over. From ten miles out the city glowed below us like some enormous fireplace full of flickering embers, reflecting the effects of over twenty-five hundred tons of high explosive and incendiaries.

As we approached, Hanover's flak batteries opened up, and since they could now concentrate on a solitary target, got in some very good shooting. Flashes all around us gave vivid testimony of their competence. Suddenly a panicky voice shouted on the intercom: "BALLOONS!" Whoever it was took ten years off my life. I wondered fearfully how the Germans could get balloons and balloon cables up to 13 000 feet.

Nothing communicates itself faster between the various scattered positions in a bomber than uncontrolled panic in someone's voice. That shout set everyone's heart racing. In a second or two the flash of more bursting shells lit the sky around us, repeatedly and rapidly, and in the momentary illumination they provided I saw that what had caused the shout was simply the billowing black smoke puffs from earlier shells. The skipper commented on it at the same time. I began breathing again, relieved, but angry with the unknown clot who had scared me so thoroughly and so unnecessarily. I know my own crew would not have reacted with such a lack of discipline, and began to feel that there was really very little I wanted to learn from this aggregation who, between them, had violated half a dozen fundamental precepts in this one operation.

The rest of the trip was a long drawn out ordeal for me. This crew was truly windy. Fright crackled in virtually all their intercom exchanges—and there were far too many of these. Putting one's life in the hands of a group of aircrew whose nerves are shot is a harrowing experience. I longed for the moment when we would reach the English coast and relative safety—at least I thought it meant relative safety.

Eventually it came to pass, we did attain that great divide, and a short time later approached our base and called for landing instructions. I thought I detected a warmer than usual note in the response of the WAAF radio operator, and assumed that our tardiness had already occasioned concern— and some tentative mental arithmetic regarding available aircraft for the next operation.

Ten minutes later we switched off Z Zebra's engines. We had been flying for five hours and twenty-five minutes, and I had never experienced a sensation of relief quite as intoxicatingly satisfying as what I felt as I climbed out the rear door and stepped onto the lovely, wonderful, marvellous, fabulous, solid old concrete of that good old dispersal. I said my twentieth brief prayer of thanks under my breath as I walked forward to where some of the other members of the crew were lighting their cigarettes.

I was about to follow suit, but deferred the act momentarily while I watched the navigation lights of another aircraft, even later than our own, rounding slowly into the funnel of the Drem system and lining up to land. We were in the first dispersal clear of the runway in use, and as this aircraft prepared to land at the far end, it was heading almost directly at us. What caught and held my attention was the sight of yet another pair of navigation lights rapidly approaching those of the aircraft about to land. They were too close, vaguely disturbing; I did not quite know what to make of it. The landing aircraft was only twenty feet in the air, almost over the end of the runway, when the puzzle was speedily unravelled.

There was a stuttering thunder of cannon as the second aircraft opened fire at point blank range on the unsuspecting Stirling. In two seconds the Junkers 88 had overtaken and passed its main target and came roaring on in our general direction, hosing streams of tracers before it like flaming strings of incredibly fast baseballs. At the first bark of the guns the adrenalin had gushed again, and I launched into a workmanlike swan dive onto the concrete. Unmindful of the shock, I lay quaking in my boots and watched the intruder sweep toward us at full throttle. It seemed to me, compressing myself industriously against the tarmac, that every round of the tracer slicing out of the darkness was going to hit me between the eyes. As though not satisfied that he had terrified me sufficiently, the Ju 88 pilot dropped a shower of butterfly bombs as he whistled across the field, and a dozen of those unpredictable and vicious little canisters, each one closer than the last, exploded with jarring blasts in the course of that fiery, roaring sweep.

In twenty seconds the whole thing was over. The noise of the Ju 88 faded as he dashed at tree-top level for the sea, and the Stirling which had been his primary target wobbled to a stop clear of the runway. (The Stirling pilot, Jake Walters—of whom more anon—and the rest of the crew, had escaped physical injury by some miracle, although their aircraft was battered almost beyond repair thanks to the close range working-over from three 20-mm cannon and three machine guns.)

I climbed slowly, and very warily, to my feet, ready to plummet to the horizontal position again at the first hint of another intruder, and found that I still had a death grip on the handle of my chest pack. My heart was still racing in overdrive, and the only possible reason I could imagine for my hands not trembling as I lit my cigarette was that the multitude of shakes, quakes, and tremors I was experiencing were cancelling each other out. For some hours I harboured a terrifying after-image of cannon spitting fire in my face to the accompaniment of an ear-shattering crescendo of Junkers Jumo engine noise and tooth-rattling blasts from butterfly bombs.

I went in for interrogation, took a cup of coffee liberally laced with Lamb's rum (which tasted terrible but worked therapeutic miracles), and went down to the officers mess to find my trunk. There was a note tied to the handle, and some kind soul who noticed the vacant stare in my eye guided me through the seas of mud adorning the neighbourhood to the correct Nissen hut and an empty bed. Sleep was a long time coming.

When I woke up, after three or four hours' fitful sleep, my first thought was to contact the crew. It transpired that the previous evening all my NCOs had been on their bicycles on a road skirting the field when the unmistakable sounds of an operational takeoff had come to them and bombers had begun climbing into view from aerodromes all around the area. They had paused to watch the Chedburgh takeoff, having a proprietary interest in some unknown aircraft amongst the procession, had seen the Stirling catch fire in the air,[2] and had witnessed its implacable descent and the mounting pall of smoke that marked its end. As I had realized, they had no way of knowing whether they had just seen their skipper die and no way of finding out for some hours. They concluded, so they told me with straight faces, that if I had been in that Stirling, I was dead and there was nothing they could do for me except hold a wake. But if I had not been in the burning Stirling, the wake would either be premature, depending upon what happened on the raid itself, or completely superfluous if I should be lucky enough to return—hence in either case the proceedings would not be in good taste. Consequently they had re-mounted their bicycles and carried on to the Sergeants Mess dance at Stradishall, whither they had been bound originally. Resplendent in his new serge uniform (compliments of Mary Stringer and a tailor who could not detect his professional touch with the coke), Stan inserted the needle a little further by assuring me that he personally had had a particularly joyous evening.

I responded in kind, saying I was touched by their concern for my well-being, and with more such banter we headed for the crew room to attend a special parade the wing commander had called for all aircrew.

Apparently one or two of the aircraft had been late taking off the previous night, and the wingco was determined that this would not happen again. He reviewed the situation in undiplomatic language and issued an edict that henceforth every crew was to be at its aircraft one full hour before takeoff. Someone pointed out, not nastily but with proper respect, that often the flying meals were not ready at the airmen's mess in time for the crews to meet that sort of deadline.

"I don't give a damn if you starve to death," McGlinn said icily, "you are going to be at your aircraft one hour before takeoff."

This was hardly the recommended Dale Carnegie approach for winning friends and influencing people. On the other hand, the wingco made his point with the desired forcefulness and of course had his way, differences of opinion being so easy to resolve under the stripe system; but he left a residue of resentment in his crews. Since this was the first opportunity I had had to draw a long breath since arriving on the station, I made a few inquiries as to the wingco's background.

He had come to Chedburgh to take command of 214 only a short time before we came over ourselves. He had had no previous operational experience, and hence was still regarded sceptically by most of the squadron's senior skippers as a handbook pilot, particularly when he was reviewing points of engine handling or tactics during briefing. The period of mutual assessment was continuing.

o

Every morning about ten o'clock the wingco received a call from Group HQ. He in turn called his two flight commanders and told them accordingly that "There is a war on tonight—maximum effort," or that "the squadron is standing down." Four times out of five it would be the first message, and pilots would hurry to airtest every serviceable aircraft so that the armourers could get on with bombing-up. Even when this message came through, however, the weather conditions were frequently so threatening, either over base or over the continent, that operations were subject to cancellation right up to the last minute. The heaviest gamble, of course, involved the meteorologists' predictions of what landing conditions would be when the huge bomber force arrived back over its bases—with rapidly emptying tanks.

This morning of 23 September 1943, the message had already gone round: there was a war on. Further, I had been alerted to fly another second dickey trip. Meantime I was ordered to take my own crew, airtest W Willie, and then do a compass swing on it. We got at it right after lunch.

Already the station was a beehive of activity. Big petrol bowsers were making their rounds, pumping thousands upon thousands of gallons into empty tanks. Trucks laden with oxygen cylinders methodically called at each dispersal. Tractors towing long rows of bomb trolleys trundled around the perimeter track. Gunners polished the perspex of their turrets, and stripped and cleaned the guns, while armourers carefully draped long symmetrical belts of ammunition that here and there reflected the oil-dulled gleam of brass and cupro-nickel. Hundreds of men concentrated on allotted tasks; there were no idlers in sight. Before I was quite ready, it was time to go to briefing again.

This trip I was to fly with a crew skippered by an NCO, a slight chap of medium height named Flight Sergeant Sellar. I knew five minutes after I met him that I was in better hands than I had been in the night before. Sellar had an air of quiet, unflappable confidence that I liked. We sat together waiting for the curtains to be drawn.

"Gentlemen, the target for tonight is Mannheim."

Mannheim, twin city of Ludwigshafen, lay at the junction of the Rhine and the Neckar, I noticed, almost as far east as Hanover but two hundred miles further south. Via the aircrew grapevine I had already learned that trips to southern Germany, because of the much longer overland routing involved, gave the night fighters a better chance to get organized against us, and that opposition in this area was usually strong. Mannheim was on Bomber Command's priority target list primarily because of its iron and steel plants, tool and die plants, and substantial petroleum storage facilities.

We went out to J Jig an hour before takeoff, in compliance with the new ordinance. The wingco had obviously taken whatever steps were necessary to reach the staff of the airmen's mess, because we had our fried egg flying meal in lots of time—and were thus deprived of the opportunity of feeling sorry for ourselves as martyrs who had to fly on ops without being fed.

The first hour of the trip passed uneventfully, at least as uneventfully as operational flights could, seemingly. For half an hour on the climb one engine threatened to overheat, which would have left Sellar with a number of critical decisions to make, decisions which he had to anticipate before the contingency actually occurred. But the needle of the cylinder head gauge finally became stationary only a few degrees above the recommended upper limit, and Sellar settled for a minor reduction in power which he was later able to make up when we levelled out and made our general reduction to cruising boost and revs.

This trip promised to be hotter than Hanover, nevertheless I felt a growing confidence as I witnessed the performance of Sellar and his crew. They could have been demonstrating, for some Air Force film, the way an operational crew ought to carry out its duties. No one wasted a word on the intercom and, when someone did pass a message, it was in the calm, matter-of-fact voice that one would use in a classroom exercise. The contrast between this crew and my flying companions of the previous night was as wine to water.

Several times, from different sectors of the black void ahead, flashing particles of fire lashed out, looking like white sparks streaming from a high speed grinding wheel. Sometimes the first stream would be answered by a puny returning stream. But all too frequently the opening stream went unanswered, and on occasion this unsettling fireworks display was climaxed by a terrible fire blooming in the darkness, or by an explosion on the ground, as a bomber perished under the guns of a night fighter. I had seen only one or two of these, at a distance, on the Hanover attack. They were noticeably more frequent now, but the laconic sighting reports betrayed no trace of the feelings we were all experiencing.

The attack opened on schedule while we were five minutes away from the target, for we were not in the first wave. Brilliant green TI's cascaded onto the aiming point and glowed fiercely as the waves of bombers soared overhead and began unloading a heavy discharge of bombs all around and through them. Before we began our run-up, German "cat's eye" fighters—day fighters not equipped with Airborne Interception radar—arrived on the scene and dropped row upon row of chandelier flares high above us. With this illumination they had no difficulty spotting the bomber stream and many combats broke out in and around the target area, a vast arena now flooded with a pitiless light.

Sellar responded to the bomb aimer's instructions with a quiet "Bomb doors open" as we began our run. As he concentrated on the run and the bomb aimer's corrections, my eye caught a movement ahead of us to port. In a moment a Ju 88 flew into plain view heading in the opposite direction. For a brief moment I was able to take in every detail in the harsh light bathing the scene. The Ju 88 was on fire; flames and smoke streamed from its port engine. On the thin tubular body the identifying black cross was clearly visible in its white frame. The pilot huddled over the controls; from his attitude one sensed that he was trying desperately, before his aircraft exploded, to guide it beyond the lethal area of illumination—to get clear of the guns and the fires below and bail out. He had no eyes for us as he concentrated solely on staying alive.

I felt no sympathy for him, only relief that he was in no position to attack us. They were killers in our book, killers who had every advantage over us, the prey they stalked.

Sellar had not so much as turned his head to look at the enemy aircraft, ignoring the flak and focusing all his attention on fine course corrections as the bomb aimer directed him with precision toward a fresh set of TI's just positioned by the Pathfinder "backers-up" slightly to the left of the original markers. To a neophyte like me at least the attack appeared to be heavy and concentrated. In an area of perhaps 150 acres around the TI's it looked to me as though every factory, every house, every building of every description was on fire. Over much of this expanse the colour of the fire had changed during the five or six minutes since the attack had opened, turning from the diamond white incandescence of the hundreds of thousands of incendiaries themselves to the deeper reddish flames which testified that the fires had taken hold in the buildings. As we left there were still hundreds of heavies behind us on their way in to blast and burn more of the target sector.[3] I glanced back for another glimpse of Mannheim as we were moving out of the area of illumination. The nethermost pit of hell itself could scarcely have appeared more frightful. The over-all spectacle was virtually indescribable, the product of bursting shells, a vast enclave billowing fire and smoke below, searchlights groping in slow frenzy, their beams rendered anemic by the glare of hundreds of flares slowly descending on their parachutes—with additional rows of fresh ones being seeded far above.

Leaving the target we still had three hundred miles before us to make the enemy coast. There was no let-up in vigilance. German night fighters would still be ranging in force, striving to render our attack as costly as possible. Confirmation was provided by three more combats that broke out in close proximity on the way back, a strong indication that there were many more taking place, for the bomber stream was strung out for many miles both in front and behind us. But we were not molested. Eventually we crossed the enemy coast outbound, and although no one relaxed his efforts, we knew our chances of getting home were now beginning to increase substantially. After a further suspenseful wait we approached our own base.

The weather had clamped down at Chedburgh, apparently just before our arrival, resulting in a diversion to Waterbeach. Arriving there, we found ourselves running a bit low on juice, with nine aircraft ahead of us in the landing pattern. I grew tense as the minutes ticked by. Traffic was heavy around the drome, many other non-Waterbeach aircraft having been diverted there like us; and with twenty-odd tired crews circling the field with us in the blackness we got two bad scares, one from a pilot who changed altitude without any clearance and practically landed on us, the other from a pilot who failed to turn on his navigation lights and apparently did not see ours. Through it all, Sellar remained imperturbable. After ten or fifteen minutes, when we had been in the air for five minutes short of seven hours, we were given Turn One and pancaked.

Again the relief of being safely down flowed over us like a healing drug. We luxuriated in the sensation as we lit our cigarettes and waited for the crew bus. There was little conversation; everyone was too tired.

At interrogation, since I was not directly involved in the questioning, I had an opportunity to study the aircrew in the room with me. There was scant similarity between the figures around me and the keen Brylcreem-ad airmen on the recruiting posters which had equated joining the Air Force with "Adventure in the Skies." Seven hours of sweating concentration in a snug flying helmet had left everyone's hair plastered to his head like wet fur. Bleary eyes, and faces etched with the imprint of oxygen masks and the weariness spawned of acute tension and lack of sleep, complemented the sagging posture and occasional sighing exhalation of cigarette smoke to present a picture of men wrung out like dish rags—men who had had enough adventure to do them for a bit.

Waterbeach had been unprepared for this inundation of surplus aircrew, and had only a handful of spare beds. I spent three weary and uncomfortable hours vainly trying to sleep in an armchair in the officers mess, then gave up and went out to see if I could rustle up a cup of coffee from one of the cooks while I waited for breakfast.

Back at Chedburgh three hours later, I learned that our crew had not been placed on the battle order for that night, although we were down to do an air test on E Easy right after lunch. I tried to sleep for a couple of hours, then rose for lunch and made my way up to the flights for the air test.

After we had landed, the NCOs told me there was to be a dance that night at the Sergeants Mess, and invited me to come. I had a much more attractive prospect in mind—about ten hours uninterrupted sleep—so I begged off. . . .

. . . on the morning of 25 September, Squadron Leader Jeffries, flight commander of "A" Flight, told me that my crew was to do a fighter affiliation exercise in E Easy. He also told me that I was to take her "Gardening" that night for my first Stirling operation with my own crew.

"Gardening" was the code name for mining operations. The RAF did an enormous amount of this work, laying mines in coastal waters and harbours all the way from Norway to the Gironde estuary. By so doing they not only kept a large number of German minesweepers working constantly in an attempt to keep shipping channels open, particularly in the "inside" waterways from Norway and Denmark down behind the Frisians, but they sank a large and strategically significant tonnage of shipping and dislocated and delayed the movement of a vast number of other important cargoes.

Mining trips were usually much less risky than main force operations. But if, when the aircraft was going in at six hundred feet to drop its mines, it happened to stray within range of one of the many German flak ships which were rotated at random to guard the most likely places, it stood an excellent chance of being blown to Kingdom Come before its crew knew what had happened.

Jake Walters—he who had been landing after the Hanover raid when the Ju 88 overtook him—was one of the few who lived to tell the tale after encountering a flak ship at close quarters. Jake told the story splendidly after a few pints: how he and his crew had navigated unerringly to the prescribed spot in the channel adjoining the Frisians, descended to six hundred feet after going through the required procedure of checking their position again on Gee, had made their run with the bomb doors open—and flown directly over a flak ship that had heard their Stirling coming and was cocked and primed waiting for them. The first thunderous salvo had been right on target—the flak ship could hardly miss at that range—and Jake and the boys had been blown completely upside down only six hundred feet over the North Sea.

At this point in the recital Jake always paused for effect, took a long draught from his pint, then looked everyone in the eye and said, straight-faced: "I wasn't afraid to die,—BUT I THOUGHT I'D FIGHT FOR THE BOYS!"—this last clause accompanied by violent foot and arm notions demonstrating a desperate winding on of aileron and a stabbing application of top rudder.

By great good fortune the throttles had been inadvertently thrust forward unevenly when Jake went for maximum power, so that full power was applied on only one side. This unintended gesture kept the aircraft rolling in the same direction and enabled it to right itself just in time to avoid plunging into the North Sea. Jake maintained, momentarily poker-faced, that the uneven application of power—and on the right side—had been no fortuitous blunder but rather consummate airmanship flowing from a most careful and unperturbed analysis of the situation performed by him whilst hanging upside down in his straps. It was a sparkling yarn, one of several in Jake's operational repertoire; but he knew, and we knew, that his miraculous escape in the riddled Stirling constituted the exception that proved the rule.

○

At briefing we found that our Gardening was to be done in the Frisians too, but with me, as I joshed Jake later, it proved to be a case of *Veni; Vidi; Vici;* and no problems. We took E Easy into the designated channel northeast of Texel and were back home safe and sound in three hours and thirty-five minutes. I wrote it into my log book next day with a circled "4" after it.

Next night there was no war on, so the wingco laid on some training flying for the junior crews, and we wound up doing a Bullseye of just under five hours. On 28 September when we reported to the flights we were sent over to Stradishall to ferry a new kite back to Chedburgh. . . .

About noon the weather clamped in and it began to drizzle sporadically. Word came through simultaneously that there was a stand-down for the squadron. I immediately thought of a few hours sleep, followed by a foray into Bury St. Edmunds. Wing Commander McGlinn had other ideas. He was clearly a charter member of that school who believed that if aircrew were allowed to lie about they would immediately get slack, and morale would decline precipitously overnight. To keep our morale sky high, he laid on a route march for the afternoon, all the way around the Drem system. I hastily guessed the diameter of the system to verge on three miles, which meant a circumferential stroll of about nine miles—three hours totally wasted. My morale collapsed.

On subsequent occasions when the squadron was stood-down the wingco came up with other happy thoughts to keep morale soaring. We collected teapot-sized boulders, whitewashed them, and arranged them in neat borders outside various buildings to set off the inspiring period architecture, i.e. Nissen huts and other austerity monstrosities. The double row circling the flagpole compound, the very epitome of originality in design, represented our ultimate triumph in this challenging field. This day, as I slogged my way around the field resignedly, suffering from intensely low morale, the wingco, who had not shirked the march himself, fell in alongside me.

He asked me how our Gardening in the Frisians had gone. I said "Piece of cake, sir," this being the accepted response for a pukka operational pilot. If one had just returned from Berlin with two engines out and pieces falling off the aeroplane all the way back, it would still be proper form to tell anyone inquiring that the show had been a piece of cake. The other alternative, one not employed when responding to a wing commander, was to magnify the exploit outrageously, in which case one's statement would likely be written into the "Line-shoot" book which most squadrons kept in the officers mess.

It quickly became apparent that what McGlinn really wanted to talk about was the second dickey trip I had done on Hanover. Having checked the navigator's log, spoken to the pilot, and, I suspect, looked at the target photos, the wingco was not at all satisfied that the performance had served its purpose as an instructive exercise for me. He finally came out and said that he was quite prepared to lay on another second dickey trip for me before I took my crew on a main target. I wanted no more second dickey trips, and hastened to assure him that I was confident I could handle a target with my own crew. McGlinn seemed satisfied and vaguely pleased with this response, and let the matter drop.

That night I decided to forego the trip to Bury St. Edmunds. Three hours of morale building, a good bit of it across muddy terrain, had taken the edge off my appetite for pleasure. I repaired instead to the mess, with my leg tendons feeling every bit as resilient as chewed string, and settled in for a quiet and sedentary evening. . . .

On Saturday, 2 October, we were briefed for Gardening again, but this time it was to be no short flip to the Frisians. The target area for these mines was a shipping channel around Anholt Island off the coast of Sweden, far up in the Kattegat. Our route would take us in over Denmark, which we were told was another sensitive area so far as night fighters were concerned, and in terms of distance the red tapes traced out a round trip which looked to be somewhere between 1300 and 1400 miles.

The weather was reasonably good over England when we took off, except that it was a particularly black night; but as we approached Denmark the visibility deteriorated steadily, with a high overcast shutting out every vestige of starlight. We flew along silently, hour after hour, in and out of unseen clouds whose presence was betrayed only after the fact by their inner turbulence. When Sam did have occasion to exchange a word or two with me—and this only occurred at widely spaced intervals—the sudden sound of his voice in my headphones made me jump. After three and a half hours we were nearing the point at which we were to start our descent preparatory to laying the mines.

Without warning the blackness surrounding us was suddenly filled with slashing white tracer coming from the starboard quarter; simultaneously Bert gave the urgent order "Corkscrew starboard!" and the aircraft vibrated to the chatter of our own guns.

I was already wrenching the Stirling into a steep starboard dive, and out of the corner of my eye watched in wild fright the hosing streams of tracer following us. Again I had the terrifying impression that the streaking cannon shells were passing within inches of my head. The firing stopped as abruptly as it had started. I kept up the corkscrew until Bert came on from the mid-upper turret a few seconds later to report that the Messerschmitt 210 had broken off.

Three minutes after we had levelled up—and well before our hearts had subsided to their normal rhythm—the Me 210 came bursting in on us a second time, from a hundred yards away on the port quarter. Again the first intimation we had of his presence was a withering hail of cannon fire, and again we dived fiercely into our corkscrew, causing parachute packs, navigation instruments, and all the other loose gear to fly wildly about the aircraft. Once more we somehow managed to stay just clear of the pursuing stream of fire. It was apparent throughout that the fighter was doing his utmost to tighten his turn and correct his deflection, but his own surplus speed and the sharpness of our turns towards him were too much; he could not obtain sufficient lead to strike home. As in the first attack, he kept up his fire as long as he could, a good four-second burst, but although his flashing tracers crept close to us, our own gunners' fire forced him to break off a second time.

My heart was beating like a frightened bird's. There are few things quite so startling as having an unseen fighter stalk you to point blank range then open up with cannons in pitch darkness. After he had broken off the second attack we kept up a mild evasive action for several minutes, but there was no further sign of the deadly twin-engined hunter.

Sam came on the intercom to point out that it was now time to commence our descent to 600 feet. At this point Stan volunteered to go up front to relieve J.B. who had been riding in the front turret. J.B.'s six-foot-four frame was about one foot longer than the turret had been designed to accommodate, with the result that spending extended periods cramped in its drafty embrace almost paralyzed him. At OTU and Conversion Unit this potential difficulty had been recognized; in fact we had feared for a time at Stradishall that J.B. was going to be taken out of our crew because of his height. We had successfully pleaded our case for keeping him with us by pointing out that our wireless operator was not just an ordinary wireless op, but a trained air gunner as well, and that he could therefore relieve J.B. as occasion required. Stanley, who was a much smaller man, now went forward to do a stint in the nose turret and let J.B. out of its torturous confines.

About ten minutes after Stan had settled himself behind the forward guns, I levelled out with the altimeter showing six hundred feet. The period of unbroken silence stretched to a quarter of an hour, and my heart had just about reached its normal cadence again when Stan set it racing with a sudden urgent call:

"Climb Skipper—FOR CHRIST SAKE!"

There was no mistaking the urgency in his voice, and I shot up four hundred feet before wasting any time checking on what the problem was.

When I did inquire, Stan had some difficulty emulating the calm tones of a BBC announcer while he described what he had seen. I had even more trouble keeping my poise when he revealed that we had just passed slightly *below* the mast-tops of what appeared to be some small fishing vessels. Visibility in the scud was next to nil; only by the grace of God had we missed descending another thirty feet and burying ourselves in a watery grave.

I realized immediately what had happened, and it had been my fault, and to a lesser extent Sam's, that the whole crew had nearly been killed. We had been warned at briefing that we would probably encounter a low pressure area in the vicinity of our target, and would therefore have to set a new QFE on the altimeter. The situation, cited in every textbook, was one of the classic weather hazards associated with aneroid barometer altimeters. The sudden upset of our fight to stay alive under the two fighter attacks had temporarily driven this vital detail from my mind as I started our descent, and for the same reason Sam had overlooked his written log note to remind me of the QFE setting recommended by our met officer.

I hastily made the correction, which we could now certify as reasonably accurate, having practically flicked our props through the water at the old setting, and we proceeded to sow our crop of 1500 pound mines after Sam had verified his position.

We then altered course and started the long trail home. I looked forward hopefully to an uneventful journey, feeling that we had earned a rest, what with abysmal weather on the way in, two heart-stopping fighter attacks, and then some unintentional night wave-hopping amongst a Swedish fishing fleet. But a quiet uneventful trip home was not to be our lot.

I climbed to 12 000 feet for the return journey; however, my hopes of finding clear air went unrealized. We were still condemned to flying in and out of invisible cloud in pitch black conditions of near zero visibility. We turned onto a long, straight leg of our route, and half an hour went by without a word on the intercom. Our earlier experience with the night fighter had removed any need for me to remind the gunners to maintain the sharpest possible vigil.

Some movement below the level of my gaze caused me to glance at the yoke of the control column. I could see nothing out of the ordinary. Moments later the sensation occurred again, and once more my quick glance downward caught nothing. The third time it happened, I kept my glance lowered for a few seconds.

A spark seemed to flit between my thumbs. I moved them, and again what looked like arcing electricity flowed from the bolt head in the centre to either side of the control yoke. As I watched in apprehensive fascination, the tempo of the discharge gradually increased, and in a few minutes it became continuous. Something prompted me to glance back over my left shoulder and my heart froze in fright once again. C Charlie was sheathed in a bright phosphorescent radiance. Around the tips of the port propellers two great circles of eerie fire, pulsing like the aurora borealis, glowed in the darkness, making a giant concentric design with the ever-present dull glow of the hot engine cowlings. I was momentarily petrified by the display, ignorant of its origin and portent, and even after several minutes had passed without anything untoward happening, I remained acutely uneasy. This shimmering corona playing across the plane's wings was not the sort of furbelow I wanted around my gas tanks. I descended several thousand feet, but the frightening aura clung to us.

I had never heard of St. Elmo's fire, let alone seen it, and what we were then flying through was St. Elmo's fire at its fearsome worst. If I had known then what I know now about the unhappy possibilities inherent in critically high charges of static electricity around aircraft, I should have been even more frightened than I was—difficult as that feat would have been. Gradually the flow diminished, faded, and disappeared, to my great relief. We had been airborne about six hours.

We landed precisely eight hours after takeoff and were soon slouching wearily in the crew bus as we headed for the parachute section. Later, when we had finished our stint with the interrogating officer, Wing Commander McGlinn came up to me while I was choking down some rum-laden coffee— I hated the stuff, but the rum unravelled the mental and physical kinks at a great rate—and began chatting in a less distant fashion than he had hitherto employed. After getting me to repeat the little I could tell him about the fighter's tactics, he said: "Well, that should give you a lot more confidence. Now you know your corkscrew can fox a fighter even at close range. This one had all the advantage, and yet you kept him from scoring a single hit on your aircraft."

I hadn't really been thinking of it that way, but in retrospect I could see that there was considerable validity in what McGlinn said. The German fighter pilot had been good; of that there was no doubt whatever. To be able to find and attack us, twice, in that black cloudy void, even with the assistance of AI radar, was no mean feat, for the attacks themselves had to be delivered visually in the final stages, and to follow us as closely as he had through our violent corkscrew bespoke a highly determined antagonist who knew his business.

Thinking it over as I went to catch up to the rest of the crew, I did feel better, and at least a little more confident. I hadn't bothered telling the wingco about forgetting to set the new QFE on the altimeter—figured I shouldn't worry him.

As we walked down to the airmen's mess for our fried egg and spam, we even found something to laugh about—(the rum was doing its job). Bill Bailey had stepped up into the astrodome for a casual look round approximately fifteen seconds before the Messerschmitt's first attack. I commented, recalling the blur of motion I had caught out the corner of my eye, that he had moved back out of the astrodome at about twice the speed of the first cannon shell.

Bill grinned: "Just remembered it was time to check the oil pressure on No. 4 again," he said, then showed us some physical evidence of just how rapidly he had moved when the Messerschmitt fired. His left hand had been resting on a light screw at the base of the astrodome. His departure in the face of those fiery cannon shells had been so abrupt that he had torn right through all three gloves on that hand, including the heavy outer leather gauntlet.

Stan weighed in with a new thought. "Well boys, there's a few bods up in the Kattegat that'll be laundering their underwear tonight I'll wager. Can you imagine bobbing around quietly on a fishing boat out in the middle of nowhere, and then having a bloody great Stirling come thundering out of the night at nought feet and just about take your toque off?" We all rejoiced mightily in the probability of someone else having gotten a bigger scare than we had.

NOTES

1. Some months earlier 214 Squadron had been enlarged from the standard two Flights to three; but on 17 June 1943, as part of the expansion program going on in Bomber Command, "C" Flight was taken away from 214 Squadron and became the nucleus of the new 620 Squadron.

2. That stricken Stirling actually appears to have been one from 90 Squadron which staggered into our circuit from the Wratting Common area while I had my attention focused on raising the undercarriage and bleeding off the flap. We lost two of our Stirlings from Chedburgh over enemy territory on the Hanover raid.

3. Of the 622 aircraft dispatched, 571 bombed, dropping 1974 tons. Thirty-two aircraft and crews were shot down, as compared with 26 on Hanover.

STRIKE HARD, STRIKE SURE: THE DORTMUND RAID OF 6–7 OCTOBER 1944✧

W.S. CARTER

○

On the morning of 6 October 1944, Air Chief Marshal Sir Arthur Harris, Air Officer Commanding-in-Chief Bomber Command, selected Dortmund as the primary target for that night's bombing operation. He chose Dortmund because its status as an industrial, commercial, and communications centre made it a vital link in Germany's war effort and, therefore, a valuable military target.

Dortmund is located in Westphalia, at the eastern edge of the Ruhr, Germany's industrial heartland. With a pre-war population of 550 000, Dortmund was the Ruhr's second largest city. No fewer than twenty-nine heavy industrial works were located in and around Dortmund, including thirteen coking plants, nine collieries, three chemical and explosives works, and four iron- and steel-works. Also present, but considered to be of lesser importance, were fourteen engineering and armaments works, a municipal gasworks, and ten power stations. In addition to its industrial significance, Dortmund was a transportation and communications centre. The city contained six railway marshalling yards and an inland harbour that served as the terminus of the Dortmund-Ems Canal, connecting Westphalia with the North Sea. The canal had handled 4 million tons of goods inward bound and 1.4 million tons outward bound in 1938, the last year of peace. This huge shipping capacity helped make Dortmund the second most important transportation centre in the Ruhr after Duisburg, and one of Germany's most important commercial centres.[1]

Consequently, Dortmund was the object of forty-nine bombing operations during the Second World War.[2] Almost half of these operations were

✧ Revised version of "Strike Hard, Strike Sure" from *Anglo–Canadian Wartime Relations, 1939–1945: RAF Bomber Command and No. 6 (Canadian) Group* (New York: Garland Publishing, Inc., 1991), 1–19.

no more than harassment raids carried out by fewer than a dozen aircraft and were intended to disrupt industrial production by driving workers into air raid shelters and depriving them of sleep. These raids were also designed to keep anti-aircraft ("flak") and night-fighter defences spread thinly throughout Germany and occupied Europe by diverting the enemy from actual main force targets. Bomber Command also launched a number of major operations against Dortmund, notably on 6–7 October 1944. This raid had additional significance for No. 6 Group of the Royal Canadian Air Force (RCAF). Never before or after did 6 Group order up as many aircraft for a single operation as it did that night.

The attack reflected the complex nature of Bomber Command's tactical planning at this stage of the war. During the early years, aircraft flew singly on their outward and homeward journeys, and followed their own routes. By contrast, bombing operations by the autumn of 1944 had become major battles whose routing and timing necessitated intricate planning for several hundred bombers. Moreover, Bomber Command was strong enough to bomb two major targets in one night, in addition to mounting "spoof" raids against others. Additional security was provided by radio counter measures (RCM), which were used to confuse the enemy by "jamming" his radar; and Royal Air Force (RAF) night fighters were dispatched on "intruder" operations over Germany for the purpose of shooting down enemy night fighters.

Once Harris had selected Dortmund as the primary target he left his staff to prepare the Command Operational Order. Upon its completion, and with Harris's approval, this order was sent by teleprinter to the headquarters (HQ) of the seven operational groups.[3] At 6 Group's HQ the staff transmitted the operational order to 62, 63, and 64 (RCAF) Bases at Linton-on-Ouse, Leeming, and Middleton St. George, and to their satellite stations at Tholthorpe, East Moor, Skipton-on-Swale, and Croft.[4] Bomber Command HQ planned the heaviest attack against Dortmund, the codename of which was "Sprat." Among the 519 aircraft detailed for this operation were 286 from 6 Group, 180 from 3 Group, and 53 from 8 (Pathfinder—PFF) Group. The purpose of the raid was the destruction of the undamaged area of the city near the aiming point.

The attack was scheduled to commence at H-Hour, 2025 hours, on the evening of 6 October, as PFF Mosquitoes of 8 Group marked the aiming point. They were equipped with "Oboe," a blind-bombing radar device that vectored the aircraft to their target using a beam transmitted by a ground radar station in England. The bomb aimers were supposed to release their bombs when a second beam from another ground station crossed the first. The Mosquito crews had instructions to bomb at H-5 and H+5 minutes, using the PFF marking method codename "Musical Parramatta." This procedure involved radar-directed ground marking of the aiming point by Mosquitoes using red Target Indicators (TI)—bombs designed to explode and burn with an intense glow that made them visible to the main force bomb aimers. Following the Mosquitoes were the "backer-up" Pathfinders whose task was to remark the aiming point by dropping green TIs that functioned in the same manner as the reds. The bomb aimers who were following the Pathfinders were ordered to aim at the red TIs if they could see them. If not, they had instructions to aim at the centre of the greens. Should the target be covered by a layer of cloud, the Pathfinders were to use their marking procedure called "Emergency Wanganui." This involved radar-directed sky marking, above the clouds, of the point at which the bombs were supposed to be released. Instead of green or red TI bombs, the Pathfinders had to use red TI parachute flares set to burst with cascading yellow stars at fifteen thousand feet. As with Parramatta, backers-up would have to remark the release point when the flares burned out.

The Pathfinders were followed by the heavy bombers of the main force. Their attack was set to take place between a maximum bombing height of twenty thousand feet and a minimum of fourteen thousand feet. The main force was divided into four waves, each containing bombers from both 6 and 3 Groups. The bombing times were carefully arranged in order to concentrate the actual bombing in as short a time as possible and thereby, it was hoped, overwhelm Dortmund's defences. The first wave was scheduled to bomb from H-Hour to H+4, the second from H+3 to H+7, the third from H+7 to H+11, and the fourth from H+10 to H+14. Each wave was arranged in the same general configuration. The first aircraft in each wave were supposed to be the Lancasters of 3 Group, followed by the Lancasters and Halifaxes of 6 Group.

The assigned route was indirect and had several course changes on the outward and homeward trips. Although the indirect route meant a longer flight time and more complex navigation, it also promised two distinct advantages. First, course changes were intended to divert and/or delay the enemy's responses by concealing the final destination of the bomber "stream." Secondly, a route with several "dog's legs" could be plotted away from any known concentrations of both enemy flak defences and night-fighter beacons. Two other important tactical aspects of the route to and from Dortmund were the plotting of the route over liberated French territory and the flight to the target at low altitude for as long as possible.[5] Both measures were intended to avoid enemy territory and flak until otherwise unavoidable.

Signals security took the form of strict instructions to aircrew about maintaining wireless transmission, radio transmission, and radar silence until they reached 0600E.[6] This precaution was to make it more difficult for the German radar operators to obtain a fix on the bomber stream. Another security measure involved the release of "Window," strips of metallic paper, down the flare chute of the aircraft in order to jam German airborne and ground-based radar. At Skipton-on-Swale the crews were ordered to begin releasing Window normally at a rate of two bundles a minute as soon as they reached the bomb line, the point beyond which live bombs could be jettisoned without risking Allied lives.[7] They were further instructed to drop four bundles a minute when thirty miles from the target and to continue until they were thirty miles beyond the target. Then the crews could reduce the rate to two bundles a minute until they reached the bomb line, at which point they could cease dropping Window. Final security instructions, consisted of the traditional warning from the intelligence officers not to reveal upon capture by the enemy any more than one's name, rank, and service number.

Outside the sphere of the Canadian Bomber Group's immediate activities, much was being done by Bomber Command to give the Dortmund operation every opportunity to succeed. Strong enemy anti-aircraft defences rendered numerous diversions a tactical necessity. The largest and most vital of the diversionary operations, almost on a scale of a major raid in its own right, was an attack on Bremen, codename "Salmon." A force of about two hundred aircraft from 5 Group was dispatched, with H-Hour planned for 2025 hours, the same time as H-Hour over Dortmund.[8] In addition to Bremen, there were diversionary operations mounted against Berlin, Ludwigshafen, and Saarbrücken. These were much smaller than the raids against Dortmund and Bremen, but they were conducted in their opening stages as real attacks so as to deceive the German defenders into believing that a main force raid was imminent.

In addition to spoof attacks, the complex tactical plan also called for RCM and intruder patrols to be carried out by 100 (Special Duties) Group. The group's RCM activities on the night of 6–7 October consisted of supporting both attacks against Bremen and Dortmund. The attack by 5 Group on Bremen was supported by six Stirling bombers carrying "Mandrel," an airborne radar device designed to jam the enemy's early warning radar equipment, thereby preventing the German ground controllers from locating the bomber stream until it was too late to disrupt the raid. Further south, fourteen Halifaxes, Stirlings, and Flying Fortresses dropped Window near Mannheim in order to cover 6 and 3 Groups' attack against Dortmund. In addition, five Fortresses sortied carrying "Jostle," an airborne radar set used to jam German radio transmissions and interfere with their air-to-ground communications. Lastly, ten Halifaxes, Mosquitoes, and Liberators made signals investigation patrols.[9]

"Serrate" and intruder patrols essentially served the same purpose, namely, the interception and destruction of enemy night fighters. There were thirty-eight Mosquitoes airborne from 100 Group equipped with Serrate, a radar set that could home in on the airborne-interception radar signals used by the German night fighters to do the same to the bombers. The Serrate Mosquitoes conducted their patrols around enemy night-fighter beacons in order to intercept and shoot down the German night fighters, and on 6–7 October they claimed one *Junker* (Ju)-88 aircraft destroyed. Another thirty-eight Mosquito intruders from 100 Group were ordered either to keep pace with the bomber stream or to patrol near the enemy's airfields in order to ambush German night fighters while they were attempting to land. In all, at least fifteen Mosquitoes made high level intruder patrols, of which one went missing; nineteen more Mosquitoes conducted sorties near enemy airfields; and one made a special intruder patrol.[10]

The balance of 6–7 October's activities included minelaying by nineteen Halifaxes and Lancasters off Heligoland, Texel, and the Weser Estuary, accomplished with no loss of aircraft. Also, six Hudsons and Stirlings flew operations on behalf of Special Operations Executive, and one Stirling was lost. Lastly, two Mosquitoes flew meteorological reconnaissance flights.[11]

After 6 Group's bases and stations had received their copy of the Operational Order, the navigation briefing took place for navigators and bomb aimers. This briefing was usually held at least thirty minutes prior to the main briefing. Besides navigators and bomb aimers, those captains of aircraft (usually pilots) who wished to be fully apprised of all aspects of their upcoming operation would also attend, even though the pilots' attendance was apparently not mandatory. The navigation officer would explain to the navigators the flight plans they were to follow, all known locations of the enemy's flak defences, the positions of route markers signalling course changes, the cities where spoof raids were planned, which emergency airfields were open to receiving returning, damaged bombers, and which navigational aids to use. Bomb aimers would receive from the bombing leader their bomb sight settings, the target height, the types of TIs to be used, and the sequence in which the bomb aimers were to aim at the TIs.[12]

Following the navigation briefing, all aircrew attended main briefings. At Eastmoor, the intelligence officer started with a description of Dortmund's importance. He then discussed the German defences, beginning with the subject of decoy fires. He warned the crews not to be fooled by the numerous decoys found in the Dortmund area and called their attention to one particular site half a mile south of the city. Next he mentioned the menacing array of anti-aircraft defences, consisting of light and heavy flak guns. Although no substantial amount of flak was expected on the outward and homeward journeys as long as the bombers stayed on course, several danger spots existed for those who strayed off track. On the outward flight both Cologne and Koblenz, about ten or fifteen miles to the north, had to be avoided, as did Münster, about fifteen or twenty miles to the east on the homeward trip. The defences at Dortmund itself were described as intense, consisting of both light and heavy flak. The extent to which the bombers would encounter enemy night-fighter opposition was unknown, but the intelligence officer warned the air gunners to stay alert. He also outlined some of the nearby landmarks that would help the crews recognize the target, including the woodland about five miles south of Dortmund, the canal, the marshalling yards, and the harbour near the aiming point. The spoof attack against Bremen was mentioned and was followed by an explanation of the PFF marking method.[13]

After the main briefing, crews went to the mess for their usual preflight meal. They then headed for their lockers, donned their flying kit, and climbed into trucks that took them to the dispersal points where their bombers stood waiting. A pre-flight inspection was conducted to ensure that all the equipment and aircraft were functioning properly. Then it was time to taxi to the runway for take-off.

o

The outward journey took place under a cloudless sky, and little flak was encountered. Even so, the flight was not uneventful, for a number of encounters with enemy aircraft occurred. One such combat involved a Lancaster X from 428 Squadron, flown by Flying Officer G.R. Pauli. Lancaster "T-Tommy" was outward bound and on course at eighteen thousand feet when the enemy night fighter was first seen. At 2024 hours Sergeant W. Harper, the mid-upper gunner, spotted the fighter four hundred yards away, visible against the light, cloudless sky. The fighter, a *Messerschmitt* (Me)-410, approached the bomber from the starboard quarter above, closing to 150 yards. The pilot threw the aircraft into a starboard "corkscrew" manoeuvre, dropping one thousand feet in the process. At the same time, Harper and the rear gunner, Sergeant A.G. Scott, began firing at the Me-410 when it was still three hundred yards away and they continued firing until the Me-410 was about 150 yards distant, at which point the German pilot broke away to the port quarter level. He had not fired a single round of ammunition at the bomber. However, an estimated two hundred rounds had been fired by Scott and 150 by Harper, causing no visible damage to the fighter. Thus, no claim could be entered in the Combat Report. The bomber itself suffered no damage and there were no casualties among the crew.[14] They bombed late at 204130 hours, aiming at the centre of the red and green TIs; and they also described the bombing as "well concentrated" and the target as "well afire."[15]

Not all encounters were as inconclusive as Pauli's. One of 408 Squadron's crews, flying in a Halifax VII and captained by Pilot Officer T.V. Barber, destroyed an Me-109 single-engined night fighter. Halifax "Z-Zebra," had successfully bombed Dortmund and was on the homeward journey when the combat occurred. The weather was cloudless with the moon "rising dead astern," and the bomber was flying on course at a height of fourteen thousand feet. The first visual contact was made at 2048 hours against a light sky.[16]

> The Rear gunner first sighted this E/A/C [enemy aircraft] making an orbit at a fighter beacon—then dived at them from dead astern up. The Rear gunner gave the order 'Corkscrew Starboard Go' also giving the mid-upper gunner the position of the E/A/C, who immediately opened fire at 400 yards. Strikes were seen to register by the skipper, rear and mid upper gunner as this E/A/C was seen to explode and disappear at 250 yards on the port side. Owing to the fact that the intercom plug in the rear turrent was U/S [unserviceable], the rear gunner had his turret centralized—doors open and intercom connected with the plug in the fuselage. As it was impossible for him to rotate his turret and bring his guns to bear on the E/A/C, he kept up a running commentary of the attack over the inter com. This is a case of very good team work between the two gunners and excellent shooting on the part of the mid-upper gunner. Two other crews from this squadron reported seeing an aircraft hit the ground in flames at the same position and time as this attack.[17]

Airborne that night as a second pilot or "second dickey" was Flying Officer Paul E. Burden of Fredericton, NB, who had arrived with his crew at 434 Squadron, Croft, on 4 October.[18] Prior to this posting, he had flown over two thousand hours with an RCAF Ferry squadron. In this respect he was, in his words, "unique." Most new pilots on front line squadrons had two hundred hours' flying time when they began their first operational tour.

Burden recalls having a feeling of "great anticipation" when his name appeared on the Battle Order for the night of 6–7 October, because "I had been so keen to get on ops [operations] for so long. . . . That day, my first op, I had no idea what I was going to experience and I was fully aware of everything that was going on . . . but I suppose the word would be 'a bit tense'. I was not frightened; I was able to control myself. As a matter of fact, I was fortunate that way. I always was."

Burden does not remember the briefing that afternoon. Even so, he recalled "being impressed that I wasn't to take along certain objects in pockets and this kind of thing, although I don't recall being told that at briefing." As far as the target was concerned, "I just knew that, when we were told to go to Dortmund, it was just a name to me; but I can remember . . . the word 'Dortmund' was mentioned, so I certainly caught onto that really rapidly."

All of the new pilots on 6 Group's front line squadrons had to do their first trip with an experienced crew, so as to learn what a nighttime raid over Germany was like. Burden flew on 6–7 October with his flight commander, Squadron Leader G. Nickerson of "A" Flight, whom he remembers as "quite an able individual." Ironically, Burden's duty with Ferry Command probably made him more experienced as a pilot because, unless Nickerson had been previously an instructor, Burden's flying time would have exceeded that of his flight commander. Even so, it was Nickerson who had the experience in bombing operations and was qualified to initiate the new pilot.

None of 6 Group's bombers was shot down by enemy night fighters on 6/7 October, but two Halifaxes were lost after being hit by flak over the target. By coincidence, both bombers crashed after their two port engines were damaged. One of them, a Halifax VII from 426 Squadron, was flown by Flight Lieutenant W.P. Scott, who went missing on his twenty-ninth operation, tantalizingly close to his thirtieth trip and the end of his tour. In retrospect, Scott appears to have been jinxed from the start because Halifax "U-Uncle" was a standby aircraft that he and his crew had to take when their own aircraft proved unserviceable. Scott's bomb aimer, Flying Officer A.F. Livingstone, recounted the drama.

> Took off 4 mins. after (our a/c/ us) [aircraft unserviceable] set course time because the spare a/c wasn't ready. Caught up to the stream over France and when climbing for height and a/c had to be coaxed up from 13000'. We got to 17500 and the skipper said she wouldn't have climbed very much higher. On the bombing run we did an S turn to port because of another a/c directly above us. Flak was very heavy and we just bounded across the target. Directly over target the Engineer was hit by flak through the left eye which took a good piece of the side of his head with it. He grabbed the WAG [wireless operator/air gunner] around the neck and tore his oxygen mask off. We let down to 11000 so we could work without oxygen. I moved from the nose to the cockpit and just then the kite [aircraft] lurched and we weren't getting any use out of the port engines. The stbds [starboard engines] were throttled back to keep

her level and she started losing height and air speed fast. The skipper asked if the gas was on and it was. Then he gave the order to bale out. Fire broke out in the port inner and I left after the Nav. [navigator] and WAG. I seemed to stay in the slip stream for a long time and did 3 complete flips. The chute opened and hit me on the forehead as it went up. Then there was a bright reddish orange flash on the ground which lasted for a second or two then died down to a small glow. I presumed that this was the a/c. In a short time which seemed less than a minute I landed in a field of cattle.[19]

The other RCAF bomber lost to flak was a Halifax III from 433 Squadron. Halifax "G-George" was flown by Flying Officer V.G.B. Valentine, who was on his first operational trip with his own crew. According to Valentine,

We set course in Halifax "G" over base at approx. 1800 hrs. Our route took us across the Channel into France until we were parallel with our target . . . The Dortmund Ems Canal. We then turned east towards the target and a few miles south of it. We were approaching the target at 20,000' when a burst of flak caused both port engines to become u/s. With the help of the engineer I feathered both engines and trim [sic] the a/c as well as possible. Even so considerable pressure was needed on the aileron controls to keep it level. The a/c began to lose height quickly (1000'/min.) at first but gradually the descent was reduced to 500'/min. The target was very near (5 mins) so I decided to bomb the target, turn due west and then bale the crew out over allied lines. However, over the target at 7–8000' we sustained several hits on the air foils and fuselage. The target bombed we turned off west. At 5000' I levelled the a/c off and it promptly stalled at 125mph. (IAS) [Indicated Airspeed] Recovery was made at 500' and Duisburg was below us. It is my idea that we crashed into a factory chimney. Four members of the crew were in crash positions when we crashed and two others were going into positions. The four in position were killed whereas the other two were badly injured but saved.[20]

Burden calls his first trip "a mystifying thing in the sense that there I was . . . classified as second pilot but with no controls; and I sat on a tin seat that folded down from the wall, which was vacated by the flight engineer for me once we got off the ground; . . . and it was . . . a ridiculous feeling being without any controls."

He remembers many details about the raid. "We had lots of opposition . . . [and] . . . even by later standards, . . . that was a rugged trip." By October 1944, radar-directed flak, not fighters, was the bomber's main enemy. As the aircraft closed on Dortmund the ground defences made their presence felt. Burden recalls that "the last three or four minutes before the target when we were building our run-up, flak was really close. . . . I can remember we were just being 'heave-hoed' all over the landscape . . . we were really bumped and crashed around from explosions. . . . We did sustain one hole from flak.

"I can remember running in. Here I was sitting on this tin seat, and with no controls, and with my arms just dangling over the side; and I thought, 'Good God, ... I could lose two arms right here, just as easily as Hell.' So, . . . the last two minutes over the target, I sat on my hands. I wasn't going to lose my arms.

"Also, when they all say that people's lives . . . flash before them when there's something critical about to occur, . . . as we were running up . . . I figured there was a good chance that this aircraft could go down, . . . and then I got wondering. I said, 'Now what did I forget that I should have remembered?' I remember, . . . my paybook was in my pocket with . . . all sorts of data in it that I was supposed to have left behind, so I kept . . . reassuring myself that . . . if I had to hit the silk, . . . the first thing I'd do is throw away this damn paybook on the way down so . . . that [it] wouldn't be tied to me."

Over a burning target at night, aircrew were often awestruck by the sights and sounds they witnessed. The constant pounding of the aircraft's engines was interrupted only by the dull "thud" of flak shells exploding nearby or the chatter of Browning .303 machine guns firing from the mid-upper or rear turret. If the flak burst was close enough the crew could hear the rattle of fragments as they bounced off or pierced the fuselage or wings. Sometimes, crews could smell burning cordite from the guns or flak. Interspersed with the sounds were the instructions the bomb aimer gave the pilot as they made their final run-up to the aiming point.

The night sky was awash in light as many colours burst brightly and faded. German night fighters dropped parachute flares that burned with an intense white glow. From the ground, searchlights rose like white columns, with the master searchlight, for unknown reasons, shining with a bluish tinge. Mixed with these colours were the red and green TIs as they fell earthward. On the ground lay the city. As the bombers flew over their target, aircrew who could see below watched the city writhe as the orange and yellow fires took hold and burned everything within reach. Often, crews saw individual explosions.

Against this background, bombers flying at lower altitudes could be observed crossing the target area, in danger of being hit by bombs dropped from aircraft above. Depending on how effective the German defences were, aircrew could witness the death of a bomber as it exploded with a brilliant flash or burned fiercely as it dived earthward, often out of control. During the later stages of the attack, much of these and other sights were obscured as smoke from the bombing and fires rose skyward.

Burden recalls that Dortmund "was a brilliantly lit-up target. We were not particularly early on it because it was . . . going real good when we got there." In addition to seeing "lots of fires and flames," he remembers that, "I was a new boy so I was all eyes, and when I saw the Pathfinders' markers . . . I was . . . tremendously impressed with the whole thing; . . . I was . . . a bit pleased with myself too, because I didn't think anybody would be wondering how . . . one would take to this; and so, when . . . we got back, I was just as keen as could be to get at it myself."

The loss of two Halifaxes was more than compensated for by the success of the Dortmund attack. According to the intelligence officer of 424 Squadron at Skipton-on Swale, the crews, in almost all cases, described the attack as a "good prang," the traditional RAF term for successful bombing operations. Most of the crews bombed the primary target between 202736 and 2037 hours, aiming at the centre of the red and green TIs. They reported the flak over Dortmund as having been moderate to heavy in intensity and ranging from fourteen to twenty thousand feet. Most crews also commented upon the presence of many fires and explosions, some of which were said to have been quite large.[21]

Not all of 424 Squadron's aircrew bombed the primary target. One crew attacked an alternate target and two others returned early to England. Halifax III "V-Victor," was captained by Flying Officer L. Wright. He and his crew were not able to locate Dortmund because their navigational aids suddenly became completely unserviceable. Instead, they bombed an alternate target consisting of a revolving beacon and a row of five lights. The two "early returns" were Halifax III "D-Dog," flown by Flying Officer W.S. Bonar and Halifax III "W-Willie," captained by Flying Officer H. Cowan. Bonar had to jettison his bombs and return to the England because of propeller trouble in the port outer engine. Cowan jettisoned his bomb load after all four machine guns in the rear turret jammed, leaving the turret unserviceable and the bomber almost defenceless.[22]

The return home to England of the group's aircraft was not uneventful. The weather had been forecast as foggy north of the Wash with a lot of stratus cloud further south, and over northern Yorkshire the weather was as predicted.[23] The group's bombers had to be diverted to southern stations. Most of 424 Squadron's Halifaxes were diverted to Mendelsham.[24] The only problem that the crews encountered was the failure of aircraft traffic control at Mendelsham to provide proper radio transmission directions for landing. Some of the pilots followed 6 Group's radio transmission procedure, whereas others reported that they were obliged to simply "muddle through." In spite of the lack of proper radio transmission directions, the landings went well; the bombers landed quickly and none experienced any serious problems. By all reports, conditions for the aircrew at Mendelsham were good. The crews almost universally praised the quality of the food there and several mentioned the movie (title unknown) shown for them. The only discordant note was some criticism regarding the quality of the beds.

Among 6 Group's diverted bombers was Nickerson's Halifax III of 434 Squadron. Burden recalls that, "we were airborne seven hours and ten minutes, and . . . couldn't get back to Croft because of weather; . . . we were diverted to Newmarket Racetrack, and . . . landed in the centre of the racetrack, with a flarepath put down, those little flare pots; and my guess is that

that didn't happen too many times. It was the only time that I ever was in an aircraft, a four-engined job, that landed on other than a paved runway."

The initial, optimistic impressions of 424 Squadron's aircrew were confirmed by the RCAF's post-operational Intelligence Appreciation.

> The attack was carried out in clear weather, no cloud with good vis[ibility]. T.I.G. [green TIs] were numerous and well concentrated with a few T.I.R. [red TIs] visible. The attack opened punctually and a good concentration of bombing resulted as it progressed. Several large explosions are reported at 2025 hrs. to 2029 hrs. followed by dense fire and smoke. Crews bombing in the latter stages of the attack report numerous fires taking hold. All reports to hand indicate an accurate and highly successful attack[.][25]

For Bomber Command the Dortmund operation was indeed an undeniable success. A total of 523 aircraft were dispatched on 6–7 October. Of these, 483 bombed the primary target, five bombed an alternate target, thirty-five aborted their operations, and only five were lost. The tonnage of bombs dropped was over 1000 tons of high explosives and 566 tons of incendiaries. 6 Group's contribution was considerable. No fewer than 293 aircraft were dispatched (45 Lancasters and 248 Halifaxes), 278 of them bombed the primary target (43 Lancasters and 235 Halifaxes), 1 Lancaster bombed an alternate target, 2 Halifaxes were missing, and 14 aircraft aborted the operation (1 Lancaster and 13 Halifaxes). The Canadian Bomber Group dropped 666.3 tons of high explosives and 146.9 tons of incendiaries.[26] On a percentage basis 6 Group's contribution to the raid was 56.03 percent of the aircraft dispatched, 57.6 percent of those crews who bombed the primary target, 40 percent of the losses, 40 percent of the aborted operations, 61 percent of the high explosives, and 26 percent of the incendiaries.

Assessing the amount of damage done by the Dortmund raid was difficult because the analysts at Bomber Command HQ had to distinguish between fresh damage and damage caused by previous attacks. Complicating the immediate task was the recent operation against Dortmund, on 5 October, by the 8th United States Army Air Force. Even so, the Interpretation Report provides a good picture of what Bomber Command accomplished on 6–7 October.

The operation caused much widespread damage throughout Dortmund, most of which was near the goods yard and main passenger station.[27] Railway facilities were also seriously damaged, especially near the main passenger station. In numerous locations the railway tracks were cut, and bombs hit the carriage sidings a number of times. These facilities were assessed as 80 percent unserviceable just after the raid. Rebuilding and the clearance of debris apparently began immediately thereafter, and photographs shot one week later revealed that 50 percent of the railway lines could still not be used.

Commercial and industrial buildings in Dortmund and its port area incurred considerable damage. Bomber Command damaged or partially destroyed five engineering plants, two of which were priority targets; and a factory making special steel was moderately damaged. In all, fifteen plants were damaged in addition to an electrical equipment factory, sawmills, breweries, and cement works.

In Dortmund's built-up sections, there was much new damage to residences and businesses alike. Of the city's built-up area, the total amount of damage was estimated at 70 percent; and 50 percent of the entire city had been destroyed. During this operation, many public buildings were also severely damaged or destroyed, including a hospital, a court house, the town hall, a number of schools, and an academy.

The bombing attack against Dortmund also caused numerous civilian casualties. According to available German sources, there were 191 people dead, 418 injured, and 38 missing.[28]

The reasons for the effectiveness of the Dortmund operation have been alluded to already. Obviously successful was the tactical plan that combined a diversionary attack on Bremen, spoof raids against Ludwigshafen, Saarbrücken, and Berlin, radio counter measures, intruder patrols, and an indirect, low-altitude route over French territory. There were several reasons why these tactics were so effective.

Bomber Command believed that the attacks on Bremen and Dortmund had gone so well that they were "worthy of special comment" in the Interception/Tactics Report.[29] Obviously, the bombers had benefited from "tactical surprise." Part of the reason for this success was the diversionary attack against Bremen and its supporting Mandrel screen. Even so, Bomber Command HQ felt that their activities in northern Germany had been unnecessary because there seemed to have been "sufficient confusion" anyway within the German fighter control system in southwestern Germany. The result was the absence of any "well organised interception."

The Dortmund bomber stream flew at a low altitude so as to evade detection until no longer possible. When the bombers reached German airspace and began to increase their altitude and change course for the Ruhr, Mosquito aircraft flew to the southeast and began a spoof raid on Ludwigshafen-Mannheim, dropping Window for effect.

British signals intelligence tracked a number of German night fighters that were diverted from the region of Mainz-Frankfurt to the area where the spoof raids occurred. From the known source of sightings, combats, and attacks, Bomber Command concluded that the only German fighters to intercept the bomber stream were freelance fighters that had been either directed to the Ruhr during the operation or sent up early. Otherwise, the main force had been relatively untouched. Either the fighters were surprisingly ineffective or only a limited number had been sent up.

o

The attack of 6–7 October was only one of several main force attacks and many smaller ones carried out by Bomber Command during the Combined Bombing Offensive. According to an Operational Research Section report, a few small raids, in which Bomber Command dropped a total of 651 tons of bombs, were launched against Dortmund in 1940, 1941, and 1942. Only minimal damage was done by these attacks and "the effect on production was negligible." The maelstrom began on 4–5 May 1943, with the war's first major raid against the city, and ended with the war's last raid on Dortmund of 12 March 1945, in which five thousand tons of bombs fell on the city, bringing production to a complete halt. The total effect was devastating. During the months from May 1943 to March 1945, Bomber Command dropped approximately 16 500 tons of bombs on Dortmund, resulting in "over 90% of the main town area being rendered uninhabitable." Since there was no evidence of a decrease in the labour force or a pronounced absenteeism rate, physical damage to industrial plants was the main reason for Dortmund's loss of war production. A second factor of equal importance was dislocation of electric, gas, and water facilities in the city. The consequences can be briefly summarized. Losses in war production amounted to about 30 percent of the production levels prior to May 1943, which equalled a loss of between six and seven months' production over almost a two-year period. Moreover, coal mining was reduced to an average of 50 percent of previous production levels from the autumn of 1944 until May 1945.[30]

The Dortmund operation was only one of thousands during one of the most controversial and attritional campaigns in military history. Even so, it should not be considered typical of the Combined Bombing Offensive as a whole. It was certainly not as costly as the raid on Nuremberg in March 1944, or as destructive as those against Hamburg in July 1943 and Dresden in February 1945. The attack on Dortmund is significant nonetheless because it was representative of the type of raid mounted during the final nine months of World War II. At the time of this raid the war had reached a stage where Bomber Command could employ great striking power and enjoyed air superiority over the German night defences. In addition, this operation marked 6 Group's maximum effort of the war. The group was at the peak of its destructive power. It had become an integral part of Bomber Command and, concurrently, a symbol of growing Canadian air power.

NOTES

1. "The Bomber's Baedeker (Guide to the Economic Importance of German Towns and Cities)," part 1, 2nd ed. (1944), pp. 142–53, Directorate of History, National Defence Headquarters, Ottawa (hereafter DHist), 181.003(D3993). Essen was the largest Ruhr city, with over one million citizens.

2. Martin Middlebrook and Chris Everitt, *The Bomber Command War Diaries* (Harmondsworth: Penguin, 1985).

3. Martin Middlebrook, *The Nuremberg Raid* (London: Allen Lane, 1973; rev. ed., Penguin Books, 1986), 96.

4. Command Operational Order, 6 Oct. 1944, Public Records Office (hereafter PRO), Air 14/3126.

5. Interception/Tactics Report no. 249/44, part 2—Night 6th/7th Oct.

1944, 12 Oct. 1944, PRO Air 20/5960, p. 3.

6. Command Operational Order.

7. "S.I.O.'s Briefing Notes," 6 Oct. 1944, DHist 181.009 (D3313).

8. Command Operational Order.

9. Night Raid Report no. 734, 15 Feb. 1945, DHist 181.003(D1518), p. 3.

10. Bomber Command Intelligence Narrative of Operations no. 920, n.d., DHist 181.003(D1998), p. 2.

11. Night Raid Report, pp. 2–3.

12. See "Briefing Procedure," 13 Dec. 1943, DHist 181.009(D5026), p. 1.

13. Intelligence Briefing Notes, 6 Oct. 1944, DHist 181.009(D2466), pp. 1–2. See also Linton-on-Ouse, DHist 181.003 (D3271), Leeming, DHist 181.003(D3267), and Tholthorpe, DHist 181.009(D3245).

14. Combat Report, n.d. DHist 181.003 (D53), pp. 1–2.

15. No. 428 Squadron Operations Record Book, p. 8, DHist batch 6, box 19, no. 155 (microfilm). In fact, KB780 was attacked twice on the outward journey. Also, the air gunners' exact positions are unknown because the Record Book shows their positions as the reverse of those shown in the Combat Report.

16. Combat Report, n.d., DHist 181.003 (D53), p. 1.

17. Ibid., 2.

18. Interview with Paul Burden, 16 Jan. 1992. All information pertaining to Burden in this article comes from this interview.

19. "Questionnaire For Returned Aircrew, Loss of Bomber Aircraft," 16 May 1945, DHist 181.001(D23).

20. "Questionnaire For Returned Aircrew, Loss of Bomber Aircraft," 8 May 1945, DHist 181.001(D23).

21. Raid Reports (handwritten), 7 Oct. 1944, DHist 181.003(D5124).

22. Raid Reports, nos. 24, 4 and 3, 6 Oct. 1944, DHist 181.009(D158).

23. Night Raid Report, 1.

24. Raid Reports (handwritten).

25. Intelligence Appreciation, n.d., DHist 181.003(D3484).

26. Bomber Command Operations Record Book, p. 1408, DHist. No file or microfilm number exists.

27. Interpretation Report no. K. 3272, 25 Oct. 1944, DHist 181.003(D1826), p. 1.

28. Middlebrook and Everitt, *Diaries*, 595.

29. Interception/Tactics Report, 2–3.

30. Operational Research Section Report no. S. 238, 28 Aug. 1945, PRO Air 14/1449, p. 1.

THE IMPLICATIONS OF TECHNOLOGICAL BACKWARDNESS: THE CANADIAN NAVY 1939–1945[*]

MARC MILNER

○

History is replete with examples of technologically backward forces suffering defeat and there are some notable examples, like the Falkland's War, of modern equipment failing to confer an advantage sufficient to win even with superior numbers.[1] But all other things being equal, it is preferable to fight with the best weapons possible—and with good reason. Israel's air war with Syria over the Bekaa Valley in June 1982 was a clear example of the annihilating potential of superior technology well used.[2] The war in Afghanistan suggests there may still be scope on land for determined men armed with a few simple weapons, but naval and air warfare are not for the halt and the lame.

Analysts have traditionally focused on the importance of technology to air warfare, in part because of the intensity of the electronic battle fought over Germany from 1940 to 1945.[3] But in a quieter, if no less profound way, navies too have struggled with the problems of electronic and high tech warfare for the last fifty years.[4] Like the air forces, navies man large, expensive pieces of equipment built to take them into a hostile environment—and back safely—and both services have developed complex instruments to extend the sensor and weapons range of those "platforms." Failure to keep abreast of developments in this electronic battle hold dire consequences. The recent history of the Royal Canadian Navy (RCN) is a case in point. Our fleet retains the ability to hit submarines at considerable ranges with its mix of sonars and helicopters, but it is otherwise utterly defenceless. Its obsolete electronic countermeasures capabilities and lack of modern long range and point defence missile systems leave the fleet vulnerable to attack. In an earlier age the fleet might have "gone down fighting," inflicting some

[*] *The Canadian Defence Quarterly* 19, 3 (Winter 1989), 46–52.

measurable damage on the enemy in the process. But in the age of missiles and electronic warfare the Canadian navy faces annihilation with no cost to a modern enemy, other than expended ordnance.

Traditionally the Canadian navy has had a defensive role, protecting shipping from attacks by enemy submariners. In the 1980s the fleet is so obsolete that it is incapable of defending even itself. Senior Canadian naval officers have had to be creative in finding a viable role, and when the fleet sails in harm's way it must be protected by ships from other NATO navies. Not since the 1920s has the gap between the requirements of modern war and the capabilities of the fleet been so great. When the subject gained some brief notoriety in 1983 the then Minister of National Defence, Gilles Lamontagne, told Canadians not to worry. In the Second World War, he pointed out, we took over some aged destroyers from the United States, put some new guns on them and it all worked out. He implied that we could obtain the needed equipment from our Allies in time of crisis and that Canada had surmounted a similar problem before under more stressful circumstances. Presumably the minister's comment was for public consumption: senior naval officers no doubt ground their teeth and muttered darkly over their coffee. Recent scholarship on the Second World War makes a nonsense of Lamontagne's assertion, and outlines clearly that there are serious consequences in falling behind technologically. It is the purpose of this paper to explore some of those consequences and to illustrate some of the problems and pitfalls of fighting a modern enemy from a state of industrial and technological backwardness—the wartime tales of Canadian gallantry and important deeds well done notwithstanding.

The navy was tiny but relatively modern in 1939. Its six British-built destroyers were well equipped by the standards of their type, although verging on obsolescence. Four home-built coal-fired minesweepers of a simple design had recently been added to the fleet. This small service, with its eighteen-hundred officers and men and two bases a continent apart, drew almost exclusively on the Royal Navy (RN) for equipment, technical and officer training, uniforms, and some key senior personnel.

By 1945 much of that had changed. The RCN had grown fifty-fold, to over four hundred warships and nearly one hundred thousand personnel, making it the third largest Allied navy—indeed the third largest in the world. This tremendous growth brought with it important new roles. By 1944 the RCN was responsible for the close escort of North Atlantic convoys between New York and Britain, commanded a key theatre of war (the Canadian Northwest Atlantic, the only theatre of war commanded by a Canadian), provided nearly half of the anti-submarine strike forces in British waters, had a cruiser off Okinawa battling *kamikazes* and another on the way, other ships in the Arctic and the Mediterranean, and aircraft carriers building.[5]

CAPTIVE OF CANADIAN INDUSTRIAL CAPABILITY

The wartime RCN was both the product and the captive of Canadian industry, for no other Canadian military service so directly reflected the state of Canada's industrial and technological development. The other services were, at the operational level, less reflective of distinctly Canadian strength and weakness. Both the Canadian army and the Royal Canadian Air Force (RCAF) engaged their principal enemies overseas as part of larger Allied formations, and, despite some minor peculiarities in equipment, fought their enemies at the end of an Allied pipeline which funneled new equipment to the front on the basis of need. Canadian-built weapons, ammunition, aircraft, and motor vehicles poured into the Allied pools and were allocated to units who were next in the rotation regardless of nationality. Those national peculiarities which did emerge, such as the use of Canadian designed and built armoured reconnaissance vehicles in First Canadian Army, had no effect on the performance of the forces that historians have seen fit to record.

The same cannot be said of the RCN. The bulk of Canada's enormous wartime fleet was built and maintained here, and indeed operated from Canadian ports or bases. It was far easier to build the hulls and man them than it was to keep pace with a rapidly changing high technology battle against German submarines. The pattern of the war was such that the RCN was thrown back on its *own* resources very early and despite the fact that it, much like the other services, functioned under higher Allied strategic direction the Canadian navy had to get on with the job as best it could with the resources at hand. Further, the navy's contribution to its war was surpassed by only the Royal and United States Navies, and in the vital North Atlantic the RCN was second only to the RN in importance. While in absolute terms (numbers of men, for example) both the RCAF and the Canadian army were much bigger than the RCN,[6] neither of the other services' contributions to their respective campaigns approached that of the navy.

The key to the convoy system, upon which *defence* primarily rested, was the *availability* of escort vessels; without them the convoys could not be sailed. The RCN filled the gap in essential numbers with home-built Flower-class corvettes, vessels which in their completed form—construction, equipment, and manpower—were neither fancy or efficient. They did not have to be, unless they were called upon to fight. Numbers were produced, the convoys sailed, and when the routing upon which defence of the convoy rested failed, a battle ensued: and if the convoy was Canadian escorted it usually suffered heavy losses. It could hardly have been otherwise.

Those simple escort vessels, built to mercantile standards, were well within the capability of Canadian industry in 1939, although much of the special equipment needed for war had to be obtained abroad. In the very early stages of the war this was a manageable problem, since much of the equipment was rudimentary or drawn from surpluses laid-up after the last war (e.g., the main 4-inch BL gun). Moreover, the fleet with which the RCN fought its most demanding battles against the wolfpacks was built for decidedly modest purposes. In 1939 the RCN needed about forty auxiliary warships for coastal patrols, minesweeping, and work off the nation's defended ports. They were to be jacks-of-all-trades, simple to build and operate, and required to stay at sea for only a few days. Although the navy wanted a naval design, it settled for the corvette, which had been adopted by the RN for emergency construction. The real thrust of *naval* expansion in

1939 lay in the building of Tribal-class destroyers—state of the art in their class—which could not be built in this country. Either the Tribals, or the expertise to build them, had to come from Britain at a time when British yards and experienced personnel were committed to their own programs. By early 1940 a scheme for bartering Canadian-built corvettes for British-built Tribals was tentatively accepted, but an equitable rate of exchange could not be agreed upon. Canada paid for its British-built Tribals, and tied up both manpower and yard space in Halifax from 1942 to 1945 building four Tribals that never fought the Germans. The corvettes ordered before the barter scheme collapsed, sixty-four in all, went ahead. The small yards needed the work (indeed, more were ordered in the summer of 1940 simply to keep the yards busy). Ten were transferred to RN accounts and the RCN thought it could make use of the rest—somewhere.

The Naval Staff of 1939–40 had no inkling that the hastily built corvettes of the first construction program would carry the burden of their war—and the navy's reputation—for the next three years, and that they would find their calling far beyond inshore waters. As basic auxiliary ships there was really little seriously amiss with the equipment of the first corvettes. They should have had a heavier secondary armament, 20mm cannon instead of the smattering of .05 and .303 machine guns, had Canada been able to provide it, but in other respects such as wireless equipment, refrigeration, main armament (supplied from war stocks by the RN), and minesweeping gear, RCN corvettes were up to standard. Indeed, in terms of radio equipment the Canadian ships were reckoned to be better fitted.[7]

TECHNICAL DEFICIENCIES OF THE CORVETTES

However, in some other respects the first Canadian corvettes left much to be desired. The navy settled for an obsolete British sonar, the type 123A, instead of the more advanced type 127 fitted in British corvettes. The reason was a shortage of gyro compasses needed for the 127 set, which Canadian industry was incapable of producing and the British were unprepared to supply. Canadian corvettes went to sea in 1940 with magnetic compasses graded in "points," not the stabilized peloruses marked in 360 degrees of modern warships. The magnetic compasses were suitable for navigation, but hardly up to the demands of modern naval warfare. The pounding of the sea, firing the weapons, or depth charges affected the alignment of magnetic compasses, while the needle's unstabilized motion made it virtually impossible to make accurate depth charge attacks on submarines or to pass bearings fast and accurately from ship to ship.[8]

The lack of a modern gyro compass was by far the greatest shortcoming of the first corvettes. It made precise navigation difficult, produced inaccurate attacks and called for high standards of training and seamanship—something unlikely given the rate of expansion. Doing without the gyro also meant that Canadian ships lacked a low-power electrical system, something essential to modernization by 1942 and which required extensive alterations to install. There were other significant problems too, some arising from the speed of construction and the unfamiliarity with marine problems of some of the yards. No historian has yet sorted out the cause of numerous equipment failures in the early days, although it seems a fair bet to lay the blame equally between shoddy construction and ineptitude of poorly trained sailors. Electrical failures were due on occasion to a too early release of depth charges, which shook the ship and rattled its electrical panels. The electrical system itself was prone to failure in the early corvettes because inexperienced shipyards fed the wiring into the *top* of circuit panels, as one would do in a home or industrial wiring application. Condensation ran along wiring and directly into the panels causing failures. The ships themselves were difficult to keep clean and rust free—a professional naval officer's guide to efficiency—because Canadian industry produced and consumed steel plate faster than it could remove the mill scale. Canada's two pickling plants were not up to the task of handling all the newly rolled plate, and construction went ahead too fast to permit weathering in stacking yards to take effect. Canadian corvettes went to sea with primer and final paint applied over the mill scale which, after several months, fell off exposing bare metal. Salt air and sea did the rest. Perhaps no image more than that of a rust-encased Canadian corvette solidified the impression of the wartime fleet as one of slack discipline and bungling incompetence.[9]

The Canadian navy had a reasonably good idea of what its corvettes were supposed to do when the ships were ordered, and their equipment was equal to the task. They can in no way be faulted for the dramatic change in the character of the war in the summer of 1940. By early 1941 submarines, which were supposed to be limited in range and mobility, began to push their attacks on Allied trade into the western Atlantic. By the early summer of 1941 there remained a short stretch of the Atlantic convoy route between Newfoundland and Iceland that still required the close protection of anti-submarine escorts, and it was that gap which the products of the first corvette program were destined to fill.

THE EFFECT OF INADEQUATE RADAR

The Newfoundland Escort Force (NEF) was formed in June 1941 to provide anti-submarine escort for mercantile convoys.[10] Apart from the weather, NEF's greatest opponent was the German submarine fleet which, since August of the previous year, had been operating like motor torpedo boats in roving "packs" against Allied convoys. By the time NEF was formed the British were already fitting their small ships with radar to locate and attack U-Boats operating on the surface at night. They discovered that the early anti-submarine radar, the type 286 with a 1.5 metre wavelength, lacked the definition needed to detect a small target close to the surface of the ocean. The cavity magnetron, invented in September 1940, made centimetric radar possible, permitting a high definition of small targets in background sea clutter. The British were making the transition to centimetric radars when the RCN first seriously considered the possibility of fitting radar to its escort fleet. In the absence of good liaison with the British the RCN opted for a 1.5 metre set, a technology already familiar to Canadian scientists. The corvette *Chambly* went to sea in May 1941 with the prototype of what became the "Surface Warning 1st Canadian," or SW1C, radar set. Ironically, in the same month HMS *Orchis*, also a corvette, was at sea off Britain with a trial radar, the type 271, the first operational ten centimetre set and a key weapon in the battle against U-Boats. Thus, even as the Canadians deployed to Newfoundland for the first time to face the German wolfpacks, they were a full generation behind in crucial radar technology.[11]

Ascertaining why the Canadians got off to a late start requires some speculation, since the documentary evidence is incomplete. It is significant that the decision to opt for the SW1C was made prior to large scale RCN involvement in anti-submarine warfare, and without good technical liaison with the RN. In March 1941 the 1.5 metre SW1C set looked adequate for a task which itself was poorly understood by senior RCN officers: it was, after all, the type then in service with RN escorts. Moreover, the type SW1C was a marked improvement over the British type 286 set with its antenna fixed to the masthead and movable only by turning the ship. The Canadian antenna could be turned by a handwheel, sweeping much like a searchlight. However, like a searchlight the cone of the radar transmission was narrow and if the target was not in the area being swept it would escape detection.

The SW1C, like the type 286, was a failure in its primary role of anti-submarine warfare, and both are credited with very few contacts.[12] The Canadian set also had serious maintenance problems, the blame for which is shared equally between the scientists who failed to design a sailor- and sea-proof set, and the RCN which trained operators not maintainers. In fact, by the time the RCN began to look seriously at the need for qualified radar personnel the country had been stripped of them to support the high-tech airwar in Europe. As late as 1943 the navy had to draft RCAF radar technicians to its corvettes in order to keep radars operating.

The operations of NEF in 1941 were a difficult experience for the RCN. The limits of the corvettes as deep ocean escorts became readily evident. Their range was short, their action in a seaway violent, and life aboard had a seriously debilitating effect on the men. At an average maximum speed of 16 knots the ships were also slow. Lack of good tactical speed led the Canadians into an arrangement with the United States Navy (USN), which was serving alongside NEF by September, that the Canadians would escort the slow convoys while the faster American destroyers (capable of 30+ knots) handled the faster ones. It was a reasonable division of labour, but one which proved costly to the Canadians since slow convoys were more vulnerable to attack. Many of the lessons of convoy battles were driven home to the RCN in 1941 in a series of convoy battles through September to November, as hastily commissioned and poorly equipped Canadian corvettes tried without much luck to defend their convoys from hunting packs.

By early 1942 the RCN realized that it desperately needed a ten centimetre radar and by late spring that it also needed two other things which Canada could not provide: high frequency direction finding (HF/DF) equipment for shipboard use, and more destroyers for its ocean escort groups. Without these assets, losses to RCN escorted convoys far outstripped those suffered by the British. As a result the RCN was forced to the sidelines in 1943, the wolfpacks were defeated by the RN, the navy failed to make the limelight just when the government needed a more positive public image, the Naval Minister charged the Chief of the Naval Staff with incompetence, the CNS was fired, and the RCN gained a dubious reputation.

The 1942 crisis is a complex one, and the actions of men must be set against a world crumbling under the onslaught of Axis powers. Under the pressures of global war and the new technologies which drove it, the Canadian navy kept the ships at sea and hoped for the best. Strategically it was the best decision, and in the end there were few alternatives. Escort operations in 1941 proved conclusively that the corvettes were not up to the task of ocean escort. Longer periods at sea, increased armament, and more equipment drove the crew size from its initial twenty-six to thirty to over eighty, requiring extensive alterations to the ship. Gyro compasses, now crucial to effective anti-submarine operations, could not be fitted until a low power electrical system was installed: rewiring required weeks of dockyard work. Modernization planning was further complicated because the industries which built the ships were on the Great Lakes and the BC coast: either too far away to be easily accessible, or beyond locks impassable to a fully fitted out corvette. The development of maintenance facilities along the Atlantic coast was neither part of the government's plan nor of the navy's. Even skilled labour to do the work on the east coast was in short supply by 1942, the result of pre-war depression, concentration on repair work in the major ports of Saint John and Halifax, conscription of qualified personnel into the army, and a lack of government capital expenditure east of Quebec. Had there not been an operational emergency in 1942 it would have been all but impossible to modernize the fleet before 1943. The failure to plan effectively for modernization speaks volumes for the RCN's early intentions for the corvette fleet.

The more urgent problems at sea in 1942 were the lack of modern radar, HF/DF, and more destroyers. All were essential in the *defence* of convoys, but none were obtainable from Canadian sources. The Canadian 10 cm radar program was struggling towards the production of the RXC, a set which entered service in 1943—a full year behind schedule—and which then proved to be an utter disaster.[13] Neither HF/DF or destroyers were available in Canada, and the RCN found that British production of these—as with radar—went to the RN first. Special pleading and the pressure of operations forced the British to divert some of their equipment to Canada by the end of 1942, but not before the RCN endured its worst period of the war.

CONVOY BATTLES: TECHNOLOGY AND EFFECTIVENESS

Convoy battles in 1942 were described by the famous British operational scientist P.M.S. Blackett as unstable equilibriums which could be tipped dramatically in favour of one side or the other depending upon who acted first. That first act derived from a battle for information. The regular and constant relay of information on convoy position, course, and speed from U-Boats in contact to shore authorities and from them back to other members of the pack through high frequency (HF) transmissions formed the basis of wolfpack operations. Once a member of the pack sighted the convoy it was usually tasked as a contact keeper until the pack was drawn in. The shadower made brief radio transmissions every hour: in the first hour an HF sighting report to shore plotters, and in the second a brief MF homing beacon for use by other members of the wolfpack. The MF homing beacon was the only direct radio communication between U-Boats. All their movements were co-ordinated by plotters ashore based on daily position reports. As each U-Boat gained contact with the convoy in turn, it too made an HF report and continued to do so periodically until the battle was over.

The HF sighting reports from U-Boats in contact were usually the first indication to the escort that it had been located. Once the position of the HF transmitter was located by triangulation from shipborne HF/DF sets, or by estimation by a lone HF/DF set (a ground wave signal indicated a U-Boat within visual range of the convoy), British escort commanders sent out one or two destroyers. Their speed (30–35 knots) allowed them to move quickly against the shadower and either attack him or force him to dive. In either event it was impossible for the U-Boat to transmit sighting reports or MF homing beacons, contact with the convoy was broken, and the convoy itself complicated the Germans' problem by an evasive manoeuvre.

The initial battle for information was crucial to what followed. Using HF/DF directed destroyer sweeps, the British could either prevent a pack from assembling around their convoys or, at worst, reduce the number of U-Boats to be dealt with when the attack finally came. In the absence of HF/DF,[14] RCN escort groups resorted to two methods of forestalling the assembly of the German subs, neither of which worked as well as the British system.

The American practice, also derived from a lack of HF/DF, pushed fast escorts to maximum visibility distance on the horizon during daylight hours, maintaining a patrol in the area where shadowing U-Boats operated. It was a less certain procedure than HF/DF directed sweeps, and risked drawing attention to the presence of the convoy. In the absence of HF/DF the RCN also attempted to use the contact U-Boat's own MF homing beacon, which could be received on the commercial MF/DF set the Canadians carried for navigation. Unfortunately, the MF signal diffused rapidly, and while it was sufficient to draw U-Boats into the general area of a convoy it was not sharp enough to permit an escort to locate a small and elusive U-Boat. Moreover, even when merchant or rescue ships in the convoy provided HF/DF bearings, Canadian escort groups usually had only one destroyer, and its fuel had to be conserved for a long crossing and unforeseen contingencies. Not surprisingly then, wolfpacks formed around RCN escorted convoys with ease.

Having lost the early battle for both position and information, RCN officers built their battle-plans on much less precise and certain intelligence than their British counterparts. And since the Canadians still escorted the bulk of the slow convoys in 1942, they had much less scope for evasive action. The RCN was thus down two strikes even before the first shots were

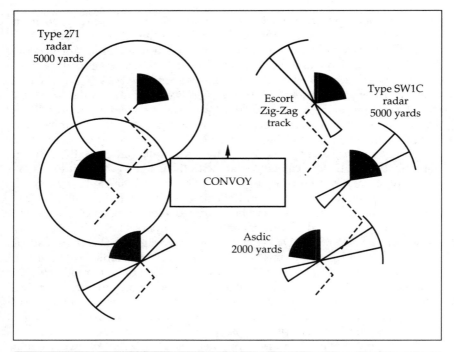

F I G U R E   1   *RADAR AND ASDIC COVERAGE FOR*
TYPICAL RCN ESCORTED CONVOY, 1942⋄

⋄ Six escorts arranged in Night Escort Screen 6 to defend against a threat from the port bow.

fired. Their final hope was to fight the pack to a standstill in the inevitable night battle which followed. For any escort group this was a daunting task. The typical convoy covered an area of five square miles and there were huge gaps between the five to six escorts which made up the screen. Those gaps could be covered well enough during daylight hours, provided the visibility was good. However, at night there was plenty of room for a U-Boat to slip into the convoy. Such an attack tipped the equilibrium in favour of the U-Boats. It drew the escorts into or astern of the convoy to search for an attacker, or to screen rescue work, thereby opening the convoy to further easy penetration.[15]

It was crucial, therefore, for the escort to respond quickly and decisively to U-boats attempting to breach the screen. British groups maintained a close fighting defence of their convoys by virtue of their 10cm radar. Its sharp definition and automated 360 degree sweeping made it possible to maintain a tight radar barrier around convoys at night. It did not always work, but on the whole the 271 radar gave British groups a fighting chance and they usually gave as good as they got.

Again it was a battle for information, and the Canadians again were not so fortunate. Their SW1C radar could only detect a U-boat under ideal circumstances, and its narrow, hand-directed cone could not provide a complete

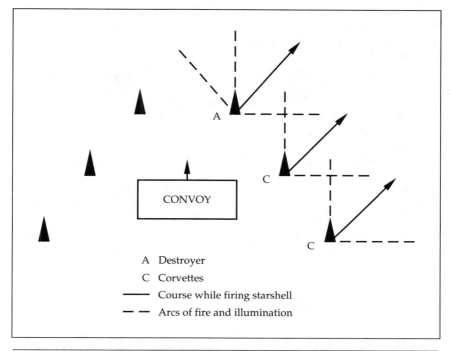

A   Destroyer
C   Corvettes
——   Course while firing starshell
— —   Arcs of fire and illumination

F I G U R E   2   *O P E R A T I O N   " M A J O R   H O O P L E "   T O*
S T A R B O A R D

radar barrier for a convoy at night. The differences in radar performance are well illustrated by Figure 1. RCN escorts therefore fought largely blind, and were forced to react to U-Boats whose presence was revealed by explosions and burning merchant ships. Canadian officers sought to regain the initiative by anticipating U-Boat actions and taking pre-emptive measures. The timing and direction of a U-boat attack could be estimated with some certainty, since submariners preferred certain light and sea conditions. Escort commanders were capable of the same calculations and could estimate when the submarine was likely to be within reach of the escort screen. If, at that moment, the escort filled the night sky with illuminants, the U-Boat might be caught on the surface before it had penetrated into the convoy. It was a gambler's tactic. Timing was crucial. Too late and the U-Boat would have the lights turned on just as he made his attack, too early and the U-Boat could veer off and lay in wait for a second attempt. And it all assumed that the U-boats were both in contact and closing to attack. If they were not in contact, the pyrotechnics might alert any U-Boat within visual range—which could be fifty miles. This illumination tactic, "Operation Major Hoople," was developed by a Canadian to suit the peculiar problems of his escorts. Its first use in November 1942 was judged a qualified success, and it was adopted for general RCN use in 1943. There is no evidence to indicate it was ever widely used, and "Major Hoople" became obsolete once Canadians got 271 radar in 1943.

The consequences of this technological gap were grave, both for the merchant ships the RCN escorted and for the service itself. Of the eleven escort groups operating in the mid-ocean against wolfpacks through the latter half of 1942, four of them were Canadian—approximately 35 percent. And yet fully 80 percent of the ships sunk from trans-Atlantic convoys between July and December were from Canadian escorted convoys. The worst "British" losses of the period fell to a largely Norwegian escort group, "B.6," which fought three major battles in which sixteen ships were sunk. All of B.6's battles were characterized by a high incidence of radar contacts and the battle for convoy HX 217 by a virtually impenetrable radar barrier.[16]

In retrospect the Canadians did extremely well, but the British ascribed their markedly higher loss rate to poor leadership and training. There was an element of truth in the British position, but RCN officers managed their battles with much less information than their counterparts—a situation that called for exceptionally high standards of co-ordination, leadership, and training. In fact, by British standards these desirable qualities were present in the single American group operating in the mid-ocean during the fall of 1942, "A.3." But its loss rate was as high as the Canadians', and its equipment was as poor.

THE RCN'S WORST PERIOD

The performance of the Canadian navy against the wolfpacks in the latter half of 1942 proved to have more than academic interest. The British were alarmed at the Canadian loss rate, and in December asked that the Canadian groups be withdrawn for additional training. The request was a major blow to RCN prestige. The Canadians believed, with considerable justification, that their recent problems were due to poor equipment, a shortage of destroyers, and, perhaps, a spell of bad luck. Indeed, the Staff Officer (Anti-Submarine) at the principal Canadian base in St John's, an RN officer, concluded that "when C [Canadian] groups are brought up technically to B [British] groups a very great increase in efficiency will result without reference whatever to training and experience."[17] He was right, but the Canadian arguments wilted in the face of the terrible losses to convoy ONS 154 which occurred even as the issue of RCN efficiency was being debated in Ottawa.[18]

The Canadians were transferred out of the mid-Atlantic in early 1943, their groups strengthened by British destroyers, new radar and HF/DF fitted, new RN group commanders assigned, and an extensive training period undertaken. When the groups returned to the mid-ocean in April they were given wide berths around U-Boat concentrations, and therefore were not in on the "kill" when the U-Boat packs were decisively beaten in the spring. Because of the transfer only two U-boat kills, and a share of another, were credited to RCN escort forces from January to May 1943: a period in which approximately one hundred U-Boats were destroyed in the Atlantic, half of them by surface ships alone. Thus, although the RCN made up half of the escorts in the Atlantic they accounted for only about 5 percent of the U-Boats sunk.

The navy's poor showing did not go unnoticed, least of all by the men at sea who found themselves playing nursemaid to the merchant ships while the Brits sank the subs. By the summer of 1943 the fleet was equipped to *defend* convoys adequately, at least by 1942 standards. However, with the defeat of the wolfpacks in the spring of 1943 the war brought an Allied counteroffensive. Escorts now had the luxury of pursuing U-boat contacts at length, giving them time to develop a good attack. And it was now that the lack of gyro compasses and low-power system came home to haunt. While the gyros were clearly essential to an accurate attack with depth charges, they were a vital component of the new ahead-throwing anti-submarine mortar called "Hedgehog," a British designed and built weapon in widespread use by the RN by 1943 and a more effective means of destroying submarines.[19]

Thus, even if the RCN had had a domestic supply of Hedgehog, the need to modernize the electrical system of its corvettes would have precluded an early solution to the lack of a state-of-the-art weapon. RN escorts were, therefore, the weapons of choice when faced with a U-Boat contact in mid-1943, and it was the relegation to second string which fired the ire of Canadian sailors and focused their attention on the technological backwardness of their ships. Believing that the channels from the operational side to the decision making staffs in Ottawa were clogged and unserviceable, and encouraged by senior British officers, a number of escort commanders appealed directly to the political head of the navy, the Minister of Defence for the Naval Service, Angus L. Macdonald. Canadian warships, they informed the minister through an intermediary, were as much as a year and a half out of date, and were relegated to secondary duties as a result. The men in the ships felt betrayed by the shore staffs and wanted action to allow them to fight on equal terms.

CRISIS IN OTTAWA

It was an extraordinary moment in Canadian naval history. The crisis in technology at sea coincided with a crisis in the Liberal government in Ottawa. By August, when the information reached Macdonald, the Liberal party had just lost the provincial election in Ontario and four federal by-elections. The government's favour had reached its lowest ebb with the electorate. Canadians were war weary and anxious to hear good news about their armed forces. On the naval side well defended convoys were not news-makers, but U-Boat kills were. The only problem was that the RCN was not sinking U-Boats. Through the late summer and fall of 1943 Macdonald probed for reasons. He asked the Chief of the Naval Staff for reports on equipment, sent his executive assistant on a secret investigation to the UK, and finally confronted Nelles in November. Macdonald charged the Naval Staff with incompetence for its failure to keep the fleet up to date in equipment, protested that he was in no way responsible for the situation, and accused Nelles and his officers of letting down the sailors and the people of Canada. Macdonald contended that had he been aware of the situation and had he not found a solution through political channels he would have withdrawn RCN escorts from operations in 1942.

The idea of the Canadian navy taking a holiday in 1942 must have seemed as absurd then as it does now, but it was Nelles who was sacked not his political master.[20] Nonetheless, Macdonald's question remains, Why was the RCN so poorly equipped? It is a question perhaps only frightened politicians and a generation raised on Canada as a "middle power" could ask. The answer lies in several areas: the rapid expansion of a previously non-technical service, the diffuse interests of the scientific establishment assigned to help the RCN, the limits of the industrial base upon which both the scientists and the navy had to draw for domestic support, the government's economic and industrial planning, and the failure to knit all of these together in order to fight a major Canadian battle in adjacent waters.

CONSEQUENCES OF TECHNOLOGICAL BACKWARDNESS

In the end, Canada's Atlantic war was fought with more than just guns—something we had the technology to produce. The main "weapons" in the war against the U-boat, the electronics and the specialized weapons, were acquired—for the most part—from our Allies after their needs had been met and the urgency at sea had passed. The consequences of that technology gap for this junior partner were grave. Canadian escorted convoys suffered perhaps the highest loss rates of the war, a distinction which has been noted by postwar critics. That rate led to the loss of operational control over our frontline forces during the crisis of the Atlantic war. The "failure" of the fleet to achieve marked success in the sinking of U-Boats provided no relief for a government which, in 1943, faced a war-weary and anxious nation, and this ultimately cost the Chief of the Naval Staff his job. As serious as all of this sounds, it is sobering to reflect that if the Canadian Navy had to go to war today it would not be so fortunate.

NOTES

1. The Argentine Army was larger and better equipped than the British, including better night fighting equipment and more modern versions of some British made equipment. See William Fowler, *Battle for the Falklands (1) Land Forces* (London, 1982).

2. The Israelis lost one fighter, the Syrians eighty-six. See Chaim Hertzog, *The Arab-Israeli Wars* (London, 1982).

3. The electronic war over Germany from 1939 to 1945 was far more intense than that fought at sea, and has generated a body of literature to match. See, for example, Alfred Price, *Instruments of Darkness* (London, 1967) and R.V. Jones, *The Wizard War* (New York, 1978).

4. The high tech side of naval warfare has been the subject of recent best-selling novels by Tom Clancy,

who presents a graphic portrait of the modern problems. A more scholarly—and historical—approach is reflected in the work of Norman Friedman. See, for example, his *Submarine Design and Development* (Annapolis, Md., 1984) and *Postwar Naval Revolution* (Annapolis, Md., 1986).

5. The best survey of the RCN's wartime activities remains Joseph Schull's *The Far Distant Ships*, originally published by The King's Printer in 1952 and recently republished in Canada by Stoddart.

6. Roughly 98 474 Canadians served in the RCN during the war, 222 501 in the RCAF, and 708 535 in the army. See C.P. Stacey, *Arms, Men and Governments* (Ottawa, 1970), app. R, 190.

7. See the Naval Staff Narrative, "Modernization of Armament and Equipment," held by the Directorate of History (hereafter DHist), National Defence Headquarters, Ottawa.

8. For details of the acquisition of this equipment see D. Zimmerman's recent, *The Great Naval Battle of Ottawa* (Toronto, 1988), which recounts the status of various Canadian equipment programs through the war.

9. The RCN's sharpest critic, Captain Donald Macintyre, in his wartime memoir *U-Boat Killer* (London, 1956), 72–82, drew on the shabby appearance of the early corvettes as evidence of their poor discipline and training, and the generally worn appearance of both British and Canadian escorts in the North Atlantic in 1941 was taken by the Americans in a similar fashion. See Patrick Abazzia, *Mr Roosevelt's Navy* (Annapolis, Md., 1975), 116–17. For details of the RCN's problems with mill scale and paint see the report of the Supervising Naval Engineer, Maritimes, of October 1942 and related correspondence in National Archives of Canada (hereafter NAC), RG 24, vol. 11695, file NSS DH 1003-2-5.

10. The account which follows is compressed from the author's book, *North Atlantic Run: The RCN and the Battle for the Convoys* (Toronto, 1985), unless otherwise specified.

11. For the most detailed account yet of how the decision on radars was made in 1941 see Zimmerman, *The Great Naval Battle of Ottawa*.

12. Only four U-Boats are known to have been detected by type 286 radar between August 1940 and February 1942, and two by SW1C during the period researched by the author. See "Summary of Analysis of U-Boat Attacks on Atlantic Convoys, August 1940 to February 1942," Public Record Office (hereafter PRO), Kew, England, ADM 199/1490, and Reports of Proceedings for ON 115, DHist, NS 8280.

13. See Zimmerman, *The Great Naval Battle of Ottawa*, for a detailed account of the RXC fiasco.

14. Rescue and merchant ships in the convoy occasionally had the equipment, although without gyro compasses the bearings they passed were seldom accurate even if they did provide an early warning of U-Boat contact.

15. It was impossible for the U-Boats to actually co-ordinate their attacks, but they did tend to arrive in waves and many Allied naval officers believed that early attacks were deliberate attempts to draw the screen off to facilitate the second wave. In practice, this is what happened.

16. These battles (SC 104, ONS 144, and HX 217) were not without losses, but they were well conducted and the information provided by the escort's HF/DF and radar allowed them to make and follow sensible battle-plans.

17. As quoted in Milner, *North Atlantic Run*, 199, original SO(A/S) to Director, Operations Division, 24 Dec. 1942, in DHist, file M-11.

18. ONS 154 lost 16 ships in a week-long battle at the end of 1942 in which no apparent damage was done to

attacking submarines. After the war it was learned that one submarine was destroyed by the escort.

19. Since the Hedgehog bombs were projected forward of the ship it did not have to run over the target to deliver the weapons, as in the case of depth charges, and therefore could retain contact with the submarine during the attack. Moreover, the Hedgehog bombs were contact fused: an explosion meant a hit, and a miss did not leave the water filled with gases from an explosion which often made regaining sonar contact difficult.

20. The extent to which Macdonald was aware of the problems with equipment in December 1942, when the groups were transferred for inefficiency, remains a point of great historical debate. Nelles's memoranda to Macdonald at the time obscure the matter of equipment and concentrate on the implications of the proposed transfer on the ongoing Canadian battle for an independent command in the Northwest Atlantic. It is possible to argue both that Macdonald was blissfully unaware of the state of the fleet—indeed that Nelles cultivated Macdonald's disinterest in the routine operations of the navy by misleading his minister—or that Macdonald was well aware of the situation (this was Nelles's position later) and that the memo dealt with matters in a general way. If the latter, then Macdonald's handling of Nelles later in 1943 displayed a willful meanness. If, as seems the case, Macdonald took little interest in the operations of the fleet and Nelles took advantage of this, Nelles reaped what he had sown. However, the extent to which Macdonald went to "get" his tired and ill Chief of Naval Staff in late 1943 reflects poorly on the minister. See Milner, *North Atlantic Run*, chap. 9.

CLOSE QUARTERS [*]

ALAN EASTON

o

The sea itself filled my thoughts as I gazed down at the dark water from the lee wing of the bridge. I marvelled at its phosphorescence and at the strange fascination a phosphorescent sea always held for me. Brilliant like boiling silver on ebony, a million drops of shining metal falling from the bow wave. The sea could be beautiful. It was tonight.

The sea fascinated sometimes. But I hated it. How long had I hated the sea? Why did I? Was it fear? God! I would hate to drown! Yes, that was one fear which had been with me constantly. The prelude to drowning must be terribly lonely. One storm stood out in my memory, one in the Roaring Forties. It came into my mind automatically with the thought of drowning.

I took my hands out of the pockets of my sheepskin and rested my elbows on the rail. No breeze touched me, sheltered there behind the dodger. The ship lifted and leaned imperceptibly, settled quietly and leaned the other way. The noise of water rushing alongside as she forged ahead would have been noticeable only if it had ceased.

There was a time when I had loved being at sea—when I was a boy, a young officer. Those had been carefree days. I had delighted in the rugged life and had wanted to see new places, new things. There was excitement in saying to myself, "Now I'm in Australia." "Is this really China?" "So this is the Land of the Rising Sun on the edge of the Far East." Those had been wonderful times. The Pacific! How lovely that ocean could be. How peaceful the water and verdant the earth; great islands with palms, brilliant flowers, gay birds and natives with their hair dyed blue and yellow and red. But I was not there now. I was on the Atlantic; nor would I wish to be any further from home. The desire to travel had worn thin. Home! That was the only place to travel to now; the one place in the world.

---

[*] From *50 North: An Atlantic Battleground* (Toronto: Paperjacks, 1980), 130–49.

How the Atlantic's grim personality, its wartime personality, brought into sharp focus those who were waiting ashore. How much dearer, more vital, they seemed to become when one was in danger. And this was not selfishness altogether. It would not be easy for them if I were lost, and I pictured with physical distress their shock at getting the news. Yes, this was what made me dislike it. I wanted to be with my family and clear of risks.

Yet there were other reasons too. Maturity had brought a hatred of discomfort. How I loathed being wet; sticky all over with salt. The dreadful jolting and tumbling when you cold not take a step without holding on. It had been fun in earlier years, but I had been softened by my years of comfort ashore. I was not really old—barely forty—but old for this job.

Why think of these things? Maybe I did not like the sea; there was no denying I hated the Atlantic, the ugliness of it, the grey dreariness, the eternal whine of the wind in the rigging. But it would not last for ever. One day the war would be over. One day, if I survived, I would be free again. Meanwhile I knew the sea better than I did the land almost and I was at home in a ship. Home! Damn that word!

Then the porpoises came. Three at first, in echelon, speeding just beneath the surface of the water towards the ship. They turned in perfect formation, like a naval squadron, and cut outward towards the curling bow wave. Then more came, fifty, a hundred, silver streaks woven in the clear black ocean. They fell in with the ship's track but at twice the speed, the young ones following their parents. They veined the water with bubbling phosphorescent pathways. They did not leap. Perhaps they would if I watched them for a while. I wondered how . . .

I came up straight . . . stood still, straining eyes and ears.

Two points abaft the beam I calculated.

"Captain, sir," came an urgent voice.

I wanted to wait a moment, to assess. Would it be in the third column, the centre column?

"Captain, sir."

"Yes, I heard it. How's your head now?"

I listened while the officer-of-the-watch asked the quarter-master.

"Two-five-six degrees, sir."

"Ring action stations."

I heard the alarm gongs ringing below and then the sound of running feet. I turned the ship towards the convoy.

"Signal from the S.O. sir, 'Operation Blueberry.'" I recognized the leading signalman's voice; he was always on his toes.

Then it was as though a hundred moons were shining on the convoy. Flare after flare burst into light high up in the sky, wavered and descended slowly, suspended by their invisible parachutes. All the water between ourselves and the ships was brilliantly lit, no submarine would escape being seen if he was under that umbrella of light.

After an interval of several minutes we turned back and stood away as we knew the others would be doing.

"*Now*," I said to the first lieutenant who was standing beside me, megaphone in hand. "Green four-oh to red four-oh, star shell, sweep."

He leaned far over the forepart of the bridge and bellowed the order to the four-inch gun's crew. There was a shrill whistle then the deep bark of the gun, then another and another between which could be heard the slam of the breech. There were the lights, like the lamps of a sloping street, spread in a neat row away ahead, each a little higher than its predecessor as they fell gently to the water. We saw our neighbouring escort coming away from the convoy's bow and we searched with glasses the water lit by her stars as well as our own. There was no submarine, no object on the sea beneath those glaring yellow orbs.

We continued for a while turning more easterly and firing star shells at intervals. Then, our distance run, we altered course to the north-west to overtake the convoy. This, we estimated, would be the best direction to take because the convoy had by now turned ninety degrees to starboard and all ships, excluding possibly those which may have been damaged, should, according to the Commodore's signals, be steering nor'-nor'-west.

We were receiving signals! This was different from the fiasco we were involved in last year when convoy movement signals never reached us.

But still we did not know what had taken place, even whether a ship had actually been torpedoed and, if one had, whereabouts in the convoy and from which direction the torpedoes had come.

"Should have word by telephone at any moment now, sir," the signal officer suggested optimistically.

"Yes," I agreed. I was glad to hear Collins say that. "But no one may know," I added, more soberly.

I had been thinking in the last few minutes what I would do. It did not take much debating because I knew at the beginning where I meant to go and only wanted to review the cons. I had been convinced for some time that in such a situation, if the U-boat was forced to dive to avoid illumination, the likely place he would go would be to the rear of the convoy. And we were in the delightful position of having steered towards the spot where the rear of the convoy had been when it was attacked.

"Not quite so dark now, is it?" Black remarked, taking his binoculars down from his eyes and looking out over the sea.

I tried to gauge it. "Perhaps not."

We were standing together on the port side of the bridge, the navigator was on the starboard side and between us were three signalmen and two lookout men. It was a small bridge to accommodate so many if we all wanted to look towards the way we were going at once, but two of the signalmen were aft a bit so there was enough room to move about a little. Collins had been coming and going between the coding office on the lower bridge and the asdic house where his second duty lay.

"The convoy'll advance a bit yet before the moon rises," I suggested.

We were endeavouring to penetrate the darkness both with our eyes and with the radar. Presently I saw something.

"Surely the convoy can't be that slow!" I exclaimed. "That's a ship I see and smoking like hell."

"Ship ahead," cried the starboard lookout.

"Yes it is, sir. A ship."

I called for a signalman to stand by with a small lamp. Half a minute passed.

"Can you see which way she's going, Pilot?" I asked. I had moved over to the starboard side to clear the foremast from my view and was now beside the navigator.

"Looks like she's crossing ahead." He spoke slowly. He was trying to define the silhouette.

"I think you're right but if she is she's not on the convoy's course."

The dim outline of a big hull beneath the thick column of black smoke pouring from her funnel, gradually became more distinct as we approached, and it soon became apparent that she was not going to cross ahead of us.

"She's stopped, Pilot, or has very little way on her."

"Signal, sir." It was West, the leading signalman.

"Yes, what is it?"

"From K129 to S.O. Believe two ships torpedoed. Am close to one still afloat. No U-boat in sight."

"Umph! I might have known he'd be there," I said, partly to the navigator and partly to myself. I knew his love for salvage work.

"He'd have been the rear escort," the navigator figured, "so would have come across any disabled ship first."

By this time we were close enough to the smoking merchantman to signal. I told the leading signalman to ask "What ship," and warned him not to use his light long in calling her up.

From where I stood I could not see any beam of light coming from the small lamp the signalman was using, so was satisfied it could not be seen far.

She lay like a black ghost as we came up and passed her a little distance off. Our eyes were used enough to the dark but, even so, we could make out little more than her shape and size and trim. No details were visible. Nor was there any sign of a corvette in the neighbourhood.

We could see she was on an even keel and had no marked list. As to damage, that was obviously hidden from us, but the huge column of inky smoke rising into the starlit sky told us of something severe below. A stopped ship at sea was always a pathetic sight to me, like a hurt and frightened animal crouching down, resigned to its fate.

Then we saw a glimmer of light from her darkened bridge and heard the signalman spelling out her name as he received the dots and dashes.

"*Loch Katrine*," the leading signalman announced.

"Make to him, 'Are you in danger of sinking.'" The message went out and before we had drawn away far the reply came back: "Think not."

We went on but not in the direction of the convoy. We would look around first; a ship torpedoed but not sunk might be attacked again. The enemy might be close by.

"Radar says he has two ships now, and one astern we've just passed and another bearing green five-five, one mile, both about the same size." The navigator had obtained the report through the voicepipe.

So neither of the two reported casualties were sunk! Unless this one was a straggler.

"Ask the radar if he can detect an escort," I said.

After a brief interval the navigator said yes, the radar operator could see something which resembled an escort near the ship on the starboard bow. This looked as though our salvage expert was investigating the condition of this other ship. I reported the name of the first we had met to the senior officer and that she was apparently not in imminent danger of sinking. I thought we would go back to her presently.

Soon matters made our course of action more definite. A further signal from the corvette K129 came in indicating that she was alongside a torpedoed ship and that another escort was in the neighbourhood picking up survivors and would render assistance, if necessary, to the ship nearby. This was the first intimation we had that another escort was in the vicinity. She was evidently the one we had recently noticed in the radar; K129 would not have been noticeable, her form would have blended into the ship alongside which she seemed to be lying.

I sent another R/T message, this time to the two ships engaged in the rescue work, "Shall screen your operations." This was plainly our duty though I would have liked, later on, to have broken off to help the cripple we had passed.

We had been warned time after time not to undertake salvage work or even rescue work without having the protection of another escort. This advice admittedly was not adhered to very closely for escort vessels were all too few and could not be spared. Not that merchant ships could be sacrificed more readily, but corvettes, if torpedoed, were almost as good as lost at once.

The injunction had obviously been disregarded by the first corvette coming on the scene and the second escort appeared to have adopted the same attitude. Placed as we were, therefore, the situation obviously demanded that we should act as their protector. So the two merchantmen were duly plotted on the chart and we commenced to circle them, passing each at about a mile distant.

The ship forged ahead at fifteen knots, faster than I would have preferred to go because of the high consumption of fuel at that speed, but we could not go slower than a quarter of a mile a minute if we were to attempt adequately to screen the ships. I sent a message to the senior officer informing him of what we were doing. I thought he would not welcome the absence of three escorts from his group but hoped he would not recall us before our partners had completed their work.

As I stood searching the sea ahead and on either side with my glasses, I wondered how the convoy was getting on, whether it had been attacked again—we had neither seen nor heard anything. I was vaguely concerned as to whether it had turned back on to its original course yet. We had had no signal that it had. It could not continue long in that formation, advancing in a long line on a narrow front. It was just past 2300 now and only an hour since the attack, so the convoy could not be more than ten miles from us. It would not be hard to overtake now but if we remained here long, we might have difficulty in finding it and quite a job to catch it, for every hour delayed would take two hours to make good. I supposed that these escorts would be finished in half an hour or so, then we would all go on. But I was not concerned really, except that I would have liked to have seen if there was any salvaging to be done. I had always had a hankering for a towing job, though likely enough these ships were past towing.

The first lieutenant went below to see that everything was in order and I asked him to inform the stations at the same time how the situation stood. He returned in about fifteen minutes to report that all was well.

"No light showing anywhere?" I asked.

"No," he said, tucking his muffler tighter into his duffle coat. Then, nodding in the direction of the ships, "Any word from these fellows yet?"

"No."

"Won't talk more than they can help, I guess."

"No."

"They have a calm enough sea for the job."

"Yes, they have."

"Damn persistent, these U-boats." Black was looking through his glasses.

"Yes, damn persistent, but what a night to wait for!"

"It amazes me how they get away with it."

"Sickening, isn't it?" I agreed.

Presently I asked Black if he had looked in the galley when he was down. He had.

"The fire was drawn, I suppose?"

"Yes, sir."

In a little while we saw on the starboard beam the black column of smoke again and the plot indicated that the derelict had not moved since we had first come upon her. The radar bearing of it was checked with the visual bearing and it coincided—the antennae was not out of alignment. We worked round it keeping a mile or so off.

I looked at the sky. Light cirro-cumulus clouds were moving slowly from the west, sometimes covering the stars and then revealing them. The night was clear, as good a night as it had been a day. I calculated the time of moonrise, it would be a little before 0100.

After some minutes the other ship came into view; she also seemed to be still. We could not see any escorts but that was hardly to be expected because they were small and their camouflage would make them less visible. But the radar could not pick them up either. They must be right in close to one or other of the merchantmen which would obliterate them from the radar. As we pressed on, the stricken ship came abeam to starboard, standing out more clearly than the first, but began to fade as we dropped her back on the quarter.

I heard the navigator acknowledge a report from the radar operator.

"Radar contact red four-oh, mile and a quarter, sir."

His voice came with a note of urgency in it.

A few paces took me to the port side. The first lieutenant followed.

"Tell him to hold it and we'll put it ahead," I called over my shoulder to the navigator, and to the rating at the wheelhouse voicepipe, "How's her head?"

I had my glasses on the smooth, dark water beyond the port bow. Almost immediately the answer came back:

"Oh seven five, sir."

"Port fifteen. . . . Steady on oh three five."

I turned my head subconsciously to the right to compensate for the quick swing of the ship to port so that I could keep my eye on the compass bearing of the reported object. Once or twice I looked over the top of my binoculars to glance at the bow of the ship to make sure I was directing my gaze ahead.

"Red one-oh, one mile" came the report from the radar. Ten degrees on the port bow.

"Steer oh-two-five."

"Object's small but getting larger," called the navigator repeating the radar operator's report.

"Can you see anything, Number one?" I asked.

"Not yet, sir."

"Ought to be showing soon. Stand by for star shell."

He passed the order and had his binoculars back to his eyes in seconds.

"Radar says about ahead now, sir, three quarters of mile. Going into the ground wave."

Curse these glasses, I thought, why can't I see through them? But it was like looking for a black spider on a dark wall.

"There it is! A bit to starboard!"

I took a quick glance at the first lieutenant to see exactly which way his glasses were pointing. Then I looked again and this time I saw it.

"Submarine, I think, sir," Black said slowly, quite steadily.

I looked hard.

"Looks more like a fishing trawler to me."

Surely, I thought, that's a trawler. High in the bow and high aft. We're on the edge of the Banks, too. No. That's not her stern, she's high amidships. It's her bridge, her conning tower! Now I can see her stern. It's low. It's a submarine! Beam on.

"Full ahead."

The order was instantly passed. Tenseness reigned. The engine-room would be tense, too. Full speed meant an emergency.

"Fire, Number One."

A shrill whistle sounded and I shut my eyes. Then the gun went off and I opened them again. After what seemed like a long wait the star shell burst. There she was! A U-boat silhouetted against the falling ball of light.

I had no need of my binoculars now. The U-boat lay broadside on, about fifteen degrees on the starboard bow, less than four hundred yards away. Her bow was pointing directly across our course and I saw a short boiling wake at her stern—she had obviously just got under-way and was working her propellers at full speed.

I altered course five degrees to starboard. Was that enough? Was it too much? Was she diving? Yes.

"Fire again."

I gripped the rail and watched the U-boat. Then a blinding flash came before my eyes. I had failed to obey my own orders. When the gunlayer blew his whistle before he pressed the trigger all eyes were to be shut. So intent had I been that I did not hear the whistle and the gunflash momentarily blinded me. I had to give up temporarily and hope that my vision would be restored quickly.

"Take over, Pilot, I can't see. She needs to come a little more to star-board, I think."

I felt for him with my left hand and touched his sleeve. He made a small alteration of course to starboard. I stared and blinked alternately and felt desperate.

"Is she going down?" I asked the navigator.

"Yes," he replied.

Then came Burley's voice close by me.

"Shall I fire a snowflake now, sir?"

"Yes," I answered.

God bless that man, I thought; he never forgets!

A moment later there was a swoosh and up went the rocket. Five sec-onds elapsed, then it was as though a great arc lamp had been switched on. The rocket had exploded ejecting its brilliant flare a thousand feet above.

I saw again. The U-boat was still before us, fine on the starboard bow, barely a ship's length away. But the upper part of her conning tower only was showing now.

"Stand by to ram!"

Then, hardly dropping my voice, "Set pattern A."

The asdic officer heard and passed the order on.

Would we make it? Would we reach her in time? We were desper-ately close.

In the pool of light shed by the flare we saw the U-boat's conning tower disappear. Our bow was almost on her, almost in the luminous whirlpool where her conning tower had been, the great white wake showing the short straight course she had steered—she had had no time to turn before she dived and she could not dive and turn as well.

In three seconds the bow cut the disturbed water. I waited for the crash. Another thirty feet . . . it did not come. The streak of foaming, whirling water was beneath the gun deck now. I heard no grind of steel nor felt the keel touch. Now it was beneath the foremast.

"Fire."

Collins caught my shouted word. "Fire one—Fire two—Fire three"—he intoned as he pressed the buzzers. Neil and his men aft would respond instantly to the ringing bells.

I looked over the port side. The disturbed water did not extend beyond the ship on that side. The flare fell into the water astern and all was blackness.

I jumped to the starboard wing of the bridge. The streak was abreast of the after gun platform, its phosphorescence making it as clear as a white line on a highway. Then there were simultaneous explosions.

Four seconds later there were two more. The ship shook violently.

I turned and looked ahead but I would not have seen anything if there had been something there. I was shaking badly and I felt rather weak and my mouth was dry. I wanted a smoke of my pipe. I had failed to ram him— even to hit him. If we had touched him we would surely have felt it; and to scrape him would have done more damage to us than to the vessel below.

The only way was to hit him squarely with the stem, and that I did not do. I felt disappointed. But mostly I felt relief.

"How far have we gone since firing?" I asked the plotting rating, speaking through the asdic house window.

"A thousand yards," he replied after a moment.

"I'll turn now and see if you can pick him up," I said to Collins.

We turned and steamed back on a more or less reciprocal course but allowing for the movement of the submarine in the direction we had last seen him going. In a minute or so the asdic officer reported he had contact. He and the operator held it and we ran in and fired five charges. We thought it was a pretty accurate attack.

But something else was more intriguing. A strong smell of diesel oil came to us. We all remarked about it at once and looked over the side to see if any oil was visible on the water. It was too dark to see anything and we soon ran out of it. This immediately started conjecture on the bridge. Obviously it was from the U-boat.

Presently we came back again and regained underwater contact. Although it was fading and uncertain we let go ten charges set to explode deep. The sweet odour of diesel oil was heavy in the air on this run in, and by the length of time we took to pass through it, it was evident that it had spread over a much wider area.

A few minutes later Neil, the torpedo officer, appeared on the bridge. He was breathing fast.

"What are you doing here?" I asked, wondering why he had left his post when we were using depth charges.

"It was the finest thing I ever saw, sir! Think we are wasting ammunition now."

"What do you mean?"

"Why! Didn't you see it?"

"See what?"

"Didn't you see what happened on the first attack?" he queried incredulously.

Then he told the story.

The depth charge from the starboard thrower sank fifty feet and then exploded, as did the others. It must have touched the U-boat's after deck as it went off, for a moment later the bow of the U-boat broke surface a few feet astern. She rose up out of the water to an angle of about forty degrees exposing one-third of her long slender hull. Her momentum was still carrying her forward at right angles to our course. As she hung for an instant poised in this precarious position, a depth charge which had been dropped over the stern rail exploded immediately beneath her and she disappeared in the huge column of water.

"She'll never surface again, sir," Neil concluded.

I was dumbfounded. What I had tried to do as a secondary action had succeeded.

We resumed the patrol.

An hour later the moon came up behind light clouds and the ships at once became clearly visible and at a much greater distance. This was not good if other submarines were about but we did not know whether the ships were abandoned or not, we had had no further word from the two escorts. If we did not hear, the only thing we could do was to continue to screen them until the morning when we would see what had been done or what there was left to do. I did not care to break silence with a signal now asking how the situation stood.

The moon made it light enough now to recognize people on the bridge and it was at this time that I saw the chief engineer emerging from the shadow of the asdic house. He had neither coat nor cap on, which was unusual for him when he came to the bridge.

"Captain, sir?" he said in his inquiring sort of way.

"Yes, Chief."

"Can you reduce speed yet, sir?"

"Why? Anything wrong?"

"I've got a hot bearing down below, sir, and it's good and hot. I've been running the fire hose on it for the last hour but that ain't good for it."

"Why, no it isn't," I said.

Lloyd was a great chap. He would keep the engines going fast if he thought I really needed it and adopt any measure within reason before admitting defeat. But I knew it was against his principles and very distasteful to him to run salt water on bearings. The bearing must be very hot! I had put half speed on the telegraph again after the emergency was over but I had kept a speed of nearly sixteen knots by ordering it on the revolution indicator.

"I'm sorry, Chief. If I'd known you had trouble I'd have gone slower. To what speed do you want me to reduce?"

"A hundred and thirty revs would do it, I think, if you don't mind," said the chief, hating to ask for it.

"Why, yes, that'll be all right. Let me know soon if it's cooling down."

I asked the navigator to decrease the revolutions accordingly.

"She'll cool down, sir. If she don't I'll tell you."

Then he burst out, "Sir, I could've touched it with me hand. That submarine, I mean. She came up that close to the stern I could've stretched out me hand and touched her. Could've spat aboard of her. Black all over she seemed to be—bottom and all."

"Close as all that? You were on deck?"

"Why, sir, I just came up from the engine-room to see what was doing and then . . . it was just happening. I thought she might've taken our rudder off as she came up. It was wonderful! Just wonderful, sir!"

He hesitated, seeming to feel that he might have expressed himself rather exuberantly.

"Well, I must get along below. Thank you, sir," and off he went.

Twice we passed through the patch of diesel oil but could see no wreckage. It could hardly be expected that we should, because small objects on the water would most likely escape the keenest eye, however bright the night.

At 0130 it became foggy and before long the visibility was no more than three hundred yards. The air grew chilly and wet and the moon, as it rose higher, spread a gloom over the ship as its light partially penetrated the vaporous ceiling. We went to the second degree of readiness which released one or two men from the various stations to fetch coats or oilskins for the others and make cocoa or soup, and it permitted the cook to light the galley fire for a short while and the gunlayer to send for his trousers—he had just finished washing down his lower half when the alarm had sounded and in his hurry could not find them. I passed word to slow down to six knots, because there would be practically no danger now to the disabled ships— fog was our greatest protector. We would jog along until daylight if the fog remained, which it probably would, and if nothing untoward developed I would perhaps send half the men below to stand by in less discomfort. It was always a question to know when it was safe to belay action-stations. This lesser speed, too, would give the hot bearing a further chance.

The slow speed was a relief to the men in the boiler rooms. Four hours at stations, most of it at high speed requiring full pressure, was trying. The stokers had sweated copiously as they tended the burners behind the blazing furnaces, changing them as they carbonned up.

There was the feed pump to watch too, and the fan. But there were still moments when a stoker could stand back from the face of the furnace and have a word with the P.O.

The stoker P.O. in Number 2 boiler room was a steady type and he knew the value of public relations. They were down in a steel compartment, a cofferdam from upper deck to keel, sealed off from the rest of the ship. They could see nothing of what was going on. But they could feel the sea in the small pendulum motion of the boiler room, and they could feel the sudden violence of exploding depth charges, as though they were just beneath the steel plates they were standing on. The stoker P.O., however, had his small means of communication.

This was a voicepipe connecting the engine-room with both boiler-rooms, and the engineers posted a man to pass any information which could be gleaned during an action through to the stokers, as long as a man could be spared. Thus when an attack was about to be made the bridge told the engine-room and they told the P.O. in the boiler-room. But the bridge sometimes forgot and then it seemed to those below that they were being torpedoed, until the multiple detonations convinced them that they were not.

We had come into the oil again and the smell of it was as strong as ever. We were supposed, according to instructions, to obtain a sample of any oil which had been expelled from a submarine and I had been speaking about it to the first lieutenant earlier. But it was not easy to pick up samples of diesel oil. However, now that we were going slowly Black thought he could get it.

"Where are you going to try it, Number One?" I asked.

"On the port side of the upper deck, I think, beneath the bridge. So if you want me I'll be right handy."

He sent for the chief bosun's mate and went below.

The navigator and I stood in the port wing of the bridge, coats buttoned up, hands in our pockets. We were talking in a desultory sort of way. He was hungry. So was I. I said that Burley usually had a sandwich for me when I was up, and a cup of cocoa.

"I don't think he will tonight," the navigator remarked. "He's hurt his hand."

"Not when he fired that snowflake?"

"No, before that. When he was coming up after the alarm went."

"Bad?"

"Broken or sprained perhaps." The navigator tucked his muffler tighter into his sheepskin. "He stayed up here just the same and passed your wheel orders and fired the rocket but he was pretty uncomfortable, I guess. Said one of the lads going down from the bridge to his station knocked him down the ladder as he was coming up—it was dark, you know—and he landed across the small arms hatch. Lucky he didn't break his back."

"Yes. Tough luck. Hope it doesn't put him out."

It was very quiet. The breeze had died out with the fog and the small bow wave could hardly be heard—an occasional lap, that was all. Heavy drops of moisture fell now and then from the rigging and made little sounds as they hit the deck. We could faintly hear the turn of the asdic wheel.

The sick-berth attendant crept on to the bridge on the other side and whispered to Leading Signalman West that he had strapped up Burley's hand. He had had a casualty!

"That's good, Tiffy. Any bones broken?"

"I don't think so but he won't be able to use the signal lamp for a while."

West looked at his friend with envy in his eyes. "Gee! I'd like to get below for a smoke."

The S.B.A. looked across the bridge and then behind him. "I've got one here," he whispered, moving a hand in his coat pocket.

"Alight? Hell! You fool! What did you come on deck for with that?"

The S.B.A. suddenly felt sensitive.

"All right. Come here," said the leading signalman in an undertone.

Behind the asdic house the S.B.A. took his hand carefully out of his pocket. West cupped the prohibited light in both hands and drew in, sucking its balm down his windpipe. He looked up at the misty vault overhead as he slowly let the thin smoke out of his lungs. Then he pushed the half-burned thing back into his friend's hand.

"Best I ever had, chum! Now you better bugger off down, quick."

The leading signalman resumed his stand. He was smiling. Tension had dropped away.

The radar operator called again. I could hear quite distinctly what he was saying to the navigator through the voice pipe from where I stood.

"I've just started up again, sir," came the voice, "and I think there's something in the ground wave. It's too close to get the direction."

I stood up against the dodger and looked ahead.

"Keep a sharp look-out there," I sang out to the look-outs and signalmen on the bridge. "Radar reports something close."

"You're not sure?" I heard the navigator say down the pipe. Then he said to me, "He's not certain at all, he just thinks." The radar was either right or wrong to the navigator.

"Tell the wheelhouse to stand by the telegraph," I said.

I peered into the fog, glasses were no use, they only magnified the vapour. I naturally looked in the direction in which we were going because that was where our greatest risk of collision lay.

Two minutes passed. I remained still, looking, listening. Then I heard a shout from the deck below.

"Submarine on the port beam."

It was Black's voice.

I turned instantly and saw it; a U-boat, fully surfaced, lying motionless, no more than a hundred and thirty yards away. She was a little before the beam and her bow was pointing almost towards us showing the fore part of her starboard side at a fine angle. A backdrop of fog hung behind her grey, shadowy conning tower.

"Full ahead! Hard aport! Port beam—submarine—open fire!" The gun was already loaded.

Then the first lieutenant was up. He was yelling at the gun's crew.

"Rain her fast. Red eight-oh. Shoot when you're on."

He looked along the bridge rail then down at the gun again.

"Red nine-oh. Swing her round!" he shouted.

"Come on! Get her on!" I called back to Black as I glanced down at the gun barrel and back at the high, blunt-nosed bow of the still, silent craft. The guntrainer was coming around but ninety degrees was a long way to wind a four-inch quickly.

The ship glided slowly on. She could not pick up headway swiftly like a destroyer. And she was too sluggish on the helm at this speed to turn fast— there was little point in it, anyway; the enemy was inside our turning circle.

The U-boat was end-on now, wraiths of mist passing over her fore deck and before her superstructure farther back. Her hawsepipes resembled great eyes staring at us.

The navigator muttered what I was thinking, "Hope she doesn't let loose."

She was drawing abaft the beam but either the gunlayer or trainer, or both, could not find her. The dimness of the foggy night made it difficult for them. Then the submarine drew just abaft the safety bearing and the gun could not reach any farther. Perhaps three-quarters of a minute had gone by since she had first been seen.

Then there was a colossal sound of escaping air, as though the top of a high pressure chamber had been blown off, and the U-boat went down like a stone.

She had made no forward movement, had obviously vented all her ballast tanks at once. One moment she was there, fully buoyant, the next she was gone. She submerged so quickly that I could hardly believe my eyes as I looked at the empty sea with the curtain of fog beyond.

The ship was at last gathering way and as she did so ten charges were dropped set to explode at varying depths. But our distance from the submarine was too great to inflict a fatal wound, the best they could have done was to have shaken her, perhaps badly, with her negative stability. An enemy report was sent out on the wireless.

We ran away for a thousand yards or more so that we could place ourselves suitably for an asdic attack but when we came back we could not establish contact. We spent half an hour around the spot where the U-boat had submerged but failed to obtain the slightest indication of her presence.

It was not that the submarine could have got out of range so quickly, it was a matter of water conditions. She was under a thermal layer which the asdic could not penetrate. We expanded our radius but still could find no trace of the enemy.

Her commander had evidently surfaced his boat not ten minutes before we had encountered her. The radar was obliged to shut down for five minutes every half-hour to cool the motor and it must have been during this interval that she had come to the surface. Had she not been submerged before the radar was switched off, she would have been detected. The German on the hydrophones obviously had not heard our propeller before she came up, and this may have been because it was turning slowly, although I would have thought that he should have heard it. Possibly he did not listen very attentively. I did not think it was a case of his hearing the beat of a propeller close to and the captain deciding to come up and torpedo the ship to which it belonged, in spite of the fact that our revolutions at this time equalled those of the average merchant vessel travelling at normal speed. Had this been his intention, we would have received the benefit of his idea. It appeared to me that he was taken completely by surprise and was intent on making a rapid escape.

Up to this time I had not known that a submarine could submerge without going ahead of her engines, which, with the hydrophones set to dive, would drive her down. I had never been told of this practice or read of it. But I knew it now. I found out afterwards, after much inquiry, that a U-boat could submerge without moving ahead if she vented all her tanks simultaneously, including her emergency tanks if a hasty descent was called for, but that this would not be done except in dire necessity. To this U-boat the necessity had been dire.

Now I knew for certain that danger lurked in the offing. If the fog lifted it would be very potent.

We had failed to sink the latest member of Admiral Doenitz' fleet, or even inflict damage on her. Could we have done either? Had I slipped up somewhere? Was it lack of preparedness? How many C.O.'s asked themselves the same questions during the war!

I thought about it for a bit, standing on the inevitable bridge staring into the fog. The only thing I could have wished was that the gun had gone off. It was a great pity the layer and trainer had been unable to bring the gun to bear, but it was not their fault. I knew that. They had to see to fire. I could not say I wished we had been in a different relative position because there was not a better one, unless it was 150 yards farther over and we had accidentally crashed into the boat. But our speed would have been too slow to have even cracked her pressure hull. It was not for want of skill or effort afterwards that the asdic ratings did not hear a submarine echo.

We would never find ourselves so near a U-boat again—or so I thought.

section 4

POST-1945

o

L ike the Great War before it, the Second World War profoundly altered Canada's position in the community of nations and the nature of its armed forces. These changes were accelerated by the general devastation of large portions of Europe and Asia, which placed the Canadian economy in an extremely powerful position, and by the polarization of the globe into two mutually antagonistic socio-economic systems.

The pre-1939 view that "Canada lived in a fireproof house far from inflamable materials" was replaced by the view—born of 100 000 dead in two wars—that what happened elsewhere was of prime interest to Canada. The Canadian government chose to exercise its influence in organizations devoted to collective security, like the UN and NATO. Such institutions permitted smaller nations, like Canada, the Netherlands, Denmark, and Australia, to balance the dominant power of Britain, France, and, more importantly, the US in issues affecting the security of the west. More practically, the post-war world called for careful management lest a spark ignite another global conflagration. It was not always possible for the lesser states to completely redirect superpower interests, but sitting at the table and being in-the-know helped.

For the armed forces this activist foreign policy resulted in the growth of standing forces and overseas activity on an unprecedented scale. Post-war retrenchment gave way by the 1950s to the largest ever peacetime expansion, until by the end of the decade the permanent professional forces eclipsed the militia in size. Participation in foreign adventures that just a generation before would have been unthinkable now became a matter of course. By 1953 the regular forces had mushroomed to over 100 000 all ranks, and over the previous three years the defence budget had quadrupled. When the dust settled, the army had twelve permanent force infantry battalions and four armoured regiments organized into brigades and— briefly—a reinstated First Canadian Division. Two of these brigades were stationed overseas with NATO and in Korea, and plans were made to reinforce the NATO commitment in the event of a general war.

The RCN and RCAF also underwent unprecedented peacetime growth. The navy found a role largely in the Atlantic within NATO doing the same anti-submarine and trade escort duties which it had performed during the war. However, this time a large modern fleet, including an aircraft carrier and state-of-the-art anti-submarine destroyers, was acquired, wartime vessels were recalled from reserve and an air service developed. Naval exercises by the early 1960s involved as many as thirty RCN warships and over 10 000 personnel at sea. But of all the services, postwar expansion brought the biggest initial gains to the RCAF. In an age when the fear of long-range bombers carrying nuclear weapons dominated, air superiority was crucial to survival and long-term mobilization. It was agreed that an air force—like the navy—could not be easily improvised in an emergency. Thus by the end of the 1950s the RCAF was, numerically, the largest of the three permanent services, with over a thousand aircraft, an air division in Germany and considerable responsibility under the recently signed NORAD agreement, all supported by a large indigenous aircraft industry.

The maintenance of such large standing forces could not last. The Canadian economy could not sustain the burden, and increasingly the object of Western defence planning was the avoidance of war, rather than preparing to fight one. As early as the mid-1950s, plans for the militia already saw them reduced to civil defence tasks, and by the 1960s, with the abandonment of large-scale mobilization plans for protracted war, a viable role for the militia had all but disappeared. A major reduction in the number of militia units and their strengths occurred in 1963 and by the 1970s what had been for hundreds of years a part of the social fabric of Canada had dwindled into obscurity. Canada's new breed of professional soldier, sailor, and flier were called upon to maintain a high level of operational readiness and competence in order to keep the threshold of nuclear war as high as possible. That same professionalism also allowed Canadian troops to quickly earn international respect for their leading role in the new task of "peacekeeping."

During the 1960s the size and relatively modern equipment of the forces gave them considerable credibility in their tasks. However, by the end of the decade they had been completely reshaped. Paul Hellyer's 1964 White Paper attempted to address the problems of shrinking budgets first by "integration" of the armed forces, a process widely supported, and ultimately through the "unification," a policy bitterly opposed. As with many unpalatable plans, unification was sold on the grounds of leaner, but better equipped forces. The Forces were unified, officially, on 1 February 1968 without much fanfare.

The net result of the re-organization and promises was a much smaller, dis-spirited and little better equipped Canadian Armed Forces. Major cutbacks followed under the Trudeau administration. Canada's commitment to NATO fell from 10 000 to half that, and the total force strength dropped to about 80 000. In addition, new "French Language Units" were introduced into the regular force structure. Two major wars, several minor ones, and an alliance dominated by the British and Americans had all but confirmed the Canadian forces as anglophone institutions for a century. At the end of the 1960s French Canadians were welcomed back into the armed forces of their country.

Implementation of the recommendations of the Bilingualism and Biculturalism Commission was only a foretaste of what the Trudeau years held in store. His revolution in defence and foreign policy turned Canadian emphasis first to sovereignty, requiring presence more than procurement. Thus the 1970s witnessed the virtually unchecked "rust-out" of the Canadian Forces. New tanks, jet fighters, and maritime patrol aircraft were purchased, but increasingly Canada's NATO forces were simply hostages to fortune: a demonstration of Canadian willingness to die in defence of Europe, but not to spend money doing so. By the 1980s the advent of new missiles and the general disbelief in the plausibility of nuclear war forced a major increase in the value of conventional deterrence in Europe. Unfortunately, the Canadian Forces were now so far behind that neither Liberal nor Tory governments could afford the equipment needed. A modest re-equipment program, including new ships for a navy that could no longer defend even itself, began in the last of the Trudeau years and was pursued cautiously by the Mulroney government. The Torys' more ambitious plans for re-equipping the Forces, announced in the 1987 White Paper, were undone by the collapse of communism at the end of the 1980s and the unification of Germany. Canadians, who had spent their "peace dividend" in the 1970s now began to balk at defence expenditures, and the government, caught in its own debt crisis, cut deeper into its own defence budget. In 1991 the government announced its intention to close bases in Germany and bring the troops home, though retaining a commitment to send a brigade to NATO in the event of an emergency. Much like the re-organization of the 1960s, that of the 1990s was sold on the potential savings which could be channelled into new equipment purchases, the promise of a leaner more mobile force, and a greater commitment to help in the brush-fire wars of the world. What the expeditionary brigade will look like, what kind of war it will be able to fight, and how it will get there all remain mysteries. The one saving grace in all this, perhaps, is the "Total Force Concept," the re-integration of the reserves into the regular force structure.

Participation in the UN-sanctioned Gulf War of 1990–91 represented a major departure from nearly a century of Canadian military expeditions. For the first time no ground forces, apart from those needed to support naval and air operations, were committed to a war. The army, eager to participate, found it hard to sit idle while their NATO colleagues prepared for battle. But in the end, Canada fought a war without a single fatality: what would Mackenzie King have thought? Ironically, the Gulf War was quickly followed by the largest and most dangerous Canadian "peacekeeping" operation yet undertaken, the dispatch of several thousand troops to the Balkans. In an unsettled post-Cold War world it seems that the demands on Canada's soldiers, sailors, and fliers are likely to increase, and the dangers they face will grow. So far they have been up to the challenge.

PEACEKEEPING: THE MID-EAST AND INDO-CHINA ⬦

J.L. GRANATSTEIN AND D. BERCUSON

○

The Korean War had been an example, not of peacekeeping, but of collective security. There is a world of difference between the two. The chief object of peacekeeping is to keep two potential combatants separated while diplomatic efforts are mounted to resolve their conflict; the aim of collective security is to stop an aggressor, by force if necessary.

There were no instances of U.N.-sponsored collective security from 1953 to 1990. As long as the Cold War divided the Great Powers into two armed camps, each jockeying to expand its theatre of influence and each deeply suspicious of the other's every move, there could not be enough agreement or trust to allow a collective-security action. But peacekeeping was possible, at least in those instances where the Great Powers were not directly involved.

Over the next forty years there were many such cases, as the U.N. tried to maintain the precarious balance of peace. In a world increasingly dominated by superpowers and military blocs armed with nuclear weapons of terrifying power, the need to control small wars before they exploded into great crises was apparent, and military observers from many nations donned sky-blue berets with U.N. badges and disinterestedly tried to damp down conflict and steer feuding opponents to the conference table.

Even these peacekeeping operations might not have been possible had the U.N. not found a way around the monopoly of the Great Powers. The Security Council had been able to take steps to deal with North Korea's aggression only because the Soviet Union happened to be boycotting the council and hence did not cast its inevitable veto. The next time there was

⬦ "The Mid-East and Indo-China," chap. 7 from *War and Peacekeeping: From South Africa to the Gulf—Canada's Limited Wars* (Toronto: Key Porter Books Ltd., 1991), 188–208.

an international crisis, however, the U.S.S.R. or some other Great Power might block any U.N. action. The answer was the "Uniting for Peace" resolution of November 1950, which authorized transfer of responsibility for collective security to the General Assembly—where the West had a clear majority at the time—when a Security Council response was blocked by a veto. At last what Pearson called the "irresponsible and unprincipled use of the veto" could be circumvented. The U.N.'s member states, and not just the Great Powers, now had the capacity to act if necessary.

Curiously, Canada's Cold War rearmament, which quadrupled the size of the armed forces within a few years of the outbreak of war in Korea, provided the country with the ability to play a major role in peacekeeping in the years that followed. Because the Canadian forces thought of war in Europe as their first priority, Canada built up a balanced mix of forces. In addition to infantry, which virtually every nation could supply, there were military engineers, communications specialists, and ordinance and supply officers capable of managing sophisticated inventories and getting them to troops in the field. The air force had pilots experienced on both light aircraft and large transports, as well as skilled ground crew technicians to keep them flying. And though the navy was largely geared to anti-submarine warfare, the fleet could carry troops and equipment long distances in a pinch. The forces also had the capacity to function in both French and English, though that skill was less developed than it would be three decades later. These were formidable advantages, and when they were combined with the high reputation Ottawa's diplomats had built around the world for a distinctive committed impartiality, they virtually guaranteed that Canada would be called on whenever the United Nations moved towards peacekeeping. In fact, Canadians are so used to seeing their troops as neutral enforcers of the peace that they tend to forget the country's role in Korea. That is one reason why Korea remains largely an unknown war to Canadians, to this day.

THE MIDDLE-EAST MORASS

Canada's first forays into U.N. peacekeeping had come before the Korean War. A few Canadian officers had served as observers along the borders between India and Pakistan, in Jammu and Kashmir, in the bloody years after those two states became independent of Britain in 1948, in the operation known as the U.N. Military Observer Group India-Pakistan (UNMOGIP). (In 1965–66 Canadians would also join the U.N. India-Pakistan Observation Mission—UNIPOM—along the rest of the India-Pakistan border.) The presence of the U.N. did not bring any lasting peace—more than four decades later, hostilities and bloodshed still erupt from time to time—yet the presence of impartial observers has lessened the violence, and has likely saved many lives.

The conflict between Israel and its Arab neighbours, and the persistent tensions between Israelis and Palestinians, have created an equally intractable situation—and a potential conflict between the Great Powers, who, in varying degrees at different points, have supported their client states. During the First World War the British had gained control of Palestine and had promised to create a Jewish national state, but by 1947 Britain was looking for a way out of Palestine, and although the U.N. tried to establish an administration that could take over, its efforts were fruitless. Fighting between Jews and Arabs began after the U.N. passed a resolution calling for the partition of Palestine; after Israel proclaimed its independence in 1948, hostilities intensified. After the opposing sides accepted a thirty-day Security Council ceasefire, Belgium, France, and the United States—three nations with consular offices in Palestine's capital, Jerusalem—sent military observers into the area, but the war carried on in fits and starts until January 1949. Subsequently, Israel signed armistice agreements with Egypt, Lebanon, Jordan, and Syria, and to monitor these agreements the Security Council set up the U.N. Truce Supervision Organization (UNTSO) with fifty officers. The idea was that Mixed Armistice Commissions (MACs) would investigate incidents. But there were far more incidents than there were UNTSO officers to investigate them, and by 1953 tension on the Arab-Israeli borders had increased as guerrilla attacks inevitably produced retaliatory strikes. A spiral of escalating violence had begun.

The answer was to increase UNTSO's strength, and at this point Canada became involved. Four army officers were seconded to the Department of External Affairs for a one-year tour of duty in February 1954, and several months later Canada agreed that General E.L.M. Burns, who had commanded the 5th Canadian Armoured Division and I Canadian Corps in Italy during the Second World War and had subsequently become deputy minister of Veterans Affairs, could become chief of staff of UNTSO.

Born in 1897, Burns had attended the Royal Military College and had served overseas during the Great War with distinction. He had stayed in the army between the wars, earning a reputation as an officer with an uncommonly good mind. Able though he was, he was a stiff man, and no inspiring commander; while his staff respected him, he won little affection. Nor was he much admired by the Israelis or the Arabs. For one thing, he set out to learn Arabic but not Hebrew. His reason? The Israelis could communicate with him in English, French, or German, but the Arab officers, for the most part, spoke no other language. There was practicality there, but perhaps a lack of sensitivity.

In fairness, however, Burns' work was a task of almost unrelieved frustration. As he wrote later, the armistice agreements "contained certain vague statements and compromises, essential to secure the signature of both sides, given the circumstances of 1949. It was hoped then that the difficult points would be settled in peace negotiations after a relatively short period. . . . " But there were no negotiations—and there would be none until after three more wars—and instead "there were disputes about the interpretation of the armistice agreements. . . . All the while, both sides violated, or failed to observe the agreements, in more or less serious ways." Burns tried to be impartial, but "before I had been long in the Middle East, I learned that no matter how hard one tried to be objective and impartial, if one accepted the views of one side on any matter, the other side accused one of partiality."

In this hornets' nest of suspicion, Burns and his UNTSO officers were caught in the middle, desperately trying to keep peace amid the shooting. In August 1955, for example, the Egyptians accepted UNTSO's requests for a ceasefire and agreed to halt *fedayeen* raids launched by Palestinians dispossessed of their homes by the Israelis. But the *fedayeen* guerrillas carried no radios and could not be reached once they had crossed into Israel, and so the raids went on. In revenge, the Israelis sent an armoured unit into the Gaza Strip, destroyed a police station and a hospital under construction, and fired indiscriminately into a village. "I had the feeling I was trying to stop a runaway truck on a steep hill by throwing stones under the wheels," Burns said. The Egyptians said thirty-six had been killed and thirteen wounded; the Israelis claimed they had hit the police station because that was the point from which the raids had been launched. All-out war was averted, but only barely.

Despite complaints from both sides, Burns' impartiality was impeccable. Whether that was true of all his officers was another question. Canadian diplomats were told repeatedly that UNTSO officers arrived in the Middle East pro-Israeli but invariably departed pro-Arab. It was also said that officers and U.N. officials "spoke in openly critical terms of Israel." As for Burns, when he wrote his book *Between Arab and Israeli* he took pains to point out in his preface that it was possible to oppose Israeli policy without being anti-Semitic.

Normally each officer spent half his one-year term on the Israel-Syria MAC and half on the Israel-Jordan MAC. Observers lived in fixed observation posts for four or five days and then had a day off; much of their time was spent conducting investigations or monitoring radio transmissions. As is often the case with military service, there was discomfort of a high order. One Canadian, returning to his quarters after being pinned down in his observation post by mortar fire, took his boots off and was promptly bitten by a poisonous snake.

By 1958, after the 1956 war between Israel and Egypt had screwed tensions higher still, there were fourteen Canadians, the largest national contingent in UNTSO, which included Swedish, American, Norwegian, French, Danish, Australian, Belgian, and Dutch officers. The next year, the number was increased to seventeen.

Their work often put UNTSO team members in peril. Two Canadian officers were injured in a mine explosion in 1956, and one of those officers, Lieutenant-Colonel George Flint, was killed by Jordanian fire two years later. The U.N. report said Flint had gone to the Israeli sector under a white flag in response to a complaint that the Israelis were firing at a Jordanian village. He died from a single shot fired by a Jordanian sniper.

UNTSO's worth is difficult to appraise. It could not prevent the Suez crisis of 1956, nor could it move the parties towards peace talks. The Israelis often complained that the observers did not stop incidents or protect Israeli citizens; moreover, they claimed, UNTSO's very existence inhibited progress towards a permanent settlement. But UNTSO did provide a medium that let the Israelis and Arabs talk to each other and reach local ceasefires. Useful or not, UNTSO continues to this day, and Canadians continue to serve in it.

PEARSON'S TRIUMPH

The Suez crisis began in Cairo, Paris, and London. The 160-kilometre Suez Canal, which connects the Mediterranean to the Red Sea and is critical for Europe's oil supplies, was owned by Britain and France. When Egypt's President Gamal Abdal Nasser nationalized the canal in July 1956 there was outrage in London; the French fighting against rebellious Algerians, similarly feared the new Arab militancy, and the leaders of the two nations began planning a joint military strike that would topple Nasser and put them in occupation of the canal. In London especially, Nasser inexplicably was seen as another Hitler—much as Saddam Hussein would be thirty-five years later—and politicians and the press talked wildly of the necessity to avoid another Munich. Egypt in 1956 wasn't Germany of 1938, but none seemed to realize this. In September the French conceived the stratagem of involving the Israelis, who looked on Nasser as the major supporter of Palestinian guerrilla activities, and members of Prime Minister David Ben Gurion's government, eager to seize the opportunity to hit their main enemy, were brought into the planning.

During the last week in October, while the United States was in the final days of a presidential election campaign and the attention of the world was fixed on the anti-Communist revolt in Hungary, Israel began to mobilize its armed forces. On 29 October the Israelis sent their armour into the Sinai desert, an action that was greeted, according to plan, by a joint British-French ultimatum to Cairo and Jerusalem for "early cessation of hostilities to safeguard the free passage of the Canal." Israel instantly agreed to halt its armoured spearheads sixteen kilometres west of the Suez Canal, but Egypt, ordered to halt its troops sixteen kilometres east of the canal and to accept temporary occupation of Port Said, Ismailia, and Suez, naturally refused. With that as justification—exactly as planned—Britain and France began air and sea operations. The Egyptian air force was eliminated quickly, while, in the Sinai, the Israelis routed Nasser's army.

At the U.N. the Anglo-French-Israeli invasion was viewed with utter horror by other Western nations. The United States introduced a motion in the Security Council that called on Israel to withdraw and on Britain and France to stop the threats of and use of force. The motion was vetoed by Britain and France. The next day, the Uniting for Peace resolution of 1950 was used for the first time, the vetoes of Britain and France were overridden by the required two-thirds majority, and the General Assembly assumed responsibility.

Ottawa's response to the attacks on Egypt was one of shock, "like finding a beloved uncle arrested for rape," *The Economist* observed. In public the government was moderate, merely expressing "regret" that Britain and France "felt it necessary to intervene with force on their own responsibility."

But in private the line was much tougher, the secret telegrams from St. Laurent to Prime Minister Anthony Eden fairly sizzling—so much so that London was said to be "aghast." The Canadians believed they had been lied to by Eden in his past promises and in his description of the reasons for the Anglo-French ultimatum, and they thought London was risking the withdrawal of the non-white Commonwealth, as India, Pakistan, and Ceylon reacted very strongly to this outright attack on a Third World nation.

But what could be done? The Cabinet discussed the idea of a U.N. police force for Suez, and when foreign minister Lester Pearson left for New York on 1 November he took with him the idea of transforming the Anglo-French invaders into such a force. But the temper of the General Assembly made this out of the question. In the early hours of 2 November, the assembly passed a resolution calling for a ceasefire and the withdrawal of troops.

Canada abstained on this resolution, and when Pearson took the podium to explain his country's vote he advanced the idea that was to win him the Nobel Peace Prize—the idea of a large U.N. army made up of national contingents. This was very different from the original post-war plan for a cadre of U.N. generals deploying international armies, which had proved unworkable. As Pearson said,

> I regret the use of military force . . . but I regret also that there was no more time, before a vote had to be taken, for consideration of the best way to bring about that kind of cease-fire which would have enduring and beneficial results. . . . I therefore would have liked to see a provision . . . authorizing the Secretary-General to begin to make arrangements with Member Governments for a United Nations force large enough to keep these borders at peace while a political settlement is being worked out. . . . My own Government would be glad to recommend Canadian participation in such a United Nations force. . . .

Meanwhile the fighting continued, and Britain and France were now demanding a U.N. force as a precondition to a ceasefire. After hasty consultations in Ottawa and with representatives of other countries, Pearson introduced a resolution asking the secretary-general, Dag Hammarskjöld, to submit a plan for establishing "with the consent of the nations concerned" an "emergency international United Nations force to secure and supervise the cessation of hostilities," and it passed in the early hours of November 4. At home, many newspapers portrayed Pearson as selling out Canada's friends and pandering to petty dictators. "Canada chose to run out on Britain," the *Calgary Herald* said, "at a time when Britain was asserting the kind of leadership the world has missed, and needed."

Nonetheless, bolstered by the support of his prime minister and convinced that he was acting in the long-term best interests of all, Pearson persisted. He had extraordinary capacities for hard work and endurance. He was persuasive, and willing to use his powerful charm to make a point. Before noon a scheme was ready, improvised by an informal planning group of Canada, Norway, India, and Colombia. There would be a U.N.

Command headed by General Burns, still chief of staff of UNTSO, and infantry would be sent by contributing countries as soon as possible. At the General Assembly that night, this resolution passed without objection. The U.N. was going into Suez.

So were the British and French. On 5 November, Anglo-French troops landed from the air and sea at Port Said. But the attack only served to demonstrate the weakness of the invaders. Why had they needed a week to get troops from their staging areas on Cyprus to Egypt? Clearly Britain and France were no longer great military powers with a worldwide reach. And then a new menace appeared in this most appalling week in post-war history: the Soviet Union, its hands still running with the blood of the people of Hungary, threatened the attackers with nuclear weapons. To Washington, Moscow proposed "joint and immediate use" of Soviet and American troops to resist the "aggression against the Egyptian people."

Though Dwight Eisenhower, the newly re-elected American president, was furious with London and Paris, he immediately rejected the Soviet suggestion. Meanwhile, Pearson and Hammarskjöld were putting the finishing touches on a report to the General Assembly. No members of the Security Council were to be permitted to contribute troops; thus the Anglo-French invaders could not suddenly put on blue berets, nor could the U.S. or the U.S.S.R. send in armies. Political control was given to the secretary-general, and the force was to be politically neutral. Furthermore, it was recognized that Egypt's consent was necessary before the U.N. could function on Egyptian territory. The General Assembly accepted the report and the United Nations Emergency Force (UNEF) came into administrative existence. To turn it into a force in being was still to be achieved.

The immediate need was for infantry, and the 1st Battalion of the Queen's Own Rifles (QOR) was picked as Canada's contribution. In addition there would be "ordnance, army service corps, medical and dental detachments to ensure that the battalion group is self-contained and can operate independently from a Canadian base." The initial plan was to fly the QOR to Egypt on RCAF aircraft and use the aircraft carrier HMCS *Magnificent* to ship the vehicles and heavy equipment—and also, as General Charles Foulkes, chairman of the Chiefs of Staff Committee said, to provide "a firm base to which we could evacuate quickly" in the event of trouble.

While the Queen's Own scurried to get ready, Ottawa sent a trio of experienced military planners to New York to sit on Hammarskjöld's newly established Military Advisory Group. How would troops get to the Middle East? What would they eat and how would food reach them? How could they communicate with New York and their home countries? What facilities were needed for transport, for supply, for maintenance? Could the United States be asked to assist in getting UNEF under way? No one had answers, but the Canadians stood out because of their experience: they were accustomed to sending troops abroad, they had unusually balanced forces, and they were scrupulous in their administration and staff work. Thus they were taken seriously when they suggested that UNEF should be a buffer force, large enough to be noticed but not one that could intervene militarily;

that the U.S. should be asked to help with stores from its large stockpiles in the area; that the headquarters and support units for all contingents should be consolidated and should function in English; and that Hammarskjöld should get Egypt to agree to let UNEF in.

The latter proved more difficult than might have been thought. Its forces had been routed, but with the ceasefire in place Egypt now wanted to see its sovereignty infringed as little as possible. The secretary-general tried to ease matters by accepting troops only from non-controversial countries—Colombia, Brazil, Indonesia, Yugoslavia, India, Denmark, Sweden, Norway, Finland, and Canada. But was Canada truly in this category? Hammarskjöld thought so; Pearson had turned his back on Britain by proposing the creation of UNEF.

Not true, the Egyptians argued. Yes, Pearson had been helpful in New York, but there were practical problems. Canada belonged to that imperial-ist alliance, NATO. Besides, its infantry looked like the British infantrymen still exchanging shots with snipers in Suez; they wore the same uniforms, and Canada's flag included the Union Jack in one corner. Even the name, the "Queen's Own Rifles," sounded hopelessly British. No, the QOR could not come into Egypt.

While the objections were not unreasonable, they were excruciatingly embarrassing for Pearson. His role in New York was being denounced at home, and now the Egyptians, though defeated on the battlefield, were imposing conditions and slighting a regiment with battle honours extend-ing back to the Fenian raids. Worse yet, the Queen's Own had been moved from their home in Calgary to Halifax with the full accompaniment of pub-lic relations fanfares. If they were rejected, the humiliation to the govern-ment would be acute.

But rejected they were, and Canada's pride was salved only slightly when General Burns found a compromise. On November 19, Burns wrote to Pearson to say that "the most valuable and urgently required contribution the Canada could make to the Force at the present time would be to supply an augmented transport squadron of the R.C.A.F." to carry troops to Egypt, and that "if the administrative elements of the army contingent could go forward at an early date" this would help get UNEF operating. With Burns' letter in hand, Ottawa could claim that military necessity alone was shaping its contribution. Whether the voters agreed was less certain; seven months later they would put Conservative leader John Diefenbaker into power. By 21 November, in any case, three hundred administrative troops were on their way.

As soon as the Canadians arrived, General Burns asked them to take hold of the UNEF rear area. This was a hard task for they were housed in squalid huts, slapped under a curfew, and obliged to adhere to a blackout. As one private put it, "I thought we was here to clear the Egyptians out of the Canal Zone. Instead damned if they aren't treating us like prisoners of war." Still, they did their prosaic but essential jobs well, and by the next month Burns was asking for more of them. Once the British and French withdrawal had been completed and a demarcation line between Israeli and Egyptian forces had been defined, UNEF's problems were administrative, and no other remotely acceptable country could be found to tackle them. What the general now wanted was a signals squadron, a field workshop to handle electrical and mechanical maintenance, two transport platoons, and an RCAF communications squadron. To make this more palatable, he also asked for a (somewhat more glamorous) reconnaissance squadron equipped with armoured cars. Meanwhile the QOR returned home to Calgary, morale much depleted; *Magnificent*, carrying 405 soldiers and a hundred tonnes of stores and with its decks crammed with 230 trucks and other vehicles, as well as a helicopter and four light aircraft, finally sailed on 29 December. When the carrier arrived in Egypt on 12 January the Canadian representation in UNEF exceeded one thousand men, or more than a sixth of UNEF's total strength.

The Canadians' tasks in UNEF were not all that dissimilar to the work they would have done with NATO or in Canada. Their administration was handled by the euphoniously named CBUME—Canadian Base Unit Middle East. The signals squadron was spread over four sites and had responsibility for communications within UNEF, using radio, telephone, teletype, and dispatch riders, and its commander was chief signals officer to the force commander. The field workshop maintained 1250 trucks, the Royal Canadian Army Service Corps transport company hauled supplies from the docks to the troops in the field, and other Service Corps officers ran the Cherif quay at Port Said. The Ferret scout cars and jeeps of the reconnaissance squadron, initially formed from officers and men of the Royal Canadian Dragoons and Lord Strathcona's Horse, patrolled the sand dunes along the desert armistice line, in serious danger from Israeli and Egyptian mines. And the RCAF's 115 Air Transport Unit, flying old Dakota transports and newer Otters, shared a desolate airfield with a squadron of MiG fighters of Egypt's air force.

Despite all the difficulties of heat, disease, and boredom, their one-year tour of UNEF duty was an education for the Canadians. There was a generalized contempt for the bribery and corruption endemic among Egyptian officialdom, but there was also sympathy for the civilians caught in this territorial impasse. In a personal letter in 1962, a lieutenant with the recce squadron of the Royal Canadian Dragoons would observe of the Israelis:

> ... there is only one kibbutz available for general study. ... The leaders are pleasant to talk with, polite and half apologetic about their younger members who on the whole are inclined to be a bit arrogant and know it all. I think this is probably because they have not had to do any fighting but would like to prove that they are just as good as their elders. Unfortunately because of the rules it is impossible to have a good bull session. ... I have the impression that they have a feeling that the 1956 war was a little too easy and they are wondering what would have happened if it had been a little tougher. Still, they are willing to do it again and they will go all out because they can't afford to lose.

The Palestinian Arab who lives in the Gaza strip is between the Devil and the deep blue Med. Jimmy Nasser is pushing on one side and Israel stands on the other waiting to kick him in the teeth at the first sign of hostility. They're an unsettled group who are afraid Jimmy will use them for shock troops if he goes after Israel and right now there is no hope of smashing Israel and taking back the land they believe is theirs.

He added that it was a "funny thing coming off the desert—everyone feels like a big party and has a tremendous itch to shoot up the local police post." In other words, the frustrations of UNEF service were severe.

Still, there were compensations. There was leave in Beirut—then a warm city of great loveliness, although in 1958 it too needed a brief peace-keeping mission—the U.N. Observation Group in Lebanon (UNOGIL)—to patrol its Syrian border. There was the chance to talk with other U.N. troops and to watch their operational style. A captain with the transport company noted that "the gun-toting Brazilians" had a "distinctive method: if they are not making headway on the local market they simply draw a .45 Colt and point it in the general direction of the shopkeeper. Very effective. Prices come down quickly. They are the bane of good Egyptian-UNEF relations." He was later made commander of the Port Said garrison, which included a movement-control detachment, a frozen-food storage depot, and a guard platoon of Indian soldiers. "I am senior U.N. officer in the Port so I am also sort of a mild 'big effendi'." That soon palled; he wrote a few months later, "Boredom is a place much like Port Said." Still, "Whatever else this force may be it does foster the belief that the U.N. is a working reality and that editorialists are both wrong and foolish to forecast its demise. Gaza HQ is a hodgepodge of more than two dozen countries. It's quite a sight on Sunday nights to see saris, turbans, business suits, fezzes, etc. A very good feeling. The brotherhood of man. . . . "

THE SIX-DAY WAR

A sense of the brotherhood of man remained notably lacking between Egypt and Israel and between Israel and Syria. There were regularly military provocations between the nations, and in 1967 the Middle East once more blew up.

Tension had been rising since 1966, with snipings, raids, terrorism, and counterterrorism forming the daily diet. IN April 1967 there were serious clashes along the Israeli-Syrian border, and President Nasser, the acknowl-edged leader of the Arab world, could not afford to be left behind. When Israel issued a warning to Syria, Nasser responded by moving troops into the Sinai desert on 15 May and asking UNEF to withdraw from its sites along the Israeli-Egyptian border and to concentrate at Gaza. Secretary-General U Thant's reply was that UNEF would leave Egypt altogether if it had no useful role to play and if it was asked, and on 18 May Nasser made that "request"; a few days later Egyptian troops occupied UNEF posts over-looking the Gulf of Aqaba, Israel's only outlet to the Red Sea. By that time Ottawa had already sent out three RCN warships to bring the Canadian contingent home. After hurried consultations in New York and with U.S. President Lyndon Johnson, and after Israel had begun its own mobilization, Prime Minister Lester Pearson said that Canada supported "the right of access to and innocent passage through the Gulf of Aqaba." Nasser's response was to call Pearson an "idiot" and then, at 1:00 p.m. on 27 May, to order Canadian troops out of Egypt within forty-eight hours.

This forced improvisation on National Defence Headquarters. The sea evacuation plan was scrapped and the RCAF's Air Transport Command was called in instead. By 30 May all the Canadians, except for a small rear-guard preparing the heavy equipment, had flown out of Egypt in eighteen flights on Yukon and C-130 aircraft, along with over 100 000 kilos of equipment. As a result, Canada was spared the casualties that fell upon the Indian (fourteen killed and twenty wounded) and Brazilian (one killed) UNEF units when Israel sent its forces against the Arabs on 5 June. Massive air attacks wiped out its neighbours' air forces, and then Israel destroyed Egypt's army in the Sinai. Jordanian troops were pushed out of old Jerusalem and back over the River Jordan, and finally Syria was whipped on the Golan Heights. It took barely six days and left Israel the supreme military power in the Middle East, its forces sitting on a large expanse of territory extending from the banks of the Suez Canal to the Jordan River and the Golan Heights.

UNEF's ten years of peacekeeping had ended in war, confusion, and embarrassment. In Canada the reaction against the humiliation of Canada's representatives, and against the United Nations and peacekeeping in general, was very sharp—for a time. In the guidance notes sent to its missions abroad, the Department of External Affairs noted that "The lesson which we must draw from this is that a peace-keeping operation such as UNEF is not an end in itself but a practical adjunct to peace-making. Hand in hand with peace-keeping there must be continuous efforts to work assiduously for a settlement and not to regard a truce as a satisfactory long-term settlement."

It would take another bloody war between Israel and Egypt, in 1973, to force those two antagonists to the peace table, and there would eventually be another UNEF, and then the Multinational Force and Observers (MFO), an American-sponsored peacekeeping force outside the aegis of the U.N. On Israel's other borders, however, there would be no peace, only a constant series of guerrilla skirmishes and air attacks interspersed with larger actions. The U.N. would be involved in these further futile pacification attempts, always with Canadians, playing their usual quiet and competent role.

INDO-CHINA

By the early 1950s, peacekeeping had become an accepted form of international action. And it was not only the United Nations that found the concept attractive. When, for example, the Great Powers and the other countries concerned with the war in French Indo-China met at Geneva in the summer of 1954, an international commission to supervise a ceasefire, monitor the transfer of populations, supervise free elections, and keep watch on subsequent developments seemed a natural idea.

Indo-China, once a federation of a French colony and several French protectorates, includes the present-day countries of Vietnam, Laos, and Cambodia. When the area was liberated from the Japanese at the end of the Second World War, the French hoped to keep these countries as virtual colonies. Laos and Cambodia accepted the idea but in Vietnam a coalition of nationalists and Communists, the Viet Minh, demanded complete independence. The result was years of bitter fighting, with the French losing ground—and heart.

In 1954, at a conference in Geneva called to resolve both this and the Korean situation, it was decided that, pending elections, a provisional line would be drawn at the 17th parallel, separating "North Vietnam" (with its capital at Hanoi) from "South Vietnam" (with its capital at Saigon). A cease-fire would allow the French to withdraw, while the Viet Minh would pull back to North Vietnam.

Although Canada had participated in the discussions that wound up the Korean War, Ottawa was unrepresented at the Indo-Chinese talks. There was, as a result, enormous surprise and not a little concern when Canada, along with India and Poland, found itself asked to be a member of an international commission to supervise the ceasefire. Ottawa learned of the request from the press, and Canada's representative at the U.N.'s Geneva headquarters told Ottawa that "The suggestion made by the Chinese delegation at yesterday's meeting that members of the Commission be India, Canada and Poland came as a complete surprise." Apparently Krishna Menon of India had suggested Canada's name to China's Chou En-lai, and the choice had seemed acceptable. The reasons were almost exactly the same as those that had made Canada palatable to India and Pakistan when UNMOGIP had been set up a half-dozen years before: it was a disinterested, non-colonial power without military commitments in the region. But there was one additional factor: the commission was to be balanced, with one Western democracy, Canada, one Communist nation, Poland, and one neutral, India. Though it was a formula for deadlock, this troika represented the reality of power in South-east Asia in a way that a wholly neutral commission could not.

One immediate complicating factor was that the United States, though it had participated at Geneva, was unhappy with the concessions made to the Communists and was trying to dissociate itself from the plan. Another was that Ottawa had little familiarity with the background and complications of the area. Still, the request could hardly be evaded. As Lester Pearson said, "Just as local conflicts can become general war, so conditions of security and stability in any part of the world will serve the cause of peace everywhere." But in view of the Americans' disapproval, Arnold Heeney, Canada's ambassador to the United States, felt obliged to mollify the State Department and assure them that "we would wish to keep the United States Government informed privately of the course of events. This we felt we could do quite properly without impinging on our international responsibilities as members of the Commission." Much later down the road, the way Canada carried out that undertaking would cause substantial embarrassment.

The Cabinet agreed to participate, but questions remained unanswered. What was the legal basis of the Geneva agreements? Which countries were committed to maintain them? How many personnel would be required of the armed forces and from External Affairs? And how many commissions would be created?

The last question was the easiest to resolve. After discussions with the Indians and the Poles, there was agreement that three separate commissions should be formed and each of the members would pay its own personnel costs, while the Great Powers would share all but the local costs, which would be borne by the parties to the agreement. Like the U.S., South Vietnam dissociated itself from the agreements, an ominous hint of difficulty to come.

By 11 August the first Canadians had arrived in Indo-China. External Affairs had provided three officers of ambassadorial rank, some eleven or twelve political advisers, and office staff. The armed forces, primarily the army, contributed eighty-three officers, including three major-generals, and thirty-one other ranks. As most of the diplomats and officers were bilingual, this was a serious drain on the officer resources of the army and on External Affairs.

The records indicate that Canada hoped to carry out its work on the three commissions, soon to be dubbed the International Commissions for Supervision and Control (ICSCs) but always known as the International Control Commissions (ICCs), with impartiality. Still, the set-up of the ICCs left no doubt that each member was expected to represent a point of view, and before long the Canadians came to the conclusion that impartiality did not work. As External Affairs told its main posts overseas, "an impartial approach on the part of the Canadians combined with the partisan attitude of the Poles and the middle-of-the-road policy adopted by the Indians did not lead to just decisions. Since early 1955, there has been an increasing tendency in the Canadian Delegation to apply pressure against North Vietnam and to defend South Vietnam when it was considered Commission action . . . was unduly harsh."

As that comment suggests, the real problem for the ICCs was in Vietnam. In Laos and Cambodia there was progress; the Cambodian government took hold of its territory with some speed, the Communists were persuaded to withdraw, the resettlement of refugees and political partisans proceeded calmly, and there were free elections in September 1955. With so little work, the members of the ICC had time to grow to dislike one another. As one Canadian officer wrote, everyone agreed not to discuss religion or politics or other topics liable to bring out deep prejudice. Language kept the Poles isolated, he added, and although initial efforts were made by Indians and Canadians to socialize, those soon foundered, and both kept to themselves. By 1956 the Cambodian ICC was essentially out of work, and it existed in only token form until complete withdrawal at the end of 1969.

In Laos the ICC supervised the release and exchange of prisoners, and teams stationed around the country investigated a number of military skirmishes. The conditions were appalling and the work was ordinarily boring, so much so that the Canadian ICC commissioner, Léon Mayrand, had time to report on the Polish contingent:

> Generally speaking our members get along quite well with the Poles in off duty hours, playing games together, entertaining on a team basis, loaning each other periodicals and books. However their dress, deportment, cleanliness and observations of local customs leaves much to be desired by our standards. Their table manners and consumption of food and drink are atrocious.

What the Poles reported about Canadian intelligence and table manners regrettably remains unknown.

By 1958 the opposing factions in Laos had formed a coalition, and the new government called for the ICC's withdrawal. But in 1961 the coalition collapsed and the Great Powers began to fight out their rivalries there. The next year the Laos ICC had to be re-established, and Canada provided a delegation of nine diplomats and nineteen military personnel. In 1969, although the Laos ICC continued, Canada withdrew its delegation; instead a member of the Vietnam ICC attended the sporadic meetings. This state of affairs lasted until 1973, when the Laos ICC was briefly revived before being finally wound down the next year.

If Laos and Cambodia were relative successes, Vietnam of course was not. In 1954 the country was divided between a Communist regime in the north, under the able Ho Chi Minh, and a "democratic" government in the south, and although elections were supposed to create a single government throughout the country, the South Vietnamese—with American encouragement—disdained the 1954 settlement and simply refused to hold them. The north, equally unwilling to see a free, supervised election, similarly ignored the Geneva accords, and both countries began arming themselves with the aid of their Great Power patrons—China, the Soviet Union, and the U.S.—again in violation of the accords. Thus the Vietnam ICC, the largest of the three from the beginning, had a hopeless task. With the co-operation of the departing French administration the ICC did supervise the regroupment of civilians, as French colonials left the north for Saigon or to return to France and as Roman Catholic Vietnamese in large numbers moved southwards. At the same time 80 000 Viet Minh troops moved north, leaving behind large cadres, soon known as Viet Cong, to begin a guerrilla war in the south. By April 1955, although the north had put obstacles in the way of the ICC and although Pearson had complained in Parliament of bureaucratic obstruction and intimidation, over 700 000 people had been moved from one zone to the other—an astonishing emigration handled in relative peace—while 75 000 prisoners of war had been exchanged.

Still, the Canadian frustration was growing. The Poles were openly partisan, winking at North Vietnamese violations of the accords but protesting even minor South Vietnamese breaches. The Indians bounced first to one side and then to the other, in a parody of neutrality. As long-time Canadian diplomat John Holmes wrote, because there was more freedom of movement in the south the ICC "was in a position to prove Southern but not Northern violations. The Southerners and Americans inevitably complained and increasingly insisted that the known if not proved disregard of the arms control provisions by the Communists not only justified but made essential their doing likewise." Moreover, the mounting tempo of the guerrilla war in the south, largely indigenous but undoubtedly supplied from China and North Vietnam, led the Americans to step up their military involvement in the early 1960s and to demand ICC action to control subversion.

By 1963 the Vietnam War was in full swing, and the United States was pressuring its allies to contribute. Australia, South Korea, and other nations sent troops, but Canada refused, citing its ICC membership as the reason: how could a country monitor a ceasefire, even a sham ceasefire, if its troops fought beside one of the belligerents? The logic was unassailable, and the ICC at least served one useful purpose for Canada.

There was precious little utility anywhere else. One analysis of ICC voting found that Poland and India had voted together forty-three times between 1954 and 1965 while Canada and India had cast similar ballots forty-two times; Canada and Poland had never voted together against the Indians. Even so, only 53 percent of Canada's votes had been cast for South Vietnam, against Poland's 84 percent for the north. Impartial Canada was not, but compared to the Poles the record looked reasonably balanced.

The commission lost all trace of usefulness as the intensifying war made the gathering of evidence more and more difficult. The mobile ICC teams that had operated in the aftermath of the Geneva accords had been disbanded, and the teams monitoring the flow of arms at major ports of entry were allowed only limited freedom. Squadron Leader Hugh Campbell, an RCAF officer who did a tour in Vietnam, talked freely to the press on his return, admitting bluntly that the Canadians had thwarted investigations of American violations of the arms provisions exactly as the Poles had earlier blocked investigations of northern violations. If the ICC team spotted jeeps being unloaded from a ship, the Canadians would claim the vehicles were South Vietnamese exports to the United States—and as long as the ICC was on the scene, the winches would dutifully load jeeps back into the hold.

In Saigon, as the *New York Times* reported in 1967, the ICC team drove each day to the airport to "look for foreign military aircraft, their type and number of engines, takeoffs and landings." Sometimes, the paper quoted one ICC member, "we stay minutes. Other days we stay hours but that is rare." In Hanoi the teams faced more sobering conditions. There was the threat of being killed in American bombing raids, food was scarce, and the suspicion of the North Vietnamese was palpable. The only entertainment possible was poker and the occasional old movie. The boredom and futility were mind-numbing.

What is significant is that virtually all the Canadian diplomats and servicemen who served on the ICC came away firm supporters of the

American intervention. A whole generation, many destined to rise high in their country's service, had their anti-Communism reinforced by Indo-Chinese service. Information collected in the north quickly found its way to the Americans; diplomatic dispatches on North Vietnamese leaders and events similarly went to Washington. Charges that this was going on were made by Squadron Leader Campbell as early as 1965 and were repeated with details by the CBC in 1967, but Ottawa's denials of impropriety were always prompt: "Members of the Canadian delegation in Viet Nam are not engaged in clandestine or spying activities," Prime Minister Pearson said in May 1967. "The Canadian delegation reports to the Canadian government and the Canadian government only; it is for the Canadian government to decide in the case of these reports . . . what use is to be made of them in the course of normal diplomatic exchanges. . . . " In other words, the ICC officers were clean but Ottawa was passing things on wholesale.

In fact Ottawa had been doing more than this. In 1964 and 1965 the Canadian ICC commissioner, Blair Seaborn, had made repeated trips to Hanoi. While doing ICC business Seaborn, a senior and able diplomat, had acted as an intermediary for the United States, or so telegrams published in the "Pentagon Papers"—a top-secret U.S. study leaked to the *New York Times*—indicated. For example, the U.S. government, though worried about Canada's increasingly negative attitude to the escalation of the war, nonetheless wanted Seaborn to warn the north that it would be "punished" if its infiltration into the south was not checked. Seaborn dutifully conveyed the message, in slightly different terms, telling North Vietnam's prime minister that the "USA did not RPT not want to carry war to north but might be obliged to do so if pushed too far by continuation of Viet Minh-assisted pressures." The responses were typically stubborn and unyielding, and soon the Americans began bombing targets in the north, and the war escalated further.

Technically there was nothing improper in Canada acting as it did. The role of diplomatic intermediary is one of long standing. Still, for a member of the ICC, presumably expected to play a monitoring and supervisory role, to carry messages, sometimes bellicose messages, from one warring state to another was surely not what had been intended in the Geneva accords. The Vietnam War, vicious and corrupting as it was, had begun to infect everything it touched.

By 1972, as the war went on without let, the ICC role had become completely pointless, but there was still no easy way for Canada to escape its commitment. Then South Vietnam refused to allow Indian ICC personnel to operate there, and ICC headquarters shifted to Hanoi. The rancour between the participants increased and in 1973, after the Paris peace accords had more or less ended the war, the ICC wound up its operations. In Vietnam, at least, peacekeeping had been a lost cause.

However, that did not prevent the establishment of a new ICC. This one—known as the International Commission of Control and Supervision (ICCS)—was a creation of the Paris peace talks, concluded in January 1973, between the United States, South Vietnam, the Viet Cong's provisional government, and North Vietnam. To monitor the new "ceasefire" in South

Vietnam and to supervise the latest exchange of prisoners of war, the parties called on Canada, Hungary, Indonesia, and Poland—for this ICCS was evenly balanced between two Communist and two non-Communist nations.

Canada's contribution was reluctantly granted by the government of Pierre Trudeau. After nearly two decades of unhappy and frustrating experiences on the ICC the government had few illusions about the possible success of the new commission, and agreed to join only if, as External Affairs minister Mitchell Sharp put it, "the provisions for the operation of the new Commission appear workable and offer some prospects for success." The minister and his officials knew that the peace being established was largely a sham, but their view was that participation was worthwhile because it would help extract the United States from the Vietnam quagmire. Therefore, Ottawa agreed to participate for only a two-month period, and the ambassador to the ICCS, Michel Gauvin, adopted what was called an "open mouth" policy. Canada was no longer playing games—if there was interference and obstruction, Gauvin would say so. Under the ambassador were 50 officials from External Affairs, and a military team of 240 headed by Major-General Duncan McAlpine; he and most of his men were on site by late January 1973.

Like the old ICC, the ICCS operated with both fixed and mobile teams, its headquarters located in the ICC's former building in Saigon. There were seven regional headquarters throughout the south, twenty-six smaller teams which monitored the inflow of war material and supervised POW exchanges—the most important aspect of the operation for the United States, and hence for Canada—and fourteen point-of-entry teams. The ICCS had access to twenty-one helicopters and four fixed-wing aircraft—ironically chartered from Air America, reputedly a Central Intelligence Agency front.

The pattern that had prevailed on the ICC very quickly reasserted itself as the ICCS bogged down under a flood of complaints, the great majority filed by South Vietnam. The Poles and Hungarians proved unwilling to criticize North Vietnamese violations of the ceasefire accords. In fact the ceasefire was an illusion, with both sides fighting major engagements. The main use of the Paris accords was to accelerate the withdrawal of American forces by providing, as an excuse, the story that the war was over.

The phony peace did not satisfy Gauvin. When he was chairing the ICCS he flatly refused to call meaningless meetings that would go on endlessly without reaching agreement; either there would be agreement, he said, or there would be no meetings. As the leading student of Canada's role noted, "A competent ICCS was anathema to the communist side. Investigators might 'discover' [North Vietnamese] troops." The ambassador, of course, knew they were all through South Vietnam, and in April he lent strong support to American charges that North Vietnam was infiltrating troops into the south. The Poles and Hungarians were most unhappy with Gauvin and went public with denunciations of his "arrogance."

Nor was Ottawa pleased when Viet Cong forces kidnapped some of its peacekeepers (they were later freed) and another was killed when his helicopter was shot down. True to its word, the government—which in March had reluctantly extended its participation for a further ninety days—announced that Canada was going to withdraw on 30 June 1973. After direct representations by American Secretary of State Henry Kissinger, the Canadians remained an additional month so replacements could be found. The decision to withdraw was Canada's toughest action ever in a peacekeeping role, the first and only time that Ottawa refused to continue its participation in a charade.

Except for a skeleton team, the Canadians duly left by the end of July. The war went on until North Vietnam's victory over the South at the end of April 1975, when—with the victors at the outskirts of Saigon—the Canadians' office and personal possessions, including the official car, were flown out. North and South Vietnam were reunited under Hanoi's control on 2 July 1976, twenty years after the Geneva accords. The Vietnam War was at last over.

THE RCN AND THE CUBAN MISSILE CRISIS [✧]

PETER HAYDON

○

The conventional wisdom on Canada's role in the Cuban missile crisis is that it was a political debacle. Yet, the military role in the crisis was much greater and more significant in terms of co-operative continental defence than is often recognized. For many reasons, some of which now make little or no sense, the military dimension has received only limited attention from scholars and the media, while the political system still tends to hide from it. More significantly, the navy and the air force have remained virtually silent on the events of October and November 1962. In part, this is because they saw their roles in the crisis as part of their routine Cold War responsibilities and, as such, relatively unnoteworthy. But in hindsight, those operations are very much more significant than usually acknowledged. Moreover, there was another side to Canadian maritime operations during the Cuban missile crisis, which evolved from confusion over command and control of Canada's military. That confusion is understandable under the circumstances because the Canadian naval and air response to the deployment of Soviet strategic missiles to Cuba evolved out of an unpredicted sequence of events that the national command structure was not designed to handle.

[✧] This paper has not been previously published. It is based on research conducted for my new book, *The 1962 Cuban Missile Crisis: Canadian Involvement Reconsidered* (to be published in 1993). I would like to thank the staffs of both DND's Directorate of History and the Government Documents Section of the National Archives for their invaluable help in doing the research. The help of the former Canadian Institute for International Peace and Security in providing some of the funding for my research trips to Ottawa is greatly appreciated. I am very grateful to participants in the crisis, particularly Vice-Admiral K.L. Dyer, Commodore James Pratt, and Squadron Leader Ed Voelmecke, for their help in filling many of the gaps in the official records. And last, but not least, I want to thank Tony German for generously sharing some of his research for his excellent book, *The Sea Is at Our Gates*.

Before delving into maritime operations at sea during the crisis, it is useful to stop for a moment and look at how various scholars, historians, and retired naval officers have treated the subject.[1] The first Canadian analyses were essentially political, with more concern shown for the NORAD response than for maritime forces and the role they played in countering a Soviet naval challenge to North American security. There were some passing references to a Canadian naval role in the crisis but without elaboration. In 1978, Jocelyn Maynard Ghent took a fresh look at the overall crisis, paying some attention to the naval aspects of the operation while focusing, understandably, on the bilateral and political issues. The next contribution came from Admiral Jeffry Brock with his views on the crisis as he saw it from Ottawa as the Vice Chief of the Naval Staff (VCNS). After that, Joel Sokolsky began to put some real flesh on the skeleton in his paper "Canada and the Cold War at Sea," and it became clear that Canadian maritime forces made a significant contribution to the related anti-submarine campaign on the eastern seaboard. Working mainly from US sources, Sokolsky realized that the fabric of operational agreements between the two navies was every bit as important as those between the air forces within NORAD, and that these naval agreements were fully tested during October and November 1962. But Sokolsky did not provide details of those operations. These began to emerge in Tony German's *The Sea Is at Our Gates*, which offers a level of detail not previously seen and gives a most interesting account of the naval side of the crisis. But there is still much more to the saga than told so far, as this paper suggests.

Far more information is available now than a few years ago, and so it is apparent that the crisis had far deeper political implications than we may have realized. Moreover, many of the military aspects of the crisis remain classified, and there are still gaps in the sequence. A few of the gaps have been filled here from the recollections of the people who took part in the crisis, but many questions remain unanswered. Nevertheless, it is important to tell the story, even with its gaps, because one of the errors of the aftermath of the crisis was that the story of the maritime role was not told. It is, in the end, a remarkable story of effective bilateral co-operation.

THE SETTING

Despite growing American concern over the military build-up in Cuba, there was initially no concrete proof that those forces were a direct threat to North America. Finding the necessary proof thus became a primary US intelligence requirement. Throughout 1962 the Americans expected some kind of Soviet diplomatic or military initiative as a prelude to another round of confrontation over Berlin. Any change in Soviet presence or military operating patterns would thus serve as warning. Cuba, however, was an unlikely location, but not out of the question. In addition to locating new strategic weapons systems, it was also vitally important to the west to monitor the movement of Soviet shipping in North American waters. The naval role in this strategic intelligence gathering was to maintain surveillance of

Soviet submarine operations and the activities of their fishing fleet.[2] Canadian and American forces shared these tasks. Thus naval operations directed at Soviet maritime activity in the western Atlantic were already well underway (indeed had been for years) when the presence of missiles in Cuba was confirmed on October 13th.

Although basic plans for joint Canada-US defence of the continent had existed for some time, they did not make allowances for the direct and confrontational way in which the Kennedy administration handled the Cuban missile crisis. The framework of bilateral defence planning was based on the assumption that co-ordination between Canadian and American forces would take place when any direct threat to North America presented itself. Canadian politicians assumed this would take the form of political consultation along lines similar to the NATO procedures. To the military staffs on both sides of the border, however, consultation was a process that would only take place within military channels of communication established by the 1946 Basic Security Plan for continental defence. Because joint maritime bilateral planning was founded on a concept of close personal contact between the command staffs in Halifax and Norfolk, Va., and those in Esquimalt and Pearl Harbour, responding to a crisis at sea was not an unduly difficult task. The air forces were also able to work together quickly and efficiently. But the ease with which the various operational staffs were able to co-operate was misunderstood in Ottawa and was later seen as a threat to political control over the Canadian military.[3] Yet the series of maritime events in which Canadian ships and aircraft co-operated with their American partners during the Cuban missile crisis is a good example of sound military planning and co-operation. But first, the events must be put into context by briefly explaining the structure of bilateral plans for the maritime defence of the continent.

PLANS AND CONCEPTS OF OPERATIONS

By the mid-1950s the increasing use of the North American continental shelf by the Soviet fishing fleet began to have strategic implications. As a result, the Newfoundland Patrol was established in the fall of 1957 to meet the need for a continuous naval presence in the Grand Banks area.[4] By the summer of the next year, both the military and the media made the linkage between the Soviet fishing fleet and covert military operations. In public, however, the navy firmly denied this linkage existed.[5] In fact, the Royal Canadian Air Force (RCAF) had been conducting surveillance of the Soviet fishing fleet since 1954, and there was a joint reporting system that included intelligence reports and assessments from closer inspection of Soviet vessels when they visited Canadian ports.

By following up on all submarine sighting reports, most of which were spurious, and by keeping close watch on the Soviet fishing fleet, ostensibly to make sure they did not fish in Canadian territorial waters, the military maintained effective surveillance. These operations involved Royal Canadian

Navy (RCN) ships supported by RCAF and United States Navy (USN) maritime patrol aircraft, and for the most part were boring employment carried out in areas of predominantly bad weather. Nevertheless, the vigilance paid off. In November 1958, a task group consisting of the aircraft carrier *Bonaventure* and seven destroyers with support from the RCAF made contact with a submarine near a large group of Soviet fishing vessels on the northeast part of the Banks. The final analysis of the operation was that it was "highly probable that submarines are operating in this area and, during replenishment periods, seek shelter beneath fishing fleets by day and surface within fishing fleets by night."[6]

Although suspicions that Soviet submarines were using the Grand Banks and the Canadian continental shelf continued to grow, solid evidence was hard to get. RCN assessments were, however, realistic in recognizing the primary threat posed by the Soviet fishing fleet was economic rather than military. Yet it was acknowledged that many of those vessels carried out a secondary function of gathering electronic intelligence.

> It has only once been possible to identify visibly a Soviet submarine in the Atlantic. A number of contacts have been made by ships, aircraft and submarines. Many sighting reports have been made by civilians. These covert operations are believed to be for intelligence collections, monitoring of NATO exercises, charting of ocean areas in which Soviet submarines may require to operate under possible wartime conditions, and for the maintenance of submarines in readiness for a possible emergency.[7]

The media continued to show periodic interest in the movements of the Soviet fishing fleet and in the RCN and RCAF surveillance. For the most part, the official responses to press queries were predictably safe and sterile. Occasionally, a more formal question came through the political system, as in the fall of 1962 when there was concern over Soviet fishing operations on both the west and east coasts, but the answers remained evasive.[8]

Concern over Soviet activities off the eastern seaboard was not exclusively Canadian. The USN had also been monitoring the Soviets, particularly from their base at Argentia in Newfoundland. Liaison between Canadian and American commanders and their staffs began in the early 1950s when the USN maintained a large force in Newfoundland. Initially that force was an air patrol group, but in 1959 it became known as the "Barrier Force, US Atlantic Fleet." The "barrier" concept of anti-submarine operations called for an integrated and layered defence across the main approach routes to North America. Under this concept, which remained in being until the mid-1960s, aircraft carriers, destroyers, submarines, maritime patrol aircraft, and fixed underwater sensors operated together under the direction of a shore headquarters with the aim of preventing enemy submarines from coming within missile firing range of North American targets.

Although the co-operation between the Pacific fleets was high, it never reached a comparable level to that in the Atlantic. Planning took place on roughly similar lines but the distance from Esquimalt to Hawaii precluded much of the close contact enjoyed by the commanders and their staffs in the

Atlantic. Moreover, the level of Soviet activity in the Northeast Pacific was much less than that in the western North Atlantic. This did not stop Canadian and American naval units from working together in many parts of the Pacific. By the 1960s, through close liaison and operational experience, the two North American navies grew to respect each other's capabilities and were able to function together effectively. Indeed, by the 1960s the level of co-operation and co-ordination between the two Atlantic navies reached a level that was probably beyond the original concepts of the 1947 Basic Security Plan.

In 1960, the Chief of Naval Operations for the US Navy summarized the threat posed to North America by Soviet submarines in stating:

> Since 1955 Soviet submarine operations at sea, outside their normal operating areas, have increased steadily. At first, these operations were limited to several hundred miles from homeport areas. Today, these operations have been extended father into the Atlantic and Pacific—some in close proximity to our coasts. These should be considered as a part of normal cold war operations.[9]

Three aspects of the Soviet submarine capability were of particular concern; submarine-launched missiles (ballistic and air breathing), world-wide operations against US and allied naval forces, and intelligence gathering. In response to this threat, US naval forces began to locate and track Soviet submarines, ensuring they knew they were under surveillance and would be subject to prompt attack if they committed a hostile act. The concept of operations gave priority to gathering intelligence on Soviet submarine operations as warning of any surprise attack launched from sea.[10] Implementing this concept of operations called for the co-ordination of all anti-submarine operations and their conduct under strict rules of engagement when in contact with Soviet submarines.[11] This concept was applied to joint Canada-US operations.

The Canadian appreciations of the threat and of Soviet submarine capability were similar to those in the United States, but expressed in more cautious terms, as a 1961 Canadian assessment shows:

> There is evidence that a number of long-range submarines have been converted, and others constructed, to fire ballistic missiles. It is expected that further types of new submarines will be built to fire missiles. The majority of SSBs can be expected to be deployed against the east and west coast of North America, where they will supplement the air attack . . . [and] By 1 January 1962 about 35 ballistic missile submarines may be available to supplement the strategic missile attack on North America. At the beginning of the period (of this Estimate), the SSB will be forced by reason of the limited range of its missile to operate within 300 nm of the American coast.[12]

The Canadians believed the sea-based threat came from submarines that would use missiles, torpedoes, and mines to neutralize military bases, warning radar stations, ports, and anti-submarine forces. They also believed the

Soviets might use northern and Arctic waters as launch areas for missile attacks against early warning radar sites, despite the inherent co-ordination difficulties. The role of the Soviet fishing fleet in wartime was thought to be one of adding to the overall confusion and disruption by breaking underwater cables and attacking isolated points on shore once the war had started. The greatest concern to Canadian and American planners alike was the growth of the Soviet submarine fleet in both size and technical proficiency.

Thus, the concepts of surveillance and naval preparedness in place by October 1962 had evolved over a period of years, essentially since the mid-1950s when the Soviet submarine threat began to generate concern. Co-ordination of operations had become routine, particularly the air patrols where the USN worked in close conjunction with the RCAF, often alternating in a patrol area. Both Canadian and American aircraft routinely co-operated with the fixed surveillance system stations in identifying contacts. Similarly, ships were always available on short notice in harbour or on patrol in the coastal areas. By 1960, keeping a continuous military presence in the North American offshore zone was a standard requirement for Canadian and American maritime commanders. As far as the Canadian commanders were concerned, they were operating within their prescribed terms of reference and needed no further authorization to change operating and training patterns within the designated Canadian area of responsibility. In simple terms, they were responsible to the Minister of National Defence, through the Chief of the Naval Staff (CNS), for the control of all units under their command. This included the movement of those units, their logistic and administrative support, and scheduling the exercises necessary to maintain their operational efficiency.[13] This power was not absolute, but included a considerable degree of latitude in controlling the fleet. The important point was that the right to direct operations had been officially delegated by the Minister of National Defence, thereby establishing that political control was only necessary for extraordinary situations. A change in the level of Soviet maritime activity or simply the requirement to schedule training exercises was sufficient justification for a maritime commander to deploy ships and aircraft on his own authority. CNS exercised a degree of control over operations through his approval of proposed fleet employment plans. There was also an indirect but effective measure of control exercised through fuel allocation. Fuel was a constant concern for operational commanders, and if they did not have sufficient funds to buy the necessary fuel they had to request additional funding from the CNS.

In 1962, joint maritime operations had become a carefully co-ordinated procedure through which the maritime patrol aircraft and warships of both nations worked with fixed hydrophone systems (SOSUS) to investigate and confirm possible submarine contacts and exchange information on the movement of the Soviet fishing fleets. Even though operationally desirable, it would have been impossible to keep all maritime forces on task. Instead, there was a "ready" system, independent of the formal alert system, by which additional ships and aircraft could be deployed quickly to a contact area when needed.

The heart and soul of the Canadian maritime defence organization was the *RCN Defence Plan*.[14] The purpose of the plan, which was issued under the authority of the CNS, was to prepare the navy for war or any other emergency, and would be activated in the event of a national General Alert or if there was a direct attack on Canada. Commanders made their own plans for their areas of responsibility. The basic concept of operations came from a requirement to keep at least 30 percent of operational forces readily available at all time to meet emergencies in the Canadian areas of responsibility in the Atlantic (CANLANT) and Pacific (ALCANUS). Commanders had to plan maintenance and refit schedules, employment programmes and leave periods to meet this requirement. They also had to ensure that their forces could be deployed quickly in an emergency to meet the assigned tasks and sustain those operations for a thirty-day period. The commanders also had to have plans for the immediate dispersal of ships and key support facilities.[15] Provision was also made for seaward defence and mine clearance at naval bases and operating ports.

The *RCN Defence Plan* functioned within the Canadian Military Alert Measures system which consisted of five stages of increasing readiness with provision for a rapid response if a situation escalated quickly.[16] Canadian Forces Headquarters in Ottawa controlled and co-ordinated the activation of the various measures in response to political direction. The commanders thus had a considerable degree of autonomy in managing their fleets, other than in taking steps that might create public concern. These, naturally, were politically sensitive and were co-ordinated by Ottawa.

One of the contentious issues within the Cuban missile crisis has always been the alerting of the fleet and RCAF units before Diefenbaker gave his permission to do so. This complex and fascinating topic is beyond the scope of this paper, but can be put into perspective for now by simply stating that in the absence of adequate direction from Ottawa, Admiral K.L. Dyer, Flag Officer, Atlantic Coast, and his counterpart in Esquimalt did what they considered necessary.[17] In Dyer's case, he and the staff simply followed the procedures in the General Defence Plan. Although the admirals and their principle staff officers talked back and forth, there was no formal direction until the crisis was well underway. Rather than cast doubt on the integrity of the Naval Staff in Ottawa for this situation, it should be made clear that the fault lay in the interface between the national military staff and its political masters. Personalities obviously came into play, particularly in the Naval Staff, but the root cause of the problem was organizational. The important point to make here is that while the crisis began on 22 October in Ottawa, it started over a week earlier in Halifax and Esquimalt.

THE CRISIS AT SEA

Operations at sea during the crisis fall into three distinct phases:

1. the prelude to the crisis from late September 1962 until Kennedy's speech to the world during the evening of Monday 22 October;

2. the period of international tension as Kennedy and Khrushchev negotiated; and

3. the disengagement phase that lasted from 29 October until almost the end of November.

Politically, the crisis is seen as a single event that essentially ended on 28 October when Khrushchev ordered the vessels carrying the nuclear warheads to Cuba to turn around. But that was not the end of the crisis. There was a final act to be played in which both the RCN and RCAF had leading and controversial roles.

In the 1960s there was no standard deployment pattern for the ships, submarines, and maritime patrol aircraft of either the Atlantic or Pacific fleets. Operations were, in fact, a condition of almost continual activity to meet two principal objectives: surveillance and training. October and November 1962 were to have been busy months for the navy and its maritime air element. One of the high points was a large joint ASW exercise, *Beagle II*, conducted off the eastern seaboard from 29 October to 9 November. The aim of the exercise was to test Canadian and American reaction to a major deployment of Soviet submarines into North American waters. The other coincidence was that a large NATO staff exercise, *Fallex 62*, had been held that September. Based on a scenario of Soviet aggression in Europe, it involved both the Naval Headquarters and Command staffs. As a result, the command staff were able to review the emergency organizations. In fact, the staffs had a head start when the crisis broke.

Although Canadian maritime operations took place in both the Atlantic and the Pacific, the focus here will be on the Atlantic because that is where the Soviets were. Contingency operations were also initiated on the West Coast, and followed a similar pattern to those in the Atlantic where joint exercises were cancelled, surveillance and readiness increased, and extensive co-ordination carried out with the USN. But the lack of a real threat gave those operations somewhat less purpose than those orchestrated by Admiral Dyer and his staff, who had evidence of an increase in Soviet submarine activity in the western Atlantic.

PHASE I—BEFORE KENNEDY'S SPEECH

Until the Soviets open up their archives and tell us how they operated their submarines in October and November 1962, there has to be some speculation on when the actual crisis started. As far as the Canadian and American ASW forces were concerned, the pattern of Soviet submarine activity changed early in October. Also, there were changes in the operating patterns of electronic intelligence (ELINT) trawlers and other Soviet surface ships. By 13 October, when the Americans obtained photographic proof of the missile sites in Cuba, it was clear that the Soviets were up to something.[18] The American admirals naturally passed their concern to Halifax through the "hot line" linking the two headquarters. Then, on Wednesday 17 October, Vice-Admiral "Whitey" Taylor, the Commander of the US Atlantic ASW Forces (COMASWFORLANT), and his senior aviator,

Rear-Admiral George Koch, flew into Halifax for what Admiral Dyer called, "discussions of immediate operational concern."[19]

That night, the first of twelve Soviet submarine contacts that Canadian ships and aircraft would prosecute during the crisis was detected. Designated as B-27, that contact was investigated by Canadian and American aircraft until 21 October without clear confirmation that it was a Soviet submarine. Because it was only about 300 miles off the Canadian coast and thus technically within range of key North American targets if it were a missile-firing submarine, B-27 was cause for concern.

Activity was not restricted to anti-submarine aircraft alone. Admiral Dyer formed a second "ready" escort group the previous week, and several ships conducted exercises in local areas. As a result, two of the three available escort squadrons were either at sea or at short notice for sea throughout the two weeks before the crisis became official. With *Bonaventure* and the 1st Escort Squadron away in European waters and the 3rd Squadron on reduced manning, Dyer and his staff could do little more than keep the three squadrons ready and increase the intensity of air patrols. The two submarines of the Royal Navy's 6th Submarine Division, based at Halifax to assist the RCN in A/S training, could not be used with the same flexibility, at least not at the beginning of the crisis.

PHASE II—THE PERIOD OF POLITICAL TENSION

Initial public reaction to Kennedy's speech of October 22nd was largely one of shock. Knowledge of the impending crisis was kept to a select few. The US military, however, was authorized to begin preparing for action against Cuba on Saturday, 20 October. The American media did not complete the link between the crisis and the preparatory US military manoeuvres until 21 October. Even then, the White House denied that such a linkage existed. For instance, a *New York Times* article speculated and referred to the exercises as a "powerful show of force" and linked it to the burning of much late-night oil in Washington by "top security officials."[20] By 21 October it was clear that secrecy was crumbling, and it was time to make the crisis and intended response public. In Canada, there had been no sign in the press of any impending incident with Cuba or of the US military movements before October 22, when the whole story was made public. The Canadian media, on the other hand, seemed disinterested in the American crisis. They were more concerned with the nuclear weapons issue, which was debated in the House on October 17, and with the proposed cuts in the Canadian Civil Defence Organization's budget.[21]

Thus, Kennedy's speech that evening was a complete surprise to the Canadian political system and to the population as a whole. The military, on the other hand, had already started to make some preparations, and all that remained to be done was for the formal order to be given to increase the level of readiness and to take the remaining steps that would begin activating contingency plans. But the necessary orders never came. It was as if the crisis had fallen into a vacuum. Admiral Dyer knew well beforehand that something was happening. The staff in Esquimalt also knew. And

Admiral H.S. Rayner, the CNS, knew because his two commanders told him. What Rayner did with that information remains somewhat of a mystery. He told the Minister the gist of what was happening. Beyond that, there are no records.[22] The net result was that political and military Ottawa did nothing despite requests from Kennedy and NORAD to put the military on alert. In the absence of direction, the onus was on the Maritime Commanders to take the necessary action.

To all outward appearances, the next day, the 23rd, was one of inactivity. Dyer waited, totally frustrated, for the Naval Staff or the Chiefs of Staff Committee to do or say something. There were phone calls, but there is no record of what was said (probably quite wisely). The problem, of course, was political. Diefenbaker would not authorize Harkness, the Minister of National Defence, to put the forces on an alert status despite US requests to match their increased readiness. However, by this time, the press had the full story and were speculating on the future sequence of events, but had not yet begun to link the Canadian military to the situation. Diefenbaker's wavering was already a source of American concern, particularly as he was pressing to have the United Nations involved in resolving the crisis. Much of his rationale was his suspicion that the Americans were not telling him the truth.[23] This too is another story, and one that has been well told by the political historians.

In Halifax, preparations continued. Some of the ships of the 7th Squadron came back from exercises for replenishment while the others remained at sea. Ships of the other squadrons were kept ready for quick deployment. The most significant event was another possible submarine contact. This one, code-named B-28, was about 300 miles southeast of Halifax and heading for North American waters. As the tempo increased, the impasse between Ottawa and the Commands was broken. The Naval Board met twice on the 24th and, in response to Harkness's direction to begin implementing a state of "Discrete Military Vigilance," began to consider how to implement the various measures. Apart from recalling *Bonaventure* and the 1st Squadron from Plymouth and the 2nd Squadron from the San Francisco area, the Naval Staff did not really do very much to support the Commanders' quest for direction. Again, the phone lines burned, but this time action was taken.

Again, there is no record that explains exactly how the decision was taken to start deploying the fleet the next day. What seems clear though is that in frustration and in the absence of direction from the national headquarters, Admiral Dyer started deploying his fleet on 25 October to increase the level of surveillance, improve readiness, and to disperse the ships. In doing this, he simply followed the defence plan.

The 9th Squadron deployed to St. John's, Newfoundland, and established a patrol area to the east of Cape Race with support from USN patrol aircraft operating from Argentia. The 5th Squadron set up a patrol area to the southeast of Halifax, with extensive support from the RCAF who were also still hunting B-28, the contact gained the night before. The 7th Squadron came back to Halifax, prepared for war, and made ready to deploy to the base in Sydney. The RN submarines based at Halifax went to patrol areas to the northeast of the Grand Banks (*Alderney* immediately, and *Astute* a few days later). The 3rd Squadron was brought to full manning and put through a short training period before deploying to Shelburne from where it patrolled Georges Bank. The tracker aircraft from Shearwater were assigned to coastal patrol with a detachment moving up to Sydney to support operations in the Cabot Strait. This was the best anti-submarine screen Dyer could provide under the circumstances.

While all this was going on, the USN began to establish an ASW barrier extending 600 miles to the southeast of the Cabot Strait. This was manned by ten American submarines supported by USN patrol aircraft (P2Vs) operating out of Argentia and by RCAF *Argus*. The speed with which this all happened on the 25th shows that the plans had been made for some time with extensive co-ordination between Dyer and his USN counterparts. Moreover, the joint RCN-USN ASW exercise, *Beaver II*, was cancelled, and two USN destroyers that had been in a Canadian port quickly returned to their home base. The cover story, to appease political sensitivities as well as to prevent the press unduly alarming the public was that, "ships are proceeding for Canadian portion of joint Canadian-USN exercise which was cancelled, and are carrying out what remains of the exercise."[24]

Bonaventure and the 1st Squadron sailed in the late afternoon of the 25th, leaving *Nootka* behind to complete some repairs and to pick up the inevitable stragglers from leave. They would not return to Halifax until 2 November. They came back at economical speed, delayed a little by poor weather, and seemed somewhat unconcerned with the crisis developing off the eastern seaboard of North America. A clue to this may lie in the fact that Naval Headquarters issued the recall. One of the Naval Staff's primary concerns was accounting for the extra fuel the crisis would require. Even after almost thirty years, it is not easy to explain adequately the conduct of the Naval Staff during the crisis. The minutes of Naval Board offer very little by way of rationale and Admiral Brock's account is not complete.

At sea, where the crisis was a reality, periodic contact was held with B-28, and by the 26th it gave every indication of being a Soviet submarine. Because the submarine seemed headed for the Georges Bank area, where there was much Soviet fishing fleet activity, Argus patrol aircraft and ships of the 5th Squadron established a barrier across its path. However, the submarine was elusive, and its identity was not confirmed even though aircraft held contact for some time. The location of Soviet trawlers, tankers, and fishery support vessels able to replenish submarines was another concern. Also, the positions of the ELINT trawlers themselves were important because they acted as communication links for submarines. Experience had proved that Soviet submarines frequently rendezvoused with these vessels and that the fishing fleet often provided cover and protection as well as logistic support. Thus, much of the Canadian and American surveillance effort was directed to building the plot of all Soviet ships. The concern was that the Soviets would try to put a missile-firing submarine within range of a major North American city for use as a bargaining chip in resolving the

Cuban crisis. Georges Bank was thus a logical place for a Soviet submarine to be. B-28, therefore, had possible strategic significance.

As possible submarine contacts were gained and lost they received new designator numbers unless a direct correlation between two contacts existed. Correlation between the various contacts was done ashore where the pattern of contacts was compared to the possible operating cycle of a submarine: the speed of advance, the track, the cycle of charging its batteries, and the proximity of other submarines and support ships. From those correlations, optimum search areas and barrier positions were developed. B-28 was one of such a series of contacts, yet its true identity was never discovered despite a considerable effort by both Canadian and American ASW forces.

The likelihood of intensified Soviet submarine activity was further suggested by the presence of the Soviet tanker *Atlantika*, a submarine replenishment vessel. She had been in Halifax at the beginning of the crisis and sailed during the afternoon of 27 October. As she left port, the *Atlantika* was shadowed by trackers from Shearwater in the hope that it would soon rendezvous with either a submarine or an ELINT trawler. But nothing happened, the tanker just moved down to the Georges Bank area to join the bulk of the Soviet fishing fleet. Meanwhile, the hunt for B-28 continued. Contact was gained again during the night of 27/28 October and was held for several hours. At that time, it was thought to be a *Whiskey* class submarine, armed with conventional anti-ship torpedoes and therefore not a strategic threat. But it continued to be elusive. It seems clear now that it was following a standard cycle for running silent for twelve to sixteen hours, then coming up to charge the battery and then going down again. This procedure allowed the submarine to make about five knots as it headed towards the coast. Contact was lost again in the early morning.

Requirements for both the Cuban quarantine and the "SUBAIR" barrier that ran southeast from the Cabot Strait stretched USN capability beyond its capacity, and the USN asked Dyer for help on ASW barrier. The support was for air patrols, particularly in the most distant patrol zones where the Argus's greater endurance made a considerable difference. Although this began to put a strain on Canadian flight operations, Dyer believed it necessary to support the Americans to the limit of his ability.[25] Moreover, the need to put so much of the US Atlantic fleet on the quarantine line around Cuba meant that the USN could not follow the normal concept for joint ASW operations. Instead, they relied on their Canadian partners to fill the gaps created by the Cuban tasking. The USN were overcommitted and asked the Canadians to take over responsibility for co-ordinating ASW operations in the QUONSET ASW area to the immediate south of the Canadian zone. This required Canadian units to operate much further south than usual,[26] and Dyer did not have enough resources to meet all the possible commitments. Without the declaration of a formal alert, when the normal accounting procedures for fuel, stores, and dockyard overtime would be held in abeyance, fleet and maritime air operations were constrained. One of Dyer's greatest frustrations was Ottawa's reluctance to recognize this problem. Having to explain the continuing requirement for ASW surveillance in the Atlantic when the politicians considered the crisis over (Khruschev agreed to withdraw the missiles on 28 October) was another of Dyer's problems. To reinforce his phone conversations with CNS and VCNS, Dyer continued to send them detailed summaries of the situation.

Unfortunately, RCN and RCAF forces had not been able to accomplish much during the political phase of the crisis. Although they held contact with several possible submarines and most of the key Soviet surface vessels, there was little indication of Soviet intentions. Moreover, there was still no real direction from Ottawa. The Naval Board had not met since their meetings on the 24th, and there was no linkage between Canadian political issues and the military situation. The Pacific was calm without any indication of Soviet naval activity. In the Atlantic, however, the submarines and the Soviet fishing fleet were very active. Despite frequent reports, Admiral Dyer could not convince the Naval Staff that he had a problem. In trying to guard against the unexpected, he was still very much on his own.

PHASE III—DISENGAGEMENT

When Nikita Khrushchev accepted Kennedy's proposal for ending the crisis on 28 October and ordered his merchant ships to return to the Soviet Union, the consensus was that the crisis had ended. Canadian politicians certainly believed so and the House returned to its normal partisan thrust and parry. The media also turned to other news items, apart from the occasional challenge of the government's handling of the crisis. But the crisis was not over. The missiles in Cuba had not been dismantled, and the Soviet submarines continued to close the North American coast. Even though the US suspended the blockade of Cuba, military concern still ran high. As a result, operations against Soviet submarines and surface ships continued in the Atlantic. Sporadic contact was maintained with B-28 (renamed B-32 by then) as it continued to close the North American coast. Even though one part of the crisis was over, the Soviet navy was apparently unaware of the change.

Dyer's problem was that he could not convince Ottawa that the Soviet submarines still presented a potential threat to North America, and he remained frustrated by Ottawa's refusal to see the situation in a tactical light. As a result, he took every opportunity to explain the complexity of the situation, to the point of making very comprehensive reports on the status of his forces. He kept emphasizing the need for extensive surveillance, including the use of the RN submarines in an advanced ASW barrier between Newfoundland and Greenland to detect submarines coming into North American waters from the Soviet Union. In each report, Dyer stated that he intended to maintain the present level of operations.

By signalling his "intentions" to both CNS and his USN counterpart, Vice-Admiral Taylor, Dyer was inviting them to disagree with and, if necessary, override his assessment of the situation and tactical plan. He was forced into this position by a lack of positive political direction from Ottawa. There are no records of the telephone calls that went back and forth between Halifax and Ottawa, but from the tone and content of the message traffic it is clear that a marked difference of opinion existed.[27]

The Naval Board met again on 30 October to re-assess the crisis in the light of official caution expressed by NATO commanders and by the Commander of the US Atlantic Fleet. Rather than being concerned over the international situation, which was again being linked to a Berlin crisis, the Board was far more concerned with administration and in not creating political problems than it was with the defence of the continent. The little direction it gave concerned fuel economy rather than continental defence.

> It was noted that it would be necessary to reduce expenditures attributable to the international situation as soon as possible to prevent an over expenditure of funds. While it was agreed that the decision on how long the current posture should be maintained was for higher authority, the Services were under direction to make no undue expenditures while maintaining the present precautionary measures and while planning for a possible worsening of the situation.[28]

Accordingly, it directed the fleet commanders to keep fuel expenditures within current fiscal year allowances. This also applied to the RCAF Maritime Air Command. To remain within those limits would have required a substantial reduction in the level of activity and meant that they could not help the Americans. To Dyer and his air commander, Air Commodore Clements, this was not acceptable as it ran contrary to the entire concept of joint continental defence.[29]

Tactically, the 31st was a better day. That afternoon, contact was made with a submarine in a position that correlated to B-32. There was also an increase in the activity of the ELINT trawlers. One was sitting just outside Halifax, another had joined the fishing fleet on Georges Bank and a third, the *Shkval*, was headed northeast towards the position of the submarine. Contact was made with a second submarine south of Sable Island in the early hours of the morning near one of the ELINT trawlers. A situation was developing for which Dyer did not have enough resources, and the USN were similarly strapped. The return of *Bonaventure* and the 1st Squadron on 2 November was thus very important. Also, it looked as if Georges Bank would be an area of particular interest, and so using the support ship *Cape Scott* to provide base support in Shelburne was equally important.

When Admiral Dyer made the decision not to reduce the level of operations, he almost certainly did so after talking to his colleague, Admiral Taylor in Norfolk. In formally acknowledging Dyer's message of intent, Taylor succinctly summarized the reasons for concern over the Soviet submarine situation and re-emphasized the need for continuing Canadian support of those operations.[30] There is no record of how the message was received in Ottawa, but Dyer's intention to continue operations went unchallenged. Nevertheless, he was caught between the proverbial "rock and a hard place" in having to balance conflicting requirements of fuel economy, operational requirements, and supporting the Americans. In frustration, Dyer had to state his problem in blunter terms and seek the necessary guidance from Ottawa to avoid an embarrassing situation should he have to reduce the level of support given to US operations.[31] The problem was aggravated by the fact that the staffs in Ottawa did not share his view of the seriousness of the potential threat posed by the Soviet submarines.

The Naval Board met at 1030 next morning (2 November) to discuss a return to normal maintenance and refit cycles. The minutes of the meeting did not mention Dyer's concerns, expressed the day before. However, CNS replied to him later that day approving his request that he be allowed to use his discretion.[32] Nevertheless, the CNS cautioned him to maintain adequate reserves of essential stores such as sonobuoys and to establish and maintain refit and training schedules. This essentially ended the dispute between Halifax and Ottawa over the control of operations. What the exchange shows is that although the Maritime Commander had certain powers delegated to him for the conduct of operations, he could only exercise that authority with one hand tied behind his back because the Naval Staff in Ottawa retained firm control of fuel and war stores expenditure.

Meanwhile, operations in the Atlantic continued without significant change. The *Bonaventure* group returned to Halifax on 2 November and started to prepare to deploy again on the 5th. For the first time in the crisis Dyer had a full slate of resources and the authority to direct operations as he thought appropriate.

Activity levels were still high, and it seemed that the Soviets were about to make a move. The ELINT trawler *Shkval* was on the move from the B-32 area and headed northeast towards the American SUBAIR barrier to the area where there had been an increase in the number of submarine contacts. Then, on the afternoon of 2 November a USN aircraft made contact with another submarine close to Georges Bank. Canadian ships were in the vicinity and joined the hunt as the submarine headed for the sanctuary of the Soviet fishing fleet.

The availability of *Bonaventure* with her aircraft on 5 November provided some much needed help. At that point the Atlantic fleet had reached the limit of its capability, and thus was probably on a full war footing. The carrier, some twenty-four escorts, and two submarines were deployed across an area over 1000 miles long and about 250 miles wide. In addition, the RCN and RCAF air squadrons were maintaining patrols over five separate parts of that area.

Then, on the morning of 7 November *Kootenay* gained contact with the submarine near Georges Bank. Aircraft also made contact. The confirmation came when two Soviet trawlers charged *Kootenay* in an attempt to drive the ship away from the submarine. The contact was later classified as a *Foxtrot* class submarine, but the Canadians did not play the scene out; instead they returned to Admiral Dyer's control while the USN continued the prosecution.

Essentially, that was the end of the active ASW operations. The ships stayed out for a few days longer, the patrol aircraft continued their surveillance. The first of the RN submarines came back from the advance patrol area on the 8th, and the fleet began to return to the normal cycle of maintenance and training.

By the 11th the crisis at sea was virtually over. There were no submarine contacts and only the ELINT trawlers remained under surveillance. *Shkval* returned to the area of B-32 after *Bonaventure* left, and the fishing fleet remained on Georges Bank. The Americans closed down their ASW barrier on the 13th and the forces went home. The end of the crisis was an anti-climax. There had been no victory. Few of the Soviet submarines had actually been seen because contact with them had mainly been electronic. It was almost as if it never happened. Even the official acknowledgments of a job well done were missing.

CONCLUSION

This of course begs the question, "How well did the RCN and RCAF do?" The crisis was, after all, a full scale test of continental defence plans. In some respects this is an impossible question to answer because the number of submarines is still unconfirmed. Although there were twelve designated contacts, some were on the same submarine while others were not submarines at all. The issue would seem to be whether or not the B-28/B-32 contact, classified as a *Whiskey* class was, in fact, the same submarine found on Georges Bank. In terms of time and distance, the contacts could have been on one submarine. However, the classification was different and the level of protection afforded the Georges Bank submarine by the fishing vessels might indicate a higher relative importance.

The *Foxtrot* class submarines had a strategic role against shipping and carried nuclear torpedoes but did not have a missile capability. Thus, it would make sense for one to be on patrol near Georges Bank where it could monitor the US submarine traffic out of New London and also the shipping out of New York. It could also be argued that the Georges Bank contact was a *Golf* class missile-firing submarine. The characteristics of the *Golf* and the *Foxtrot* were similar. One fact is certain, whatever the classification the submarine had started its patrol long before the crisis and remained in North American waters throughout. It is also possible that the Georges Bank submarine was also the contact B-27 that was gained some 300 miles off the Nova Scotian coast on 18 October. We may never know.

It seems, in fact, that there were only ever two submarines in the Canadian area. One was B-28/B-32, which had a patrol area some 300 miles to seaward of Cape Cod. This may have been a missile-firing submarine. The other submarine was the one caught on Georges Bank on 3 November. This submarine may have been assigned the task of watching Halifax. The movements of the ELINT trawlers also tend to support this theory. Moreover, if both submarines had been on station for that length of time it would explain, at least in part, the need for contact with the replenishment vessels.

The defensive system consisted of layers of submarines, ships, and aircraft deployed along the most likely approach route from the Norwegian Sea. Theoretically, it should have been difficult for any submarine to pass through those defences without being detected. Assuming there were just two Soviet submarines in the Canadian area and that they were in place before the defences were activated. It is not surprising they were hard to find. This is a consequence of trying to conduct ASW operations in a huge area without sufficient forces. Thus, one of the lessons of the Cuban missile crisis was that without a permanent network of ASW defences and surveillance systems, the submarine has a distinct advantage. Open ocean surveillance is an expensive and time-consuming task if there is to be any degree of reliability.

On the positive side, co-operation between RCN/RCAF and USN forces and commands was good, and contingency plans were implemented quickly. One cannot find fault with Admiral Dyer's decision to take action without direction from Naval Headquarters; he merely did what he believed was in the best interests of the fleet and national defence. That the national headquarters was frozen with inaction was a systemic problem.

Although basic plans for joint Canada-U.S. defence of the continent had been drawn up for some time, they did not make allowances for the way in which the Kennedy administration initially chose to handle the Cuban missile crisis. Nor did they anticipate the failure of the Canadian command structure. Nevertheless, the bilateral defence planning framework assumed that extensive co-ordination would take place when any direct threat to North America presented itself. When this did not happen at the political level, the operational level automatically took over. Thus, the uniqueness of the Cuban missile crisis required initiative and improvisation. Because of the close contact between the command staffs in Halifax and Norfolk, Virginia, as well as those in Esquimalt and Pearl Harbour, meeting the challenges of the crisis was not unduly difficult. Years of joint training paid dividends. But the ease with which the various military staffs were able to co-operate was misunderstood in Ottawa and seen as a threat to political control over the Canadian forces. This compounded the effects of the command system failure.

By isolating himself and his government from the Canadian military, Diefenbaker changed the basic nature of civil-military relations in Canada. Rather than integrating the military into the fabric of Canadian society, as one would expect in a liberal democracy, he widened the gulf between them. The 1964 reorganization of the national headquarters restored effective civil control of the military and allowed the military to become part of society again. The Cuban missile crisis thus became a turning point in Canadian civil-military relations. Had the military dimension of the Cuban missile crisis been analysed rather than banished to obscurity as soon as the crisis was over, some useful lessons could have been drawn.

NOTES

1. At the moment, the most widely known works that refer directly to the Canadian naval role in the crisis are: Joel J. Sokolsky, "Canada and the Cold War at Sea," in W.A.B. Douglas, ed., *RCN in Transition, 1910–1985* (Vancouver: University of British Columbia Press, 1988), 209–32; Tony German, *The Sea Is at Our Gates* (Toronto: McClelland and Stewart, 1990); Rear-Admiral Jeffry V. Brock, *The Thunder and the Sunshine* (Toronto: McClelland and Stewart, 1981) chap. 7; and Jocelyn M. Ghent, "Canada, the United States, and the Cuban Missile Crisis," *Pacific Historical Review* 48, 2 (May 1979), 159–84, which has since been revised and published as, Jocelyn Ghent-Mallet, "Confronting Kennedy and

the Missiles in Cuba, 1962," in Don Munton and John Kirton, eds., *Canadian Foreign Policy: Selected Cases* (Scarborough: Prentice-Hall Canada Inc., 1992), 78–100.

2. The linkage between Soviet submarines and their fishing fleet had been recognized for some time, and fishing vessels had been seen replenishing and occasionally sheltering submarines.

3. The complex interrelationship of the two themes: effective military co-operation and political distrust, is a separate but fascinating part of the story, many of whose lessons are still valid today. Unfortunately, that story is beyond the scope of this short paper.

4. In his "Report of Proceedings" for November 1957, the Flag Officer Atlantic Coast, Rear-Admiral H.F. Pullen, said, "The numerous reports being received of submarine sightings around the Newfoundland coast, particularly in areas of strategic interest, convinced me that some positive action was required." Canada, Department of National Defence, Flag Officer Atlantic Coast, *Reports of Proceedings*, file AC: 1926-102/1, 28 Nov. 1957.

5. A *Globe and Mail* (Toronto) feature article, "Russian Vessels Off Grand Banks Puzzle U.S. Navy," 1 June 1958, p. 1, triggered considerable reaction from both the USN and RCN. A series of staff memos, starting on June 2, played down any hint of covert operations. Department of National Defence, Directorate of History (hereafter DHist) File No. 83/1132.

6. DHist file no. 73/1132 "Naval Intelligence."

7. Canada, Royal Canadian Navy, NSS 1884-1, NSS 1950-4-146/37-1 of 28 July 1960, paragraph 3, DHist file no. 73/1132.

8. Canada, Royal Canadian Navy, NSS 1888-7, memos dated 27 Sept. 1962 and 4 Oct. 1962, DHist file no. 73/1132.

9. Government of the United States, Department of the Navy, letter Op-605D4/cd Ser 00474P6 dated 15 Jan. 1960, "The Strategic Concept for Antisubmarine Warfare," p. 4.

10. In addition to deploying US submarines into Soviet operating areas, the tactical requirements were for a capability to intercept electronic emissions, the use of barriers (fixed and mobile) across principal submarine routes into the Atlantic and Pacific, and maintaining offshore surveillance systems capable of detecting and locating submarines entering a zone around the United States at distances corresponding to estimated missile ranges. Ibid, 6–7.

11. A copy of the prevailing rules of engagement can be found attached to the Naval Board Minutes for 8 April 1959, item no. 592-6.

12. Canada, Joint Intelligence Committee Report JIC 428/2(61) dated 13 Dec. 61, "The Maritime Threat to Canada 1962–1972," p. 5, DHist file no. 80/205.

13. Abstracted from the *Queen's Regulations and Orders for the Royal Canadian Navy* (Ottawa: The Queen's Printer, 1962).

14. Canada, Department of National Defence, Royal Canadian Navy, *RCN Defence Plan*, CBCN 6904(59) (Ottawa, 1959), PAC, RG24, Acc. 83-4/167, vol. 11 147, file no. 1400-1 (vol. 1).

15. Sydney, N.S., St. John's, Nfld., Shelburne, N.S., Prince Rupert, and Port Alberni were designated as dispersal bases.

16. Three measures were formal "Alert" states in which military and civilian preparations for attack on Canada were to be made, progressively, these were: Simple Alert, Reinforced Alert, and General Alert. In addition, there were two purely "in-service" conditions of Military Vigilance: a "Discrete" phase when war plans and organizations were reviewed and forces were quietly made ready for intensified operations, and a "Ready" phase in which preparations were made for deployment and dispersal.

17. At the start of the crisis Rear-Admiral Finch-Noyes was the designated Flag Officer Pacific Coast, but he was absent from his headquarters due to ill health. Rear-Admiral W.L. Landymore assumed command of the Pacific fleet on 1 Nov. 1962.

18. *CINCLANT Historical Account of Cuban Crisis–1963*, Headquarters of the Commander in Chief, Atlantic Command, Norfolk, Virginia, pp. 120–22.

19. Flag Officer Atlantic Coast, *Reports of Proceedings* for October 1962, file no. AC: 1926-102/1, 13 Nov. 1962.

20. "U.S. Forces Maneuver off Puerto Rico—Links Denied," *New York Times*, 22 Oct. 1962, p. 16.

21. According to the *Globe and Mail* (Toronto) on October 19, the Civil Defence budget was due to be cut by $1.8 million.

22. Correspondence with The Hon. Douglas Harkness.

23. On 23 Oct. 1962, the *New York Times* contained a sceptical article by Raymond Daniell, "Canada Asks Inspection of Cuba; Britain Supporting Quarantine," in which Diefenbaker was quoted as saying he wanted to know the full facts before committing himself. The innuendo was that the Soviets would also want to know the facts. An *Ottawa Citizen* article of the same day, "Study Alert for RCAF and RCN" contradicted the *New York Times* in saying that Diefenbaker claimed to be fully supportive of Kennedy.

24. Flag Officer Atlantic Coast message, CANFLAGLANT 251848Z Oct. 62.

25. CANCOMARLANT Msg P 271615Z Oct. 62.

26. CINCLANT Report, p. 122.

27. In discussing this period with Admiral Dyer and his Chief of Staff, Commodore Pratt, both remember it as an extremely frustrating situation in which they could not get Admiral Rayner (CNS) to make a decision or give Dyer formal authority to continue supporting the Americans.

28. Naval Board Minutes for 30 Oct. 1962, paragraphs 3 and 4.

29. This concern is well explained in CANAIRLANT's messages of 30 Oct. (DTG 301630Z and 301920Z) to the Vice Chief of the Air Staff. From RG24, acc. 83-4/216, vol. 47, RCAF file S-003-114.

30. COMASWFORLANT message of 1 Nov., DTG 010121Z, RG24, acc. 83-4/216, vol. 47, RCAF file no. S-003-114.

31. CANCOMARLANT message of 1 Nov., DTG 012045Z, RG24, acc. 83-4/167, vol. 267, RCN file no. 1480-146/10 pt. 5.

32. CANAVHED message of 2 Nov., DTG 022016Z, RG24, acc. 83-4/216, vol. 47, RCAF file no. S-003-114.

FROM OCTOBER TO OKA: PEACEKEEPING IN CANADA, 1970–1990◇

DAVID A. CHARTERS

◦

If there is a Canadian "Picture of the Year," the one for 1990 was undoubtedly a striking image: a masked Mohawk "Warrior" and a stone-faced young Canadian soldier staring each other down across a barrier of razor wire. That image, which perhaps evoked comparisons with Lebanon or Northern Ireland, probably said a great deal about the troubled state of the Canadian nation in the summer of 1990. More important for this essay, however, it illustrated graphically the Canadian army's approach to internal security (IS) operations in the current era. That approach is characterized less by the use of lethal force than by the establishment of a firm, purposeful, visible, even intimidating *presence*, the aim of which is to defuse confrontation by wearing down an opponent psychologically. This approach has long historical roots in the Anglo-Saxon tradition of military aid to civil authorities; the "minimum force" principle is notable in this regard. This essay will argue that there is another dimension to the Canadian context of this tradition: that of international peacekeeping. The aim of this chapter is to demonstrate the extent to which IS and peacekeeping operations in the Canadian tradition have come to share a common doctrine and practice.

Before proceeding further, a brief discussion of methods and sources is in order. First, the paper will examine the Canadian army's operational doctrine for IS and peacekeeping: the principles and practices that guide training and operations. Second, it will show how those concepts were applied in three IS operations: the October Crisis (1970); the Olympics security operation (1976); and the Mohawk Warriors' barricades standoff (1990). Finally, the conclusions will suggest that the doctrine, the training, and the oper-

◇ From David R. Jones, ed., *Military Aid to Civil Authorities in the Anglo-Saxon Tradition* (forthcoming).

ations discussed illustrate how these two "traditions" of conflict management have become intertwined; and that the experience of one type of operation provides a doctrinal "institutional memory" which serves to prepare troops for the other.

The proposition that there is a link between IS and peacekeeping is not entirely novel; retired Major-General Dan G. Loomis makes the connection in his book *Not Much Glory: Quelling the FLQ*, published in 1984. Loomis argues, in effect, that Canada's involvement in international peacekeeping was actually part of a pre-conceived "strategy" to prepare the army to suppress the Front de Libération du Québec (FLQ), the Québec extremist separatist movement that was active from 1963 to 1970. The authors of this alleged—and in Loomis's view, farsighted—"strategy" were Canadian Prime Ministers Lester Pearson and Pierre Trudeau and General Jean V. Allard, the Chief of the Defence Staff.[1] While the Loomis book is problematic in its interpretation both of the organisation and intentions of the FLQ and of Canadian government intentions and decisions,[2] the suggested convergence of IS and peacekeeping doctrine and practice opens the door to an intriguing intellectual exercise. In fact, this essay represents an expansion and further development of themes and ideas advanced in one of the author's earlier collaborative works.[3]

This chapter relies mainly on secondary sources, with all the limitations that ensue. With respect to the 1990 incidents, the author is relying mainly on the media coverage which, although extensive, was not necessarily accurate, well-informed, or unbiased. These sources have been supplemented by testimony presented to the parliamentary committee that examined the 1990 crisis and that committee's final report, and by a briefing paper and several interviews with officers who took part in the army's operations. But source problems are not confined to the most recent events. It is striking that even after twenty years, little of substance has been written about the October Crisis, particularly its military aspects. Because until recently the key cabinet documents remained closed, the secondary literature was incomplete and unsatisfactory.[4] But documents released in 1991 shed some light on the extent of the Québec and federal governments' knowledge of the situation and how and why they made important decisions. Some of these are cited in this text, along with a few unpublished documents on army training for aid to the civil power (IS). A number of published primary sources have also been consulted. Nevertheless, this essay falls short of being a definitive work on the subject, although the evidence to support the line of argument is strongly suggestive.

DOCTRINE AND TRAINING

In his 1977 study of Canadian defence policy, Brian Cuthbertson asserts that in Canada, aid to the civil power had "always been predicated on using troops to deal with riots and disturbances."[5] Others, however, suggest the need for a wider interpretation of the army's role, redefining it as "keeping the peace."[6] Cuthbertson's interpretation is nonetheless consistent with

Army doctrine of the 1970s. A 1971 training pamphlet on aid to the civil power focused almost exclusively on "unlawful assembly and riot." It also enunciated clearly the fundamental, long-standing principles that guide Canadian internal security operations: supremacy of the civil authority; the application of only the *minimum force* necessary to achieve the aim; compliance with the law; impartiality; the use of force as a *preventive* tactic, that is, to prevent worse disorders, *not* as a *punitive* tactic; there must be justification for each separate act by the army; troops will operate only under *command* of their officers; and, the use of the army as a *last resort*—only when the police can no longer contain the situation.[7] Both public statements and unpublished data from the 1990 operation indicate that these basic principles are still considered to be valid.[8]

Moreover, they are almost identical to those applied to peacekeeping operations. The basic principles of United Nations (UN) peacekeeping operations include: supremacy of the authority of the United Nations (the international equivalent of the civil power); application of the minimum force principle; impartiality; the use of armed force to prevent further violence; troops operating only under orders from the designated commander of the force; and the use of armed force only as a last resort.[9] This similarity is hardly accidental. Although neither the UN nor Canada invented peacekeeping, Canadian forces have been involved in most operations under UN auspices, as well as others.[10] The secondary literature indicates clearly that Canada has contributed to the development of peacekeeping doctrine.[11] What the literature does *not* say is that the Canadians drew upon their doctrine for aid to the civil power to create a similar body of principles for peacekeeping. Nevertheless, given the considerable body of evidence that such principles evolved over time in the British/Canadian experience of aid to civil authority, the early Canadian involvement in interpository peacekeeping operations, and the explicit similarity between the two bodies of doctrine, it seems fair to infer that some "cross-fertilization" did take place. However, the limitations of existing literature on the subject suggest that this is an area that requires more research.

Moreover, it is important to emphasize that IS and peacekeeping are *not completely* analagous. This is particularly clear with respect to the notion of "impartiality." In international peacekeeping operations, the forces usually do represent a genuinely "disinterested" third party (such as the UN), which is not a belligerent or partisan to the conflict, and thus can be presented as and expected to remain neutral. In IS operations, the notion of impartiality is framed in a somewhat different context. In these cases, *the army is explicitly an arm of government*, and the government may in fact be a party in the conflict. Constitutionally, the army cannot pretend to be neutral between the government and those who have or are threatening to mount violent opposition to it.[12] What it *can* do is try to avoid taking sides or giving the appearance of doing so in conflict situations where the civil authority is trying to restore peace between two or more factions within the wider community. Of course, as the Northern Ireland situation illustrates,[13] this is much easier said than done. So, although the *intent* of IS and peacekeeping operations differ significantly, they do appear to share a common body of principles. The appearance of similarities is sustained when the focus of scrutiny shifts from doctrine to training.

The operational tasks of peacekeeping consist largely of four activities: observation, patrolling, reporting, and interpositioning (the latter refers to the placing of peacekeeping forces between groups or forces who have been fighting or who might be expected to do so). In addition, peacekeeping troops may be expected to engage in negotiation and mediation as a means to prevent localized disputes from escalating into major incidents or crises.[14] The Canadian approach to preparing troops for these duties has changed over time. In 1958, Canada designated a specific infantry battalion (on a three-year rotational basis) to be the "stand-by" force for UN peacekeeping operations. The battalion received two to six months of specialized training for peacekeeping, and was exercised annually in co-operation with the Royal Canadian Air Force (RCAF) to test its readiness and procedures for airlift to overseas destinations. Only in the case of Cyprus in 1964 was the designated battalion called upon and deployed. Since that time, peacekeeping requirements have varied so widely that little advance preparation of a highly specialized nature could be done. More often, Canada was called upon to provide technicians and specialists in the fields of signals, logistics, and engineering. Consequently, the idea of a "stand-by" force had to be expanded from a battalion to a contingency force brigade, from which the required units or specialists could be drawn. But, the limited resources of the army meant that designating training and equipping units specifically for peacekeeping was never a realistic option for Canada. Such a course was explicitly rejected in the 1964 Defence White Paper.[15]

In any case, although they did require a different *attitude*, peacekeeping operations did not require entirely new tactics. So, the army developed standardized briefing and training packages that integrated peacekeeping into the army training program as a whole.[16] Writing in 1978, Brigadier-General Clay Beattie, who had commanded the Canadian force in Cyprus, commented that:

> In general, we have found that by training personnel for the 'worst case situation' . . . in defence of Canada or NATO environments, we can easily modify that training to adapt personnel to the peace-keeping environment. . . . such special training emphasizes the constabulary approach, the exercise of restraint, the use of minimum force as necessary, and the importance of self-discipline, tact, impartiality and negotiating skills in the resolution of conflict situations. In the case of formed units or formations, field exercises are conducted to practise personnel in procedures for preparation, mounting, movement, and tactical deployment . . . in the theatre of operations.[17]

Canadian practice, then, has been to expose all army headquarters, formations, and units to at least two weeks of training in peacekeeping each year. This is supposed to be sufficient to allow any unit to be ready at short notice for peacekeeping duty. In addition, some units would be exposed to refresher courses on subjects of particular value, and selected unit members are designated for refresher training on air movements. The units and soldiers themselves are trained in the following skills:[18]

1. crowd control and dispersal;

2. use of batons and shields;

3. protection of VIPs, convoys, buildings;

4. establishing military control of an area;

5. road blocks;

6. cordon and search, and area search;

7. urban patrols; and

8. mounting guards and pickets.

Refresher training might include sub-unit (platoon and section) tactics, unarmed combat, communications, military engineering, map-reading, first aid, hygiene and sanitation, security of stores and equipment, and orientation to specific operational environments. The troops would take part in exercises, from sub-unit to full-scale deployment, at least annually. That was the status of peacekeeping training in 1970, in the months just prior to the October Crisis.[19]

It does not require a major leap of logic or faith to recognize that this kind of training dovetails neatly with that required for IS operations, or even for counter-insurgency as it was envisaged at that time.[20] For example, training exercises carried out by the Canadian Guards regiment in the mid-1960s blurred the distinction between training for peacekeeping, for internal security, and for counter-insurgency and anti-terrorist operations.[21] The government of the day, to its credit, displayed unusual candour when questioned in parliament as to whether such exercises were a possible prelude to sending Canadian troops to intervene abroad as counter-insurgency forces, as the United States had done in the Dominican Republic. Defence Minister Leo Cadieux emphasized that Canadian troops had to be trained to deal with all types of civil unrest *in Canada* (author's emphasis), and that this type of training was also necessary for Canadian soldiers serving on peacekeeping operations, such as Cyprus or the Congo [now Zaire].[22]

Around 1980, the Department of National Defence (DND) lowered the priority of IS training. G. Davidson Smith suggests that this reflected the fact that the army had not been required to use lethal force during either the October Crisis or the Montreal Olympics.[23] By this time as well, the RCMP, provincial police, and major municipal forces had created riot squads and tactical units, so it was plausible to argue that a significant military commitment to IS was no longer necessary. Moreover, the Canadian Forces had other commitments with higher priorities in terms of personnel and expenditure. Consequently, the amounts of time and money spent on IS training were reduced, and IS equipment, such as riot shields, were withdrawn from army inventories. If the army was called out again for riot control, it would deploy with its regular weapons, as the "force of last resort." The army was expected to retain capabilities to provide protection for vulnerable points, and to provide special skills and equipment for tasks considered to exceed police capacity—for example, providing an armoured vehicle to assist police in subduing a barricaded sniper. The army's declining role in this field was underlined further in 1986, when even the barricade/assault counter-terrorism task was assigned to a newly-created RCMP Special Emergency Response Team (SERT). After six years without an incident, however, the government decided in 1992 to disband SERT as a cost-cutting measure, and to re-assign the task to the army, where many felt it should have been in the first place.[24]

The reduced scale of 1980s IS preparation was readily apparent in the training of the 2nd Battalion Royal Canadian Regiment (2RCR), based at Canadian Forces Base (CFB) Gagetown, New Brunswick. In the period 1979–81, 2RCR carried out several exercises in a series known as ROYAL RESPONSE. The first of these, in March 1979, involved the deployment of the full battalion on a five-day field exercise in Hartland, New Brunswick. The last in the series, held in Kentville, Nova Scotia, in March 1981, was a command post exercise only, held indoors with limited live action, designed to test planning and staff duties.[25] Both exercises tested the troops and their officers in the same tasks:

1. protection of vulnerable points and VIPs;

2. patrolling;

3. road blocks;

4. cordon and search operations;

5. joint civil/military and police planning and operations;

6. hostage-taking incidents;

7. convoy and route protection; and

8. searches for explosives.

While the setting of these involved the containment of a fictitious terrorist campaign, the overlap with peacekeeping tasks is obvious; they are virtually identical.

The 1981 exercise plan said explicitly that "Internal security operations and aid of the Civil Power is a subject that is not included in the normal military curriculum."[26] It went on to stress that units and personnel would require initial or refresher training.[27] The significance of ROYAL RESPONSE III in 1981 is that it was the last major IS training undertaken by 2RCR before it deployed to Quebec in 1990, nine years later.[28] Yet, this battalion's situation was not unique. A DND report dated 1 June 1990 and based on assessments done in 1989 stated that the armed forces as a whole were not capable of handling a major breakdown of public order, and that they were no longer carrying out training for "riotous crowd control with shields and batons."[29] No new equipment (for such tasks) had been purchased for several years, and the DND assumed that if troops were deployed into such situations, it would be only when "the situation is beyond the club and shield stage."[30] During the Mohawk Barricade standoff, the army "rose to the occasion" and adapted to the changing and complex situation, but some of the limitations mentioned above were readily apparent.

The foregoing seems to establish a clear link between IS and peacekeeping in theory and training. Yet it is one thing to demonstrate that link at the theoretical level and quite another to demonstrate it at work in actual operations. This essay will now attempt to do so by examining three army IS operations: the October Crisis; the Olympics security operations; and the Mohawk Warriors' barricades standoff.

PEACEKEEPING IN CANADA: THREE OPERATIONS

It is worth bearing in mind at the outset an important fact; between the end of the Korean war in 1953 and the outbreak of the Persian Gulf War in 1991, peacekeeping duties and IS tasks comprised the sum total of the Canadian army's *military operational* experience. United Nations–sponsored and other peacekeeping operations have been the most frequent and prolonged commitments. In Cyprus, for example, Canadian troops have been deployed on peacekeeping duties for more than twenty-five years. In many cases, the Canadian Forces provided administrative and technical support. But, in Cyprus, the Golan Heights, the Sinai (1956–67), and recently along the Iran-Iraq border, Canadian troops have served "on the front line," patrolling, observing, and mediating. Moreover, because these operations tend to be "personnel-intensive" and the Canadian army has been relatively small, most units and a larger proportion of the army's personnel have served in at least one peacekeeping operation, and many have done several.[31] Although the various Canadian governments have assigned different priorities to peacekeeping within Canadian defence policy over time,[32] it has remained the most consistent *operational* tasking. The dominance of the peacekeeping "paradigm" in Canadian military experience, virtually to the exclusion of traditional "warfighting," is such that one officer concluded that Canadian troops were forever destined to be "Voyeurs of War."[33]

At home, the armed forces have been called out frequently in aid of the civil power to fulfill a wide variety of requirements since 1945. Most of these, however, did not involve a requirement for actual or potential use of force. Instead, they needed personnel or special skills and equipment for activities such as search and rescue, flood control, fighting forest fires, and other forms of disaster relief. A small number of events involved the deployment of *armed* forces: prison disturbances; hostage barricade situations; and a police strike in Montreal. Only three operations required the deployment of large numbers of *armed* troops (i.e., formations consisting of more than a single battalion).[34] These operations are examined in turn.

1. THE OCTOBER CRISIS (1970)

In October 1970, troops were deployed during a period of crisis arising from the kidnapping of a foreign diplomat and a Quebec government cabinet minister by two small cells of the FLQ terrorist separatist movement.[35] The official public rationale was that the army was called in to assist the police who, it was alleged, were stretched to the limit by the intensive investigative duties arising from the kidnappings. In his own account of the crisis Gérard Pelletier, then Secretary of State, explained the use of troops as a response to fears of the federal and Quebec governments that further incidents or other acts of violence might occur, and that the police did not have the staff to protect all personnel and to deal with other disturbances at the same time.[36] There clearly was a crisis atmosphere at the time, and it was not confined to Quebec. Political leaders and activists from both sides were contributing to the tension, either by throwing their political weight and rhetoric behind the aims, if not the methods, of the FLQ, or by painting the FLQ and the threat it posed in "larger than life" dimensions.[37] But since that time, observers and critics from perspectives as diverse as those of General Loomis and Pierre Vallieres (then a pro-FLQ activist and ideologue) have challenged the official version of events. They assert that the real intention in using the army (which, they allege, was reorganized in the mid-1960s specifically for this eventuality), in concert with the other measures that followed, was to deliver a stunning psychological shock that would stop the armed separatist movement in its tracks and discredit both the movement and its methods once and for all.[38]

Documentary evidence now available to the author casts doubt on the official version, and lends weight to the psychological shock thesis, although not to the underlying premeditated "strategy" or conspiracy that Loomis and Vallieres assume. First, although the police forces were described on 12 October as "already strained," two days later RCMP Commissioner Len Higgitt told the cabinet committee on Security and Intelligence (which served as the policy-making body during the crisis) that " . . . there was no shortage of manpower, from a police point of view."[39] Moreover, when Lieutenant-General Michael Dare, the Vice-Chief of Defence Staff, presented the cabinet committee with the plan for use of troops, it was described first and foremost as "a symbolic 'show of force' against the FLQ."[40] Freeing up the police for other tasks seems to have been a secondary concern. Second, the "show of force" role envisaged by General Dare coincided neatly with the concerns of Prime Minister Trudeau. Under mounting pressure from the government of Quebec to do something dramatic to resolve the crisis, Trudeau felt that the federal government would have to take action to prevent the mood of dissent in Quebec from being transformed into a "popular movement"; otherwise the government might lose the power to act at all.[41] It was undoubtedly this line of thinking that prompted his now-famous exchange with reporter Tim Ralfe on 13 October. When pressed on how far he would go to defend Canadian society against the emergence of a "parallel power," Trudeau replied, "Well, just watch me."[42]

Regardless of intent, the October deployments actually involved two distinct operations. The first was Operation GINGER, which commenced on 12 October, two days after Pierre Laporte's abduction. Strictly speaking, this was not an "aid to the civil power" operation, in which a *province* requests the deployment of the armed forces. Rather, the troops were called out under regulations which allow the *federal* government to deploy them to "assist civil authorities"; that is, one federal agency (in this case DND) was providing "armed assistance" to another federal agency (the RCMP). Between five hundred and one thousand troops from the 2nd Combat Group, based at CFB Petawawa (about 150 km west of Ottawa) relieved the RCMP from guard duties on VIPs, government buildings, and other vital points in the Ottawa area. They also assisted the police in sweeps and searches. GINGER lasted until 21 November.[43]

The operation in Quebec, code-named ESSAY, was larger and more complex. An "aid to the civil power" operation, it commenced on 15 October, with a written request from the Quebec justice minister (attorney general) for armed forces to "help the police protect the public and public buildings."[44] Operation ESSAY involved some five thousand to six thousand troops of the 5th Combat Group, the Canadian Airborne Regiment, elements of the 2nd Combat Group, and supporting arms and services. The forces had been placed on warning orders at the outset of the crisis, so when the request for aid came (at 1245 hours, 15 October), the response was rapid: the first troops landed in Montreal by helicopter at 1405. The entire 5th Combat Group and the paratroops (who were flown from Edmonton, Alberta) were deployed across the province by 2250 the same day. The buildup of the remainder of the forces in the province took several days. ESSAY ended on 4 January 1971.[45]

As the troops were being summoned, the Quebec provincial cabinet passed an order-in-council placing all police and military forces under the command of the director of the Quebec Provincial Police. Therefore, all armed forces operations were undertaken at the request and under the direction of the civil authorities. The chain of command went from the police director, to the commander, Mobile Command (the army) to the commander, 5th Combat Group, which was the conducting formation. Units and troops thus received their orders through the normal military chain of command. To facilitate co-operation the army established a joint operational headquarters at the offices of the Quebec Provincial Police. On 16 October the federal government proclaimed the War Measures Act, giving soldiers and police sweeping powers of arrest, search and seizure without warrants, and detention without trial.[46]

In fact, the armed forces carried out no arrests on their own; that task was left to the police. Most of the troops were deployed on static guard duties in Montreal, Quebec City, and at other locations across the province. When required to assist the police in sweeps and raids, the Airborne Regiment provided helicopter- or vehicle-borne tactical teams which mounted the cordons around the search sites. They did not participate, however, in house-to-house searches themselves. Deployment and subsequent operations entailed, as well, extensive airlift and other air activities, including reconnaissance flights by CF-5 jet fighters. During the entire period of active duty the forces fired only ten shots, all warnings; there were no casualties from any of the incidents.[47]

These activities were quite different from those anticipated in legislation covering aid to the civil power. But, as noted earlier, they were completely in tune with the kind of training and peacekeeping operations in which the army was engaged at that time. The activities of one unit are particularly instructive in this regard. The 1st Battalion, Royal Canadian Regiment was deployed on rotation from Cyprus straight into the crisis. Sub-units moved to the Ottawa–Hull–Western Quebec region within days of arrival in Canada. One company protected VIPs in Ottawa, another the hydro-electric grid serving the capital. The remainder carried out "show the flag" patrols throughout the battalion area, which covered some 3200 square miles. The army and police forces in the area established a joint headquarters in Hull. When not on operations, the troops were kept busy on training.[48] This one example would seem to support the proposition that IS and peacekeeping doctrine, training, and operational experience were interchangeable to a considerable degree. It is important to emphasize, however, that at no time during the crisis did soldiers confront rioters or terrorists. From a military operational standpoint, the October Crisis was singularly uneventful, and could not be considered comparable to, for example, the situation prevailing in Northern Ireland at that time.

So, if the October Crisis was a watershed in Canadian history, it would be for its political consequences rather than for its military aspects. But it was not without its impact in the security domain. First, for the next few years, the armed forces gave higher priority to internal security. Second, General Dare carried out a review of the Canadian government's crisis management capabilities. The government did act on the report, tabled in 1972; it established the "Lead Minister" concept, designating specific departments and their heads to be responsible for handling domestic or external crises. Additionally, a security planning group was created within the Ministry of the Solicitor General, the "Lead Agency" for domestic crisis management.[49] These developments helped to prepare the government and the armed forces for the next major IS tasking, the 1976 Olympics security operation.

2. THE MONTREAL OLYMPICS (1976)

Unlike the October Crisis, which took the government by surprise, the Montreal Olympics security operation was a planned event, and the Canadian forces were involved in security planning from the earliest stages. In February 1972, National Defence Headquarters established an Olympics project office, under the direction of a lieutenant-colonel. Later that year, he and his assistants attended the Munich Olympics, where the Black September terrorist attack and the bungled rescue attempt provided an object lesson in the consequences of inadequate security planning. For the purpose of developing the National Security Plan for the Olympics, the

Solicitor General of Canada had been designated the "lead ministry." As in Operation GINGER, DND was to provide "armed assistance" to the other federal ministry, and worked in close co-operation with it in preparing the security plan.[50]

In May 1973 the Principal Committee of Public Safety for the Olympic Games (known by its French abbreviation CPSPJO) was formed, consisting of a police chairman, two representatives from the Canadian forces, and representatives from the four police forces immediately and directly involved in security operations for the Olympics—the RCMP, the Quebec and Ontario provincial police forces, and the Montreal Urban Community Police. This, the principle executive committee, was responsible for developing, co-ordinating, and executing the security operation plan, and it reported to two higher committees, one of more senior officers, and the other of political ministers—municipal, provincial, and federal.[51] Again, as in all Canadian internal security operations, the civil authorities retained ultimate authority.

The Olympic games involved twenty-four competition, fifty-nine training, and three accommodation sites in two provinces, although concentrated in and around Montreal, Bromont (about 50 miles southeast of Montreal), and Kingston, Ontario (175 miles west). Some twelve thousand athletes would have to be protected and surveillance and security provided for the hundreds of thousands of spectators, including large numbers of VIPs. The security task was formidable, involving site security at the above locations, escort of athletes in transit, VIP protection, security at points of entry and along the Canada–United States border, and security of vulnerable points in and around Montreal and at other points in Quebec and Ontario. Original plans had envisaged the use of only two thousand troops, but as the scope of the task emerged, it became clear that a much larger force would be needed.[52]

In September 1974 Major-General Roland Reid was appointed Chief of DND Olympic Co-ordination for Operation GAMESCAN, as the military operation came to be known. Mobile Command was designated to provide the major formed units for the security role at all Olympic locations. There they would work in close co-operation with the police forces and would have the powers of peace officers in order to enforce the law. Security afloat at Montreal and Kingston was assigned to Maritime Command while Air Command provided aerial security and airlift. DND also provided personnel and materiel support for non-security operations. In all, DND provided 15 763 personnel, 9085 of whom were deployed on security or security-related tasks.[53]

These functions were shared mainly between four "Task Forces." Task Force 1, based on the 5th Combat Group and augmented by an infantry battalion and an airborne Commando (company), was responsible for: perimeter security at the Montreal Olympic Village and the Olympic Park; security of athletes in transit (which included searching the vehicles beforehand, route security and armed escort of the vehicles); security at various decentralized competition and training sites; protection of vulnerable points across the province of Quebec; and security patrols along the Quebec–United States border. Some four thousand troops were required to carry out these operations. Task Force 2, drawn from elements of the 2nd Combat Group and totalling about nineteen hundred troops, provided security at Montreal's two international airports, protection of VIPs and their baggage at hotels and in transit, and security at several training and competition sites in the Montreal area. Task Force 3 was made up of the airborne regiment (minus the commando in TF1). They were to provide a commander's reserve for rapid response to incidents anywhere within the security forces' areas of responsibility. Task Force 4, consisting of eight hundred troops from the 2nd Combat Group, protected the Olympic Village, vulnerable points and VIPs at the Kingston, Ontario site. They also provided border security forces, vulnerable point protection in Toronto, and a standby force in Ottawa. Separate from the other task forces, one infantry battalion was assigned to protect Canadian Forces installations in Montreal, to augment security along the New Brunswick–Maine border, and to provide additional security forces during the royal visit. Helicopter and jet fighter aircraft from Air Command provided airspace security over Olympic sites, route surveillance within the security corridor, and road convoy escort. At Montreal and Kingston, ships and helicopters of Maritime Command provided security and rescue forces for nautical events. To handle any terrorist incidents the various police forces provided between them about a dozen tactical assault teams, as well as trained negotiators and explosive ordnance disposal personnel. Nonetheless, the armed forces maintained a company-size assault force at the Olympic Park, in case a substantial assault capability was required.[54]

Mobile Command exercised operational control of all land and air elements of the armed forces, but any action by the troops requiring the use of lethal force would have to be requested by the civil authorities, in short the police forces. Security Intelligence was the responsibility of the RCMP Security Service. They conducted threat assessments over a long period prior to the Olympics, ran a Joint Intelligence Centre prior to and during the Olympiad, and conducted technical surveillance operations during the games. The intelligence cell at Mobile Command headquarters liaised with the RCMP for operational intelligence. Communications, on the other hand, were almost totally in military hands. The armed forces set up and operated the Olympic radio system and message centre and provided telecommunications support at a number of competition sites. In addition, Canadian Forces Communications Command, with the assistance of the Signals Regiment, Communications Squadrons, and signals personnel at headquarters, formation, and unit level provided secure communications for the security forces.[55]

Contingency planning was a joint government-police-military responsibility. The CPSPJO developed the basic security plan with input from all levels. Specific plans were developed for handling terrorist incidents (hostage-takings in particular) by means of negotiation, deception, and assault. The basic plan and its sub-components were tested in April 1976 in a major command post exercise (CPX) devised and directed by the Police and Security Branch of the federal Solicitor General's Department. The results of the CPX led the CPSPJO to modify the plan, which was also adjusted as deemed necessary during the actual operation.[56]

There were no terrorist incidents associated with the Montreal Olympics. Perhaps the larger security effort had the desired deterrent effect, although it is not clear whether any terrorist groups or individuals had actually planned to attack the games.[57] More important for this study, however, is the fact that Operation GAMESCAN demonstrated clearly the overlap of peacekeeping and IS tasks: patrolling, observation, reporting, VIP and VP protection, route security, and convoy escort. The units on duty included some (such as the Airborne Regiment) which had been on peacekeeping duties recently, so the tasks would have been familiar to most of the soldiers. However, they would not be tested again on such a scale for another fourteen years. And in the meantime, while peacekeeping tasks continued, IS training and duties all but disappeared from the army's "institutional memory."

3. THE MOHAWK WARRIORS' BARRICADES STANDOFF (1990)

At time of writing, the 1990 barricades standoff was barely one year into history. While the passage of time has allowed more information about those events to enter the public record, the story remains incomplete. Moreover, the fundamental issues which underlay the crisis—the relationships between indigenous and non-native peoples of North America, and disputes over the distribution of power and land—remain largely unresolved. These issues, however important, lie beyond the scope of this essay, and thus will not be addressed here. What this portion of the chapter will provide is an outline of events, including the army's operations, and an analysis of the army's role and how it relates to the central theme of the paper.

In March 1990, a land claim dispute, relatively minor in comparison with some past and present disputes elsewhere in Canada, led to a confrontation at the town of Oka, Quebec, a short distance northwest of Montreal. The Mohawk people of the nearby settlement of Kanesatake were trying to prevent the town of Oka from expanding the resort town's golf course onto land the Mohawk considered theirs and scared as well (the disputed land contained a cemetery). The Kanesatake Mohawk then barricaded a small track leading into the area (known as "The Pines"), and defied a Quebec Superior Court order (issued 30 June) to remove it. The mayor of Oka then requested that the Sûrété de Quebec (the provincial police) remove the barricade. The SQ's attempt to do so on 11 July led to an exchange of gunfire in which one police officer was killed; the police retreated and the barricade remained.[58] Within a short time, sympathy barricades were erected on the Kahnewake Reserve southwest of Montreal, blocking access to the Mercier bridge, one of the principal commuter routes into the city of Montreal. The blockade was mounted by the Mohawk "Warriors Society," an unofficial, unelected tribal faction known for its militancy on Native land claims issues, but also reputed to be involved in illegal activities on the reserves, such as gambling and cigarette smuggling.[59] The

standoff stretched through the summer, in spite of intermittent, but unsuccessful, efforts to negotiate an end to the confrontation. By early August,
tensions between the Kahnewake Mohawk, the SQ, and the residents of the
nearby town of Chateauguay (who felt greatly inconvenienced by the blockade, which added hours to their daily commuting), manifested itself in ugly
riots. On 6 August, Sam Elkas, the Quebec minister of public security (the
provincial cabinet member responsible for policing) issued a written requisition for troops in aid of the civil power, under the terms of Part 11, Section
277 of the National Defence Act.[60]

Army-police consultation had, in fact, begun much earlier. On 11 July,
the day of the violent clash at Oka, the SQ requested that the armed forces
provide night vision equipment, automatic rifles, flak vests, and eighteen
armoured vehicles. Since this was a request for technical help that did not
involve personnel (other than drivers for the APCs), this was not treated as
a request for military aid to the civil power in the formal sense.[61] By early
August DND had issued warning orders to place units on stand-by to
move. But in anticipation of a prolonged deployment requiring the support
of units in the field, administrative and support troops had begun to move
to CFB Longue Pointe in Montreal on 25 July. On 8 August the Canadian
prime minister announced that the army would be sent to replace the police
at the barricade sites. The prime minister's statement was consistent with
the practice that a province's request will not be refused. But, in fact, DND
did not act on Quebec's requisition immediately, apart from deciding which
troops would be used. It was not until 10 August, when the Chief of the
Defence Staff (CDS) General John de Chastelain returned from overseas,
that the operation was truly set in motion. At that time the CDS conferred
with Québec Premier Robert Bourassa to clarify the nature of the task the
provincial government wished the army to undertake. Three days later, the
province requested that the army begin to deploy its forces closer to the
barricade locations; four days later (17 August), the province requested the
army to relieve the police at the barricade sites. The handing over of responsibility was completed by 20 August. Seven more days passed before the
army was ordered to remove the barricades, and throughout this period
(and after) there were mediation efforts between different levels of government and representatives of the Mohawk communities. On 29 August, as
the army prepared to remove the Kahnewake barricades by force, the
Warriors agreed to a joint effort to remove them peacefully. Over the next
few days, all obstacles were removed on the roads leading to the Mercier
Bridge, which reopened for traffic on 6 September. This resolved the principal source of inter-communal conflict at that location, and tension there
eased considerably. Meanwhile, at Oka, some sixty kilometres away, the
army removed the barricades on 1–2 September without the co-operation of
the Warriors, who were pushed back and then surrounded on the grounds
of the community Treatment Centre. They remained there under close
observation by the army until 26 September, when they abandoned the
position and were taken into custody.[62] That ended the standoff, and the
troops withdrew shortly thereafter. But, at the time of writing the legal proceedings arising from the events were still on-going.

The army operation was code-named SALON. The conducting formation was the 5th Mechanized Brigade, based at CFB Valcartier, near Quebec
City, and including units from CFB Gagetown, New Brunswick. The
brigade deployed with a nearly full complement of units, troops, and equipment (except for the 12th Armoured Regiment—all but its Rear Party was
overseas). Some reservists were also called up to flesh out supporting elements. While the brigade comprised 3700 troops at peak strength, only
about half of that total were engaged in IS operations: three infantry battalions, one artillery regiment, a composite armoured reconnaissance unit
(made up from the 12th Armoured Rear Party and the Armoured Corps
School at Gagetown), plus combat engineers and military police. The
remainder fulfilled normal military support functions: planning, intelligence, logistics, transport, communications, clerical, troop welfare and medical support, and public relations. A helicopter squadron provided air
mobility, while fixed-wing aircraft were used for photo reconnaissance. The
troops were deployed as follows: 2nd Battalion, Royal 22nd Regiment, and
5th Light Artillery (in an infantry role) operated in the Oka/Kanesatake
area; 3R22eR and 2RCR in the Kahnewake area.[63]

As in all "aid to the civil power" operations, final political authority
remained in civilian hands. Within the Quebec provincial government, the
cabinet was the locus of civil responsibility for the army's operations; the
key figure in cabinet was Sam Elkas, the Minister of Public Security. His
link to the armed forces was direct, to the CDS himself. While acting at the
request of the civil power, the army operated through its own chain of command: from the CDS, through Lieutenant-General Kent Foster (Commander
Mobile Command/Eastern Region), to Brigadier-General Armand Roy
(Commander 5th Brigade), then to all units and personnel. General Foster
had responsibility for the operation as a whole; operational planning was
delegated to General Roy, his staff, and subordinate unit commanders. The
army maintained contact with the police at all levels, although contact was
not identical at each level. For example, 2RCR initially had only an SQ
Liaison Officer (L/O), who served as a conduit for intelligence and inter-
agency consultation. Later an RCMP L/O was assigned. At higher levels,
however, both forces were not necessarily represented; apparently, the SQ
was represented at brigade level, and the RCMP at Mobile Command, and
the two forces did not share the same perceptions of the situation. Given
this, and the complex and politically sensitive nature of the situation, there
was frequent consultation up and down the civilian and military chains of
command before any action was taken.[64]

The Army's mission, defined in consultation with the provincial government, was straightfoward:[65]

1. the removal of the barricades at Kahnewake and Kanesatake;

2. the restoration of freedom of movement on all roads and bridges in the
   disputed areas;

3. the removal of all strong points; and

4. restoration of normal conditions of public order and security.

From the outset, however, it was clear that this would not be a "routine" IS operation. The information available to the army at the beginning of Operation SALON, based on police and media reports, indicated that they confronted a highly motivated, heavily armed, dug-in, and tactically skilled opponent, who would use force to resist the army's efforts to carry out its mission tasks. The Warriors reportedly included a number of Vietnam veterans and former Canadian soldiers, who were knowledgeable in tactics, fieldcraft, and use of weapons. They were thought to have as many as five hundred weapons of different types, sited in fortifications so as to provide interlocking fields of fire. The Warriors or their spokespersons also warned that they would "bring down" the Mercier Bridge if attacked, so the army assumed that it had been booby-trapped with explosives.[66] Once the army deployed in late August and carried out reconnaissance on the ground and by air, the earlier estimates were scaled back (the "booby-traps" on the bridge, for example, turned out—upon examination—to be convincing fakes). Based on the early reports, however, initial planning, training, and preparation was founded on the assumption that the army would have to breach, capture, and remove defended obstacles, by force and under fire. It was for this reason that the brigade deployed with its full complement of combat equipment, including the Leopard tanks. The latter were included not for their firepower, but for the fact that their armour protection and dozer blades would permit troops to remove the barricades under fire. As events turned out, of course, they were not required.[67]

Once the barricades had been removed, Operation SALON reverted to the more traditional IS pattern. Army tasks then included: guard duties, road blocks, patrolling, arms searches, and crowd control. In addition, the army was directly involved in negotiations with the Warriors and other Mohawk leaders over terms for resolving the standoff.[68] But, it was these "routine" activities, rather than the removal of the barricades, that created the most tension and led to the most violent clashes between the army, the Warriors, and other Mohawk people. Army patrol tactics, the use of trip flares and searchlights, clearly aggravated the Native people surrounded at the Treatment Centre. There were frequent disputes with the army and the SQ over matters such as access to the area for outside observers, the seemingly arbitrary and petty obstacles and arguments over food and medical supplies, and controls on the ability of the media to report on the situation. The tension "along the razor wire" at Oka was manifest in the constant undercurrent of mutual taunting by individual soldiers and Warriors. However, in spite of a few "dramatic" incidents in which shots were fired (by whom it is not clear), and an army recce patrol inside the Warriors' perimeter that ended with one Warrior captured and slightly injured, there were no serious clashes at Oka. If the actions of some individual Warriors seemed to be deliberately provocative, the army at least did not overreact; quite the contrary, under the very trying circumstances, army discipline was exemplary. The famous picture says it all.[69]

It was the arms searches at Kahnewake that produced two of the most serious clashes, at the Longhouse on 3 September, and on Tekakwitha Island on the 18th. The latter resulted in the worst incident of the whole period. Acting on a tip arising from an arrest, the army and the SQ decided the search the island (located just offshore from the Reserve) for weapons. The SQ provided about 60 officers and 2RCR created a composite reinforced company of some 240 troops, made up from the battalion's infantry reserve plus support personnel and militia. The operational plan included phone calls to the Reserve leaders to advise them that the search was taking place. It also assumed that there would be enough troops in place at the outset to seal off the bridge connecting the island to the Reserve, thereby preventing anyone from Kahnewake from interfering with the search. For reasons which are not clear, the plan went awry; either the phone call was made too early, or the troops arrived too late (or perhaps both). In any case, by the time the troops arrived by helicopter at about 1445 hours, a crowd of some 300 angry Mohawk had already crossed the bridge onto the island. They tried to disrupt the search and a riot resulted, that lasted several hours. The crowd attacked the troops with fists, kicks, rocks, and Lacrosse sticks. About 140 troops from the search team tried to contain the riot, using tear gas, rifle butts, and warning shots. Seventy-five Mohawk and 22 soldiers were injured in the fighting. The army-police search of the island yielded forty-eight weapons, carefully wrapped and hidden (some loaded), and five thousand rounds of ammunition. The last troops withdrew from the island about eight hours after the search began.[70]

One other incident bears mentioning in a similar context. On the evening of 26 September the siege at Oka ended in confusion. Some of the Warriors tried to evade capture, while others, family members, and media personnel were being taken into custody. Encountering some resistance, the troops used force to physically subdue some of the detainees. The ugly scene was broadcast live on TV, enraging the Kahnewake Mohawk. A short time later, 350 of them advanced on an army checkpoint, which at that moment comprised only six soldiers. The Mohawk attacked the soldiers with lead pipes and baseball bats; the troops responded with tear gas, but that did not stop the crowd, some of whom had gas masks. The soldiers then fixed bayonets, and fired warning shots. Another twenty-five troops arrived, but since the rioters showed no signs of backing off, the army officer on the scene ordered the soldiers to prepare to fire at specific individuals thought to be the ringleaders of the riot. No further shots were fired; the preparations were sufficient to cause the rioters to withdraw.[71]

Operation SALON differed from the other two IS operations in several key respects. First, it was dynamic. The public order situation changed over time. As a result, while the army's mission remained constant, the tasks it was required to perform were modified. The task for which the army had prepared—an assault on defended obstacles—was not what it actually did; the functions the army did perform, of a routine IS nature, were not the ones it had prepared for. Nor was it equipped for certain IS tasks; army units did not have their own riot shields, helmet visors, or riot batons, only tear gas and personal weapons. The army did adapt to the changing situation, adjusting its tactics and improvising as circumstances dictated. Yet, clearly it was operating at the outer margins of "minimum force." If these methods had failed to deter, then lethal force was the next step. This came *very* close to happening during the final incident at Kahnewake. It is not to cast aspersions on the performance of the army to reflect how close the situation came to tragedy and the very real likelihood of escalation and further violence, at the very moment the original standoff was coming to an end. Yet, this clearly illustrates the dynamic nature of the situation. It is worth noting, as well, that while this crisis was almost unique in modern Canadian history, there are parallels in other countries; the Northern Ireland conflict, for example, evolved in a similar dynamic form in the 1969 to 1972 period.[72]

The violence that occurred is the second difference that sets the Oka operation apart from the other two. The army did not encounter violent opposition to its actions during either the October Crisis or the Olympics; nor was it called upon to use force. From the outset, the prospect of violence set an entirely different tone for the 1990 standoff. The army's role in securing the Olympic games is likely to fade from public memory, if it has not already. The October Crisis still evokes powerful images of troops on the streets. But unlike that case, from which the *image* has achieved *symbolic* status, it is the *actions* of the army at Oka and Kahnewake that are likely to be retained in the collective memory.

This feature is linked directly to the third, the extensive media coverage of the crisis. The media recorded and reported as much as it could on the crisis, and the army's role in it. Every actual or potentially controversial army action was subjected to commentary and critique. In the difficult and politically sensitive atmosphere of the crisis, this raised the stakes of every army action, and put a great deal of pressure on individual soldiers. Some, including members of the media themselves, have suggested since that reporting was biased toward the Warriors (or the Mohawk communities as a whole) and thus inevitably favoured them.[73] But, it is also clear that the army made a significant public relations effort, one which largely paid off in terms of praise for the army's performance and restraint.[74] Moreover, the army was able to use the media coverage for psychological advantage. The CDS's televised speech of 27 August was perhaps the best example in this regard. In what was a sobering, even chilling, performance, he explained exactly what the army was going to do and how, what the army knew about Mohawk capabilities, the options facing them (the Warriors), and the consequences of resistance. He emphasized that the army *would not fail* in its mission.[75] The fact that the Kahnewake barricades came down voluntarily two days later, just before the army moved to forcibly remove them, suggests that the CDS got his message across. If so, it was a skilful use of the media to intimidate an opponent.

This immediately raises the question of whether the army actually tried to "manipulate" media coverage to its advantage. Any lingering suspicions in this regard may have been given added force by the remarks of Jean-Claude Cloutier, a psychologist who worked for the armed forces as a civilian adviser on public relations. At a journalists conference in October, Cloutier was quoted as saying, in effect, that the army had "pre-scripted" their management of the crisis and that the Mohawk had played right into their hands.[76] While the CDS's speech could be seen as a key component of just such a carefully crafted media strategy, the dynamic evolution of events during the standoff suggests otherwise; the army was not always in control of the situation. The final confrontation at Kahnewake is a case in point. It is hard to imagine that anyone could have "pre-scripted" the confusing and violent denouement at Oka—which did not reflect well on the army's otherwise benign image—and the spontaneous angry riot that resulted at Kahnewake. For if the army's aim was to bring about a peaceful resolution of the standoff, employing minimum force to do so, then taking the confrontation to the brink of tragedy would hardly have been in the script. Privately, some officers have dismissed Cloutier's comments as a vast and personal overstatement of his own rather modest contribution to the army's public relations effort.[77] And to keep perceptions in perspective, it is important to take note of the fact that not all of the media coverage of the army was favourable. It was criticized in and by the media for preventing food and medical supplies from reaching the Treatment Centre, for interfering with media coverage of the Oka siege (by cutting off the media's phone communications); it was even accused of lying.[78] The fact that these charges do not appear to have tarnished the army's image permanently probably says more about the substance of the charges than it does about the army's public relations skills.

If these features clearly set Operation SALON apart from earlier IS operations, they also render it distinct from peacekeeping actions. In particular, the resort to force is rare in the latter. The only significant instances involving Canadian Forces occurred in 1974, during and after the Turkish invasion of Cyprus.[79] And, if the army initially acted as an impartial, interpository force between the SQ and the Mohawk, that impartiality was at best qualified and, in any case, temporary. Both in legal fact and in appearance the army was acting *on behalf of the civil authority*—the government of Quebec— which was one of the parties to the dispute. So, any similarity to peacekeeping should not blind one to the fact that the *intent* of the army's mission was to end the standoff on the *government's* terms, *by force* if necessary.

That said, it might be argued in the context of this paper that it is possible to distinguish between the *intent* of army operations—which is essentially a political consideration—and the *character* or *style* of those operations, that is, the way they are carried out at the tactical level. The latter is a question of doctrine, training, and experience, which is the perspective that provides the framework for this essay. When seen from this "operational" standpoint, the parallels appear, just as they did in the operations described earlier. They were apparent even to the soldiers themselves, at least one of whom remarked that the situation reminded him of Cyprus.[80] Just as in Cyprus, the soldiers found themselves mounting patrols, road blocks, vehicle searches, and OPs—familiar routine peacekeeping duties. Similarly, officers and NCOs were engaged in delicate, politically-charged mediation efforts and other negotiations to secure the removal of barricades peacefully and to de-escalate the crisis—the same skills required for "tactically-similar" peacekeeping situations. But, as one officer suggested, perhaps more than any particular skill, the link between the two types of operations comes down to a question of *attitude*; both require discipline, cool-headedness, impartiality, and adherence to the "minimum force" principle.[81]

CONCLUSIONS

The evidence presented regarding the experience of aid to the civil power in Canada over the last twenty years suggests a direct link or an overlap between peacekeeping and internal security operations. While the intentions and objectives of military activity differ in key respects for these two forms of conflict management, they do share a common body of tactical doctrine, training, and operational techniques. The extent of this overlap was readily apparent during the October Crisis and the Mohawk Warriors' barricades standoff. Indeed, as a corollary to the main conclusion, the experience of those two cases in particular indicates that, in the absence of extensive, routine training and preparation for IS, peacekeeping experience provides a relevant and effective substitute.

The very preliminary nature of this exploration of the subject probably raises more questions than it answers. It does not, for example, address the question of the *origins* of peacekeeping doctrine. The limited evidence presented here appears to indicate that it evolved from the Anglo-Saxon tradition of aid to the civil power, but perhaps other influences were at work. And if the Anglo-Saxon tradition did not influence the development of peacekeeping doctrine, then who did? This question bears exploration, so the essay closes with the observation that this subject offers important and intriguing avenues for further research.

NOTES

1. Dan G. Loomis, *Not Much Glory: Quelling the F.L.Q.* (Toronto: Deneau and Wayne, 1984), preface, 46–47, 51, 54–65, 70–71, 73, 76, 89–95, 123–26.

2. Ibid., preface, 17–23, 29–30, 38, 46–47, 51, 54–65, 70–71, 73, 76–77, 89, 112–25, 135–36, 140, 154–56. John Oliver Dendy, "The Canadian Armed Forces and the 'October Crisis': A Historian's Perspective," in *Acta* 14 [Proceedings: 14th International Military History Colloquium] (Ottawa: International Commission of Military History, 1989), 325 dismisses the Loomis thesis as "a form of conspiracy theory." At the very least there are alternative explanations for the restructuring of the armed forces in the mid-1960s, most of which are founded on financial considerations.

3. David A. Charters and James LeBlanc, "Peace-Keeping and Internal Security: The Canadian Army in Low-Intensity Operations," in David A. Charters and Maurice Tugwell, eds., *Armies in Low-Intensity Conflict: A Comparative Analysis* (London: Brassey's, 1989), 139–68.

4. Jean-François Duchaîne, *Rapport sur les événements d'Octobre 1970* (Quebec: Ministère de la Justice, Gouvernement du Québec, 1981), which provides (in French) a day-by-day chronology and analysis of issues, probably comes closest to being a comprehensive "history." John T. Saywell, *Quebec 70: A Documentary Narrative* (Toronto: University of Toronto Press, 1971), is the best of the "instant history"

genre that emerged. Louis Fournier, *FLQ: Anatomy of an Underground Movement* (Toronto: NC Press, 1984), is the most authoritative history of the FLQ, but readers should also see Ronald D. Crelinsten, "The Internal Dynamics of the FLQ During the October Crisis of 1970," in David C. Rapoport, ed., *Inside Terrorist Organizations* (London: Frank Cass, 1988), 59–89. The crisis was also the subject of memoirs by former cabinet ministers and former FLQ members alike, as well as journalistic accounts, while its legal and constitutional aspects have been dissected in the professional literature. This author cautions the reader not to treat this brief note as anything remotely resembling a complete survey of the literature on the October Crisis.

5. Brian Cuthbertson, *Canadian Military Independence in the Age of the Superpowers* (Toronto: Fitzhenry and Whiteside, 1977), 251.

6. This was, in fact, the terminology used by the British in the 1950s and 1960s: see, for e.g., the British army's manuals, *Keeping the Peace: Duties in Aid of the Civil Power* (1957); and *Keeping the Peace* (1963). Desmond Morton, "Bayonets in the Streets: The Canadian Experience of Aid to the Civil Power 1867–1990," *Canadian Defence Quarterly* 20, 5 (April 1991), 33 and note 61, explicitly links peacekeeping and "low intensity conflict" with reference to the 1963 manual.

7. Canadian Forces Officer Candidate School, *Basic Officer Training Précis: In Aid of the Civil Power* (CFOCS, April 1971), 1, 15. The list of references at Annex I of the Précis includes both parts of the 1963 British manual cited in note 6. See also, Lieutenant-Colonels R. McLean and A. Desroches, "The Canadian Forces in Internal Security Operations," in *The Management of the Police Response to Crisis Situations: The Proceedings of the Tactical Unit Workshop* (Ottawa: Canadian Police College, 1982), 61, 63.

8. "OPSALON," briefing presentation, 2nd Battalion, Royal Canadian Regiment (CFB Gagetown, 1990), 14; Lieutenant-Colonel Greg Mitchell, Officer Commanding, 2RCR, interview with author, 12 March 1991; Address by General John de Chastelain, Chief of the Defence Staff, 27 August 1990, recorded by CTV.

9. United Nations, Aide Memoire of the secretary-general concerning . . . function and operation of the United Nations Peace-Keeping Force in Cyprus, 10 April 1964, repr. in Robert C.R. Siekmann, *Basic Documents on United Nations and Related Peacekeeping Forces*, 2nd ed. (Dordrecht: Martinus Nijhoff, 1989), 152–53; International Peace Academy, *Peacekeeper's Handbook* (New York: Pergamon, 1984), 28–29, 33–34, 38.

10. Fred Gaffen, *In the Eye of the Storm: A History of Canadian Peacekeeping* (Toronto: Deneau and Wayne, 1987). Since Gaffen's book was published Canada has participated in five more peacekeeping missions: Afghanistan; Iran/Iraq; Namibia; Central America; and Iraq/Kuwait.

11. On this, see, for e.g., Charles C. Moskos, Jr., *Peace Soldiers: The Sociology of a United Nations Military Force* (Chicago: University of Chicago Press, 1976), 25–28, 87–89, 93–96; Michael Harbottle, *The Impartial Soldier* (London: Oxford University Press, 1970), 46, 123, 189; see also Fred Gaffen, *In the Eye of the Storm: A History of Canadian Peacekeeping* (Toronto: Deneau and Wayne, 1987), passim.

12. This is implicit in the very notion of military aid *to the civil power*. See the *National Defence Act*, Revised Statutes of Canada, 1985, Part 11, sections 275, 277. See also, Harbottle, *Impartial Soldier*, 46–47; and John Gellner, *Bayonets in the Streets: Urban Guerrilla at Home and Abroad* (Toronto: Collier Macmillan, 1974), 153.

13. See Desmond Hamill, *Pig in the Middle: The Army in Northern Ireland,*

1969–1984 (London: Methuen, 1985), Prologue and Phases one to four.

14. International Peace Academy, *Peacekeeper's Handbook*, 34–35, 38, 55.

15. John McLin, *Canada's Changing Defence Policy 1957–1963* (Toronto: Copp Clark, 1967), 208; Canada, Minister of National Defence, *White Paper on Defence* (Ottawa, 1964), 16; The Rt. Hon. Lester B. Pearson, Lecture at Carleton University, 7 May 1964, cited in Larry R. Stewart, ed., *Canadian Defence Policy: Selected Documents, 1964–1981* (Kingston, ON: Queen's University Center for International Relations, 1982), 156–57; Larry L. Fabian, *Soldiers Without Enemies: Preparing the United Nations for Peacekeeping* (Washington, DC: Brookings, 1971), 134–35.

16. Harbottle, *Impartial Soldier*, 123, 189; Moskos, *Peace Soldiers*, 95–96.

17. Brigadier General Clayton E. Beattie, "Preparations for Peacekeeping at the National and International Level," *Canadian Defence Quarterly* 8, 2 (Autumn 1978), 29; Captain Lorimer Joudrey, "The Military Peacekeeper Before—During—After—a Canadian Armed Forces View," unpublished conference paper (Acadia University, 1989), 6–8.

18. Canada, House of Commons, Standing Committee on External Affairs and National Defence, "Eighth Report to the House— Subcommittee on United Nations and Peacekeeping," 31 (21 May 1970), 73–74.

19. Ibid., 75.

20. In fact, the British manual *Land Operations*, vol. 3, *Counter-Revolutionary Warfare* (London: Ministry of Defence, 1969), grouped counter-insurgency, peacekeeping, and internal security doctrines together under the rubric of Counter-Revolutionary Warfare.

21. "Exercise New Crusader," *The Canadian Guardsman* [Regimental journal] (1966), 59–60; "Exercise Park Bandit," *The Canadian Guardsman* (1967), 86, 88–89.

22. John Walker, "What was the Exercise About?" *Montreal Gazette*, August 1969; see also, Loomis, 25, 144–45.

23. G. Davidson Smith, *Combatting Terrorism* (London: Routledge, 1990), 66, 70–71, 202–203, 248.

24. On the status of police tactical units in 1980, and the impact of their existence on the change of IS policy, see David A. Charters, *Police Tactical Unit Study: Issues and Lessons from Crisis Incidents* (Ottawa: Canadian Police College, 1980), 90; and testimony of General John de Chastelain, Chief of the Defence Staff (CDS), to House of Commons, Standing Committee on Aboriginal Affairs, in *Minutes of Proceedings and Evidence* 55 (19 March 1991), 98. See also, Mitchell, interview with author. In private discussions and correspondence, a number of officers confirmed the reduction in army IS training and the disposal of specialized IS equipment.
On the creation and disbandment of SERT see, The Hon. Perrin Beatty, "Counter-Terrorism: The Role of the RCMP," *RCMP Gazette* 48, 3 (1986); and *Globe and Mail* (Toronto), 17 February 1992.

25. The first exercise is described in a series of reports in the *Daily Gleaner* (Fredericton) and the *Telegraph Journal* (Saint John), 19–23 March 1979. Details of the 1981 exercise from the exercise planning précis: Canadian Forces, Atlantic Region Headquarters, *Exercise ROYAL RESPONSE III* (Halifax, NS, 1981), 1.

26. *Exercise ROYAL RESPONSE III*, 2.

27. Ibid. Several officers indicated that refresher training in the period since 1980 has consisted of no more than 1–2 days of lectures per year.

28. Interview with Colonel Mitchell and two of his officers. Others questioned informally could not recall any other major exercise since that one.

29. *Globe and Mail* (Toronto), 24 May 1991. The information in the news

report was based on documents obtained through an Access to Information request.

30. Ibid.

31. R.R. Byers and Michael Slack, eds., *Canada and Peacekeeping: Prospects for the Future* (Toronto: York University Programme in Strategic Studies, 1983), 15–17. For more detail about specific operations, see Gaffen, *In the Eye of the Storm*. On p. 253, he observes that peacekeepers constitute only a minority within the forces as a whole, which is probably correct. But, within the army, they probably constitute the majority.

32. Compare, for e.g., DND's *White Paper on Defence* (1964) and *Defence in the 70s* (1971). Both placed peacekeeping fourth in the lists of priorities (see pp. 24, 16 respectively). But the 1964 White Paper devoted much more attention to the subject and committed the forces to a high degree of readiness and capability for the task (see pp. 15–16, 24–25). The 1971 policy statement explicitly downplayed the prospects for "useful and effective peacekeeping" (p. 5) and set political and military limits on Canada's future participation in those operations (pp. 39–40).

33. Quote courtesy of an officer colleague who probably would prefer to remain unnamed.

34. McLean and Desroches, *Canadian Forces in Internal Security Operations*, 63; de Chastelain testimony, 101–102.

35. For a chronology of the October Crisis, see James Stewart, *The FLQ: Seven Years of Terrorism* (Montreal: Montreal Star, 1970), 57–82; and Richard Dalton Basham, *Crisis in Blanc and White: Urbanization and Ethnic Identity in French Canada* (Cambridge, MA: Schenkman Publishing, 1978), 175–91.

36. Gérard Pelletier, *The October Crisis* (Toronto: McClelland and Stewart, 1971), 135; see also Saywell, *Quebec 70*, 78, 81; *Montreal Star*, 13 October 1970.

37. Denis Smyth, *Bleeding Hearts . . . Bleeding Country* (Edmonton: Hurtig, 1971), 27–28, 33–34.

38. This was the central thesis of Loomis's book. See also, Pierre Vallieres, *The Assassination of Pierre Laporte: Behind the October '70 Scenario* (Toronto: James Lorimer, 1977), which reaches virtually the same conclusion, although by a different route and from a completely different political perspective.

39. Cabinet Committee on Security and Intelligence (hereafter CCSI), Minutes of Meetings, 12, 14 (morning) October 1970, pp. 3, 2 respectively. (At this time, I should like to acknowledge and thank Mr. John Starnes, who acquired these documents under an Access to Information request, and graciously provided copies to me.) It is noteworthy that Higgitt's comments to the CCSI regarding police activity at the time do not support the assertion of the later McDonald Royal Commission on police action. Canada, Commission of Inquiry Concerning Certain Activities of the Royal Canadian Mounted Police, *Third Report: Certain RCMP Activities and the Question of Governmental Knowledge* (Ottawa: Supply and Services, 1981), 201–206, points out that a directive to the police to follow up every lead overtaxed investigative staffs and swamped them with masses of information and there were also problems of co-ordinating the investigations of several police agencies. While acknowledging the lack of progress and the large volume of information being received, Higgitt insisted that—at that stage of the crisis at least—co-operation between the three police forces was good.

40. CCSI Minutes, 14 October (evening), 6.

41. Ibid. (morning), 3. The pressure from the Quebec government is readily apparent in the minutes.

42. Quoted in Smyth, *Bleeding Hearts*, 32–33.

43. Major Guy Morchain, "Peacekeeping at Home," *Canadian Forces Sentinel* (February–March 1971), 2.

44. Ibid., 2–3.

45. Ibid., 3–4.

46. Ibid., 3. Saywell, *Quebec 70*, 81; powers under the War Measures Act cited in Ron Haggart and Aubrey Golden, *Rumours of War* (Toronto: New Press, 1971), app. C, 283–86.

47. Morchain, "Peacekeeping at Home," 4–6, 9. One soldier was killed when his own rifle discharged accidentally. The fact that his weapon had a round "chambered" was probably a violation of procedure. General Dare had told the cabinet committee that magazines would be loaded, but chambers would be empty. CCSI, 14 March (evening), 7.

48. Cuthbertson, *Canadian Military Independence*, 250–51; Loomis, *Not Much Glory*, 144–45. In an earlier manuscript version of the book, Loomis described the on-site training for IS. Dendy, "The Canadian Armed Forces and the 'October Crisis,' " 326, emphasises the relevance of peacekeeping experience to all of the troops deployed during the crisis; and Morton, "Bayonets in the Streets," 33, credits the smooth deployment to the prior "peacekeeping" planning.

49. Davidson Smith, *Combatting Terrorism*, 67–68, 178, 202.

50. Captain Bill Aikman, "The Beginnings," *Canadian Forces Sentinel Olympic Triple Issues* 13, 1 (January 1977), 5; Lieutenant-Colonel Pierre Senecal, "La Securité aux jeux Olympiques 76," *Canadian Defence Quarterly* 5, 2 (Autumn 1976), 26.

51. Arthur B. Fulton, *Countermeasures to Combat Terrorism at Major Events: A Case Study for Senior Seminar on Foreign Policy* (Washington, DC: Department of State, 1976), 41.

52. Ibid., 40; *Toronto Star*, 19 July 1975.

53. Aikman, "The Beginnings," 6; Senecal, "La Securité aux jeux Olympiques 76," Department of National Defence, *Defence 1976* (Ottawa: Department of Supply and Services, 1977), 64 (annual report).

54. See Task Force and other accounts in *Sentinal Olympic Issue*, 13–44 passim, 48–50; Fulton, *Countermeasures to Combat Terrorism*, 42, 46–47. A brief but colourful account may be found in: Lieutenant Andy Pittendrigh, "Portrait of the Life of a Paratrooper in Montreal," *Junior Officer's Journal* 1, 1 (January 1977), 14–15.

55. Fulton, *Countermeasures to Combat Terrorism*, 44–45; *Sentinel Olympic Issue*, pp. 66–73; *Montreal Star*, 8 June 1976.

56. Canada, Department of the Solicitor-General, *Annual Report 1975–1976* (Ottawa: Supply and Services, 1976), 8; see also Senecal, "La Securité aux jeux Olympiques 76," 28; Fulton, *Countermeasures to Combat Terrorism*, 45–46; and Aikman, "The Beginnings," 9.

57. A report in the *Globe and Mail* (Toronto), 7 August 1976, says that security authorities claimed to have forestalled at least one planned terrorist attack, but provided few details.

58. Craig MacLaine and Michael Baxendale, *This Land is Our Land: The Mohawk Revolt at Oka* (Montreal/Toronto: Optimum Publishing International Inc., 1990), 13–14, 17–19, 22–24, provides a detailed chronology of the standoff. A journalistic account, it is unashamedly pro-Mohawk.

59. Ann Charney, "The Last Indian War," *The Idler* 29 (July–August 1990), 14–22; Maurice Tugwell and John Thompson, *The Legacy of Oka*, Mackenzie Paper 21 (Toronto: The Mackenzie Institute, 1991), 3–20. Both works are sympathetic to the plight of Native peoples, but are critical of the activities of the Warriors.

60. MacLaine and Baxendale, *This Land is Our Land*, 24–45; de Chastelain testimony, pp. 84–85.

61. Testimony by de Chastelain, Lieutenant-General Kent Foster, and Brigadier-General Armand Roy, 88–89.

62. MacLaine and Baxendale, *This Land is Our Land*, 35, 45–92; de Chastelain testimony, 85–86.

63. Ibid., 51–53; Foster testimony, 94; 2RCR Briefing text, 2, 9–10, 17. DND's *Defence 90* (Ottawa: Supply and Services, 1991), 30, indicates that intelligence support included No. 1 Intelligence Company and No. 2 Electronic Warfare Squadron from Kingston. The latter unit would have provided a communications intercept capability and thus a SIGINT product to the forces.

64. 2 RCR Briefing Text, 1–2, 14, 15–16; Mitchell, interview; a DND Memorandum published in October 1991 states that a new joint staff system for handling operational matters was initiated at NDHQ during Operation SALON. In a published interview, General Foster described his role in the consultations with provincial authorities: see "The Mohawk crisis . . . from the top," *Sentinel* 6 (1990), 6–7.

65. De Chastelain testimony, 85.

66. 2RCR Briefing text, 6–8; Mitchell, interview; de Chastelain and Foster testimony, 84, 86, 94, 97, 99; MacLaine and Baxendale, *This Land is Our Land*, 23, 28; *Globe and Mail* (Toronto), 29 Aug. 1990. In his press conference, 28 August, General Foster and his staff provided details of the Warriors' fortifications and the weapons believed to be in their hands.

67. Mitchell, interview; de Chastelain testimony, 99.

68. 2RCR Briefing text, 10–13; on negotiations, see *The Gazette* (Montreal), 21, 30 Aug. 1990; *Globe and Mail* (Toronto), 29, 30 Aug., 20 Sept. 1990; *Ottawa Citizen*, 1 Sept. 1990; "CDS Announces Initiative for Resolution to Oka Crisis," *News Release* (Ottawa: Department of National Defence), 6 Sept. 1990; MacLaine and Baxendale, *This Land is Our Land*, 78–79.

69. De Chastelain testimony, 87, 103–104; representatives of the Native communities also brought to the committee accounts of abusive behaviour by the troops: see the testimony of Linda Simon, Gordon Oke, and Joyce Nelson, in *Minutes of*

Proceedings and Evidence 46 (31 Jan. 1991), 38, 45–47, 56–57; *Globe and Mail* (Toronto), 20 Sept. 1990. A report by two Iroquois negotiators on the crisis, presented to the Iroquois Confederacy Grand Council in June 1991, alleges that some of the Warriors wanted to provoke a violent confrontation with the army, so that the Quebec and federal governments would be pressured into conceding the warriors' main bargaining point: total Native sovereignty. Report quoted on CJAD Radio News (Montreal), 5 p.m., 22 June 1991. The report was discussed in greater length in *The Gazette* (Montreal), 23 June 1991, but the newspaper article dwelt on other aspects and did not address the provocation issues. On the tensions and taunting, see also, *The Gazette* (Montreal), 5 Sept. 1991; *Globe and Mail* (Toronto), 8 Sept. 1991.

70. Major Gérald Baril, "Mission Accomplished," *Sentinel* 6 (1990), 7–8; 2RCR Briefing Text, 12–13; MacLaine and Baxendale, *This Land is Our Land*, 80–81; *Globe and Mail* (Toronto), 19 Sept. 1990.

71. 2RCR Briefing Text, 13; MacLaine and Baxendale, *This Land is Our Land*, 92.

72. See Randall W. Heather, "The British Army in Northern Ireland, 1969–72" (unpublished M.A. thesis, University of New Brunswick, September 1986), esp. chaps. 2–4, which illustrates well the dynamic nature of the situation and the resultant transformation of the army's role in the conflict, from interpository peacekeeper to counter-insurgency participant.

73. The best evidence for this comes from members of the media themselves. Some, like Lorainne Pindera, a CBC reporter who spent several weeks "behind the wire" at Oka, were honest enough to admit (as she did on "As It Happens") that they came to identify with the Mohawk and that this influenced their reporting. The enforced close confinement probably produced a kind of psychological "bonding" similar to the

"Stockholm Syndrome" associated with hostage situations. André Picard, of the *Globe and Mail*, reported as early as July on the techniques the Warriors used to enforce media compliance with their "rules," but stated that the journalists had "made themselves at home" at the Oka site. *Globe and Mail* (Toronto), 30 July 1990. He did not criticize the Mohawk for threatening the media with weapons or exposing their film. At the end of the crisis, after spending much of the period inside the Warrior's camp, he reported that "Warrior's win war of image— soldiers looked like bad guys." *Globe and Mail* (Toronto), 28 Sep. 1990.

74. See, for e.g., Winnipeg Free Press, 5 Sept.; The Gazette (Montreal), 6 Sept.: Globe and Mail (Toronto), 11 Sept.; Ottawa Citizen, 15 Oct. 1990. See also, comments by members of the commons committee to General de Chastelain, 88, 96, 111.

75. The CDS's speech was broadcast live on both CBC and CTV. The text was published as a DND *News Release*, AFN 49/90, 27 August 1990.

76. *Ottawa Citizen*, 25 Oct. 1990.

77. Some background information on Cloutier's public relations duties was conveyed to the author privately.

78. *Globe and Mail* (Toronto), 20 Sept. 1990.

79. Rosalynn Higgins, *United Nations Peacekeeping: Documents and Commentary*, vol. 4, *Europe* (London: Oxford University Press, 1981), 139–40, 196–97; see also Major K.C. Eyre, "The Future of UN Interpository Peace-Keeping under the 1956 Pearson–Hammarskjold Formula: Conclusions Drawn from Personal Experiences in Cyprus, in the Tragic Summer of 1974," *Canadian Defence Quarterly* 12, 1 (Summer 1982), 31–36; Brigadier F.R. Henn, "Guidelines for Peacekeeping—Another View," *British Army Review* 67 (April 1981), 35–36; Gaffen, *In the Eye of the Storm*, 97–105; *Toronto Star*, 30 July 1974.

80. *The Gazette*, 23 Aug. 1990.

81. Mitchell, interview; see also, Brigadier-général J.A. Roy, "Operation SALON," *Canadian Defence Quarterly* 20, 5 (April 1990), 15–19.

FURTHER READING

o

What follows concentrates on operational history and is, of necessity, highly selective. Several guides to sources in Canadian military history are available, among them O.A. Cooke's *The Canadian Military Experience 1867–1967: A Bibliography*, and the essays on Canada in Robin Higham's *Guide to Sources in British Military History* and Gerald Jordan's *Supplement* to the Higham Guide. A review of sources can also be found in Desmond Morton's *A Military History of Canada*. Those interested in policy matters are also referred to the further reading section of B.D. Hunt and R.G. Haycock's *Canada's Defence: Perspectives on Policy in the Twentieth Century*.

In addition to Morton's survey history, several other general works warrant mention. These include G. Stanley's *Canada's Soldiers* and D.J. Goodspeed's *The Armed Forces of Canada, 1867–1967*. The army's professional development to 1939 is covered in S.J. Harris's *Canadian Brass* and its history since 1867 in John Martienson's lavish *We Stand on Guard: An Illustrated History of the Canadian Army*. On a less grand scale, Tony German's *The Sea Is at Our Gates: The History of the Canadian Navy* is the only one-volume history of the navy. The necessary illustrations—of ships at least—are in a much underrated work by K. Macpherson and J. Burgess, *The Ships of Canada's Naval Forces, 1910–1981* (1981), which contains a mountain of invaluable data. Edited collections by J.A. Boutilier, *The RCN in Retrospect* and W.A.B. Douglas, *The RCN in Transition* also cover the whole sweep of RCN history. Larry Milberry's *Sixty Years* covers the history of the air force up to the mid-1980s.

Operations during the Fenian Raids, the Northwest Rebellions, and the Boer War are described in some excellent work by individual historians. Among the standards for this period are two contemporary works: R.H. Davis, *The Canadian Militia: Its Organization and Present Condition* (1873), and G.T. Denison, *Soldiering in Canada* (1900). Modern standards include Desmond Morton's *The Canadian General: Sir William Otter* and *The Last War Drum: The Northwest Campaign of 1885*, and George Stanley, *The Birth of Western Canada*. Carmen Miller's monograph on the Canadian role in the Boer War, *Painting the Map Red*, fills a tremendous void.

The study of Canadian military operations after 1914 rightly begins with the official histories, which in this country are written to a uniformly high standard. The First World War is covered in three official histories: G.N. Tucker, *The Naval Service of Canada: Its Official History*, Volume 1; G.W.L. Nicholson's *The Official History of the Canadian Army in the First World War: Canadian Expeditionary Force, 1914–1919*; and S.F. Wise, *Canadian Airmen in the First World War: The Official History of the Royal Canadian Air Force*, Volume 1. Wise is a nice corrective to the popular view that the air war was all silk scarves and Sopwith Pups. Nonetheless, Canada produced more than her share of aces. W.A. Bishop's biography of his famous father, *Courage of the Early Morning*, remains captivating reading, as does R. Collishaw's exploits in *Air Command*, co-authored by R.V. Dodds. The most thorough and scholarly accounting of RCN operations up to 1918 is by M. Hadley and R. Sarty, *Tin-Pots & Pirate Ships*. Much has been written on the Canadian Corps. The old standards, D.J. Goodspeed's *The Road Past Vimy* and John Swettenham's *To Seize the Victory* remain useful. A more comprehensive look at the corps' battles has been published in a trilogy by Dan Dancocks, *Legacy of Valour, Spearhead to Victory*, and *Welcome to Flanders Fields*, while Pierre Berton has produced a fresh look at *Vimy*. The success of the corps as an elite formation on the Western Front is explored in Bill Rawling's *Surviving Trench Warfare*. That success was due in no small measure to Sir Arthur Currie, whose life is outlined in recent biographies by Dan Dancocks, Jeffrey Williams, and A.M.J. Hyatt. Among the best war memoirs are Will R. Bird's *Ghosts Have Warm Hands* and Reginald Roy's *Diary of Private Fraser*.

The Second World War is well served by an excellent three-volume *Official History of the Canadian Army in the Second World War*; C.P. Stacey's *Six Years of War: The Canadian Army in Canada, Britain and the Pacific*, and *The Victory Campaign: The Operations in North-West Europe, 1944–1945*; and G.W.L. Nicholson's *The Canadians in Italy 1943–1945*. At present the other two services are less well served by official histories. Tucker's *The Naval Service of Canada*, Volume 2, covers activities ashore, leaving a popular history, *The Far Distant Ships* by Joseph Schull, to cover the war at sea. Until 1986 the RCAF had no official history for the Second World War at all. W.A.B. Douglas's *The Creation of a National Air Force: The Official History of the Royal Canadian Air Force*, Volume 2, covers the interwar years and operations by the Home War Establishment from 1939–1945, including the Aleutian campaign and the Battle of the Atlantic. Brereton Greenhous's forthcoming third volume of the RCAF official history will cover operations overseas.

Books on the army's operations from 1939–1945 abound, but some of the most recent and noteworthy include T. Copp and R. Vogel's *The Maple Leaf Route*, a series of volumes dealing with operations from Normandy to the Elbe, Dan Dancocks's *The D-Day Dodgers*, Denis and Shelagh Whitaker's two books, *Tug of War* and *Rhineland*, Reginald Roy's *1944*, J.L. Granatstein and Desmond Morton's *Bloody Victory*, Jack English's *The Canadian Army and the Normandy Campaign*, and Brian Villa's *Unauthorized Action*. D.S. Graham's forthcoming biography of General Guy G. Simonds will shed light on the Second World War's most successful Canadian general, and J.L. Granatstein's forthcoming book on Canadian generals of the Second World War will provide a valuable reference. George Kitching's memoir, *Mud and Green Fields*, provides the best insights into the rise—and fall—of a general officer under the stress of war. The most evocative army memoirs have come from the Italian campaign, where the fighting was like the Western Front in the First World War. Farley Mowat's *The Regiment* and

Fred Cedarberg's *The Long Road Home* capture the essence from the perspective of a young officer and an NCO respectively. A unique view of the army's problems of coping with modern war is available from T. Copp and W. McAndrew, *Battle Exhaustion*, which looks at battlefield stress and neuro-psychiatric medicine. D. Pearce's *Journal of a War* provides an illuminating first-hand account of what battle exhaustion meant.

Much less has been written on air and naval operations. S. Dunmore and W. Carter's recent *Reap the Whirlwind* remains the only scholarly monograph published on the RCAF's war—if one excludes Terry Melnyk's neglected *Canadian Flying Operations in South East Asia, 1941–1945*. L. Milberry and H. Halliday, *The Royal Canadian Air Force at War, 1939–1945*, nonetheless provides a popular and reliable one-volume account of all aspects of the air war. Operational flying was less glamourous—and more a campaign of attrition—than in the First World War, and this is reflected in the memoir literature, such as Olmstead's *Blue Skies*, Murray Peden's *A Thousand Shall Fall*, and W. Thompson's *Lancaster to Berlin*. Even the RCAF's most successful fighter ace, G.F. "Buzz" Beurling, was cool and aloof, as B. Nowlan's biography suggests. A more typical Canadian fighter pilot's war can be gleaned from H. Everard's *A Mouse in My Pocket*.

The RCN's story from 1939 to 1945 has fared little better. M. Hadley's *U-boats Against Canada* covers German operations inshore from both sides, while M. Milner's *North Atlantic Run* assesses the RCN's role in the battle against the wolf packs offshore. D. Zimmerman's *The Great Naval Battle of Ottawa* wrestles with the difficult story of the employment of science and technology by the RCN during the war. As for memoirs, Alan Easton's *50 North* remains a classic: perhaps the best memoir of the Atlantic war. H. Lawrence's *A Bloody War* and J. Lamb's *The Corvette Navy* also capture the flavour of young officers in the small ship navy at war, as does Frank Curry's unique lower deck account, *War at Sea*. No creditable biography or memoir by a senior wartime RCN officer has ever appeared.

The only two post-war official histories of operations deal with the Korean War: H.F. Wood's *Strange Battleground* covers the army while T. Thorgrimsson and E.C. Russell produced *Canadian Naval Operations in Korean Waters, 1950–1955*. J.D.F. Kealy and E.C. Russell authored an official *A History of Canadian Naval Aviation* and a popular official history of the Gulf War of 1990–91 by R. Gimblett and J. Morin is forthcoming.

Most writing on the post-1945 period deals with policy issues, but some sense for operations can be obtained from chapters in the previously cited Martienson, *We Stand on Guard*, Boutilier, *The RCN in Retrospect*, Douglas's *The RCN in Transition*, Goodspeed's *The Armed Forces of Canada 1867–1967*, Milberry's *Sixty Years*, and also from the memoirs of J.V. Allard, Jeffry V. Brock, H.D. Graham, and from numerous articles in the *Canadian Defence Quarterly*. E.L.M. Burns's *Between Arab and Israeli* looks at the origins of Canada's peacekeeping role, while such operations are examined in considerable detail by F. Gaffen in *In the Eye of the Storm* and J.L. Granatstein and D. Bercuson in *War and Peacemaking*.

An honest attempt has been made to secure permission for all material'used, and if there are errors or omissions, these are wholly unintentional and the Publisher will be grateful to learn of them.

G.F. Stanley, "The North-West Rebellion, Part 2," from The Birth of Western Canada (Toronto, University of Toronto Press, 1966), 350–73. Reprinted by permission of University of Toronto Press.

Desmond Morton, "Canada's First Expeditionary Force: The Canadian Contingent in South Africa, 1899–1900," Canadian Defence Quarterly 15, 3 (Winter 1985/86), 41–46. Reprinted with the permission of the journal.

S.J. Harris, "The Permanent Force and 'Real Soldiering,' 1883–1914," chapter 2 of Canadian Brass (Toronto: University of Toronto Press, 1988), 22–39. Reprinted by permission of University of Toronto Press.

Ronald G. Haycock, "Recruiting, 1914–1916," chapter 12 of Sam Hughes: The Public Career of a Controversial Canadian, 1885–1916, Canadian War Museum Historical Publication No. 21 (Waterloo, ON: Wilfrid Laurier University Press in collaboration with the Canadian War Museum, The Canadian Museum of Civilization, and the National Museums of Canada, 1986), 198–224. Reprinted with the permission of the Canadian War Museum and of the authors.

"The Journal of Private Fraser," from Reginald H. Roy, ed., The Journal of Private Fraser, 1914–1918: Canadian Expeditionary Force (Victoria, BC: Sono Nis Press, 1985), 199–215. Reprinted with the permission of Reginald H. Roy.

A.M.J. Hyatt, "Corps Commander: Arthur Currie," chapter 5 of General Sir Arthur Currie: A Military Biography (Toronto: University of Toronto Press in collaboration with the Canadian War Museum, The Canadian Museum of Civilization, and the National Museums of Canada, 1987), 68–89. Reprinted with the permission of the Canadian War Museum.

S.F. Wise, "The Aerial War, 1917," from Canadian Airmen in the First World War: The Official History of the Royal Canadian Air Force, vol. 1 (Toronto: University of Toronto Press and the Department of National Defence Canada, 1986), 395–419. Reprinted with the permission of the Minister of Supply and Services Canada, 1991.

Roger Sarty, "Hard Luck Flotilla: The RCN's Atlantic Coast Patrol, 1914–1918," chapter 6 of The RCN in Transition, 1910–1985, ed. W.A.B. Douglas (Vancouver: The University of British Columbia Press, 1988), 103–25. Reprinted with the permission of the publisher.

C.P. Stacey, "The Raid on Dieppe, 19 August 1942," from Six Years of War: The Army in Canada, Britain and the Pacific, vol. 1 of The Official History of the Canadian Army in the Second World War (Ottawa: Department of National Defence Canada, The Queen's Printer, 1957), 363–86. Reprinted with the permission of the Minister of Supply and Services Canada, 1991.

Farley Mowat, "Crossing the Moro," from And No Birds Sang (Toronto: McClelland and Stewart, 1979), 215–29. Reprinted with the permission of the author.

D. Graham and S. Bidwell, "Operation Olive," chapter 23 of Tug of War: The Battle for Italy, 1943–1945 (London, UK: Hodder and Stoughton, 1986), 347–66. Reprinted with the permission of D. Graham.

Reprinted by permission of Greenwood Publishing Group, Inc., Westport, CT, from The Canadian Army and the Normandy Campaign: A Study of Failure in High Command by John English. Copyright by John A. English and published in 1991 by Praeger Publishers.

J. Terry Copp, "Battle Exhaustion and the Canadian Soldier in Normandy," The British Army Review 85 (April 1987), 46–54. Reprinted with the permission of the journal.

W. Denis Whitaker and Shelagh Whitaker, "The Guns of Woensdrecht," from Tug of War: The Canadian Victory that Opened Antwerp (Toronto: Stoddart Publishing Co. Limited, 1984), 179–201. Reprinted with the permission of Stoddart Publishing Co. Limited of Don Mills, Ontario.

Murray Peden, "Operational Flying—Apprenticeship," chapter 11 of A Thousand Shall Fall (Toronto: Stoddart Publishing Co. Limited, 1988), 242–62. Reprinted with the permission of Stoddart Publishing Co. Limited of Don Mills, Ontario.

W.S. Carter, "Strike Hard, Strike Sure: The Dortmund Raid of 6–7 October 1944," *revised from the prologue of* Anglo–Canadian Wartime Relations, 1939–1945: RAF Bomber Command and No. 6 (Canadian) Group *(New York: Garland Publishing, Inc., 1991), 1–19. Reprinted with the permission of the author.*

Marc Milner, "The Implications of Technological Backwardness: The Canadian Navy 1939–1945," Canadian Defence Quarterly *19, 3 (Winter 1989), 46–52. Reprinted with the permission of the journal.*

Alan Easton, "Close Quarters," *chapter 10 of* 50 North: An Atlantic Battleground *(Toronto: Paperjacks, 1980), 130–49. Reprinted with the permission of the publisher.*

Reprinted with permission from War and Peacekeeping: From South Africa to the Gulf— Canada's Limited Wars *by J.L. Granatstein and David Bercuson, published by Key Porter Books Limited, Toronto, Ontario. Copyright © 1991 J.L. Granatstein and David Jay Bercuson.*

David A. Charters, "From October to Oka: Peacekeeping in Canada, 1970–1990," *from* Military Aid to Civil Authorities in the Anglo-Saxon Tradition, *ed. David R. Jones (forthcoming). Reprinted with the permission of the author and editor.*